Working

FIFTH EDITION

Larry J. Bailey

SOUTH-WESTERN
CENGAGE Learning·

Australia · Brazil · Japan · Korea · Mexico · Singapore · Spain · United Kingdom · United States

SOUTH-WESTERN
CENGAGE Learning®

Working, Fifth edition
Larry J. Bailey

Vice President of Editorial, Business:
  Jack W. Calhoun

Vice President/Editor-in-Chief: Karen Schmohe

Associate Acquisitions Editor: Michael
  Guendelsberger

Senior Developmental Editor: Enid Nagel

Consulting Editor: Marce Epstein

Editorial Assistant: Anne Merrill

Marketing Program Manager: Linda Kuper

Media Editor: Mike Jackson

Rights Acquisition Director: Audrey Pettengill

Rights Acquisition Specialist, Text
  and Image: Amber Hosea

Manufacturing Planner: Kevin Kluck

Art Direction, Production Management,
  and Composition: PreMediaGlobal

Senior Art Director: Michelle Kunkler

Cover Designer: Grannan Graphic Design Ltd.

Cover Image: ©Radius Images/Alamy;
  ©Blue Jean Images/Alamy; ©Radius Images/
  Alamy; ©Stephen Coburn, Shutterstock;
  ©Radius Images/Alamy. (bottom, left to
  right): ©Yuri Acurs, Shutterstock;
  ©luckyraccoon, Shutterstock;
  ©Jose Luis Pelaez Inc, Jupiter Images.

For product information and technology assistance, contact us at
Cengage Learning Customer & Sales Support, 1-800-354-9706

For permission to use material from this text or product,
submit all requests online at www.cengage.com/permissions
Further permissions questions can be emailed to
permissionrequest@cengage.com

Exam*View*® is a registered trademark of eInstruction Corp. Windows is a
registered trademark of the Microsoft Corporation used herein under license.
Macintosh and Power Macintosh are registered trademarks of Apple
Computer, Inc. used herein under license.
© 2013 Cengage Learning. All Rights Reserved.

Library of Congress Control Number: 2011945435

ISBN-13: 978-0-8400-6856-9

ISBN-10: 0-8400-6856-5

South-Western
5191 Natorp Boulevard
Mason, OH 45040
USA

Cengage Learning products are represented in Canada by
Nelson Education, Ltd.

For your course and learning solutions, visit www.cengage.com/school
Visit our company website at www.cengage.com

About the Author

Larry J. Bailey attended Ball State University on an academic scholarship and taught high school
industrial arts prior to attending graduate school at the University of Illinois where he completed the
Doctor of Education degree in Vocational Education at age 26. He held faculty research positions at
the University of Illinois and the University of Iowa before joining Southern Illinois University in 1969.
Dr. Bailey is the author of eight books and more than 100 other publications. During his tenure, he was
appointed to the National Advisory Council on Career Education and the Illinois Advisory Council on
Adult, Vocational, and Technical Education. He retired from his professorship at SIU in 2004 after 35 years
of service.

Printed in the United States of America
5 6 7 8 9 10 22 21 20 19 18

Contents

UNIT 4 FEATURES

UNIT 5
MANAGE YOUR MONEY 336

Chapter 14
The Economic World 338

Chapter 15
The Consumer in the Marketplace 360

Chapter 16
Banking and Credit 384

Chapter 17
Budget, Save, and Invest Money 410

Chapter 18
Insure Against Loss 434

UNIT 5 FEATURES

UNIT 6
INDEPENDENT LIVING   484

UNIT 6 FEATURES

Helping You Prepare for Your Next Step!

Discover career exploration and life preparation with *Working, 5e!* As this text spans the entire work/life cycle, you will find everything you need for independent success as you explore career options and plan a successful career. You will gain personal finance advice, leadership skills, knowledge to manage money, and plan for retirement.

Let's Get Started!

Each UNIT opener addresses Career Clusters with a profile of someone who participated in a co-op program, graduated, and is now employed full-time.

Each CHAPTER opens with a **PREVIEW** to introduce and reinforce concepts by providing a thought-provoking introduction to each lesson.

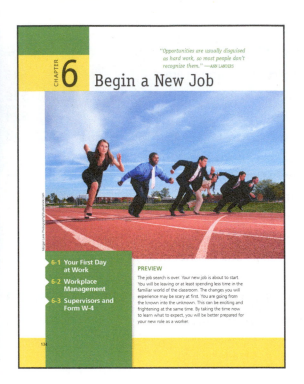

presents a real-life case study to help you understand how the chapter topics are related and important to you.

Each LESSON begins with a list of objectives and key terms to help focus your reading.

OBJECTIVES
outline the main goals of the lesson.

KEY TERMS
list the new vocabulary defined in the lesson.

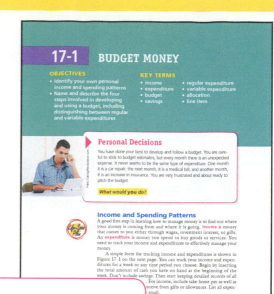

17-1 BUDGET MONEY

OBJECTIVES
- Identify your own personal income and spending patterns
- Name and describe the four steps involved in developing and using a budget, including distinguishing between regular and variable expenditures

KEY TERMS
- income
- expenditure
- budget
- savings
- regular expenditure
- variable expenditure
- allocation
- line item

Personal Decisions

You have done your best to develop and follow a budget. You are careful to stick to budget estimates, but every month there is an unexpected expense. It never seems to be the same type of expenditure. One month it is a car repair; the next month, it is a medical bill; and another month, it is an increase in insurance. You are very frustrated and about ready to pitch the budget.

What would you do?

Income and Spending Patterns

A good first step in learning how to manage money is to find out where your money is coming from and where it is going. **Income** is money that comes to you either through wages, investment interest, or gifts. An **expenditure** is money you spend to buy goods or services. You need to track your income and expenditures to effectively manage your money.

A simple form for tracking income and expenditures is shown in Figure 17-1 on the next page. You can track your income and expenditures for a week or any time period you choose. Begin by inserting the total amount of cash you have on hand at the beginning of the week. Don't include savings. Then start keeping detailed records of all ... . For income, include take-home pay as well as ... receive from gifts or allowances. List all expen... ... enditures. Say your initial cash on hand is $75.

Decisions features allow you to check **decision making** skills for: Career, Ethical, Interpersonal, Personal, and Workplace situations.

Glen Jones/Shutterstock.com

Ethical Decisions

Your employer asks you to work a few extra hours on Saturday to help catch up on an important order. Even though you have already put in 40 hours this week, you agree to do so. The next week, you discover that you have been paid straight time for 45 hours. You call this to the boss's attention. He says that he does not pay overtime and that you should be glad that you have a job. You are not satisfied with his explanation.

What would you do?

Focus on . . .
provides information on a variety of **real-life workplace topics** related to the chapter.

Focus on the Workplace

High Performance Work Organizations

Historically, many kinds of work in America have been patterned after the mass production system made famous by Henry Ford in the early 1900s. In mass production, jobs are broken down into a number of simple tasks. Each worker specializes in one task, which is done over and over.

Managers do the thinking and planning for the organization. Supervisors direct the work of frontline employees. Workers under this system need only be reliable, steady, and willing to follow directions.

The mass production system has helped make the United States a great economic power. It has also resulted in a high standard of living for workers. This system still determines the way most factories, offices, banks, hospitals, and schools are organized.

In the twenty-first century this nation faces increasing global economic competition. Increased productivity and improved quality are necessary for the United States to remain competitive. The solution adopted by many companies is called a high-performance work organization.

The basic idea of a high-performance work organization is to give greater authority to frontline workers. Layers of managers disappear as teams of workers take over such tasks as quality control and production scheduling. Workers are asked to use judgment and make decisions at the point where goods and services are produced.

This type of work organization requires retraining of workers and managers. The high cost of retraining, however, is offset by gains in quality and productivity. High-performance work organizations are becoming the model for a successful future.

THINK CRITICALLY
1. Why do you think the mass production system helped make this nation a great economic power?
2. Give some examples of ways in which a high-performance work organization might help improve quality and productivity.

Some organizations give frontline workers more authority.

6-3 Supervision and Teams HE 6 147

High Growth Occupations
FOR THE 21ST CENTURY

includes a description of a **fast-growing occupation** needing workers in the future.

High Growth Occupations
FOR THE 21ST CENTURY

Physical Therapist Assistants and Aides

Health Science

Do you like working with people? Do you want to help people improve their quality of life? You might find the occupation of *physical therapist assistant* or *physical therapist aide* a good fit for you. Both assistants and aides support the physical therapist in a variety of tasks that aid in the treatment of patients.

Treatment and services provided by a *physical therapist* may include helping patients who have injuries from an accident, relieving patients' pain, and preventing or limiting permanent physical disabilities of patients who suffer from injuries or disease. Patients may include individuals injured in accidents and individuals with cerebral palsy. They also include individuals with disabling conditions such as lower back pain, arthritis, heart disease, fractures, and head injuries.

Responsibilities for *physical therapist assistants* may include assisting patients with exercise, or performing massage, electrical stimulation, paraffin baths, hot and cold packs, traction, or ultrasound treatments. All treatments performed by assistants are under the direction of the physical therapist. Assistants also record how the patient responds to, and the outcome of, treatments. *Physical therapist aides* also work under the direction of a physical therapist. Responsibilities may include keeping the treatment area clean and organized. Aides prepare the treatment area for each patient and help patients move from one treatment area to another, either by pushing a patient's wheelchair, or by lending a shoulder for the patient to lean on. Duties also include clerical tasks, such as ordering supplies, answering the phone, or filling out insurance forms and other paperwork. *Physical therapist assistants* usually require state licensing. Programs offering certification are available through community colleges or private schools. *Physical therapist aides* do not require licensing. They receive on-the-job-training. About two-thirds of the assistants and aides work in hospitals or private medical offices. Others work in nursing and personal-care facilities, out-patient rehabilitation centers, offices and clinics of physicians, and home health agencies.

Physical therapists help patients regain strength and relearn physical skills.

446 CHAPTER 18 Tenure Against Ever

Focus on Features...

Exciting FEATURES help you use self-understanding, self-acceptance, goal setting, team building, and career information to set and achieve realistic career and life goals.

Workplace Innovations

emphasize the growing importance of technology in the career world.

Workplace Innovations
ASSISTIVE TECHNOLOGY

The same types of hardware and software technologies commonly used by individuals and business are being widely used in education and training. Students with special needs are benefiting particularly from *assistive technology*. This term refers to those applications of technology that provide ways for students with sensory, cognitive, or physical disabilities to better access classroom instruction.

The number of students with disabilities has steadily increased. Depending on their type of disability, special needs students typically require more individualized instruction. Assistive technologies can free a teacher to help more students, while at the same time helping provide a disabled student with a sense of accomplishment and inclusion.

Among the most common assistive technology products are alternative computer input devices. These include electronic pointing devices used to control the cursor on the screen without the use of hands. Wands and sticks can be worn on the head or held in the mouth to press keys on the keyboard. Trackballs on top of a base can be used to move the cursor. And, touch screens allow activation of the computer directly without using any other device.

For visually-impaired students, Braille embossers transfer computer-generated text into Braille output and translation programs convert scanned-in text into Braille. Speech recognition programs allow students to give commands and enter data using their voices to create text documents, browse the Web, and navigate among applications. Screen readers can be used to translate everything on the screen into a computerized voice that is spoken aloud. These are among the many types of assistive technologies that are available to help disabled students become successful learners.

NET FOLLOW-UP

Use a search engine to explore the Web for additional information about assistive or adaptive technologies. Have you observed any students at your school using any adaptive technologies? If so, what impact have the technologies had on the students and teachers? Be prepared to discuss your observations in class.

Search the Net

The cloud can help businesses save costs by eliminating the need for purchasing expensive computers. Flexible usage allows businesses to pay just for the computing time they need. Access **www.cengage.com/school/working** and click on the link for Chapter 13. Watch the video that explains cloud computing. Research cloud computing. What businesses do you currently use that provide services on the cloud? What other uses do you envision for the cloud?

www.cengage.com/school/working

Search the Net

provides **Internet activities** that allow you to expand your knowledge of career topics and hone your research skills.

demonstrates how important **effective communication** skills are to find a job and be successful.

Communication at Work
GET INFORMATION

You will sometimes need to get information from others in order to make good personal choices. Deciding on a health insurance plan is an example. Suppose you have several plans to choose from. You have carefully read the information about each plan. You have made a checklist to compare the plans. Still, you have questions and need advice.

Find out who can help you. Make up a brief list of specific questions, and contact the person. Organize your list and outline important points. For telephone calls, follow the advice in Chapter 4 on using the telephone.

If you think you can get the information you need over the telephone, begin by explaining the purpose of your call and asking if this is a good time. If it is not, arrange a time that is. Other people are usually glad to give you information if you are considerate of their time.

THINK CRITICALLY

1. What types of people could you call to get information about health insurance?
2. Why should you write a list of questions before calling someone for help?

Life-Span Plan Project links all aspects of personal finance to your life within a challenging capstone project that prepares you for future financial independence.

Focus on Features...

FIGURE 4-2 This is a job application form that has been filled out correctly.

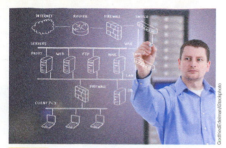

FIGURE 13-2 This diagram shows the various places information travels on the Internet.

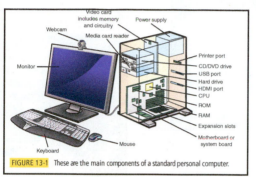

FIGURE 13-1 These are the main components of a standard personal computer.

Diagrams, forms, and photos help you connect to content covered in each chapter.

Math Connection

presents typical problems and solutions to reinforce and review your **math skills.**

Math Connection

Suppose you work for the government. Your supervisor has told you to order 4,000 cubic meters of concrete for a building job. At a concrete batch plant, concrete is sold by the cubic yard. To order the correct amount, you need to convert cubic meters to cubic yards. How many cubic yards should you order?

SOLUTION

To calculate the number of cubic yards in 4,000 cubic meters, multiply 4,000 cubic meters by the conversion equivalent of 1.31 cubic yards per cubic meter (see the conversion chart in Figure 10-6 on the next page).

$$4,000 \times 1.31 = 5,240 \text{ cubic yards}$$

You should order 5,240 cubic yards of concrete.

Access to Gale's online Career Transitions, available with each text at no extra charge, provides hands-on guidance and immediate access to key job search activities.

Career Transitions Connection

activities and exercises guide you through the online program allowing you to immediately apply what you've learned in the class.

Career Transitions Connection

Transferable Skills

Click on *Match Experience to New Careers*. In the dialogue box for "I've worked as a(n)" fill in a job, either paid or unpaid, that you have worked in. When related careers are offered in the drop down menu, click the one that is the closest match to the job title you are describing. After you have selected a position for the dialogue box, a list of similar positions will appear beneath the dialogue box. From that list, click on the job that is of most interest to you. Read through the typical activities of the job that you selected. Make a list of skills you already have that you could use in the selected job.

Focus on Assessment...
End of Lesson

End of Lesson assessment gives you a chance to check your understanding before moving to the next lesson.

2-3 Assessment

1. Identify and briefly explain the three kinds of work experience education programs.
2. How does cooperative career and technical education differ from other forms of career and technical education?
3. The term *exploratory* describes one type of work experience education. Explain why.
4. How can work experience education help you discover career interests and goals?
5. What is the benefit of establishing a work record?
6. Give an example to show how knowledge of work histories can help you think about and plan a career.

15-1 Assessment

1. How are the goals of a buyer and a seller different?
2. What is a need? A want?
3. The process of consuming has three stages. Name and briefly describe them.
4. Give three reasons why Bill Martinez is a wise consumer.
5. Why should you use and care for a product properly?
6. Planned obsolescence is often referred to as "designed for the dump." Explain what this means.
7. Who benefits the most from retailer buy back programs—consumers or retailers? Explain your answer.

Focus on Assessment...
End of Chapter

End of Chapter Assessment provides a summary of the main points. Activities and questions test your knowledge.

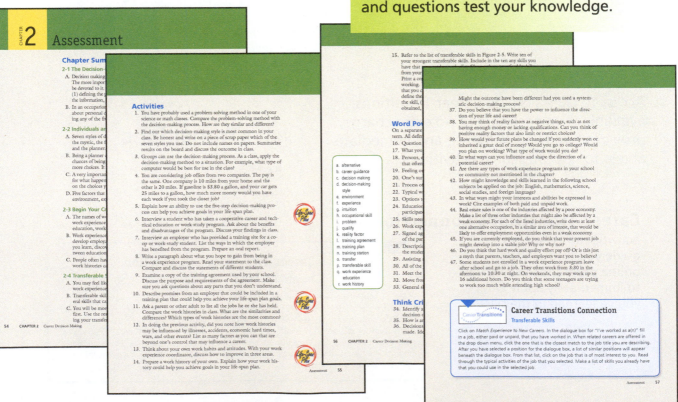

Career Transitions

Explore Career Interests. Achieve Employment Goals

You now have instant access to the most valuable, complete career exploration and job-seeking resources available online with this one-of-a-kind application. *Career Transitions* guides you through the entire career process—from individualized assessment of personal strengths and corresponding career opportunities to focused, effective activities that will help you discover a career of your choice.

Effective Career Exploration

- **You define and determine ideal career paths** using intuitive, engaging activities.
- **Individualized assessments** help you candidly evaluate personal abilities, test skill sets, and determine career opportunities that most closely align with your *P*A*T*H to Success:* your *Passions, Attitudes, Talents,* and *Heart.*
- **Clear, reliable information** highlights green, new economy, and high growth occupations.
- **Candid videos** provide realistic glimpses into daily job and career choices.

Practical Job-Seeking Expertise

- **Expert, professional guidance** helps you establish and realize employment goals
- **Unmatched, practical job-seeking tools** provide the broadest expanse of job postings online and drawn from reliable sources such as *indeed®. com, monster®, CareerBuilder®,* and thousands of company websites.
- **Interactive interview simulation** provides you with strategies and real practice for excelling in interview situations.
- **Professional resources** help **you create** resumes, cover letters, and presentations.

For more information visit www.gale.cengage.com/careertransitions

Life-Span Plan Project

The fact you are reading *Working* shows some things about you. It shows you are interested in learning how to pursue a career that will bring you income and satisfaction. You may have asked yourself questions such as, "Why do some employees advance in their careers while others are unable to keep a job?" or "What types of people are best suited to self-employment?" You may have wondered whether a career in marketing, production, or the skilled trades is right for you. Becoming a successful storeowner, computer operator, or professional caregiver may already be a basic goal you have set for yourself. Whether or not this is true of you, this book will provide you with knowledge and skills you may use to make better decisions throughout your life, both as an employee and in your personal life.

YOUR PERSONAL GOALS

Goals are things people want most to achieve in their lives. They hold the greatest value to them. Most people set a wide range of goals for themselves. Some are *short-term goals* that they hope to achieve within a year. Others are *long-term goals* that will require many years to attain. A person's goals are likely to involve family, living conditions, education, careers, community, and many other aspects of their lives. The goals you set are based on your personal values, your hopes, and your dreams.

There is no way to judge most goals as right or wrong, or better or worse. Your most important goal may be to study to become a computer operator while your best friend might want to own a farm and grow vegetables. Your brother may want to start a family at a young age while you prefer to put off marriage and family responsibilities until well into the future. The point is, a person's goals should be based on what she or he really wants from life. There is no reason for your goals to be the same as other people's goals.

Almost every important goal you could set is related to the topics in this textbook. Suppose your most important personal goal is to have a happy and secure family life. You might think this goal has little to do with what you will learn about working this year. But, if what you learn about working helps you make a better career choice, then you may be able to earn a greater income and be more satisfied with your life. This also will allow you to provide a better standard of living for a family.

A LIFE-SPAN PLAN

Today you might believe that owning a nice car is your most important goal. In ten years you may be more concerned with having a rewarding career, buying a home, or saving for your children's education. Even later you will want to have a satisfying retirement. Important events in you life, such as preparing for a career, raising a family or enjoying retirement are parts of your *life cycle*.

Your *life span* is the time from your birth to your death. It includes the events that make up your life cycle. When you are young, you set long-term goals that you want to achieve over a period of years during your life span.

The *life-span timeline* shown on the next page can help you understand the relationship between a life span and events in a person's life cycle. It shows a life span as a straight line along the top of the figure. Events in the life cycle appear beneath the time in a person's life when they might happen. If you construct a figure like this for yourself, it is likely to have different events taking place at different times because your life will not be exactly the same as anyone else's.

Life-span goals are the long-term goals that you want most to reach during your life. They shape many of the most important decisions you will make. Examples of life-span goals include completing a training program, owning a business, raising a family, or achieving financial security. For most people, life-span goals don't just happen. Successful people create plans for how

Your Life Span

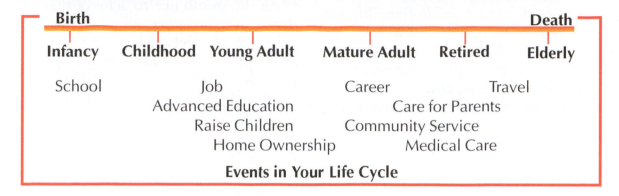

Birth						Death
Infancy	**Childhood**	**Young Adult**	**Mature Adult**	**Retired**		**Elderly**
School		Job	Career		Travel	
		Advanced Education		Care for Parents		
		Raise Children	Community Service			
		Home Ownership		Medical Care		

Events in Your Life Cycle

they can achieve their life-span goals. These plans are called *life-span plans*. Later in this class you will be asked to choose life-span goals that you will use to create a life-span plan of your own. Life-Span Plan icons, like the one here, are placed near parts of the text that can help you in setting your life-span goals and preparing a life-span plan for yourself. Life-Span Plan icons are placed in various lessons throughout the text. For each icon, a related activity is listed at the end of the chapter. By completing these assignments and saving them, you may prepare to construct your life-span plan.

GABRIELLA'S PLAN

To help you prepare your own life-span plan, consider the example of Gabriella. Gabriella is fifteen years old and a high school sophomore. Jessie, a senior at her school, is her steady boyfriend. They have talked about their future and getting married someday, but have agreed to wait until they both graduate, get jobs, and save some money.

Gabriella's favorite subject in school is marketing. She has signed up for all the marketing classes she could fit into her schedule. She was particularly interested in a class that taught her about creating websites and marketing on the Internet. Although she loves marketing, she has learned that she is not good at other aspects of running a business. She has trouble keeping financial records and finds it difficult to direct other people.

Experience has convinced Gabriella that she will never be a successful business owner unless she shares the responsibility with someone else.

Gabriella has decided that her best alternative is to find a job that allows her to carry out Internet marketing functions for a business owned by someone else. She thinks that she might eventually form a partnership to produce advertisements for the Internet with someone who has other business skills.

One of the reasons she chose to take this class was to learn about ways she can gain firsthand experience in marketing. During the class, Gabriella finished assignments that helped her learn many things about herself. She saved these assignments in a file and used them to help her complete her life-span plan by taking these steps.

FIRST THINGS FIRST

To begin her life-span plan, Gabriella identified six central life-span goals that she most wants to achieve over the next 50 years. These goals fit in well with her values, interests, and personality. They are to

1. Gain training and experience needed to have a successful career in Internet marketing.
2. Help organize and own a successful Internet marketing business.
3. Get married, have children, and own a house in a nice neighborhood.
4. Become financially secure.

5. Be active in her community.
6. Be able to retire and take up other interests by the age of 65.

Gabriella realizes that achieving these life-span goals will involve careful planning and many trade-offs. Almost all life-span goals people set require money. To pay for her training, a business of her own, a home, and a secure retirement she will need to save and invest part of the income she receives during her working life. At times, she may need to borrow funds from others. She will need to construct and follow a budget that allows her to do this. Gabriella may decide not to spend as much of her income on new clothes so she can save to pay for training later. Gabriella also needs to identify short-term goals that can help her achieve her more-important life-span goals in the future.

RELATED GOALS

Gabriella's central life-span goals are related. Saving and investing to achieve financial security will help her pay for training and later to start a business. If her business is successful, she will be able to afford the house she wants to own. Financial security will allow Gabriella to enjoy a few luxuries. Gabriella's parents immigrated to the United States from Brazil. Gabriella would like to visit Brazil. If her business is a success, she will be able to take this trip.

Gabriella wants to achieve many short- and long-term goals that are not central goals in her life. These include buying cars and furniture. Although these goals are important, they aren't the things Gabriella cares most about, so they are not listed in her life-span plan. In preparing her life-span plan, Gabriella listed and evaluated her goals to decide what was most important to her.

USING A TABLE FOR ORGANIZATION

Gabriella organized her life-span goals in a table as shown on the next page. Across the top she placed six categories to represent her six central life-span goals. On the left side she placed periods of time. These started with the next two years at the top and went 50 years into the future at the bottom. She then placed her goals according to when she would like to achieve them and how they contribute to her central life-span goals.

Gabriella feels a sense of satisfaction with her work. She created a life-span plan that she believes will help her accomplish what she wants most in life. She knows that she will almost surely revise her plan in the future, but she has a foundation on which to build. She can use her plan to help make decisions now. When she selects classes for next year, she will sign up for advertising, computer design, and another marketing class. She knows what type of part-time work to look for and how to spend and save her earnings. Because she has definite goals, she is better able to choose not to spend money for things she doesn't really need.

Gabriella's life-span plan is right for her. It fits her values, personality, and family situation. Her plan, however, would not be right for most students, including you. You aren't Gabriella. You have other values, abilities, and interests. Her personality is not your personality. Her family is not your family. You need to make your own life-span plan.

YOUR LIFE-SPAN PLAN

Near the end of this class you will be asked to prepare a life-span plan for yourself. To do this, you should reflect on what you've learned throughout this course. You will study numerous topics and finish many activities that you can use to help you complete this assignment. You also will want to consider things about yourself that were not directly covered in this course. The type and size of family you want to have is important, but will not be discussed in this course. The same is true of where you want to live and the role you wish to play in your community. Preparing your life-span plan will require you to consider all of your values and goals, not just those that are related to your career choice.

After you gather as many useful resources as you can, use these materials to help you write a list of your goals. Base them on what you want from life for yourself, your family, and your community. Sort them according to whether they are short- or long-term goals, and then classify them into overall life-span goals. Place your goals on a grid similar to Gabriella's to construct your life-span plan.

When you have finished your life-span plan, it would be helpful to ask an experienced person to review your plan with you. A teacher, counselor, or other adult you respect would be a good choice. Discuss your choices and the feasibility of your plan. This person can offer advice and encouragement for achieving your goals.

Making a life-span plan is an important first step. But, it is only a first step. Putting your life-span plan into action can make the difference between just thinking about your future and actually achieving the life-span goals that are most important to you. If you fail to act on your life-span plan, it will only be a piece of paper.

Gabriella's Life-Span Plan

Time	Training	Career	Family	Financial	Community	Retirement
Next 2 years	Complete high school and apply to a marketing trade school	Find a part-time job in marketing	Help parents with younger children	Save $2,500 each year to help pay for training	Be an active church member	Nothing yet
5 years from now	Graduate from marketing trade school	Work for a business in Internet marketing	Find a nice apartment in a good location	Save and invest income to buy a home	Serve as a leader of a community center youth group	Buy life insurance
10 years from now	Take advanced classes in Internet marketing	Work in a Web design position as an Internet marketer	Get married and buy a small home; have one child	Save and invest to finance a own firm	Teach night computer marketing classes at a local college	Open an individual retirement account
15 years from now	Learn more about small business management	Help start an Internet marketing business	Have another child; buy a larger house	Start a fund for children's education	Continue teaching Internet marketing	Add to IRA and look for investments to make
30 years from now	Take art classes so I can take up drawing or painting when I retire	Build a successful business that I can eventually sell when I retire	See children graduate from college; spend time with grandchildren	Increase savings and investments now that children have moved out	Run for town council or participate in government in some other way	Investigate volunteer work I might enjoy when I retire
50 years from now	Take classes in cooking, art, and history	Sell business; take part-time job in art store	Buy a retirement home in a warm climate	Manage investments carefully	Volunteer to advise people who own small businesses	Take one or more long trips each year and visit grandchildren

Life-Span Plan Activities

Chapter	Page	Activity
1	11, 29	Make lists of your interests, aptitudes and work values. Explain how these lists can help you create a useful life-span plan.
1	18, 30	Explain how an understanding of employment trends in the United States can help you create a life-span plan that has goals you can reasonably expect to achieve.
2	34, 55	Explain how an ability to use the five-step decision-making process can help you achieve goals in your life-span plan.
2	44, 55	Describe several promises from an employer you would hope to find in a training plan that could help you achieve goals you could set in your life-span plan.
2	47, 56	Prepare a work history of your own. Explain how your work history could help you achieve goals in your life-span plan.
3	67, 85	List several short-term goals that you might hope to achieve by accepting employment now. Describe how these job goals could help you achieve goals in your life-span plan.
4	88, 110	Explain how studying the personal data sheet you created in Activity 2a (on page 109) can help you identify things you can do now to improve the likelihood of achieving goals in your life-span plan.
5	122, 131	Evaluate your ability to communicate successfully with others. Describe how this ability is likely to help you attain goals in your life-span plan.
6	145, 149	Evaluate your ability to follow directions. Explain how this ability could help you attain goals in your life-span plan.
7	153, 170	Explain how you choose the clothes you wear. Describe how your choices could affect your ability to achieve goals in your life-span plan.
7	162, 170	Consider your feelings about always doing the best job possible. Describe how your attitude toward doing quality work may impact your ability to achieve goals in your life-span plan.
8	174, 195	Identify a job you either currently hold or could accept. Make a list of benefits you believe your employer would owe you as an employee. Discuss how these benefits could help you achieve goals in your life-span plan.
8	185, 196	Describe the relationship between your current earnings and your ability to eventually achieve goals in your life-span plan.
9	205, 231	Evaluate your ability to speak and write in standard English. Explain why this ability can help you achieve goals in your life-span plan.
9	221, 232	Evaluate your ability to work as a member of a team. Explain the importance of this ability to achieving goals in your life-span plan.
10	236, 255	List and describe several goals you might set for yourself in your life-span plan that would be easier to achieve if you are able to solve basic mathematical problems. Evaluate your mathematical skills. Should you work to improve them?
11	262, 281	Consider several goals you might set in your life-span plan. Describe how your ability to achieve these goals might be affected by your health and therefore by your diet. Do you eat a healthful diet? Should you change your diet to protect your health?

11	268, 282	Imagine that you suffered a serious injury in an accident. How might such an injury affect your ability to achieve goals in your life-span plan? Describe what you can do now to protect your personal safety.
12	288, 311	List leadership skills that you think you currently possess. Explain how these skills can help you achieve goals in your life-span plan. Do you think you should work to improve your leadership skills? Describe how you might accomplish this.
12	307, 313	Consider several goals in your life-span plan that might best be achieved through self-employment. Do you believe you are personally suited to being self-employed. Explain why, or why not.
13	326, 334	Evaluate your ability to use the Internet. Explain how this ability can help you achieve goals in your life-span plan. Do you believe you should work to improve your ability to use the Internet? Describe how you might accomplish this.
14	341, 357	Divide goals you might set in your life-span plan into two lists: (a) goals that concern consumption, such as buying a house, and (b) goals that concern production of goods or services, such as working as an electrician. Explain how these lists show we are all consumers and producers in the economy.
15	364, 381	Evaluate your ability to consume wisely. Explain why this skill is essential to achieving many goals in your life-span plan.
16	403, 409	Identify a goal you might set in your life-span plan that could only be achieved through the use of credit. Discuss things you could do now that would improve your ability to borrow funds in the future.
17	412, 431	Describe how you decide to use your earnings. Explain why creating and following a budget can improve your chance of achieving many goals in your life-span plan.
18	437, 454	Consider goals you might set in your life-span plan. Explain how health insurance can improve the likelihood of your achieving these goals.
19	458, 483	Make a list of taxes you currently pay and those that you expect to pay in the future. Evaluate how these taxes, and the government services they support, will affect your ability to achieve goals in your life-span plan.
19	468, 483	Identify a goal you might set in your life-span plan that you would expect to achieve in your later years—after the age of 67. Discuss how Social Security benefits might make this goal easier to achieve.
20	488, 499	Identify and explain a goal you might set in your life-span plan that will be easier for you to achieve because of our system of civil law.
21	502, 513	Consider the housing alternative that you think you would set as a goal in your life-span plan. Explain why other people may set different housing goals in their individual life-span plans.
22	516, 535	Explain why you would, or would not, include being a good citizen as a goal in your life-span plan. Describe how practicing good citizenship might help other people achieve goals in their life-span plans.
22	526, 536	Identify types of education or training you expect to complete after you graduate from high school. Explain how this advanced training can help you achieve goals in your life-span plan. Also explain why it is unreasonable to think you can learn everything about an occupation.

UNIT 1 — Match Your Interests to Occupations

Bill's future occupation was clear to anyone who knew him as a toddler. Bill enjoyed playing in the dirt and building with Lincoln Logs and Legos. Is it surprising that he started his own construction company as an adult?

Bill started getting paid for his construction efforts while he was a sixteen year old high school student. His mom, who sold homes for a large builder, helped him obtain his first job. While still in high school, Bill was able to learn a great deal about building homes. He learned how to frame a house, how to install and finish dry wall, and how to apply moldings. Although he was too young to do electrical and plumbing installations, he was able to observe licensed professionals while they did installations. Through these observations, as well as through casual discussions with professionals in the field, Bill was able to get a solid foundation on all aspects of building.

Watching site supervisors, who oversee each home's construction, provided Bill with a good overview of another side of the home construction business. Site supervisors need very good people skills. They oversee all the workers building the homes and interact with the customers.

Although Bill was a good high school student, he balanced his life by doing activities he enjoyed. He played the tuba in his high school band. After they both finished high school and college, he even married a fellow band member. After teaching himself to play the drums, he put together a garage band that he got together with weekly to play songs. Camping and fishing were other activities he enjoyed with both family and friends.

Bill enjoyed construction so much that he was a little conflicted about going to college. Finally, with the encouragement of friends and family, he decided he would have more job opportunities with a college education. While in college, Bill worked during vacations and summers in construction. This enabled him to keep his building skills up-to-date and helped him develop a wide network of sub-contractors including drywallers, brick layers, plumbers, and electricians.

Upon graduating from college with a degree in business, Bill received numerous job offers. He accepted a position as a site supervisor with a large builder. After spending a few years working as a site supervisor for various builders, Bill decided to start his own construction company.

As an independent business owner, Bill has learned a great deal. He deals with everything from securing bank financing, to hiring competent subcontractors, to keeping customers happy. With the recent recession, he's learned to be flexible in his business plans. Prior to the recession, he focused on new home construction. When the recession hit, fewer new homes were being built. Bill decided to focus his resources on renovations to existing homes. When the economy improves, Bill hopes to begin building new homes—including homes that have high energy efficiency.

Bill Kirtland
Owner, Kirtland Construction Inc.

CHAPTER 1

Learn About Work

"Work and play are words used to describe the same thing under differing conditions." —MARK TWAIN

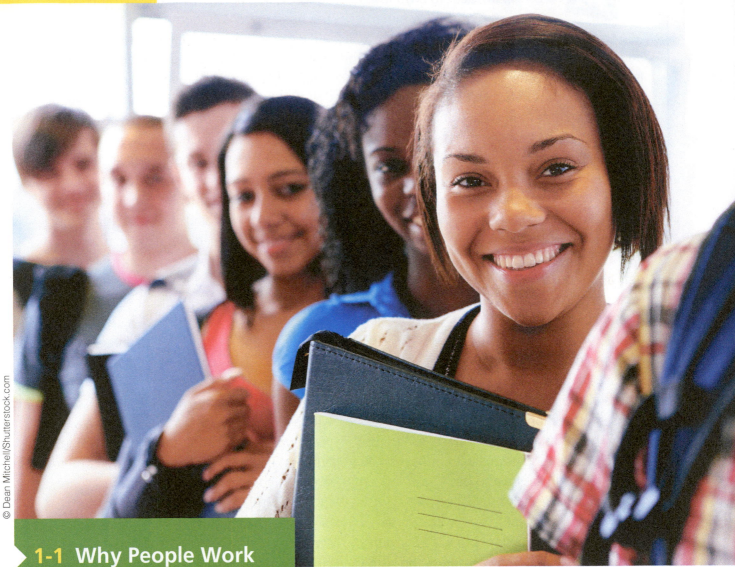

© Dean Mitchell/Shutterstock.com

PREVIEW

Most young people look forward to finishing school, leaving home, and starting out on their own. An important part of the transition from youth to young adult is getting a job. Working will enable you to establish your independence and define your own life. As a working person, you will find that other people will see and respond to you in new ways. This can be an exciting and enjoyable time of your life.

Taking/*Action* Research Occupations

The school guidance counselor gave Mel an interest inventory because Mel was uncertain which occupations would best suit him. The results suggested several occupations that Mel might like. These were electrician, aircraft mechanic, refrigeration mechanic, and tool and die maker.

These occupations do appeal to Mel, but he does not know very much about them. He wonders what workers in these occupations actually do. He has many other questions as well. What are the skills necessary to succeed in each of these occupations? If he doesn't have the skills, where could he get training? How much education or training would he need to get a good job? Do the occupations have a good outlook for the future? How much money do people in such occupations earn? Would he need to join a union?

To answer his questions, Mel needs to collect information about these occupations. Learning how to use resources on occupational information is an important part of career decision making. The school guidance counselor had a number of resources to help Mel answer these and other questions. After researching the occupations on his interest inventory, Mel has a much better idea of what it would be like to work in each of them.

Based on his research, Mel chooses the occupation of electrician. Mel has learned that job opportunities for skilled electricians are anticipated to be good and that the income he can expect to earn is more than he hoped.

After graduating from vocational school, he plans to take a job with a large company and complete an apprenticeship program. Perhaps one day he will have his own business.

THINK CRITICALLY

1. What questions do you have about occupations that you are considering?

2. What kind of information about these occupations would you need to make an informed decision?

© Artpose Adam Borkowski/Shutterstock.com

WHY PEOPLE WORK

OBJECTIVES
- Discuss reasons why people work
- Distinguish among the terms work, occupation, job, and career

KEY TERMS
- work
- occupation
- job
- career

© NinaMalyna/Shutterstock.com

Career Decisions

You have been working for about a year at a small nursery and garden center. You enjoy the informality, the variety of work, caring for plants, and being out-of-doors. You have learned about a job opening in the garden department of a large discount store. Your primary duties would be waiting on customers and operating the cash register. The job pays quite a bit more than you presently earn, but you do not think you would enjoy the new job as much as your present one. You cannot decide whether to give up a satisfying job for the opportunity to make more money.

*What would **you** do?*

Reasons to Work

People's views about work vary greatly. It would be untrue to say that all people value and enjoy their work. For most Americans, though, work is an important part of a well-rounded life. They generally like what they do. Many studies have shown that most people would work even if they didn't have to. This view of work is not limited to adults. The interest of young people in learning about and preparing for work has never been greater. People work for many different reasons. The reasons vary from person to person. The most common reasons for working follow.

Earn Money

The major reason why people work is to earn money. Earnings are needed to buy food, shelter, clothing, and other necessities. Beyond meeting basic needs, money is used to purchase goods and services that provide comfort, enjoyment, and security.

Social Satisfaction

People are social creatures. Working gives people a chance to be with others and to make friends. In the work environment, people can give and receive understanding and acceptance.

Positive Feelings

People get satisfaction from their work. For instance, your work may give you a sense of accomplishment. Think of how you feel when you finish a school project or a difficult job task. Working also gives people a feeling of self worth. Often, the feeling comes from knowing that other people will pay you for your skills.

Prestige

Some people work because of the prestige or status they enjoy. *Prestige* is the admiration of society. Some occupations have more prestige than others. What occupations do you consider to have prestige?

Personal Development

Many people have a drive to improve themselves. Work can provide an opportunity to learn and grow. Work can often be a great teacher.

Contributions to Health

Work can be very important for mental and physical health. This results from the work itself as well as the physical activity involved. People who are active and happy in their work tend to feel better.

Self-expression

You have interests, abilities, and talents. Work can be a way in which you express yourself. It does not matter what kind of work it is as long as it suits the worker and is not illegal or immoral.

In addition to the financial benefits of working, many people enjoy their work.

Work, Occupation, Job, and Career

People often use the terms *work, occupation, job,* and *career* interchangeably. They do have a number of similarities. In this book, however, the terms will be used in different ways.

Work

Work can be defined as activity directed toward a purpose or goal that produces something of value to oneself and/or to society. For instance, work can provide you with money and a sense of accomplishment. Work by a teacher or nurse provides benefits to society. Another characteristic of work is that it may be paid or unpaid. If you volunteer at a local food bank or at a blood drive, it is still considered work, even though you are not paid for it.

Occupation

All occupations carry out work. An **occupation** is the name given to a group of similar tasks that a person performs for pay. For example, keyboarding, filing, maintaining records, placing phone calls, sending email, and scheduling meetings are tasks performed in the occupation of administrative assistant. Carpenter, salesclerk, attorney, truck driver, and chef

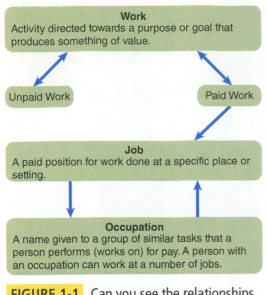

Work
Activity directed towards a purpose or goal that produces something of value.

Unpaid Work

Paid Work

Job
A paid position for work done at a specific place or setting.

Occupation
A name given to a group of similar tasks that a person performs (works on) for pay. A person with an occupation can work at a number of jobs.

FIGURE 1-1 Can you see the relationships among work, job, and occupation?

are examples of common occupations that involve groups of similar tasks. Most occupations require specific knowledge and skills. Occupations are learned on the job or in various kinds of education and training programs. A person in an occupation can work at a number of different jobs.

Job

A **job** is a paid position at a specific place or setting. A job can be in an office, store, factory, farm, or mine. For example, a nurse can work at jobs in a doctor's office, clinic, hospital, home, school, factory, or nursing home. The relationships among work, occupation, and job are illustrated in Figure 1-1.

The typical relationship between occupation and job is that an occupation is acquired first. That is, an occupation is learned through education and training, after which a job is secured. Some jobs require no previous training. When these types of jobs are obtained, occupational training may follow.

Many employers offer some training for entry-level jobs, as well as more training with new equipment or new technologies. Ongoing training will help you keep your skills sharp and help you acquire new skills, making you a more valuable employee.

Most people change jobs a number of times throughout their lives. For instance, Lionel, an administrative assistant, might leave a job at State Insurance to work at Merchants Bank. Later, he might leave Merchants Bank to work as an administrative assistant at Mercy Hospital.

Sometimes, people change both occupations and jobs. An example would be if Lionel leaves his administrative assistant position at Mercy Hospital to become an office manager for Suburban Realty Company.

Communication at Work

INTERPERSONAL RELATIONS

In any workplace, you will find it easy to get along with some coworkers and difficult to get along with others. The following tips will help you work better with many different kinds of people.

Try to communicate clearly. Many disagreements can be avoided by clearly communicating what you have to say and then taking the time to make sure the other person understands.

Try to communicate politely. If you are polite to coworkers, they are more likely to treat you politely in return. Being polite fosters an atmosphere of cooperation.

Try to understand your coworker's point of view. Have you ever snapped at someone even though he or she didn't deserve it? Remember this if a coworker ever snaps at you for no apparent reason. Don't take it personally. Try to understand.

THINK CRITICALLY

1. Give an example of each of the three tips.
2. Which tip do you think offers the best advice? Explain your answer.

During a career, occupations and jobs may change.

Career

A **career** is the combination of all the occupations and jobs held throughout your work life. Kareem began teaching in high school immediately after finishing college. He took evening courses at a nearby university earning a graduate degree, which led to his becoming a school principal. Later, he moved up the career ladder to become an Assistant School Superintendent. A number of years later he moved to another state and took a job as Superintendent of a large, urban school district where he later retired. Kareem spent his entire career in the field of education.

Some people have multiple careers or mixed careers. And some people who have a variety of occupations and jobs in many different fields cannot be said to have a career, but only a work history. At this stage of your life, it may be hard to predict what your entire career will involve. But, you can begin to plan for a career in a field of interest.

Spend some time researching possible occupations and the jobs within each occupation. Suppose you are interested in an occupation in health services. After researching health services occupations, you realize that you don't like the job opportunities or don't want to complete the necessary training. Knowing what you don't like helps you rule health services out as a possible career field. Now you can spend time researching other occupations that are of interest to you.

1-1 Assessment

1. Name two reasons why people work.

2. Name two positive feelings that you can get from working.

3. Explain the difference between an occupation and a job.

4. Have you ever done volunteer work? If so, which of the specific reason(s) discussed earlier explained your reasons for volunteering?

High Growth Occupations
FOR THE 21ST CENTURY

Dental Assistants and Dental Hygienists

 Dentists require a team of workers to help them carry out their important job. Two of these occupations are dental assistant and dental hygienist. Both occupations are expected to grow faster than average due to demand for dental services and a growing emphasis on preventative dental care.

Dental assistants work closely with, and under the supervision of, dentists. Assistants make patients comfortable in the dental chair and prepare them for treatment. Dental assistants sterilize and disinfect instruments and equipment and prepare and lay out the instruments and materials required to treat each patient. During dental procedures, they hand instruments and materials to dentists and keep patients' mouths dry and clear by using suction hoses or other devices. They also instruct patients on what to do following a procedure and provide general information on oral healthcare.

In addition to dental assistants, a large dentist office might employ one or more full-time *dental hygienists*. Often, however, a dental hygienist may work for several dentists and at different locations. Hygienists work closely with dentists, but they generally perform their duties independent of the dentist.

The primary task of a dental hygienist is to clean and polish teeth. They use a variety of hand and rotary instruments to remove deposits from teeth. Hygienists use x-ray machines to take dental pictures. They also teach patients how to practice good oral hygiene.

Dental hygienists must be licensed by the state in which they practice. Nearly all states require candidates to graduate from an accredited dental hygiene school and pass both a written and clinical examination. Most dental hygiene programs grant an associate degree, although some also offer a certificate, a bachelor's degree, or a master's degree.

In contrast, dental assistants often learn their skills on the job. In most states, there are no formal education or training requirements to become an entry-level dental assistant. But, many dentists prefer to hire assistants trained in dental-assisting programs offered by community colleges, trade schools, technical institutes, or the Armed Forces. Most programs take one year to complete.

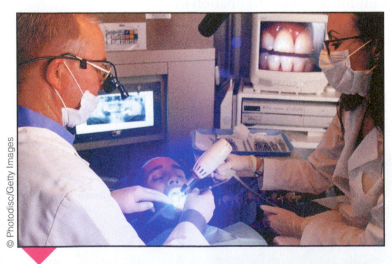
© Photodisc/Getty Images

Dentists rely on dental assistants to help with dental procedures.

GET SELF-INFORMATION

OBJECTIVES

- Discuss how self-information can help you make more satisfying occupational decisions
- Describe the three types of self-information and how they are measured

KEY TERMS

- self
- self-information
- interest
- aptitude
- work value

Career Decisions

In going over the results of a work values measure with your counselor, you learn that your highest-rated values are financial success, independence, and prestige. It is true. You would like to be wealthy and independent and have people look up to you.

"Big deal," you think. "Now all I have to do is go out and find someone who will give me an important job and pay me a lot of money. That is a joke. Work values measures are a waste of time. I will probably end up working in the mines like the rest of my family."

What would you do?

© RiverRockPhotos/iStockphoto.com

Learning About Your Self

If you are in your teens, you can look forward to 40 or more years of working. That is a long time—especially if you work at an occupation that you dislike. Wouldn't you rather have an occupation that you enjoy doing, that you are good at, and that involves work that is important to you? This lesson will show you how to gather information about your self that can help you make a satisfying occupational decision.

Before you select an occupation, you should first answer the question, "Who am I?" This means that you should learn more about your *self*. Your **self** includes your physical characteristics, your behavior, how you think, and your belief systems. Self is the sum of everything you are including the unique combination of qualities that define you. Knowledge about your self is **self-information**. This information can help you make a more satisfying occupational decision.

Your **interests** are activities and ideas you enjoy exploring. **Aptitudes** are what you are good at doing. Your **work values** reflect what is important to you about the work you do. Exploring these components of self-information will help you make better choices about your career.

Types of Self-information

When making an occupational decision, you should have information about your interests, aptitudes, and work values.

Interests

You make choices based on your likes and dislikes. You choose different types of food, music, clothes, hobbies, and so on because you enjoy one thing more than another. For instance, if you enjoy Chinese food, you may choose to go to Chinese restaurants when eating out. If you dislike Greek food, you probably won't go to many Greek restaurants.

Floral designers are likely to have creativity as a work value.

William, for instance, enjoys hunting, fishing, camping, and hiking. His interests relate to outdoor activities.

Your interests can lead to occupations that might suit you. William likes outdoor activities. This suggests that he might do well in occupations such as forester, game warden, or recreation worker.

Debbie likes working with electronic media. On her tablet computer she enjoys reading newspapers and streaming video. On her laptop computer she enjoys creating computer graphics and designing web pages. Debbie is also experimenting with an app that will play music. Which occupations would allow Debbie to use and expand her computer skills?

By thinking about your likes and dislikes, you are taking the first step toward learning about your self. Do you prefer indoor or outdoor activities? Would you rather work alone or with people? Do you like to work with tools and machines or data and figures? Do you enjoy music or art?

School courses and activities can offer clues to occupations that might be of interest. What school subjects do you like best? Think about school activities, such as clubs, plays, concerts, and fundraising events. Don't forget about hobbies. What do activities and hobbies reveal about your interests?

Vera, for example, belongs to the Journalism Club and works on the yearbook and school newspaper. English has always been her favorite subject. All Vera's interests point in the direction of a career in the communications field.

In addition to thinking about your interests, you might want to complete an occupational interest inventory. Your teacher or career counselor can introduce you to many different types of interest inventories. These inventories consist of dozens of statements describing various work activities. "Plan, budget, and keep records" or "Solve technical problems" are examples of typical statements in the interest surveys. The activities may be listed randomly throughout the inventory or similar activities may be grouped together. Figure 1-2 on the next page provides a sample of a portion of an interest survey. To complete this inventory, place a checkmark in front of those work activities that you think you like or might like to do. Some inventories list work activities followed by a scale which asks whether you "like," "dislike," or are "not sure" about the activity.

An interest inventory is not a test. There are no right or wrong answers. However, responses to the items need to be carefully interpreted.

The goal of all interest inventories is to provide you with information to help you explore occupations. Look at Figure 1-2. If you took the survey and indicated you liked all or nearly all of the seven activities listed, occupations contained within the Leisure and Hospitality industries would be a good fit to match your interests. You could then investigate occupations in the Leisure and Hospitality industries using print and online occupational information.

The results of an interest inventory do not mean that the occupations suggested are the only ones for you. They simply represent alternatives that you should investigate. Learn more about these occupations and others as well. Also learn more about your self. Don't base your occupational choice solely on the results of an interest inventory.

FIGURE 1-2 Sample Interest Survey Questions

Activities that describe what I like to do:

- Use tact and kindness when interacting with people
- Work at times that are convenient to me
- Learn about ways of life in other countries
- Arrange fun activities for groups of people
- Travel on buses, trains, or airplanes
- Help people get to know each other
- Provide people with information about interesting activities

Aptitudes

Are there occupations in which you are interested, but you wonder if you would do well in them? Karen thinks that she might like to be an architect. She isn't sure if she has the ability to become one. She needs to look at her aptitudes. An aptitude may be a natural talent or a developed ability. When you are good at doing something, you have an aptitude for it.

Karen can get some idea about her aptitudes by looking at her grades. She has taken algebra and geometry and has done well in both. Architects need math ability. Her art teacher has said that Karen has a talent for designing and illustrating. Karen thinks about the two mechanical drawing courses she took. She got an A in both. Overall, it seems that Karen might do well in her occupation of interest.

Aptitude tests can help you find out if you are suited for a certain occupation. These tests measure how well you might do in a certain field. The six most common aptitudes covered by such tests are as follows:

- Verbal aptitude—using words well
- Numerical aptitude—doing math quickly and accurately
- Clerical speed and accuracy—picking out letters or words quickly and arranging number and letter combinations in order
- Manual dexterity—moving the hands easily and skillfully
- Mechanical reasoning—understanding mechanical principles, how things work, and how tools are used
- Spatial visualization—forming mental pictures of the shape, size, and position of objects

The types of questions included in an aptitude test vary widely depending on the aptitude being measured. Several different examples are shown in Figure 1-3 on the next page. Each question has only one correct answer.

1. Which two words have the same meaning?
   (a) open   (b) happy   (c) glad   (d) green

2. Which two words have the opposite meaning?
   (a) old   (b) dry   (c) cold   (d) young

3. Add (+) the two numbers below and then select the correct answer (a, b, c, or d).
   766   (a) 677   (c) 777
   11   (b) 755   (d) 6561

4. Julie works 8 hours a day, 40 hours a week. She earns $8.40 an hour. How much does she earn each week?
   (a) $240.00   (c) $303.60
   (b) $267.60   (d) $336.00

5. At the left is a drawing of a flat piece of metal. Which object at the right can be made from this piece of metal?

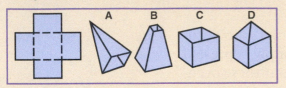

Which pairs of names are the same (S) and which are different (D)?

6. W. W. Jason . . . W. W. Jason
7. Johnson & Johnson . . . Johnson & Johnsen
8. Harold Jones Co. . . . . Harold Jones and Co.

For questions 9 through 12, find the lettered figure that is exactly like the numbered figure.

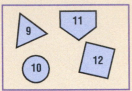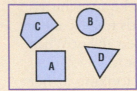

FIGURE 1-3 Sample Aptitude Test Questions

Source: "Doing Your Best on Aptitude Tests," GPO

A separate score is given for each aptitude that is being tested. The scores are often reported as percentile ranks. For example, Joe received a percentile rank of 85 on mechanical reasoning. This means that Joe scored better than 85 percent of the people who took the test.

Your teacher or counselor will help you interpret your aptitude test results. After you speak with him or her, the rest will be up to you.

Work Values

Values are attitudes and beliefs about things you think are important in life. For instance, Americans believe strongly in the right of free speech. This is a basic democratic value.

Values that relate to work and career are called work values. These are feelings about the importance or worth of an activity or occupation. Suppose you would like to have an occupation in which you could help other people. Helping others would be a work value for you. You would want this value to be part of or expressed by the work you do.

Work values can be thought of as needs you try to meet in your work. For example, Fredrico gave up a good job with a large insurance company to start his own business. He did so because he wanted to make his own decisions. For Fredrico, the need for independence was not being met in his former job. Following are examples of work values.

- Altruism—helping other people
- Creativity—inventing things, designing products, or developing new ideas
- Achievement—having feelings of accomplishment from doing a job well
- Independence—being able to work in your own way
- Prestige—wanting to be admired
- Financial success—earning enough to buy the things you want
- Security—having a steady job even in hard times
- Surroundings—being in a pleasant work environment
- Variety—having the opportunity to do many types of tasks

You can identify your work values by taking a work values inventory. Sample items in a work values inventory are shown in Figure 1-4 on the next page. The work value "Independence" is reflected in statements 1, 3, and 5. The work value "Security" is reflected in statements 2, 4, and 6.

The ratings are interpreted by adding the results. Based on three statements, scores can range from a low of 3 to a high of 9. The higher the number, the more important the work value is to you. Rating a number of statements associated with various work values can give you a better understanding of what type of work is important to you.

Unlike interest inventories and aptitude tests, the results of a work values inventory are not as easily related to specific occupations. Work values come from feelings that are more personal. Most occupations involve several work values. Work values scores are not as useful in helping to identify which occupations to explore. A work values inventory is better used to help you make a choice from among a small number of desirable occupational alternatives. Knowledge of work values can help you make final occupational choices that will lead to your future goals.

Work values tend to change more than interests and aptitudes. Things that are important to you at age 18 may not be the same things that you value at age 23. The values you hold when you are single may not be the same values you hold after you marry. Having children also changes your values.

Earl took a work values inventory. The results suggested that altruism, security, and surroundings are important to him. These results tend to confirm his interest in becoming a technology education teacher.

Norma found out that creativity and variety are the most important values for her. She is leaning toward becoming either a floral designer or an interior designer.

FIGURE 1-4 Sample Work Values Inventories Items

Read each statement and decide how important it is in choosing the type of work you would like to do. Rate the statements as follows:

3 = Very important   2 = Important   1 = Unimportant

1. Planning your own activities. _____
2. Not getting laid off. _____
3. Being your own boss. _____
4. Knowing your job is permanent. _____
5. Deciding things yourself. _____
6. Being able to count on having a job. _____

1-2 Assessment

1. What question should you ask yourself before choosing an occupation?

2. There are three types of self-information used in career decision making. Name them.

3. What can participation in school activities reveal about your self?

4. Why is it incorrect to call an interest inventory a test?

5. Without taking an aptitude test, how can you find out about your aptitudes?

6. If you are good at diagnosing and repairing auto engines, what two aptitudes do you have?

7. Name three suitable occupations for a person who values independence.

8. At what point in the career decision-making process is knowledge of work values important? Explain.

OBJECTIVES

- Explain how occupations and industries are grouped
- Describe trends in the growth of goods and service industries
- Describe employment trends in occupations

KEY TERMS

- world of work
- Standard Occupational Classification (SOC) system
- *Occupational Outlook Handbook (OOH)*
- North American Industry Classification System (NAICS)
- industry
- Bureau of Labor Statistics (BLS)
- service-providing industry
- goods-producing industry

© FuzzBones/Shutterstock.com

▶ Career Decisions

You know you would like to have a family and a stable job someday. You have given the choice of an occupation some thought. You have identified about a half-dozen or so occupations that appeal to you. But, you don't know very much about any of them. You wonder, for example, what are the typical earnings, how much education or training is required, and in what types of places can you find employment. It all seems so complicated. In discussing this with one of your friends, he said, "Don't worry about it, that's what I am doing."

What would you do?

Occupations and Industries

You may already have a good idea of what occupation you will pursue. Maybe you are interested in more than one occupation. Or you might have no idea of where to get occupational information. In this lesson, you will learn about occupations, how they are classified, and how you can use this information to conduct research on occupations that interest you.

By the year 2018, it is estimated that 154 million people will be employed in the United States workforce. People work in hundreds of different types of offices, stores, factories, mines, farms, and other workplaces. Workers are employed in thousands of different occupations. This network of occupations and workplaces is often called the **world of work**.

Because of the large number of occupations and industries, special grouping systems are used to make it easier to collect and publish information about the world of work. A *group* is a collection of two or more things that are alike in some way. For example, fruits, vegetables, and grains are groups of food. Groups are sometimes called categories, classifications, families, or clusters.

About a dozen different systems are used to classify information about the world of work. The two most important classification systems are occupational and industrial.

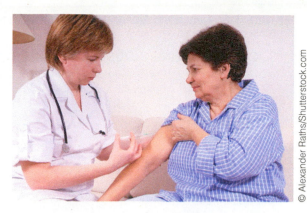

Service industry jobs, including health care, are projected to have a higher rate of growth than goods producing jobs through 2018.

Classifying Occupations

The Office of Management and Budget has developed a grouping system called the **Standard Occupational Classification (SOC) system**. The SOC classifies occupations based on the type of work performed. For instance, the Installation, Maintenance, and Repair group includes workers who maintain and repair various kinds of machines and equipment. These include motor vehicles, home appliances, communications equipment, electrical and electronic equipment, and related equipment and machines.

The SOC consists of the divisions shown in Figure 1-5. These divisions form the basis for the *Occupational Outlook Handbook (OOH)*. The *OOH* is a reference source produced by the federal government that provides occupational information and data. It is an excellent resource for occupational information.

Classifying Industries

Another important grouping system is the **North American Industry Classification System (NAICS)**. The NAICS system basically describes where people work. It is a grouping of different workplaces according to the type of product produced or service provided. The Manufacturing sector, for instance, includes industries that use machines or chemical processes to change materials or substances into new products.

In the NAICS, all places of employment are called **industries**. Hospitals, schools, grocery stores, restaurants, banks, and hundreds of other types of workplaces are industries. The NAICS is divided into two divisions and twenty industry sectors as shown in Figure 1-6 on the next page.

It is important to understand the SOC and NAICS systems. They are government systems for collecting and reporting information about occupations and industries.

Tomorrow's Jobs

The **Bureau of Labor Statistics (BLS)** is a federal agency that measures labor market activity and

FIGURE 1-5 Standard Occupational Classification System (SOC)

1. Management Occupations
2. Business and Financial Operations Occupations
3. Computer and Mathematical Occupations
4. Architecture and Engineering Occupations
5. Life, Physical, and Social Science Occupations
6. Community and Social Services Occupations
7. Legal Occupations
8. Education, Training, and Library Occupations
9. Arts, Design, Entertainment, Sports, and Media Occupations
10. Healthcare Practitioners and Technical Occupations
11. Healthcare Support Occupations
12. Protective Service Occupations
13. Food Preparation and Serving Related Occupations
14. Building and Grounds Cleaning and Maintenance Occupations
15. Personal Care and Service Occupations
16. Sales and Related Occupations
17. Office and Administrative Support Occupations
18. Farming, Fishing, and Forestry Occupations
19. Construction and Extraction Occupations
20. Installation, Maintenance, and Repair Occupations
21. Production Occupations
22. Transportation and Material Moving Occupations
23. Military Specific Occupations

FIGURE 1-6 New North American Classification System (NAICS)

GOODS-PRODUCING INDUSTRIES
1. Agriculture, Forestry, Fishing, and Hunting
2. Mining, Quarrying, and Oil and Gas Extraction
3. Utilities
4. Construction
5. Manufacturing

SERVICE-PROVIDING INDUSTRIES
6. Wholesale Trade
7. Retail Trade
8. Transportation and Warehousing
9. Information
10. Finance and Insurance
11. Real Estate and Rental and Leasing
12. Professional, Scientific, and Technical Services
13. Management of Companies and Enterprises
14. Administrative and Support and Waste Management and Remediation Services
15. Educational Services
16. Health Care and Social Assistance
17. Arts, Entertainment, and Recreation
18. Accommodation and Food Services
19. Other Services (except Public Administration)
20. Public Administration

working conditions. The BLS publishes a variety of reports including monthly analyses of employment levels and earnings.

To project future job trends, the BLS analyzes population patterns, economic and social change, and technology. By their nature, job projections are only educated guesses. However, such projections can help you know about future opportunities in industries and occupations of interest. You may not want to train for an occupation that will be in little demand.

Employment Trends in Industries

Since about 1960, employment in service-providing industries has been increasing at a faster rate than employment in goods-producing industries. **Service-providing industries** are those companies and businesses that produce or provide some type of personal or business service, such as health care, education, transportation, financial activities, and wholesale and retail trade. **Goods-producing industries** are those companies and businesses such as manufacturing, construction, and mining which produce some type of product. About eight of every ten jobs are in service industries, as are nearly all new jobs. And, this trend is expected to continue.

Rising incomes, higher living standards, and an aging population have helped contribute to the rapid growth of service industries. The result has been greater demand for health care, entertainment, and business and financial services. People with higher incomes may spend more heavily on eating out, personal fitness, recreation, and the like. The large group of "baby boomers" born between 1946 and 1964—about 76 million people—also are using more health services. In addition, the growth of cities and suburbs has brought a need for more local government services.

Through the year 2018, employment will increase faster in service-providing industries than in goods-producing ones. In fact, service-providing industries are expected to account for nearly all of the approximately 15 million new wage and salary jobs anticipated over the 2008–18 period.

Within industries, growth will vary widely, see Figure 1-7 on the next page. Note that a number of NAICS sectors have been combined. Growth will be the greatest in the Professional and Business Services and Health Care and Social Assistance Services sectors. These two sectors are expected to generate about 8.2 million jobs over the period, more than half the increase in total employment. In the goods-producing division, Construction is the only sector that is expected to grow.

Sandra is interested in a job in the Information sector. She was discouraged to read that jobs in this sector will only increase by about

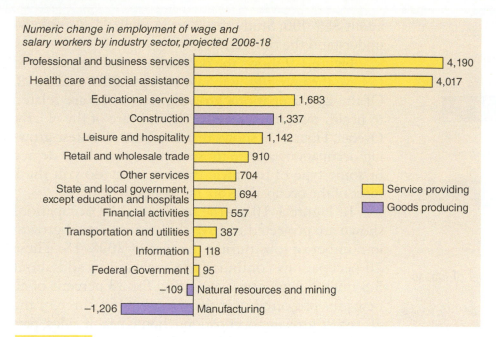

Numeric change in employment of wage and salary workers by industry sector, projected 2008-18

Industry sector	Value
Professional and business services	4,190
Health care and social assistance	4,017
Educational services	1,683
Construction	1,337
Leisure and hospitality	1,142
Retail and wholesale trade	910
Other services	704
State and local government, except education and hospitals	694
Financial activities	557
Transportation and utilities	387
Information	118
Federal Government	95
Natural resources and mining	−109
Manufacturing	−1,206

Service providing
Goods producing

FIGURE 1-7 Some industries will grow more rapidly than others.
Source: *Occupational Outlook Quarterly,* Winter 2009-10, Volume 53, Number 4

118,000 over the next decade. Upon further reading, however, she found out that the Information sector contains many of the fastest growing industries such as data processing, Web and applications hosting and streaming, Internet publishing and broadcasting, and other computer related industries. As the areas of growth overlap with Sandra's strongest interests, she is optimistic about obtaining a job within the information sector.

Employment Trends in Occupations

Future employment among occupational groups, like that within industries, will vary greatly. The fastest growth will be in professional and related occupations, which include computer, healthcare, and education occupations. Growth also will vary within a specific occupational group. Therefore, it may be better to examine the outlook for specific occupations than for various occupational divisions.

Information about projected trends is useful in several ways. It might, for instance, suggest to a person planning a career that he or she select an occupation for which employment is expected to grow. On the other hand, it might suggest to a worker in a declining occupation that he or she consider retraining for a different occupation.

For a complete picture of occupational trends, you will need to know two things. One is the rate of growth, or percentage increase, of an occupation. The other is the numerical increase of workers. The relationship between rate of growth and size of change for two occupations is shown in Figure 1-8 on the next page.

From the chart, you can see that between 2008 and 2018, the rate of growth for financial examiners will increase by 41 percent. Yet, the number of new jobs for financial examiners between 2008 and 2018 will only be about 11,000. On the other hand, the growth rate for general office clerks will increase about 12 percent. But the actual number of new jobs for general office clerks between 2008 and 2018 will be

Workforce Trends

Most job growth since 1960 has been in the service sector. One force driving this growth has been a shift in household tasks from busy household members to service workers. Family members do some tasks, other work is bought from third parties (day-care workers, housekeepers, takeout restaurants, accountants, and the like), and some is simply left undone.

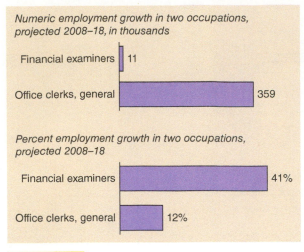

Numeric employment growth in two occupations, projected 2008–18, in thousands

Financial examiners 11

Office clerks, general 359

Percent employment growth in two occupations, projected 2008–18

Financial examiners 41%

Office clerks, general 12%

FIGURE 1-8 Comparing total number of jobs to percent growth in jobs

Source: *Occupational Outlook Quarterly*, Winter 2009-10, Volume 53, Number 4

about 359,000. Study the chart in Figure 1-8 until you understand the difference.

Figure 1-9 shows the occupations that are projected to have the fastest growth rate between 2008 and 2018. Of the 20 occupations growing fastest, 13 are related to health care, medical research, and care of the elderly. Overall, Figure 1-9 shows that 17 of the 20 fastest-growing occupations will be those requiring a college degree or some type of technical training. Why do you think most of the occupations are in the health field?

In Figure 1-10 on the next page, the occupations shown are projected to have the greatest actual growth in number of jobs during the period 2008–18. These 20 occupations combined are expected to add about 5.8 million new jobs, accounting for 38 percent of all new jobs projected over the decade. Only three of the 20 fastest-growing occupations (home health aides, personal and home care aides, and computer software applications engineers) also are projected to be among the 20 occupations with the largest numerical increases in employment. This illustrates why

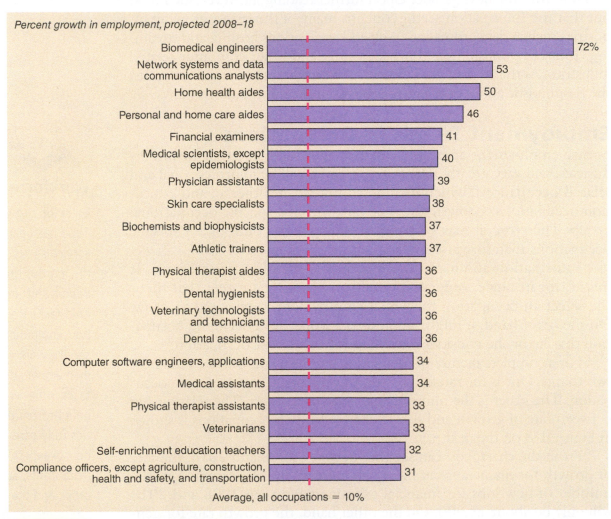

Percent growth in employment, projected 2008–18

Occupation	Percent
Biomedical engineers	72%
Network systems and data communications analysts	53
Home health aides	50
Personal and home care aides	46
Financial examiners	41
Medical scientists, except epidemiologists	40
Physician assistants	39
Skin care specialists	38
Biochemists and biophysicists	37
Athletic trainers	37
Physical therapist aides	36
Dental hygienists	36
Veterinary technologists and technicians	36
Dental assistants	36
Computer software engineers, applications	34
Medical assistants	34
Physical therapist assistants	33
Veterinarians	33
Self-enrichment education teachers	32
Compliance officers, except agriculture, construction, health and safety, and transportation	31

Average, all occupations = 10%

FIGURE 1-9 Fastest Growing Occupations

Source: *Occupational Outlook Quarterly*, Winter 2009-10, Volume 53, Number 4

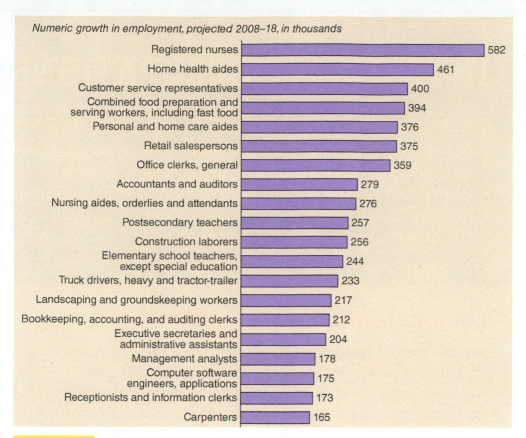

Numeric growth in employment, projected 2008–18, in thousands

Occupation	Value
Registered nurses	582
Home health aides	461
Customer service representatives	400
Combined food preparation and serving workers, including fast food	394
Personal and home care aides	376
Retail salespersons	375
Office clerks, general	359
Accountants and auditors	279
Nursing aides, orderlies and attendants	276
Postsecondary teachers	257
Construction laborers	256
Elementary school teachers, except special education	244
Truck drivers, heavy and tractor-trailer	233
Landscaping and groundskeeping workers	217
Bookkeeping, accounting, and auditing clerks	212
Executive secretaries and administrative assistants	204
Management analysts	178
Computer software engineers, applications	175
Receptionists and information clerks	173
Carpenters	165

FIGURE 1-10 Most New Jobs

Source: *Occupational Outlook Quarterly*, Winter 2009-10, Volume 53, Number 4

it is important for you to understand the relationship between "percent growth in employment" and "numeric growth in employment."

Another interesting fact shown in Figure 1-10 is that about 70 percent of the occupations projected to have the greatest job growth require only on-the-job or short-term vocational training. This contrasts sharply with the occupations shown in Figure 1-9, which mostly require a college or technical degree.

1-3 Assessment

1. Why are classification systems used to organize information about work?

2. In the SOC system, how are occupations grouped? In the NAICS system, how are industries grouped?

3. What types of industries are projected to grow the fastest? Explain why.

4. Study Figure 1-8. How many more projected job openings will be available for general office clerks than financial examiners?

5. How can projections about future occupational trends help people in making occupational decisions?

6. To understand future occupational trends, you must know two types of information. Name them.

OBJECTIVES

- Use the *Occupational Outlook Handbook* to conduct an occupational search
- Use O*NET to supplement information
- Explain Career Clusters
- List other sources of career information

KEY TERMS

- occupational search
- occupational description

© telesniuk/Shutterstock.com

Personal Decisions

You have identified three occupations that you want to investigate. You get an *Occupational Outlook Handbook* and look up the first occupation. You copy down important facts and data for later study. You follow the same procedure for the second occupation. For the third occupation, however, no information is available in the *OOH*.

What would you do?

Using the *OOH*

With the information you now have about your self and employment trends, you are ready to start an **occupational search**. You will collect information about an occupation of interest using one or more printed resources or databases. There are many helpful resources. One of the best and easiest to use is the *Occupational Outlook Handbook (OOH)*.

The *OOH* is available in guidance offices and public libraries nationwide. It is found on the Web at www.bls.gov/oco/. The *OOH* is revised every two years, so the information is up-to-date. The *OOH* lists occupations in fields that are growing. Most require some education or training beyond high school. Employment in the more than 250 occupations in the *OOH* accounts for about 90 percent of jobs in the economy.

An **occupational description** tells you what the work in an occupation is like—the tasks involved, the working conditions, the earnings, and so on. The *OOH* descriptions are organized into eight categories.

1. Significant Points
2. Nature of Work
3. Training, Other Qualifications, and Advancement
4. Employment
5. Job Outlook
6. Earnings
7. Related Occupations
8. Sources of Additional Information

OCCUPATIONAL SEARCH FORM

TITLE OF THE OCCUPATION _____

SIGNIFICANT POINTS _____

_____

_____

NATURE OF THE WORK

List five major tasks that workers in this occupation perform.

1. _____

   _____

2. _____

   _____

3. _____

   _____

4. _____

   _____

5. _____

   _____

TRAINING, OTHER QUALIFICATIONS, AND ADVANCEMENT

What is the preferred or required level of education or training?

_____

List any licensure or certification requirements. _____

List any special abilities or qualifications recommended or required. _____

What opportunities are there for advancement? _____

EMPLOYMENT

Number of jobs in the occupation _____ Year provided _____ In what types of industries or locations do people in this occupation work? _____

JOB OUTLOOK

Check the statement in each column below that best describes the future outlook for this occupation.

Change in Employment	Opportunities and Competition
____ Faster than average growth	____ Very good to excellent opportunities
____ Average growth	____ Good opportunities
____ Slower than average growth	____ May face competition
____ Little change	____ Keen competition
____ Decline	

EARNINGS

Write down the average yearly starting salary, if available._____

Range of average yearly earnings _____ Year provided _____

RELATED OCCUPATIONS

List the titles of related occupations.

1._____   5._____

2._____   6._____

3._____   7._____

4._____   8._____

SOURCES OF ADDITIONAL INFORMATION

List names and addresses of places where further information may be obtained.

_____

_____

_____

_____

_____

_____

Source of information: *Occupational Outlook Handbook* 20___/20___ Edition, pages _____

FIGURE 1-11 This form allows you to summarize information from the eight parts of the typical *OOH* occupational description.

FIGURE 1-12 Using a checklist can help you evaluate alternatives.

**CHECKLIST FOR EVALUATING POSSIBLE
OCCUPATIONAL ALTERNATIVES**

Name of occupation _____

	Yes	No	Not Sure
1. The work involved in this occupation is the type of work I'd like to do.			
2. I believe I have the ability to do well in this occupation.			
3. This occupation involves doing work that is important to me.			
4. The typical working conditions for this occupation are acceptable to me.			
5. I'm willing to complete the necessary education or training requirements to qualify for this occupation.			
6. I have the educational background to be admitted to any required education or training program.			
7. The future employment outlook for this occupation is good.			
8. I would be satisfied with the amount of earnings that is typical for this occupation.			
9. There are other related occupations in which I could work after learning this occupation.			
10. I believe I have enough information about this occupation to make a decision.			

On a scale of 1 (low) to 10 (high), I'd give this occupation a final ranking of _____

Assume you have identified a short list of occupations that might suit you. You are now ready to do an occupational search to learn more about each of your choices. In doing a search, you will find it helpful to use a form like the one shown in Figure 1-11 on the previous page. That way you can organize information from each of the occupational descriptions. You can download a copy of this form at www.cengage.com/school/working.

Get a copy of the most recent edition of the *OOH* or go to the *OOH* website. At the top of the form, write the name of the occupation that interests you. If you are using the print *OOH*, turn to the Index of occupations near the end. This will give you page numbers for where your chosen occupation is discussed. In the online *OOH*, you can find the occupation through the search feature or the A–Z Index. If you do not get good results in searching for the singular form of an occupation (for example, cabinetmaker), search for the plural form (cabinetmakers).

As you read the occupational description, fill out your downloaded search form. Feel free to make notes on the form or add other information that you think is important. Repeat this process for as many occupations as you want to research. After you have finished collecting information, compare and evaluate it. For help in doing this, refer to Figure 1-12, which can be downloaded at www.cengage.com/school/working.

O*Net OnLine

The Occupational Information Network (O*NET) is a system used by state employment service officers to classify applicants and job openings. It is also used by career information centers and libraries to access occupational information. O*NET can be used separately or in addition to the *OOH*. If you use the Internet version of the *OOH*, you will discover that at the end of each occupational description there are links to O*NET information related to the particular occupation.

You can use O*NET to search for occupations that match your skills, or you may search by keyword or O*NET code. For Loan Officers the code is 13-2072.00. The code for a Carpenter is 47-2031.00. For a Registered Nurse, the code is 29-1111.00. You can search for information using either the occupation name or the code for the occupation.

For each occupation, O*NET reports information about different aspects of the job, including tasks performed, knowledge, skills, abilities, and work activities. It also lists interests, work styles, such as independence, and work values, such as achievement, that are well suited to the occupation. O*NET ranks and scores the descriptors in each category by their importance to the occupation.

If all of this suggests that O*NET is slightly more difficult to use than the *OOH*, it is true. This should not discourage you from learning to use it. You might begin by going to the O*NET website and conducting a simple search. Using the Occupational Search feature, type in the name of an occupation of interest and click the search arrow. If you wish, print out the information displayed for future reference.

Career Clusters

An additional source of career information is the National Career Clusters Framework developed by the U.S. Department of Education to help students transition from school to work. Career Clusters group occupations based on knowledge and skills that are the same among the occupations.

There are sixteen career clusters which incorporate the occupations identified by O*NET. The clusters are shown in Figure 1-13.

There are multiple Career Pathways within each Career Cluster. A Pathway lists occupations that require a common set of knowledge and skills. For example, pathways within the Architecture & Construction cluster are Design/Pre-Construction, Construction, and Maintenance/Operations.

Other Sources of Career Information

Many organizations produce resources for occupational exploration and decision making. Your teacher or career counselor may introduce you to such materials, or you may find them on your own. The section on "Sources of Career Information" in the online *OOH* is a good place to start.

The greatest change in the use of occupational information is the development of electronic databases available on CD-ROM and the Internet. Many high schools, community and junior colleges, career centers, and state offices have access to such resources. Most of you have used or will be using a computer or other electronic tool at some point in your decision making.

It does not matter whether you use a book or a computer to find occupational information. The important thing is that you find it. A thorough occupational search will open up many possible choices to you. From these, you can make your decision. Good decisions, like the one you are trying to make, result from using complete, up-to-date information.

Search the Net

Access **www.cengage.com/school/working** and click on the link for Chapter 1. You will be directed to O*NET OnLine, the U.S. Department of Labor's database of occupational information. In Find Occupations, choose a category that interests you. Read the descriptions for three jobs in that category. Write a paragraph about one of the three jobs. Describe what you like about the job and why you think you could be successful in it.

www.cengage.com/school/working

FIGURE 1-13 Career Clusters

- Agriculture, Food & Natural Resources
- Architecture & Construction
- Arts, A/V Technology & Communications
- Business Management & Administration
- Education & Training
- Finance
- Government & Public Administration
- Health Sciences
- Hospitality & Tourism
- Human Services
- Information Technology
- Law, Public Safety, Corrections & Security
- Manufacturing
- Marketing
- Science, Technology, Engineering & Mathematics
- Transportation, Distribution & Logistics

Workplace Innovations

MANUFACTURING: 3D PRINTING

Manufacturing machines are used to shape metals and other raw materials into various component parts. The parts are assembled by workers on a production line to produce a completed object. Today, some manufacturers are using a technology called 3D printing to produce objects.

The 3D printing process works similar to an ink-jet printer. The image of an existing object is scanned into a computer. Or, for a new object, special design software is used to create a three-dimensional model. The computer sends instructions to a specially designed printer which sprays a very thin layer of plastic, metal, or other material to begin creating the object. Layer after layer of material is sprayed until the object is completed.

Much 3D printing is used for automobile and aircraft parts as well as common consumer products like jewelry, furniture, lampshades, and mobile phone cases. The product produced is limited by the material required and the size of the printer. Several companies are working on large printers that fit on a tractor-trailer and squirt out layers of special concrete to build walls. One of the most amazing applications is the use of human cells and tissue to produce body parts such as a human ear or a functioning kidney.

NET FOLLOW-UP

Use a search engine to explore the Web for additional information on the topic of "3D printing" or "additive manufacturing." Present your results.

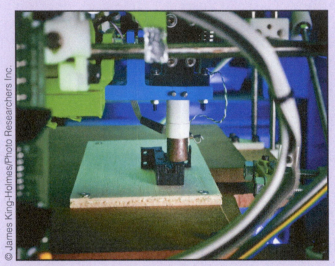

© James King-Holmes/Photo Researchers Inc.

New technology enables producing products without assembling component parts.

1-4 Assessment

1. Why is it useful to know how to use the *OOH*?

2. Each *OOH* occupational description contains eight types of information. If you want to know how many people work in a certain occupation, where would you look?

3. Are links to O*NET contained in the print version of the *OOH*, the online version of the *OOH*, or both?

4. What has been the greatest change in the use of occupational information?

5. What are the three Pathways for the Architecture and Construction Career Cluster?

Focus on the Workplace

The Changing Workplace

When this country was founded, most people lived and worked on small, family-owned farms. The farm family raised livestock, poultry, and grain.

As trading increased, small villages grew along rivers and other transportation routes. The growth of towns provided new jobs for shop owners, bankers, blacksmiths, and others. Agriculture, however, remained the base of the economy.

In the second half of the 1800s, industry in the United States expanded rapidly. Growing towns and cities needed more and more goods. Typical workers in the early 1900s had factory jobs. They produced steel, machinery, and other manufactured goods.

Growing industry and a growing population needed many kinds of business, transportation, communication, personal, and government services. In response to these demands, service industries began to expand. Typical service occupations included assistant, clerk, salesperson, and manager. In 2010, more than 80 percent of all workers were employed in services.

This service economy, however, is undergoing change. A new economy is evolving based on knowledge and information. Computers are the backbone of this information society. Influencing almost all industries and occupations, computers and related technologies provide new ways of dealing with information.

Computers have also introduced many new occupations into the workplace. These include laser nurse, computer animator, fiber-optics technician, app developer, and robotics repairer. "High-tech" industries will generate millions of new jobs into the next century. Many of you may work at some of these jobs.

THINK CRITICALLY

1. What do you think your family would have done for a living if you lived around the time of this country's founding?
2. How prepared are you for this "high-tech" workplace?

© Digital Vision/Getty Images

Computers and related technologies will continue to influence the workplace in the future.

Chapter Summary

1-1 Why People Work

A. For most people, work is an important part of a well-rounded life.

B. People work for many reasons, including money, social satisfaction, positive feelings, prestige, personal development, contributions to health, and self-expression.

C. The terms work, occupation, job, and career have different meanings. Work is activity directed toward a goal that produces something of value. It may be paid or unpaid. An occupation is the name given to a group of similar tasks that a person performs for pay. A job is a paid position at a specific place or setting. A career is the combination of all the occupations and jobs held throughout your work life.

1-2 Get Self-Information

A. Self-information can help you make a more satisfying occupational decision. When making an occupational decision, you should have information about your interests, aptitudes, and work values.

B. You can identify your interests by thinking about your likes and dislikes or by taking an interest inventory.

C. An aptitude is a natural talent or a developed ability. When you are good at doing something, you have an aptitude for it.

D. Work values are your feelings about the importance or worth of an activity or occupation. You can identify your work values by taking a work values inventory. Work values can help you make a final choice from among a number of desirable occupational alternatives.

1-3 Understand Industries and Occupations

A. The network of occupations and industries is the world of work. Grouping systems are used to organize information about the world of work. Two important grouping systems are the Standard Occupational Classification (SOC) and the North American Industry Classification System (NAICS).

B. The SOC classifies occupations according to the type of work performed. The SOC divisions are used as the basis for the *Occupational Outlook Handbook*. The NAICS describes where people work. In the NAICS system, all places of employment are called industries.

C. About eighty percent of jobs are in service industries. Through the year 2018, employment is expected to increase faster in service-providing industries than in goods-producing ones.

D. Both rate of growth and numerical increase of workers contribute to occupational trends. The fastest-growing occupations are healthcare, medical research, and care of the elderly. Occupations having the greatest increase in number of jobs include registered nurses, home health aides, and customer service representatives.

1-4 Investigate Occupations

A. The *Occupational Outlook Handbook* is an important resource. The *OOH* contains detailed occupational descriptions for about 300 occupations.

B. An occupational search is used to collect information about an occupation of interest using a variety of resources.

C. The Occupational Information Network (O*NET) is an electronic system used by state employment service officers to classify applicants and job openings. It is also used by career information centers and libraries to access occupational information. The O*NET can be used separately or as a supplement to the *OOH*.

D. Career Clusters and Pathways group occupations based on knowledge and skills that are the same among the occupations.

Activities

1. Ask your guidance counselor if you have taken any type of interest, aptitude, or work values inventory or test. If you have, ask the counselor to interpret the results for you.

2. Make lists of your interests, aptitudes, and work values. Explain how these lists can help you create a useful life-span plan.

3. Use an *OOH* and copies of Figure 1-11 to conduct an occupational search. Summarize your results to share with the class.

4. Ask your teacher or counselor to help identify a person who works in your occupation of interest that you can interview. Try to arrange to visit his or her place of employment. Before the interview, work with classmates to develop an interview form. After the interview, report to the class on what you have learned. Discuss whether the interview confirmed or changed your interest in the occupation.

5. O*NET has an online site called "My Next Move" that includes an occupational interest survey. The survey contains 60 questions similar to those shown in Figure 1-2. Complete the survey by locating the survey at the O*NET homepage and following the instructions. The survey results will show how you score in relation to six interest areas: Realistic, Investigative, Artistic, Social, Enterprising, and Conventional. Your teacher will explain how these interest areas relate to the 16 Career Clusters.

6. Invite your school guidance counselor to class. Ask the counselor to describe and demonstrate any additional career information resources in your school's guidance office, library, or career center.

7. Explain how an understanding of employment trends in the United States can help you create a life-span plan that has goals you can reasonably expect to achieve.

Word Power

On a separate sheet of paper, match each definition with the correct term. All definitions will be used, and a definition will be used only once.

8. Information about a specific occupation that explains what the work is like—the tasks involved, the working conditions, the earnings, and so on

9. Name given to a group of similar tasks that a person performs for pay

10. A system of grouping occupations based on the type of work performed

11. The sum of everything you are, including physical characteristics, behavior, how you think, and many other things

12. A company or businesses, such as manufacturing, construction, mining, and agriculture, which produces some type of product

13. Activity directed toward a purpose or goal that produces something of value to oneself and/or to society

14. Something that you are good at doing; a natural talent or developed ability

15. A company or business that produces or provides some type of personal or business service, such as transportation, finance, insurance, and trade

16. An informal phrase used to describe the network of occupations and industries that exists within the American economic system

17. A federal agency that measures labor market activity and working conditions

18. A reference source produced by the federal government that provides occupational information and data

19. Knowledge about your self, particularly in relation to career decision-making

20. In the NAICS system, a place of employment, such as a factory or a hospital

21. Attitude or belief about the importance of various work activities

22. A system of grouping industries according to the type of product produced or service provided

23. The process of collecting information about an occupation of interest using one or more printed resources or databases

24. Something that you like to do

25. The sum of all the occupations and jobs held throughout one's work life

26. Paid position at a specific place or setting

a. aptitude
b. Bureau of Labor Statistics (BLS)
c. career
d. goods-producing industry
e. industry
f. interest
g. job
h. North American Industry Classification System (NAICS)
i. occupation
j. occupational description
k. *Occupational Outlook Handbook (OOH)*
l. occupational search
m. self
n. self-information
o. service-providing industry
p. Standard Occupational Classification (SOC) system
q. work
r. work value
s. world of work

Think Critically

27. How would your future plans be changed if you suddenly won or inherited a great deal of money? Would you go to college? Would you plan on working? What type of work would you do?

28. In what ways might your interests and abilities be expressed in work? Cite examples of both paid and unpaid work.

29. This chapter explained self-information in relation to occupational decision making. Discuss how self-information may also be used to help guide educational decision making.

30. As you mature, new interests develop and old ones are left behind. Think of examples of how your interests have changed from the time when you were younger. What does this suggest in terms of your occupational interests?

31. Self-information can help you identify occupations that you might wish to have. Discuss why it is important to investigate and explore these occupations prior to making a final decision.

32. If you are really interested in a particular occupation, how concerned should you be about its future job outlook?

33. To make a good occupational decision, you should consider several types of information including the nature of the work, working conditions, job outlook, earnings, and other relevant facts. However, there are very few perfect occupations. Most occupational decisions involve a compromise among various factors. Provide examples and discuss how occupational decision making involves compromise. Do these findings contradict one another? Can you draw any conclusions from them?

34. In what ways can you influence and shape the direction of your career?

35. How might knowledge and skills learned in the following school subjects be applied on the job: English, mathematics, science, social studies, and foreign language?

Career Transitions Connection

Determine Your Interests

Click on *Assess Your Career Interests*. Take the interest survey. After obtaining your results, see which careers are recommended for you. Do any of the recommendations appeal to you? Which Career Cluster are they in? What other jobs of interest are in the same cluster?

2

"Hard work spotlights the character of people: some turn up their sleeves, some turn up their noses, and some don't turn up at all." —SAM EWING

Career Decision Making

Andresr/iStockphoto.com

PREVIEW

You make many decisions every day. Some are more important than others. A simple five-step process can help you make better decisions. When you are making an important decision, be thorough and weigh all the information. Accept responsibility for what happens to you.

Taking/*Action* Make Decisions

During the past year, Terrance has worked part-time at a local clothing store as part of a cooperative career and technical education program. Because the store is rather small, Terrance has had the opportunity to do different kinds of work there. As a result, he has learned many new skills.

Of course, Terrance sells merchandise. He is adept at operating the cash register and rarely makes an error. Terrance also has become knowledgeable about the different kinds of clothes the store sells. When a customer asks for recommendations, he can always provide them. Terrance is also good at helping people make purchasing decisions. Quite a few customers prefer to deal with Terrance when they shop at the store.

Terrance prices merchandise as well as selling it. From time to time, he also helps with payroll records and tax reports. He has spent some time learning how to use the payroll system.

Terrance has even had the chance to prepare advertising. He has written copy for newspaper and radio ads as well as flyers. His window display for an Easter sales promotion brought many compliments from customers and coworkers. Terrance's most interesting experience to date was going with the store manager, Mrs. Enrico, on a buying trip to New York City.

Terrance has found that he likes his job very much. In fact, he would like to work in some area related to business after graduation. On the way back from the buying trip, Mrs. Enrico offered Terrance a full-time job after graduation. "You are one of the best workers I've ever had," she told him. "You have a promising future with our store."

Terrance had not intended to stay at the store. He had planned to go away to college. He cannot decide whether to accept the offer of a full-time job or go to college.

THINK CRITICALLY

1. What do you think Terrance should do?
2. How should Terrance go about making his decision?

OBJECTIVES
- List and summarize each step in the decision-making process
- Understand how to use the decision-making process in making an occupational choice

KEY TERMS
- decision making
- alternative
- problem

Career Decisions

You are attending a two-year technical institute, majoring in automotive technology. After two semesters you decide to change your major to machine tool technology. The counselor says you can make the change, but you will have to take overload hours and attend an extra semester. You are anxious to finish school and begin work. You cannot decide whether the additional time and effort will be worthwhile.

*What would **you** do?*

A Five-Step Process

Decision making involves choosing between two or more **alternatives**, or options. Some people make no effort to identify the choices available to them. Choosing not to decide is also a choice. Most everyday decisions, such as "What shall I wear today?" are made without much thought. Decisions like the one facing Terrance are not as easy to make. He needs to follow a systematic decision-making process that will help him organize important information and make the decision that is best for him.

A simple five-step decision-making process is shown in Figure 2-1 on the next page. The same steps are followed whether you are making a decision about a career, choosing a college, or buying a used car. The more important the decision, the more time and effort should be devoted to it.

Define the Problem

The term **problem** here refers to a question in need of a solution. The decision-making process begins when you become aware of a problem and see the need to make a decision. Perhaps the problem is broad and long-range, such as "What are my goals in life?" Maybe it is an intermediate-range problem, such as "For what occupation do I want to prepare?" A problem like "How can I earn some money to pay for Saturday's date?" is an immediate one.

Terrance has partially solved the long-range problem of setting goals in life by determining that he would like to work in some area related to business after graduation. He still must solve the more immediate problem of whether to continue working at the clothing store. After making a choice, he may have to decide on future educational plans.

Gather Information

Once the problem is known, gather the necessary information. You cannot make a good decision without it. How do you know how much information is enough? You don't. The amount of information you gather and the time you spend gathering it should be related to the importance of the decision. The more important the decision, the more information is needed.

To help decide whether to continue working at the clothing store, Terrance made an appointment with Mrs. Enrico. He explained that he likes retail sales and his job at the clothing store. He also explained that he wants to go to college. Mrs. Enrico was very understanding and encouraging. She told Terrance what he could expect over the next several years in terms of responsibilities and salary at the store. She also gave Terrance the choice of working at the store part-time while he attends college.

Evaluate the Information

In this step, you organize the information you have gathered into categories. You then identify the pros and cons of each possible choice and eliminate any unacceptable choices. A rating scale or checklist may be of help as you do this.

After talking to Mrs. Enrico, Terrance wrote down his three choices.

1. Work full-time at the store and not go to college
2. Quit the job at the store and go away to college
3. Go to the nearby community college part-time and work at the store part-time

For each alternative, Terrance wrote down advantages and disadvantages. For instance, if he chose the first alternative, Terrance would have a full-time salary. He could probably buy the car he wants. On the other hand, he might want to change jobs someday. In that case, a degree would be a strong advantage. He also reviewed the alternatives with his parents to see if they could add any information.

Step 1: Define the Problem.
Become aware of a problem and see the need to make a decision.

Step 2: Gather Information.
Obtain information about the problem.

Step 3: Evaluate the Information.
Organize the information into categories. Identify the pros and cons of each possible choice. Eliminate any unacceptable choices.

Step 4: Make a Choice.
Select the alternative that leads to the most desirable result and has the highest possibility of success.

Step 5: Take Action.
Put your choice into action and commit yourself to making the decision work.

FIGURE 2-1 Learning this five-step process can help you to plan your career better.

koun/iStockphoto.com

When many choices are available, it is helpful to have a structured method of decision-making.

Make a Choice

At this point, you choose one of your alternatives. Making a choice is often difficult because rather than choosing between desirable and undesirable alternatives, you must choose from among several desirable alternatives. Look for the alternative that leads to the most desirable result and has the highest possibility of success.

It was time for Terrance to choose. He decided on Choice 3, which was working part-time and going to college part-time. By working, he could pay for his education without having to borrow money. A community college would also be cheaper than a four-year school because he could live at home. And who knows? Maybe he will want to transfer to a four-year college in two years.

Take Action

At this point, you begin to carry out the alternative you chose in Step 4. Suppose that you have weighed alternatives and decided to seek a job in a distant city. The best thing to do before you leave home is to find a job in the new city. Or at least try to identify several promising job leads.

Taking action also involves committing yourself to making a successful decision. If you are moving to a new city, for example, it might be a while before you find a job there. It would be easy to give up. Stick with your job search plan, but make sure your expectations are realistic.

Having made his choice, Terrance informed his parents and Mrs. Enrico. They all agreed with Terrance's decision and thought that he was wise to have made it. Terrance felt good about having put the decision behind him. Now it was time for him to start deciding what courses to take in school.

Occupational Decision Making

How can the decision-making process be used in making an occupational choice? As each step is explained, refer to Figure 2-2. The first step is defining the problem. In this case, the question is, "Which occupation should I choose?"

In Step 2, you collect information. In choosing an occupation, you must gather information about your own (self) characteristics and about occupations. The three major types of self-information are interests (things you like to do), aptitudes (things you are good at), and work values (attitudes and beliefs about the importance of work activities). You will use the information you have gathered about your interests and aptitudes to develop a preliminary list of occupational alternatives. You will then explore each occupation on the list.

In the third step, you organize the information and identify the pros and cons of each possible choice. Refer to Figure 2-3, "Occupational Alternatives Checklist". Download a copy of Figure 2-3 at

Step 1: Define the Problem.
Which occupation should I choose?

⬇

Step 2: Gather Information.
• Identify interests and aptitudes.
• Develop a list of occupational alternatives based on self-information.
• Collect occupational information.

⬇

Step 3: Evaluate the Information.
• Organize the information.
• Compare and evaluate occupational information.
• Evaluate your own feelings and attitudes.
• Eliminate unacceptable occupational alternatives.

⬇

Step 4: Make a Choice.
Based on your work values and career goals, choose the occupation that seems best to you now.

⬇

Step 5: Take Action.
Begin a job search or enroll in an appropriate education program that will prepare you for the occupation.

FIGURE 2-2 This is how the decision-making process is applied to making an occupational choice.

www.cengage.com/school/working. You consider the information carefully and eliminate those occupations that are unacceptable.

By the fourth step, you have only a few alternatives left. Each of the choices seems equally desirable. You may be happy with any one of the choices. What you try to do, though, is choose the one alternative that seems best at this time. There is no guarantee that your choice will work out. You must choose based upon your best judgment. Considering your work values may be helpful in this step.

Once you have made a decision, you are ready to put your choice into action. Starting a cooperative education program is an example of taking action. Perhaps you are not sure what type of educational program will meet your needs. If this is the case, you should start the decision-making process again. This time the problem is, "What type of educational program should I choose?"

During any of the five steps, you may wish to seek help from a counselor, teacher, parent, or other adult. Talking about goals and alternatives often helps people make decisions. The final decision, though, will be yours.

OCCUPATIONAL ALTERNATIVES CHECKLIST

Name of occupation_____

	Yes	No	Not Sure
1. The work involved in this occupation is the type of work I'd like to do.			
2. I believe I have the ability to do well in this occupation.			
3. This occupation involves doing work that is important to me.			
4. The typical working conditions for this occupation are acceptable to me.			
5. I'm willing to complete the necessary education or training requirements to qualify for this occupation.			
6. I have the educational background to be admitted to any required education or training program.			
7. The future employment outlook for this occupation is good.			
8. I would be satisfied with the amount of earnings that is typical for this occupation.			
9. There are other related occupations in which I could work after learning this occupation.			
10. I believe I have enough information about this occupation to make a decision.			

On a scale of 1 (low) to 10 (high), I'd give this occupation a final ranking of_____.

FIGURE 2-3 Using a checklist like this one can help you evaluate alternatives.

2-1 Assessment

1. When is a systematic decision-making process best used?
2. Name and briefly explain each step in the decision-making process.
3. In choosing an occupation, you collect two types of information in Step 2. Name them.
4. Following a systematic decision-making process increases your chances of making a good decision but does not guarantee it. Explain.

Athletic Trainer

Few young athletes are able to go on and be successful in professional sports. However, one way to remain involved in sports is to work as an athletic trainer. Individuals in this occupation specialize in the prevention, treatment, and rehabilitation of muscle and bone injuries and illnesses. Athletic trainers are recognized by the American Medical Association as allied health professionals. They should not be confused with fitness or personal trainers who are not healthcare workers.

When injuries occur during training or competition, athletic trainers are often the first healthcare providers on the scene. They must be able to recognize and evaluate injuries and provide immediate care. By training athletes about how to reduce their risk for injuries, athletic trainers seek to reduce the frequency of injuries. They advise athletes on the proper use of equipment, exercises to improve balance and strength, and home exercises and therapy programs. They also help apply tape, bandages, and braces to prevent or protect injuries.

Physicians often direct the work of athletic trainers. Physician supervision ranges from discussing specific injuries and treatment options to providing treatment and rehabilitation plans. Sometimes athletic trainers have business responsibilities which include dealing with budgets and purchasing.

Work schedules vary by the type of work setting. Athletic trainers who work in hospitals, clinics, and corporate wellness programs, for example, usually average a 40–50 hour workweek. Those who work in sports settings have schedules that are usually more varied. Athletic trainers must be present for team practices and competitions and often work long hours, including evenings and weekends.

The employment outlook for athletic trainers is expected to grow much faster than average because of expanded opportunities in the healthcare industry and in high schools. But, heavy competition is expected for positions with professional and college sports teams, which tend to require advanced degrees and considerable experience.

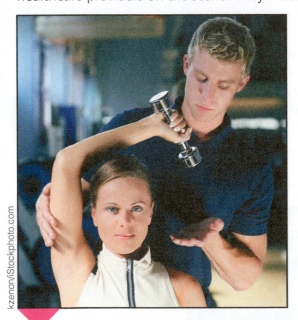

kzenon/iStockphoto.com

Athletic trainers help people improve fitness levels.

INDIVIDUALS AND DECISION MAKING

OBJECTIVES

- Identify and describe different decision-making styles
- Discuss the need to accept responsibility for career planning
- Explain four factors that can influence decision-making

KEY TERMS

- decision-making style
- intuition
- environment
- experience
- reality factor

Career Decisions

You plan to go to a business school next year. You have already applied and been accepted. Now, you are using a decision-making process to choose a program of study. You have collected information and given the problem a great deal of thought. The difficulty is that you like two programs (specializations) equally well.

What would you do?

kutaytanir/iStockphoto.com

Decision-Making Styles

The decision-making process is a tool. How well you use this tool depends largely on your style of decision making and your willingness to accept responsibility and take action.

In watching a baseball game, you will notice that players have different batting styles. For example, one batter will move quickly into the batter's box, crowd the plate, and swing at the first ball that comes near the strike zone. Another batter will delay stepping into the box, stand deep in the box, step out of the batter's box if the pitcher is too slow, and not swing until the pitch is exactly right. People also have different **decision-making styles**, or typical ways of making decisions. These styles are gained over a long period of time. Seven styles of decision making are most common.

- **The agonizer**   These people collect information and spend a lot of time evaluating it. In fact, they spend so much time doing this that they end up not knowing what to do! They get overwhelmed with all the data.

- **The mystic**   Have you heard someone say a decision was made because it "felt right"? Such a decision is based on **intuition**, which

Making the right choice can be difficult.

is a feeling or hunch. Some people make most of their choices this way.

- **The fatalist** These people do not believe that they have much control over their choices. So, they do not spend much time gathering information. Leon is an education major. His parents insist that he live at home and attend the local university. They will pay his tuition and expenses if he does this. However, the school's education department is weak. State University, 200 miles away, has a strong education department. Leon, an excellent student, would like to go there. But he is convinced he has no choice.

- **The evader** John is a junior in high school. He has taken a general program of study because he has made no career decision. He hopes that if he delays long enough, the problem will go away. In its worst form, this style of decision making is known as "the ostrich style." Ostriches stick their heads in the sand. John is behaving like an ostrich. He hasn't made any career decision at all.

- **The plunger** These people eagerly make decisions. In fact, they are usually too eager to do so. The plunger frequently chooses the first alternative that comes to mind.

- **The submissive** "What do you want me to do?" Sound familiar? Such people always want someone else to make a decision for them. If no one will make the decision for them, submissives will make it themselves based on what they think someone else would want them to do.

- **The planner** These people are likely to use a good decision-making strategy. They are thorough and weigh all the information. Such people seek to maintain a balance between facts and emotions. Is this your decision-making style?

Being a planner can have several benefits. For instance, it can increase your chances of being satisfied with your decision. By collecting information about a number of alternatives and carefully weighing the facts, you increase the chances of choosing an alternative that is best for you.

In addition, being a planner will provide you with more choices. A skilled decision maker usually develops many alternatives from which to choose. Having several alternatives gives you more freedom than if you had only one or two. Planning will help you gain greater control over your life.

Take Charge of Your Life

The benefits of successful decision making are achieved only if the process is used. Using the process depends on your willingness to accept responsibility for making decisions and for taking action to carry them out.

Part of becoming a mature person is accepting responsibility for what happens to you. This does not mean that luck, natural ability, family advantages, or discrimination do not play a part. It is clear that they do. For instance, the election of George W. Bush as the 43rd President of the United States was certainly helped by the wealth and name he inherited from his family. The success of Ted Williams at baseball was influenced positively by his nearly perfect eyesight.

It is possible to identify many examples of famous or successful people who did not have such advantages or who had only average ability. Success and happiness depend largely on the choices you make.

Too many people blame someone or something for what happens to them. For example, in conversations about grades, students often say things like, "Mr. Anderson gave me a D in English." In truth, teachers do not give grades at all. Teachers simply assign grades to students' work. If you receive an A, you earned it. The same is true if you receive a D.

Other Influences On Decision Making

Information, decision-making style, and willingness to accept responsibility all influence decision making. Three more factors related to decision making are previous decisions, environment and experiences, and real-world restrictions.

Previous Decisions

One decision may influence later ones. To illustrate, consider Dee Dee, a tenth-grade student who is deciding what courses to take next year. She picks a health occupations course. By making this decision, Dee Dee will begin to move toward a health career and away from other fields such as business or food service. Her decision, however, isn't final. Dee Dee may change direction later—even as an adult. Important choices that influence later career decisions include selecting school courses and college majors, gaining work experience, marrying, and joining the military.

Environment and Experiences

Your **environment** is your surroundings. It includes your family, neighborhood, friends, school, church, and the like. Your **experiences** are what you do and what happens to you in your environment. Environmental and experience factors may strongly influence your choices.

Luis, for example, decided to become a veterinary assistant. His decision was heavily influenced by three environmental and experience factors. He grew up on a farm where he developed a love for animals. He enjoyed part-time work at his uncle's animal hospital. And he lived near a college that offers the only veterinary assistant's program in the state.

Real-World Restrictions

There are a number of **reality factors** over which you have little control that often influence decisions. These can be people, events, or situations. Sam would like to be a musician, but the reality is that he would have trouble supporting himself. So he chooses another occupation and plays for parties on weekends. Someday he may be able to work as a musician full-time.

Often factors that appear to be real-world restrictions are not. For instance, Sarah didn't think she would have enough money to attend a

Workforce Trends

The BLS defines the labor force as the number of people aged 16 or older who are either working or looking for employment. It does not include active-duty military personnel or institutionalized people, such as prison inmates. Putting a figure on this total supply of labor is a way of determining how big the economy can get. Labor force figures are often confused with overall employment figures. For example, the labor force is expected to reach 167 million people by 2018. But, the actual number of employed workers is expected to be 154 million.

Search the Net

Access **www.cengage.com/school/ working** and click on the link for Chapter 2. Read the information on the web page, and then click on the link for the Decision-Making Worksheet. Apply the worksheet to a career-related decision you are facing. Share your results.

www.cengage.com/school/working

certain school. She was happy that her application for a scholarship was approved. The scholarship, together with a student loan, would help her pay for her schooling.

Other reality factors include age, experience, qualifications, abilities, and physical characteristics. In making career decisions, everyone faces real-world restrictions. When you face such a situation, either try harder or choose another alternative.

Economic Conditions

Changes in economic conditions may impact life decisions. When there is nearly full employment in a country most workers who want a job have one. In a full employment economy workers will buy luxury items, go to restaurants, and buy larger homes. However, when unemployment is high, workers will buy only essential items, eat at home more often, and stay in their current housing.

Changes in the economy affected Denzel's career plans. Denzel enjoyed making deals. In his younger years, he was known as the king of the lunch time trade. He often traded his home-made peanut butter and jelly sandwiches for his friends' cafeteria purchased food. He also got along well with others. He'd always thought it would be fun to work in residential real estate, selling homes to individual buyers.

Then the recession which began in 2008 started to take its toll. House sales fell. As earnings in real estate sales were based on commission, if no houses sold, no money was earned. As Denzel had heard that eighty percent of new jobs were in service occupations, he decided to explore customer service jobs that would provide a steady paycheck. If he took a customer service job, he would gain valuable experience satisfying customers. Then, when the economy improved, he could obtain a real estate license and pursue his dream of becoming a real estate agent.

2-2 Assessment

1. Match these characteristics with decision-making styles: (a) delaying a career decision, (b) being overwhelmed with all the data, (c) choosing the first alternative that comes to mind.

2. Which is the best decision-making style to use?

3. Being a planner can have several benefits. Name three.

4. Explain what is meant by "accepting responsibility for what happens to you."

5. Give an example of how previous decisions may influence later ones.

6. Name three reality factors that can limit career decisions.

7. How can economic conditions affect career choices?

BEGIN YOUR CAREER

OBJECTIVES

- Name three types of work experience education
- Identify the benefits of work experience education
- Explain work histories and how they can help with career planning

KEY TERMS

- work experience education
- occupational skill
- training station
- training agreement
- training plan
- career guidance
- work history
- qualify

Personal Decisions

Your school has both school-based and co-op career/technical education. You cannot decide which one meets your needs. The advantages of the school-based program are that you know the teacher, you are familiar with the equipment, and you would be taking the course with your friends. In the co-op program, you would meet new people, earn some money, and work on more advanced equipment. Other students have told you that in co-op you will work harder and that more will be expected of you.

*What would **you** do?*

ktaylorg/iStockphoto.com

Work Experience Programs

During the last several decades, many kinds of education programs have been developed to help young people learn about and prepare for work. Programs of this type are called **work experience education**. Their purpose is to provide opportunities for students to explore or participate in work as an extension of the regular school environment. Unlike many countries, the United States does not have a national system of education. As a result, state and local work experience education programs are called by many different names. Whatever it is called, a work experience program is probably one of the following.

Career and Technical Education

Career and technical education is a program in which students learn specific occupational skills for employment. **Occupational skills** are skills needed to perform tasks or duties of a specific occupation. One kind of career/technical education is school-based education, which is taught in classrooms, shops, and laboratories. Instruction may be provided in occupational areas such as agriculture, business, marketing, family and consumer science, industrial-technical, and health.

Another kind of career/technical education is cooperative (co-op) career/technical education. This is a cooperative program between a secondary school or community college and a local employer. Most co-op education students attend classes at their school campus for part of the day. They spend the rest of the day working at a training site in a local business or industry. Students receive both pay and school credit for their co-op jobs.

In co-op career/technical education, the student learns and applies occupational skills on the job rather than only in a school shop or laboratory. Another part of co-op career/technical education is a related class. This is taught at the school to reinforce skills used at a job site. Students study topics such as job seeking, consumer skills, independent living, and career planning.

Co-op career/technical education follows certain guidelines and procedures. A cooperative education teacher/coordinator employed by a school system usually manages the program. The coordinator reviews and approves student applications for the program. The coordinator also approves each student's place of employment, called the **training station**. The training station may be any type of workplace that relates to the student's career objectives. Common training stations include stores, offices, hospitals, restaurants, and auto repair shops. At the training station, the student is under the direction of a supervisor.

The cooperative education program is a three-way relationship involving the student, the employer-supervisor, and the cooperative education coordinator. Early on, all three parties sign a **training agreement** outlining the relationships and responsibilities of the parties. See the sample training agreement in Figure 2-4 on the next page. All three parties also participate in the development of a step-by-step training plan. A **training plan** describes the knowledge, attitudes, and skills to be developed by the student.

Work-Study

Work-study programs, sometimes called general work experience education, are similar to co-op career/technical education in several ways. Both allow students to attend school part-time while working part-time. For these jobs, students receive pay and school credit. A work experience coordinator supervises each program.

Unlike co-op career/technical education, work-study is not a program of on-the-job training for a specific occupation. Rather, the program helps students develop *employability skills*, which are the general work habits and attitudes required in all jobs. They include, for example, punctuality, dependability, and cooperation. Many students find that the combination of school and work is more interesting than school alone. Also, the opportunity to earn money keeps some students in school who might otherwise drop out before graduation.

Some students are motivated to stay in school by participating in a work-study program.

Photodisc/Getty Images

SAMPLE TRAINING AGREEMENT

Trainee _____   Training Station _____

Employer _____   Supervisor _____

Employment start date _____   Employment end date _____

Work schedule _____   Compensation rate: $ _____ (per hour)

(days/hours of employment) _____

EMPLOYER RESPONSIBILITIES

1. Complete quarterly on-the-job evaluation reports to help determine the student's grade.
2. Give trainee duties that provide knowledge and skill in this job.
3. Notify the coordinator of employment problems. If termination is pending, please provide two weeks notice.
4. Provide worker's compensation insurance for the student.
5. Do not discriminate against student based on race, color, national origin, sex, or handicap.

STUDENT RESPONSIBILITIES

1. Adhere to school attendance policies for school times and work times. A student must attend school to attend work and must attend work while participating in program. Student absences need to be reported to both the coordinator and the employer.
2. Provide advance notice of planned absences from school or work. Will follow the school's policy for providing information for excused absences.
3. Student must meet job requirements of training station or risk failing the course.
4. I must follow all published school rules and government laws while at the workplace.
5. Participation in the program is a year long commitment. I must keep my job and stay a full-time student for the year. I will try to resolve problems as they arise. Only the coordinator can give me permission to quit the job. If I lose my job, it is my responsibility to find a new job within two weeks. If I am without a job for more than two weeks, I will not be allowed to continue in the program.
6. The coordinator and employer are responsible for making job changes.
7. I will go to study hall if I am briefly without a job.
8. Receiving full credit for cooperative education means that I must work at the job for the entire school year.

COORDINATOR

1. Work with employer to determine required skills. Teach students skills that will help them be successful at the job.
2. Provide training station with guidance regarding supervision of a student learner.
3. Make quarterly visits to the job site to provide ongoing support and to obtain student evaluations.

PARENTS

1. Support the student to successfully fulfill both school and work assignments.
2. If student experiences troubles at the job site, notify the school coordinator. The coordinator will work with student and employer to help resolve issues. Parents should not contact the employer.

PARTICIPANT SIGNATURES:

Student Signature _____   Date _____

Employer Signature _____   Date _____

Parent Signature _____   Date _____

Coordinator Signature _____   Date _____

Administrator Signature _____   Date _____

FIGURE 2-4 Sample Training Agreement

Many skills can be learned from experienced coworkers.

Thomas_EyeDesign/iStockphoto.com

Exploratory Work Experience Education

Many schools provide exploratory work experience education for junior high and beginning high school students. The purpose of this type of program is to provide students with opportunities to observe work and to try out various work tasks. Students explore various occupations in order to discover or to confirm occupational interests. Thus, the program is concerned with career guidance rather than the development of occupational or employability skills. **Career guidance** is assisting students in career planning and decision making. Exploratory programs may last only a few days or a few weeks. Students receive no pay for the work they do, but they usually receive school credit.

Benefits of Work Experience

Depending on the type of program in which you are enrolled, work experience can benefit you in the following ways.

- **You can learn occupational skills.** You can acquire skills through on-the-job training in an actual work setting. These skills will make you more desirable to potential employers in the future. These skills may also qualify you for higher starting pay than another candidate who has not learned these skills yet.

- **You can develop employability skills.** Success on the job requires more than occupational skills. Work experience provides opportunities to develop the types of work habits and attitudes that employers expect.

Communication at Work — SELF-TALK

From high school basketball players to Olympic gymnasts, many athletes are taught to use positive self-talk to help themselves succeed. "I can make this free throw." "I can see myself doing every step of my routine perfectly." The running commentary that cycles through a person's mind is self-talk. "I studied hard for this test and I know I can figure out the answer" is an example of self-talk that would help you while taking a test.

Research has shown that positive self-talk can do more than help people win at sports. It can help them ward off illness, reduce stress, and cope with medical problems. Positive self-talk can help

you manage yourself at work. It can also help you become what you want to be.

Ralph was a camera operator for a public television station. After a while, he decided that he wanted to become an airline pilot. Ralph was not sure that he could do this. When he encountered something difficult in his training, Ralph would talk himself through it in his head. This technique helped give Ralph confidence that he could achieve his goals.

THINK CRITICALLY

1. Apply self-talk to a situation in your school life.
2. Apply self-talk to an issue in your personal life.

- **You can establish a work record.** It is often hard to get a job if you lack previous experience. Completing a work experience program will make it easier for you to get a job later because you can use your work experience as a reference.

- **You can earn while you learn.** Earning your own money will give you a sense of accomplishment. You will be able to save money, buy things that you might not otherwise be able to afford, or both. For some students, the money they earn can be the difference between staying in school and dropping out. You may also be able to save money for future expenses, such as living on your own or getting additional training for your occupation.

- **You can discover career interests and goals.** Work experience can help you find out what type of career you want. You may either confirm your present interests and goals or find new ones. You may still have time in your high school career to explore other occupations in a work experience setting.

- **You can recognize the relationship between education and work.** Work experience can provide something that may be missing at school. Education can take on new meaning as you come to recognize a greater connection between what you are learning in school and what you would do at a job.

- **You can remain employed after graduation.** Many students in work experience jobs are offered permanent jobs after graduation. This benefits both students and employers. If you are pleased with your job, you won't have to look for a new one. Hiring a work experience student saves the employer both interviewing and training time. Some students continue in co-op jobs while obtaining further education after high school.

On-the-job training occurs in many trades.

What is a Work History?

Your **work history** is all of the jobs that you will hold during the course of your working lifetime. The four work histories that follow illustrate how jobs can serve different purposes at different times in a person's life. Jobs are often used as a way to achieve something else. One purpose may be to learn occupational skills. Another purpose may be to earn money for college. Some jobs are used to gain experience in order to **qualify**, or meet the preliminary requirements, for a better job. For most people, first jobs are only stepping stones. Knowing about different work histories can help you think about and plan for your own career.

Example 1 Terry

Terry got a co-op job in a small electronics sales and repair shop. After he graduated, he took a full-time job in the electronics department of a large discount store. He often did small repair jobs for friends and neighbors. His next job was a job repairing televisions and installing satellite dishes. He took this job to save enough money to open his own business. Terry now has a stable job as owner-manager of an electronics supply firm.

Example 2 Maria

After high school graduation, Maria was unemployed until she got a full-time job as a salesclerk in a clothing store. Maria discovered that she enjoyed retail selling and had a talent for it. After two years, she quit her job and enrolled in college to major in marketing. During college, Maria had a part-time job in a clothing store. After earning her diploma, she took a job as a sales manager for a national department store. She worked at that job for five years before staying at home for two years with young children. Maria just started working again at a job that is similar to the one she left earlier.

Example 3 Cindy

Cindy was an outstanding athlete who never worked while attending high school or college. Her first job was as a high school teacher and coach. After six years, a friend in the sporting goods business offered Cindy a job. Cindy enjoyed the challenge of the job. After a year, she took a job in school athletic sales with a sporting goods manufacturer. She believes increasing sales will help her earn a promotion to manager.

Example 4 Ricardo

Ricardo never liked school and could not wait to graduate. After high school, he got a job stocking shelves in a grocery store. He worked for a couple of months before getting into an argument with the store manager. Ricardo was fired. His next job was working as a service station attendant. After working at that job for about a year, Ricardo decided that he should learn a skill. He enrolled in a technical school to learn computer programming. He had heard this was a growing field. While going to school, Ricardo took a part-time job at another service station. He quit school after six months because he had to study too hard. Now Ricardo has another job driving a delivery truck while he decides whether to join the Armed Forces or start his own business.

2-3 Assessment

1. Identify and briefly explain the three kinds of work experience education programs.
2. How does cooperative career and technical education differ from other forms of career and technical education?
3. The term *exploratory* describes one type of work experience education. Explain why.
4. How can work experience education help you discover career interests and goals?
5. What is the benefit of establishing a work record?
6. Give an example to show how knowledge of work histories can help you think about and plan a career.

TRANSFERABLE SKILLS

OBJECTIVES

- Define transferable skills and why you need them
- Identify your transferable skills

KEY TERMS

- transfer
- transferable skill

Career Decisions

One of the options that Chuck is considering is joining the military. He prefers doing hands-on activities and knows that the military services have many trade and technical jobs. But, he doesn't know whether he would like wearing a uniform, following strict military rules, and other aspects of a military lifestyle. He is also concerned about leaving the military after his enlistment commitment is fulfilled. Will all of his military training be wasted?

What would you do?

MTMCOINS/iStockphoto.com

What Are Transferable Skills?

In the previous lesson, Terry, Maria, and Cindy moved successfully from school to work, from one job to another, and from being unemployed back to employment. One of the reasons for their successes is that they were able to **transfer** skills learned in one setting to another. Cindy is a good example. Her experiences as an athlete and a coach gave her the background to interact effectively with school officials who purchase athletic equipment and apparel.

You may be feeling like you are not prepared to move into a real job because you lack previous work experience. You have more training than you think. Everyone has dozens of skills and each one can be related in some way to a job. Without ever having a job, without ever being trained for a job, you are potentially qualified to perform many types of jobs.

When asked in a job interview about their skills and experience, many people have little or nothing to say. Some people hesitate to write a resume because they do not know how to define their skills and abilities. To be a successful job hunter, you must be able to tell employers, clearly and in detail, what you can do.

Skills for all Situations

Unlike occupational skills, which tend to be used only in one type of job, **transferable skills** are skills that can be used in many occupations and jobs.

- Analyze facts
- Artistic
- Build
- Calculate
- Confidence
- Construct
- Cooperate
- Creative
- Delegation
- Detail-oriented
- Editing
- Ethical behavior
- Facilitate problem-solving groups
- Forecasting
- Goal setting
- Helpful
- Inspire others
- Integrity
- Interpret data
- Listening
- Manage money
- Multilingual
- Musical
- Negotiation
- Nurturing
- Operate equipment
- Persuading
- Presentation abilities
- Project management
- Punctual
- Raw material planning
- Reading body language
- Reconcile expenses
- Responsible
- Safety training
- Self-starter
- Selling
- Sensitive to others
- Speak effectively
- Speak Spanish
- Team builder
- Time management
- Use spreadsheet software
- Use word processing software

FIGURE 2-5 Examples of Common Transferable Skills

They are general skills that can transfer from one type of work to another. These skills do not require additional education or training from the employer. For this reason, your transferable skills are often more important than your job skills. This is especially true if you are changing jobs or making the transition from school to work.

Jacob saw a job announcement for an appliance repair assistant to help disassemble, clean, repair, adjust, and reassemble household appliances. His only previous experience was helping his dad rebuild small gasoline engines. In an interview with the employer, Jacob discovered that the employer was primarily interested in hiring a person who could use hand tools, follow instructions, observe safety rules, troubleshoot, and repair mechanical devices. Jacob now has a new part-time job while he completes his education.

Why You Need Transferable Skills

Estimates vary regarding the number of job changes individuals have over the course of their working lives. Some estimates range between seven and ten different jobs and may involve multiple occupations. The Bureau of Labor Statistics notes that seventy-five percent of workers age 16 to 19 and fifty percent of workers between ages 20 to 24 have been at their current jobs for less than a year.

Occupation and/or job changes may occur for a variety of reasons including earning a promotion, sale of a company or a division, a change in personal circumstances, poor economic times, and new competition in the market. Being able to convince a potential employer that you are right for the job, including drawing upon skills that were developed outside of the workplace, is critical to obtaining new employment.

Workers who have a genuine interest in the job and industry they work in are more likely to be enthusiastic and energetic when performing their work duties. Oftentimes people have developed skills while pursuing hobbies or volunteer work that will help them obtain jobs of personal interest. It is very important that you identify and convey your transferable skills to a potential employer.

Gina enjoyed helping out in her family's backyard garden. She liked learning about the nutrients contained within each vegetable and how the nutrients promoted good health in people. She enjoyed experimenting with new recipes that used the freshly grown vegetables. When interviewing for a job as a chef's assistant, Gina was able to speak enthusiastically about growing fresh produce, understanding the nutritional value of each ingredient in a recipe, and how all the fresh flavors blended together for delicious meals. Her transferable skills and knowledge prompted her interviewer to offer her a job as a chef's assistant at the conclusion of the interview.

Your Transferable Skills

In the next unit, you will learn how to conduct a systematic job search. You will be more effective in this effort if you have done a skills analysis first. Get to know yourself better by taking a personal inventory. Skills gained from home, school, extracurricular, volunteer, and paid work should be examined as well as those skills gained from hobbies and other life experiences. These skills go beyond your interests, aptitudes, and work values. Skills are portable abilities that you take with you from job to job. To help you get started, take a look at the transferable skills listed in Figure 2-5 on the previous page.

Every worker must continually engage in job training.

Once you have identified your transferable skills, you need to develop them into statements that you can make in an interview. Consider

- What your transferable skill is
- How you obtained your skill
- How the skill will help you perform your job duties

Math Connection

Suppose you are deciding between two jobs that will pay exactly the same. One factor you are considering is the cost of commuting. One job is at a company that is 15 miles away. The second is at a company that is 5 miles away. If gasoline is $3.40 a gallon, and your car gets 20 miles to a gallon, how much extra money per week would you have if you took the second job?

SOLUTION

1. Multiply the number of miles you would drive by two to determine how far you would drive each day.
2. Multiply this number by the number of workdays per week.
3. Divide the product by the number of miles to a gallon your car gets.
4. Multiply the dividend by the cost per gallon of gas.
5. Subtract the cost of gas for the second job from the cost of gas for the first.

Weekly cost of gas (Job 1):
(1) 15 mi × 2 = 30
(2) 30 × 5 = 150
(3) 150/20 = 7.5
(4) 7.5 × $3.40 = $25.50

Weekly cost of gas (Job 2):
(1) 5 mi × 2 = 10
(2) 10 × 5 = 50
(3) 50/20 = 2.5
(4) 2.5 × $3.40 = $8.50

Amount of extra money you would have if you took the second job = $25.50–$8.50
= $17.00

You would have $17.00 extra per week if you took the second job.

Title of job being interviewed for	Housekeeper for patients staying at Children's Hospital
Transferable skill	Speak Spanish
Declaration about transferable skill	"I can speak Spanish"
Brief personal summary of how skill was obtained	"All four of my grandparents, who often took care of me while my parents worked, spoke Spanish as their native language."
Explain how skill will help job performance	"Many of the hospital's patients speak Spanish as their primary language. I will be able to explain to them why I am entering their rooms. I will also be able to chat with them while I clean. This may make the patients feel more relaxed."
Title of job being interviewed for	Construction worker
Transferable skill	Built wood structures and operate power tools
Declaration about transferable skill	"I can use tools to build things."
Brief personal summary of how skill was obtained	"We had two dogs that the family loved but then my sister developed an allergy to them. So, instead of getting rid of the dogs, I built them each a dog house."
Explain how skill will help job performance	"I can draw and interpret simple blueprints, calculate how much lumber to order, and operate power tools."

FIGURE 2-6 These are examples of how to highlight transferable skills during an interview.

When you think about how you obtained your skill, consider whether the skill was developed by taking a course in school, by self-learning out of school, by volunteering, or by helping someone else. When you weave together a brief story explaining your skill, how you obtained it, and how it will benefit the prospective employer, you are demonstrating to the employer that you are someone who can pull together past experiences to build new skills.

Sharing just a brief summary of how you obtained the experience helps the employer get to know you as a well-rounded person. Employees who are well-rounded can often get along well with others because they have more common experiences to share with others.

Refer to Figure 2-6 for sample statements about transferable skills. Each statement is followed by an example and a connection to a specific job. Sometimes multiple transferable skills can be combined into one statement. Using this technique will show employers that you are a motivated job candidate who can think well and adapt to new situations.

2-4 Assessment

1. Why are transferable skills often more important than specific job skills? Explain and give an example.

2. Have you ever been asked in a job interview to name your strongest skills? How did you respond?

3. Is the skill "manage time" a job skill or a transferable skill? How about "replace spark plugs"?

4. Why should you identify your own transferable skills before going into a job interview?

Focus on the Workplace

Envy in the Workplace

Success and happiness depend on your own efforts. This does not mean, however, that other people cannot help or hinder you. In her book, *The Snow White Syndrome*, Betsy Cohen points out that envy is often a by-product of success. Envy is dissatisfaction or dislike at the success or good fortune of another. In the fairy tale, Snow White's beauty led the Wicked Queen to try to kill her.

Unfortunately, envy exists in the workplace. The more successful you are, the more envy you are likely to arouse. In the workplace, an envious person can hurt you. This is because your success often depends on others' cooperation. If someone is envious, he or she can make you look bad. Here are some ways that envy is expressed:

- "Forgetting" instructions or deadlines
- Gossiping or lying behind your back
- Being continually late, stubborn, or resistant
- Clever put-downs
- Excessive compliments and flattery
- Outright destruction of your work

Envious people act to control you. They want to bring you back to their level. To avoid being a victim of envy, learn to recognize it. Try to develop a tolerance for it. Do not make it worse by flaunting your strengths. Be considerate toward coworkers. Build on other people's achievements. Remember that envy reflects what other people may see, not the real you.

If you are ambitious and aspire to be successful, be prepared to face envy. It exists in many workplaces. If you achieve success, someone is probably going to be envious.

THINK CRITICALLY

1. Think of a time when you or someone you know was envious of another person. How did you or the person you know act toward this person?
2. Look at the list of ways that envy is expressed. List strategies for dealing with three of them.

Recognize and tolerate envy.

dottyjo/iStockphoto.com

Chapter Summary

2-1 The Decision-making Process

A. Decision making involves choosing between two or more alternatives. The more important the decision, the more time and effort should be devoted to it. Decision making involves the following five steps: (1) defining the problem, (2) gathering information, (3) evaluating the information, (4) making a choice, and (5) taking action.

B. In an occupational decision, Step 2 involves collecting information about personal characteristics and occupational alternatives. During any of the five steps, you may wish to seek help from an adult.

2-2 Individuals and Decision Making

A. Seven styles of decision making are most common: the agonizer, the mystic, the fatalist, the evader, the plunger, the submissive, and the planner. The planner is the preferred style.

B. Being a planner can have several benefits. It can increase your chances of being satisfied with your decision. It can provide you with more choices. It will help you gain greater control over your life.

C. A very important part of growing up is accepting responsibility for what happens to you. Your success and happiness will depend on the choices you make.

D. Five factors that influence decision making are previous decisions, environment, experiences, real-world restrictions, and the economy.

2-3 Begin Your Career

A. The names of work experience programs vary by state. Types of work experience education include cooperative career and technical education, work-study, and exploratory work experience education.

B. Work experience programs allow you to learn occupational skills, develop employability skills, establish a work record, earn while you learn, discover career interests, recognize the relationship between education and work, and remain employed after graduation.

C. People often have very different work histories. Knowing about work histories can help you think about and plan your own career.

2-4 Transferable Skills

A. You may feel like you are not prepared for a job because you lack work experience. Everyone has dozens of transferable skills.

B. Transferable skills can be used in many occupations. They are general skills that can be transferred from one type of work to another.

C. You will be more effective in a job search if you do a skills analysis first. Use the results of the analysis to prepare statements explaining your transferable skills to potential employers.

Activities

1. You have probably used a problem-solving method in one of your science or math classes. Compare the problem-solving method with the decision-making process. How are they similar and different?

2. Find out which decision-making style is most common in your class. Be honest and write on a piece of scrap paper which of the seven styles you use. Do not include names on papers. Summarize results on the board and discuss the outcome in class.

3. Groups can use the decision-making process. As a class, apply the decision-making method to a situation. For example, what type of computer would be best for use in the class?

4. You are considering job offers from two companies. The pay is the same. One company is 10 miles from your home and the other is 20 miles. If gasoline is $3.80 a gallon, and your car gets 25 miles to a gallon, how much more money would you have each week if you took the closer job?

5. Explain how an ability to use the five-step decision-making process can help you achieve goals in your life-span plan.

6. Interview a student who has taken a cooperative career and technical education or work-study program. Ask about the benefits and disadvantages of the program. Discuss your findings in class.

7. Interview an employer who has provided a training site for a co-op or work-study student. List the ways in which the employer has benefited from the program. Prepare an oral report.

8. Write a paragraph about what you hope to gain from being in a work experience program. Read your statement to the class. Compare and discuss the statements of different students.

9. Examine a copy of the training agreement used by your school. Discuss the purpose and requirements of the agreement. Make sure you ask questions about any parts that you don't understand.

10. Describe promises from an employer that could be included in a training plan that could help you achieve your life-span plan goals.

11. Ask a parent or other adult to list all the jobs he or she has held. Compare the work histories in class. What are the similarities and differences? Which types of work histories are the most common?

12. In doing the previous activity, did you note how work histories may be influenced by illnesses, accidents, economic hard times, wars, and other events? List as many factors as you can that are beyond one's control that may influence a career.

13. Think about your own work habits and attitudes. With your work experience coordinator, discuss how to improve in three areas.

14. Prepare a work history of your own. Explain how your work history could help you achieve goals in your life-span plan.

15. Refer to the list of transferable skills in Figure 2-5. Write ten of your strongest transferable skills. Include in the ten any skills you have that may not be on the list. Choose three transferable skills from your list that you think will interest most potential employers. Print a copy of Figure 2-6 from www.cengage.com/school/working. Use the worksheet to develop the skills into statements that you can make in an interview. Use the five-step process: (a) define the job title (b) list the skill, (c) make a declaration about the skill, (d) give a brief personal summary about how the skill was obtained, and (e) explain how the skill will help job performance.

Word Power

On a separate sheet of paper, match each definition with the correct term. All definitions will be used, and a definition will be used only once.

16. Question in need of a solution or an answer
17. What you do and what happens to you in your environment
18. Persons, events, or situations over which you have little control that often influence decisions
19. Feeling or hunch
20. One's surroundings, including neighborhood, family, and friends
21. Process of choosing between two or more alternatives or options
22. Typical ways in which people make decisions
23. Options to choose from in making a decision
24. Education programs that provide opportunities for students to participate in work as an extension of school
25. Skills needed to perform tasks or duties of a specific occupation
26. Work experience student's place of employment
27. Signed agreement outlining the relationships and responsibilities of the parties involved in a work experience education program
28. Description of knowledge, attitudes, and skills to be developed by the student participating in a work experience education program
29. Assisting students in career planning and decision making
30. All of the jobs that one holds during the course of a working lifetime
31. Meet the preliminary requirements, as for a job or position
32. Move from one place to another
33. General skills that can transfer from one type of work to another

a. alternative
b. career guidance
c. decision making
d. decision-making style
e. environment
f. experience
g. intuition
h. occupational skill
i. problem
j. qualify
k. reality factor
l. training agreement
m. training plan
n. training station
o. transfer
p. transferable skill
q. work experience education
r. work history

Think Critically

34. Identify and discuss a variety of situations in which a systematic decision-making process should be used.
35. How is an occupational decision different from a job decision?
36. Decisions are influenced by previous decisions made and not made. Identify some of the important decisions you have made.

Might the outcome have been different had you used a systematic decision-making process?

37. Do you believe that you have the power to influence the direction of your life and career?

38. You may think of reality factors as negative things, such as not having enough money or lacking qualifications. Can you think of positive reality factors that also limit or restrict choices?

39. How would your future plans be changed if you suddenly won or inherited a great deal of money? Would you go to college? Would you plan on working? What type of work would you do?

40. In what ways can you influence and shape the direction of a potential career?

41. Are there any types of work experience programs in your school or community not mentioned in the chapter?

42. How might knowledge and skills learned in the following school subjects be applied on the job: English, mathematics, science, social studies, and foreign language?

43. In what ways might your interests and abilities be expressed in work? Cite examples of both paid and unpaid work.

44. Real estate sales is one of the industries affected by a poor economy. Make a list of three other industries that might also be affected by a weak economy. For each of the listed industries, write down at least one alternative occupation, in a similar area of interest, that would be likely to offer employment opportunities even in a weak economy.

45. If you are currently employed, do you think that your present job might develop into a stable job? Why or why not?

46. Do you think that hard work and quality effort pay off? Or is this just a myth that parents, teachers, and employers want you to believe?

47. Some students not enrolled in a work experience program leave after school and go to a job. They often work from 3:30 in the afternoon to 10:30 at night. On weekends, they may work up to 16 additional hours. Do you think that some teenagers are trying to work too much while attending high school?

Career Transitions Connection
Transferable Skills

Click on *Match Experience to New Careers*. In the dialogue box for "I've worked as a(n)" fill in a job, either paid or unpaid, that you have worked in. When related careers are offered in the drop down menu, click the one that is the closest match to the job title you are describing. After you have selected a position for the dialogue box, a list of similar positions will appear beneath the dialogue box. From that list, click on the job that is of most interest to you. Read through the typical activities of the job that you selected. Make a list of skills you already have that you could use in the selected job.

UNIT 2 Prepare for Work

CHAPTERS
3 Search for a Job
4 Apply for a Job
5 Interview for a Job

Photographer's Choice/Getty Images

Co-op Career SPOTLIGHT

Hospitality & Tourism

Aurora Patag and her family love food. Some of Aurora's fondest family memories involve cooking food with her mother, uncles, and grandparents. Aurora estimates that when her family travels, about 60% of family photos focus on food. Aurora's food interests have an international flair. Her Mom, who immigrated to the U.S. as a young adult, often cooked traditional Filipino dishes. During the time she lived in Italy, Aurora became well acquainted with Italian food.

While still in high school, Aurora provided content for a food website. She wrote posts, developed recipes, and reviewed cookbooks. She earned money based on the amount of traffic that the site generated. This ongoing interest in food compelled Aurora to enroll in a dual admit program at Cincinnati State Technical and Community College and at the University of Cincinnati. Her first degree, which was earned June 2011, is an Associate Degree in Culinary Art's Technology from Cincinnati State. The studies for her Associate Degree focused on food preparation, food safety, and restaurant work. Most of these classes were hands-on classes in classroom kitchens. The courses she is taking while working on earning her Bachelor's Degree at the University of Cincinnati focus more on the chemistry side of food including the nutritional aspects of food. Most of these classes are held in classrooms.

While earning her Associate Degree, Aurora participated in the co-operative education program. In one of her positions, she worked 32 to 45 hours per week while maintaining a full-time

Aurora Patag
Certified Culinarian

student status. Aurora had a number of strategies that enabled her to succeed in school while working full-time. Her first priority was to maintain self-awareness. She stayed attuned to when she felt to stressed out and to when she needed help. Aurora also set clear priorities for herself. To maintain these priorities, she learned to say no to certain requests–like when coworkers would ask for help in covering some of their workload. Effective time management was Aurora's third strategy. Sometimes she would multitask, like when she would try to memorize information while washing dishes.

Aurora lives at home and contributes some of her co-op earnings to her educational expenses. She was awarded multiple partial scholarships to help pay for tuition. Aurora's parents encouraged her to use her money for educational expenses. To avoid car expenses, Aurora carpooled with her father. For two years, Aurora woke up every morning at 4:45 a.m. to drive her father to work before heading to campus. After classes were complete, she would pick her father up from work on her way home. Depending on traffic, her commute time in each direction was between 30 and 90 minutes.

Although Aurora works very hard, she believes firmly that everyone needs and is entitled to leisure time. Aurora has used her leisure time to earn a black belt in karate, to learn to play the recorder, piano, violin, and guitar, and to participate musically at her place of whorship. She also enjoys hosting the occasional potluck dinner for friends. One of her friends summarized these potlucks as a place where "culinary people like to show off, and we non-culinary people get to sit back and just enjoy."

3 Search for a Job

"People forget how fast you did a job, but they remember how well you did it." —HOWARD NEWTON

FuzzBones/Shutterstock.com

PREVIEW

In this chapter and Chapters 4 and 5, you will learn how to find a job. If you do not have a job, you will be able to use the information right away. If you are working now, the material will help you in your next job search.

Taking/*Action* Look for Work

Jonita Johnson was anxious to start working and earning some money. She went to Mr. Sandoval, her work experience coordinator, to ask him what she needed to do to be ready to look for a job.

"First, you'll need to be very clear on what you want from a job," Mr. Sandoval said.

"I know I want to be a hair stylist eventually, but I don't have the qualifications to be a stylist now," Jonita said. "The classes I'm taking in school will get me ready for the state licensing exam. Also, I'll need to earn some money to help out at home."

"Okay. You just said two things. First, you are looking for a job in a beauty salon that is paid. Second, this position should help you gain valuable experience so you can get a good job once you pass the state licensing exam. Do you know anyone who works in a hair salon?" he asked.

"Well, one of my teachers mentioned that she knew someone who owned her own shop. She might be hiring," she replied.

"That's great!" Mr. Sandoval said. "Do you think your teacher will put in a good word for you?"

"I think so. My grades are good in her class and she likes my work."

"Write down all the information your teacher can give you about this job lead. Next, look for job openings both in the newspaper and online. The Sunday paper usually has the most help-wanted ads. For ads that sound promising, cut out the ones from the newspaper and print out the ones from the Web. Reply to each ad that you are interested in," Mr. Sandoval instructed.

"I have no idea how I'm going to keep all that information straight, Mr. Sandoval," she said.

"Let me show you how job-lead cards can help."

Parris Blue Productions/Shutterstock.com

✻ Success Tip

Ask your friends, family, and teachers for job leads.

THINK CRITICALLY

1. What was the first step to finding a job that Mr. Sandoval discussed?

2. In your chosen field, do you know anyone who might give you a job lead?

OBJECTIVES

- Discuss how different work histories can lead to a stable job
- Describe how adapting to change leads to job stability
- Explain why it is important to follow and anticipate workforce trends

KEY TERMS

- stable job
- self-direction
- promotion
- obsolete
- technology
- monitor

Diego Cervo/Shutterstock.com

Ethical Decisions

A fellow employee approaches you at work with some advice. "Listen," he says. "You are working too hard. Slow down a little bit. You are making the rest of us look bad. You do not want us all to be angry with you, do you?" The comments upset you. You are just trying to do the job the best way you know how. You are not trying to show anyone up. But now you wonder if you should slack off a bit.

What would you do?

Work Histories and Stable Jobs

Different work histories can lead to a stable job. In Lesson 2-3, you read how Terry, Maria, and Cindy followed different paths to a stable job. One route is not necessarily better than another. Some work histories like Ricardo's, however, only lead to detours and dead ends.

A **stable job** is one that you consider to be permanent and that may last several years. This does not mean, however, that you stay in the job forever. Remember Cindy's example (see page 48). You may have a stable job at any time in your work life. Following are additional characteristics of stable jobs. Being aware of them can help you gain greater control over your work history.

Self-direction

Gaining a stable job does not usually happen by accident. Most successful careers come from hard work and **self-direction**, which means setting goals and taking steps to get there. Part of being self-directed is developing your skills through education or training.

Once you get a job, you need to work hard to keep it. This means performing your job tasks proficiently. Your employer pays you to do all of your job tasks carefully and correctly. You need to learn and grow on the job. You need to keep up-to-date with what is going on in your field.

Advancing in a job usually requires doing more than your share. To become eligible for **promotion**, or advancement to a higher-level job or position, you may also need to get more education or training. Sometimes, advancing in a career involves taking risks. A willingness to take a risk, though, often leads to greater personal and career success.

Effort Pays Off

Not enough jobs are available for everyone who wants one. This is especially true for young people. If you want to work, you may have to accept any job that you can get. It may be low-paying, boring, or undesirable in some other way. But a job is a job! Many adults started their careers this way.

Many jobs are physically demanding.

It can be argued that there are no bad jobs as long as they are not illegal, immoral, or otherwise harmful. A job is a beginning. It is a way to earn money, get experience, learn skills, and prove yourself. Your first job may lead to a better one if you are cooperative, follow rules and directions, take an interest in what you are doing, and do your best. Getting along with coworkers and customers is also important. Employers tend to recognize and reward good work.

Stable Jobs Adapt to Change

The world of work is continually changing. Some industries and occupations become **obsolete**, or no longer exist, as new ones are created. For example, the number of communications equipment operators has steadily decreased because of increased use of voicemail. This technology, however, has created a need for new types of workers who can install and maintain new equipment and software. **Technology** is the application of scientific knowledge to practical uses. During your work life, you will have to adjust to many changes due to *technological changes*.

People who are more successful are generally those who anticipate and adapt to change. Eva and Mario are good examples. Eva and

In addition to working hard at a current job, workers also need to consider how they will obtain their next job.

Workforce Trends

Life expectancy is projected to rise from 77 years in 2005 to 82 years in 2050. Increased life expectancy will probably have little direct effect on the composition of the workforce. However, the impacts on families, jobs, and the marketplace, such as demand for medical services, will likely be significant.

Mario own a keyboarding and printing service. Most of their clients are small business owners and college students.

A few years ago, they began to get requests for desktop publishing. They initially had to decline the business. To meet the needs of clients, they purchased desktop publishing software, scanners, color laser printers, and binding equipment. They also installed free Wi-Fi, created a business website, and joined both Facebook and LinkedIn. And, they began to offer discounts to college students. Mario, Eva, and the office staff took extra time to learn how to use the new software and equipment. They are glad they did. They now have more business and have been able to pay for the new equipment with the increased earnings.

Part of your preparation for a career should include planning for change. Try to develop the skills you will need in tomorrow's workplace.

Monitor Workforce Trends

In Lesson 1-3, you read about future employment trends in various industries and occupations. This kind of information can help you make better educational and occupational decisions. But, it doesn't stop there. It is also important that you continue to **monitor**, or keep track of, such information throughout the course of your career. This is because most workers experience multiple job and/or occupational changes during their working lives. But, how do you keep up-to-date?

The Bureau of Labor Statistics updates its long-term industry and occupation projections every two years. The projections are then published and circulated widely on the BLS website, in the *Occupational Outlook Handbook, Occupational Outlook Quarterly, O*NET*, and in many national newspapers and news magazines.

Taken together, Figures 1-7, 1-9, and 1-10, from Lesson 1-3, show which industries and occupations are projected to experience the greatest future employment growth. Now, take an opposite view and look at projected job losses.

Figure 3-1 on the next page shows the number of jobs that are projected to be lost during the 2008–18 period in specific industries. Declines in industry employment are usually the result of falling demand for specific goods and services, increased imports that reduce domestic production, or the use of technology that increases worker productivity. Declining employment may lead to unfavorable job prospects, but the need to replace workers who leave an industry often creates some job openings.

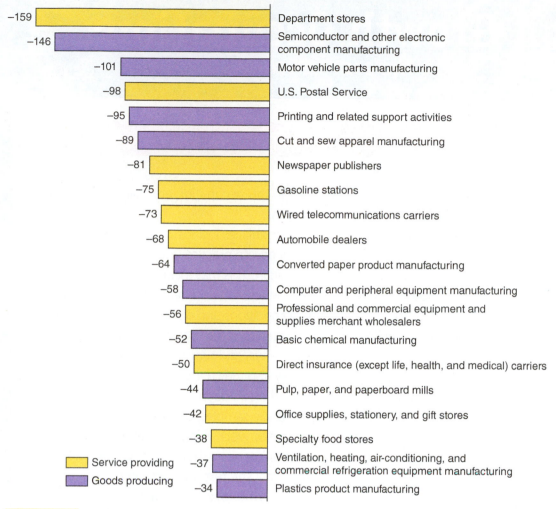

Numeric Decline in Employment of Wage and Salary Workers by Detailed Industry, Projected 2008–18, in Thousands

Value	Industry
−159	Department stores
−146	Semiconductor and other electronic component manufacturing
−101	Motor vehicle parts manufacturing
−98	U.S. Postal Service
−95	Printing and related support activities
−89	Cut and sew apparel manufacturing
−81	Newspaper publishers
−75	Gasoline stations
−73	Wired telecommunications carriers
−68	Automobile dealers
−64	Converted paper product manufacturing
−58	Computer and peripheral equipment manufacturing
−56	Professional and commercial equipment and supplies merchant wholesalers
−52	Basic chemical manufacturing
−50	Direct insurance (except life, health, and medical) carriers
−44	Pulp, paper, and paperboard mills
−42	Office supplies, stationery, and gift stores
−38	Specialty food stores
−37	Ventilation, heating, air-conditioning, and commercial refrigeration equipment manufacturing
−34	Plastics product manufacturing

Service providing
Goods producing

FIGURE 3-1 Projected Job Losses from 2008–2018

Source: *Occupational Outlook Quarterly*, Winter 2009–10, Volume 53, Number 4

3-1 Assessment

1. Name three reasons why a person might voluntarily leave a stable job.

2. Jobs can serve different purposes at different times in a person's life. Give three examples.

3. Give an example to show how taking a risk can lead to greater success in a career.

4. How can technological change influence a career? Give one positive and one negative example.

5. Refer to Figure 3-1. Why do you think large job losses are projected in department stores, the U.S. Postal Service, and newspaper publishers?

High Growth Occupations
FOR THE 21ST CENTURY

Veterinary Technologists and Technicians

Agriculture, Food & Natural Resources

Do you like animals? Do you want to help pets and their owners? If so, consider the occupations of *veterinary technologist* and *technician*. Both work closely with veterinarians to provide care for owners of pets, farm animals, and animals in the care of humane societies and other animal shelters. With the exception of education differences, veterinary technologists and technicians perform many of the same duties, so most workers in this occupation are called technicians or vet techs.

Responsibilities include conducting clinical work in a private practice under the supervision of a veterinarian. This may include performing medical tests on animals and treating and diagnosing medical conditions and diseases. Vet techs also may obtain and record the animal's case history, prepare X-rays, and provide specialized nursing care. They also may perform lab tests such as urinalysis and blood counts, assist with dental care, prepare tissue samples, or take blood samples.

Vet techs work in private veterinary clinics, animal hospitals, humane societies and other animal shelters, and research facilities. For people who love working with animals, the work may be satisfying. Some of the work, however, may be physically and emotionally demanding. Vet techs may need to clean cages and lift, hold, or restrain animals who may bite or scratch. The work setting may be noisy with dogs barking or other animal sounds.

Education requirements are different for veterinary technologists and technicians. Technologists require a four-year program. Technicians require a two-year program. Many community colleges offer a two-year associate degree for technicians. Usually people entering as a technician are expected to work as a trainee with on-the-job training under a veterinarian. State exams and certification are required by every state for both technologists and technicians. Exams and certification requirements differ from state to state.

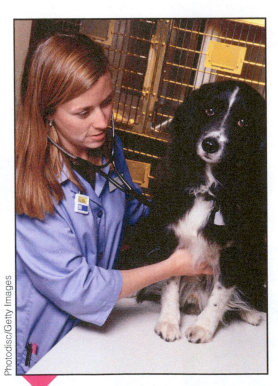

Photodisc/Getty Images

The veterinary technologist and technician occupations may be very satisfying for people who love working with animals.

JOB SEARCH PREPARATION

OBJECTIVES

- Describe the importance of clarifying job goals before looking for employment
- Explain how to get a Social Security number and work permit

KEY TERMS

- Social Security
- Social Security number
- minor
- work permit

Career Decisions

You learn about a job opening for a part-time custodian at the shopping mall. The hours are good and the pay is decent for a beginning job. You cannot decide whether to apply. You really do not want to empty wastebaskets and mop floors. You wonder how you will feel if your friends see you working there.

What would you do?

snapphoto/iStockphoto.com

Job Goals

Students enrolled in work experience education programs get jobs in several ways. In cooperative career and technical education, the coordinator plays a major role. The coordinator usually "sets up" training stations in the community and interviews and selects qualified students for admission to the program. The coordinator then takes into account students' interests, aptitudes, and job goals. These are matched with suitable jobs. It is up to the student, however, to interview with the employer and get the job.

In work-study programs, a student may get a job before or after entering the program. Some students will already have a job and ask to continue it for school credit. This may be done as long as the coordinator approves the training station. Students who do not have jobs when they enroll in a work-study program will need to find one.

Think About Job Goals

Why do you want a job? Be prepared to answer this question. You will be hearing it often. Your work experience coordinator will certainly ask it. The coordinator wants to help you find a job that suits your interests and abilities. By getting to know you better, your coordinator can help you get a job you will enjoy. Counselors, placement officers, and others you approach for job leads will ask you about your job goals. And, of course, an interviewer will probably ask the question during a job interview.

Thinking about your job goals will help you, too. What you want out of a job will influence how and where you look for one. Since you are now enrolled in a work experience program, you have probably already done some thinking about your goals.

Benefits of Work Experience

Reviewing the benefits of work experience education covered in Chapter 1 can help you clarify your job goals. Typical goals are:

- Learn occupational skills
- Develop employability skills
- Establish a work record
- Earn while you learn
- Discover career interests and goals
- Recognize the relationship between education and work
- Remain employed after graduation

You may want to rank the benefits in order of their importance to you. Doing this can help you focus on your most important goals.

It was not difficult for Rachel to decide what she wanted out of a job. She became interested in interior design after taking courses in textiles and home furnishings and equipment. She learned about a co-op position at a large furniture store that has an interior design department. She interviewed for the job and was hired. Rachel loves what she is doing. She hopes that the company will hire her permanently after she graduates. Can you name Rachel's job goals?

Get Required Documentation

Federal law requires every person regardless of age to have a Social Security number to be claimed as a dependent on Tax Form 1040. If you do not have a Social Security number, you should get one before you start a job search. You may also need to get a work permit.

Search the Net

Access an application for a Social Security card by clicking on the link for Chapter 3 at **www.cengage.com/school/working.** You can use the application to obtain an original, duplicate, or corrected card or to report information changes. Fill out the form. If you don't have a card, submit the form to your nearest Social Security administration office, following the directions on the form.

www.cengage.com/school/working

Social Security Number

Social Security is a national program of social insurance. Your employer will withhold money from your paycheck for this. The money will go to the Social Security system. Social Security was designed to provide income payments to retired workers. Sometimes Social Security benefits are available to families prior to retirement if there is a loss of income due to either illness or the untimely death of a family member. You will learn more about Social Security in Chapter 19.

In order for the government to keep a record of your earnings, you will need a **Social Security number**. This is a number that specifically identifies you for Social Security, tax, and employment purposes. The number will remain with you for life. The number is unique to you; no one else has the same number. An employer will ask for your number when you apply for a job or start work. Your Social Security number may have other uses. For example, you may be required to provide your Social Security number to prove your identity when you apply for a driver's license.

You can apply for a number at any Social Security office. You can also download an application form from the Web. You must fill out the application form and provide proof of your date of birth, identity, and U.S. citizenship. Noncitizens that have been approved to work in the United States by the Department of Homeland Security (DHS) are required to have a Social Security number. After your application is processed, you will receive a Social Security card in the mail.

Work Permit

At one time, employers were free to hire workers of any age for any type of job. It was not uncommon for young children to work long days in factories, mills, and mines.

Many occupations have experienced workers train younger workers.

Various federal and state laws now protect the health and safety of **minors**, or people who have not reached the full legal age. Such laws regulate working conditions and working hours of students under the age of 16 or 18. For instance, the Fair Labor Standards Act states that a person under the age of 16 may not be employed during school hours. Some states have stricter child labor laws than others. The Department of Labor has a website, YouthRules, which explains child labor laws. You can determine the laws in your state by going to the Youth-Rules website (youthrules.dol.gov).

A **work permit** is a form issued by school officials that gives a student legal permission to work during school hours as part of a work experience education program. A work permit restricts the number of hours worked and the types of jobs a student can perform. School officials issue work permits for students under a certain age. In some states, the age is 16. In other states, it is 18.

In addition to a work permit, your state or school district may require other kinds of approval before you can work. Ask your school counselor or work experience coordinator about such rules.

3-2 Assessment

1. Takeesha has a part-time job. She is starting a work experience program. How can she keep her job and get school credit?

2. Why is it important to clarify your job goals before beginning the job search?

3. Why must you get a Social Security number before you start work?

4. Are foreign workers required to obtain a social security number?

5. A work permit allows a student to work during school hours. Who issues it?

APPRENTICESHIP PROGRAMS

OBJECTIVES

- Describe the nature and operation of an apprenticeship program

KEY TERMS

- apprenticeship
- apprentice
- journey worker
- apprenticeship register

nadirco/Shutterstock.com

Career Decisions

"I learn new things every day," says Elizabeth, who is training as an electrician apprentice. "I get to use my hands and my mind. I'm practically guaranteed a great job in a few years in an occupation that I know I will like and that pays very well."

In fact, Elizabeth earns full-time pay while she learns. "It's better than any scholarship," she says. Elizabeth is describing a few of the benefits of apprenticeship. She was looking for a low-cost education in a highly skilled field. Like thousands of others, she found what she wanted in apprenticeship.

Elizabeth is so enthusiastic about her apprenticeship program that you have begun to think that this might be a good alternative. You want to find out more about apprenticeship programs, but you don't know where to start.

What would you do?

Job Training with a Paycheck

An **apprenticeship** is a formal on-the-job training (OJT) program during which a worker (called an **apprentice**) learns an occupation. Extensive OJT and related instruction are involved. Apprenticeships usually last from one to six years. During this time, the apprentice works under a skilled, experienced worker called a **journey worker**. Upon completion of the apprenticeship program, the apprenticeship becomes a journey worker.

Under the journey worker's guidance, the apprentice gradually learns a trade and performs the work under less and less supervision. Apprentices are full-time employees. An apprentice's pay generally starts out at about half that of an experienced worker and gradually increases throughout the apprenticeship. Many programs are cosponsored by trade unions that offer apprentices union membership.

Registered Apprenticeships

Some high schools offer pre-apprenticeship programs that are quite similar to co-operative education and work study. However, almost all apprenticeship programs begin after high school graduation and are operated according to formal guidelines established by the U.S. Department of Labor. Programs which meet certain government standards of fairness, safety, and training are called *registered apprenticeships*. Any occupation can be registered as apprenticeable if it meets the following four criteria.

- It is clearly defined
- It is customarily learned on the job
- It requires manual, mechanical, or technical skill
- It requires at least 2,000 hours of work experience and, usually, at least 144 hours of related instruction

Over 1000 occupations within the United States have registered apprenticeships. Growth in apprenticeship programs is ongoing. Construction and manufacturing apprenticeships are most common, but apprenticeships are available for all sorts of occupations. Possibilities range from telecommunications, environmental protection, and pastry making to healthcare, childcare, and the arts.

The number of apprenticeable occupations may seem overwhelming, but not every occupation is available at a given time. Programs open and close depending on the number of new workers in an occupation, which varies from state to state.

A journey worker teaches an apprentice how to safely perform job duties.

auremar/Shutterstock.com

It often takes many years of skilled supervision for an apprentice to learn all aspects of a job.

Find an Open Program

After selecting a preferred occupation, the next step is to look for openings in apprenticeship programs. Finding open programs can be a challenge, especially in occupations with small numbers of workers. A good place to start is the U.S. Department of Labor Office of Apprenticeship Sponsors Website (oa. doleta.gov). You can look for apprenticeship opportunities within your state and county.

Joining the military is another way to participate in apprenticeships. People who enlist in certain occupations, including cook and engine mechanic, can complete registered apprenticeships during military training. Local military recruiters can provide additional information.

Qualifications for Entrance

Employee associations, employers, or labor unions manage apprenticeship programs. As program sponsors, they choose apprentices, develop training standards, and pay wages and other expenses.

For all registered apprenticeships, there is a standard application procedure. First, applicants fill out the required forms. Next, applicants take any required tests. Finally, those who meet preliminary requirements are asked to complete an interview. All qualified applicants are placed on an apprenticeship waiting list called an **apprenticeship register**. The most qualified applicants are listed first.

Apprenticeships in some occupations are highly competitive, with more applicants than openings. If you want to work in a competitive apprenticeship program, you may have to wait weeks or months before an opening becomes available.

3-3 Assessment

1. Apprenticeship is often compared to co-operative education. How are they similar and different?

2. Can a local high school offer registered apprenticeships? Why or why not?

3. Where can you find out about open apprenticeship programs?

4. What is the required procedure to get on an apprenticeship register?

Focus on the Workplace

Labor Unions

A labor union is a group of workers who have joined together to protect their rights. The two main types of unions are craft and industrial. A *craft union* is made up of skilled workers in a craft or trade, such as plumbers, musicians, or barbers. Workers in the same industry often belong to an *industrial union*. Perhaps you have heard of the United Auto Workers or the United Mine Workers. These are industrial unions.

Throughout its history, organized labor has fought for three main goals. These have been improvements in

- Wages, hours, and benefits
- Job security
- Safe and healthful working conditions

Unions also provide apprenticeship programs that teach work skills to young union members. Some unions have hiring halls where workers can go to find out about job openings.

Most unions in the United States are in the Midwest and Northeast. These areas have traditionally had large construction, manufacturing, transportation, and mining industries.

An employer that has an agreement with a union is called a union shop. In a union shop, the employer can hire whomever he or she chooses. However, the employee must join the union within a certain period of time. About 22 states have so-called "right- to-work" laws that do not allow union shops. These states have open shops in which an employee does not have to join a union.

When you start a job, a coworker or supervisor may ask you to join a union. Members of the local union must vote on your membership. Usually, though, anyone who applies is accepted. You will probably pay an initiation fee to join, and you must pay regular dues. You can learn more about unions on the Internet. Many unions have websites for news and membership information.

THINK CRITICALLY

1. Do you think labor unions are needed today? Why or why not?
2. What might be some advantages and disadvantages of union membership?

Photodisc/Getty Images

This pastry chef is a union member. Does she belong to a craft union or an industrial union?

OBJECTIVES

- Identify job lead sources
- Demonstrate how to prepare a job-lead card

KEY TERMS

- entry-level job
- referral
- advertisement
- One-Stop Career Center
- fee
- job bank
- job portal
- social network
- job-lead card

Feng Yu/Shutterstock.com

► Ethical Decisions

A schoolmate approaches you and says he heard you were looking for a job. He has a buddy who needs some people to deliver packages on weekends. The work is easy. You simply ride the bus around town and drop off packages at various places of business. The pay is $15 per hour in cash. You are told not to ask questions or to discuss the job with other people. You are concerned about taking the job because it sounds "fishy."

What would you do?

Sources of Job Leads

It was the first day of the new school year. Sally was on the way to her work experience education class. "I wonder what job they will have for me," thought Sally.

The bell rang and students turned their attention to Mr. Amed, the teacher-coordinator. He took attendance and then began to explain about work experience education.

"A requirement of this program," he explained, "is that each of you must have a job. Some of you already have jobs. For the rest of you, your first 'job' will be to get a job. I do not have any jobs to assign."

Sally was somewhat surprised. She raised her hand to ask some questions. "Mr. Amed, I do not know where to get a job," she said. "Where do I look for jobs? And if I find one, what do I have to do to apply for it?"

"Don't worry," said Mr. Amed. "I will help you learn about sources of job leads and how to apply for a job."

If you do not yet have a job, you will need to plan how to get one. At this point in your life, you will probably apply for an **entry-level job**. An entry-level job requires little or no experience. The following sources of job leads are those through which you are most likely to find a job. Some of these sources are traditional ones that have been used for decades. However, you will also be introduced to newer approaches made possible through use of the Web.

Family and Friends

Start your job search by making a list of your relatives, neighbors, and friends. They may know of job leads from their own job searches. Do not forget places where you and your family do business. You may want to have a family member review your final list. Do not hesitate to ask family or friends for help. However, do not expect them to find a job for you. Getting a job lead is the most you should hope for. It will be up to you to pursue the lead.

In-School Sources

Three good sources of job leads may be available within your school. One is your cooperative career and technical education or work experience coordinator. He or she is probably already involved in helping you. Do not sit back and wait for the coordinator to find you a job.

Most schools also have a guidance office or guidance counselor. It is common for local employers to contact counselors when looking for workers. The counselor will usually keep a list of job openings or post them on a bulletin board. Ask the counselor for information available about job openings.

A third source is job placement offices or career centers. Interested students gener-

Sharing information with friends, including contact information of people you know who might have information about specific jobs, is a good way to get job leads.

ally register with the office. Job counselors may provide job counseling, help match students with job openings, and facilitate interviews. **Referrals**, which provide students with specific job or contact information, are given to direct a student to employers who are hiring.

Advertisements

When employers have jobs to fill, they often use **advertisements** (ads), which are written descriptions of jobs, to look for workers. Ads may be posted on a store window, published in the classified section of a newspaper, or posted online. Five common kinds of ads are shown in Figure 3-2 on the next page.

The first kind is an *open ad*. It tells about the job requirements, identifies the employer, and tells how to apply. The second kind is the *blind ad*. The name, address, and phone number of the employer are not shown. Employers post blind ads to keep from being bombarded with phone calls. Employers screen applicants to determine which qualified applicants to interview.

ZUMBA INSTRUCTOR

Fitlslt, a leading corporate fitness company, is seeking a Zumba instructor for downtown Boston class on Thursdays from 6:30pm–7:15pm. Certification required. $21 per class. Applications accepted through 1-15-2012. Apply in person at Fitlslt, 417 North Main St., Boston, MA, 02110

OPEN AD

OFFICE ASSISTANT

Travel company seeks friendly person to perform various office duties. Must have computer knowledge and customer service skills. Benefits available. $8/hour. Send cover letter and resume to:

Office Assistant, P.O. Box 737, Boulder, CO, 80306

BLIND AD

ASSEMBLER (Toledo, OH)

Date: 2011-04-08, 11:45 AM EDT

Reply to: job-xxexj 2413747638@joblistings.org

Injection Molding company in Toledo, OH has an opening in our Assembly department for: Assembler. First shift (6:00 am to 2:30 pm) Duties include: Line Assembly of plastic automotive parts. Eligible for benefits after 90 days of employment. Experience in Assembly preferred.
- Compensation: $9.12/hr.
- Principals only. Recruiters, please don't contact this job poster.
- Please, no phone calls about this job!
- Please do not contact job poster about other services, products or commercial interests.
PostingID: 2312740038

POSTED BLIND AD WITH ELECTRONIC REPLY

EARN
$400–$800

Email for details to:
Greatjobsareus@greatjobsareus.com

CATCH-TYPE AD

DRAFTER
$28,000

Fee Paid

At least 2 years' experience. CAD skills required. Call us or bring in your resume to compare your experience with our company requirements.
JOLEEN EMPLOYMENT AGENCY
17 Plaza Offices, P.O. Box 671
Palestine, TX 75901-2837
555-0192

AGENCY SPOT AD

FIGURE 3-2 Examples of Job Advertisements

An electronic version of the blind ad, often found on electronic job boards, is the *posted blind ad with electronic reply*. When you click on the "reply to" hyperlink, an email to the employer is automatically prepared with the job title in the subject line. By using an email address specifically developed for the particular job listed, the identity of the employer is disguised.

A *catch-type* ad is the fourth kind. It tends to promise good pay and downplay the qualifications needed for the job. The "catch" is that the job is usually for door-to-door salespeople or similar sales jobs.

The last kind of ad is the *agency spot ad*. Note that the ad omits the name of the employer. It is used by private employment agencies to advertise jobs available only through the agency.

CareerOneStop

Every state has a system of public employment offices usually called **One-Stop Career Center** or something similar. More than 1,800 of these centers are located throughout the country. These offices provide free services such as job counseling and training, help with resumes, and job listings. The primary purpose of the career centers is to help workers who have lost jobs or been laid off find jobs. Services are also provided to first-time job seekers, but preference is usually given to previously employed workers.

Some offices have a youth counselor who works mainly with young people. Career center counselors often cooperate closely with local high school work experience programs and community job training projects.

Registration is required to use the career center. Online registration is available. A counselor will interview you to find out your interests and qualifications. You might be asked to take an interest inventory or aptitude test. If a job is available, the counselor will arrange for you to have an interview. You can find the location of One-Stop Career Centers in your state by going to the CareerOneStop website (www.careeronestop.org) sponsored by the U.S. Department of Labor.

Private Employment Agencies

These are businesses that find people jobs for a fee. The **fee** is a sum of money charged by a private employment agency for helping someone find a job, and it is paid by either the employer or the employee. If you use a private employment agency, be sure that you understand the financial arrangements before signing a contract or accepting an interview. Private agencies do not generally deal with clients under 18 and those who are looking for part-time, entry-level jobs.

Direct Employer Contact

A help-wanted sign posted in a business is the oldest method of announcing a job opening and is still commonly used. If you see such a sign, ask the employer for an application. Many large employers such as McDonalds, Walmart, and Lowe's have an in-store computer kiosk where you fill out a job application online.

FIGURE 3-3 Examples of the Most Common Occupations for Workers Ages 16–24

1. Cashiers
2. Cooks
3. Stock handlers and baggers
4. Waiters and waitresses
5. Custodians and cleaners
6. Secretaries/administrative assistants
7. Construction and other laborers
8. Retail sales workers
9. Receptionists
10. Child-care workers
11. Food counter and rental clerks
12. Nursing aides, orderlies, and attendants
13. Bank tellers
14. Delivery truck drivers
15. Service station attendants
16. Carpenters
17. Bookkeepers and accounting clerks
18. General office clerks
19. Groundskeepers and gardeners
20. Computer operators and repairers
21. Animal care workers
22. Fitness workers
23. Stock clerks and order fillers
24. Couriers and messengers
25. Production machine operators

Employers often have unadvertised job openings. Figure 3-3 on the prior page lists 25 of the most common occupations for workers ages 16–24. Study this list to get an idea of the types of employers that hire large numbers of young workers. You might use the *Yellow Pages* to make a list of companies to contact.

Another means of direct employer contact is to visit a company employment office. Go dressed as you would for an interview. Be prepared to fill out an employment application form. Check bulletin boards outside the personnel office, too. Available jobs are often listed there. Some companies also have a separate telephone number that provides prerecorded messages about openings.

Web-Based Job Banks and Portals

The Internet has changed the way that most public and private institutions announce job vacancies. For example, school guidance offices and career centers often list job leads on a web page. Many newspapers, particularly those in large cities, provide online listings of job vacancies. **Job banks** provide an electronic data base of jobs searchable by computer. CareerOneStop provides links to job banks for states.

Private employment agencies typically have a website that explains their services to job seekers. Finally, thousands of public and private employers list job opportunities online. Many of these listings also provide online job application forms and accept electronic resumes.

In addition to listing job vacancies at individual companies and institutions, the Internet has a number of sites devoted entirely or in part to jobs and job seeking. *Web portals*, or Internet sites that provide access to a wide variety of web-based content, are familiar to many

Communication at Work — ASKING FOR JOB LEADS

By current estimates, the average American will change jobs at least seven times in his or her career. The job-change process can be made easier if you get job leads. How can you gather job leads effectively?

Be clear about what you want. Most people want to help you, especially close friends and family members. But they can only help if they know exactly what you want. Make sure you can communicate your work history and career goals.

Ask for what you want. Asking for job leads can be awkward. Don't get discouraged. The person you are asking probably had the same feelings at one time.

Be polite and grateful for information. Have you ever heard the expression "information is power"? When you ask for job leads, you are asking someone for important information. The more polite you are, the more information you may receive, and that may help you get a good job!

THINK CRITICALLY

1. What can you do to thank someone who gives you a job lead?
2. Why is it important to show your appreciation for job leads?

Internet users. A **job portal** is a website that provides access to online job information. CareerOneStop has a listing of twelve of the most common job banks and job portals. You need to recognize that web-based job banks and job portals may be less useful to young people looking for entry-level jobs than more traditional sources.

Use Social Networks to Find Jobs

A **social network** is an online site that allows individuals and businesses to interact with family, friends, acquaintances, and other businesses. The growth of social networks such as Facebook, Twitter, My Space, and LinkedIn has provided other important tools for job searches. Social networks are primarily used to keep up with friends and family and make new connections with people who have common interests. You should get familiar with the different forms of social media and their approaches. Each one is slightly different in the kinds, formats, and delivery methods of information shared through their user network.

Workplace Innovations

SMARTPHONE AND TABLET APPS

According to MarketWatch, the business news and information website, the "app revolution" is the biggest market in the history of the planet. What is meant by "apps" are mobile computer software applications, for smartphones and tablets. In 2010, more than 250 million people bought an app-enabled smartphone. By the end of 2013, it is estimated that there will be more than one billion app-enabled smartphone users worldwide. Tablet use is increasing rapidly.

There was only a small market for apps prior to July 2008 when Apple opened the App Store with 500 free and purchasable apps. In May 2011, Apple reported having more than 500,000 apps and having reached over 15 billion app downloads. These figures do not include several billion more app downloads based on the Android operating system and those of other manufacturers.

A smartphone operates as a wireless mini-computer with a touch screen. Tablets operate in a similar way. The capabilities of smartphones, tablets, and computers are becoming increasingly similar.

When you download an app such as Facebook, a small icon will appear on your screen. To connect, you simply touch the icon and are sent to the Facebook website. Most, but not all apps connect to the Internet and consume data when in use.

There are approximately 20 different categories of app software. The five most popular and their percent of total sales in 2011 were: games (15%), books (14%), entertainment (11%), education (8%), and lifestyle (7%). The average price paid for an app in 2011 was $3.64, although 37% of all apps were free. What was the number one app in 2011? You guessed it—"Angry Birds." What is your favorite app?

NET FOLLOW-UP

Use a search engine to explore the Web for additional information on the topics of "smartphone applications" and "best mobile apps." Are there job search apps that could assist you with finding a job?

Using social networks for a job search is not as simple as posting a resume on a job portal site. The correct use of a social network can take a considerable amount of time. It is generally more effective to spend extra time and energy maintaining a high profile on one site, than trying to juggle different platforms on multiple sites.

Some sites offer the opportunity to have jobs sent to your email or phone account as soon as they are posted. When using this type of service, you can narrow the job postings that are sent to you by selecting specific criteria to identify the jobs of most interest to you. For example, you could register on the site for jobs in lawn care that are located in Miami, Florida. With that criteria selected you would not receive job postings for lawn care jobs in Detroit, Michigan or for sales jobs in Miami, Florida. Just as it is important to be courteous in face-to-face interactions, it is also important to be courteous when using social networks for business purposes. It is important to build a connection with contacts before asking them for information or business contacts.

Keep Track of Job Leads

"Hey, Steve," said Carlos. "I got my first job lead yesterday. I was eating lunch when I noticed the manager putting up a sign. It was for a part-time kitchen helper. So I wrote the information down."

"Great! What did the sign say?" asked Steve.

"Let me see," answered Carlos. "I have the information here someplace."

Carlos continued to search his backpack for the scrap of paper on which he took notes. Finally he said, "Darn, I must have lost it. Oh well, I will go back this weekend and get the information again."

Carlos is off to a shaky start in his search for a job. He was alert to notice the sign and to write down the information. Carlos was careless, though, in misplacing his notes. He also showed poor judgment in not going back or calling right away. When he returned during the weekend, he found the job was filled.

Competition for jobs is fierce. It is important to act quickly when a job of interest is available. If you don't act quickly, someone else may get the job you want.

Prepare Job-lead Cards

Whenever you learn about a job lead, make a job-lead card. A **job-lead card** is a card used to record information and notes about a job lead. An example is shown in Figure 3-4 on the next page. A 5-inch by 8-inch card works best because it gives you enough room to record information and make notes. The card has two parts.

On the Job Lead part (Side 1), record all important information about the job. If you have an ad, tape it onto the card. Write the source, date, type of position, and person to contact. Record the company name, address, phone number, and URL, if the organization has one.

On the Action Taken part (Side 2), record what you did to follow up the job lead. Write the date when you contacted the employer and the name of the person with whom you talked. Also write the results of the contact. If you get an appointment, record the date, time, and place. If you need directions, be sure to ask. Write the directions on the back of the card. Any follow-up you will do after your appointment should also be noted.

Benefits of Job-lead Cards

What are some benefits of using job-lead cards? They keep you from forgetting important information. They save you time. By being organized, you make better use of your time. Can you name other benefits?

Follow Through

You face stiff competition for jobs. Do not hold back. As soon as you learn about a job lead, follow through with quick action. The early applicant usually gets the job. If you do not get the job immediately, call or go back a few days later. Let the employer know that you are really interested in the job. Motivation and persistence, so important in finding a job, are also qualities that make you a good employee. Employers recognize this. Demonstrating motivation and persistence in pursuing a job lead increases your chance of being rewarded with a job offer.

JOB LEAD

Source: *Daily Gazette*
Date: *1/20/--*
Type of Position: *Packing Clerk*
Person to Contact: *Steve*
Company Name:
Address: *Lindbergh & Olive*
Phone Number: *555-0151*
URL:

PACKING CLERKS
PART-TIME JOB OPENINGS

Please: These are not full-time jobs. We have peak business seasons in Jan., Feb., Apr., Oct. Hours will vary from 0 to 40 a week. Also may have late afternoon (3 p.m.–7 p.m.) shift available. Job requires standing & using manual dexterity while preparing and packing women's clothing, shoes, and gifts for UPS shipment. Perfect job for stay-at-home moms or dads or students. Again—not a full-time job! Near Lindbergh & Olive. No smoking. $8.10 per hour. All applicants must pass a written test.

CALL STEVE, 555-0151

ACTION TAKEN

Call Made To: *Steve (555-0151)*
Date: *1/21/--*
Contact Made With:
Date:
Results: *Asked to come in and fill out job application and take a written test.*
Date, Time, and Place of Appointment: *1/23/--, 9:30 a.m. Mid-West Packaging Inc. Use main entrance.*
Follow-up: *After test, call back (ask for Steve) on 1/28/-- for possible interview.*

FIGURE 3-4 Sample Job-lead Card

3-4 Assessment

1. Andrea says she would "feel funny" asking friends and family for job leads. Do you agree with her? Why or why not?

2. Your school may have job lead sources. Name three.

3. Name five common types of help-wanted ads.

4. What is the purpose of the One-Stop Career Centers?

5. What are the main differences between a public and a private employment agency?

6. Name three reasons why job banks, job portals, and social network sites are valuable job search tools.

7. Explain the purpose of a job-lead card.

8. Why should you follow through with quick action on a job lead?

Chapter Summary

3-1 Obtain a Stable Job

A. A stable job is one you consider to be permanent. It may last for several years. Many different routes can lead to a stable job. One route is not necessarily better than another.

B. Most stable jobs result from hard work and self-direction. Quality effort on a job usually pays off. People with successful, stable jobs are generally those who anticipate and adapt to change.

C. Most workers experience multiple job and/or occupational changes during their lifetimes. Therefore, it is important for you to monitor how industries and occupations grow and decline over time.

3-2 Job Search Preparation

A. What you want out of a job will influence how and where you look for it. Therefore, think about your job goals before beginning the job search. Do this by reviewing the seven benefits of work experience education.

B. Apply for a Social Security number as soon as possible. An employer will ask for your number when you apply for a job or start work. In some states, you may also need to get a work permit.

3-3 Apprenticeship Programs

A. An apprenticeship is a formal on-the-job training (OJT) program during which an apprentice (worker) learns an occupation. Extensive OJT and related instruction are involved under the supervision of a journey worker.

B. Most apprenticeship programs begin after high school and are operated according to formal guidelines established by the U.S. Department of Labor. Programs which meet certain government standards are called registered apprenticeships.

C. Applicants to an apprenticeship program must follow a standard process consisting of an application, testing, and an interview. Qualified applicants are then placed on a waiting list called an apprenticeship register.

3-4 Job Search in the Digital Age

A. To be enrolled in cooperative career and technical education or work-study, you must have a job. If you do not already have one, your first "job" will be to get a job.

B. The most common sources of entry-level jobs are (a) family and friends, (b) in-school sources, (c) advertisements, (d) One-Stop Career Centers, (e) private employment agencies, (f) direct employer contact, (g) job banks and job portals, and (h) social networks.

C. The Internet has changed the way that most public and private institutions announce job vacancies and the way that job seekers look for jobs. In this new digital age, it is essential that you learn how to use job banks, job portals, and social networks to look for jobs.

D. Whenever you learn about a job lead, make a job-lead card. It will help you remember important information, save you time, and help you get more positive results. After recording all important information about a job lead, follow through with quick action.

Activities

1. Conduct a search on the Internet and collect information regarding how to use a business networking site, like LinkedIn, to conduct a job search. Working in small teams, compile a list of "do's" and "don'ts" for generating an online business profile. As a group, develop the characteristics and background of a pretend student. Pick an industry or job the pretend student wants to work in.

   a. Follow the guidelines developed by the group to create an online profile for the pretend student. Share the results as a class.

   b. Using each team's list of "do's" and "don'ts," develop a set of guidelines that the class thinks is appropriate for developing online profiles.

   c. Compare the class guidelines to guidelines published online. Revise the class guidelines to include helpful ideas from the online search.

   d. Use the revised class guidelines to develop your own online profile. Submit the profile to your instructor.

2. Find examples of the five types of ads described earlier in the chapter. You can find the examples either online or in a newspaper. (The Sunday paper often has the most help wanted ads.) Print out any examples found online. Tape the examples onto a sheet of paper and label each type of ad. Then give the paper to your instructor. When you get your paper back, discuss your ads with the class.

3. There are many online sources available to help with the job search process. Access www.cengage.com/school/working. Then click on *Web Links* to find links for the following.

   a. **YouthRules! by State**   Review the types of information available. Click on YouthRules by State to find the requirements in the state where you live or plan to work. Find out your state's rules on student employment during school hours. If a work permit or other type of approval is required, take the necessary steps to complete the approval process.

   b. **Apprenticeship Videos**   Watch an introductory video describing apprenticeships. Then click on Apprenticeship Sponsors.

Follow instructions to find open programs in your county. Make a list of the apprenticeships that are of interest to you.

c. **Use Social Networks to Look for Jobs** Read three articles from the sites. List ten key points to consider when using social networks to find jobs. Share your list with the class.

4. Select an industry from Figure 3-1, in Lesson 3-1, that is of interest to you. Use the *Occupational Outlook Handbook* to identify five jobs from that industry. Consider local business opportunities where you live. Prepare a list of the selected jobs and possible local employers. Compare your list with classmates and discuss whether these jobs should be pursued given that jobs in these industries are expected to decline.

5. Using the job-lead card shown in Figure 3-4 as a sample, make your own job-lead card. Create new categories of information that you think might be helpful to have on the card. Exchange cards with a partner and give suggestions for improving his or her card.

Word Power

On a separate sheet of paper, match each definition with the correct term. All definitions will be used, and a definition will be used only once.

a. advertisement
b. apprentice
c. apprenticeship
d. apprenticeship register
e. entry-level job
f. fee
g. job bank
h. job portal
i. job-lead card
j. journey worker
k. minor
l. monitor
m. obsolete
n. One-Stop Career Center
o. promotion
p. referral
q. self-direction
r. social network
s. Social Security
t. Social Security number
u. stable job
v. technology
w. work permit

6. Direct students to employers who are hiring
7. Skilled, experienced worker who teaches an occupation to and supervises the work of apprentices
8. Advancement to a higher-level job or position
9. Type of formal occupational program combining on-the-job training with related instruction
10. Application of scientific knowledge to practical uses
11. Waiting list on which the names of qualified apprenticeship applicants are placed
12. Electronic data base of jobs searchable by a computer
13. Job boards or company website containing job banks and various kinds of job search information
14. People who have not reached the full legal age
15. Online site that allows individuals to interact with family and friends as well as being a useful tool for job searches
16. Outdated; no longer in use
17. Worker participating in an apprenticeship program
18. Setting goals and working toward them
19. To keep track of; check continually
20. Beginning job that requires little or no previous job knowledge
21. Job considered to be permanent; may last several years
22. State system of public employment offices that helps unemployed people find jobs

23. National program of social insurance
24. Number assigned to qualified people by the Social Security Administration
25. Form issued by school officials that gives a student legal permission to work during school hours as part of a work experience education program
26. Card on which to record information and notes about a job lead
27. A written description providing notice of a job that needs to be filled
28. The money charged by a company to help job seekers find jobs

Think Critically

29. What role does the teacher-coordinator play in helping students find jobs in work experience education programs?
30. Why have state and federal laws been passed restricting the hours of employment and regulating the working conditions of minors?
31. Eight major sources of job leads are discussed in this chapter. Can you think of other sources in your city or community that have not been mentioned?
32. The ease or difficulty of finding a job may be influenced by where you live, for example, whether you live in a city or rural area. What other environmental, economic, or occupational factors influence job availability?
33. What benefits do employee associations, employers, and labor unions receive from sponsoring apprenticeship programs?
34. How can you utilize all the job search methods identified in this chapter to research current job openings for five jobs you may be interested in pursuing?
35. Why do some states require you to register before accessing the state's job bank?
36. List several short-term goals that you might hope to achieve by accepting employment now. Describe how these job goals could help you achieve goals in your life-span plan.

Career Transitions Connection

Find a Job

Click *Browse Career Paths*. From the *Get a Job* tab, click *Search Jobs, Internships, & More*. Specify if the job you are searching for is an apprenticeship, temporary, or entry level. Complete the requested fields and then click on *search*. Review the information for three jobs that are of the most interest. You may need to enter alternate job titles if the particular job you are seeking does not have any openings in your geographic area. List the jobs, in order of preference, on a sheet of paper. Be prepared to participate in a class discussion regarding the best way to obtain these jobs.

"Genius is one percent inspiration and ninety-nine percent perspiration." —THOMAS A. EDISON

Apply for a Job

Andresr/Shutterstock.com

PREVIEW

Finding job leads may seem to take a long time. It does indeed take a great deal of time to contact family and friends, search newspaper and online ads, search job banks and job portals, develop an online profile, and identify other leads. Once you find a good job lead, however, things can speed up very quickly.

Taking/Action   Work Experience Education

Ricardo learned from his Uncle Geraldo about a bowling buddy who was expanding his hardware store. Uncle Geraldo thought his friend might be hiring some new employees and suggested Ricardo should call him.

The next day Ricardo called Mr. Tamaka at the hardware store. He explained that he was looking for a job and that his uncle had told him to call. Mr. Tamaka said that he had already received several inquiries about the job.

"However," he went on to say, "I would be happy to have you fill out a job application form. Why not stop by and see me after school tomorrow?"

"Thank you very much," said Ricardo. "I will be there at four o'clock tomorrow afternoon."

Ricardo went to see Mr. Tamaka the next day after school. He made sure that he was neatly dressed. He went with notes he had prepared about his work history. He asked for the job application and filled it out.

Donna is also on the trail of a job lead. She read an ad in the newspaper for a Hair Stylist/Shampoo Assistant. "Experience helpful but not necessary," the ad said. "Full training available. Forward a resume to The Hair Performers, 638 North Walnut St., Muncie, IN 47308-9372 or hairstylist@hairperformers.com."

"This sounds like what I am looking for," Donna told her family. "I'd better write a cover letter and put my resume in the mail at once."

Ricardo and Donna were ready to take quick action on job leads. Ricardo already had a personal data sheet prepared to assist him in filling out a job application form. Likewise, Donna had a stack of resumes ready and waiting. She also knew how to write a cover letter. Ricardo and Donna have learned some valuable skills needed to apply for a job.

iodrakon/Shutterstock.com

* Success Tip

Follow up on job leads quickly by having the information you need.

THINK CRITICALLY

1. What were some good steps that Ricardo took in pursuing the hardware store job?

2. Why did Donna want to get her cover letter and resume in the mail quickly?

DATA SHEETS AND JOB APPLICATIONS

OBJECTIVES
- Prepare a personal data sheet
- Complete a job application form

KEY TERMS
- reference
- personal data sheet
- job application form

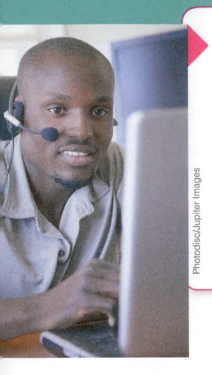

Photodisc/Jupiter Images

Career Decisions

You see an ad in the newspaper for a computer operator. The job is exactly what you are looking for. However, the ad states that "prior work experience is required." You have not had any prior employment as a computer operator, but you have been operating your own computer for many years. Plus, you have been volunteering your time at the Senior Center helping with computer instruction and repairs. You are confident that you can do the job. Should you ignore the stated requirement and apply for the job?

What would you do?

Personal Data Sheet

Suppose that you are in Ricardo's shoes and have to fill out a job application form tomorrow. Will you be prepared? Can you, for example, remember the name, address, and telephone number of each employer for whom you have worked? Do you know your high school class rank and grade point average (GPA)? **Reference** are individuals who are qualified and willing to provide information about you to a potential employer. Do you have a few people in mind who could serve as references for you?

Most employers require job seekers to fill out an application form. To be ready, you need to prepare a personal data sheet. A **personal data sheet** is a summary of personal, educational, and employment information. You will not give it directly to an employer. Rather, you will use it to assist in filling out an online application form. Or, take it with you to a place of business and use it to fill out a printed job application form.

A personal data sheet contains four primary types of information. A sample data sheet is shown in Figures 4-1A and 4-1B on the following pages. You can add or delete parts to meet your own needs. Download a copy of the Personal Data Sheet at www.cengage.com/school/working.

PERSONAL DATA SHEET

IDENTIFICATION

Name _____ Soc. Sec. # _____

Address _____

Telephone (___) _____

Email Address _____

Hobbies/Interests _____

Honors/Awards/Offices _____

Sports/Activities _____

Other _____

EDUCATIONAL BACKGROUND

	Dates Attended	
School Name and Address	From:	To:
High School:		
Course of Study _____ Rank _____		GPA _____
Favorite Subject(s) _____		
Other (College, Trade, Business, or Online Courses):	From:	To:
Course of Study _____ Rank _____		GPA _____
Favorite Subject(s) _____		
Other (College, Trade, Business, or Online Courses):	From:	To:
Course of Study _____ Rank _____		GPA _____
Favorite Subject(s) _____		

FIGURE 4-1A Follow this general outline when you prepare a personal data sheet. Use it to fill out a job application form and create a resume. (The sample data sheet continues on the next page.)

A. **Identification**   Included in this part is personal identification information. In-school and extracurricular activities, interests, and awards are listed. The intent is to provide information that explains who and what type of person you are.

EMPLOYMENT HISTORY

(Start with present or most recent employer.)

1. Company _____ Telephone (___) _____
Address _____
Employed from Mo. _____ Yr. _____ /to Mo. _____ Yr. _____ Supervisor _____
Position/Title _____
Last Wage _____ Reason for Leaving _____

2. Company _____ Telephone (___) _____
Address _____
Employed from Mo. _____ Yr. _____ /to Mo. _____ Yr. _____ Supervisor _____
Position/Title _____
Last Wage _____ Reason for Leaving _____

3. Company _____ Telephone (___) _____
Address _____
Employed from Mo. _____ Yr. _____ /to Mo. _____ Yr. _____ Supervisor _____
Position/Title _____
Last Wage _____ Reason for Leaving _____

REFERENCES

1. Name _____ Title _____
Address _____
Email _____
Relationship _____ Telephone (___) _____

2. Name _____ Title _____
Address _____
Email _____
Relationship _____ Telephone (___) _____

3. Name _____ Title _____
Address _____
Email _____
Relationship _____ Telephone (___) _____

FIGURE 4-1B Personal Data Sheet (Continued)

B. **Educational Background**   Record data about your high school and any colleges, technical schools, online courses, or any other formal training. Repeat the basic information for each school. The type of student you are will be of interest to employers.

C. **Employment History** List information about all previous employment. Although it is acceptable to list volunteer jobs, paid employment should be listed first. Start with present or most recent employment. Add employers as necessary.

D. **References** List the names of people who can provide favorable information about your personal, school, and employment background. Examples include teachers, coaches, club advisors, and previous employers. Be sure to ask their permission to be used as a reference.

Job Application Form

Employers ask for information about job candidates in a variety of ways. When reading a job ad, pay special attention to any instructions about how to apply, and make sure to include any documents the employer requests. Some employers will only accept information electronically. Others will only accept completed paper job applications. Some will not accept phone calls about openings. Other employers will want additional material, like work samples or references. Don't be disqualified for an opening because you didn't follow the instructions.

A **job application form** is used by employers to collect personal, educational, and employment information from a job applicant. The information provided on the form helps employers to sort out the best-qualified persons for the job. After screening the application forms, the employer will invite a few people for an interview.

If you have prepared a personal data sheet, you will have taken a big step toward filling out a job application form. You will be able to copy facts and information from the data sheet directly onto the job application form. Take your personal data sheet with you each time you contact an employer or employment office.

The type of job application form used will differ from company to company. A typical form is shown in Figure 4-2 on the next page. Follow these tips in filling out a job application form.

- Before you begin to fill out the form, read it over carefully. Study the instructions so you will know what information to provide. Note which parts are "for employer use only."

- If you fill out a paper application, you may want to get an erasable ballpoint pen. This will allow you to correct mistakes easily. Be as neat as possible.

- You will probably be asked to print the information. It is a good idea to print even if it is not required on the form. Be sure to sign your name in those places that ask for your signature. Use your correct name, not a nickname.

Workforce Trends

Demographics refer to the physical characteristics of a population. There are three major demographic trends that are changing the U.S. labor force. Slowing growth, aging, and increasing diversity are contributing to changes in today's and tomorrow's workforce. These changes make it necessary for workers of all ages and backgrounds to learn how to work with people who are different from themselves.

Sometimes it is necessary to ask a few questions when filling out a job application.

APPLICATION FOR EMPLOYMENT
(PRE-EMPLOYMENT QUESTIONNAIRE) (AN EQUAL OPPORTUNITY EMPLOYER)

PERSONAL INFORMATION

DATE _April 15, 20--_

NAME _Morales Ronald R._

SOCIAL SECURITY NUMBER _351-44-5751_

PRESENT ADDRESS _6428 Valley Rd._ _Payne_ _Ohio_ _45880-1482_

PERMANENT ADDRESS _same_

PHONE NO. _419-555-0127_

ARE YOU 18 YEARS OR OLDER? YES ☒ NO ☐

ARE YOU EITHER A U.S. CITIZEN OR AN ALIEN AUTHORIZED TO WORK IN THE UNITED STATES? YES ☒ NO ☐

EMPLOYMENT DESIRED

POSITION _Engine and power train mechanic_

DATE YOU CAN START _May 1_

SALARY DESIRED _open_

ARE YOU EMPLOYED NOW? _yes_

IF SO, MAY WE INQUIRE OF YOUR PRESENT EMPLOYER? _yes_

EVER APPLIED TO THIS COMPANY BEFORE? _no_

WHERE? ___ WHEN? ___

REFERRED BY _Ken Jenkins_

EDUCATION	NAME AND LOCATION OF SCHOOL	NO. OF YEARS ATTENDED	DID YOU GRADUATE?	SUBJECTS STUDIED
HIGH SCHOOL	Memorial High School	4	yes	vocational curriculum automotive
COLLEGE	Hillside Community College	2	yes	automotive technology
TRADE, BUSINESS, OR CORRESPONDENCE SCHOOL	NA			

FORMER EMPLOYERS (LIST BELOW LAST THREE EMPLOYERS, STARTING WITH LAST ONE FIRST.)

DATE	NAME AND ADDRESS OF EMPLOYER	PAY	POSITION	REASON FOR LEAVING
FROM June 20-- TO present	Goodman's Tire & Auto Center 219 E. Sycamore, Payne, OH 45880-1475	$18.50 hr.	service technician	currently employed
FROM June 20-- TO May 20--	Hunter's Auto Repair 2025 W. Walnut, Paulding, OH 45879-5923	$13.10 hr.	general auto repair	part-time only
FROM Aug. 20-- TO May 20--	Millcroft Service Station 436 Main St., Payne, OH 45880-1485	$9.70 hr.	auto maintenance	co-op student learner

WHICH OF THESE JOBS DID YOU LIKE THE BEST? _Hunter's Auto Repair_

WHAT DID YOU LIKE MOST ABOUT THIS JOB? _engine diagnosis_

REFERENCES (GIVE THE NAMES OF THREE PERSONS NOT RELATED TO YOU, WHOM YOU HAVE KNOWN FOR AT LEAST ONE YEAR.)

NAME	ADDRESS	POSITION	YEARS ACQUAINTED
Earl Thompson	Goodman's Tire & Auto Center 219 E. Sycamore, Payne, OH 45880-1475	Service Manager	1.5
Yvonne Hunter	Hunter's Auto Repair 2025 W. Walnut, Paulding, OH 45879-5923	Owner/Manager	2.0
Leroy Hopkins	Hillside Community College 24 Given Rd., Paulding, OH 45879-5826	Automotive Instructor	2.0

FIGURE 4-2 This is a job application form that has been filled out correctly.

- Answer all questions on the form. If a question does not apply to you, put "NA" for "not applicable." Do not leave a blank space; the employer might think you forgot to answer the question.

- Answer all questions honestly. Giving false information can catch up with you later. If you do not have the information or do not know the answer, write "unknown."

- List the specific position or job for which you are applying. Do not write "anything" in the space. Although you may be willing to accept any job, you want to convey that you are interested in and qualified for a specific job.

- Misspelled words give a poor impression of your ability. Take a small pocket or electronic dictionary with you and use it.

A job application can be difficult to complete without having a personal data sheet.

- You may be asked to name the "wages or salary expected." It is best to discuss salary in a personal interview with the employer. Write "open" in the space provided.

- In the employment history section, you may be asked to give the reason for leaving a previous job. Do not put down anything that criticizes a past employer or shows that you were not an acceptable employee. Examples of appropriate reasons for leaving a job are "returned to school," "left for a better job," and "job terminated."

- After you have filled out the form, check it carefully before mailing it or handing it in.

What happens after you submit the job application form? Do you wait to hear from the employer? Some employers collect job applications for a position that begins on a certain date. Other employers, who may have no jobs available at the moment, collect applications for future use. Make sure you find out what to do next. Write the information down on your job-lead card.

4-1 Assessment

1. What are the two main uses for a personal data sheet?
2. What kinds of people might you give as job references?
3. Why do employers use job application forms? Give an example.
4. If a question on a job application form does not apply to you, how should you answer it?
5. Why have many employers switched to using online job application forms?

WRITE A RESUME

OBJECTIVES

- Understand the parts of a resume
- Explain the two common forms for preparing a resume
- Prepare a resume

KEY TERMS

- resume
- qualification
- character
- chronological resume
- functional resume
- portable document format (pdf)

Leah-Anne Thompson/Shutterstock.com

Personal Decisions

Last year in English class, one of the writing assignments was to prepare a resume. The teacher provided brief instructions and gave guidelines. You followed the guidelines and thought you did a pretty good job. However, the teacher assigned a grade of B- and noted that the resume "contained careless spelling and grammatical errors and omitted some required information." You read about an interesting job opening today that requires a resume to be submitted. "I wonder if I can use the resume that I already have," you think to yourself. "An employer probably isn't going to read the resume as critically as an English teacher."

What would you do?

Parts of a Resume

When applying for a job online or in person, you will probably be asked for a resume. A **resume** is typically a one-page description of a job seeker's work history and qualifications for employment. A **qualification** is the background, knowledge, or skill that makes one eligible for a job. A resume provides a way to show an employer how your qualifications match a job's responsibilities. If a resume is well-constructed, you have a better chance of landing an interview and a job.

If you have prepared a personal data sheet, you already have the basic information to be included in your resume. You will need to choose which parts of that information to use. Then you will have to arrange the information into a neat, organized format. The format will vary depending on your background and qualifications and the type of job being advertised. A resume provides the following five kinds of information.

A. **Personal Information** Personal information is given at the top of the page. Your name, home address, email address, and phone number are all that is needed. Your voicemail message should sound professional.

B. **Career Objectives** Give a short statement of your career objectives. Be specific about the type of job you are seeking. Think in terms of how you can help a prospective employer. Make your objective general so that it can be used for multiple employers. Some general objectives typical for entry level workers are:

- To obtain training and acquire experience in retail sales
- To gain practical work experience while saving money for college
- To further develop my skills as a licensed practical nurse

To distinguish yourself from your competition, consider wording your objectives in terms of how you can help a prospective employer. An employer will hire you because they believe you will help them earn a profit. Review the statements in Figure 4-3. *Your Personal/Career Goal* lists why you are interested in this job and what you hope to achieve. *Objective Stated on Resume* phrases your personal goal in a way that is appealing to employers. These statements could help you get a job that would meet your needs and also show a prospective employer that you would help their business be profitable.

FIGURE 4-3 Sample Objectives

Your Personal/Career Goal	Objective Stated on Resume
Work in retail sales at home supply store	Help satisfy customers by assisting them with the selection of the proper tools for their home repair and home improvement projects
Learn more about proper care of trees and lawns	Give customers pride in their yards by fertilizing, weeding, mowing and trimming their yards
Stay fit and burn calories while earning money working as a fitness instructor	Help class participants improve their physical fitness while having fun

C. **Educational Background** List all high schools, colleges, technical schools, online courses, and any other relevant training. Begin with the most recent and work backward. List any diplomas, degrees, licenses, and certificates you earned. Mention any honors or awards you received. If you have specific computer, foreign language, or technical skills, be sure to include them. For example, Ronald Morales' performance in an engine troubleshooting contest demonstrates he has good diagnostic and mechanical skills.

D. **Work Experience** Begin with your present or most recent job. Identify each employer, the time period worked, and the type of job duties performed. Include co-op or work-study jobs here rather than in the section on educational background. If you have limited paid work experience, list unpaid experience, such as baby-sitting, yard work, and home maintenance. Other activities might include participation in organizations, associations, student government, clubs, or community activities. You can also mention volunteer work experience, such as being a junior volunteer, camp counselor, or campaign worker.

E. **References** Two or three references are satisfactory. Present and previous employers and supervisors are best. A prospective employer will probably contact the references to inquire about your work habits, attitudes, and skills. If you are a recent graduate, you can list instructors who are familiar with your schoolwork. **Character** is the combination of qualities and traits that defines who you are. A personal reference, such as a family friend, who can comment about your character may be listed as one of the references.

Choose a Format

There are two main resume formats—*chronological* and *functional*. Each is defined by the way it organizes your experience. Choose the one that shows your experience to the best advantage.

About 1″

Ronald R. Morales

6425 Valley Road, Payne, OH, 45880-1482, (419)555-0127, rrmorales@buckeye.com

OBJECTIVE My immediate objective is to obtain a job at a new car dealership as an engine and power train mechanic. My long-range goal is to become a shop supervisor or service manager. I am willing to complete additional training as required.

> *Typical entry level objective*

EXPERIENCE Auto Mechanic

June 20 to present, Goodman's Tire & Auto Center Payne, OH

> *About 1″*

> *Listing benefits to employer*

- Ensured customer safety and satisfaction by providing thorough tune-ups, general engine repair, front wheel alignment, and brake work

Auto Mechanic

June 20-- to May 20-- Hunter's Auto Repair, Paulding, OH

- Earned college tuition while working part-time

> *Bullets highlight training and achievements*

- Performed engine diagnosis, general engine repair, tune-ups, and transmission repair

Cooperative Vocational Education Student-Learner

August 20-- to May 20-- Milcroft Service Station, Payne, OH

- Performed routine auto maintenance and minor engine repair

About 1″ **EDUCATION** Hillside Community College, Paulding, OH

August 20-- to June 20--

- Associate of Applied Science Degree in Automotive Technology
- Team member of first-place team in regional engine troubleshooting competition

State Licensing Board, Ohio
July 20--
Earned license as a state auto and truck inspector

Memorial High School, Payne, OH
August 20-- to June 20--

- High School Diploma
  Two years of career and technical auto education
  One year of cooperative career and technical education
  President of local SkillsUSA Chapter

> *Highlights leadership*

INTEREST Hybrid cars

REFERENCES References are available on request

> *About 1″*

FIGURE 4-4 Sample Chronological Resume

Chronological Resume

A chronological resume organizes your experience around the jobs you have held. This format is an excellent choice for people with steady work histories or previous jobs that relate closely to their career objective. A sample chronological resume is shown in Figure 4-4 on page 96.

To create a chronological resume, list each position you have held, starting with the most recent. For each position, give the title of the job, name of the organization you worked for, and years you worked there. Next, relate the duties and accomplishments of that job.

---

14 E. West Street, Phoenix, AZ, 85019, (417)555-2222, bortzv@phoenix.com

Vita Bortz

OBJECTIVE   Help exercise class participants improve their physical fitness while having fun

EXPERIENCE   **Skilled at performing choreographed routines for large groups**

- Helped initiate enthusiastic responses from large groups
- Designed new dance routines
- Performed dance routines as part of group performance

Caring for children with medical needs means, as an instructor, you will be alert to medical needs of class participants

Capitalized bold letters designate significant headings

Experienced in dance and theatrical performances

- Served in cast of three school plays

Job related skills are listed

Effective group organizer

- Organized high school team for annual Leukemia and Lymphoma Society walk

Responsible care giver

- Provided supervision, entertainment, and nutrition for three siblings, including children with medical needs
- Drove children to and from activities
- Maintained employer confidentiality

Keep sufficient margins on every side of resume

SKILLS
- AFAA Certified Kickboxing Instructor
- AFAA Certified Personal Trainer
- Certified Zumba Instructor
- Hands-only CPR Trained

EMPLOYMENT HISTORY

Kickbox Instructor	Phoenix Fit Center, Phoenix, AZ	September, 2013 to present
Nanny	Johnson Family, Phoenix, AZ	March, 2010 to present
Cast Member	Happy Amusement Part, Phoenix, AZ	Summers, 2012 and 2013
Cheerleader	Thunder High School, Phoenix, AZ	September, 2011– June, 2013

Work history and education at bottom

EDUCATION   High School Diploma   Thunder High School, Phoenix, AZ   June, 2013

REFERENCES   References are available on request

FIGURE 4-5 Sample Functional Resume

When describing jobs, use action statements, not sentences. Instead of writing "I managed the magazine subscription department," write, "Managed a magazine subscription department." Begin each statement with strong verbs. If you were able to improve your employer's business in some way, be sure to include that information. Writing "Managed a magazine subscription department. Reduced subscription billing costs by ten percent." shows a potential employer that you are able to go beyond performing standard duties and to think of ways to improve the business. Three to five statements are usually sufficient for each job.

Functional Resume

Because the chronological format emphasizes dates and job titles, it is often a poor format for frequent job changers, people with inconsistent work histories, or new entrants to the work force. For these applicants, the functional resume is a better choice. The functional resume organizes your experience around skills rather than job titles. This format is better for students who have some work history, but not in positions that relate directly to the job they want. Organizing experiences around skills can connect less relevant jobs to career qualifications. For example, a job waiting tables can be combined with other responsibilities to show organizational and customer service skills. To create a functional resume, identify three or four skills required for your target job. For each skill, identify three to five concrete examples to demonstrate that ability. Use action phrases when writing your list.

The last part of the functional resume is a brief work history. Write only job titles, company names, and employment years. If you have gaps in your work history, you could use the cover letter to explain them, or you could fill them by adding volunteer work, community activities, or family responsibilities to your job list. A sample functional resume is shown in Figure 4-5 on page 97.

Prepare the Resume

An advertisement for a single job opening can generate hundreds of responses. Busy reviewers often spend as little as 30 seconds deciding whether a resume deserves attention. To help you pass the 30-second test, your resume must be attractive, easy-to-read, and error free.

Most students and recent graduates use a one-page resume, while experienced workers may use one or two pages. If you can't limit your resume to one page, it probably contains unnecessary words or irrelevant information. Eliminate anything that does not help prove you are qualified for the job.

Resume *templates,* or preformatted forms that allow you to fill in your information in a pre-existing document, are available in many word processing packages. Using a template will allow you to create an attractive resume. You can also design your own resume from scratch. Using a resume template is the easiest method and it is perfectly acceptable for students entering the workforce.

Generally, resume writing guidelines include using one-inch margins and blank lines between sections. A traditional type font such as Times New Roman or Arial sized at 10 point or above makes resumes easy to read. Always use a spell checker. Proofread your resume carefully. Be particularly careful to make sure all of your personal contact information is correct. A spell checker will not know if you have incorrectly listed your phone number or address. Ask your instructor and/or a family member to proofread the final product before it is mailed or transmitted electronically.

For resumes that will be printed and sent through the mail or dropped off at an employer location, consider the quality and color of the paper used. Investing in a box of heavier weight or textured linen paper with matching envelopes could be a small investment that will help add a quality feel to your resume. Use a bland color for the paper. White, beige, and light grey are all good choices.

You should save the resume file electronically for future use. If you send it to a different employer, you may need to revise it slightly to meet different job requirements. Develop an organized system for changing the file name of resumes that you save. For example, "Resume_landscaping_050713" would designate a resume that was developed for a landscaping job on May 7, 2013. "Resume_store sales_100413" would designate a resume developed for a retail sales job on October 4, 2013.

A **portable document format (pdf)** is a software file that looks and prints the same across a variety of platforms. It can be put in a *protected* status which prohibits anyone from making changes to the document. Create a protected pdf document before you send it to a prospective employer or post it online. This keeps accidental errors from occurring if your resume is forwarded within a company or by an agency.

Search the Net

Access **www.cengage.com/school/working**. Click on the link for Chapter 4. Use the Internet to learn more about writing your resume. Read the article entitled "Resumes, Applications, and Cover Letters." After reading the article, compose your resume. Organize your resume using either the chronological or functional method. Format the resume using the general guidelines provided. Consider what type of job you would use your resume for. Now consider how you would modify your resume for a different job.

www.cengage.com/school/working

4-2 Assessment

1. Name the five kinds of information provided in a resume.
2. How are chronological and functional resumes organized?
3. Which resume format is the better choice for a student or new entrant into the work force? Why?
4. Why is it important that your resume make a good first impression?
5. Name three reasons why it is essential to prepare your resume using a computer and word processing software.
6. Would it be a good idea to print your resume on purple paper so that it captures a reader's attention?
7. Why is it important to develop a unique naming system when storing electronic versions of resumes?

High Growth Occupations
FOR THE 21ST CENTURY

Receptionists, Information Clerks, and Customer Service Representatives

 Do you have good interpersonal and communication skills? Do you like finding solutions to a problem? If so, you might like working in an office as a receptionist and information clerk or as a customer service representative.

Receptionists and information clerks usually work in business settings that require a front-office greeter. Medical centers, office buildings, and educational facilities typically use receptionists and information clerks to greet and assist visitors. Courteousness and professionalism are important in this occupation. Providing helpful information about the organization, directing visitors to their destination, answering phones, routing calls, and responding to inquiries from the public are typical duties. Some receptionists coordinate mail into and out of the organization and aid security by monitoring the access of visitors.

Receptionists often have multiple tasks to perform during the workday.

Receptionists and information clerks provide customer service. However, many retail, manufacturing, financial, insurance, and service industries employ specialized *customer service representatives*. Workers in this occupation are responsible for helping customers who have problems and questions, and making sure that customers are satisfied with their goods or services.

Customer service representatives receive specific training in order to interact with customers, provide information about products, and handle and resolve complaints. In larger companies, they may receive training in one area and only interact with customers in that area of business. For example, some customer service representatives for credit card companies are trained to answer only questions about replacing lost or stolen credit cards. Many customer inquiries are routine and customer service representatives simply look up the answer on a computer.

Good interpersonal, communication, and problem-solving skills are essential for receptionists and information clerks and customer service representatives. Basic to intermediate computer skills are also important for most jobs. For workers who communicate through email, good typing, spelling, and grammar skills are necessary.

Receptionists and information clerks and customer service representatives generally need only a high school diploma as most of their training is received on the job. Applicants who have had some formal office experience may be in the greatest demand.

CONTACT EMPLOYERS

OBJECTIVES

- Explain four methods to contact employers about a job
- Describe the two most common types of pre-employment tests

KEY TERMS

- cover letter
- pre-employment test
- civil service test

Personal Decisions

There is an opening at a business owned by your best friend's mother. You are not sure how to apply for the job. Should you call her at home or at work? Should you have your friend ask his mother for you? Should you give her a resume even though she already knows you? Should you address her as Ramona, which you normally do, or as Mrs. Cruz?

What would you do?

Leah-Anne Thompson/Shutterstock.com

Four Methods to Contact Employers

Methods to apply for a job include applying in person, by phone, by letter, and online. In all four approaches, do everything you can to present yourself and your qualifications in the best possible light.

Apply in Person

A help-wanted sign often contains the statement "apply in person." The sign may give the name of a person to contact or it may say to "ask for the manager." Sometimes the ad only lists the name of the company.

When you apply for a job in person, first impressions are very important. Some employers judge an applicant's appearance, self-confidence, and social skills this way. You want to be well-groomed and appropriately dressed. Introduce yourself and explain who you are. You may want to say you are a work experience education student.

If you have been referred by a placement counselor, teacher, or employment agency, share this information. A referral can give you an immediate edge over other applicants.

State your interest in the job advertised. If the first meeting goes well, the employer may ask you to fill out a job application or to leave a resume. Be prepared. Take your personal data sheet and your resume.

Apply by Telephone

Skillful use of the telephone is very important to a successful job search. By using the telephone, you can make many contacts in the time it takes to make one personal visit.

The purpose of telephoning is to convert a job lead into an appointment for a job interview. In some cases, you may be following a suggestion from a family member or friend. An opening might not exist. For other leads, you know a certain opening is available. Perhaps you are answering a help-wanted ad. Whatever your reasons for making the call, the following guidelines should help you:

- **Get organized before you call.** Have your job-lead card, pen, and paper ready. Know the purpose of your call. Plan what you are going to say. If you are nervous, consider preparing a short script. Include the key points you want to cover in the call. Rehearse the script prior to the call. Keep the script handy during the call.

- **Call from a quiet place.** You do not want any background noise during the call.

- **Make sure your phone equipment is working prior to the call.** If you are using a wireless handset, make sure the battery is fully charged and the reception is clear. If you are uncertain about how clear your phone sounds, call a friend prior to making the business call. Ask you friend how the reception sounds. If you use a cell phone, ensure the reception is as good as possible. This includes making sure your battery is fully charged, your cellular carrier provides good reception in your area, and that you decide whether to use an ear piece or speaker function. You want the call to go smoothly and to have clear communication. A dropped call or garbled conversation would frustrate both you and the person you are calling. Do not have anything in your mouth when you talk.

- **Give your name and briefly state your business.** Use the employer's name several times during the conversation.

- **Be courteous, friendly, and interested.** Speak with a pleasant, even tone of voice. Put a "smile" in your voice, but talk naturally.

- **Write down information quickly.** Try not to ask the person to repeat what was said.

- **Ask for an appointment, but do not be pushy.** If you get an appointment, record the time, the place, and the interviewer's name.

Apply in Writing

Another way to act on a job lead is to write an application letter. You might do this when acting on a suggestion from another person or responding to a newspaper help-wanted ad. A **cover letter** is a letter of application accompanied by a resume that is sent to a potential employer. The cover letter and resume may be mailed, emailed, or faxed.

Cover letters are an opportunity to convey your focus and energy. Especially for students who may not have a lot of work experience, the cover letter is a way to show enthusiasm. Following up with a phone call shows the employer drive and interest. An example of a cover letter is shown in Figure 4-6 on the next page. It should have four parts.

In the first paragraph, explain your reason for writing. Name the job for which you are applying. Explain how you learned about the job. Use the second paragraph to briefly list your qualifications. Give the facts, but do not brag. Employers will look carefully at this paragraph.

The third paragraph calls attention to the resume. It may also be wise to give a date when you will be available for employment. The term *enclosure* is used beneath your typed name to let the person reading the letter know to look for other documents that were mailed with your letter. In the last paragraph, ask for an appointment. Tell how you can be contacted. Close the letter with a courteous comment or a thank you.

Notice that the sample letter is short and to the point. The purpose of the letter is to attract and hold the reader's interest. It should not attempt to give facts that are better stated in a resume and job interview. If you are qualified for the job, the letter and resume should make the employer want to invite you for an interview.

The form and appearance of the letter are very important. Write several drafts of the letter until you feel it is correct. Have a teacher or

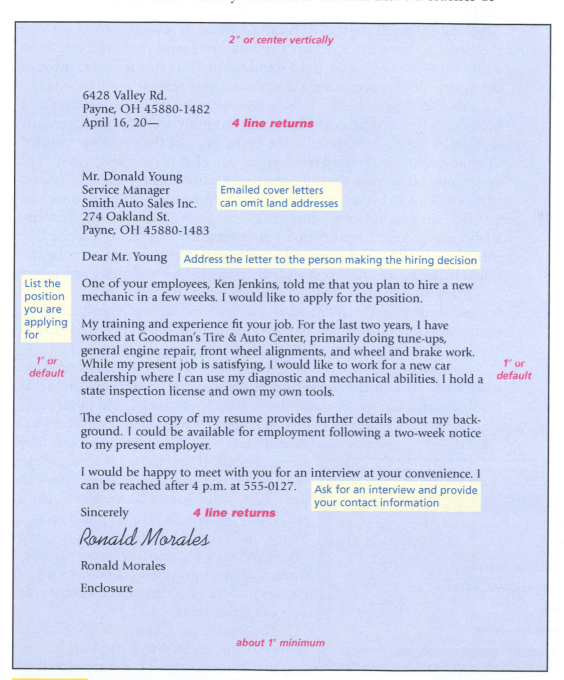

FIGURE 4-6 Sample Cover Letter

parent review it for correct spelling and grammar. Key the letter neatly, following a standard personal-business letter format. If you are using word processing software, use the spell check function. For printed cover letters, make sure the paper used is the same as the paper and envelope selected for your resume.

If you will be mailing printed copies of your resume, make sure all addresses on the envelope are printed neatly. It is preferable if this printing occurs with a computer printer, but if you do not have one available, print neatly by hand.

Proofread the letter carefully to check for errors. Ask a friend or family member to do the same. Save the file electronically. You will be able to use it in the future as a guide in writing additional letters.

Apply Online

Applying for a job on the Web can be done in several ways. One way is to write a cover letter, attach a resume, and send them directly to an employer by email rather than standard mail. If this is done, most of the same rules for preparing a cover letter and resume are followed.

Another type of online job application is one in which an employer provides a form to be completed and submitted electronically. Many companies have a hyperlink on the home page of their website entitled "Employment" or a related term. When you click on this link, a new page opens, providing some type of online application form. Figure 4-7 shows an example of an online application form. Most forms consist of various text fields in which data are entered. For example, at the top of the form, a label may ask for "Your Name." A rectangular box called a single-line text field usually follows into which the required information is keyed. Often larger boxes called text areas are provided for multi-line text input.

After all required information has been provided, a click of the mouse transmits the form to the employer. Before submitting an online application form, it is a good idea to print a copy and read it carefully for spelling, grammar, and factual errors.

Another way to use the Web is to post a resume to an online database. There are numerous government agencies and private companies that provide such a service. Resumes are collected, organized, and made available to employers for review. Employers initiate contact with applicants in whom they are interested. If you have a resume, it can often be emailed. You might be asked to scan the resume and transmit an image file, like a pdf. When you are planning to post a resume online, make sure the resume is formatted simply. When a resume is transmitted electronically, word processing features such as indents, boldface, bullets, and different type sizes can cause errors.

To increase the chances of your online resume being selected in a database search, you may want to replace the statement of career goals with a summary containing

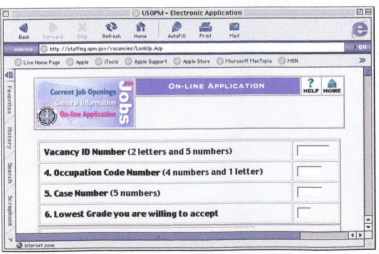

FIGURE 4-7 Sample Online Job Application

keywords relating to the position you want. For example, for a customer service job, your summary might say, *Strong communication and telephone skills; excellent keyboarding, computer, and Internet skills; and good organizational and interpersonal skills.*

Some agencies and companies provide resume development software online. Information is keyed into a form that the software converts into a standard resume style. It is very important to proofread such information carefully before submitting it to a digital database.

Pre-Employment Tests

Mei-ling lives in the city that is her state's capital. A large state university is nearby. The state government and university are two of the city's major employers. Because they hire many employees, Mei-ling applied for work at both offices. She was surprised to learn that she would have to take a test before she would be asked to interview for a job. Mei-ling found something that is very common. To apply for almost all state and federal government jobs, applicants must take one or more pre-employment tests. A **pre-employment test** is a test or performance test administered by an employer as part of the job application process.

One type of pre-employment test is the **civil service test**. This test is given to a job applicant seeking a government job. The intent of civil service testing is to promote fairness in employment. Job applicants with the highest civil service test scores are given preference in hiring.

Private employers may also administer pre-employment tests. Large employers often give them as part of the job application process. For entry-level jobs with the government or private employers, the most common types of tests are general ability tests and performance tests.

General Ability Tests

A general ability test measures basic learning skills such as reading, spelling, vocabulary, and arithmetic. These written tests are similar to the types of tests that you have taken throughout your school years.

Math Connection

You are applying for a position that requires each candidate to be able to key an average of 30 words per minute. The last three times you tested yourself, you keyed 30, 28, and 35 words per minute. Do you fit the requirements for this position?

SOLUTION

To calculate the average words per minute, add the test rates together and divide the sum by the number of times you tested yourself.

Average words per minute = (30 + 28 + 35) ÷ 3
= 93 ÷ 3
= 31

Because your average is higher than 30 words per minute, you fit the requirements for this position.

Performance Tests

In a performance test, you are asked to demonstrate skills needed for a specific occupation. An example would be a clerical skills test that requires you to proofread a business letter for possible errors.

Many performance tests are hands-on tests. They require you to use actual tools or machines. Suppose you are applying for a job as a data processing operator. Before being considered, you might be tested on a computer. By testing your skills now, employers avoid possible surprises later.

Take a Test

You should not let the thought of taking a pre-employment test scare you away from a possible job. You will do better on the test if you do not spend time worrying about it. You may be surprised to learn that mild test anxiety can be good. Studies have shown that mild stress actually improves the performance of athletes, entertainers, and test-takers.

Most tests don't require any advance preparation. If you have not used your skills recently, you may want to practice before you take a test. Prepare yourself mentally and physically. Be positive. Think of the test as a chance to show what you know and can do. During the days before the test, try to exercise, relax, eat well, and get plenty of sleep.

Many tests have time limits. You will be told how much time you have. Listen carefully to the instructions. If you do not understand what you are expected to do, be sure to ask questions before the test begins. After you start the test, work steadily and carefully. Do not spend too much time on any one question. If math is required, double-check each answer. If you finish ahead of time, use the remaining time to go back and complete unanswered questions or recheck answers.

Once the test is over, do not worry about it. Employers do not expect perfection. They just want some idea of whether or not you can do the work. Do not leave until you know what the next step will be. Ask when and how you will be told the test results. Some employers hold an interview immediately after a pre-employment test. The test may even be scored then. Other employers invite applicants back after they have examined the job application and the test results.

4-3 Assessment

1. Name four ways to contact potential employers.
2. Why should you use the telephone in a job search?
3. What should be in the last paragraph of a cover letter?
4. What are the two most common types of pre-employment tests? What is the purpose of each?
5. In the days preceding a pre-employment test, what is the best type of preparation?
6. If you finish a pre-employment test before the time limit is up, what should you do?

Focus on the Workplace

Lie Detector and Honesty Tests

If you apply for a job in which money, merchandise, or drugs are handled, you may have to take an "honesty test." One type is a polygraph, or lie detector, test. A polygraph is an electronic machine that is connected to the body of a subject. The person is asked a series of questions, while the machine records electronic impulses and other data on a graph. If the person tells a lie, the device supposedly detects slight changes in the person's breathing rate, pulse, blood pressure, or perspiration.

Many experts in the field question the accuracy of polygraph tests. As a result, Congress passed a law in 1988 to restrict the use of such tests. The law prohibits polygraph tests for screening job applicants. An exception is for those seeking jobs in government, as security guards, or handling narcotics. The law also limits the use of polygraphs for workers already on the job. Managers cannot ask employees to take the test unless there is a "reasonable suspicion" that they have committed a crime. Even then, the test is voluntary. An employee cannot be fired for refusing to take it.

To avoid the problems and cost of polygraph tests, some companies use written honesty tests. These have multiple choice or yes-no items, such as:

- Have you every stolen anything from an employer?
  Yes   No
- Have you ever cheated in school?
  Yes   No
- Have you ever lied to a teacher or boss?
  Yes   No

The written test is interpreted by comparing an applicant's answers to those of persons already judged to be honest. Whether honesty tests help screen out dishonest job applicants is open to debate. But unless laws are passed restricting their use, millions of job applicants will probably be required to take these tests.

THINK CRITICALLY

1. What jobs do you think should require lie detector or honesty tests?
2. Would you apply for a job that required a lie detector or honesty test?

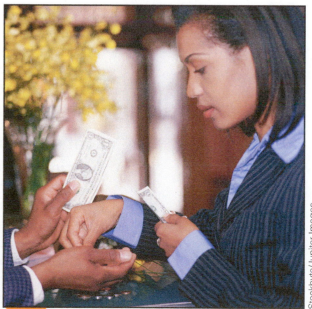

If a job involves handling money, you may be required to take an honesty test.

Stockbyte/Jupiter Images

Assessment

Chapter Summary

4-1 Data Sheets and Job Applications

A. The four sections of a personal data sheet are identification, educational background, employment history, and references. This document contains the types of information most often requested by employers. You should complete a personal data sheet prior to filling out a job application or preparing a resume.

B. Job application forms are used by employers to help sort out qualified individuals from a pool of applicants. Follow the guidelines in this chapter to increase your chances of being selected for an interview. After you submit the job application form, make sure you find out what to do next.

4-2 Write a Resume

A. The five kinds of information included in a resume are personal information, career objectives, educational background, work experience, and references. A resume is often used when applying for a job in person, by letter, or by email.

B. There are two main resume formats—chronological and functional. A chronological resume organizes your experience around the jobs you have held. A functional resume organizes your experience around skills rather than job titles. Choose the one that shows your experience to the best advantage.

C. Most students and recent graduates use a one-page resume. It is acceptable to use a template to prepare a resume. For resumes that will be dropped off or sent through the mail, consider the quality of the paper and envelopes that will be used. The resume should have a neat, error-free, and professional appearance. Develop an organized system for storing electronic versions of your resume.

4-3 Contact Employers

A. You can contact an employer about a job in person, by phone, by letter, or online. Applying in person usually also serves as a job interview. When contacting an employer by phone, make sure that your phone battery is charged and the reception on both ends is clear. A cover letter is required when applying by mail. Online applications can be completed by sending an email with an attached resume or by completing an online application. The purpose of phone, letter, and online contacts is to gain an interview. In all four approaches, do everything you can to present yourself and your qualifications in the best possible light.

B. Many employers administer pre-employment tests to job applicants. The most common are ability tests or performance tests.
Government jobs may require the completion of a civil service
test. Test anxiety is normal. Practicing for a test is a good idea.
After beginning a test, work steadily and carefully.

Activities

1. You want to apply for a job that requires you to have an average score of 70 on four pre-employment tests. You score 60, 72,
69, and 75 on the four tests. What is the average of the four test
scores? Did you meet the requirement for the job?

2. Each of the following activities requires you to access links that
can be found at www.cengage.com/school/working.

    a. Click on Forms to download a copy of the Personal Data Sheet.
    Complete a personal data sheet following the model shown in
    Figure 4-1. Ask your instructor to look over your rough draft.

    b. You have been advised to convert your resume to a pdf document
    before sending it to a prospective employer. There are a number
    of free software applications that allow you to do this. Click on
    Web Links for a link to a free PDF Converter. Review the web-
    site. Your instructor will give you guidance regarding whether to
    download a copy of the application. (There are also a number of
    free pdf readers. The most widely used is Adobe Reader.)

    c. There are many types of pre-employment tests you may be
    asked to take. Click on Web Links for Pre-employment
    Tests to learn about whether these tests are legal.

    d. Click on Forms for Sample Objectives Template and download
    a template of Figure 4-3. Complete three of your goals and
    objectives. Exchange the completed chart with another student.
    Give each other feedback regarding how well the listed objec-
    tives would meet both your needs and the needs of an employer.

    e. Click on Web Links for Online Application Example to view a
    demonstration of how to complete an online application.

    f. Click on Web Links for Job Applications. This link will
    provide access to downloadable job applications. Using your
    personal data sheet, practice filling out several sample job
    application forms. If you choose to do so, these forms can be
    submitted to the actual companies.

3. Prepare a resume according to the format shown in Figure 4-4 or
4-5. Choose the format that seems best for your experience. Your
instructor may ask you to develop both types. Turn the resume in
to your instructor for evaluation.

4. Many recruiters use software to automatically sort through resumes. Revise the objective of one of your resumes to list key words that would help your resume be matched to the position you are most interested in. Exchange revised resumes with a classmate. Discuss how effective the revised objectives would be at surviving the automatic sort process.

5. After you have finished preparing a resume, write a sample cover letter following the format shown in Figure 4-6. Turn the cover letter in to your instructor for evaluation.

6. Practice role-playing in class how you would use a telephone to contact an employer for a job interview. One student can be the applicant and one the employer. Follow the guidelines on telephone use given earlier in this chapter.

7. Explain how studying the personal data sheet you created in Activity 2a can help you identify things you can do now to improve the likelihood of achieving goals in your life-span plan.

Word Power

On a separate sheet of paper, match each definition with the correct term. All definitions will be used, and a definition will be used only once.

8. A form used by employers to collect personal, educational, and occupational information from a job applicant

9. A letter of application accompanied by a resume that is sent to a potential employer

10. The combination of qualities and traits that defines who you are

11. Organizes your experience around skills rather than job titles

12. Names of individuals listed on a personal data sheet, job application form, or resume who are qualified to provide information about the applicant

13. The background, knowledge, or skill that makes one eligible for a job

14. A one-page description of a job seeker's history and qualifications for employment

15. A pre-employment test that is administered to a job applicant seeking a government job

16. Organizes your experience around the jobs you have had

17. A software file that looks and prints the same across a variety of platforms.

18. A paper-and-pencil test or performance exercise administered by an employer as part of the job application process

19. A summary of personal, educational, and employment information used to help fill out a job application form and to prepare a resume

a. character
b. chronological resume
c. civil service test
d. cover letter
e. functional resume
f. job application form
g. personal data sheet
h. portable document format (pdf)
i. pre-employment test
j. qualification
k. reference
l. resume

Think Critically

20. During a phone conversation, what are some clues that there is not clear phone reception during the call?

21. People sometimes make mistakes during their lifetime. These might include getting into trouble at school, getting arrested for a minor infraction, or getting fired from a job. If a question is asked about things like this on a job application, how should you respond? What if it means that your answer will keep you from getting the job?

22. If you had an option to apply for a job in person, by letter, or by email which would you choose? Discuss the advantages of each and why you chose the option you did.

23. What do you think about the practice of requiring an honesty test as part of the job application process? Discuss both your and the employer's point of view.

24. Would you prefer for your resume to be screened by a person or electronically by a computer? Which method would give you the best chance of being selected for an interview? Explain your answer.

25. Why is it important to get the permission of people you plan to use as references before giving their names to an employer?

26. Why does listing your career objective in a way that provides a benefit to the employer give you a competitive edge?

27. Despite following the guidelines in this chapter and careful attention to detail, it is possible to submit a resume to a prospective employer that may contain typographical, grammatical, or factual errors. Discuss what actions (if any) you might take should this happen.

28. Students who write and speak in English as a second language may have challenges at various times in the job application process. What are some of the things that might be done to overcome language barriers in the process of filling out a job application, preparing a resume, and writing a cover letter?

29. Some people have a resume posted on Facebook or another social network. Discuss the advantages and disadvantages of doing this.

Career Transitions Connection

Write Your Resume

Click on *Write a Resume*. From the *Resume Home* list, you will be prompted to complete information for each section of your resume. Make sure to hit the green save button after filling in information for each section. Each saved section will have a green checkmark in the *Resume Home* list. Preview your resume. You can change the order that information is presented in and you can also edit information. Download and save an electronic copy of your resume.

"If you do not feel yourself growing in your work and your life broadening and deepening, if your task is not a perpetual tonic to you, you have not found your place." —ORISON SWETT MARDEN

Interview for a Job

Kzenon/Shutterstock.com

5-1 Before the Interview

5-2 During the Interview

5-3 After the Interview

PREVIEW

The interview is the best chance you have of convincing potential employers to hire you. You should prepare yourself for the interview. Practice answering questions and research the company. You must also act appropriately during the interview. Remember how important first impressions are. Finally, you must follow up to make sure that the interviewer remembers who you are and that you want the job.

Taking/*Action* Get an Interview

Ron Morales had just gotten home from work when his cell phone rang. He answered it.

"Hello, Ron Morales speaking."

"Hello, Ron, this is Donald Young at Smith Auto Sales. I have your letter of application and resume in front of me. It seems as if you would like to get out of your present job."

"No, sir, 'getting out' is not the main reason I am looking for a job," Ron replied, pleasantly but firmly. "I like my job at Goodman's, but most of our work involves doing routine repairs on older cars. I have some training and skills that I am not able to use there. I would like to work on newer cars and be able to specialize in diagnostic work."

✱ Success Tip

Be ready to talk about what you want from a job.

"That is good to hear," Mr. Young said. "As you know, new car models are becoming more high-tech all the time. It is essential that technicians have the confidence and ability to do diagnostic work. This is one of the primary skills that I am seeking in hiring new technicians. I called Leroy Hopkins at Hillside Community College and he said this is one of your strong areas."

"Yes, it is. Diagnostic work is often very simple if you know how to use testing equipment."

"I agree," said Mr. Young. "If I hired you, would you have any interest in becoming a peer trainer? I think some of our less skilled technicians might benefit from having a fellow mechanic help them learn how to better use testing equipment."

"Yes, I think that I would enjoy teaching," replied Ron. "My mother is a teacher and she has always said that I have a talent for teaching."

"Ron, I would like to talk further with you and show you around our shop. Could you come in Saturday morning at 9:00?"

"Yes, I would be happy to. I will see you on Saturday at 9:00, Mr. Young. Thank you for calling."

THINK CRITICALLY

1. How did Ron handle the question of why he wanted a new position?

2. What do you think Ron said that made Donald Young want to interview him?

auremar/Shutterstock.com

OBJECTIVES
- Explain the purpose of a job interview
- Identify barriers to attending a job interview or performing a job
- Name and briefly describe six steps of job interview preparation

KEY TERMS
- job interview
- appraise
- commitment
- barrier
- reprimand
- hypothetical
- confirm

ra2 studio/Shutterstock.com

Personal Decisions

You have an allergy to various food products. Occasionally, you unknowingly eat something that causes an allergic reaction. An unpleasant-looking skin rash appears on your face and hands. The day before a job interview you have such a reaction. You are very upset and discouraged. You don't want to go to the interview like this.

What would you do?

Purpose of the Interview

The job interview is a face-to-face meeting between you and an employer. It is generally the last and most important step in the job-seeking process. An interview for an entry-level job usually lasts about 15 to 30 minutes. You will not be invited for an interview unless the employer thinks you may be qualified for the job. The employer wants to find out in person if you have the skills for the job. Another purpose is to help the employer decide if you will be able to work well with supervisors and coworkers.

An interview gives you a chance to "sell" what you can do for the employer. During the interview, an employer will judge your qualifications, appearance, and behavior. Equally important, the interview gives you a chance to appraise, or evaluate, the job and the company. It enables you to decide if the position meets your job goals and interests and whether this is the type of company for which you want to work.

Overcome Barriers to Employment

A commitment is an obligation to perform a task at a specified time and place. Accepting an invitation for a job interview is a big commitment on your part. It means that if you do well in the interview, and are offered a job, you should be ready and able to go to work.

A **barrier** is any condition that makes it difficult to achieve an objective. You should have already given thought to and made plans to overcome any barriers that might interfere with attending the interview or might later interfere with carrying out the responsibilities of a job. For example, do you have dependable personal or public transportation available? Do you have to care for any family members in a way that might interfere with a job? Do you have scheduled commitments that will require you to miss work? If you are going to school, can you successfully combine school work and employment?

These are not minor issues which you can ignore and hope to work out later if you are offered a job. They are part of the planning and preparation for a job interview. You owe it to an employer to be able to meet the expectations of a job if one is offered. Barriers to employment can often be overcome, but they need to be identified and resolved early in the job-seeking process.

Prepare for the Interview

Before each interview, you should take the attitude that the job you are applying for is the one you want. To present yourself in the best possible light, you will need to do several things to prepare for the interview.

Review Your Online Reputation

Social network sites like Facebook, MySpace, Twitter, and others can be enjoyable ways to connect with family and friends and share common interests. Social networks can also help you find a job. It is important to have an online presence where you can display your skills and experience. Your online profile can help you connect with others who can possibly assist in your job search and career advancement.

What you may not know, however, is that many companies are using social networks as part of their interviewing and background checking process. A large proportion of companies that do online searches indicate that they have rejected applicants as a result of information found online.

Employers want to find and hire a candidate who will be successful on the job and one who will not embarrass them or tarnish the company's reputation. The primary things that recruiters look for online are (a) information on drinking and drug use; (b) offensive language or inappropriate pictures; (c) discriminatory remarks about race, gender, religion, and sexual orientation; and (d) unprofessional screen names. In short, your media presence can make you extremely attractive or unattractive to an employer. Follow these guidelines to present and maintain a positive image online.

Clean up your image as needed. Look at all your online information including your profile, blogs, wall posts, groups, and photos. Remove anything that is or might be considered to be inappropriate. In addition Google your name and see what you find. If you find something you would rather an employer not see, ask the website to remove the content about you.

Your friends may, without your knowledge, post information or pictures about you. If they *tag*, or electronically label a picture of you with your name on it, your picture may be found during an online

Workplace Innovations

ONLINE REPUTATION MANAGEMENT

Negative information or bad publicity on the Web can damage reputations, ruin careers, and result in untold dollar amounts of lost business. As a result, a new type of company has emerged called *online reputation management (ORM)*. Such companies began originally to help parents protect their children from damaging their reputations through embarrassing postings and photos on social media websites. Later, company services expanded to assist adults and businesses.

ORM's offer subscription services to businesses for monitoring and managing the online reputation of the company. Or, an ORM may be called in to deal with a single case or threat. When damaging content is found, the ORM works to get the information removed from the offending website. If they are unable to get the content removed, ORMs have ways to neutralize the content and promote a positive image for the client.

Some types of information, however, cannot be removed from the Web such as legitimate news stories and certain court documents and records.

The fees that ORMs charge for their services vary from a few dollars a month for a basic individual report to hundreds of thousands of dollars a month for a large multi-national company. As an alternative, there are a number of free tools available online which individuals can use to monitor their reputation.

NET FOLLOW-UP

Use a search engine to explore the Web for additional information on the topics of "online reputation management" or "online reputation management tools." After doing your research, jot down your thoughts regarding the amount of time and effort that is required to monitor the online reputation of an individual or a business. Be prepared to participate in a class discussion regarding the value ORMs provide to customers.

search by an employer. Because a picture can be tagged instantly at any time, you should consider frequently checking your online profile. It would be unfortunate if, after cleaning up your online image for the first time, someone posted new, unflattering information about you that a potential employer discovered.

Understand how to use privacy settings. Most social networks allow you to decide which parts of your site are open to the public and which parts are private. You might, for example, limit access of your photos to family only. But, privacy settings are often misunderstood and misused. The best approach is to eliminate anything from your site that could cause embarrassment.

Be consistent. Does your online profile match your resume? It is okay to rework your resume for different job descriptions. But, basic employment history such as job titles, previous employers, employment dates, and job responsibilities should be consistent.

Know your friends. People often connect on their social network with "friends" whom they barely know. Not only can the information that you post damage your reputation, but also what others post on your page can be damaging as well. Remove postings by others that may get you in trouble and consider removing them as a friend.

Employer monitoring of your social network site often does not end after you are hired. Your boss may look online occasionally to see if you are maintaining responsible behavior or to see if you are saying anything negative about the company or its employees. Carla should have known this. She called her company one morning to say that she was sick and would not be coming to work. Her boss checked her Facebook page later in the day only to discover that she was chatting with her friends about "partying too much last night and having to call in sick." Fortunately for Carla, her boss only gave her a **reprimand**, which is a formal statement of misconduct, rather than fire her.

Practice Your Interview Skills

You may be a little nervous when you think about going for a job interview. That is normal. To reduce your anxiety and help build your confidence, you may want to role-play some practice interviews. Something as important as a job interview deserves advance preparation.

You may be able to set up a classroom interview situation. Arrange a desk and a couple of chairs the way you might find them in an office. The instructor or a fellow student can play the role of an employer. Take turns being interviewed for a **hypothetical**, or imagined, job.

Before you practice the interview, though, work together as a group to develop a list of questions for the interviewer to ask such as the following.

- Tell me something about yourself.
- Do you like school?
- What is your favorite subject? Why?
- What do you do in your spare time?
- Tell me why you applied for a job with us.
- How much do you know about the type of work we do here?
- Why do you think you would like this kind of work?
- Have you ever worked on this type of equipment before?
- If I hired you, how long would you expect to stay with us?
- How much do you expect to make?
- What would you want to be doing in five years?
- When will you be available to start work?
- Do you have any questions?

By practicing the interview, you will become aware of what is involved in answering a question out loud. It can be a valuable learning experience to discover, for example, how much you stumble and hesitate. Do not try to memorize answers, but do practice until you can respond easily. Make special efforts to rid your speech of "uhs," "you knows," and similar responses.

In addition to participating yourself, you can learn a great deal by watching others during practice interviews. Devin, for example, noticed how some individuals pause for long periods before answering a question and repeatedly change positions in their chair. He has made a mental note to try to avoid these behaviors.

Learn About the Company

Find out as much as possible about the job and the company before your interview. Start by asking people you know who might have information. From personal contacts, you may learn inside information. For example, you might find out about the working conditions or the turnover rate of personnel.

Further information may be available from the company itself. Check to see if they have a website. If so, read all of the posted material and look to see if descriptive information is available about the person who will be conducting the interview. The interviewer might be favorably impressed if you happened to mention something personal that you read on the Web.

Managing an online profile can be difficult for a company. Be very careful if you stumble onto negative comments about the company. You will need to figure out who posted the negative comments and why he or she posted the comments. Is it a disatisfied customer or a disgruntled former employee? Negative comments are not necessarily accurate. It is best not to mention negative comments during the interview.

If the company does not have a website, ask about getting copies of any brochures, catalogs, annual reports, or other types of descriptive materials that would help you learn more about them. Some facts to look for include products produced or services provided, growth rate, and standing in the industry.

If the potential place of employment is a restaurant, retail store, or similar public place, it may be possible to get firsthand information. Visit the establishment to get a feel for the atmosphere. You can observe the type of work done and perhaps ask employees a few questions.

If information about the company is not available, find out something about the industry. Imagine you are going to interview for a job in a property management firm. Find out what services this type of firm provides.

When you finish your research, write up a list of questions that you would like to ask about the job or the company. For example, you might ask, "Why did the job become vacant? Will any more training be required? What are the working hours? Who will my supervisor be if I get the job?"

It is generally best to avoid asking about salary or benefits in the job interview. If the information is not provided by the interviewer, you can ask after you have been offered the job.

Assemble Needed Materials

Have the materials you plan to take to the interview ready. These include the job-lead card, the personal data sheet, the resume, copies of any correspondence, a pen, a notebook, a list of questions you will ask, and a work permit, if needed. Also, take samples of your work if possible. Carry all the materials in a large envelope or briefcase.

Consider Your Appearance

Your grooming and dress will influence the interviewer's final decision. Choose clothes that are appropriate for the job setting. Ron, for example, has an interview for a job as an auto mechanic. It is not necessary that he wear a coat and tie, but jeans and a T-shirt are too casual.

Workforce Trends

Deciding how far to go in school is one of the most important decisions an American worker makes. Educational attainment plays a critical role in job placement, earnings, and how long people work or are unemployed. On average, the more education individuals have, the more likely they are to seek and find jobs, earn higher wages, and retire with a pension.

If you are not sure what to wear, ask your work experience coordinator or counselor for advice. Or visit the company ahead of time to see how people dress. Remember, though, you are dressing for an interview, not the job you will be doing.

Whatever clothes you decide to wear, they should be clean, pressed, and in good condition. Clothes do not have to be expensive to look neat. Clean your shoes. Avoid too much jewelry and accessories. Conceal tattoos if you can. Remove any unusual body piercings.

Careful grooming is also very important. If you need a haircut, plan ahead to get it done. On the day of the interview, a shower or bath is a must. Wash your hair, clean your nails, and brush your teeth. Men should shave or trim beards and mustaches. No heavy-smelling colognes or aftershaves. Women should use makeup and perfume sparingly.

Be sure to have a healthful, easy to digest meal or snack before the interview. You will need energy to stay focused. You do not want your stomach growling from hunger or making loud digestive noises during the interview.

Check Last-Minute Details

Going to an interview at the wrong place or time may seem dumb. But people do it all the time. It will help if you write the date, time, and place of the interview on a job-lead card. Double-check the information.

You should make a trial run so you will know where the company is located and how long it takes to get there. *Global Positioning Systems (GPS),* which are used to generate electronic directions, are not always accurate. Rush hour traffic and construction can affect travel time. Use GPS directions as a guideline, but do a trial run.

If more than a week goes by between the time you made the appointment and the interview, call to **confirm**, or verify, it. Plan to arrive at the interviewer's office five to ten minutes ahead of schedule. Introduce yourself and tell why you are there. Do not bring anyone with you. You do not want to give the impression that you cannot do things on your own.

5-1 Assessment

1. From the interviewer's standpoint, what is the purpose of the job interview?

2. What two things can you do in a job interview?

3. Name four common barriers to carrying out a job.

4. Name the six things that you should do to prepare for a job interview. Why is each important?

5. Why would an employer care about the information you have on a social network site?

6. If you can't find background information about a specific company, what should you do?

7. Why do a trial run to the interview site?

High Growth Occupations
FOR THE 21ST CENTURY

Do you want to work outdoors? Do you like working with plants or want repetitive work, such as mowing? If so, think about the occupation of grounds maintenance worker. These workers are responsible for creating and maintaining attractively designed, healthy lawns, gardens, and grounds. They take care of both indoor and outdoor lawns and gardens in private, commercial, and public facilities, such as business complexes, malls, hotels, apartment houses, and even private residences.

Stockbyte/Getty Images

Flowers and plantings that decorate public facilities such as shopping malls and hotels were planted by a grounds maintenance worker.

Grounds maintenance workers include landscaping and groundskeeping workers. Although the two often overlap, *landscaping workers* install and maintain landscaped areas and *groundskeeping workers*, also called groundskeepers, maintain the landscaped areas, grade the land, and install lighting and sprinkler systems. They also build walkways, terraces, patios, decks, and fountains. Groundskeepers maintain the land for a variety of facilities, including athletic fields, cemeteries, schools, college and university campuses, parks, and other businesses and residential facilities. Grounds maintenance workers who maintain golf courses are called *greenskeepers*.

Jobs for grounds maintenance workers often are seasonal. The highest demand for workers is in the spring, summer, and fall, which is when most of the planting, mowing, trimming, and cleanup are done. Workers must be willing to work in all kinds of weather, including rain and heat. The work is physically demanding, involving bending, lifting, and shoveling.

A high-school diploma is required for some jobs. However, no minimum education is required for entry-level positions. On-the-job training is provided to teach workers safety and how to operate equipment, which may include lawnmowers, trimmers, leaf blowers, and small tractors. Entry-level workers need to be able to follow directions and learn proper procedures for mowing and planting. Employers prefer self-motivated, responsible workers who can work with little supervision. Wages are low, so employers usually are looking for good workers who can handle the physical demands.

DURING THE INTERVIEW

OBJECTIVES

- Describe acceptable behavior while waiting for a job interview
- Discuss guidelines regarding proper conduct during a job interview

KEY TERMS

- compatible
- body language

Creatas/Jupiter Images

Personal Decisions

You arrive at the interview location about 15 minutes prior to the interview. Since it is a nice day, you decide to sit outside the main entrance a few minutes before entering the building. As you are waiting, a person comes out of the building about your age. She takes out her cell phone and places a call. You overhear part of a conversation in which she says that the interview is over and she is ready to be picked up. You assume that the person may have interviewed for the job that you are seeking. You would really like to ask the person some questions, but are not sure if it would be appropriate.

What would you do?

While You Wait

Before entering the office, make sure that your cell phone is turned off. You may have to wait a short time in an outer office or reception area. During that time, you should relax, read, or look over your list of questions. Be pleasant toward others in the reception area. Do not smoke, chew gum, or do anything distracting. The interviewer may later ask for the receptionist's opinion of you.

You may wonder what type of person the interviewer will be. Unfortunately, you have no way of knowing. If you have five job interviews, you will probably find five completely different personalities.

It is not necessary for you to like the interviewer or for the interviewer to like you. The interviewer is looking for the best person to fill a job. You are not there to be social. You are looking for a job.

Prepare yourself to deal with whatever you may find. Remain calm and do your best. If you have prepared well for the interview, you have done your homework up to this point.

Phil Date/Shutterstock.com

FIGURE 5-1 By leaning forward, these workers demonstrate with their body language that they are interested in what the speaker is saying. With his smile, the speaker indicates that he is pleased with the work.

Interview Behavior

Let the interviewer set the tone and pace. Adjust yourself to the style of the interviewer. For example, if the interviewer is serious and business-like, your style should be similar. If the interviewer is cheerful and out-going, you may need to brighten up a little. Try to establish a **compatible** relationship, or a relationship that is pleasant, with the interviewer.

Communication skills, which are important at every step of the job search, are more so in the job interview. Be sure to listen carefully and speak clearly. Answer each question briefly, but do not give one-word or one-line answers. If you think that the interviewer has not understood your answer or that you have not made yourself clear, try again. Stay on the topic until you are sure that the interviewer has understood your message.

Answer a question only after the interviewer is completely finished. Otherwise, you risk making a bad impression. You may also never find out the exact question or hear information added to the question.

Listening to the interviewer is as important as speaking thoughtfully and clearly. The ability to listen shows your attentiveness and reflects on your interest in the job. At times, you may want to ask the interviewer the meaning of a word or phrase. Do so. You must understand a question before you can answer it.

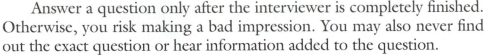

Communication at Work — ILLEGAL INTERVIEW QUESTIONS

There are certain questions that interviewers cannot legally ask you. These include questions about marital status, plans for children, child-care arrangements, disabilities, and health. If an interviewer asks you a question on one of these topics, how should you respond?

"Answer" a question that wasn't asked. Don't answer the question directly. Instead, give the interviewer some positive information that relates to your ability to do the job. For example, suppose an interviewer asks, "Do you have any disabilities?" You might respond, "I can assure you that there is no reason that I could not do a great job for you. Look at my work record, for example."

THINK CRITICALLY

1. Why do you think some questions are illegal in a job interview?
2. What would you do if an interviewer presses you for a direct answer after you answer a question indirectly?

FIGURE 5-2 Rolling eyes upward and avoiding eye contact convey disinterest and disrespect.

FIGURE 5-3 With his glasses off, eyes shut, and yawning, this worker's body language indicates he is too tired and disinterested to even try and see what is going on around him.

Nonverbal Communication

Body language may help or hinder communication. **Body language** is unspoken communication through physical movements, expressions, and gestures. During the interview, sit comfortably, but do not slouch. Keep your hands on your lap. Do not look at your hands or feet. Maintain good eye contact throughout the interview, but do not stare. Keep a pleasant expression on your face.

Also be aware of the interviewer's body language. Watch for nonverbal clues. If the interviewer's body language conveys something negative, think about what you are doing or saying. Modify what needs to be changed. Refer to Figures 5-1, 5-2, and 5-3. Which examples of body language would you use in an interview? Which examples would you avoid?

Ask Questions

An interview involves two-way communication. The interviewer will ask you questions. The interviewer will also expect you to ask questions. It is wise to refer to the list of questions you made beforehand. Hold the list near your lap so you can glance at it as you talk.

Search the Net

Asking good, thoughtful questions in your interview can help you make a good impression. Access **www.cengage.com/school/ working** and click on the link for Chapter 5. Read the list of Sample Job Interview Questions. With a partner, take turns being the interviewer and the job applicant. Practice asking and answering the questions. Give particular thought to how you would respond to any of the illegal questions listed. Make up at least five questions of your own.

www.cengage.com/school/working

It is a good idea to ask questions during an interview in a polite and pleasant manner.

Do not be in a hurry to ask questions. Wait until the interviewer invites them. A pause in the conversation once the interview is well under way may be the time for you to bring up your questions. Be careful, though, not to interrupt the interviewer. Request an opportunity to ask your questions before the interview ends. Your questions should indicate a sincere interest in the company and the job and that you have prepared for the interview.

For example, you might ask, "What opportunities are there to advance within the company?"

Use good judgment in deciding how much time to take with questions. Try to sense whether or not the interviewer is on a tight schedule. If time seems pressing, ask only your most important questions.

Conclude the Interview

The interview is almost over and the employer has not told you when a decision will be made about the job. What do you do? Ask about it. If the interviewer asks you to call back or supply more information, note it on the job-lead card.

Try to get a feeling for when the interview has run its course. The interviewer may stand or simply say, "Well, I think that I have enough information about you at this time." To help bring an interview to an end ask, "Are there any more questions I can answer?"

SOUTHWEST REALTY COMPANY APPLICANT EVALUATION

Name_____ Interview date_____

Position applied for_____

Criteria	Poor	Good	Excellent
1. Appearance	☐	☐	☐
2. Poise	☐	☐	☐
3. Responses	☐	☐	☐
4. Grammar and speech	☐	☐	☐
5. Background	☐	☐	☐
6. Knowledge of job requirements	☐	☐	☐
7. Interest in company	☐	☐	☐
8. Potential	☐	☐	☐

Strengths:_____
_____
_____

Weaknesses:_____
_____
_____

Based on interview, review of application, and follow-up, should an offer of employment be made?   Yes ☐   No ☐

Date _____ Interviewer _____

FIGURE 5-4 Some employers use forms like this to help them rate a job candidate.

Some jobs, like for a student orientation leader, might require that you be interviewed by a group of people. What does the body language of the yawning interviewer tell you? Why might he choose to yawn during an interview?

Many job applicants fail to ask for the job. Tell the interviewer if you want the job. Say something like, "I know I can do the work, Mr. Young. I would like to have the job."

Seldom does an interviewer make a job offer or reject an applicant at the conclusion of an interview. Usually the interviewer wants to think about and compare all applicants before making a decision. In some cases, the interviewer's role is to evaluate and make recommendations only. See the bottom of Figure 5-4. The actual employment decision may be made by another person.

If you do learn that the company cannot use you, ask about other employers who may need a person with your skills. Thank the interviewer, shake hands, and leave. On the way out, thank the assistant or receptionist.

5-2 Assessment

1. What impression does it give if you are text messaging or listening to music while waiting to be called into an interview?

2. Is it necessary that you like the interviewer? Why or why not?

3. Explain what it means to "adjust your interview style to that of the interviewer."

4. Give examples to illustrate "negative" body language and "positive" body language.

5. What is a major mistake that applicants often make at the end of a job interview?

OBJECTIVES

- Name and describe the two things to do after a job interview
- Discuss how to respond to a job offer

KEY TERMS

- follow-up letter
- conditions of employment

Monkey Business Images/ Shutterstock.com

Career Decisions

You have to decide between two job offers. One is a traditional job for a person of your gender. The other is a nontraditional job. You would be the only person of your gender out of eight employees. You feel confident that you can do the job, but are concerned about being harassed and accepted.

What would *you* do?

Steps to Take

You can benefit from every interview, no matter what the outcome. Take time to think about the experience as soon as possible after the interview. Review any mistakes you think you made and consider how you could have avoided them. Could you have been better prepared? Did you mention everything about yourself that the employer needs to know? Think about what you did well. Would these things help you in other interviews?

Promptly send a **follow-up letter**, or a thank-you letter, to the interviewer. Such a letter may accomplish the following things:

- It helps to build a courteous relationship.
- Having your letter keeps your name in front of the interviewer.
- Taking time to write a letter tells the interviewer of your continued interest.
- The letter allows you to reinforce key points you discussed during the interview.
- If you forgot to mention something important during the interview, you can put it in your follow-up letter.

A sample follow-up letter is shown in Figure 5-5 on the next page. Suppose the interviewer told you that you would not be hired. Or, perhaps you are no longer interested in the job. Send a letter to thank the interviewer for considering you.

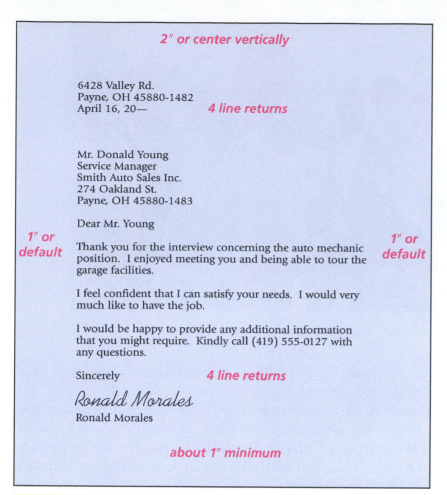

2″ or center vertically

6428 Valley Rd.
Payne, OH 45880-1482
April 16, 20— **4 line returns**

Mr. Donald Young
Service Manager
Smith Auto Sales Inc.
274 Oakland St.
Payne, OH 45880-1483

Dear Mr. Young

1″ or default

Thank you for the interview concerning the auto mechanic position. I enjoyed meeting you and being able to tour the garage facilities.

I feel confident that I can satisfy your needs. I would very much like to have the job.

I would be happy to provide any additional information that you might require. Kindly call (419) 555-0127 with any questions.

Sincerely **4 line returns**

Ronald Morales
Ronald Morales

1″ or default

about 1″ minimum

FIGURE 5-5 Sample Follow-up Letter

When writing a follow-up letter, refer to the guidelines for preparing a letter of application in Chapter 3. The rules are similar for both types of letters. If someone helped arrange your interview, send a note of appreciation to him or her. This should be a simple, handwritten thank-you note.

After completing these steps, wait and try to relax. Continue to pursue other job leads in the meantime. If you have not heard from the company in a week, get in touch. You can do so sooner if the interviewer indicated that a decision would be made in less than a week.

Respond to Job Offers

You may be hired or rejected during an interview. Usually, though, the employer makes a decision later. Employers like to interview several people for a job before making a choice.

A job offer is generally made by telephone or in person. This gives the employer and the applicant a chance to discuss the details of the job offer. If the conditions of employment were not discussed earlier, ask about them before accepting. **Conditions of employment** are the specific details of a job offer, such as working hours, salary or wages, and fringe benefits. You will want to know when you start work and if there is anything special that you need to bring or be prepared to do

Accepting a job offer is gratifying.

the first day. For example, you might need to pick up a uniform. You may also receive a job offer by letter.

It is possible to be considered for a job at different places at the same time. Within the same week you have been interviewed for jobs at both Burger Barn and Chicken Shack. If Burger Barn offers you a job and you accept it, you should phone Chicken Shack and explain that you have taken another job.

What if a company offers you a job you do not want? Be polite. You never know when you may be contacting the company again. Give a brief explanation of your reasons for rejecting the offer. Regardless of your reasons, do not criticize the employer.

Not all of your interviews will result in job offers. In fact, most of them probably will not. Dealing with rejection is something we all must learn to do. Being disappointed is normal. Do not, however, react with anger toward an employer. By accepting rejection gracefully, you keep alive your chances for a future job. In all companies, employees come and go. New jobs open. If you are good enough to have been invited for an interview, then you are qualified for a job. Do not get discouraged. Whether at that company or somewhere else, a job will open up for you.

5-3 Assessment

1. You can benefit from every interview, no matter what the outcome. Explain.
2. What five things may a follow-up letter accomplish?
3. You are being considered for two jobs. You receive one job offer and accept it. What should you do next?
4. Why is it important to accept a job rejection gracefully?

Focus on the Workplace

Drug Tests

During the job interview, Akira was surprised to learn that his potential employer has a drug-testing program. After the first month of employment, all workers at Allied Receiving are subject to random drug testing. The purpose of such tests is to identify employees who use illegal or illicit drugs, such as marijuana and cocaine. Not only is the use of such drugs illegal and dangerous, but the drugs have also been linked to accidents, injury, absenteeism, health problems, theft, lower productivity, and job loss.

To identify drug users, employers often require each employee to submit a urine or hair sample for analysis. The urinalysis can detect traces of cocaine up to five days after the drug was taken. Marijuana can show up in the urine for several weeks after use. Hair analysis can detect drug use for approximately the previous 90 days.

Currently, a majority of the nation's 500 largest corporations have drug-testing programs. Testing may be required for job applicants, employed workers, or both. Some employers test workers for "cause"; for instance, if they notice a worker is not performing well. Others test randomly, without announcement and without even suspecting wrongdoing.

Even though drug testing is widely used, the practice remains controversial. Some people claim that the tests are often inaccurate. Others claim that the tests violate a person's right to privacy. But, the U. S. Supreme Court has held that both blood and urine collection are minimally intrusive and not harmful to job applicants when conducted properly.

Each state has its own laws governing employment drug testing which employers should follow. Generally these laws allow for drug testing of job applicants provided the applicant knows that the testing is part of the hiring or retention process for all employees. Most employers have fairly wide latitude regarding drug testing and the current emphasis on drug free workplaces encourages this.

THINK CRITICALLY

1. What jobs do you think should require candidates to be screened for drug use? Why?
2. If you were an employer, would you require drug testing of your employees? Why or why not?

Photodisc/Getty Images

Unpleasant as it might be, employers have the right to test applicants and employees for illegal drug use.

Chapter Summary

5-1 Before the Interview

A. An interview is the final important step in the job-seeking process.

B. Part of the planning and preparation for a job interview includes identifying and resolving any barriers to employment. One of the most common barriers is reliable transportation to and from work.

C. In preparation for an interview, you should review your online reputation, practice your interview skills, learn about the employer, assemble needed materials, consider your appearance, and check last-minute details.

5-2 During the Interview

A. Before entering the office, turn off your cell phone. Be polite and pleasant while you wait for the interview.

B. During the interview, adjust yourself to the style of the interviewer. Be sure to listen carefully, speak clearly, and use appropriate body language. An interview isn't just one way. Be prepared to ask the interviewer questions. If you want the job, tell the interviewer near the end of the interview.

5-3 After the Interview

A. After the interview, take time to think about the experience. Review any mistakes you think you made and consider how you could have avoided them. Promptly send a follow-up, or thank-you, letter to the interviewer and anyone else who helped you obtain the interview.

B. A job offer may be made following the interview or later by phone or letter. Before accepting the offer, make sure you understand the conditions of employment. If you are rejected for a job, accept it gracefully. Don't do anything to close the door on a possible later offer or opportunity.

Activities

1. Research the website of a well-known company that you might like to work for. Determine if the site has information about employment opportunities. Use your research to prepare for a hypothetical interview at the company. Write down five questions that you would ask during an interview and turn it in to your instructor.

2. Websites are not available for all companies. In this case, you should learn about the type of industry in which the company is classified. Select one of the following industries and do a web search to find out what it produces or what service it provides: brokerage office, courier service, diagnostic imaging center,

hydroelectric power generator, and terrazzo contractor. Or, your instructor may assign a different industry to research. Write a summary paragraph and turn it into your instructor.

3. In class, practice role-playing a job interview. Each student should have the opportunity to be interviewed. The instructor will initiate the interview with a couple of questions. Class members can then participate with additional questions.

4. If equipment is available, record the role-playing interview. View and discuss the recordings later. Seeing yourself in a recording can often be quite informative.

5. Prepare a follow-up letter to a hypothetical job interview. Turn it in to your instructor for evaluation.

6. Evaluate your ability to communicate successfully with others. Describe how this ability is likely to help you attain goals in your life-span plan.

Word Power

On a separate sheet of paper, match each definition with the correct term. All definitions will be used, and a definition will be used only once.

7. Pleasant or agreeable

8. The specific details of a job offer, such as working hours, salary or wages, and fringe benefits

9. A face-to-face meeting between a job seeker and a potential employer

10. Any condition that makes it difficult to achieve an objective

11. A thank-you letter sent to an interviewer following a job interview

12. Imagined or pretended

13. To verify or make firm, such as calling to check on an appointment

14. A formal statement or expression of misconduct

15. Unspoken communication through physical movements, expressions, and gestures

16. A duty or obligation to do something

17. To evaluate someone or something, such as a potential employer

> a. appraise
> b. barrier
> c. body language
> d. commitment
> e. compatible
> f. condition of employment
> g. confirm
> h. follow-up letter
> i. hypothetical
> j. job interview
> k. reprimand

Think Critically

18. Despite your best planning efforts, an unexpected emergency or problem arises that prevents you from attending a job interview. How should you handle a situation like this?

19. A person with advanced education or highly marketable skills can often negotiate favorable conditions of employment following a job offer. Discuss realistically how much bargaining power a person has in applying for an entry-level job.

UNIT 3 On the Job

Blend Images/Getty Images

Co-op Career SPOTLIGHT

Jake Mendoza, a co-operative education student at Skyline High School in Dallas, TX, was very interested in the political process. He learned about politics by participating in many activities. Jake participated in Youth in Government, which is a model government program, through his local YMCA. The program gave Jake the opportunity to be part of a team that competed in areas of legislative and judicial law making. The team that Jake was on during his sophomore year focused on legislative issues. On that team, he learned how to propose a bill and get it passed. In his junior year, Jake was on a judicial team. On that team, he learned about the roles of a witness and an attorney.

Jake also volunteered on a variety of political campaigns, including races for a judge, a mayor, a state governor, and a state representative. He supported these campaigns by distributing campaign literature and by making phone calls in support of the campaigns. Sometimes Jake went block walking to contact potential voters at various locations to provide information that supported candidates. He spent time working as an election clerk and as a poll greeter.

While still in eighth grader, Jake's political passion had compelled him to apply to a high school that offered a combination curriculum of advanced social sciences and co-operative education. After earning a spot at Skyline High School, Jake began his studies in the Law Career cluster. It took three years to fulfill his educational requirements before he was allowed to participate in the co-operative education program.

Jake interviewed for a job as an intern at a law firm. The knowledge he gained through Youth in Government and by being a campaign volunteer enabled Jake to demonstrate his understanding of the political and legal systems. Jake's qualifications were so impressive that the law firm hired him as an intern.

Jake Mendoza
Legal Intern

As a senior, Jake works 20 hours per week at the law firm. Each day he attends school from 9:15 a.m. until 1:05 p.m. He then travels to the law office where he works from 1:30 p.m. until 5:30 p.m. He gets home from work at 6 p.m. He then has dinner and starts on his homework.

His duties at the law firm are varied. He is responsible for contacting clients to remind them of their court dates. He helps assign attorneys to the court cases they will pursue. Sometimes he contacts the courts to confirm which cases are on the *docket*, or schedule, of the court. He also answers telephones, greets guests, and files. Jake earns $7.50 per hour. The minimum wage in Texas is $7.25 per hour.

During his spare time, Jake enjoys playing basketball and working out. He also likes to take his four year old and two year old nephews to play in the park. Sometimes he helps his Uncle Lupe build showers and frame glass mirrors.

Jake recently took the SAT, a college entrance exam. He plans to attend a four year college with a political science major and a marketing minor. He then plans to attend a three year law school. After his schooling is complete, he hopes to work as a lobbyist, as a political consultant, or as an attorney.

CHAPTER 6

"Opportunities are usually disguised as hard work, so most people don't recognize them." —ANN LANDERS

Begin a New Job

Morgan Lane Photography/Shutterstock.com

PREVIEW

The job search is over. Your new job is about to start. You will be leaving or at least spending less time in the familiar world of the classroom. The changes you will experience may be scary at first. You are going from the known into the unknown. This can be exciting and frightening at the same time. By taking the time now to learn what to expect, you will be better prepared for your new role as a worker.

Taking/*Action* Begin Work

Denny Liu was hired as a salesclerk at Rogers', a small men's store in North Plaza Mall. Denny learned about the job opening at Rogers' while he was working as a cooperative education student at another mall store. He applied for the job in person. After a short interview with Bob Brown, the manager, he was hired on the spot. Denny agreed to report for work after giving the other store two weeks' notice.

Three weeks later Denny arrived for his first day at work. Bob was unlocking the entrance. After greeting each other, Bob and Denny walked to the rear of the store. Along the way, Bob flipped on the lights. Denny smiled to himself. He was amused at how different the back of the shop looked compared to the shop's front display area.

Denny and Bob exchanged small talk as Bob sorted the mail. A few minutes later Courtney and Evan, two other employees, came into the shop. Bob introduced Denny to them. They all chatted for a few minutes. Courtney and Evan then went to get the shop ready for its 10:00 a.m. opening.

Bob gave Denny a few forms to sign and a payroll card. He told Denny how to keep track of the number of hours he worked. They then walked around the shop while Bob explained procedures and pointed out features of certain merchandise.

Bob told Denny that he wanted him to begin working at the ties and accessories counter. If the other salesclerks got busy, he was to leave the counter area to help out.

"Denny, you know what goes on in a men's store," Bob said. "If you have questions or need help, ask us. We'll just play it by ear."

By 10:10 a.m., Denny had waited on his first customer and made his first sale. He was so busy that it was almost 1:30 p.m. before he had time for lunch. Business during the afternoon was also good. He even waited on several customers whom he knew from his previous sales job. Overall, Denny had a good first day. He had to ask a few questions, and Bob made a few suggestions. Denny knew he was going to like working at Rogers'.

THINK CRITICALLY

1. Do you think Denny had a typical first day on the job? Why or why not?

2. Why do you think the first day went so well for Denny?

OBJECTIVES

- Recognize that anxiety about beginning a new job is normal
- Describe what to expect from an employer when beginning a new job

KEY TERMS

- anxiety
- employee orientation program

Cultura/Jupiter Images

Personal Decisions

You have just been hired as a clerk at a grocery store. Your new supervisor tells you to report for work tomorrow at 4:00 p.m. sharp. You agree to do this and leave the store. Later, you remember that you have to take a makeup exam at school tomorrow afternoon.

What would you do?

Pre-Employment Anxiety

Anxiety is the state of feeling worried or uneasy, usually about something that may happen in the future. You may have feelings of anxiety about beginning a new job. Try to relax. Remember the employer chose your job application from among many others. You were hired because the employer believed you were the best person for the job. Your employer wants you to succeed. Your employer understands you are going through a stressful time. He or she understands it will take time for you to learn the company's rules, its procedures, and any other policies.

Report for Work

What you do on the first day of work depends on the company you have joined. Denny Liu's first day on the job, at a small company, went smoothly due to his past experience. Francine Gordon's first day of work, at a large corporation, was much different.

Two weeks after her interview, Francine was offered a job as an equipment operator at Northeastern Electric Power Company. Because this was the job Francine wanted, she accepted right away. Francine was told to report to work at 9:30 a.m. on Monday for a new **employee orientation program**, at which she would learn about company policies and procedures. She was also told that a parking decal for her car and a map showing the location of the meeting room would be sent to her in the mail.

Francine arrived at the plant about 9:15 a.m. on Monday. A uniformed guard at the entrance motioned for her to stop. Before Francine could say anything, the guard asked her if she was a new employee. The guard pointed out the building entrance and the parking lot she needed to use. Francine used her map to find the correct meeting room. There, Mr. Walsh, the Director of Human Resources, welcomed her and gave her a name tag. She was then directed to a seat.

At 9:35 a.m., a woman went to the front of the room. Mr. Walsh introduced her as Mrs. Ramos, the Public Relations Specialist. Mrs. Ramos welcomed the 12 new employees and introduced several staff members. She distributed handouts of a slide presentation. Mrs. Ramos encouraged the new employees to take notes on the handouts. Then she gave a 15-minute slide presentation about the company. Francine took notes on the handouts. Before seeing the presentation, Francine had not thought much about the number of people and businesses that depended on Northeast Electric Power Company.

Mr. Walsh then took over the meeting and explained the purpose of his office and the services it provides to all employees. After answering some questions, he passed out a folder to each person. The folder contained an "Employee Handbook" which explained company policies and rules. It also had a number of different forms to be completed.

Some large companies, such as Northeast Electric Power Company, have a very formal employee orientation program. Because of the large number of employees that Northeast Electric Power Company hires, such a program is efficient. The company can orient several new workers at once. This kind of detailed program ensures that all employees have received the same information. Many problems can be prevented when all employees are following the same set of rules.

Unique First Days at Work

What a difference between Francine's and Denny's first days! Denny spent most of his first day waiting on customers. Francine spent much of her first day learning about Northeast Electric Power Company. Francine didn't actually start work until two weeks later. She spent the first two weeks in class learning how to be an equipment operator. Clearly, one person's first day at work may be quite different from another person's first day at work.

6-1 Assessment

1. Name two ways to relieve pre-employment anxiety.
2. What are two reasons companies conduct formal employee orientation programs?
3. What are some ways that Francine's and Denny's first days were similar?

Workforce Trends

Between 2008 and 2018, the number of women in the labor force will grow at a slightly faster rate than the number of men. The male labor force is projected to grow by 7.5 percent (from 82.5 to 88.7 million) compared with 9.0 percent (from 71.8 to 78.2 million) for the female labor force. By 2018, about 71 percent of men and 59 percent of women are expected to be in the labor force.

High Growth Occupations
FOR THE 21ST CENTURY

Executive Secretaries and Administrative Assistants

Executive secretaries and *administrative assistants* provide high-level administrative support for an office and for top executives of an organization. Office automation and organizational restructuring have led executive secretaries and administrative assistants to increasingly assume responsibilities once reserved for managerial and professional staff.

Word processing, writing, and communication skills are still essential. Knowledge of computer software applications, such as desktop publishing, project management, spreadsheets, and database management, is also required.

Executive secretaries and administrative assistants generally perform fewer clerical tasks and have more information management responsibilities. In addition to supervising clerical staff, they may handle tasks such as reviewing incoming memos, submissions, and reports and planning for their distribution. Preparing agendas and making arrangements for meetings of committees and executive boards are other duties. Conducting research and preparing statistical reports may be required.

Employers look for good customer service and interpersonal skills because executive secretaries and administrative assistants must be tactful in their dealings with people. Discretion, good judgment, organizational skills, initiative, and the ability to work independently are especially important for higher-level administrative positions.

High school graduates who have basic office skills may qualify for entry-level secretarial positions. But to move up the career ladder and become an executive secretary and administrative assistant, additional training, experience, and maturity are required.

Employers of executive secretaries increasingly are seeking candidates with a college degree, as these secretaries work closely with top executives. A degree related to the business or industry in which a person is seeking employment may provide the jobseeker with an advantage in the application process.

Employment is projected to grow about as fast as the average occupation. However, executive secretaries and administrative assistants will have among the largest number of job openings due to growth and the need to replace workers who transfer to other occupations or leave this occupation.

Administrative assistants need strong computer and interpersonal skills.

WORKPLACE MANAGEMENT

OBJECTIVES

- Describe the purposes of an organization chart
- List areas for which employers have policies and rules

KEY TERMS

- authority
- responsibility
- delegate
- supervisor
- morale
- employee handbook
- reimburse
- due process
- confidentiality
- probation

Ethical Decisions

Upon beginning a new job, you may know very little about a company or its management. This can happen despite your best efforts to research the company and ask thoughtful questions in a job interview. Suppose that during the orientation meeting you discover things about the company that disturb you. Perhaps the company manufactures products that are in conflict with your moral or religious beliefs. Perhaps the company officials have an attitude that is completely different from your own. You begin to wonder if this is the right job for you.

What would you do?

CREATISTA/Shutterstock.com

Organizational Structure

During your first days on a new job, you will find out how the company is organized and what the written rules are. You will also begin to learn about the unwritten rules. The company will want to know more about you, too. You will have to fill out many forms. The most common one is Form W-4.

There are many important details that workers need to learn during their first day on the job. Francine and Denny learned many of the same things during their first day on the job. They learned how the workplace was laid out, where they would be working (their workstations), how to keep track of hours worked, where to look for posted notices such as work schedules, and what to do if they needed help or had questions.

All organizations, including companies and schools, have lines of authority and responsibility. **Authority** is the power or rank to give orders and make assignments to others. For instance, a teacher has authority in the classroom. **Responsibility** deals with the duty to follow an order or carry out an assignment. As a student, you are responsible for completing your assignments. Your teacher is responsible for evaluating your completed assignments. A sample *organization chart,* which shows the flow of authority and responsibility for a small kitchen equipment manufacturing company, is shown in Figure 6-1.

In a corporation, stockholders have the ultimate authority. But stockholders cannot manage a company. So, the stockholders elect a board of directors. A board of directors is normally comprised of people both inside and outside of the company. They meet regularly to review management, establish policy, and make business recommendations.

The board hires a president to manage the company. The president **delegates**, or assigns, tasks to lower-ranking executives who are responsible for various operations. The company president has the greatest authority and the greatest responsibility in an organization.

As you can see in Figure 6-1, each person or group of workers in an organization does different tasks. Note how each level in the organization is responsible to another level. For most organizations, the lower you are on the organization chart, the less authority you have.

You will be given a job title. Where will your job fit into the overall organization? If you start out in an entry-level job, you will probably have a lot of responsibility and little or no authority. A **supervisor** is a boss who gives directions and orders and oversees the work of others. You will probably report to a supervisor who will assign work to you. Answering to a supervisor or boss is called *reporting to authority*. You may do this in two ways. One is *formal reporting*, which is based on rank or the chain of command. For example, Figure 6-1 shows that the production workers formally report to the plant manager.

Another way of reporting to authority is *informal reporting*. This usually involves reporting to a specific person for a short time or for a certain work assignment. Suppose you work on the accounting staff for the company in Figure 6-1. Your regular supervisor, the vice president for finance, assigns you to help the sales manager on a project. Your

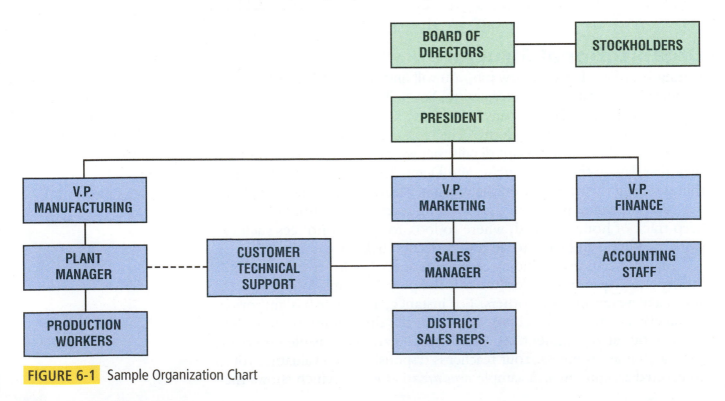

FIGURE 6-1 Sample Organization Chart

regular supervisor directs you to do what the sales manager tells you. In this case, you will be informally reporting to the sales manager.

Sometimes an organizational chart shows dotted lines as well as solid lines. Multiple lines mean that the department, or the workers in the department, report to multiple managers. In Figure 6-1, customer technical support reports to the sales manager. This reporting relationship is represented by a solid line. The customer technical support group is also responsible to the plant manager. This relationship is represented by a dotted line. If multiple customer complaints are received for broken toaster ovens, the technical support group must provide updates to both the sales and plant managers.

It is important to follow your company's lines of authority, both formal and informal. Take time to become familiar with these by listening, watching, and asking questions.

Policies and Rules

Most companies have written policies and rules. These help the organization run smoothly. Imagine what would happen to production if large numbers of workers took their vacations at the same time. Or, imagine how disruptive it would be if people came to work and left whenever they wanted.

Policies and rules ensure that all employees receive fair and equal treatment. Some policies and rules are required by federal and state laws. Others are desirable simply to promote good morale and positive working relationships among employees. **Morale** is a mood or spirit, such as the attitude and emotion of employees.

The formal rules often appear in a company's **employee handbook**, which is a booklet given to new employees that contains explanations of company policies and rules. If your company has an employee handbook, you will be given a copy when you start work.

Some companies have employees who are union members. A *union* is a group of workers in a similar line of work who unite with the intent of obtaining improved working conditions by negotiating as a single group. If the workplace is unionized, the employee handbook may contain both the employer's and the union's rules.

An employer may also present policies and rules in several other ways. Rules may be explained at a formal meeting or program for new employees, as was done in Francine's orientation. In some cases, important rules appear on a sign or bulletin board or are sent as email. Figure 6-2 is an example of a policy that was distributed by email. Your supervisor or coworkers may also be useful sources of such information.

SUBJECT: NO-SMOKING POLICY
DATE: Wed, 1 Aug 20-- 9:26:26-0500
FROM: "Hector Diaz" <hdiaz@stateins.net>
TO: "All Employees" <list1@stateins.net>

State Insurance has established a No-Smoking Policy aimed at protecting the health of our employees and our workplace environment.

Smoking is not permitted by any person anywhere within State's portion of the building. This rule applies to all State employees, temporary employees, visitors, and customers.

All potential new hires must be advised of this policy and must abide by it as a condition of employment.

Employees in violation of this policy will be subject to the following:

First offense: Written reprimand
Second offense: 30 days' probation
Third offense: Two weeks' suspension without pay
Fourth offense: Immediate dismissal

FIGURE 6-2 Employees learn about company policies and rules in many different ways.

Cities and states need to carefully organize workers just like businesses need to organize workers. Access **www.cengage.com/school/working** and click on the link for Chapter 6. Read the organizational chart for New York City. Are you surprised to see that the Mayor reports to the voters? How is that the same or different than the president of a company reporting to customers or shareholders? Why do the police and firefighters have both a straight line and a dotted line on the chart? How do you think this chart differs from the organizational chart for your city?

www.cengage.com/school/working

Some of the most common items for which employers have written policies and rules are:

- **Salaries, wages, and benefits**   Many employers outline in writing how pay rates, benefits, and raises are decided.

- **Attendance, absences, and punctuality**   You must report to work on time every workday unless you have a good reason not to. If you are going to be late or absent, follow your employer's policy for reporting in. Learn whether a medical excuse is needed for sick days. Find out company policy regarding reporting for work during extraordinarily bad weather.

- **Leave**   Most employers provide time off, with and without pay, for various reasons. Find out your employer's policies for sick leave, vacation, jury duty, and other time off.

- **Work schedule and records**   You must follow company rules for hours worked, meals, breaks, and overtime work. This often means clocking in and out on time in person. Don had a friend, Kim, clock in for him on mornings he wanted to sleep late. When the boss found out, both Don and Kim almost lost their jobs.

- **Expenses and reimbursement**   If you travel on company business or buy materials for company use, those expenses are considered company costs. The company should reimburse you for them. To **reimburse** is to pay back money that has already been spent. Company policy will explain what expenses you can be reimbursed for and how to go about getting reimbursement.

- **Due process**   Suppose you have a complaint about something or your boss has a complaint about you. The company may have formal procedures for solving this problem. **Due process** is the legal right to be notified of a complaint against you and to state your case or point of view before a decision is made.

- **Standards of conduct**   Most companies have conduct and discipline policies regarding such issues as sexual harassment, alcohol and drug use, and use of computers and the Internet.

- **Protect personal information of customers**   Keeping a person's identity, financial, and health information private is referred to as **confidentiality**. For some businesses, it is necessary to explain employee's legal obligations to protect customer data and confidentiality.

- **Safety and security**   Every company is concerned with maintaining a safe and secure workplace. You may be given information on potential safety hazards and how to deal with and report accidents and injuries. Information may also be provided dealing with personal safety, handling money, and keeping computers and company records secure.

Some companies conduct employee orientation with groups of employees.

- **Probation and review**   As a new employee, you may work for a period of time on probation. **Probation** is a trial period during which one's performance is being observed and evaluated. During this time, supervisors will carefully evaluate your work and attitude. At the end of your probation period, the employer will decide whether or not to employ you permanently. Once you are a permanent employee, a supervisor will review your performance from time to time.

Read and carefully study your company's employee handbook. If you can't find rules covering these items or other items of interest, ask your supervisor about them. You are responsible for obeying all policies and rules. Not knowing the policies and rules is not a good excuse for not obeying them. You may be asked to sign an "I agree" form that says you have read and understand the contents of the employee handbook.

Not all of a company's rules are written down. You will gradually learn rules that are not in the employee handbook. Some of these rules relate to appearance, work habits, attitudes, and job performance.

Victor was planning to do some home repairs over the weekend, so he took his toolbox home with him. He left for work Monday morning with his toolbox, but forgot that several of his tools were still lying in the garage. Later in the morning when he reached into his toolbox for a screwdriver, he remembered where it was. He had to ask another crew member to borrow one. The look on his coworker's face suggested that there is an unwritten rule about borrowing tools.

One unwritten rule relates to how people deal with each other in daily activities. In some cases, managers, supervisors, and employees are very casual. Everyone is on a first-name basis. In other cases, the workers are more formal. All workers may be addressed by last names. Ann Morales, for instance, is called Mrs. Morales.

Some organizations have a formal way of getting work done. Ways of doing things that differ from the accepted way may be frowned upon. In less formal organizations, the most important thing may be getting the work done. How the work gets done may be left to each worker. Pay attention to learn your company's expectations.

6-2 Assessment

1. Which is usually greater for beginning workers, level of authority or level of responsibility?

2. How do formal reporting and informal reporting differ?

3. What two purposes do written policies and rules serve in a company?

4. Name five ways that a company may communicate policies and rules.

5. Why would employees be required to sign an "I agree" form after reviewing the employee handbook?

6. Give an example of an area that is often covered by unwritten rules.

SUPERVISORS AND FORM W-4

OBJECTIVES
- Identify ways to work effectively with a supervisor
- Understand how to fill out a Form W-4

KEY TERMS
- allowance
- exempt

ilkeryuksel-/iStockphoto.com

Interpersonal Decisions

You are enjoying your new job and your fellow workers are pleasant and cooperative. Everyone seems to get along and work together to get the job done. Of course, each person has his or her own personality. One of the crew members, however, seems quite strange. You notice that he seems to be watching you constantly. You try to ignore it, but occasionally your eyes meet after which you smile and return to the task at hand. This has continued for a number of days and you are getting increasingly uncomfortable. You have lost some of your initial enthusiasm for the job and a couple of coworkers have asked you if there is anything wrong. You feel like talking to your supervisor, but you don't want to get anybody in trouble or have your supervisor think you are overreacting.

What would you do?

Working Under Supervision

In the workplace, every employee is responsible to someone else. This is not unlike school. In your job as a student, you are responsible to your teachers. They, in turn, report to the principal or department head. On the job, unless you are self-employed, you will work under the direction of a supervisor.

Although self-employed workers do not have direct supervisors, they have customers. Guidance regarding expectations and job requirements are given by customers. Failure to meet the expectations of a customer can result, not in a reprimand, but in a loss of business income.

Your supervisor will be responsible for training you and seeing that you learn company rules. He or she will also observe how well you perform on the job. Your success as an employee relates strongly to

Math Connection

You have just started working in the returns department. Your supervisor says 1 out of every 36 sets of china shipped arrives with broken pieces. In a shipment of 900 sets, how many sets are likely to have broken pieces?

SOLUTION

To calculate the number of sets that will probably have broken pieces, set up the equation as fractions. Cross-multiply the numerator and denominator that are known and divide by the other denominator.

$$\frac{1}{36} = \frac{?}{900} \qquad 1 \times 900 = 900 \qquad 900 \div 36 = 25$$

In a shipment of 900 sets, you can expect 25 sets to contain damaged pieces.

how well you work under supervision. Some suggestions for getting started on the right foot with your supervisor follow.

- **Use the supervisor for communication**   If you want to send messages to someone higher in the organization, go through your supervisor.

- **Ask the supervisor for direction**   Your supervisor is responsible for your work, training, and safety. Before performing tasks for the first time, go over them with the supervisor. For example, you might say, "After I get these cartons unpacked, then I should come and see you, right?" Understanding beforehand what you are to do saves everyone time. If you are ever unsure of how to do something, ask for help. Most supervisors respect people who know when to ask for help.

- **Don't ask for or expect special treatment**   Most supervisors are responsible for many workers. All should be treated the same, so don't ask for special favors.

- **Accept and use the supervisor's suggestions**   Your supervisor is more experienced at the work than you. Carla thought she had a better way of doing a job task. Because she was a new worker, though, she kept quiet. Later she learned that there were good reasons, such as safety, for following standard procedures.

Your supervisor is there to direct and assist you. Be aware, however, that your supervisor has other work to do. Your goal should be to learn your job quickly and perform it well with only a minimum of supervision.

It is a good idea to ask for help if there is something you do not understand.

Lisa F. Young/Shutterstock.com

Payroll Withholding

Every worker must pay federal income tax. The tax system operates on a pay-as-you-go basis. This means that the employer takes income tax out of each paycheck. The amount of tax the employer withholds depends on

- The amount of money you earn
- Whether you are married or not
- The number of **allowances**, or tax exemptions, you are entitled to claim. For instance, a single person is entitled to one allowance.

Your employer will keep track of how much money you earn. On Form W-4, you will provide information about your marital status and the number of allowances you are entitled to claim. John Pate is single and only claims one allowance. His completed Form W-4 is shown in Figure 6-3.

Christina Comito is a single parent with two children. She claims three allowances—one for herself and one for each child. Based on each employee's earnings, marital status, and allowances, an employer looks at a table to find how much tax to withhold.

Some people may be exempt from tax withholdings. Being **exempt** means that they do not have to pay taxes. People who earn less than a certain amount of money in a year are usually exempt.

Form **W-4** — Department of the Treasury, Internal Revenue Service

Employee's Withholding Allowance Certificate

▶ Whether you are entitled to claim a certain number of allowances or exemption from withholding is subject to review by the IRS. Your employer may be required to send a copy of this form to the IRS.

OMB No. 1545-0074 **2013**

1 Type or print your first name and middle initial. Jack V. | Last name Pate | 2 Your social security number 315 20 4024

Home address (number and street or rural route) 1612 Fredrick St.

3 ☒ Single ☐ Married ☐ Married, but withhold at higher Single rate.
Note. If married, but legally separated, or spouse is a nonresident alien, check the "Single" box.

City or town, state, and ZIP code Carbondale, IL 62901-1482

4 **If your last name differs from that shown on your social security card, check here. You must call 1-800-772-1213 for a new card.** ▶ ☐

5 Total number of allowances you are claiming (from line **H** above **or** from the applicable worksheet on page 2) — 5: 1

6 Additional amount, if any, you want withheld from each paycheck . . . . — 6: $ 0

7 I claim exemption from withholding for 2013, and I certify that I meet **both** of the following conditions for exemption.
- Last year I had a right to a refund of **all** federal income tax withheld because I had **no** tax liability **and**
- This year I expect a refund of **all** federal income tax withheld because I expect to have **no** tax liability.

If you meet both conditions, write "Exempt"here . . . . ▶ 7

Under penalties of perjury, I declare that I have examined this certificate and to the best of my knowledge and belief, it is true, correct, and complete.

Employee's signature (Form is not valid unless you sign it.) ▶ *Jack V. Pate* — **Date** ▶ March 6, 2013

8 Employer's name and address (Employer: Complete lines 8 and 10 only if sending to the IRS.) | 9 Office code (optional) | 10 Employer identification number (EIN)

FIGURE 6-3 Your employer will ask you to fill out one of these forms. A worksheet is provided to help you figure withholding allowances.

6-3 Assessment

1. **How is the job of a student similar to that of a paid employee?**
2. **What are four ways to start a good relationship with an employer? Briefly explain each.**
3. **What three things determine how much tax is withheld from your paycheck?**

Focus on the Workplace

High Performance Work Organizations

Historically, many kinds of work in America have been patterned after the mass production system made famous by Henry Ford in the early 1900s. In mass production, jobs are broken down into a number of simple tasks. Each worker specializes in one task, which is done over and over.

Managers do the thinking and planning for the organization. Supervisors direct the work of frontline employees. Workers under this system need only be reliable, steady, and willing to follow directions.

The mass production system has helped make the United States a great economic power. It has also resulted in a high standard of living for workers. This system still determines the way most factories, offices, banks, hospitals, and schools are organized.

In the twenty-first century this nation faces increasing global economic competition. Increased productivity and improved quality are necessary for the United States to remain competitive. The solution adopted by many companies is called a high-performance work organization.

The basic idea of a high-performance work organization is to give greater authority to frontline workers. Layers of managers disappear as teams of workers take over such tasks as quality control and production scheduling. Workers are asked to use judgment and make decisions at the point where goods and services are produced.

This type of work organization requires retraining of workers and managers. The high cost of retraining, however, is offset by gains in quality and productivity. High-performance work organizations are becoming the model for a successful future.

THINK CRITICALLY

1. Why do you think the mass production system helped make this nation a great economic power?
2. Give some examples of ways in which a high-performance work organization might help improve quality and productivity.

kali9/iStockphoto.com

Some organizations give frontline workers more authority.

Chapter Summary

6-1 Your First Day at Work

A. It is normal to experience some anxiety when beginning a new job. Many companies provide an orientation to help new employees get started properly. Your employer wants you to be successful on the job.

B. One person's first day at work may be quite different from another person's first day. However, most new employees do similar things and are provided with similar kinds of information.

6-2 Workplace Management

A. An organization chart shows the flow of authority and responsibility within an organization. It is important to follow your company's formal and informal lines of authority and responsibility.

B. Companies have written policies and rules to help them run smoothly. You are responsible for obeying all policies and rules. Companies also have unwritten rules that you will need to learn.

6-3 Supervisors and Form W-4

A. On the job, you will probably work under the direction of a supervisor. Use the supervisor for communication and direction. Accept and use the supervisor's suggestions, but don't ask for or expect special treatment.

B. Employers are required to withhold money from your paycheck for federal income tax. The amount withheld is based on information that you provide on Form W-4.

Activities

1. As a group activity, develop an organization chart for the employees in your school. At the top of the chart, start with the school district's board of education. How many levels are there? Suppose a teacher has a complaint about a board policy. With whom would he or she file a complaint? Discuss the process the teacher should follow.

2. Obtain an example of a company employee handbook. If you do not have one from your own job, ask to borrow one from a friend or search the Web. Look through the handbooks in class and discuss examples of each of the types of policies and rules explained in Lesson 6-2. Do the handbooks contain types of policies and rules that are not explained in the chapter? If so, discuss the merits of these policies and rules.

3. Does your school give students a written code of conduct that outlines policies and rules? If so, discuss how it is like a company

employee handbook. If not, discuss possible policies or rules that could go into such a handbook.

4. The supervisor at your new job expects you to assemble 15 cases every two hours. In an eight-hour shift, how many cases should you assemble?

5. Evaluate your ability to follow directions. Explain how this ability could help you attain goals in your life-span plan.

Word Power

On a separate sheet of paper, match each definition with the correct term. All definitions will be used, and a definition will be used only once.

6. A trial period during which one's performance is being observed and evaluated

7. Training for a new employee on the company and its policies and procedures

8. At work, the duty to follow an order or carry out a work assignment

9. Assign a task or responsibility to others

10. A booklet given to new employees that contains an explanation of company policies and rules

11. The number of tax exemptions to which one is entitled

12. The power or rank to give orders and make assignments to others

13. To pay back money already spent

14. To be free of something, such as not having to pay taxes

15. A feeling of concern, worry, or unease

16. The legal right to be notified of a complaint against you and to state your case or point of view before a decision is made

17. A boss who gives directions and orders and oversees the work of others

18. A mood or spirit, such as the attitude and emotion of employees

19. Keeping a customer's or patient's data or information private

a. allowance
b. anxiety
c. authority
d. confidentiality
e. delegate
f. due process
g. employee handbook
h. employee orientation program
i. exempt
j. morale
k. probation
l. reimburse
m. responsibility
n. supervisor

Think Critically

20. What are some of the reasons why employers want new employees to make a quick and successful transition from school to the workplace?

21. Think of an instance in your life in which your anxiety about a situation turned out to be worse than the situation itself. What might this suggest regarding anxiety toward beginning a new job?

22. Some supervisors try not to get too friendly or informal with employees whom they supervise. Do you think this is a good or bad idea? Why?

23. Under what circumstances might someone choose to specify an additional amount of withholding on line 6 of Form W-4?

"The secret of joy in work is contained in one word—excellence. To know how to do something well is to enjoy it." —PEARL BUCK

Expectations of Employers

Konstantin Chagin/Shutterstock.com

PREVIEW

Everyone needs time to adjust to a new job. After that, you will need to meet the same expectations as other employees. Accepting a job means you make a contract with an employer. You agree to perform certain duties in return for a certain salary or wage. Your responsibility is to do the tasks you were hired to do, in the way and at the time the employer wants them done.

Taking/*Action* Work Attitudes

Art is an insurance agent. He also serves as secretary of the area's youth soccer association. Over the weekend, he needed to prepare a mailing for the group. So, after work on Friday, he loaded up his briefcase with supplies from the company's storeroom. He picked up a couple of pens, a legal pad, a ream of printer paper, a roll of tape, and a box of envelopes.

Art didn't consider taking a few office supplies to be stealing. "They won't miss this stuff," he thought. "The company made $350 million last year." Later that week, Art heard that Janice, a coworker, was fired after her supervisor found out that she had let slip some confidential company information in an email to a supplier. Art thought this was too harsh and said something to his supervisor about the firing.

"Art, giving away confidential company information is stealing," his supervisor said. "Whether it's a box of paper or a computer or a trade secret, it's all the same thing. Any employee who is caught stealing can be fired, as our employment handbook states."

"Stealing is a violation of the company's trust," his supervisor continued. "Even if an employee who stole was kept on, that person's chances for future advancement in the company would be lessened."

Art was upset. Usually his company was very lenient with employees and gave second chances. The conversation made him worry that he might be fired if someone saw him take the supplies from the storeroom.

You have a promising future. Don't risk it by being like Art. Do not take anything owned by the company, regardless of its worth.

racnus/iStockphoto.com

Success Tip

Honesty is the ONLY policy!

THINK CRITICALLY

1. Do you think that what Art did and what Janice did are the same thing?

2. If Art had been fired, do you think it would have been easy for him to find another job?

JOB PERFORMANCE AND ATTITUDES

OBJECTIVES

- Name and summarize the five things that employers expect regarding job performance
- Name and summarize the nine things that employers expect regarding work habits and attitudes

KEY TERMS

- productivity
- judgment
- punctuality
- cooperation
- interest
- enthusiasm
- honesty
- loyalty

Andresr/Shutterstock.com

Workplace Decisions

You have been instructed to call a supplier and order replacement parts for several broken pieces of equipment. You are careful to provide all important information on quantities, part numbers, prices, and so on. After you finish, the supplier asks, "How do you want this shipped?"

"Gee, the boss did not tell me," you think. There is no one else in the office to ask.

What would you do?

Employer Expectations

Work organizations produce goods or provide services. Employers in all industries have expectations of workers.

Productivity

Employers expect employees to complete a certain amount of work. The output of a worker is **productivity**. Suppose Worker A does more work than Worker B. This means that Worker A is more productive.

Productivity is usually thought of in terms of goods-producing occupations such as welder, bricklayer, or factory worker. Productivity is also important in service occupations. Service-producing occupations include barber, flight attendant, salesclerk, and nurse. Whether you hammer nails or wait tables, you will be expected to give a day's work for a day's pay.

Quality of Work

An employer expects you to do your work carefully, accurately, and thoroughly. Quality of work means how well a job is performed. Poor work quality may cancel out high productivity. For example, a secretary who keys fast but makes a lot of errors is not doing the job well. Likewise, a production worker who solders many electrical components but whose soldered joints do not hold is performing poorly.

Quality of work is very important to a company's success. Customers who receive high-quality goods or services come back for repeat business. This is why employers want their workers to do the best job possible.

Good Judgment

Has anyone ever told you to "Use your head"? This saying means to think about what you are doing or figure it out yourself. You cannot run to a boss every time you have a problem or must make a decision. **Judgment** is thinking about a problem and making the right decision. Your employer will want you to use your judgment.

Using good judgment is a sign of maturity that employers look for when promoting people to better jobs. If you are known as someone who makes quick decisions and has poor judgment, your time with the company may be short.

Safety Consciousness

Many jobs involve working with tools, machines, and equipment, some of which may be dangerous. For your benefit as well as that of coworkers, the employer will expect you to work safely. Part of being a safe worker is knowing how to do a job. You will have learned this through education or on-the-job training.

Your employer will expect you to perform your job in the way that you have been trained. In addition, the company will probably have safety rules that you will be expected to follow. For example, workers in certain areas of a plant may need to wear a hard hat or safety glasses.

If an accident or emergency does happen, you will be expected to follow certain steps. Consider what you would do if a machine part gets stuck in a punch press. Your boss has told you that when this happens you should turn off the machine right away and go for help. Do what you are told. Do not try to fix the problem yourself.

Learn your company's safety rules and procedures by reading and studying printed company material. If you have any questions, be sure to ask your boss. Once you know the safety rules, practice them. Knowledge of them alone is not enough.

Care of Equipment

An employer often has money invested in expensive tools and equipment. You will be expected to take care of them and use them properly. Damaged tools and equipment cost money in two ways. First,

Search the Net

Access the OSHA website through **www.cengage.com/school/working** and click on the link for Chapter 7. Choose one topic in the list of Safety and Health Information Bulletins. Read the information about the topic and then write a paragraph summarizing what you learned.

www.cengage.com/school/working

the item must be repaired or replaced. Then, while the repairs are in process, work time is lost. Should you have questions about tools or equipment, ask them. Not doing so could cause serious problems.

Suppose you are working summers as a farm laborer. The boss asks you if you know how to drive the tractor. You say that you do. The tractor has some features that are unfamiliar to you. You decide to drive it anyhow. After a few minutes, the tractor stops dead. The mechanic says that your mistake caused several thousand dollars' worth of damage to the tractor. Even though the boss fires you, it could have been worse. In some cases, improper use of tools and equipment injures and kills workers.

Work Habits and Attitudes

Another type of employer expectation has to do with work habits and attitudes. These are the ways employees behave on the job. Poor work habits and a negative attitude are the main reasons most people lose their jobs. You may, for example, be a great hairstylist. You will not keep your job, though, if you cannot get along with your boss, coworkers, or clients. Figure 7-1 provides a list of ten problems noted by employers for young workers.

Attendance and Punctuality

To avoid work delays or interruptions, employers expect workers to be on the job regularly. At a construction site there were negative consequences when a worker made a habit of "taking off."

A crew was building townhouses. Most of the workers showed up unless they had a good reason not to. Yvonne, however, frequently missed work. When she was absent, the other workers covered for her. Sometimes, though, the others were too busy with their own work to do hers. Yvonne's work did not get done on those days. The boss told Yvonne that if other crew members missed work as she did, the job could shut down. Yvonne got the point and changed her ways.

Punctuality is also necessary. **Punctuality** means being on time. Workplaces that are open at certain times need employees there to deal with business. An employer's profits and public image may suffer if employees are not there. Suppose a restaurant opens for business at 6:00 a.m. If some workers do not arrive until 6:30 a.m., customers will get poor service. They will eat elsewhere and tell others to do the same. Be ready to work at starting time, stay until quitting time, and take only the time set aside for lunch periods and breaks. Most workers are not paid for time they miss when they are absent or tardy.

If you must be absent or late, try to tell your supervisor as far ahead of time as possible. If you have a doctor's appointment scheduled during work hours, notify your boss as soon as you make the appointment.

FIGURE 7-1 Interviews with employers have indicated that these are among the most serious problems of young, entry-level workers.

1. Absent from work too frequently or for questionable reasons
2. Has to be supervised too much of the time
3. Takes no initiative when something needs to be done
4. Isn't very observant; fails to recognize errors or problems
5. Doesn't listen well
6. Arrives late or leaves early too often
7. Doesn't consider the consequences of decisions or actions
8. Too much socializing with other workers or visitors
9. Can't accept suggestions or criticism
10. Doesn't seem to care about doing a job well

Workplace Innovations

NASA INVENTIONS

In 1958, the National Aeronautics and Space Administration (NASA) was created to run the civilian space program. To accomplish such things as landing a man on the moon and exploring the surface of Mars with unmanned robotic vehicles, NASA employs many top-notch scientists and engineers. Their talents range from astronomy and physics to chemistry, biology, and materials science.

Because no one had ever gone to the moon or explored Mars, NASA had to invent all sorts of high-tech equipment and materials to solve the special problems of space exploration. Once developed, NASA is required by law to disseminate that technology for private use. Since 1976, there have been more than 1,600 commercial applications of NASA technologies. A number of science and technology related websites have produced lists of their selections for top NASA "spinoffs." The website science.howstuffworks.com lists its top five NASA inventions as follows:

1. Scratch–resistant eyeglass lenses
2. Cochlear ear implant hearing aid
3. ArterioVision video imaging software
4. Anti-corrosion protective coating
5. Memory foam

There have been so many inventions, that NASA produces an annual publication entitled *Spinoff* featuring an average of 50 technologies each year. An accompanying website is maintained containing a searchable database of these technologies. The website also contains a "spinoff game" and an interactive learning tool that are worth your time to investigate at www.sti.nasa.gov/tto/.

A number of commercial products, like cordless power tools, have been used in NASA programs. As a result, NASA has incorrectly been given credit for the invention. Other product inventions incorrectly attributed to NASA include Tang, Teflon, and Velcro.

NET FOLLOW-UP

Use a search engine to explore the Web for additional information on the topic of "NASA spinoffs."

Cooperation

"He or she just refuses to cooperate" is a common employer complaint about a worker. **Cooperation** means getting along with others. One aspect of cooperation is following orders or doing what you are told to do. As a beginning worker, you will probably receive many orders.

Your job may include boring tasks, such as sweeping floors or cleaning equipment. After all, someone has to do these tasks. If you won't, your employer will hire someone who will. Accept your assignments cheerfully, or at least willingly, and do your best. If you do, the employer will notice.

Cooperation also means being able to take criticism. When you accept wages, you agree to do the job the way the employer wants it done. The employer has a right to criticize or correct you. The employer

EDHAR/Shutterstock.com

It is important to work cooperatively on teams.

wants you to improve your work performance. You should, too. Accept and profit from constructive criticism. Thank the employer, tell him or her you will improve, and then do so.

Interest and Enthusiasm

Employers like employees who show interest and enthusiasm toward their work. Such people are often the most productive and cooperative workers. **Interest** is a feeling of excitement and involvement. **Enthusiasm** is eagerness or a strong interest in something. Few people, of course, find everything about their job to be interesting and enjoyable. Show your enthusiasm for those parts that you like.

Your company and your coworkers also deserve your interest and enthusiasm. Keep up-to-date on the company's plans. Read any employee newsletter, company magazine, or website that is available. Try to take part in company social events and activities. You and the company will benefit.

Honesty

Employers expect honesty of their employees. **Honesty** is a refusal to lie, steal, or mislead in any way. Stealing is a serious problem in many businesses and industries. Most employees caught stealing are fired. They may face criminal charges as well. Honesty also means obeying all laws related to company business practices and policies such as not overcharging customers or accepting personal gifts or favors from a client, if prohibited.

Loyalty

Your employer would like you to feel a sense of loyalty to the company. **Loyalty** means believing in and being devoted to something. This means, for example, that you should not criticize the company when talking with coworkers, friends, or strangers. It is being proud of what you do and where you work.

This does not mean, however, that you should never leave a job for a better opportunity elsewhere. You should use judgment regarding switching jobs. A substantial pay raise, the chance to learn something new, or greater opportunities for advancement are all good reasons to change jobs. However, frequently changing jobs for a raise of a few cents per hour could give you a bad reputation in the workplace.

Communication

Most newly hired workers have a mobile phone or similar device. These, of course, are convenient and useful tools for communicating with family and friends. They may also have an important role in certain types of businesses.

Mobile phone use, especially texting, actually interferes with communication between workers and their bosses and between coworkers. Texting is simply sending information to a receiver. Communication is not only about talking, it is also about listening. It is about exchanging information so that everyone gets something valuable out of the exchange.

If you don't understand an instruction given by the boss, ask a question. When there is work-related information that the boss needs to know, tell her or him personally. Talk and listen to your boss and coworkers and take the time to cultivate these conversations.

The Web

Many jobs also incorporate Internet use. If required to use the Web for work, learn your employer's guidelines for Web use at the workplace. Many businesses discourage or forbid employees from surfing the Web for non-work related searches. You should not log on to personal accounts, either for email or social networks, while at work.

While you are at work, your employer pays you for your time, attention, and effort. For many businesses, the inappropriate use of mobile phones and the Web *steal time*, or allow a worker to be paid by an employer while pursuing a personal interest. Mobile phone and Internet use at work also lower performance, detract from customer service, and threaten workplace safety. For these reasons, many companies ban or restrict mobile phone and Internet use in the workplace.

7-1 Assessment

1. What five things do employers expect regarding work performance?

2. How is productivity different in a goods-producing occupation and in a service-providing occupation?

3. Name three things that an employee can do to perform a job more safely.

4. Give an example of how a broken piece of equipment costs a company money, in addition to the cost of repair or replacement.

5. List four ways that an employee can be cooperative on the job.

6. Being an honest employee involves more than not stealing from the employer. Explain.

7. How does the personal use of mobile phones by employees interfere with good workplace communication?

8. Why do employers care about how you use the Internet while at work?

High Growth Occupations
FOR THE 21ST CENTURY

Bookkeeping, Accounting, and Auditing Clerks

Bookkeeping, accounting, and auditing clerks are financial record keepers. These workers have a wide range of skills from "full-charge" *bookkeepers*, who can maintain an entire company's books, to *accounting clerks* who handle specific tasks. All these clerks make numerous computations each day and must be comfortable using computers to calculate and record data.

In small businesses, bookkeepers and bookkeeping clerks often have responsibility for some or all of the accounts, known as the general ledger. They also produce financial statements and prepare reports and summaries for supervisors and managers. Bookkeepers prepare bank deposits by compiling data from cashiers, verifying and balancing receipts, and sending cash, checks, or other forms of payment to the bank. Additionally, they may handle payroll, make purchases, prepare invoices, and keep track of overdue accounts.

In large companies, accounting clerks have more specialized tasks. Their titles, such as accounts payable clerk or accounts receivable clerk, often reflect the type of accounting they do. In addition, their responsibilities vary by level of experience.

Auditing clerks verify records of transactions posted by other workers. They check figures, postings, and documents to ensure that they are mathematically accurate, and properly coded. They also correct or note errors for accountants or other workers to fix.

Many bookkeeping, accounting, and auditing clerks use specialized accounting software, spreadsheets, and databases. Most clerks now enter information from receipts or bills into computers, and the information is then stored electronically. The widespread use of computers also has enabled clerks to take on additional responsibilities, such as payroll, procurement, and billing.

Most bookkeeping, accounting, and auditing clerks are required to have a high school degree at a minimum. However, having some postsecondary education is increasingly important and an associate degree in business or accounting is required for some positions. Once hired, bookkeeping, accounting, and auditing clerks usually receive on-the-job training. Under the guidance of a supervisor or another experienced employee, new clerks learn company procedures. Some formal classroom training also may be necessary, such as training in specialized computer software.

Monkey Business Images/Shutterstock.com

Bookkeepers are responsible for organizing large amounts of data.

GROOMING, APPEARANCE, AND PROPER DRESS

OBJECTIVES

- Explain why good hygiene and grooming are important on the job
- Understand the importance of dressing appropriately at work
- Summarize guidelines for proper dress at work

KEY TERMS

- personal hygiene
- grooming
- posture
- wardrobe

Career Decisions

You just started a co-op job at a large savings and loan association. You are aware of how important it is to look good on the job. Everyone at work dresses nicely. But you only have a couple of decent outfits. You do not have the money for new clothes. You feel very self-conscious at work. You know you look more like a student than an employee. You are thinking about looking for a new job where you could wear a uniform or more casual clothes.

What would you do?

Tracy Whiteside/Shutterstock.com

Appearance Matters

An appropriate appearance on the job begins with **personal hygiene**, which means keeping one's body clean and healthy. Good **grooming**, which means having a neat and attractive appearance, is also necessary. Rules for personal hygiene apply to everyone. What is considered to be attractive or good grooming varies from person to person and job to job. A hairstyle that looks good on one person may not suit another. What is considered to be proper makeup in one job setting may be inappropriate in another.

Tips for Grooming and Appearance

Some of the following tips may apply to you and your job situation. Others may not.

Hairstyle

For most jobs, hair should be neat, trimmed, and not too faddish. Hair dyed in crazy colors and funky hairdos on both males and females are out of the question for most jobs. Beyond this, how you wear your hair is up to you. Whatever style you choose, hair should be neatly combed or brushed.

A hairstylist can help you choose a style that goes well with your features and hair type. When deciding on a hairstyle, be sure to think about how much care it will need.

Shaving

A grooming choice for men is whether to be clean-shaven or to grow a mustache or beard. Going to work with a growth of stubble is not a good choice. Should you decide to grow facial hair, start during a vacation. If you do grow a mustache or beard, shave your neck and the uncovered parts of the face. Weekly trims are necessary.

Deodorants and Antiperspirants

Even after bathing, underarm perspiration odor can develop quickly. Many people use a deodorant for odor or an antiperspirant for wetness. Choose whatever fits your needs.

Wendy, a realtor, has always perspired heavily. Moving to Texas made her problem worse. Deodorant was no longer enough. Perspiration stains on her clothing embarrassed Wendy, especially when she was with clients. Antiperspirants reduced her perspiration and embarrassment.

Skin Care and Cosmetics

Your skin may need care beyond daily bathing. The most common problem is dry skin. In colder climates, heated homes and low humidity cause skin to become dry and itchy. In such cases, moisturize your skin often with lotion. Hands may need special attention. Abused hands get rough and sore and look bad. To help heal them, use hand lotion often. This applies to both men and women.

Many women choose to use cosmetics or beauty aids to improve their appearance. If you do, don't overdo them. Too much makeup can dry out the skin and cause irritation. Cosmetic counters in large department stores or specialty cosmetic stores often have people who can advise you on cosmetic use.

Posture

Matthew is always clean and well groomed. His poor posture, however, ruins his appearance. **Posture** is the way you stand, walk, and sit. People with poor posture have a stooping head and shoulders and a belly that sticks out. Their body language makes them look lazy and lacking in self-confidence. This may be untrue, but poor posture sends out the wrong message.

A person with good posture appears poised and self-confident. Good posture, like good grooming, is necessary to make a good impression on the job. It also makes you feel better and helps fight fatigue.

Paying attention to your appearance helps create a good impression at work.

Tattoos and Body Piercings

The use of tattoos and body piercings by professional athletes, film stars, and musicians has resulted in such practices being widely imitated and more accepted by people of all ages and genders. Greater acceptance by society, however, does not mean that a majority of people and employers approve.

You should, however, give consideration to the standards or customs within your industry and within your part of the country. A worker who frames pictures in a specialty art store might be able to have a different appearance than a worker who works as an administrative assistant at a law office. Appearance standards that may be acceptable in Los Angeles, CA may not be acceptable in Dayton, OH. If you are uncertain about the standards of a new employer, err on the side of being cautious.

The basic issue for employers is that they want their employees to present a professional appearance and to represent the company in a positive way. An employee may think that this is unfair, but the courts have generally ruled that an employer has the right to specify certain appearance standards as long as they don't discriminate among employees. For example, an employer cannot prohibit a female from having a tattoo, but allow a male to do so.

There are many things to consider as you begin a new job and try to be successful at work. It is generally best not to get a tattoo or body piercing. If you have one or both, you should remove body piercings while on the job and cover tattoos with clothing, if possible. Later, you may discover that your employer and coworkers do not consider either to be an issue.

Dress for Success

Clothes are important to your overall appearance on the job. Some jobs require a uniform. If yours does, make sure the uniform you wear is always clean and pressed.

If your job does not require a uniform, deciding how to dress will be more difficult. On most jobs, however, the employer expects workers to dress in a certain way. A bank teller, for instance, is supposed to look professional. For a man, this might mean nice slacks and a dress shirt. A jacket or tie might be needed as well. In some situations, a suit might be required. For a woman, professional dress includes nice slacks and a dress shirt. Sometimes you may choose to wear a skirt or dress. If so, make sure the length is long enough to cover your thighs when you sit down. Both men and women should wear subdued colors. Navy, brown, black, and grey are always safe choices for pants or skirts. White, beige, and light blue are often reasonable choices for shirts. Dress shoes should be

Workforce Trends

The Great Recession was an eighteen month recession between December 2007 and June 2009. It was the longest and deepest recession since the Great Depression. Men and women were affected differently during the downturn. Construction and manufacturing, industries which predominately employ men, were hit hard by the recession. The service sector, which predominately employees women, did slightly better during the recession.

Most jobs have an expectation regarding how workers will dress for work.

VR Photos/Shutterstock.com

You know that appearance is very important in American culture. How often do you draw conclusions about others based on things like length or style of hair, grooming, fitness, and style or quality of clothes?

At work, you are likely to come in contact with people whose personal appearance is very different from what you are used to. Suppose you have a transportation job. One of the drivers might be a Sikh American man who wears a turban. Some of your customers might be Muslim women who wear the traditional veil.

Do not draw conclusions about people whose culture you do not understand. Show people from other cultures the same courtesy and respect you show to everyone else.

THINK CRITICALLY

1. Think of some other examples of clothing that people from other cultures wear while working.
2. Why do you think some people in the United States from other cultures wear clothing that represents their cultures?

worn. Athletic shoes should not be worn. If in doubt, notice what the other employees wear. If you have any questions, ask your boss.

If you do not own a watch, consider buying one of a conservative style. Wearing a watch allows you to subtly check the time. Using a cell phone to check the time might make coworkers or bosses think you are checking your phone for personal messages or texts.

Generally speaking, clothing worn for recreation, lounging about, or hanging out with friends is not appropriate on the job. Can you think of a job where wearing flip-flops or a t-shirt emblazoned with your favorite grunge band would be acceptable? Okay, you may be able to think of a few places, but they are probably very few in number.

Clothing Guidelines

Here are several guidelines that will help you choose clothes for work and care for them properly.

- **Wear what fits your job**   Think about your job. Will you get dirty and greasy? Will you need protection from sun, wind, rain, or cold? Will you be handling food? Would dangling belts, flowing clothing, or oversized jewelry be likely to get tangled in equipment? Do you need steel-toed shoes to protect your feet in a manufacturing environment? Buy clothing that is well suited for the work you will do.
- **Wear what looks good on you**   Within the expectations or requirements for the job, wear clothes that look good on you. Choose clothes that match your physical features and personality.
- **Plan your wardrobe carefully**   You will probably not be able to buy your entire wardrobe, which is the clothing that you wear, all at once. So build around a number of basic items. For instance, a pair of grey slacks will go with many different shirts, blouses, or sweaters.

- **Learn how to coordinate clothes** Teach yourself to mix and match your clothes. For instance, do not wear a plaid shirt or blouse with different plaid slacks. Libraries have magazines and books that can help you learn about fashion. A variety of websites have fashion suggestions and shopping guidelines.

- **Choose quality, well-made clothing** The most expensive clothes are not always the best quality. Nor are clothes with a popular name or label always the best. Compare clothes and prices in many different stores before you decide to buy.

- **Take proper care of your clothes** Think about clothing care before you buy. Easy-care fabrics are more practical than ones that require ironing or dry cleaning. To prevent heavy wrinkling, hang up or fold clothes properly. Iron wrinkled clothes. Clothes have tags that tell how to care for them. Follow the instructions carefully.

- **Accessories** You may need to bring a lunch box, a messenger bag, or a purse to work. Structured accessories look better than baggy accessories. A lunch box with structured sides looks neater than a floppy sack. Select accessories that are practical, durable, and conservative.

zulufoto/Shutterstock.com

It is important to take care of stains quickly so that your clothing conveys a neat appearance.

Michele's clothes are well chosen and fit her nicely. She is careless, however, in taking care of them. Her winter coat has been missing buttons for two years. Today, she wore a dress that has a ripped arm seam. In spite of her nice clothes, Michele often looks sloppy. Her coworkers joke about her appearance.

The way you look influences how other people see you and will greatly affect your job success. Everyone can look good. Remember that a winning appearance depends more on knowledge and effort than it does on physical beauty.

7-2 Assessment

1. For most jobs, what is the basic rule about hairstyles?
2. Suppose Kyle, a surveyor, wants to grow a beard. When should he start?
3. What is the purpose of a deodorant? An antiperspirant?
4. How does good posture help you to make a good impression on the job?
5. If you aren't sure about how to dress on the job, what two things might you do?
6. List six basic rules for clothing choice, wear, and care.
7. People who are physically attractive, almost always look well dressed. Do you agree or disagree with this statement?

RATE WORK BEHAVIOR

OBJECTIVES
- Describe the purposes of a performance evaluation
- Explain the two-step evaluation process

KEY TERM
- performance evaluation

ruzanna/Shutterstock.com

Personal Decisions

You have always wanted long, polished nails. One Saturday you go to a salon for artificial nails. You think they are gorgeous. At work on Monday, things are not so good. The longer nails interfere with your keyboarding. Your work has slowed and you are making more mistakes. The supervisor notices and suggests you have the nails trimmed. "I cannot," you think. "I paid a lot of money for these nails."

What would you do?

Purposes of Evaluation

Instructors have been evaluating your work as a student for many years. On the job, your employer will also evaluate your work. A **performance evaluation** is the process of judging how well an employee is doing on the job. The employer rates your job performance, your work habits, and your attitudes.

Employee evaluation allows employers to determine how well workers are doing their jobs. Performance evaluations have several purposes. One purpose is to decide if you deserve a pay raise and how much to give you. Employers provide pay raises as a reward for good work.

Evaluation also helps employees become better workers. This benefits both the employee and the employer. The feedback helps the employee learn and improve. For the employer, the evaluation may suggest places the employee needs more on-the-job training.

Finally, evaluation provides a basis for future job assignments. When filling an opening for a department supervisor, management might review employee evaluations to see which employees are candidates for promotion. Or, suppose your evaluation results suggest that you would do better in a different job. The employer might then transfer you to another department.

How You Are Evaluated

The way you will be evaluated differs from company to company. Daksha, who works for a very small company, does not often realize that her boss is evaluating her. From time to time, she and her boss discuss Daksha's work. All feedback is verbal, no forms are used, and no records are kept.

Most large firms, however, have a standard procedure for employee evaluation. The evaluations usually take place once a year, although every six months is not uncommon.

Most evaluations are done in two steps. Your boss or supervisor fills out an evaluation form. A sample form is shown in Figure 7-2. Then you meet with the supervisor or boss. The two of you go over the form and discuss your strengths and weaknesses. The tone of this meeting should be positive and constructive, unless you are doing a really poor job.

Student-Trainee Evaluation Sheet
COOPERATIVE EDUCATION PROGRAMS
Swinburn Public Schools
Student's Name _____
Training Station _____

Reporting Month _____
Please Return By _____
Supervisor's Name _____

INSTRUCTIONS: Please rate the student by circling the number on each scale below at the point that most accurately describes the student learner's progress to date. (Please feel free to make comments on the back of this paper.)

CATEGORIES	OUTSTANDING	ABOVE AVERAGE	AVERAGE	BELOW AVERAGE	UNSATISFACTORY
Personal Appearance	5	4	3	2	1
Attendance and Tardiness	5	4	3	2	1
Rate of Progress	5	4	3	2	1
Follows Directions	5	4	3	2	1
Job Judgment Decision Making	5	4	3	2	1
Attitude Toward Job	5	4	3	2	1
Ability to Get Along with People	5	4	3	2	1
Initiative (Does Things Without Being Told)	5	4	3	2	1
Safety	5	4	3	2	1
Dependability (Overall)	5	4	3	2	1

OUTSTANDING	ABOVE AVERAGE	AVERAGE	BELOW AVERAGE	UNSATISFACTORY
☐	☐	☐	☐	☐

Supervisor's Signature _____ Date _____ Letter Grade _____
Student's Signature _____

FIGURE 7-2 Sample Performance Evaluation Form

Most employees are formally evaluated at least once a year.

The discussion between you and your boss or supervisor will not be one-sided. You should have a chance to discuss what you like and dislike about your current position. This is a good time for you to discuss your future goals. Do not use the time, however, to complain about the job or your coworkers.

An evaluation is not just a once-a-year event. Your boss is continually watching your job performance, work habits, and attitudes. The ratings you receive in an evaluation result from a process that goes on all the time. This is why it pays to do your best work each and every day.

If you get a negative evaluation, you will need to accept your shortcomings. Make sure you understand what you can do to correct the problem. Your future in the company will depend on showing that you can improve your work behavior before the next evaluation. If you ignore what your boss tells you, your next evaluation could be your last.

7-3 Assessment

1. For employers, what are the three purposes of employee evaluation?

2. How does a performance evaluation benefit an employee?

3. Describe the two-step evaluation procedure that most companies follow.

4. If you get a negative performance evaluation, what should you do?

Focus on the Workplace

Military Occupations

The largest employer in the country is the military services, which provides training and work experience for more than 2.4 million people. More than 1.4 million people serve in the active Army, Navy, Marine Corps, and Air Force. More than 1 million serve in their Reserve components, and the Air and Army National Guard. The Coast Guard is now part of the U.S. Department of Homeland Security.

The major occupational groups in the military are similar to those in the civilian sector. More than 75 percent of military occupational specialties have civilian counterparts. Nearly 25 percent of enlisted persons are involved with electrical, electronic, mechanical, and related equipment. This reflects the highly technical and mechanical nature of the military. Officers (about 1.8 percent of all military personnel) are concentrated in administration, medical specialties, and directing combat activities.

Military life is more disciplined and structured than civilian life. There are dress and grooming requirements. Certain formalities, such as saluting officers and obeying military laws and regulations, must be followed.

Hours and working conditions vary. Most military personnel usually work 8 hours a day, 5 or 5 1/2 days a week. Some assignments, however, require night and weekend work or being on call at all hours. All may require travel and periodic relocation.

About 184,000 personnel must be recruited each year to replace those who complete their commitment or retire.

So, opportunities (technical and nontechnical) are usually plentiful. The five services offer hundreds of schools and thousands of courses of instruction. A section on "Job Outlook" may be found in the *Occupational Outlook Handbook*. A compendium of military occupational, training, and career information entitled Military Career Guide Online is available on the Web at www.todaysmilitary.com.

THINK CRITICALLY

1. Are there some military jobs that appeal to you? If so, what are they?
2. How do civilian occupations differ from those in the military?

Aviation continues to be a large part of the U.S. Armed Forces.

Photodisc/Getty Images

Chapter Summary

7-1 Job Performance and Attitudes

A. After a short period of adjustment, you will need to meet the same expectations as other employees. Your responsibility is to do the job tasks in the way and at the time the employer wants them done. Your employer will expect the following in terms of your job performance: productivity, quality of work, good judgment, safety consciousness, and care of equipment.

B. Another type of employer expectation has to do with work habits and attitudes. Your employer will expect the following: attendance, punctuality, cooperation, interest, enthusiasm, honesty, loyalty, communication, and appropriate use of the Internet.

7-2 Grooming, Appearance, and Proper Dress

A. No matter what your job, remember your employer will expect you to groom and dress properly. What is considered to be a good appearance, however, will vary from job to job.

B. In addition to personal hygiene, grooming is important on the job. Hair should be neat, trimmed, and not too faddish. Men should decide whether to be clean-shaven or to have facial hair. Underarm odor and wetness can be controlled by deodorants and antiperspirants. Women should use cosmetics and beauty aids that are appropriate for the job. Use good posture to show confidence. Avoid tattoos and body piercings.

C. How you dress is important to your overall appearance on the job. If in doubt, notice what other employees wear or ask your boss.

D. Wear clothing that fits the type of job you have. Wear what looks good on you. Plan your wardrobe carefully and learn how to coordinate clothes. Choose quality, well-made clothing and take proper care of them.

7-3 Rate Work Behavior

A. An employer will evaluate your job performance, your work habits, and your attitudes. Employee evaluation allows employers to determine how well workers are doing their jobs. Evaluation results are the basis for pay raises and promotions.

B. Most evaluations are done in two steps. First, your boss or supervisor will fill out an evaluation form. Next, he or she will meet with you to go over the ratings. If you get a negative evaluation, you will need to improve your performance before the next rating.

Activities

1. Figure 7-1 lists reasons that often make employers unhappy with young workers. Access www.cengage.com/school/working and click on the link for Chapter 7. Download the form Work Behaviors of Concern. Save the spreadsheet with the title "Class Ranking of Concerning Behaviors." As a class, assign a rank to each behavior, with one signifying the most concerning behavior and ten signifying the least concerning behavior. Save the original spreadsheet with the title "Supervisors Ranking of Concerning Behaviors." Sort the behaviors in any order you select. Print out copies of this blank, newly sorted spreadsheet. Ask a few experienced workers or supervisors to rank the behaviors by assigning a rank to each behavior, with one signifying the most concerning behavior and ten signifying the least concerning behavior. Ask them to add other behaviors they consider important. Be sure the people who complete the form provide information on the industry and jobs they work in. Tally your results. As a class, tally all the results. Review the results and compare them with Figure 7-1. Discuss the results in class. Does the type of job and industry impact the behaviors that are considered most important?

2. Assume you are an employer. What would you do or say to an employee who (a) puts the wrong kind of lubricant in a chain saw, causing it to burn up; (b) calls in sick, but on your way to lunch, you see the person playing tennis; (c) makes personal long-distance calls on company phones; (d) criticizes the company to coworkers; (e) works out during lunch and comes back to work without showering? Think of an answer for each situation. Discuss your answers in class.

3. Laws governing who can perform tattoos and piercings and who can receive them vary from state to state. Some states have no laws or requirements while others are quite specific and stricter. Search the Web to find out the rules in your state.

4. Prepare a bulletin board that shows dress and appearance for different occupations. Each person in the class should contribute something from a magazine or other source. Focus on occupations of interest to students in the class.

5. There are many sites on the Web where you can create a "virtual hairstyle" and experiment with different hairstyles. Other sites allow you to become a "virtual clothing shopper" and try different clothing combinations. Search the Web for "virtual hairstyles." and "virtual clothing shopper." Determine which sites best meet your needs. Form small groups of classmates. Perform the following tasks.
   a. Develop two well-groomed, well-dressed characters. One should be male and one should be female. It may be necessary to compile the groomed head on one site and the wardrobe on another site.

b. Write how you decided what would make your characters well groomed.

c. Select three tops and three bottoms for each of the characters. The colors and styles selected should enable you to mix and match to make nine outfits. Make a list of the nine outfits for each character. Your instructor will provide you with an outline for the list.

d. Share your results with the class.

6. Explain how you choose the clothes you wear. Describe how your choices could affect your ability to achieve goals in your life-span plan.

7. Consider your feelings about always doing the best job possible. Describe how your attitude toward doing quality work may impact your ability to achieve goals in your life-span plan.

8. In small groups, make a list of what can be stolen from a place of work. There should be two categories. One category is for things you can touch and feel. Another is for things supplied at the workplace but which you cannot see or touch. Which type of theft is easier to monitor? Why? What would you do if you witnessed a coworker stealing from your employer?

Word Power

On a separate sheet of paper, match each definition with the correct term. All definitions will be used, and a definition will be used only once.

9. Maintaining a neat, attractive appearance

10. Wearing apparel; one's clothing

11. The process of judging how well an employee is doing on the job

12. Getting along with and working well with others

13. The position of a person's body while standing, walking, or sitting

14. Eagerness; a strong interest in something

15. Being on time

16. Faithfulness; believing in and being devoted to something

17. Keeping one's body clean and healthy

18. The output of a worker; how much a worker produces on the job

19. A feeling of excitement and involvement

20. Thinking about a problem and making the right decision

21. A refusal to lie, steal, or mislead in any way

a. cooperation
b. enthusiasm
c. grooming
d. honesty
e. interest
f. judgment
g. loyalty
h. performance evaluation
i. personal hygiene
j. posture
k. productivity
l. punctuality
m. wardrobe

Think Critically

22. During the last decade or so, many U.S. manufacturers have moved their plants overseas, claiming U.S. workers are often less productive and less concerned about quality than foreign workers. Do you think this is true?

23. Some companies make employees pay for any tools or equipment they damage or lose. Do you think this practice is fair?

24. Suppose you and two other employees work as clerks at a convenience food store. One afternoon you notice that a co-worker lays $2 from a customer's purchase beside the cash register. You think it is odd that he does not ring it up. When you look again, the money is gone. Over the next several days, you watch him more closely. You discover that he is stealing money. Would you say something to him, tell your boss, or keep quiet? Why?

25. Are you aware that many people are injured, suffer serious infections, and even die as a result of tattoos and body piercings? If you should decide to get a tattoo or piercing, how can you protect yourself from injury or infection?

26. What are your feelings toward someone who has poor personal hygiene or an inappropriate appearance? Pretend that you have a friend or coworker with such a problem. Discuss your feelings and how you might go about telling the person.

27. Good appearance varies from job to job. Discuss some examples. Give examples that illustrate both different grooming practices and different types of dress.

28. Some companies have what are called "casual Friday" dress days. Some students probably work for such a company or know a family member or friend who does. Discuss advantages and disadvantages of this practice.

29. As an employee, which would you rather receive: (a) a guaranteed four percent annual raise or (b) the possibility of a raise between zero and eight percent, based on the results of an annual evaluation of your performance? Why?

30. While grabbing some coffee this morning at your group's coffee station, you heard that your supervisor recently had software installed that provides a daily report of all websites visited during the day in your department. The name of the employees who visited the sites are included in the daily report. Why do you think this software was purchased? How will it affect your job?

Career Transitions Connection

Interview Practice

Click *Interview Simulation*. STAR describes a method of answering interview questions that focuses on the Situation, Task, Action, and Result. Click on the gold star to learn more about STAR. As a class, go through the interview simulation process for a candidate with "little work experience." For each question, vote on the correct answer. Review the simulation feedback. What did you learn from the feedback?

8

Worker Rights and Protections

"Great works are performed not by strength, but perseverance."
—SAMUEL JOHNSON

Rob Kints/Shutterstock.com

PREVIEW

Employees have certain responsibilities to employers. An employment contract, however, isn't a one-way deal. Employers also owe certain things to their employees. Workers are entitled to fair and honest treatment regarding wages, hours, and equal pay, as well as a safe and healthful workplace.

Taking/*Action*   Employer-Worker Relations

Throughout its history, the American labor movement has fought to improve working conditions and have a voice in how jobs are performed. This has resulted in periodic confrontations between management and labor.

One such event occurred in 1971 at the Lordstown, Ohio, General Motors assembly plant. The Lordstown assembly line was producing 104 cars per hour. The industry average was 55 per hour. To increase productivity, GM officials cut back workers on the line and increased the number of jobs each person had to do. The result was that many workers could not keep up with the pace. Some workers were literally riding down the line with the cars as they tried to bolt on parts. The company took several other unpopular actions including eliminating shop safety rules and laying off employees. Workers complained. They filed more than 10,000 grievances. But GM officials ignored them.

Out of frustration, workers began intentionally leaving pieces off cars and inflicting costly damage. Many cars came off the line with broken windshields, missing parts, torn upholstery, keys broken in the door, or other damage.

The company responded with measures that included refusing emergency breaks and increasing disciplinary layoffs. It would not add a third shift to help with the increased work.

The workers went on strike. Between March 3 and March 24, 1972, approximately 8,000 workers participated in the strike. After three weeks and $150 million in lost production, workers and management agreed to a settlement. Some 700 workers who had been laid off returned to their jobs. Workers who had lost their jobs in disciplinary layoffs received full back pay, and their records were cleared. The union dropped thousands of grievances and did not challenge the company's authority over production.

*Success Tip

Understand that progress in employer–worker relations is always possible.

THINK CRITICALLY

1. Why did the GM workers go on strike?
2. How does the case of Lordstown illustrate an employer's lack of respect toward workers?

DUTIES OF EMPLOYERS

OBJECTIVES

- Describe the duties of employers
- List three fair employment practices
- Explain workers' rights regarding protections against discrimination

KEY TERMS

- employment practices
- minimum wage
- youth minimum wage
- standard workweek
- discrimination
- equal employment opportunity
- affirmative action

Glen Jones/Shutterstock.com

Ethical Decisions

Your employer asks you to work a few extra hours on Saturday to help catch up on an important order. Even though you have already put in 40 hours this week, you agree to do so. The next week, you discover that you have been paid straight time for 45 hours. You call this to the boss's attention. He says that he does not pay overtime and that you should be glad that you have a job. You are not satisfied with his explanation.

What would you do?

What Employers Owe Workers

Employers owe certain things to their employees. One of these is payment for their work. Other responsibilities include the following:

- **Training and supervision**   An employer should provide necessary on-the-job training. Once the worker starts the job, the employer should give proper supervision and feedback.
- **Orientation to the workplace**   Workers need to know information about company policies and rules. When these change, the employer should tell its workers.
- **Honesty and respect**   An employer owes all its workers honesty and respect.
- **Fair employment practices**   Laws cover child labor, work hours, and payment of wages. An employer who wants to avoid legal problems must obey such laws.
- **Protection from discrimination**   Laws prohibit discrimination against workers.
- **Safe working conditions**   Years ago, employers did not have to provide safe working conditions. Many workers paid with their lives. Employers now must follow certain health and safety standards.

Honesty and Respect

An employer who pays your salary has a right to tell you what to do as long as it is not unlawful. Most employers, however, realize that honesty and respect toward their employees are essential. Workers are not robots. They are human beings with pride and self-worth.

The Lordstown story illustrates that employers cannot always force workers to do what they want them to do. The best relationship is one in which employers treat workers as they wish to be treated. Honesty and respect are the foundation for a good relationship between employers and workers.

Search the Net

Access **www.cengage.com/school/working** and click on the link for Chapter 8 to learn more about federal child labor laws. What were the FLSA child labor provisions designed to do?

www.cengage.com/school/working

Fair Employment Practices

Employment practices are the manners and methods by which employers deal with their employees. Many state and federal laws cover employment practices. A very important federal law is the *Fair Labor Standards Act (FLSA)*. It applies to employers or companies that do business in more than one state and have annual sales above a certain amount. The FLSA covers child labor, wages and hours, and equal pay.

Child Labor

The FLSA includes laws covering workers under the age of 18. People 15 years old and younger cannot work in factories or during school hours. Nor can people under 18 work in dangerous occupations such as mining. Each state has its own child-labor laws. If both federal and state laws apply to a situation, the employer must obey the stricter standard.

The law is flexible to allow students to take part in work experience education programs. In most states, schools issue work permits to those between 14 and 17 years of age. This allows students to work during school hours. The program helps protect the health and welfare of minors. It regulates the types of work they may do and the hours they can work. How can a work permit benefit employers as well?

Wages and Hours

The FLSA sets standards for minimum wages and maximum hours for most workers in the United States. The **minimum wage** is the lowest hourly wage the law permits employers to pay workers. Not all employers are covered by this law. In 1938, the national minimum wage was $0.25 an hour. By July 2009, the figure rose to $7.25 an hour. Congress periodically raises the minimum wage. Many states have laws regarding workers' pay. When there is a difference between state and federal laws, the higher standard applies. For example, if the minimum wage in your state is $8.00, eligible workers would receive the $8.00 wage.

There are some exceptions allowed. A **youth minimum wage**, also called a sub-minimum wage, is set at 75% of the minimum wage for student-learners and 50% for handicapped students. A youth minimum wage can be paid to work experience student-learners and handicapped students as long as the student is enrolled in a work training program.

Another exception is the Full-time Student Program that allows employers in retail or service establishments, agriculture, or institutions of higher education to pay full-time students under 20 years of age any wage above $4.25 for the first 90 calendar days of employment. After 90 days they must be paid not less than 85% of the minimum wage and can work a maximum of 8 hours daily or 20 hours weekly.

The wages for apprentices are less than those for more established workers. Actual wages and benefits paid to apprentices vary widely.

The FLSA sets the length of the **standard workweek**, which is, by law, the completion of 40 hours of work during a seven-day period. Time worked beyond 40 hours is *overtime*. For overtime hours, employers must pay workers a rate of 1½ times their regular rate.

Equal Pay

Jose and Ruth are assistant managers for a small hotel chain. They have equal qualifications and equal seniority. After learning Jose makes a lot more money than she does, Ruth is trying to determine why there is a difference in the pay. Although workers may receive different salaries because of shift work, skill level, and seniority, Ruth has ruled out all those reasons. The only difference Ruth can name is that she is a woman. Ruth knows the Equal Pay Act of 1963 outlaws different wage scales for equal work. This means workers doing the same job must receive the same wage. What should Ruth do?

Laws protect workers with a disability from discrimination by employers.

Protection from Discrimination

Laws protect workers from being discriminated against. **Discrimination** means favoring one person as compared to another. If an employer will not hire you only because of your race, that is discrimination. Other examples include being "passed over" for promotion because of your gender or being fired from your job because of your age. Equal treatment is legally required in such areas as hiring, promotion, and job security. Laws deal with equal employment opportunity and affirmative action.

Equal Employment Opportunity

The passage of the *Civil Rights Act of 1964* gave the government a strong legal tool to prevent job discrimination. It paved the way for **equal employment opportunity**, which means that unions and employment agencies cannot discriminate against people because of race, color, religion, sex, or national origin. The *Equal Employment Opportunity Commission (EEOC)* administers the Civil Rights Act and related laws.

In 1964, Warren Johnson lost his job as a landscaper when his employer went out of business. Warren was 56. With his experience, he figured he would easily find a job. The first two employers to whom he applied told him he was "too old." Warren was upset. At the time, he could not legally fight the employers. Today, Warren could take action against them. The *Age Discrimination Act of 1967* was passed to prohibit discrimination against people between 40 and 70 years of age.

Goodluz/Shutterstock.com

The *Rehabilitation Act of 1973* extended protection to those with physical or mental disabilities.

The *Americans with Disabilities Act (ADA)*, which took effect in 1992, gives civil rights protections to individuals with disabilities similar to those provided on the basis of race, sex, national origin, age, and religion. In 2010, the ADA law was expanded to prohibit discrimination against individuals suffering from "invisible disabilities" such as multiple sclerosis, post-traumatic stress disorder, epilepsy, and many other conditions. The EEOC also administers these laws.

The *Family and Medical Leave Act (FMLA)* took effect in August 1993. It requires employers with 50 or more workers to grant up to 12 weeks of unpaid leave a year. This allows workers to take time off to help care for a new baby or an ill family member without fear of losing their jobs. The law was expanded in 2009 to allow eligible employees to take leave due to a family military member being called to active duty or to help care for an injured or ill service member.

Employers sometimes advertise that they are an equal opportunity employer, as shown in Figure 8-1.

FIGURE 8-1 Some companies advertise that they are an "Equal Opportunity Employer."

SALES

NEWSPAPER SALES REP

A national newspaper is seeking a sales representative for St. Louis/Kansas City. Responsibilities include the development of retail, vending, corporate, and college sales. Excellent salary and benefits. Car provided. Send resume and salary history to:

ARC INC.
78 W. FIFTH ST
STE. 100
SHAKER HEIGHTS, OH 44120-5849
ATTENTION: ERIC NEANG

Equal Opportunity Employer

Affirmative Action

Equal employment opportunity laws forbid job discrimination. There are people, however, who have been victims of past discrimination. For instance, many women and members of minority groups have been unjustly passed over for job promotions. This is an example of a condition that affirmative action tries to correct.

Affirmative action is a set of policies and programs designed to correct past discrimination. It is not a single federal law, although many federal regulations and laws require affirmative action in hiring and promotions. Most affirmative action programs include special efforts to hire and promote women, members of minority groups, people with disabilities, and veterans.

8-1 Assessment

1. What types of responsibilities do employers owe workers?
2. Why should employers treat employees with honesty and respect?
3. Name three areas that the FLSA covers.
4. Are state minimum wages the same as the federal minimum wage?
5. For what five things does the Civil Rights Act of 1964 prohibit discrimination? What was added in 1967, 1973, 1992, 1993, 2009, and 2010?

High Growth Occupations
FOR THE 21ST CENTURY

Truck Drivers

Have you noticed how many large trucks travel the highways? As the population and economy grows, the demand for goods increases, which leads to having more trucks hauling goods across the country. Truck driving is a large occupation with numerous job openings.

Slightly more than half of all truck drivers are heavy truck and tractor-trailer drivers. These are drivers of the big "over-the-road" or "long-haul" rigs, meaning they deliver goods over intercity routes that may span several states. Some drivers have regular routes or regions where they drive the most, while others take on routes throughout the country or even to Canada and Mexico.

Long-haul drivers are often responsible for planning their own routes. In most cases, drivers are given a delivery location and deadline, and they must determine how to get the shipment to its destination on time. This can be difficult, as drivers must find routes that allow large trucks, and must work within the rules imposed by the U.S. Department of Transportation. Drivers must fill out logs to show that they have followed these rules, which mandate maximum driving times and rest periods between shifts.

Although most trucks have comfortable seats, good ventilation, and ergonomically designed cabs, driving a truck is still a physically demanding job. Driving for many hours at a stretch, loading and unloading cargo, and making many deliveries can be tiring. Making the decision to work as a long-haul driver is a major lifestyle choice. Drivers may be away from home for days or weeks at a time, and they often spend a great deal of time alone. Local truck drivers usually return home in the evening.

Drivers who operate heavy trucks or tractor-trailers need a commercial driver's license (CDL). Most prospective truck drivers take driver-training courses at a technical or vocational school to prepare for CDL testing. Driver-training courses teach students how to maneuver large vehicles on crowded streets and in highway traffic. These courses also train drivers how to properly inspect trucks and freight for compliance with regulations.

Truck drivers are often responsible for planning their own routes.

WORKER SAFETY AND HEALTH

OBJECTIVES

- Explain the roles of employers and workers regarding safety and health in the workplace
- Identify agencies that deal with workers' complaints

KEY TERMS

- Occupational Safety and Health Administration (OSHA)
- musculoskeletal disorder (MSD)
- ergonomics

Workplace Decisions

The production machine on which you work was repaired over the weekend. As you begin work on Monday morning, you notice that the safety guard has not been replaced. You immediately go to the supervisor. He tells you to go ahead and get started and he will replace the guard when he gets time. You do not want to work on the machine unless the safety guard is in place.

What would you do?

Alistair Cotton/Shutterstock.com

Safe Working Conditions

Have you ever seen workers wearing hard hats and safety glasses? Perhaps you have worn this gear yourself. Safety equipment helps protect workers from injury. Years ago, many employers were often unconcerned if their employees failed to use safety equipment or otherwise acted unsafely. Some employers made employees work under unsafe or unhealthful conditions. If workers complained, they sometimes lost their jobs.

In 1971 working conditions became safer. That year marked the beginning of the **Occupational Safety and Health Administration (OSHA)**. This government agency sets and enforces standards for safe and healthful working conditions. OSHA has developed and published literally thousands of standards and regulations for dozens of different industries. Below are examples of how OSHA regulates conditions.

- Each high-radiation area shall contain a sign having the radiation caution symbol and the words: CAUTION, HIGH- RADIATION AREA.
- Tools and other metal objects shall be kept away from the top of uncovered batteries.

Math Connection

You work in a medical laboratory. OSHA requires that all biological hazardous waste be weighed before it is sent to the hazardous waste management company. The limit per week that the waste management company can handle is 400 pounds. You have six containers with the following weights: 75 lb, 85 lb, 70 lb, 80 lb, 62 lb, and 60 lb. Based on the weekly limit, how many of the six containers will the waste management company take this week?

SOLUTION

You must first calculate the total weight of the six containers.

Total weight of the six containers = 75 + 85 + 70 + 80 + 62 + 60 = 432

The total weight of the six containers is more than the waste company will take. Since the weight of any of the containers will put the total weight over the limit, only five of the six containers will be taken.

- Exposed hot water and steam pipes shall be covered with insulating material whenever necessary to protect employees from contact with them.
- Safety shoes shall conform to certain standards.
- All workplaces shall be kept as clean as the nature of the work allows.

All employers, except the self-employed, having at least one employee must obey OSHA standards. Federal, state, and local government workers are covered by a special OSHA program. To help employers, OSHA offers free on-site visitations. Most employers welcome suggestions that will create a better work environment. Exceptions exist, though. To discourage these, OSHA makes random inspections as well. If inspectors find hazards, the employer can be fined and the business shut down.

A restaurant server complained to her employer that it was too hot in the restaurant's kitchen area. The employer ignored her complaint. She took her complaint to OSHA. When the employer found out, he threatened her, began giving her the least desirable work, and rearranged her work schedule. The server tried to reason with the employer but finally quit because of the harassment.

The server filed a complaint with OSHA. After investigating, OSHA ordered the employer to pay the server back wages and to remove all papers about the case from her files. (Most employers keep records on each employee.) OSHA also required the employer to post a notice that advised other employees of the settlement.

Protect New Workers

New employees have a much higher risk of injury than experienced workers. Various articles and reports published over the years indicate that a majority of all work-related injuries occur during the first few years of employment. Why are new workers more likely to be hurt?

Studies show that new workers often do not know enough to protect themselves. Following are examples that illustrate this problem.

- Of 724 workers hurt while using scaffolds, 27 percent said they had received no information on safety requirements for installing the kind of scaffold on which they were hurt.
- Of 868 workers who suffered head injuries, 71 percent said they had no instruction about hard hats.
- Of 554 workers hurt while servicing equipment, 61 percent said they were not informed about lockout procedures. Lockout means that any energy source (electrical, hydraulic, mechanical, or other) that might cause unexpected movement must be disengaged or locked.

In nearly every type of injury studied by safety experts, the same story is repeated. Workers often do not receive the safety information they need. Or, if they do, they do not apply it.

What Workers Can Do

During on-the-job training, your employer is responsible for your safety education. You, too, play an important role. Before starting to work, be sure that you understand all necessary safety measures. If an explanation is unclear, ask again. Practice and use what you have learned. Do not take shortcuts that could endanger your health or safety. Following are some general safety rules.

Workers need to use precautions to avoid injuries.

- Never use a tool or piece of equipment that lacks a safety guard or has a non-working one.
- If earplugs or other personal protective devices such as gloves or aprons are required, use them at all times.
- Do not "horse around" or play practical jokes at the workplace.
- Be especially careful when you get tired. This is when accidents are more likely to happen.
- If you work where dangerous substances are used, find out what something is before you handle it.
- Accept responsibility for your own safety on the job.

Besides taking care of their own safety and health, workers should be on the lookout for possible dangers. Employers should correct any problems that employees call to their attention. If an employer does not correct a problem, it is up to the employee to call on OSHA for help if needed. OSHA protects your right to complain to your employer, your union, and OSHA itself. It is illegal for your employer to punish you for exercising this or any other OSHA right.

Design a Safer Workplace

Many of you have experienced fatigue, sore and aching muscles, and perhaps injury from overexertion in sports, recreation, or work activities. So have millions of American workers who are employed in a wide variety of industries and occupations. **Musculoskeletal disorder (MSD)** is a broad term used to describe a variety of diseases or injuries to bones, muscles, tendons, joints, nerves, and blood vessels. Musculoskeletal disorders are

Workstation Review

1. **Monitor Screen Top**
   Slightly below eye level

2. **Body**
   Centered in front of the
   monitor and keyboard

3. **Forearms**
   Level or tilted-up slightly

4. **Lower Back**
   Supported by chair

5. **Wrists**
   Should not rest
   while typing

6. **Legs**
   Horizontal

7. **Feet**
   Resting flat on the floor
   or footrest

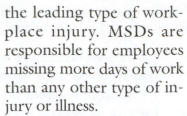

FIGURE 8-2 Sample of Ergonomic Considerations for Computer Work

the leading type of workplace injury. MSDs are responsible for employees missing more days of work than any other type of injury or illness.

Common symptoms include aches, pains, tingling, swelling, and loss of joint movement and strength in the affected area. Work activities that are frequent and repetitive and lead to fatigue and overuse can cause these disorders. An example is repetitive motion injury found among people who work long hours at a computer. A less familiar but painful overuse injury is trigger finger syndrome, which is frequent among assembly line workers.

A common characteristic of most MSDs is that they involve simple physical activities such as keyboarding, lifting, bending, reaching, stretching, and using hand or power tools. The problem occurs when these simple tasks are done over and over again every day until they eventually cause stress to the muscles and tendons. The problem is made worse when poor posture is involved and/or poor working conditions are present.

Even though MSDs are costly to both employers and employees, many of them can be prevented through the application of ergonomics. **Ergonomics** is the scientific study of people at work and how the work is performed. The goal of ergonomics is to reduce stress and eliminate injuries and disorders associated with the overuse of muscles, bad posture, and repeated tasks. This is accomplished by designing tasks, work spaces, controls, displays, tools, lighting, and equipment to fit the employee's physical capabilities and limitations. An example of ergonomic practices applied to the correct use of computers is shown in Figure 8-2.

Ergonomic experts have developed guidelines for the safe performance of most jobs. It is likely that your employer will be familiar with such guidelines and will teach you them as part of your on-the-job training. You can also find them on your own by doing a Web search using the term ergonomics and the name of your occupation. To illustrate, you could search for "ergonomics and electricians."

Agencies Provide Services to Workers

What should you do if you have a work problem dealing with fair employment practices, discrimination, or health and safety? If you are a work experience student, contact your school coordinator. He or she can help solve the problem. Apprentices and union workers can speak to the union representative.

Civil service employees also have representatives they can turn to for help. Wherever you work, follow any procedures that appear in your company's policy manual.

If you do not have certain procedures to follow or anyone else to help you, try to work out the problem with your boss or employer. Ask for a meeting to informally discuss your complaint. Present your point of view and then listen patiently to the other person's side of the story.

If an informal meeting does not work, file a formal complaint. Write a letter to the proper company official. State your complaint clearly and briefly. Ask for an answer by a reasonable date. Be polite and businesslike in your letter. Do not make demands. Ask that the problem be solved. Keep a copy of the letter for your files.

FIGURE 8-3 These are the primary federal agencies that handle complaints regarding fair employment practices, discrimination, and health and safety.

Type of Complaint	Federal Agency
Child labor Wages and hours Minimum wage Migrant workers Family and medical leave	Wage and Hour Division U.S. Department of Labor 200 Constitution Ave., NW Washington, DC 20210 www.dol.gov/whd/
Equal pay Discrimination based on race, color, religion, sex, national origin, age or disability	U.S. Equal Employment Opportunity Commission (EEOC) 131 M Street, NE Washington, DC 20507 www.eeoc.gov/
Safety and Health	Occupational Safety and Health Administration (OSHA) U.S. Department of Labor 200 Constitution Ave., NW Washington, DC 20210 www.osha.gov/

State and local offices for the three federal agencies listed above can be found on their websites or in your telephone directory for "Government" listings.

If all your efforts to solve the problem meet dead ends, you can turn to outside help. Many federal laws and government agencies protect the rights of workers. A summary of the major types of complaints and the agencies that handle them appears in Figure 8-3. Ask for help at a public library if you have trouble finding the contact information you need.

Most employers support and respect laws and rules that protect workers. Employers may sometimes overlook a law or rule. Other times, though, an employer may violate a law on purpose. In either case, it is up to you to identify and then to report any violations you find. Learn your rights so you can be in control of your health, safety, and welfare.

8-2 Assessment

1. To which employers do OSHA standards apply?
2. Why are new employees more likely to be hurt on the job than more experienced workers?
3. To protect your health and safety, what four things should you do before you start to work?
4. Why do many simple work tasks often lead to later injuries?
5. What is the goal of ergonomics? Give an example.

Focus on the Workplace

Collective Bargaining

Labor (workers) and management (owners/managers) both want to see a company grow and succeed. Occasionally, the two groups may disagree regarding wages, benefits, working conditions, or other matters. If the workers are union members, the two sides engage in collective bargaining to settle their differences.

Collective bargaining is an important right of union members. Because of the unequal bargaining power between an individual employee and a company, federal law permits workers to group together and negotiate common terms and conditions. The main body of law governing collective bargaining is the National Labor Relations Act.

In typical collective bargaining, union representatives present demands. Management may accept or reject the demands. It may also make a counteroffer. The two sides often negotiate for days or even weeks. Eventually, the two sides usually agree. The agreement, called a labor contract, is put into writing. The union membership must then vote on the agreement. As a legal document, the labor contract can be enforced in a court of law. The contract usually covers a specified time period, such as three years.

After a labor contract is signed, the agreement is put into practice. A contract presents certain rules that labor and management are to follow. Sometimes, though, a complaint or grievance arises over what the rules mean or how they are carried out. For instance, a grievance might result from the firing of a worker or the violation of a safety practice.

The procedure for settling grievances is an important part of the labor contract. An employee with a grievance, along with the union representative, usually discusses the matter with the boss. Most problems are resolved at this level. If the problem is not resolved, the employee may file a complaint with a higher level of management.

In recent years, particularly after the 2008 elections, public employee unions in several states have come under attack. For example, in Wisconsin the Governor cut the bargaining rights and benefits of public workers. Similar efforts also began in Ohio, Tennessee, Indiana, and other states.

THINK CRITICALLY

1. Why would a group of workers have more bargaining power with an employer than a single worker would?
2. Do you think it is important to have a procedure for settling grievances in labor contracts? Why or why not?

Photodisc/Getty Images

Collective bargaining is a process in which workers and management meet to resolve differences.

OBJECTIVES
- Identify and describe different forms of compensation
- Describe paycheck calculations
- Discuss the purposes of raises and how to ask for one

KEY TERMS
- compensation
- overtime pay
- gross pay
- deduction
- net pay
- statement of earnings
- automatic raise
- merit raise

Ethical Decisions

Each payday you carefully go over your check. Several times, you have found mistakes in which you were underpaid. The boss always apologizes and makes the correction. This payday, however, you discover you have been overpaid by $20. You share this information with a coworker. He tells you to forget it, since you have probably been cheated out of more than $20 by the company. You have been thinking about this all weekend.

What would you do?

moshimochi/Shutterstock.com

Your Job Earnings

When you get paid, you will receive a paycheck and an attached statement of earnings. Some people cash or deposit their paycheck and throw away the pay statement. This is not a good idea. You may have lost money because of an error. Or too much money may have been withheld for certain deductions.

The amount of your paycheck depends on how you are paid and on the deductions taken out. How do you know if your paycheck is accurate? Read on.

The total amount of income and benefits you receive for your job is your **compensation**. Employees are compensated in many ways.

- **Wages** Most workers receive a set hourly wage. To arrive at the amount of pay, an employer multiplies the hourly wage by the number of hours worked. For example, if Sean receives $8.60 an hour and he works a 40-hour week, his weekly wages are $344.00 ($8.60 × 40). Most hourly workers are paid weekly.

- **Overtime**   For working more than 40 hours a week, most hourly workers get **overtime pay**. The overtime wage is usually 1½ times the normal hourly wage. Sean works in a garden store. With spring planting starting, Sean worked 45 hours one week. His pay is $8.60 an hour for the first 40 hours and $12.90 an hour ($8.60 × 1.5) for the 5 extra hours. His weekly wages are $408.50 ($344.00 + $64.50).

- **Salary**   Some workers receive a salary instead of an hourly wage. Salaried workers are paid a set sum of money per week, month, or year, instead of by the hour. Teachers' salaries are usually a certain amount for nine or ten months. Some salaried workers are paid weekly. Others receive checks every other week. Some people must really plan ahead! They get paid only once a month.

  Salaried workers may put in more than 40 hours a week. Even so, they usually do not receive any extra pay. Do you think this is fair?

It is important to make good use of your paycheck.

- **Piece rate**   In this method, the worker is paid for the amount of work performed. A sewing machine operator, for example, might be paid $.90 for each piece of goods completed. If 112 such pieces were done in one day, the worker would get $100.80 (112 × $.90) for that day.

- **Commissions**   Most sales workers receive all or part of their pay through commissions. A commission is an amount of money the worker receives for making a sale. Real estate agents and insurance brokers are some workers who receive commissions. Can you name others?

  Most commissions are a certain percentage of the total sale. Rita Yang, for example, is a real estate agent. She gets a 2 percent commission on each house she sells. Last week, Rita sold a house for $210,000. This meant a $4,200 commission ($210,000 × 0.02). She does not do that every day, though.

- **Tips**   Some workers receive a minimum hourly wage and earn the rest of their compensation from tips. Examples include restaurant servers, porters, and cab drivers. Can you think of any others? A tip or gratuity is an amount of money given in return for a favor or service. Tips is an acronym for the phrase "to insure prompt service."

- **Bonuses**   A bonus is extra money a company gives workers as a gift or a reward for good work. Most bonuses come from employers that are willing to share some of the company profits. Auto manufacturing companies, for example, often distribute annual profit-sharing amounts of several thousand dollars to each worker.

- **Fringe benefits**   Fringe benefits are indirect forms of compensation. That is, they are given instead of cash. Do you or members of your family get company-paid insurance? How about paid holidays, vacations, and sick days? These are the most common fringe benefits. If you do not get fringe benefits, don't be discouraged. Most entry-level and part-time jobs offer few fringe benefits. Chances are you will get some later.

Your Paycheck

When you get your first check, look it over carefully. Make sure that your name is spelled right and your address and Social Security number are correct.

Your first paycheck may surprise you. Most new workers don't take home the pay they expect because the employer has taken money out for certain reasons. There are many factors that contribute to how the employer figures your earnings.

The amount of salary or wages that you earn during a certain time period is **gross pay**. For example, if you work 20 hours a week at $8.10 an hour, your gross pay is $162.00 (20 × $8.10). From this amount, deductions are made for taxes, retirement, and so on. **Deductions** are amounts that are withheld from your paycheck. After deductions are subtracted from your gross pay, you are left with **net pay** or take-home pay. A pay statement or **statement of earnings** attached to your paycheck shows your gross pay, deductions, and net pay. A sample pay statement for a person paid weekly is shown in Figure 8-4.

Payroll deductions are of many types. The employer must withhold some of them. Other deductions depend on what you request the employer to withhold. Some common types of payroll deductions are the following:

PERIOD FROM 02/18 TO 02/24 20--				
NAME				
20	REG. HR. @ 8	10	162	00
	OT. HR. @			
TOTAL EARNINGS ➜			162	00
F.I.C.A.	12	39		
WITHHOLDING U.S. INCOME TAX	5	00		
STATE INCOME TAX	3	15		
TOTAL DEDUCTIONS ➜			20	54
NET PAY			141	46

FIGURE 8-4 Always examine your paycheck and statement. Ask your supervisor about any figures you do not understand.

- **Income taxes**   Your employer must withhold federal income tax from your earnings and send it to the federal government. When you start your job, you will need to fill out a Form W-4. Based on your answers and what you earn, the employer figures the amount of federal tax to withhold each payday. Depending on where you live, the employer may withhold state and local taxes, too.

- **FICA**   The acronym FICA stands for Federal Insurance Contributions Act. The FICA tax is better known as the Social Security tax. Most jobs in the United States are part of the federal Social Security program. Both you and your employer pay into this fund. Notice in Figure 8-5 that the employer withheld $48.41 during this pay period for Social Security from Esther Roberts's paycheck.

FIRST TRUST CORPORATION 2 COMPUTER DR. TROY, NY 12179-5483						**Pay Statement**				
Co. Code 5XQ	Department 301712	File No. 35637	Clock No./ID 05502	Name Roberts, Esther		Pay Period Ending 01/17/--		Pay Date 01/24/--		
Hours/Units	Rate		Earnings		Type	Deduction	Type	Deduction		Type
40	632	80	632	80	REG B	3 68	DENTAL	23	73	HEALTH

This Pay	Gross		Fed. With. Tax		Social Security		State With. Tax		City With. Tax		Sui./Dis.		Net Pay	
	632	80	70	00	48	41	21	08				84	465.06	
YTD	1,898	40	210	00	145	23	63	24			2	52		

FIGURE 8-5 Sample Statement of Earnings

It is always gratifying to receive a pay raise.

If Ester Roberts was self-employed, she would have to pay both the "employer" and "employee" portion of FICA. Sometimes FICA withholdings change. For example, in 2011, FICA was reduced temporarily to 13.3%. FICA may change again in the future.

- **Insurance**   Many employers offer group life and health insurance programs to full-time employees. Employers may pay all, part, or none of the insurance cost. If you must pay, the employer may withhold the premium from your paycheck. Esther Roberts's employer contributes 70 percent toward health insurance and provides free life insurance. Esther pays $23.73 per week for health insurance, $3.68 for dental insurance, and $0.84 for supplemental income and disability coverage.
- **Union dues**   Sometimes union members can pay their dues through payroll deductions.
- **Charity**   Many workers donate to charity through payroll deductions. A common example of a charity is United Way.
- **Savings**   Do you find it hard to save? If so, see if your employer can withhold money for savings. For instance, the employer may be willing to deduct money for a savings account or U.S. Savings Bonds.

When you start a job, the employer should explain your deductions to you. If no one does, ask. After all, the deductions are your money.

Pay Raises

Alice had been working in the claims department of an insurance agency for three years. Alice was often praised for her productivity and her skill. Her boss said she was the most valuable employee in the department. Alice thought her annual raise should be higher than everyone else's. It wasn't. Alice's boss said that if she gave Alice a larger raise then everyone else, it would upset other workers. Because she was not rewarded for her excellent performance, Alice interviewed for a job at another company and accepted a similar position at a higher pay rate.

Pay raises benefit both employees and their employers. The idea of a pay raise may be an incentive for you to do a good job. An *incentive* is a potential reward to work toward. After getting a raise, you may feel better about your job. This may make you continue to improve your work. Improved work makes employees more valuable to the company.

Most companies want to keep good employees, so they give them raises. Good workers who do not get the raises they think they deserve may go elsewhere.

In many jobs, employees receive automatic raises every 6 months, 12 months, and so on. An **automatic raise** is a regular pay raise received by all employees. All employees may get the same dollar amount or the same percentage amount. In some cases, the amount of the raise depends on the type of job. Production employees may get higher raises than office workers, for instance.

Some employers give merit raises instead of, or in addition to, automatic raises. A **merit raise** is based on the amount and quality of an employee's work. Most of these employers use a performance evaluation to determine merit raises.

Not all employers have a set policy on pay raises. In such cases, it may be up to the employer to decide when an employee deserves a raise. Or the employee may be expected to ask for a raise. This type of situation is common in small businesses.

Suppose you decide to ask for a raise. If you are a new employee, do not expect one until after you have learned the job and shown you can do it well. You must earn a raise. Some workers want a raise because they are not making as much money as they would like.

Before you speak to your boss about a raise, plan what you will say. Think about what you have done well. Make a list of specific examples.

Ask for a raise when the company is doing well and the boss has had a good week. Do not ask for a raise during a time when you should be working. Ask for an appointment to discuss a raise during break, at lunch, or after work. When asking for a pay raise, tell the boss why you deserve one. Steve, for example, pointed out to his boss that sales had increased 18 percent since he had started working in the department.

Ask your boss what workers must do to get a pay raise. If you have done all those things, tell the boss. Be clear. Talk about exactly what you have done. If the boss says there is no rule for granting raises, present your case. When asking for a raise, show confidence and respect. If you are turned down, do not argue with the decision. Just say that you will keep working hard and hope that you get a raise later. If you feel strongly that you deserve a good raise, you may want to follow Alice's example.

Pay Raises Are Not Always Possible

Most employers support the practice of giving workers a pay raise because this generally means that the company is doing well and has the resources to share with employees. It may also mean that the company recognizes and appreciates the hard work and productivity of its workforce. However, the economy goes through good and bad times. Between December 2007 and June 2009, the United States experienced a very bad economic downturn, called the Great Recession. Companies went out of business, laid-off workers, froze or reduced wages, or asked employees to take unpaid leave several days a month. During times like this, a pay raise is usually out of the question. Many employees feel lucky to just keep a job.

8-3 Assessment

1. The amount of your paycheck depends on what two things?
2. Why is it important to check your pay statement often?
3. List and briefly explain each form of compensation.
4. What is the difference between gross pay and net pay?
5. What is the more common name for the FICA tax?
6 Describe how you should go about asking for a raise?
7. Why might it be necessary for an employer to freeze or reduce your wages?

OBJECTIVES

- Identify the most common reasons for changing jobs
- Explain what to do when voluntarily leaving a job

KEY TERMS

- letter of resignation
- slander

Career Decisions

You have been working at a farm implement dealership since your senior year in high school. You like the job and the people who work there. The business, however, is barely making enough profit to stay alive. You have only had one small raise in three years. You have been laid off for a couple of months each winter. The prospects for additional raises or promotions do not look good. You understand the dealer's financial problems, but you have your future to think about.

What would you do?

Reasons for Job Changes

Most people start working in a low-paying, entry-level job. An entry-level job is a good way to earn money and gain valuable experience. Usually, though, an entry-level job is not one that you want to keep forever. You may want to advance within the company or move to a better job in another company.

Job Promotions

A *promotion* is advancement to a higher-level job within a company. The new position usually brings a new title, more money, and more responsibility. Some promotions also bring the chance to supervise others. Opportunities for promotion differ among occupations and industries. For example, most workers in skilled trades have less chance for promotion than do sales representatives. Large businesses offer more chances for promotion than do small ones.

Promotion opportunities occur for two reasons: a new position is created within the company or a vacancy occurs because someone was promoted or left the company. How can you put yourself in line for a promotion? You can begin during the job interview. Ask, "What are my chances for advancement if I perform well?" Suppose you work where you can advance. Do the best work you can every day. Employers notice workers who do their jobs well and get along with others.

Even if you are a good employee, remember that promotions take time. Employers want to watch you over a period of time. Even when an employer thinks you are ready, an opening may not yet exist. Or a worker who has the same job as you may have more seniority. If so, the person with seniority will probably get promoted first.

While many people want promotions, not everyone wants to be the boss or have a better job. A higher-level job is not for everyone.

When the job of office manager opened up, Ramon's coworkers encouraged him to apply. He was the most experienced accounting clerk in the company, got along with everyone, and knew the business well. He applied for the job and got it.

Ramon soon found out that being an office manager was different from what he expected. He had to assign work, manage the office budget, make on-the-spot decisions, and do many other things. To get everything done, he began to come to work earlier and stay later. Once he started giving orders, Ramon sensed tension between himself and the other employees. His most painful moment was when his boss ordered him to fire one of the clerks.

Ramon is not alone. All businesses have people like him. They are great workers but are not suited to be supervisors. No matter what your job, try to work toward something you will like. For many workers, that is the job they have now.

Temporary and Contract Workers

Some employers hire temporary workers for relatively short-term needs. Workers may be hired directly by the company or the company may use workers provided by an employment agency. Temporary workers may be hired for seasonal needs, when a regular employee is on medical leave, or when a specific business need arises. Hiring workers to help with the holiday shopping rush or to cover for an employee who will be out due to surgery are some examples of when temporary workers might be needed.

Many people choose to be self-employed. They take jobs on a project-by-project basis. Instead of receiving a paycheck from an employer, they receive payment from the person who has hired them to complete a project.

Although self-employed workers have a great deal of flexibility when determining how and when they will work, they also have responsibilities that employees of a company do not have. Self-employed workers need to be accountable for filing quarterly taxes, obtaining health insurance, keeping track of business expenses, and determining how to calculate the cost for their services. Home remodeling workers, house cleaners, and Web designers are positions that are frequently filled by self-employed workers.

Due to the nature of their job assignments, temporary and contract workers change jobs frequently.

Workforce Trends

Total employment can be divided into two main segments: wage and salary workers and self-employed workers. In 2008, approximately 9 of every 10 jobs were held by wage and salary workers, the remainder being held by the self-employed. Whereas wage and salary employment is expected to grow by 10.5 percent over the 2008-18 decade, self-employment is projected to increase only 5.5 percent.

Other Reasons

Years ago, most people stayed on a job for most of their working lives. Things have changed since then. While some people stay on the same job, most people do not. The most common reasons for changing jobs are as follows:

- **Lack of opportunity with present employer**   You may be in a dead-end job that offers little chance for pay raises and promotions.

- **Better opportunity elsewhere**   Perhaps you like the job you have but another company offers you an even better job. Often such a change involves a pay raise.

- **Dislike for present occupation or job**   Not everything looks as good up close as it did from afar. Perhaps you thought you would really enjoy your present occupation. After doing it for a while, though, you see that it's just not what you want to do for the rest of your life. You may want to train for another occupation. Or you may like your occupation (what you do) but dislike your job (where you work). If so, changing jobs is probably the answer.

- **Change in personal or family situation**   You may need to quit a job because of such things as illness or a move to a new area.

- **Loss of job**   *Downsizing* occurs when an employer reduces the workforce because of a business slow down, a corporate reorganization, or the sale of a company. Sometimes jobs are lost when an employer goes out of business. These things are not your fault. Being fired probably is, though. Either way, you are out of a job.

If You are Fired

Being fired is much different from leaving a job on your own. Some employers may ask you to leave but give you the chance to resign. Resigning will make it easier to find another job. If you are fired or must resign, try to turn disaster into a learning experience. Never make the same mistake twice.

- Phyllis was fired but was not sure why. It would have been easy for her to never go back. Instead, she made an appointment with her former boss to find out why she was fired. After learning about some of her poor work habits, she decided to improve on her next job.

- Theo was let go because he did not have the skills for the job. He decided to start classes at the community college and work toward a degree.

- Sharlene lost her job because of too many absences. She did not think the boss would fire her. When the boss did, Sharlene was shocked. She will do her best to make sure it will not happen again.

- Ed was told that he had a bad attitude. It was true. He could not get along with the boss, coworkers, or customers. Ed talked with a good friend who helped him understand what he was doing wrong. Ed now sees that he was carrying a chip on his shoulder.

Leave a Job

No matter why you are changing jobs, plan the change carefully if you can. Do not make a quick decision. Some workers get angry and quit. Later, most of these people regret what they did.

When Alice was upset about her low pay raise, she did not immediately quit. She knew it would have been a mistake to quit on the spot. Instead, she made sure she had a new job first. Another mistake would have been to say, "If you don't give me a raise, I'm going to quit." What do you think would have happened then?

Once you have decided to leave, find out if the company has rules about quitting a job. If so, follow them. If not, give your employer at least two weeks' notice. Tell your boss before you mention it to your coworkers.

A **letter of resignation** is a letter written by an employee notifying an employer of the intent to quit a job. Follow up your verbal notice with a written letter of resignation. Figure 8-6 provides a sample resignation letter. Such a letter should contain the following points: (a) the fact that you are leaving, (b) a date when you plan to leave, (c) the reason you are leaving, (d) an offer to help train your replacement, and (e) a thank-you for the chance to work there.

Once you have told your employer you are leaving, do not let up. Do your job as best you can through the last day. Do not criticize your boss or brag to your coworkers about your new job. Your employer will watch and evaluate you through your last day. Your boss's good opinion may be valuable to you in seeking future jobs. Therefore, try to leave on good terms with your employer.

When you leave an employer, you need to be respectful of the employer. If you have been fired from a job or if you leave voluntarily, do not post anything online that is critical of a company, boss, or coworker. Such behavior shows a lack of maturity and could hurt you in obtaining another job. **Slander** is a false statement that is harmful to a person's reputation. You could even be sued for slander if the comments are particularly hurtful or untrue.

FIGURE 8-6 Sample Letter of Resignation

893 N. Rigeway St.
Statesboro, GA 30458-1347
August 8, 20—

Ralph W. Wilson, Manager
Hoags Drugs, Inc.
416 Webster Dr.
Statesboro, GA 30459-3820

Dear Mr. Wilson

This is to inform you that I have decided to resign from my present position and return to college. I plan to continue working through August 30. I would be happy to do whatever I can to help train a replacement.

Hoags is a fine company with many wonderful employees. I have enjoyed my job and have learned a great deal from you and the rest of the shipping department crew. Thank you very much for the opportunity to have worked here.

Sincerely
James R. Long
James R. Long

8-4 Assessment

1. Name two reasons why promotion opportunities occur.
2. Is promotion for everyone? Why or why not?
3. List five common reasons for changing jobs.
4. Why is it best to leave a job on good terms with your employer?
5. What could happen to you if you posted something online about a boss or coworker that is not true?

Chapter Summary

8-1 Duties of Employers

A. An employer who pays your salary has a right to give you orders as long as they are not unlawful. Most employers, however, realize that honesty and respect toward their employees are essential.

B. A very important federal law is the Fair Labor Standards Act (FLSA). The FLSA covers child labor, wages and hours, and equal pay.

C. Laws exist to promote equal employment opportunity. It is illegal for employers, unions, and employment agencies to discriminate against people because of race, color, religion, sex, national origin, age, or physical or mental disabilities. The Family and Medical Leave Act allows workers to take time off to care for a new baby, an ill family member, or to help meet the needs of family members who are in the military.

D. Many affirmative action policies and programs have been established to help victims of past discrimination.

8-2 Worker Safety and Health

A. The Occupational Safety and Health Administration (OSHA) sets and enforces standards for safe and healthful working conditions. Workers can file a complaint with OSHA if an employer refuses to correct unsafe or unhealthful working conditions.

B. New employees have a much higher risk of injury than experienced workers. These workers often do not receive the safety information they need or they do not apply the information. The ergonomic impact of how work will affect a worker's body is an important consideration for employers.

C. If you have a problem at work regarding fair employment practices, discrimination, or health and safety, try to solve it informally. If this does not work, file a formal complaint with the proper company official or turn to outside agencies for help.

8-3 Your Job Earnings and Paycheck

A. The amount of your paycheck depends on how you are paid and on the deductions taken out. Employees are compensated in many ways. These include wages, salary, piece rate, commissions, tips, bonuses, and fringe benefits.

B. The total amount of salary or wages that you earn is your gross pay. From this, certain deductions are made leaving you with net pay. The major types of deductions are income taxes and FICA tax.

C. Pay raises benefit both employees and employers. Some workers receive automatic raises. Merit raises may be given instead of, or in addition to, automatic raises. Reasons that an employer might not provide a raise include tough economic conditions.

8-4 Job Changes

A. A promotion is advancement to a higher-level job within a company. Earning a promotion usually takes time and is based on outstanding performance.

B. Most people do not stay in the same job all their lives. Some people work as temporary or contract workers. There are many different reasons for changing jobs.

C. Some people are fired or given a chance to resign. If this happens to you, try to learn from the experience.

D. Plan job changes carefully. Follow company guidelines for leaving, try to leave on good terms, and do not criticize any part of the company.

Activities

1. Find out your state's laws on two or more of these topics: child labor, minimum wage, wages and hours, and equal pay. You can usually find such information on the Web by doing a search using the name or your state followed by the "Department of Labor." Report your findings to the class.

2. Find out who is covered under the Americans with Disabilities Act (ADA) and what the "reasonable accommodation" requirement of the act means. The ADA home page at www.ada.gov/ is a good resource. Report and discuss your findings in class.

3. Write an imaginary letter to an employer complaining of a work-related problem. Follow the guidelines presented in this chapter.

4. Identify a job you either currently hold or could accept. Make a list of benefits you believe your employer would owe you as an employee. Discuss how these benefits could help you achieve goals in your life-span plan.

5. As a class, watch "Teen Workers: Real Jobs, Real Risks" available online at www.cdc.gov/niosh/talkingsafety/video.html. The video is an excellent summary of worker safety and health information. Discuss what workers said that indicated they had received safety training and make a list of how you could avoid unsafe work conditions.

6. You earn $7.20 an hour on your job. One week, you work 48 hours. You are paid the normal rate for the first 40 hours and time and a half for overtime. What is your gross pay for the week?

7. With a partner, role-play a conversation you might have with your supervisor to ask for a raise. Plan out what you are going to say beforehand.

8. Nat earns a salary of $280 a week plus a 5% commission on his total sales. This month his sales amounted to $26,000. His deductions are as follows: Federal income tax, $294.00; Credit union, $65.00; State tax, $52.44; Charity, $35.00; FICA, $185.13.

   Based on these figures, what is Nat's gross pay for the month? How much are his total deductions? What is his net pay?

9. Describe the relationship between your current earnings and your ability to eventually achieve goals in your life-span plan.

Word Power

On a separate sheet of paper, match each definition with the correct term. All definitions will be used, and a definition will be used only once.

a. affirmative action
b. automatic raise
c. compensation
d. deduction
e. discrimination
f. equal employment opportunity
g. employment practice
h. ergonomics
i. gross pay
j. letter of resignation
k. merit raise
l. minimum wage
m. musculoskeletal disorder (MSD)
n. net pay
o. Occupational Safety and Health Administration (OSHA)
p. overtime pay
q. slander
r. standard workweek
s. statement of earnings
t. youth minimum wage

10. A false statement that is harmful to a person's reputation
11. A regular pay raise received by all employees
12. A wage rate paid to student-learners set at 75% of the minimum wage
13. The government agency that sets and enforces standards for safe and healthful working conditions
14. The amount on a paycheck; the take-home pay of an employee after deductions are subtracted from gross pay
15. Favoring one person as compared to another
16. The idea, supported by law, that employers, unions, and employment agencies cannot discriminate against people because of race, color, religion, sex, or national origin
17. A set of policies and programs designed to correct past discrimination
18. The wage received for working more than 40 hours a week, usually 1½ times the normal hourly wage
19. A letter written by an employee notifying an employer of the intent to quit a job
20. The scientific study of people at work and how the work is performed
21. The total amount of income and benefits received for a job
22. A broad term describing a variety of workplace injuries and illnesses caused by repetitive motion, fatigue, and overuse of muscles and joints
23. A pay raise based on the amount and quality of an employee's work
24. A certain amount that is withheld from an employee's paycheck
25. A pay statement; the attachment to a paycheck that shows your gross pay, deductions, and net pay
26. By law, the completion of 40 hours of work during a seven-day period
27. The amount of salary or wages earned during a certain time period, before deductions are withheld
28. By law, the lowest hourly wage that can be paid to an employee
29. The manners and methods by which employers deal with their employees

Think Critically

30. Federal law and some state laws permit employers to pay student-learners, full time students, and apprentices less than the minimum wage. What is the justification for this? Do you think this is fair?

31. Affirmative action programs give special advantages to groups that were discriminated against in the past. Discuss in class the pros and cons of such programs.

32. Have you ever had a work accident or an injury on the job? If so, how might it have been prevented? Discuss your answers in class.

33. If you were a salesperson, would you rather be paid a salary or a straight commission? Discuss the advantages and disadvantages of each.

34. In recent years, workers in a number of industries have been forced to take pay cuts and give up benefits in order to save their jobs. Would you be willing to take a pay cut to keep a job?

35. Do you think that you would like to be a supervisor? Why or why not?

36. Why do you think the Family and Medical Leave Act was amended in 2009 to include family needs arising from family members who are on active military duty? Do you think any other amendments should be made to the act? Discuss your ideas as a class.

37. You have just joined a start-up company. You are very excited about the products the company makes and the opportunities that you will have at your job. Because cash is tight, your office furniture has been put together from whatever sturdy used equipment the company owners found at used furniture warehouses. Your computer screen is about a foot and a half above your eye level and your non-adjustable chair is so tall that your feet dangle. You expect to spend about four hours each day at your computer. What should you do?

38. Access www.cengage.com/school/working and click on the Web Links for Chapter 8. Go to the link entitled Youth Worker Rules and Rights. Select a topic of interest (or your instructor may assign a topic), read the information, and summarize key points. Be prepared to discuss your assigned topic and to present the strengths and weaknesses of how the laws and policies are written.

Career Transitions Connection

Salary Negotiations

Click on *Tips & Advice*. Click on *Negotiating*. Review the article on Job Offer Negotiating. Many people are uncomfortable asking for things or discussing money issues. Look for guidance in the article regarding the best way to prepare for salary negotiations. If more money is not available from the employer, think about what else you might want to negotiate for. Determine a way to ask for more money but to still be in a favorable position to accept the job even if additional wages are not available.

UNIT 4 Success Skills

Yuri Arcurs/Shutterstock.com

198

Co-op Career SPOTLIGHT

After graduating from high school, Katriel England took a job working thirteen hour days in a warehouse that filled orders for a variety of products ranging from athletic wear to dvds. Workers had to prepare boxes for shipment by placing the products ordered into boxes. Workers had a *quota*, or a company defined minimum, of 90 boxes in a given time period. If workers did not meet their quota on a daily basis, they would be given a point. Any worker who accumlated six points was automatically fired. Workers could acquire points for other reasons, including leaving work early – even if the cause of leaving was due to illness. The rigid production quotas and demerit system inspired Katriel to consider ways to improve her work environment.

Katriel had had experience with other work. While still in high school, she worked weekends bagging groceries. She eventually was promoted to cashier. After being promoted, her pay went from $6.50 per hour to $7.50 per hour. She had also worked as a census taker. She particularly enjoyed that job as the hours were flexible and the pay, at $17.50 per hour, was very good.

Creative pursuits had always been among Katriel's interests. She enjoyed painting and writing poetry. She also enjoyed the challenge of putting together unassembled furniture.

Katriel thought working in cosmetology would be a way to stay creative while earning a living. There was one cosmetology school that particularly caught her eye. When visitng the school, she noticed that the students and the staff had a variety of personal styles – including hair of many different vivid colors and a variety of hair styles. She felt quite at home at this school that encouraged personal creativity. Katriel registered on the spot for this school.

Katriel England
Cosmetology Student

Although she spent the first six weeks of the the eleven month curriculum learning the basics, she then began working with guests. During this time she learned about theory, color, texture, makeup, and cutting. As she prepares to graduate, Katriel will fine tune her skills while trying to develop a clientele. Guests who come for services at Katriel's school learn who she is and what her abilities are. If she successfully establishes a business relationship with the guests, and if they like the way she provides hair services, they may follow her to her job site and become her regular clients.

One of the things Katriel enjoys most about her work is satisfying her customers. When a customer sees their final look in the mirror for the first time and their face lights up, Katriel knows she's done her job well.

Katriel has volunteered for numerous charity events, including fashion shows, as part of her education. She really enjoys preparing models to walk down the runway. She hopes that, upon graduation, she will be able to work in the fashion industry.

"All labor that uplifts humanity has dignity and importance and should be undertaken with painstaking excellence." —DR. MARTIN LUTHER KING, JR.

Workplace Communication

StockLite/Shutterstock.com

PREVIEW

Typical workers spend a large proportion of their workday hours communicating through listening, speaking, reading, and writing. These are four basic skills for communication. Technological advances have changed the way communication occurs. Workers communicate by phone, email, instant messaging, and texting. The devices used to communicate include PCs, notebooks, tablet computers, and mobile phones.

Taking/*Action* Communicate at Work

Joan was excited about her first day of work as a clerk at an auto dealership. Marion, who was training her, took time to show her how to answer the phones. "Good morning (or afternoon). Midwest Motors, Joan speaking. How may I help you?"

Next, Marion showed Joan the list of do's and don'ts for answering customer questions and transferring calls. The list was ten pages long! Marion said that it was very important for Joan to read the list carefully and to learn how to answer customer calls as quickly as possible. Joan would need to be very professional on the phone. "After all," Marion told her, "first impressions of a business tend to stay with customers."

Marion advised Joan that the best way to handle customer calls was to listen carefully. "Customers usually tell you what they need. If they don't, then ask a few questions and listen again."

Later, Marion showed Joan how to use the office email system. She explained that the different departments within the dealership frequently used email to communicate with each other. Joan was pleased that the spell checker worked in the same way as the software she had used for school projects. She always liked to check her spelling before she sent out anything written.

Finally, Marion showed Joan how to use the computer's printer. The printer had scanning, faxing, and copying capabilities.

A few weeks later, Marion stopped by Joan's desk one day to talk to her. "I just wanted to let you know that the quality of your work is being noticed," she said. Marion continued, "You are friendly and professional with customers, and your emails and faxes are clear and error-free. Keep up the good work!"

THINK CRITICALLY

1. For which tasks does Joan use her communication skills?

2. Why is it important to have good communication skills at work?

✳ Success Tip

Almost every profession will require you to use different types of communication.

Andresr/Shutterstock.com

OBJECTIVES
- Identify three types of skills required to be successful on the job
- State guidelines for effective listening
- Discuss rules for effective speaking

KEY TERMS
- pronunciation
- enunciation
- standard English
- grammar

SusanHSmith/iStockphoto.com

Career Decisions

Joyce works at Meadows Garden Center as a stock handler. She loves her work and takes excellent care of the plants. But, Joyce's boss Mrs. Ramirez, often has to correct her grammar, spelling, and math. Mrs. Ramirez is very complimentary of Joyce's work with the plants, but tells her that the garden work itself isn't enough. Joyce listens to her boss patiently even though she doesn't actually agree with her. "I bet I can get easily get another job taking care of plants at a place where they appreciate my work," Joyce thinks to herself.

What would you do?

Communication Skills

To be successful on the job, you need three types of skills: (a) occupational skills, (b) employability skills, and (c) basic academic skills. *Occupational skills* are the technical or manual abilities unique to a certain occupation. People learn these skills through career and technical education or other types of education and training programs.

Certain skills, such as honesty, good grooming, and a positive attitude, are required in all jobs. These are examples of *employability skills*.

Workers need basic *academic skills*, too. This chapter deals with communication skills, one set of academic skills. Communication involves sending information, ideas, or feelings from one person to another. This is done through language. Language may be spoken or written. Before communication can take place, a receiver must understand the language. Communication, therefore, involves listening, speaking, reading, and writing.

Listen

Communication links the working world. Listening may be its weakest link. It has been said that poor listening costs employers billions of dollars every year.

Poor listening takes many forms. For instance, the boss told Murray to include price lists with the report he was about to mail out to the district sales managers. Murray was not listening carefully and sent out just the report. A couple of days later, the phones started ringing. The agents wondered where their price lists were. Murray knew he had goofed. He sent out a second mailing right away. By not following directions, Murray cost the company time and money. Common causes of poor listening include distractions, prejudging, over stimulation, and partial listening.

It is important to give your full attention to the person who is speaking.

samotrebizan/iStockphoto.com

Distractions

Have you ever thought of something else while someone was talking? It's often hard not to do this. Most people talk at a rate of about 125 words per minute. The average mind can handle about 600 to 800 words per minute. This means that there is a gap between the rate at which people are able to speak and the rate at which listeners are capable of thinking. Therefore, the mind tends to wander.

A *distraction* is something that diverts your attention. For instance, suppose you are talking to the boss and someone turns on a noisy machine. Perhaps the workplace lighting flickers on and off. Your mind might focus on the distraction. Other common distractions are telephone calls, changes in temperature, and new smells. What kinds of problems could being distracted cause later?

Prejudging

Sometimes listeners try to outguess the speaker. This is called *prejudging*. Here is an example. Mrs. Krause asked to meet with the salesclerks before the store opened. Carla began to feel nervous. She thought that Mrs. Krause was going to criticize her for something she had done. She started to think what her answer would be. But Mrs. Krause just wanted to review check-approval policies. Carla had prejudged what Mrs. Krause was going to say. As it turned out, Mrs. Krause complimented Carla. She was the only one who was doing that task correctly!

Over Stimulation

Another cause of poor listening is *over stimulation*, which occurs when a listener becomes too eager to respond to the speaker. Mr. Costa was demonstrating to Lee and the other apprentices how to adjust an air compressor and spray gun. He said that enamel requires a higher air pressure than lacquer. He misspoke—lacquer requires higher air pressure. Lee caught the error and could not wait to correct him. He was so eager to point out the mistake that he didn't pay attention to the rest of the demonstration.

Partial Listening

Partial listening can take several forms, including *fragmented listening* and *pretend listening*. Fragmented listening occurs when the listener listens only for certain things. For example, Harold works as a graphic artist for a large department store. Twice a year, the store manager talks to all employees about company goals. The only time Harold pays attention is when the manager says something about the art department.

Pretend listening is when the listener either doesn't care what is going on or is waiting for a turn to talk. Margo is a maintenance worker for the same company as Harold. She thinks it is a waste of time for maintenance workers to attend the manager's presentation. Though she pretends to listen, she thinks about everything but company plans and goals. By not concentrating on the message being delivered, Harold and Margo miss very important information.

The following are some guidelines for good listening. Rate yourself in terms of how good a listener you are. You should

Music devices should be turned off during a conversation.

- Have a questioning attitude. Good listeners want to understand what is being said.
- Concentrate on what is being said. Listening requires effort and active participation.
- Eliminate distractions by turning off noisy machines, shutting doors, closing your notebook computer, and moving closer to the speaker.
- Use your eyes as well as your ears and mind. Observe the facial expressions and body language of the speaker. These are often as important as what is said.
- Listen between the lines for what the speaker does not say. The Coldwell Company's president told workers that someone had bought the company. Though he did not say so, it sounded as if the plant might be relocated.
- Get all the facts before evaluating or reacting to them.
- Write down important things before you forget them.
- Ask questions if you do not understand something.

Speak Clearly

Effective speaking requires correct pronunciation, clear enunciation, use of standard English, and good grammar.

Correct Pronunciation

Pronunciation is the way in which words are spoken. Most words have several syllables. For instance, the word candidate has three syllables: can-di-date. Correct pronunciation means saying the proper sound for each syllable and accenting the right syllable. In this word, the second syllable often is mispronounced without the "d" as candidate. Note also that the first syllable should be accented: can'-di-date.

Clear Enunciation

Enunciation refers to how distinctly or clearly you speak. Many people, for instance, don't clearly enunciate contractions such as we're. That is, they say "wer" instead of "we're." How do you say we're?

Poor enunciation and bad pronunciation often go together. As a result, words like *are* and *our* often sound alike. The same is true for *fire* and *far*. Say these two pairs of words out loud to find out how clearly you enunciate.

Use Standard English

American English takes many forms. One is the informal slang that many teenagers use. Can you give some examples? It's fun to speak like this with friends. Informal slang is nonstandard English. So is poor grammar. **Standard English** is the usual form of language used by the majority of Americans. Most employers will expect you to use standard English on the job.

Good Grammar

Since grade school, you have studied grammar in language arts and English classes. **Grammar** is a set of rules about correct speaking and writing. All languages have dozens of rules.

Grammar rules are pretty easy to understand. Even so, many people continue to say things like "they ain't here" instead of "they aren't here." Can you think of reasons why people break so many grammar rules when they speak?

Why should you use good grammar? Well, your ability to get and keep a job may depend on it! How you speak makes an impression on an employer. Suppose you are interviewing people for a job. Two applicants have strong

Speaking clearly with good grammar leads to pleasant conversation.

job skills. One says things such as "I done it" and "I couldn't find it nowhere." The other person speaks correctly. Which applicant would you hire? Poor grammar may cause an employer to doubt your ability. It can also turn away customers.

9-1 Assessment

1. What three types of skills are needed to succeed on the job?
2. Name and provide an example of each of the four common causes of poor listening.
3. What does having a "questioning attitude" when listening mean?
4. What are the four things required to be an effective speaker?
5. Why is good grammar important for job success?

High Growth Occupations
FOR THE 21ST CENTURY

Self-enrichment Education Teachers

Do you have a special skill or talent such as playing a musical instrument, drawing or painting, or perhaps skill in a foreign language? If so, you might consider teaching your skill or talent to others as a self-enrichment teacher.

Self-enrichment education teachers provide instruction on a wide variety of subjects that students take for fun or self-improvement. Some teach classes that provide students with useful life skills, such as cooking, personal finance, and time management. Others provide group instruction intended solely for recreation, such as photography, pottery, and painting. Many others provide one-on-one instruction in a variety of subjects, including singing, or playing a musical instrument.

Some teachers conduct courses on academic subjects, such as math, grammar and composition, and foreign languages, in a nonacademic setting. The classes taught by self-enrichment teachers seldom lead to a degree and attendance is voluntary. At the same time, these courses can provide students with useful skills which make them more attractive to employers.

Many of the classes that self-enrichment educators teach are short in duration, some finish in one or two days or several weeks. These brief classes tend to be introductory in nature and generally focus on only one topic, such as a cooking class that teaches bread-making.

Most self-enrichment teachers are self-employed and work part time. Some have several part-time teaching assignments, but it is most common for teachers to have a full-time job in another occupation.

Many classes for adults are held in the evenings and on weekends to accommodate students who have a job or family responsibilities. Similarly, self-enrichment classes for children are usually held after school, on weekends, or during school vacations.

In general, there are few educational or training requirements for a job as a self-enrichment teacher beyond having knowledge and skill in the subject taught. Business skills are also required to market services, attract students, collect fees, and maintain account records.

CREATISTA/Shutterstock.com

Self-enrichment teachers often provide individualized instruction.

READ AND WRITE

OBJECTIVES

- Describe ways to improve reading skills
- Identify different forms of written business communication
- Explain newer communication technologies

KEY TERMS

- information communications technology (ICT)
- paperless office
- barcode
- QR code
- radio frequency identification

Personal Decisions

You come home from school grumbling about the grade you received on a written assignment. The teacher always marks off for misspelled words regardless of how good the paper is otherwise. You tell your sister Amy that you do not think it is fair.

"If I were you, I would not worry about it," says Amy. "You do not have to be concerned about spelling when you get out of school. At work, we use word processing software that automatically identifies and then corrects any spelling errors."

What would you do?

Protomorphic/iStockphoto.com

Read

Like listening, reading is a way to receive information. Both require concentration and understanding. More so than listening, however, reading requires recognizing words before you can understand their meaning. Language is like a code. Unless you can recognize and attach meaning to it, you can't understand it.

Can you recognize and understand these English words: glabella, larrikin, neap, and scrieve. Are any of them familiar to you? Probably not. The words might as well be written in Italian (unless, of course, you know that language). This points out the importance of vocabulary. Your vocabulary is the total of all the words you know. You cannot understand what you read unless you know the meaning of the words used.

Improve Your Vocabulary

Your vocabulary already consists of thousands of words. Keep adding new words to your vocabulary. Do not just pass over words that you don't know. As you find new words, look up their meanings in a printed or online dictionary. Small electronic dictionaries are very convenient as are mobile phones with an internet connection. After you learn a word, use it in your speaking and writing. Vocabulary building is a lifelong task.

Practice Reading

Because reading is a skill, people can improve it through practice. Reading newspapers, magazines, and online content is a good way to practice. So, too, is reading material in your field. You will improve your reading and learn at the same time. Sometimes you need to read some things that are not interesting to you. On your own time you can read about your interests, hobbies and other topics of interest. If you don't want to spend money, check out materials from a public library, or take advantage of the many newspaper and magazine sites on the Web.

Write

Workers often spend less time writing than listening, speaking, or reading. Even so, writing is probably the most important form of business communication. This is because good business practices require that permanent records be kept of all business operations, transactions, and agreements. Denny learned this the hard way.

Denny was asked to answer the phone while the boss went out. He took two calls and left messages on her desk. A few moments after she returned, Denny saw the boss approaching.

"Who are these messages from?" she said. "I can't read them."

What could Denny say?

Written communication takes place within a company and between organizations. Internal communication takes the form of notes, business forms, and memorandums. External communication mainly takes the form of business letters. Increasingly, electronic mail is being used for both internal and external communication.

Handwritten messages should be written neatly.

Mastertasso/Shutterstock.com

Notes and Business Forms

A note is the most informal type of written business communication. A note may be a short handwritten message or an email. Business forms are another type of written communication. Most of these forms are provided as templates on a computer. Businesses use forms to record business operations. Here are some examples of common business forms:

- Petty cash form
- Quotation form
- Packing list
- Sales call report
- Job work order
- Receiving form
- Purchase order
- Stock requisition
- Invoice

Notes and business forms are usually simple to complete. However, they need to be readable and accurate. For a message to be readable, write or key it neatly. Spell words correctly. If you aren't sure about the spelling of a word, check a dictionary. Always check messages for possible errors before transmitting them.

If you are using software to compose a message, run the spelling and grammar checkers before sending it. Then proofread the message for errors the spelling and grammar checkers may have missed (for example, if you keyed hat instead of that).

Email

Within companies, email is the main form of written communication. Email carries messages upward, downward, and across departmental lines. For example, a stock clerk may write an email to a boss. The boss may respond with an email to the department. Or you may send an email to someone in another department. Email is convenient and inexpensive. It allows a user to electronically send, receive, and store messages 24 hours a day. Messages can be easily organized and stored in electronic files for future reference. A major advantage of email is that multiple copies of a message can be transmitted as easily and inexpensively as a single copy.

Emails deal with most business matters. They are usually brief. Their tone tends to be rather informal. Emails are used to communicate four types of information:

- Instructions or explanations
- Announcements and reports
- Requests for information, action, or reaction
- Answers to requests

Little introductory information is necessary in an email. The first paragraph is used to explain the purpose of the email. Emails should be limited to one main topic. Headings, underlining, or capitalization of words can be used to call attention to key points. When you use email, the information fields such as To, Cc, and Subject, appear automatically. See Figure 9-1 for a sample email.

A *signature block* is a few lines of text that may be automatically added to the end of every email you send. The signature block contains your name, your title (if you have one), your company name, and contact information not already listed in the email. Phone numbers are an example of contact information that may be included in signature blocks.

In emails sent to only one person, include a brief salutation at the beginning such as the receiver's first name. If you don't have a signature block, key in your contact information. Do not send an email with a blank subject line as some email screening software may automatically send it to the junk mail folder or the receiver might not open it.

FIGURE 9-1 Sample Email

From: Carl Roark
Sent: Tuesday, September 13, 2012 3:59 PM
To: Marketing Department
Cc: Carol Evans
Subject: Part-time temp

Good morning everyone

We have a part-time temp, Kelly Jones, starting today who will be working with us the next several weeks. She will be working Monday through Wednesday each week. Kelly will be located in a center cube near the copy room. She will be working closely with Anne.

Please welcome her.

Carl Roark
Assistant to Carol Evans
Jefferson Company
888-888-8888

FIGURE 9-2 Email Policies for a Business

Email Policies

1. The company email system is for business use only. Personal use of email is strictly prohibited.
2. Check for messages at the start of your shift and several times throughout the day.
3. Do not use email for information that is sensitive or confidential. Consult with your supervisor beforehand if you have any doubts about whether to send an email.
4. Do not forward a message to another party without permission of the original sender.
5. Copy your message only to those who need to receive the message or reply.
6. When using the Reply feature, put your comments at the top of the message. Avoid including the entire message with your response.
7. To conserve storage space on the server, delete files you no longer need on a regular basis. Be aware, however, that deleted messages still exist on backup tapes.
8. Don't send email messages just because you can. This is a waste of your and your coworkers' time.
9. Although email is often informal, keep in mind that the email reflects on you and the company. Correct spelling, grammar, and punctuation are still important.
10. Write descriptive subject lines to help direct the reader's attention.
11. An email should have a good appearance. Do not key in all caps or all lowercase letters.
12. Use of standard acronyms is permitted, such as ASAP. But do not overuse acronyms or use acronyms that are more appropriate for personal communications, such as ROFL (rolling on floor laughing).
13. Do not send jokes, political cartoons, articles, offensive photos, chain emails, links to social media or videos, or anything else that is in violation of the company's employee handbook.

Companies provide email policies to their employees. Figure 9-2 shows typical email policies.

Memos may be created in word processing software using the templates provided in the software. Such memos are sent by email.

Business Letters

Business letters are used when more formal writing is needed. The average worker is more likely to write notes and emails on the job than business letters. However, it is important to know how to write a good business letter. Job searches and insurance claims are two business areas that still use business letters. A business letter should:

- Communicate a clear message.
- Convey a professional, businesslike tone.
- Be well organized.
- Use correct grammar, spelling, and punctuation.
- Have an attractive appearance.

A sample business letter with its major parts labeled is shown in Figure 9-3. The letter uses block style. In block style, all lines (except the printed letterhead) begin at the left margin. The letter uses *open punctuation*, which means there is no punctuation after the salutation or complimentary close. An alternative is mixed punctuation. *Mixed punctuation* means using a colon after the salutation and a comma after the complimentary close.

FIGURE 9-3 The Main Parts of a Business Letter

2" or center vertically

Northern University
2134 Central Avenue
Albany, NY 12201-4396
(518) 555-0100

Date August 29, 20—   **4 line returns**

Letter address
Cooperative Education Student
Central High School
1900 W. Main St.
Muncie, IN 47302-1416

Salutation Dear Student

1" or default
Business letters should be keyed on good-quality, white, standard-size (8½- by 11-inch) paper. They should be single-spaced. Double spacing should be used between paragraphs, before and after the salutation, and before the complimentary close. Four line returns should be used between the date and the letter address. Four line returns should also be used between the complimentary close and the keyed writer's name to provide space for the writer's signature.

1" or default

Body Center letters vertically or set a top margin of 2 inches. If you use your word processor's center page feature, insert two line returns below the last keyed line to put the letter in reading position. Set side margins at 1 inch or use the default settings for your word processor. The bottom margin should be at least 1 inch.

Most businesses have letterheads that include their address. If your employer does not, key the business's address (the return address) before the date, as in the letter on page 103.

Preparing a letter correctly and keying it neatly help make a favorable impression on the reader. A proper business letter shows evidence of a sincere and serious interest in the subject being conveyed. Use a business letter for all of your important written communication.

Complimentary close Sincerely   **4 line returns**
John J. Burns

Writer John J. Burns
Writer's title Professor

about 1" minimum

Many individuals and companies use templates for business letters. A template will already include the major format elements shown. This saves time and maintains a uniform style for the organization. Also, most word-processing software has templates for business letters.

When writing a business letter, make a draft copy first. Then rewrite the letter as necessary. Before sending it, read the letter carefully for errors. As a final step, save your letter. Remember to back up electronic files regularly.

Communication Technologies

The evolution of computers, software, electronic business equipment, and new forms of digital and radio frequency coding have changed business communications in very significant ways.

Electronic Equipment and Devices

Among the most significant technological developments in history are the computer, the Internet, and various types of devices based on computer chip and laser technologies. These technologies have forever changed personal communication, what workers do, and how business is conducted. Several decades ago, business communication was considered to be the exchange of knowledge and information within and outside the organization to achieve goals of the business. Traditional forms of communications were printed, written, verbal, or auditory.

Information communications technology (ICT) refers to electronic tools and equipment that store, retrieve, manipulate, transmit, or receive information electronically in digital form. ICT is replacing many traditional forms of business communication. Devices that provide ICT include computers, mobile phones, cameras, handheld games, multifunction copiers and printers, cash registers, magnetic stripe card readers, and ATM machines.

Workers still communicate through spoken or written words. But, more and more of their time is spent keyboarding, clicking a mouse, using a touch screen, and interacting in numerous ways with stationary and mobile electronic devices.

Email allows businesses to communicate and send information to remote locations worldwide. Information and data are stored in electronic files rather than in file cabinets. Mobile smart phones and tablet computers allow workers to communicate and conduct business anywhere and at anytime.

A **paperless office** is a work environment in which the use of paper and traditional forms of communication are eliminated or greatly reduced. Many offices are on the way to becoming paperless.

Benefits of a paperless office include increased productivity, cost savings, reduced need for storage of printed documents, improved speed for retrieving and sharing information, and reduced damage to the environment.

Goodluz/Shutterstock.com

Many workers use multiple communication devices at the same time.

Digital Communications

Less familiar but extremely important types of digital communication technologies use laser and imaging technology and radio frequency identification to collect and manage data. You have seen barcode labels printed on food packages that are used to automate supermarket checkout systems. The simplest type of **barcode** consists of varying widths and spacings of parallel lines. Figure 9-4 displays a variety of common bar codes.

The primary purpose of a barcode is to quickly and accurately access information through the code using some type of reader or scanner. A handheld or stationary scanner uses a light source to illuminate the bars and spaces on the barcode. A sensor reads the reflected light from the barcode and generates a digital signal. Finally, a decoder using special software decodes the signal into readable text that is displayed on a monitor. Some of the most common applications of barcode technology include:

- Almost every type of consumer product available from a commercial retail store has a UPC barcode on it.
- Retail membership cards issued by "big box" retailers, grocery stores, health insurance companies, and even driver's licenses have bar codes to identify consumers.
- Hospitals and clinics use barcode wristbands for patient identification and to access patient data and history instantaneously.
- The movement of various items such as mail, package delivery, airline luggage, and rental cars are tracked using barcodes.
- Library checkout of books is easier and faster using barcodes on books, magazines, DVDs, and other materials and media.
- Airlines use barcoding on boarding passes and even send barcodes to passenger's mobile phones to allow electronic self check-in.
- Barcoded event tickets allow customers to more quickly enter sporting events, concerts, theaters, and other entertainment locations.

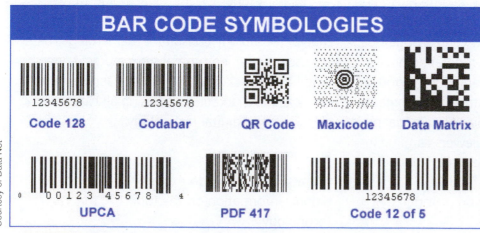

Courtesy of Data Net

FIGURE 9-4 These are common types of bar codes.

One of the newer types of barcodes is the QR code (or Quick Response code). The **QR code** is a two-dimensional code consisting of black modules arranged in a square pattern on a white background. The coded information can be a website, text, or other type of data.

The increasing use of QR codes, especially in advertising, is due to greater availability and use of mobile smart phones. The QR code can be read by a special barcode reader or camera phone. Because more people now use smart phones and tablet computers, it is very easy to use the phone or computer camera to click on an image of the code which then directs you to an online destination. See Figure 9-5 on the next page for an advertisement containing a QR code.

Workplace Innovations

USING WEBSITES IN NEW WAYS

The funeral home industry is usually thought of as very traditional and conservative. However, funeral homes are now incorporating technology in all phases of the funeral process. Many companies provide websites that offer preplanning services for families or individuals to plan and personalize a later funeral. For example, one can write his or her obituary, upload photos or videos, share special memories with family and friends, select favorite music and writings, choose a casket or cremation urn, and design a headstone. All of this can be done free online without ever visiting a funeral home.

After a death occurs, funeral homes work with families to send out death announcements quickly via various social media. A memorial page can be posted online where viewers can find information about scheduled services, sign a guestbook and share condolences, and view a video tribute and/or other information provided by the deceased.

At the visitation, a photo slideshow with accompanying music is often shown. Printed materials passed out at the visitation or funeral may contain a QR code linked to a Web obituary or tribute. QR codes may also be used on the cemetery headstone. Family members or friends are often unable to get to the funeral for a variety of reasons. So, some funeral homes offer real-time webcasts of the funeral for people who cannot attend. Later, the webcast can be posted online as a permanent memorial.

To assist funeral homes in learning to use technology, a new type of entrepreneur called a *funeral technology consultant* is emerging. These are usually certified funeral service practitioners who have a background in funeral services and are skilled in marketing and using all types of electronic and digital technology.

NET FOLLOW-UP

Use a search engine to explore the Web for additional information on the topic of "funeral technology".

There is no question that grocery line checkouts have been accelerated due to the use of UPC barcodes. Even with barcodes, however, the checkout line sometimes gets quite long. But, soon such lines could disappear due to a newer technology called **radio frequency identification (RFID)**. This is a type of system that transmits the identity of a product using radio waves.

Think how cool it would be to go to the grocery store, fill up your cart, and then walk right out the door. Instead of having a clerk scan each item, each of the products in your cart having an RFID tag will automatically communicate with an electronic reader. The reader will calculate your bill and notify your bank, after which the amount of your grocery purchase will be deducted from your checking account.

RFID technology is not yet as common as barcodes, but it is currently being used for EZPass through toll road booths and to pay for gasoline purchases at stations having SpeedPass. Currently, some of the largest retailers such as WalMart, Target, and Best Buy are using RFID in supply chain management. It is probably only a matter of time until they start using the technology for consumer transactions.

FIGURE 9-5 QR codes may be included in advertisements.

COREY LOWENSTEIN/MCT/Landov

9-2 Assessment

1. In what ways are listening and reading the same?

2. List two ways to improve reading skills.

3. Why is writing probably the most important form of business communication?

4. Email is used to communicate four types of information. Name them.

5. What four steps should be followed in writing a business letter?

6. What are three advantages of using electronic mail?

7. What new forms of "writing" have emerged as a result of ICT?

8. What is the primary purpose of barcode technology?

9. What is the difference between barcodes and RFID?

OBJECTIVES

- Understand rules for effective communication
- Discuss how face-to-face communication can help avoid and solve workplace conflicts
- Identify ways to participate effectively in a task group

KEY TERMS

- discretion
- videoconferencing (VC)
- task group
- virtual team

Paul Matthew Photography/
Shutterstock.com

▶ Interpersonal Decisions

You enjoy being in the club and are always eager to help out. In fact, you probably do more than anyone else. It is getting to the point that whenever something needs to be done, club members look to you. You have been asked a number of times recently to substitute for someone who has other plans. Some members seem to be taking advantage of your willingness to always pitch in.

What would you do?

Communication Using Technology

Have you ever played "telephone tag" with another person whom you fail to reach by phone and are forced to leave a message on their voice-mail? The person returns your call later only to discover that you are unavailable, so a message is left for you. This can continue for several cycles before you are finally able to connect with the other person.

Today, telephone tag is much less common because electronic communication using email and text messaging is becoming the preferred means of personal and business communication. In fact, now voicemail can be emailed to your computer. Businesses are finding this more convenient and less expensive. Electronic communication changes interpersonal relations. It does not change the need for good interpersonal skills.

Telephone Skills

Using the telephone is part of a job search. Proper use of the telephone is also required on the job. An employee represents the company in a business transaction. An employee's time also costs the business money. Therefore, an effective speaker conducts telephone conversations with courtesy and efficiency.

Answer a Business Call

When answering a business call, you should observe these guidelines:

- Answer in a pleasant, helpful tone of voice. Identify the company at once. For example, you might say, "Hello, Edwards and Company" or "Edwards and Company, may I help you?"

- Listen attentively as the caller gives the reason for calling. Be prepared to record a phone message. If you take a message, record complete information: the date, the time, the caller's name and number, the nature of the call, and any follow-up action required.

- Route the call to the person best able to meet the caller's need. An appropriate response would be, "Thank you, I'll transfer you to Mr. Weber, our sales manager."

- If the caller wants to talk to a specific person, you might ask, "May I tell her who is calling?"

- Often, the desired person will not be able to accept the call. In this case, your response might be, "I'm sorry, Mrs. Knight is away from her desk. Would you like me to take a message or do you prefer her voicemail?"

- Always fulfill your promise to the caller. Pass on the message, track down the correct information, return the call yourself, or do whatever else is required.

- Don't cut off a conversation with a statement like "I've got to hang up so that I can take another call."

- Pleasantly conclude all calls; for example, "Thank you for calling."

Place a Business Call

Similar courtesies should be used when placing a business call. Follow these rules:

- Before placing a call, write down the points you want to cover.

- If you are placing an order, complete a written order form beforehand.

- Identify yourself at once and state your reason for calling. For example, you might say, "Hello, this is Arnold Swartz at Midwest Publishers. I'm calling to inquire if our order is ready to be picked up."

- Name the person or department you are trying to reach. After identifying yourself, say something like, "I would like to speak with Mr. Sullivan in the service department."

- If you anticipate having more than a brief conversation, ask whether it is a convenient time to talk.

- Talk in a warm and friendly tone. Be direct and businesslike.

Polite Telephone Behavior

Some businesses or organizations have special rules or requirements for telephone use. For example, you should always ask permission from the other party in a conversation before switching to a speaker phone. **Discretion** is behaving or speaking in a way that avoids causing offense or revealing private information. Individuals who work in attorney's offices, financial institutions, medical facilities and other workplaces where private matters are discussed need to use discretion and be aware of the volume of their phone conversations.

Polite behavior also applies to things you might happen to overhear from someone else's conversation. Don't repeat information you were not meant to hear and resist the temptation to butt into a phone conversation in an effort to be "helpful." Usually, any special rules or guidelines regarding phone behavior that is required will be a part of your on-the-job training or new employee orientation.

Text Messages

Text messaging, or texting, is the exchange of brief written messages over a network. Most texting is done between mobile phones, but messages can also be sent and received by some fixed-line phones and many other types of electronic devices. The maximum length of a cellphone text message is 160 characters of the English alphabet. Spaces between words count as a character.

While texting is used mostly for personal communication, it has become increasingly popular as a method of business communication. Appropriate ways to use texting in business include communicating to sales reps a change in the meeting room location, to update outdoor workers of changing weather conditions, or to notify a shipper of the receipt of an important package. Whenever it is necessary or desirable to communicate with a customer, client or coworker instantly and easily, a text message may be the appropriate means.

Although texting is by nature more casual, the rules for clarity and professionalism apply to business texting. Rules for correct grammar, spelling, and punctuation also apply. Following are additional guidelines for business texting:

You should maintain a professional tone for business texts.

- Never text when operating a motor vehicle or other type of equipment. It is unsafe and may also be illegal, depending on your locale.

- Texting should only be used for brief communications. If a topic is complicated or requires more than a short message, send an email or ask when would be a good time to call.

- Make sure you are texting to the correct phone number. It is easy to make a mistake using a small keyboard. Select the phone number from your contacts list if possible and always double-check the number for accuracy before sending.

- Think about the timing of your message. Even though many people keep their mobile phones with them at all times, sending texts at non-business hours may be frowned upon.

- Do not text while in a meeting, in the presence of others, or any other time when you are expected to be engaged in what is going on around you.

There are some jobs and some industries that may not allow texting. Individuals who sell financial products are sometimes not allowed to text clients to avoid misinterpretation regarding the amount of financial risk or reward of a product.

Voicemail

When you place a call, you often hear a message like this: "Hello, this is Graham Bell. I am away from my desk for a short time. Please leave a message following the beep." Many businesses use computerized telephone answering systems known as voicemail. These systems can direct calls to a specific individual or extension and also allow callers to leave messages. Often these messages are sent to the email of the person you are calling.

Voicemail is best used to communicate a short message. You might use it, for example, to remind a patient of a forthcoming appointment or to request that a client return your call. Messages left on a voicemail system should be brief, clear, and complete. Follow these guidelines:

Business voice messages should be clear, brief, and complete.

- Greet the recipient and identify yourself and your company. State your telephone number, even if you are not asking that the call be returned. For example, you might say, "Hello, Mrs. Cristobel. This is Julian Curtis at Cyberworks. My number is 555-0129."

- Provide a brief message, such as "I'm calling to confirm our meeting on Thursday afternoon at 3 P.M."

- Invite the listener to contact you if necessary. Say, for example, "If you have questions prior to the meeting, please give me a call."

- Conclude the call in such a way that the recipient will know you have completed the message. Say, for example, "I am looking forward to meeting you tomorrow."

You may hear a recorded message that includes a statement saying that "I am available by mobile phone at 123-1231." By providing an alternate mobile phone number, you have been given permission to call the number.

A message recorded for the voicemail system at work should be businesslike. A workplace message may also be changed frequently to reflect your appointment and travel schedules. Here's an example: "Hello, this is Jenny McCormack. I will be traveling most of the day on Tuesday, October 17, but will be checking messages frequently. Please leave a message and I will return your call as soon as possible."

Remote Communications

Many businesses have multiple locations throughout the United States, and even internationally. Bringing employees from different sites together for a meeting or conference can involve much expense, travel time, and lost productivity. As a result, companies use various types of communication technologies to interact with employees at remote locations.

Videoconferencing (VC) is technology that allows two or more locations to interact via two-way audio and video transmissions. As an entry-level employee, it is likely that your participation in a VC would be for training purposes or perhaps as part of a new employee orientation program. To participate in a VC, follow these guidelines:

- Review any preconference material that was provided. For example, you might be given recommendations for what type and color of clothing to wear. Or, to avoid wearing big, shiny, clanking jewelry.

- Turn off your mobile phone during the conference.

- If there is a chairperson, pay attention and show respect as the chair's role is to coordinate the meeting.
- Be ready to respond if you are asked to introduce yourself.
- If an agenda is provided, study it to get an overview of the conference. Take note of any opportunities to ask questions.
- Do not carry on any side conversations.
- Behave and act naturally. You are looking and being looked at as you would in any normal meeting.
- If you do speak, look at the camera and be aware of the positions of microphones and speak clearly in your normal tone of voice.

Historically, VC began as two-way televised sessions in which one site was designated as the local site and the other as the remote site. They were conducted using expensive dedicated equipment in special rooms and required major technical know-how to set up and operate.

Since the late 1990s, the use of *switched circuit communication lines (ISDN)* has gradually given way to Internet-based systems. Network bandwidth has increased as costs have decreased. Advances in computers, peripherals, and software have improved considerably. Web-based computer systems provide more features than traditional VC systems. These include chat areas, shared software applications, whiteboards, web browsing, PowerPoint presentations, and recording and playback capabilities.

Many corporations, universities, and other institutions still conduct VC in special dedicated rooms to conduct training and large meetings. Increasingly, however, the trend is toward conducting VC using desktop and mobile computers. The terms *webcast* (one-way communication) and *webina*r (two-way communication) are often used to describe these newer approaches to web conferencing.

Face-to-Face Communication

A simple definition of communication is the verbal or non-verbal exchange of information. There are many types of communication technologies that allow information to be sent and received instantly and at anytime and anyplace. Even though technology makes the exchange of information easier and quicker, there are a number of workplace situations where face-to-face communication is much more effective.

Conflicts occur in the workplace just as conflicts occur in our personal lives. They are a normal and natural part of work and life. Sources of workplace conflicts might include personality clashes, unclear definitions of responsibility, competition, cultural differences, and conflicts between personal goals and organizational goals. Although workplace conflicts may appear to be very different, they often share a common characteristic, which is that communication is both the cause and the solution of the conflict.

When managers, employees, and coworkers rely too much on technology for communication, misunderstandings can occur. For example, the following text message was sent from a team leader to a team member: "Thanks for your input today; you should speak more often in meetings." The team leader intended the message to be a compliment, but the team member interpreted it as a criticism for lack of participation in previous meetings. What was missing in this instance was the face-to-face interaction. Think how different the interpretation would have been if the team leader said this in person with a warm tone of voice, a smile on her face, and a handshake.

Nonverbal communication is often essential to communicating accurately and effectively. What is said in a message certainly matters, but so does voice inflection, eye contact, posture, facial expressions, and body language. When a person shows sincerity in her or his conversation and body language, the listener can see and feel the sincerity of the speaker. Face-to-face communication helps reduce gaps in communication and helps lead to resolution of a variety of workplace problems.

🔍 Search the Net

Access **www.cengage.com/school/ working** and click on the link for Chapter 9. Read the NASA press release. What do you think is the purpose of the Stafford-Covey Return to Flight Task Group? Surf the Web to find the conclusions of this important task group.

www.cengage.com/school/working

Task Groups

Most people, at least some of the time, work in groups. These are called task groups or work groups. A **task group** is a work group formed to accomplish a particular objective.

Purposes of Task Groups

Groups are often formed to brainstorm a new product, discuss quality control problems, or plan a new sales strategy. There is a trend in business and industry to use more and different types of task groups. But do groups really perform better than individuals?

Groups are generally superior to most individuals at many but not all tasks. A school newspaper, for example, benefits by having different people write columns on events, club activities, and sports. It would be hard for one person to write about all these things. For tasks requiring a lot of effort, groups are faster than individuals. An example is fund raising for a class trip.

Work in Task Groups

The following guidelines will help you work effectively in a group:

- **Show your readiness to help the group.** A group depends on the willingness of each member to accomplish its work. Do your share of the work on a regular basis, and volunteer your efforts from time to time for special group projects.

- **Accept the role the group gives you.** Groups have leaders and followers. Followers are often in greater demand. Pitch in and do whatever the group needs, whether it is recording minutes, stuffing envelopes, or cleaning up after a meeting.

- **Carry out your role as best you can.** Sports teams often have role players who go into the game to do certain things. Role players make a valuable contribution to a team or a group. Do your job well. The group and you will both benefit.

- **Share your views.** Do not hold back on a good idea or suggestion. Your solution may be perfect. Offer your feelings and opinions, even if they differ from what others think. Groups sometimes make poor decisions or choices. If you believe this is the case, say so.

- **Do not dominate meetings.** Someone who talks too much irritates other members. Do not overpower others, even though you may have the right answers or the best ideas.
- **Accept group decisions.** Offer your views during a discussion. But do not argue once the group makes a decision.
- **Encourage other members.** Doing your best on a job will encourage others to do so, too. A kind word from time to time always helps. Remember to pass out compliments and congratulations for a job well done.
- **Think of solutions, not past problems.** Suppose you have a fight with a family member. Dwelling on the problem will not help. Thinking of how to solve it will. The same is true in task groups. Focus on finding solutions to problems.
- **Be proud of group success.** Completing a hard task is very satisfying. Should success come, enjoy it with fellow group members.

As a young worker, your participation in a work group will probably be face-to-face with other group members. At some later point in your career, however, you may be part of a virtual team. A **virtual team** is a small, temporary work group that is separated geographically and who participate in a group project online. Virtual teams communicate electronically and may never meet in person.

Working as part of a virtual team employs the same rules and guidelines discussed above. In addition, you will need to learn new ways of working across boundaries using electronic information and new communication technologies.

9-3 Assessment

1. Name two reasons why proper use of a telephone is important in business.
2. Provide an example of polite telephone behavior that may be unique to a certain business situation.
3. How are the rules for texting similar to other forms of business communication?
4. When is a voicemail message best used?
5. Why are companies using more videoconferencing?
6. How can communication be both a cause and a solution of workplace conflicts?
7. Groups are generally superior to most individuals at many tasks. Give an example.
8. An informal text with a friend might say "C U @ 9 @ mall" or "lol on fouled ball." Would this be an appropriate business text? Why or why not?

BOSSES, COWORKERS, AND CUSTOMERS

OBJECTIVES

- Explain the importance of human relations to success on the job
- Understand how knowledge about different generations can improve the workplace environment
- Discuss ways to get along with bosses and coworkers
- Identify three reasons why customers patronize a particular business

KEY TERMS

- human relations
- interpersonal attraction
- seniority
- territorial rights
- patron
- goodwill

Interpersonal Decisions

You have been cutting and styling Mrs. Laird's hair for about six months. You are beginning to dread her coming into the shop. You like Mrs. Laird, but her young son is a terror. You wish she would not bring him along. He is loud, obnoxious, and disturbs the other customers. He always cries when he does not get his way. You do not want to make Mrs. Laird angry, but something has to be done about the boy.

What would you do?

CandyBox Images/Shutterstock.com

Human Relations

You deal with people every day of your life. You talk, joke, plan, study, and argue. Some of these dealings are more important than others. When you go into a store to buy a quart of milk, your conversation with the clerk will not influence much. A talk with your boss, coworkers, or teacher just might. Your dealings with others influence your happiness and success. They also affect others. Ask Carlos. Guy was supposed to pick up his friend Carlos on the way to school. Guy got up late and, in his hurry to get to school, forgot Carlos. So an unhappy Carlos had to walk two miles to school. He got to school late, missed a test, and had to go to detention after school. Guy's mistake caused problems for Carlos.

Some human relations are pleasant. Others are very difficult. Human relations are interactions among people. Unless you become a hermit, you cannot get away from other people. So you need to develop human relations skills. This is especially true for workers. Many fired workers lose their jobs because they cannot get along with others.

Communicate Across Generations

People are shaped by family heritage and the environment in which they grow up. The *time period* during which an individual is born and raised has an influence on her or his later attitudes, values, and behaviors. A group of individuals born and living at about the same time is a generation. Different generations have been reared, educated, and trained differently. They have learned to work differently and to use tools and technology in certain ways. Specific characteristics of generations often interfere with communication, and this can create problems.

Today's workplace may have workers from four generations. Each generation has been given a unique name and has been described as having certain common characteristics. There is general agreement on the characteristics and behaviors that define each generation.

Understanding different generations can make the work environment less stressful and more productive. However, not all individuals of a particular generation think and act the same. Generational differences do not mean that one generation is better than another.

Traditionalists

This generation was born before 1946. Significant events that occurred during the years of their birth were the Great Depression (1929-1939) and World War II (1939-1945). The parents of traditionalists suffered through the Great Depression and WWII. These parents made great personal sacrifices. The traditionalist generation lived through and may have participated in the Korean and Vietnam Wars. Most of them graduated high school, but few attended college. Their primary access to technology was the radio and a telephone. They communicated largely with paper, pen, and manual typewriters. Traditionalists tend to be private, hard working, cautious, disciplined, and self-sacrificing.

Baby Boomers

World War II ended in 1945. As a result, millions of Americans who fought in the War and who supported the war effort at home returned to more normal lives. This meant marriage and family and the birth of the largest generation of Americans ever. Between 1946 and 1964, 76 million babies were born. This generation has had a tremendous influence on all aspects of American life. Television came along during this generation. They became the first computer literate generation. Many baby boomers attended college and were very career-oriented. They tend to be motivated, competitive, and team-oriented. They have also been called the "Me" generation and the "rock and roll" generation.

Generation X (Gen X)

Members of Gen X were born during the years 1965-1980. Many were raised by career and money-conscious Boomers in comfortable surroundings. Getting a good education was encouraged and going to college was expected. But, many were children of divorced parents and grew up in blended families. They watched color TV and video movies, and played games on personal computers. They are comfortable with

Workforce Trends

Except for older workers, the share of the labor force among age groups is expected to decline during the period 2008–2018. Workers aged 16 to 24 are expected to decrease from 14.3 percent to 12.7 percent. The primary working-age group, those between 25 and 54 years old, is projected to decline from 67.7 percent to 63.5 percent. Workers aged 55 years and older, by contrast, are anticipated to leap from 18.1 percent to 23.9 percent of the labor force during the same period.

most forms of entertainment and business technology and were the first generation to embrace the mobile phone, Internet, email, and text messaging. They tend to marry late, value access to information, work hard to have more time for family and leisure activities, are independent and creative, and are often short on loyalty to an organization.

Generation Y (Gen Y)

Members of Gen Y were born during the years 1981-2000. This is the first generation to grow up in a high tech environment. They have been surrounded at home and school with all forms of high speed entertainment and communications technology. They watch large flat-panel TVs with hundreds of cable channels. The TV may be connected to a game console, a computer, and a digital video recorder. They constantly use mobile phones for talking, texting, taking photos, finding directions, and surfing the Web. They have grown up with more cultural diversity than previous generations. They value technology, are used to being entertained, seek instant gratification, and are social and peer oriented. They face a more pessimistic economic and environmental future than previous generations.

Communication Styles

Members of these four generations have been influenced differently by technology and forms of communication as shown in Figure 9-6. These differences carry over into the workplace. Under the best of circumstances, communication between employers and employees and between coworkers can be difficult. When four different generations of workers are at work, the communication challenges increase.

Individuals from different generations may have different values, different ideas, different approaches to accomplishing a task, and different ways of communicating. All four groups also have much in common. For example, there are few workplaces today and few workers who do not use computers and information technology. Nonetheless, different generations have preferred ways to communicate.

Traditionalist (Before 1946)	Baby Boomer (1946–1964)	Generation X (1965–1980)	Generation Y (1981–2000)
Uses traditional media (TV, newspapers, etc)	Face-to-face communication	Interactive communication style	Comfortable using electronic technologies
Formal written or oral communications	Computer and technology literate	Adapts quickly to new technology	Prefers email, voice mail, and texting
Letters, memos, and phone calls	Uses phone or email to set up meetings	Email and Internet are primary tools	Asks for and gives regular feedback
Face-to-face communication	Body language important	Likes direct, immediate communication	Stays connected electronically and networked
Clear and straightforward style	Open, direct style	Wants information shared on a regular basis	Multi-tasking comes naturally

FIGURE 9-6 Different generations often prefer different communication methods.

Get Along with People at Work

Suppose you and a student whom you do not like find yourselves in the same class. You will probably not need to work closely with that student. On the job, if you need to work closely with someone whom you really do not like, you will need to put your personal feelings aside.

At work you have to deal with all kinds of people. These include bosses, coworkers, and customers. You may like some people more than others. Even so, you must try to get along with everyone. Understanding bosses, coworkers, and customers can make this task easier.

You need to form a good working relationship with your boss. Try to understand the boss's position. Being a boss is not easy. How would you feel if you had to fire someone? Bosses sometimes must do this. They must provide workers with instructions and helpful criticism. Good bosses act in the interest of the company, not out of friendship. Sometimes, workers and bosses become friends. This should not influence their work behavior. The company should come first. If you and your boss are not friends, that is fine. You can still have a good relationship. Some bosses make it a policy not to be friends with people they supervise.

Strong friendships depend on **interpersonal attraction**. Interpersonal attraction is a tendency to be drawn to another person, often because of similar characteristics and preferences. You enjoy being with people who are like you in some ways. You choose such people for friends, and they choose you. At work interpersonal attraction is not as important. What is important is doing your share of the work and following rules.

As a new worker, coworkers will be watching you. They will expect you to do your share of the work. Your coworkers probably will not mind helping you from time to time. They will expect you to do the same when they need help. But your coworkers will not put up with doing their work and yours, too—at least, not for long.

Rules make sure that employees in similar jobs receive equal treatment. If you ignore the rules, you are indicating that you are different or better than the other workers.

Communication at Work

COMMUNICATE WITH BOSSES

- **Keep your boss informed about what you are doing.** Make sure your boss knows how you are progressing on your assignments. If a problem arises, provide the details in a timely way.
- **Speak your boss's language.** Find out how your boss likes to communicate. Some supervisors like brief conversations. Others prefer email.
- **Be considerate of your boss's time.** Supervisors are busy. If you must speak to your supervisor, arrange a convenient time for him or her.

THINK CRITICALLY

1. Is it ever appropriate to discuss personal matters with your boss? If so, when?
2. What is another way to improve your communication with your boss?

Be aware of how long coworkers have been in their jobs. **Seniority** refers to the length of time someone has worked for a company. Workers with the most seniority have the most privileges. Respecting seniority rules helps you get along with coworkers.

Territorial rights are unwritten rules concerning respect for the property and territory of others. Some workers feel that they control a certain office, area, or sales territory. When you are on their turf, they expect you to behave as they wish. An example might be that you are not supposed to use someone's tools without asking permission first. Be alert for such things. Try to respect others' territorial rights.

Doing your share of the work and following the rules lead to good feelings among coworkers. Other ways to maintain good relationships with coworkers include the following:

- **Appearance** Maintain good hygiene and dress appropriately.
- **Courtesy** Be pleasant, friendly, and courteous. Do not force relationships with coworkers.
- **Attitude** Be positive. Do not complain about your job.
- **Interest** Show interest in the job. Pay attention to what coworkers are doing and show them you feel their interests are important.
- **Loyalty** Do not criticize the company or gossip about coworkers.
- **Tolerance** Try to tolerate the opinions, habits, and behaviors of coworkers. Being different is all right. Marta is a vegetarian. From her, some coworkers have learned more about good eating habits.
- **Maturity** Be agreeable, avoid arguments, and talk through conflicts.
- **Dependability** Always do what you say you will do. Quinn agreed to work overtime on Saturday afternoons. Last Saturday would have been a great sailing day. Quinn went to work because he had given his word. He would have preferred to have gone sailing.
- **Openness** Be open to suggestions and change. Ask coworkers for advice. Offer to help them.
- **Ethics** Do not try to get ahead at the expense of others. Yolanda is the department's most creative layout artist. She lets her work speak for itself. Yolanda never criticizes the other artists' work to make herself look better.

Get and Keep Customers

The purpose of a business is to make a profit. Some businesses sell goods, such as clothing, hardware, or autos. Others sell services, such as insurance, haircuts, or dry cleaning. A business sells its goods or services to customers.

Customers are called by many names. An accountant may speak of clients, and a nurse, of patients. Clients are the business customers of a professional worker. Patients are persons under treatment or care by a medical practitioner. What about users of library services? In a sense, they are customers, even though

Providing superior customer service can help a business develop loyal customers.

they do not pay for their service directly. They are **patrons**, which are customers of certain service-producing businesses or institutions.

Relationships between employees and customers are important to the success of a business. There are reasons why a customer deals with a certain business. Employees can behave in a way that encourages customers to return. One reason customers patronize a business is they like the product or service provided. To *patronize* means that you trade with or give your business to a certain individual or company. Customers who patronize a business have certain wants or needs. A competent worker who treats customers well encourages business.

Darcy is a landscaper for Sunrise Nursery. Mr. Clements, a client, said he wanted more flowers and shrubs around his house. He did not have anything special in mind. Darcy said she would think about it and call him. She did so and made an appointment with Mr. Clements. Darcy brought design sketches, catalogs, and a price estimate. She had everything Mr. Clements would need to make a decision. Darcy's efforts paid off. She got that job and other new customers in the neighborhood.

Businesses that provide services after a sale also encourage customers. The services may include product repairs and refunds.

A third reason customers return to a business is **goodwill**—acts of kindness, consideration, or assistance. These are the little things about a business. Examples include reputation, honesty, and attitude toward customers. Employees promote goodwill in many ways.

- Shaheen calls as many customers as possible by name. She also knows which ones like to be called by their first names and which by their last.

- Ingmar knows that people often come into the store just to look around. He makes them feel welcome and then stays back until they ask for or seem to need help.

- Some customers at the ice cream shop where Cleveland works have trouble deciding on a flavor. He offers them free samples.

9-4 Assessment

1. What is a major reason why many workers get fired?
2. Attitudes, values, and behaviors are shaped by two major influences. Name them.
3. Identify generational differences in communication styles.
4. How important is it for you to be friends with the boss?
5. Name two ways to get along with coworkers.
6. How should you relate to a coworker whose opinions, habits, or behaviors are different from yours?
7. What should you do if a coworker offers suggestions?
8. What are three reasons why customers deal with a certain business?

Focus on the Workplace

Relate to Workaholics

At some point in your career, you may work for or with a workaholic or become one yourself. Understanding and getting along with workaholics is a special case in human relations. Workaholics are people who are addicted to their work.

Americans are among the hardest working people in the world. In a web article entitled "Are You a Workaholic?" ABC News reported that Americans work an average of 205 more hours a year than Italians, 270 more than the French, and 473 more than Norwegians.

The website *Workaholics Anonymous* has a list of twenty questions that indicate whether you might be a workaholic. For example, is work the activity you like to do best and talk about most? Have your long hours hurt your family or other relationships? Do you work or read during meals?

Workaholics exist in every occupation. It is not necessary to be employed to be one. Many home-makers are workaholics. Workaholics are surprisingly happy. They are doing what they love. If they are in the right job, they can be extremely productive.

More than thirty years ago, Marilyn Machlowitz was one of the first to write about the problem of workaholics. Her early writings are still true today. She pointed out that worka-holics may be among the world's worst workers. They suffer few ills themselves. But they often wind up doing damage to their companies. They frequently create a pressure-cooker atmosphere.

Workaholics often have difficulty delegating work to others. They are critical of coworkers and are ill suited to be good team players. Even their high energy level causes problems. Workaholics may try to do everything themselves. They tend to be perfectionists and nothing is ever good enough for them.

It can be difficult to work with a workaholic. The truth is, says Machlowitz, that workaholics are better suited to be business owners than employees. They do not do well in a business organization working with or managing people.

THINK CRITICALLY

1. Do you think you may be a workaholic? Why or why not?
2. Would you want to work for a workaholic? With a workaholic?

Yuri Arcurs/Shutterstock.com

Workaholics expect a lot from themselves and from others.

Assessment

Chapter Summary

9-1 Listen and Speak

A. In addition to occupational and employability skills, basic academic skills are required for job success.

B. Communication links the working world. Listening may be its weakest link. Common causes of poor listening include distractions, prejudging, over stimulation, and partial listening.

C. Effective speaking requires correct pronunciation, clear enunciation, use of standard English, and good grammar.

9-2 Read and Write

A. Reading requires recognizing words before you can understand their meanings. Therefore, effective readers need a large vocabulary. Because reading is a skill, it can be improved through practice.

B. Writing is probably the most important form of business communication. It is good business to keep records of business dealings. Internal communication (communication within a company) takes the form of notes, business forms, and memorandums. External communication (communication between organizations) mainly takes the form of business letters.

C. Digital communication technologies have significantly changed the way individuals and businesses communicate. Email is becoming the preferred method by which business communicate internally and externally.

9-3 Effective Communication and Group Participation

A. Even though electronic communication is increasing, effective telephone skills and polite telephone behavior are still important in business communication. Text messaging and voicemail should be used in a businesslike manner.

B. Videoconferencing is used to interact with employees in remote locations.

C. Even though technology makes the exchange of information easier and quicker, there are a number of workplace situations where traditional face-to-face communication is often more effective.

D. Learning to work effectively in groups is important.

9-4 Bosses, Coworkers, and Customers

A. Human relations are very important to job success. Many fired workers lose their jobs because they cannot get along with others.

B. The workplace of today has workers from four generations: Traditionalists, Baby Boomers, Generation X, and Generation Y. Members of different generations have been influenced differently by technology and, as a result, often prefer to communicate differently.

C. At work, you will have to deal with all kinds of people. Understanding bosses, coworkers, and customers can make this task easier and more pleasant.

D. Relationships between employees and customers are important to the success of a business. Providing good products or services, treating customers well, and providing service after a sale are the ways to attract and retain customers.

Activities

1. Keep a list for one day of slang words and phrases that you hear. The next day, share the list with the class. Discuss what words and phrases of standard English could be substituted for them.

2. You are in charge of organizing the annual company picnic. Compose a memo to company employees. The memo should provide all of the important details about the picnic.

3. List several of your hobbies or recreational interests. Go to the school or public library and find out what books are available on these subjects. Choose a book and read it. Make a short oral report to the class.

4. Technology has provided a number of new tools that allow you to download a book and read or listen to it on a variety of electronic devices. Search both the library and the Web for free ebooks. Make a list of at least three books that you are interested in reading. Share the list with the class including why the book is of interest.

5. QR codes are used in a variety of print advertising. Each member of the class should find and post on a class bulletin board examples of advertising that uses QR codes. An instructor or student with a smartphone can demonstrate how they are used. As a follow-up activity, the instructor might also ask you to bring in samples of less common uses of QR codes such as business cards, wedding invitations, and temporary tattoos.

6. Evaluate your ability to speak and write in standard English. Explain why this ability can help you achieve goals in your life-span plan.

7. The class will be divided into two task groups. One group should develop a short script for how to place a business call. The other group should develop a script for how to answer a business call. Using mobile phones with the speakers turned on, two members of group one should conduct the simulated placing of a business call. Do the same thing with members of the second group answering a business call. Try to make the simulations as real as possible. Class members not participating should listen quietly to the conversations. Following the simulations, discuss how the calls

were conducted and note any parts of the conversations that need improvement.

8. Identify a human relations problem that you have had with another student or coworker. What was the nature of the problem? Based on what you have learned in this chapter, how could you have helped avoid the problem? Share your answers in class.

9. This chapter gave several reasons why customers deal with certain businesses. Think about your favorite businesses. Can you add any reasons to those the text gives? As a class, list the reasons.

10. Evaluate your ability to work as a member of a team. Explain the importance of this ability to achieving goals in your life-span plan.

Word Power

On a separate sheet of paper, match each definition with the correct term. All definitions will be used, and a definition will be used only once.

11. When two or more locations interact via two-way video and audio transmissions simultaneously

12. A two-dimensional matrix bar code that is used to identify products or provide information

13. The usual form of language used by the majority of Americans

14. Unwritten rules concerning respect for the property and territory of others

15. A work group that is separated geographically and who participates in a group project using electronic technologies

16. A work environment in which the use of paper and traditional forms of communication are eliminated or greatly reduced

17. A work group formed to accomplish a particular objective

18. Acts of kindness, consideration, or assistance

19. How distinctly or clearly one speaks

20. Behaving or speaking in such a way as to avoid causing offense or revealing private information

21. The length of time someone has worked for a company

22. Interactions among people

23. Customers of certain service-producing businesses or institutions

24. Technology that transmits a product's identity using radio waves

25. A tendency to be drawn to another person, often because of similar characteristics and preferences

26. Lines of varying width that can be read by an optical scanner

27. The way in which words are spoken

28. Electronic tools and equipment that store, retrieve, manipulate, transmit, or receive information in digital form

29. A set of rules about correct speaking and writing

a. barcode
b. discretion
c. enunciation
d. goodwill
e. grammar
f. human relations
g. information communications technology (ICT)
h. interpersonal attraction
i. paperless office
j. patrons
k. pronunciation
l. QR code
m. radio frequency identification
n. seniority
o. standard English
p. task group
q. territorial rights
r. videoconferencing
s. virtual team

Think Critically

30. In addition to preferences for specific types of communication, each generation has different ideas regarding privacy. As a class, list the following topics on the board: annual household income, the number of household pets, favorite vacation spots, and the most recent illness causing an absence. Discuss how much information each generation would be inclined to share on each of these topics. Include in your discussion allowances for personality differences as well as generational differences.

31. There are geographic differences in the way people use language. You may have lived or traveled in areas different from where you now live. Discuss some of the interesting and colorful words and phrases that people use in different parts of the country.

32. If someone opened and read a letter you had written, that would violate the law and your privacy. The same cannot be said of email. Contrary to what many people believe, the email that you write at work is not private. Employers can read email that their employees have written. People have been fired for including in email sensitive or unethical information. Do you think employers should be allowed to read employee email?

33. Human relations skills are also important for bosses. What does it take beyond being a good coworker to be an effective boss?

34. Many people see themselves as getting along well with others. Yet you have read that many fired workers lose their jobs because they cannot get along with others. What are some causes of "bad attitudes" and conflicts among people at work?

35. Certain occupations like police officers, nurses, and attorneys deal with people who are often emotionally upset. What types of special human relations skills do these people need? What other occupations require these skills?

36. You are probably a member of Generation X. Does the information in Lesson 9-4 accurately describe your generation? Discuss why or why not. Are there other characteristics that you think should be added?

Career Transitions Connection

Interacting With Your Boss

Click on *Tips & Advice*. Click on *Negotiating*. Watch the videos How to *Talk to Your Boss* and *How to Deal with a Difficult Boss*. Just as your boss is responsible for managing you, you are responsible for managing interactions with your boss. A strategy that will help you have a successful relationship with your boss is to always behave professionally and not take any negative interactions personally. Why was protecting your own self-esteem stressed in the video?

"Nobody ever lost his shirt when his sleeves were rolled up." —ERIK HOFFER

Math and Measurement Skills

VikramRaghuvanshi/iStockphoto.com

10-1 Basic Math

10-2 Basic Measurement

PREVIEW

Like communication skills, math is also important on the job. Some occupations use math more than others. Math is taught from early grade school through high school. The purpose of this chapter is not to introduce new math content. Rather, the chapter illustrates how basic math and measurement skills previously learned are used in the workplace.

Taking/Action Math Skills

Jamal was looking for a job in the retail industry. He wasn't great at math, but he thought that the skills he had would enable him to get a good job. He had also worked previously at a video rental store. Jamal went to a music store at a nearby mall and filled out an application.

The manager, Mr. Rodriguez, called Jamal to schedule an interview. On the day of the interview, Jamal made sure he was neatly dressed, and he had prepared answers to the usual interview questions. Jamal showed up for the interview on time and politely greeted the store manager.

Mr. Rodriguez interviewed Jamal and gave him an overview of the entry-level position available. After a brief tour of the store, Mr. Rodriguez handed Jamal a sheet of paper. It was a math test with ten problems. The problems had to do with totaling purchases and figuring discounts and sales tax.

"When you are ringing up sales, the cash register will total purchases and compute discounts and sales tax for you," the manager said, "but I am looking for employees who can think on their feet and make these computations on paper or in their heads. Sometimes you will need to do this."

Mr. Rodriguez continued, "You are a strong candidate for the position, but you must get at least eight of the ten questions correct on this test. You have 15 minutes." Mr. Rodriguez then left the room.

Jamal was scared. He wanted the job. He had no idea that math skills would be so important. At first, his mind went blank. Then, he carefully read each question. He had an easy time with the questions about adding sums and figuring sales tax, but the discount questions were tougher. He finished the test with two minutes to spare and checked his answers.

The store manager returned and reviewed Jamal's test. Jamal had gotten nine of the ten problems correct. "Congratulations," said Mr. Rodriguez, extending his hand. "When can you start?"

THINK CRITICALLY

1. Why do you think math skills are important in retail sales?

2. What are some other retail occupations that require knowledge of total purchase amounts, sales tax, and discounts?

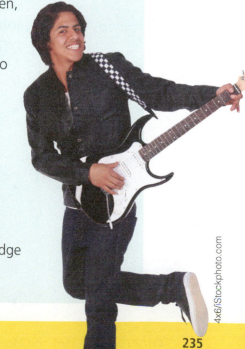

4x6/iStockphoto.com

BASIC MATH

OBJECTIVES

- Recognize that occupations require different levels of math skills and that all 16 career clusters include occupations requiring some math skills
- Apply math skills to the computation of total purchase amount, trade discount, cash discount, markup, sales tax, and markdown

KEY TERMS

- invoice
- trade discount
- terms
- cash discount
- markup
- markdown

Phase4Photography/Shutterstock.com

Workplace Decisions

In observing your boss, you are surprised at the amount of math that she uses. She seems to constantly be analyzing sales data and entering numbers into a notebook computer. You would like to be able to move up in the company or perhaps own a small store of your own someday. However, math has always been your weakest subject. You wonder whether you would be able to perform the math part of the business.

What would you do?

Who Uses Math?

In 2018, about 3,000 mathematicians are projected to be employed in the U.S. labor force. However, millions of additional workers will have jobs in which mathematics is a necessary part. And, millions more will require some understanding of basic math. The *Occupational Outlook Quarterly* has classified occupations in four groups according to the level of math skills required: advanced, applied, practical, or general.

- **Advanced** Occupations in the advanced or theoretical math skills category require an understanding of more complex math concepts such as calculus and linear algebra. Occupations in this skill category include architects, chemists, engineers, math teachers, and social scientists.

- **Applied** The applied math skills category includes those in which workers need to understand mathematical concepts and be able to apply them in their work. Knowledge of statistics and trigonometry may also be needed. Occupations in this skill category include accountants, computer programmers, financial managers, physicians, and science technicians.

- **Practical** Occupations in the practical math category may require algebra and geometry, in addition to general math skills.

Workplace Innovations

HIGH-PERFORMANCE CONCRETE

Concrete, one of the oldest and most basic building materials, has become high-tech. About 1,900 years ago, the Romans built the Pantheon. It continues to be the largest unreinforced solid concrete dome in the world. The secret to its survival, which was probably unknown to the builders, was that the lightweight concrete used to build the dome had set and hardened from the inside out. Because the concrete cured internally, it resisted shrinking and cracking and developed greater strength and durability.

Standard concrete is made from a mixture of Portland cement, sand, gravel, and water. It is typically cured from the outside for a week or so by maintaining the proper temperature and dampness. In recent years, construction engineers have discovered that replacing some of the sand with a light-weight, pre-wetted absorbent material produces lighter and more durable concrete. As a result, internally-cured concrete is now being widely used in the construction of highway pavement, bridge decks, water tanks, and other concrete structures.

Compared to standard concrete, internally-cured concrete increases the cost of a project by about 10 to 12 percent. Studies have shown that bridge decks made with internally-cured, high-performance concrete are estimated to have a service life of 63 years as compared to 22 years for standard concrete. The advantages of reduced cracking, better protection against salt damage, and reduced disruption to the traveling public far outweigh the additional construction costs.

NET FOLLOW-UP

Explore the Web for additional information on the topic of internally-cured concrete. Do any of the articles reference any other manufacturing improvements that cost more initially and save money in the long term? Be prepared to share your findings during a class discussion.

Occupations in this skill category include automobile mechanics, carpenters, machinists and tool programmers, ophthalmic laboratory technicians, and purchasers and buyers.

- **General**   The general math skills category requires basic arithmetic such as addition, subtraction, multiplication, and division. Occupations in this skill category include bank tellers, cashiers, order clerks, roofers, and secretaries.

Occupations Using Math

Another way of grouping occupations is according to the sixteen career clusters described in Chapter 1. The sixteen clusters are shown in Figure 10-1 on the next two pages. Typical occupations are given for each cluster showing how math is used in those occupations.

There are two important characteristics of math on the job: (a) the level of math skills required in a particular occupation or job may vary from general to advanced, and (b) all sixteen career clusters include occupations that require some degree of math skills.

CAREER CLUSTER ICON	CAREER CLUSTER	SAMPLE OCCUPATIONS WITHIN EACH CAREER CLUSTER THAT USE MATH
	Agriculture, Food & Natural Resources	*Farmers and ranchers* maintain financial, tax, production, and employee records. *Foresters* count timber, determine the timber's worth, negotiate the purchase price, and create purchasing contracts.
	Architecture & Construction	*Architects* prepare and administer construction contract documents. *Carpenters* study specifications in blueprints, prepare project layouts, and determine required materials.
	Arts, A/V Technology & Communications	*Photographers* use formulas to estimate light levels, distances, and the number of exposures needed. *Broadcast technicians* monitor and log transmitter readings.
	Business, Management & Administration	*Accountants* compute taxes and prepare tax returns. *Marketing managers* evaluate product development costs including budgets, research and development needs, and profits.
	Education & Training	*Fitness and wellness coordinators* prepare budgets and develop strategic, operational, purchasing, and maintenance plans. *Teachers* grade tests and assignments and maintain accurate and complete student records.
	Finance	*Insurance claims clerks* calculate and transmit claims for payment. *Loan officers* analyze applicants' financial status, credit, and property evaluations to determine whether the applicant is a good credit risk.
	Government & Public Administration	*Economists* collect and process economic and statistical data. *Urban and regional planners* conduct field investigations to compile and analyze facts affecting land use.
	Health Science	*Medical and clinical laboratory technicians* analyze and record test data to issue reports that use charts, graphs, and summaries. *Opticians* make lenses, verify that finished lenses are ground to specifications, and maintain records of customers' prescriptions.
	Hospitality & Tourism	*Chefs* estimate amounts and costs of required supplies, such as food and ingredients. *Lodging managers* collect payments and record data concerning funds and expenses.

CAREER CLUSTER ICON	CAREER CLUSTER	SAMPLE OCCUPATIONS WITHIN EACH CAREER CLUSTER THAT USE MATH
	Human Services	*Sociologists* analyze and interpret data in order to increase the understanding of human social behavior. *Property managers* prepare detailed budgets and financial reports for properties.
	Information Technology	*Database administrators* review project requests describing database user needs to estimate the time and cost required to complete the project. *Document management specialists* analyze, interpret, and distribute system performance data.
	Law, Public Safety, Corrections & Security	*Loss prevention specialists* conduct store audits to identify problem areas or procedural deficiencies. *Immigration and customs inspectors* determine duty and taxes to be paid on goods.
	Manufacturing	*Biomass plant technicians* calculate, measure, load, or mix biomass feedstock for power generation. *Machinists* produce parts to specifications and measure, examine, and test completed parts to ensure conformance to specifications, using precision measuring instruments.
	Marketing, Sales & Sevice	*Customer service representatives* determine charges for services requested, collect payments, and arrange for billing. *Wholesale and retail buyers* analyze sales records, trends, and economic conditions to anticipate consumer buying patterns and how much inventory is needed.
	Science, Technology, Engineering & Mathematics	*Hydrologists* measure and graph lake levels, stream flows, and changes in water volumes. *Industrial engineers* perform mathematical calculations to determine manufacturing processes, staff requirements, and production standards.
	Transportation, Distribution & Logistics	*Airline pilots and flight engineers* check passenger and cargo distributions and fuel amounts to ensure that weight and balance specifications are met. *Supply chain managers* analyze inventories to determine how to use inventory efficiently while optimizing customer service.

Regardless of which occupation you choose to prepare for, you should expect that part of your occupational preparation will include some understanding of math concepts and skills. And the more math that you take, the more likely you are to get a better job and to earn more money throughout your working life.

Common Uses of Arithmetic

Business math involves common ways in which arithmetic is used on the job. Business math includes calculation of total purchase amount, trade discount, cash discount, markup, sales tax, and markdown.

Total Purchase Amount

Most of your purchases involve single items. For instance, you buy a pair of running shoes for $54.95. The total amount of your purchase is easy to determine: 1 × $54.95 = $54.95. In most states, you must add sales tax, too.

Businesses often buy large numbers of the same item. A sporting goods store, for example, might buy dozens of pairs of running shoes. To find the total amount of the purchase, multiply the number of items by the price of one item (the unit price). This skill is important for people who prepare invoices. An **invoice** is a bill for goods. An example of an invoice is shown in Figure 10-2.

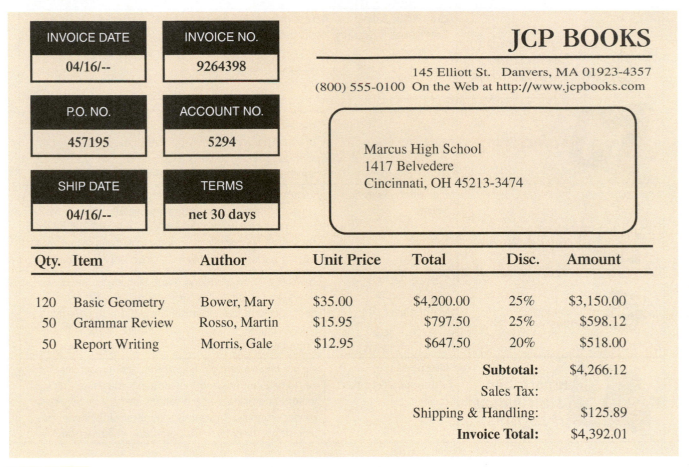

INVOICE DATE	INVOICE NO.
04/16/--	9264398

P.O. NO.	ACCOUNT NO.
457195	5294

SHIP DATE	TERMS
04/16/--	net 30 days

JCP BOOKS

145 Elliott St. Danvers, MA 01923-4357
(800) 555-0100 On the Web at http://www.jcpbooks.com

Marcus High School
1417 Belvedere
Cincinnati, OH 45213-3474

Qty.	Item	Author	Unit Price	Total	Disc.	Amount
120	Basic Geometry	Bower, Mary	$35.00	$4,200.00	25%	$3,150.00
50	Grammar Review	Rosso, Martin	$15.95	$797.50	25%	$598.12
50	Report Writing	Morris, Gale	$12.95	$647.50	20%	$518.00
				Subtotal:		$4,266.12
				Sales Tax:		
				Shipping & Handling:		$125.89
				Invoice Total:		$4,392.01

FIGURE 10-2 A common use of math in business is to fill out invoices.

Problem Determine the total amount of a purchase of 24 pairs of shoes at $42.95 each, 15 pairs of socks at $1.85 each, and 3 dozen packages of shoelaces at $.89 each.

Solution

	Quantity × Unit price	= Amount
Shoes	24 × $42.95	= $1,030.80
Socks	15 × $ 1.85	= 27.75
Laces	36 × $ 0.89	= + 32.04
Total amount		$1,090.59

Trade Discount

A **trade discount** is a deduction from the catalog (list or suggested retail) price of an item. Trade discounts are usually given to retailers to enable them to sell merchandise at a greater profit. In some cases, buyers get special discounts when ordering large quantities of something. The trade discount is a percentage of the list or selling price.

Problem An office desk is listed in a catalog at $680. Business customers can buy the desk at a trade discount of 30%. How much will a business have to pay for the desk? (The business pays the net purchase price.)

Business customers can often save money when buying large quantities of an item.

Solution   30% = 0.30

$$
\begin{array}{r}
\$680.00 \\
\times \quad 0.30 \\
\hline
\$204.00 \quad \text{Discount}
\end{array}
$$

$$
\begin{array}{r}
\$680.00 \\
- \quad 204.00 \\
\hline
\$476.00 \quad \text{Net purchase price}
\end{array}
$$

Cash Discount

Every sale between a business buyer and seller involves terms. The **terms** state the time limit within which the buyer must pay. A common term of sale is "net due in 30 days." This means that the buyer has 30 days in which to pay the bill. After 30 days, the buyer must pay the price plus interest. Note the terms shown in Figure 10-2 on the previous page.

To encourage prompt payment, the seller may offer a cash discount. A **cash discount** is a reduction in price, often of several percent, offered to a buyer to encourage early payment on an account. A cash discount benefits both the buyer and the seller. The buyer saves money, while the seller has a paid account.

Problem An invoice for $510 has terms of net due in 30 days with a 3% discount given for payment within 10 days. What is the sale price if the buyer pays within 10 days?

Solution   3% = 0.03

$$
\begin{array}{r}
\$510.00 \\
\times \quad 0.03 \\
\hline
\$15.30 \quad \text{Discount}
\end{array}
$$

$$
\begin{array}{r}
\$510.00 \\
- \quad 15.30 \\
\hline
\$494.70 \quad \text{Net amount of payment}
\end{array}
$$

Workforce Trends

Between 2008 and 2018 the BLS projects that 37.6 million workers will enter the labor force and 25 million will leave. New entrants into the labor force are anticipated to be around 1.6 million more than in the previous decade. Many people will leave the labor force because of aging and retirement. More men are expected to leave the labor force because the male labor force has greater numbers of older workers than the female labor force.

Comparing similar products involves deciding what price you can afford to pay.

Markup

A retailer buys goods from a supplier to resell. Remember the running shoes? The price the store paid is the cost price. **Markup** is the amount of money that the retailer added to the cost price in order to earn a profit on the product.

Selling price = Cost price + Markup

Problem An item costs $28.00; its selling price is $35.00. How much is the markup?

Solution

$35.00	Selling price
− 28.00	Cost price
$ 7.00	Markup

Problem Based on the cost price, what is the percent of markup? (Percent of markup = Markup ÷ Cost price)

Solution

Markup ÷ Cost price = Percent of markup
$7.00   ÷ $28.00   = 0.25 or 25%

Businesses know how much markup will give them enough money to cover expenses and make a fair profit, so they add the markup to an item before trying to sell it.

Problem A radio costs $42.00 and will be sold at a markup of 30% of the cost price. What is the selling price?

Solution

$42.00	Cost price
× 0.30	Markup
$12.60	

$42.00	Cost price
+ 12.60	Markup
$54.60	Selling price

Sales Tax

Most states and cities have sales tax on goods and services. Sales taxes usually range between 1 and 7 percent. The sales tax is added on to the purchase price of goods and services. Why is no sales tax shown on the invoice in Figure 10-2 on page 240?

Problem Someone buys a sweater for $38.00 and a pair of pants for $46.00. A 5% sales tax is added to the purchase price. What is the total amount of the purchase?

Solution

$38.00	
+ 46.00	
$84.00	Purchase price
+ 4.20	Sales tax is $84.00 × 0.05
$88.20	Total amount

Markdown

Most retail stores have periodic sales to move slow-selling merchandise, clear out end-of-season goods, or attract customers to the store. A reduction in the selling price of a product is called a **markdown**. The markdown is usually expressed as a percent.

Problem   A merchant is having a sale on all summer dresses at 40% off (markdown). What is the sale price of a dress that was originally priced at $55.00?

Merchandise usually goes on sale at the end of the season.

Solution

$55.00	Original price
× 0.40	Markdown
$22.00	

$55.00	Original price
−22.00	Markdown
$33.00	Sale price

10-1 Assessment

1. What level of math skills is typically required for each of the following occupations: machinists and tool programmers, science technicians, bank tellers, and engineers?

2. What is the relationship between the amount of math you have taken and your future job opportunities and job earnings?

3. Calculating total purchase amount, trade discount, markup, sales tax, and so on, is often called "business math." Why?

4. How does a cash discount benefit a buyer? A seller?

5. A company is billed $1,850 with a cash discount of 5% offered for payment within ten days. How much could it save?

6. What is the difference between cost price and selling price?

7. What is the selling price of a dress that costs $60 and is marked up 40%? If the dress is later put on sale at a markdown of 25%, what is the new selling price of the dress?

High Growth Occupations
FOR THE 21ST CENTURY

Do you like to help other people? Would you like to be part of the medical community? You might like a career as a medical assistant. People in this occupation assist physicians, podiatrists, chiropractors, and optometrists with patients and with office duties. In smaller offices medical assistants may have only clinical duties, but in large offices they may have both clinical and administrative duties.

Clinical responsibilities of medical assistants may include any of the following: take medical histories, record vital signs, explain treatment procedures to patients, prepare patients for examination, and assist the physician during the examination. They may collect and prepare laboratory specimens or perform basic laboratory tests in the office laboratory, dispose of contaminated supplies, and sterilize medical instruments. They also may instruct patients about medication and special diets, prepare and administer medications as directed by a physician, authorize drug refills as directed, phone in prescriptions to a pharmacy, draw blood, prepare patients for x-rays, take electrocardiograms, remove sutures, and change dressings. Duties may vary from state to state.

Administrative responsibilities of medical assistants may include any of the following: answer the office phones, greet patients, update and file medical records, fill out insurance forms, answer correspondence, schedule appointments, arrange for hospital admission and laboratory services, and do the billing and bookkeeping.

Medical assistants also may keep the instruments and equipment in order in the examination rooms, purchase and maintain supplies, and keep the examination and the waiting rooms neat and clean. Some medical assistants specialize, which may increase their duties.

Medical assistants work in clean, well-lit medical offices. Most employers prefer graduates of a program in medical assisting, which may be acquired through vocational-technical high schools, or post-secondary vocational schools, and community and junior colleges. Postsecondary schools may offer an associate degree.

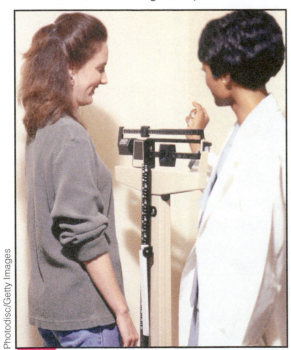

Photodisc/Getty Images

Before patients see the doctor, medical assistants may be responsible for weighing them and recording the result on their chart.

BASIC MEASUREMENT

OBJECTIVES

- Calculate surface measures and volume measures
- Convert measures from one unit to another

KEY TERMS

- measurement
- perimeter
- circumference
- area

Workplace Decisions

You have just finished preparing the site for pouring a concrete patio. You overhear the boss saying that the job will probably require about 10 yards of concrete. That does not sound right to you, so you make a quick calculation. You come up with 12 yards. You want to tell the boss he is wrong, but you are not sure how he will react.

What would you do?

Rob Marmion/Shutterstock.com

Surface and Volume Measures

Measurement is the act of determining the dimensions, quantity, or degree of something. The object can be volume, area, distance, temperature, time, energy, or weight. Measurement answers the question "How much?" It does so in a uniform and standardized way. This means, for example, that all inches are the same length. Many workers use basic measurement skills on their jobs. This is sometimes called "vocational math" or "shop math."

Surface Measurement

Being able to calculate the surface measures of areas and perimeters is necessary on many jobs. Construction workers, for example, must measure perimeters and areas in order to know how much concrete, lumber, and other materials to order. Workers in the printing industry must measure perimeters and areas to cut specific sizes of paper stock.

Perimeter

The **perimeter** of an object is the distance around it. Perimeter is measured in standard linear units, including miles, feet, inches, kilometers, meters, centimeters, and millimeters. You find the perimeter by adding together the lengths of the outer edges of the figure for most shapes. For circles and some irregular figures, you will need to use simple formulas.

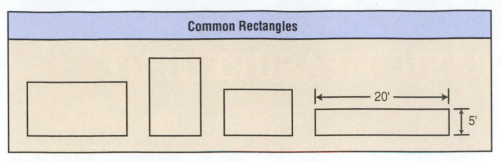

FIGURE 10-3 The rectangle is a familiar geometric shape.

Knowing how to calculate measurements will enable you to build many useful projects.

A rectangle is a four-sided object having a right angle (90 degrees) at each corner. The page you are reading is a rectangle. Most walls and floors are rectangles. Even a square is a rectangle. Some common rectangles are shown in Figure 10-3.

Rectangles have two pairs of sides. Each pair is equal in length. To find the perimeter, you add together the lengths of all sides. Suppose you are building a fence to enclose a dog kennel. Using the measurements shown in Figure 10-3, you add the length of the two 20-foot sides together with the length of the two 5-foot sides to find that the perimeter is 50. Thus, you need 50 feet of fencing to build the kennel. If all sides were of equal length, you could have found the perimeter by multiplying the length of one side by four.

Circumference

The perimeter of a circle is called the **circumference**. To find the circumference, you must know the diameter or the radius of a circle. A circle with a radius of 8 inches and a diameter of 16 inches is shown in Figure 10-4.

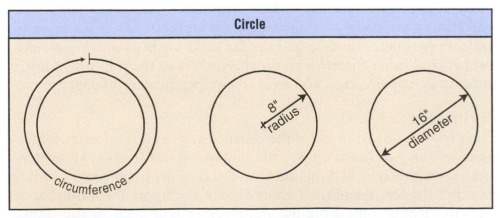

FIGURE 10-4 The main parts of a circle are circumference, radius, and diameter.

To determine the circumference, you must use a formula. The formula is as follows:

Circumference = 3.14 × diameter
or $C = 3.14 × D$ Note: The 3.14 does not change.

Say that you are going to form and install an exhaust duct in a wood-working shop. Using the dimensions shown in Figure 10-4, how wide of a piece of sheet metal will you need to roll it into a cylinder that is 16 inches in diameter?

Step 1   Set up the equation.
$C = 3.14 × D$

Step 2   Place values into the formula and multiply.
$C = 3.14 × 16$ inches
$C = 50.24$ inches

You will need a piece of sheet metal 50.24 inches wide plus a little extra for the seam.

The same process in reverse will help you determine the diameter or radius of a circle, if you know the circumference. To find the diameter, you divide the circumference by 3.14. For example, a circle with a circumference of 35 feet has a diameter of 11.15 feet ($D = 35 ÷ 3.14$).

Area

The **area** is the number of square units of space on the surface of a figure enclosed by the perimeter. Area calculation uses several simple formulas, each of which is suited to a certain geometric shape. Areas are given in units of square measure such as square feet, square inches, or square meters.

For rectangles, the formula for determining area is as follows:

Area = length × width
or $A = l × w$

For example, the area of a rectangular room that is 8 feet long and 12 feet wide is 96 square feet ($8 × 12 = 96$). If the room were square with each side being 12 feet, then the area would be 144 square feet ($12 × 12 = 144$).

To find the area of a circle, you again use a formula that contains the constant 3.14, as well as the value of the radius. The formula is written as follows:

Area (A) = $3.14 × r^2$

The r^2 means the radius is squared. In other words, you multiply the radius of the circle by itself before multiplying it by 3.14. The symbol for squaring is a small 2 that is placed slightly above and following the number to be squared. For example, suppose a circle has a radius of 4. The square of the radius (r^2) would be $4 × 4$, or 16.

A rectangular concrete pad is used as a base for an above ground swimming pool.

Suppose you are going to pour a round concrete pad for a storage tank. To determine how much concrete is needed, you first must figure the area. The radius of the pad is 8 feet. You would work the problem in the following steps:

Step 1 Set up the equation.
$A = 3.14 \times r^2$

Step 2 Place values into the formula and multiply.
$A = 3.14 \times 8^2$
$A = 3.14 \times 64$
$A = 200.96$ square feet

Before ordering the concrete, you would need to calculate the volume of concrete needed. This is explained in the next section.

Volume Measurement

Like perimeters and areas, volume measures are often used on the job. Volume is the amount of space an object occupies. It can be expressed in units of cubic measure such as cubic inches, cubic yards, and cubic feet. It can also be given in units such as gallons, quarts, ounces, and bushels.

To determine the volume of a figure that contains all right angles, such as a rectangular figure or cube, the formula is as follows:

Volume = length × width × height
or $V = l \times w \times h$

For example, to find the volume of a rectangular box that is 4 feet long, 2 feet wide, and 1 foot high, you multiply $4 \times 2 \times 1$, which equals 8 cubic feet.

If the dimensions are in different units, they will have to be converted to the same unit of measurement before multiplying. How would you calculate the amount of fill gravel to lay a 6-inch base in a ditch before installing a sewer pipe? The ditch is 30 inches wide and 150 feet long.

Many jobs require workers to perform precise measurements.

Step 1 Set up the equation.
$V = l \times w \times h$

Step 2 Place values into the formula.
V = 150 feet × 30 inches × 6 inches

Step 3 Convert all measures to the same units. In this case, use feet.
V = 150 feet × 2.5 feet × 0.5 foot

Step 4 Multiply.
V = 187.5 cubic feet

You would need 187.5 cubic feet of gravel. However, because gravel is usually sold by the cubic yard, you would need to divide 187.5 by 27 (1 cubic yard contains 27 cubic feet). How many yards of gravel would you need?

Linear Units	Time Units
1 foot = 12 inches	1 minute = 60 seconds
1 yard = 3 feet or 36 inches	1 hour = 60 minutes
1 mile = 5,280 feet or 1,760 yards	1 day = 24 hours

Weight Units
1 pound = 16 ounces
2,000 pounds = 1 ton
1 pint = 1 pound

Volume Units
1 gallon = 231 cubic inches
1 cubic foot = 7.5 gallons
1 cubic foot (water) = 62.5 pounds
1 gallon (water) = 8.3 pounds
1 bushel (struck) = 2,150.4 cubic inches
1 bushel (heaped) = 2,747.7 cubic inches
1 cubic foot = 1,728 cubic inches
1 cubic yard = 27 cubic feet

Area Units
1 square foot = 144 square inches
1 square yard = 9 square feet
1 square mile = 3,097,600 square yards

FIGURE 10-5 These are conventional units of measure.

Systems of Measure

To be effective on the job, you should be able to work with the basic units of measure in the conventional (or English) and metric systems. You should be familiar with procedures for converting measures from one unit to another within the same system. You also need to be able to convert measures from the conventional system to the metric system and vice versa.

You are probably most familiar with the conventional system of measure. It is the one used most often in the United States. Some conventional units of measure and their relationship to each other are shown in Figure 10-5.

Math Connection

Suppose you work for the government. Your supervisor has told you to order 4,000 cubic meters of concrete for a building job. At a concrete batch plant, concrete is sold by the cubic yard. To order the correct amount, you need to convert cubic meters to cubic yards. How many cubic yards should you order?

SOLUTION

To calculate the number of cubic yards in 4,000 cubic meters, multiply 4,000 cubic meters by the conversion equivalent of 1.31 cubic yards per cubic meter (see the conversion chart in Figure 10-6 on the next page).

4,000 × 1.31 = 5,240 cubic yards

You should order 5,240 cubic yards of concrete.

Linear Units	Area Units
1 millimeter = 0.001 meter	1 square centimeter = 100 square millimeters
1 centimeter = 0.01 meter	1 square meter = 10,000 square centimeters
1 decimeter = 0.1 meter	1 square kilometer = 1,000,000 square meters
1 meter = 1,000 millimeters, 100 centimeters, 10 decimeters	
1 kilometer = 1,000 meters	**Volume Units**

Weight Units

Weight Units	Volume Units
1 milligram = 0.001 gram	1 milliliter = 1 cubic centimeter
1 centigram = 0.01 gram	1 milliliter = 0.001 liter
1 decigram = 0.1 gram	1 centiliter = 0.01 liter
1 gram = 1,000 milligrams, 100 centigrams, 10 decigrams	1 deciliter = 0.1 liter
1 kilogram = 1,000 grams	1 liter = 1,000 milliliters, 100 centiliters, 10 deciliters
	1 kiloliter = 1,000 liters

FIGURE 10-6 These are metric units of measure.

Within the same unit or type of conventional measure, conversion to equivalent measures usually involves division or multiplication. For example, to find the number of cubic feet required to hold 20 gallons of water, you would divide the 20 gallons by the conversion equivalent of 7.5 gallons per cubic foot:

$$20 \div 7.5 = 2.67 \text{ cubic feet}$$

To find the number of square feet in 20 square yards, multiply 20 square yards by the conversion equivalent of 9 square feet per yard:

$$20 \times 9 = 180 \text{ square feet}$$

Most of the world, except for the United States, uses the metric system of measure. However, Congress passed a trade bill in 1988 that required all federal agencies to convert to the metric system by 1992. This means, for example, that if the Justice Department wants to buy paper, it must be measured in centimeters, not inches. If the Department of Defense wants to buy gasoline, it must do so in liters, not gallons.

This law will not force private companies to convert to the metric system. It seems likely, however, that it will encourage them to do so. Some occupations and industries use the metric system a lot. The fields of medicine, engineering, and science are examples. Metric units of measure are shown in Figure 10-6.

A variety of math skills are required in the workplace.

Conversions between and across units of measure in the metric system are in whole numbers and are divisible by 10. This is a major advantage over the conventional system of measure. For example, a centimeter is 10 millimeters and 20 cubic centimeters is equal to 20 milliliters. To find the number of meters in 86.2 kilometers, simply multiply by 1,000:

86.2 kilometers $\times$ 1,000 = 86,200 meters

There will be times on the job when you will work with both conventional and metric units of measure. It often becomes necessary to convert measurements from one system to another. To do so, you can use the conversion chart shown in Figure 10-7 on the following page or use conversion calculators found on the Web.

Suppose you want to express 30 square feet (ft^2) in terms of square meters (m^2). Since 1 square foot is about 0.09 square meter, you must multiply the number of square feet by 0.09:

30 ft^2 $\times$ 0.09 = 2.7 m^2

The conversion chart is very useful for making quick and easy conversions from metric to conventional and from conventional to metric. However, keep in mind that the converted values are only approximate. If greater accuracy is needed, consult a table that has the conversion values listed to three decimal points.

🔍 Search the Net

A number of sites on the Web provide calculators that can be used to make conversions from metric to conventional and from conventional to metric. Access **www.cengage.com/school/working** and click on the link for Chapter 10. Do the following conversions using the calculator tool:

1. You need 20 yards of fabric to make curtains for your bedroom. How many meters of fabric would you need?
2. You just bought 5 pounds of coffee beans at Starbucks. What is the weight of the coffee beans in kilograms?
3. You need 20 liters of soda for a party. How much soda is this in quarts and gallons?

www.cengage.com/school/working

10-2 Assessment

1. Why are uniform and standardized measures necessary in business and industry?

2. How many 4- by 8-foot sheets of plywood are needed to cover a 16- by 32-foot roof?

3. How many cubic feet of storage space is contained in a warehouse that is 40 yards long and 15 yards wide and that has 12-foot ceilings?

4. Which system of measure is used by most countries in the world?

5. The temperature is 78 degrees Fahrenheit. How many degrees Celsius is this?

FROM METRIC TO CONVENTIONAL

Symbol	When You Know	Multiply by	To Find	Symbol
LENGTH				
mm	millimeters	0.04	inches	in
cm	centimeters	0.39	inches	in
m	meters	3.28	feet	ft
m	meters	1.09	yards	yd
km	kilometers	0.62	miles	mi
AREA				
cm^2	square centimeters	0.16	square inches	in^2
m^2	square meters	1.2	square yards	yd^2
km^2	square kilometers	0.39	square miles	mi^2
ha	hectares (10,000 m^2)	2.47	acres	
MASS (weight)				
g	grams	0.04	ounces	oz
kg	kilograms	2.2	pounds	lb
t	tonnes (1,000 kg)	1.1	short tons	
VOLUME				
ml	milliliters	0.03	fluid ounces	fl oz
l	liters	2.11	pints	pt
l	liters	1.06	quarts	qt
l	liters	0.26	gallons	gal
m^3	cubic meters	35.31	cubic feet	ft^3
m^3	cubic meters	1.31	cubic yards	yd^3
TEMPERATURE (exact)				
°C	Celsius temperature	9/5 (then add 32)	Fahrenheit temperature	°F

FROM CONVENTIONAL TO METRIC

Symbol	When You Know	Multiply by	To Find	Symbol
LENGTH				
in	inches	2.54	centimeters	cm
ft	feet	30.48	centimeters	cm
yd	yards	0.91	meters	m
mi	miles	1.61	kilometers	km
AREA				
in^2	square inches	6.45	square centimeters	cm^2
ft^2	square feet	0.09	square meters	m^2
yd^2	square yards	0.84	square meters	m^2
mi^2	square miles	2.59	square kilometers	km^2
	acres	0.41	hectares	ha
MASS (weight)				
oz	ounces	28.35	grams	g
lb	pounds	0.45	kilograms	kg
	short tons (2,000 lb)	0.9	tonnes	t
VOLUME				
tsp	teaspoons	4.93	milliliters	ml
Tbsp	tablespoons	14.79	milliliters	ml
fl oz	fluid ounces	29.57	milliliters	ml
c	cups	0.24	liters	l
pt	pints	0.47	liters	l
qt	quarts	0.95	liters	l
gal	gallons	3.79	liters	l
ft^3	cubic feet	0.03	cubic meters	m^3
yd^3	cubic yards	0.77	cubic meters	m^3
TEMPERATURE (exact)				
°F	Fahrenheit temperature	5/9 (after subtracting 32)	Celsius temperature	°C

FIGURE 10-7 These are approximate conversion charts.

Focus on the Workplace

Calculator Review

The calculator is an essential tool in the workplace. Most desktop, notebook, and tablet computers include calculators. A majority of cellphones have calculators as well. A calculator has number buttons and command buttons. The arrangement of the buttons and which command buttons are included will vary among different models.

Push CE if you make a mistake in your last entry.

Push C if you make a mistake and want to redo the problem.

Turn on the calculator. To add 34 and 57, push 34 + 57 =. The answer appears on the screen: 91.

Subtraction (64 − 8 =), multiplication (27 × 6 =), and division (135 ÷ 7 =) are done in a similar manner. Simply enter the first number in the calculation; press −, ×, or ÷; enter the second number; and press =.

The calculator has no commas and no dollar signs. To add $3,618 and $4,192, push 3618 + 4192 =. The screen shows this total: 7810. When you write the total, include the dollar sign and comma: $7,810.

Many calculators have these additional buttons:

- The MR button reads or displays the memory number.
- The MC button clears the memory to zero.
- The M+ button enters or adds to the memory number.
- The M− button subtracts from the memory number.

Placing a number in memory is useful for figuring sales tax, markup, and markdown. (The steps on your calculator may vary slightly. Read the directions.) If you want to add a sales tax of 3.5%, push 3.5 M+. To calculate the tax on $54.95, push 54.95 × MR %. Push the equal sign. The answer is 1.92325 or $1.92.

If the tax increases from 3.5% to 4.0%, the actual increase is 0.5%. To increase the tax by that amount, push .5 M+. To decrease the tax by 1.25%, push 1.25 M−. Push C to clear the memory when you have finished.

THINK CRITICALLY

1. For what tasks at work could or do you use a calculator?
2. Calculators, computers, cash registers, and other devices automatically perform many math calculations on the job. This being the case, how important is it that you be able to do math by hand?

There is often a need to do calculations in the workplace.

Chapter Summary

10-1 Basic Math

A. Occupations can be classified according to the level of math skills required: Advanced, applied, practical, or general. All sixteen career clusters include occupations that require some degree of math skills. Strong math skills increase your lifetime earning potential.

B. Business math involves being able to figure total purchase amount, trade discount, cash discount, markup, sales tax, and markdown.

10-2 Basic Measurement

A. Basic measurement skills involve being able to perform surface measurement (perimeter and area) and volume measurement.

B. Most countries and some occupational fields use the metric system. Making measurement conversions within the same system and between the conventional and metric systems is a necessary skill.

Activities

1. List all the ways you use math and measurement skills in your co-op or work experience job. Compare your list with other students' lists. What skills does the class find are the most common?

2. Test your skills in reading a ruler by playing "The Ruler Game." Access www.cengage.com/school/working and choose chapter 10. Click on the Web Links for The Ruler Game. Follow the instructions. Compare your score and time with those of your classmates.

3. For the classroom in which you are meeting, perform the necessary measurements and calculations to answer the following questions:

   a. What is the perimeter of the classroom?
   b. How much area of floor space is contained within the classroom?
   c. How much area of wall space is taken up by window and door openings?
   d. How much volume is contained within the classroom?

4. To find the average of a set of numbers, you can add them on a calculator and divide by the number of items. Here is an example:

   $(140 + 145 + 146 + 149 + 144 + 146) \div 6 = 145$

   The average is 145. Another way to find the average is to pick a "benchmark" number less than or equal to the smallest number. In the example, 140 would be the benchmark. Now, add the difference between each number and the benchmark. Then find the average of the difference: $(0 + 5 + 6 + 9 + 4 + 6) \div 6 = 5$.

The average of the difference is 5. Add this to the benchmark and you get 145. This shortcut can save you considerable time. Often, you can add the numbers in your head without using a calculator. Using benchmarks, find the averages of the following numbers:

a. Prices of $200, $220, $210, $215, and $230
b. Lengths of 47, 46, 51, 45, 52, 46, and 49 inches
c. Temperatures of 80, 72, 75, 74, 73, 77, 81, and 76 degrees Fahrenheit

5. List and describe several goals you might set for yourself in your life-span plan that would be easier to achieve if you are able to solve basic mathematical problems.

Word Power

On a separate sheet of paper, match each definition with the correct term. All definitions will be used, and a definition will be used only once.

6. The distance around the outside of an object
7. A bill for goods
8. An amount added by a retailer to the cost price of goods that allows it to cover expenses and make a fair profit
9. The act of determining the dimensions, quantity, or degree of something
10. A deduction from the suggested catalog price of an item
11. The number of square units of space on the surface of a figure enclosed by the perimeter
12. A reduction in price, often of several percent, offered to a buyer to encourage early payment on an account
13. The perimeter of a circle
14. That part of an invoice that states the time limit within which a buyer must pay for merchandise received from a seller
15. A reduction in the selling price of a product

a. area
b. cash discount
c. circumference
d. invoice
e. markdown
f. markup
g. measurement
h. perimeter
i. terms
j. trade discount

Think Critically

16. Should the U.S. require all businesses to use the metric system?
17. In "rough carpentry" work, measurements within ¼ inch are considered accurate. Other jobs, such as installing cabinets, require more accurate measurement. Discuss and give examples of how standards of accuracy in measurement vary among different occupations.
18. How much is the sales tax in your state? What types of goods and services does it cover?

11 Health and Safety

"I never did anything by accident, nor did any of my inventions come by accident; they came by work." —THOMAS A. EDISON

skynesher/iStockphoto.com

PREVIEW

Good health is essential for success as a student and worker. Eating right, exercising, and finding ways to manage stress will improve your health, appearance, and attitude. Many fitness activities involve some risk of injury. Accidents have multiple causes. There are many ways to avoid accidents.

Taking/*Action* Eat Right

Janine and Manuela were roommates in their first apartment. As soon as they had unpacked all of their belongings, they realized they were hungry and there was no food in the kitchen.

The young women went to the local grocery store. They had never lived away from their parents, so they decided to get all the junk food and snacks that they liked. The cart was soon filled with candy, chips, soft drinks, and other junk food.

Janine and Manuela enjoyed being able to eat whatever they wanted. They ate ice cream for dinner. They ate chips and salsa for lunch. They ate cookies for breakfast.

After about a week of eating this way, Janine sat down with Manuela one morning. She said, "You know, I do not feel very good. I think it's the food we're eating. I hate to say this, but I think I want a home-cooked meal with a big salad."

"You're right," Manuela replied. "Let's make a list."

The two young women got out a cookbook that Janine's mother had given them. They made a list of basic items that their kitchen should have. Janine and Manuela decided that they would each prepare a good dinner three times a week that they would share. They would eat out or cook for themselves the other night.

Manuela called her father and wrote down recipes for several of her favorite meals. Janine found some recipes in the cookbook that sounded great. A coworker of Manuela recommended a website that provided weekly menus including weekly ingredient shopping lists. Manuela subscribed to the list. She thought it would be good to have some new recipes handy for after they'd tried the interesting cookbook recipes.

Janine and Manuela went to the grocery store again. On the way, they saw a lot of people in the community center parking lot. The center was hosting a farmers' market where local farmers could sell their produce. Janine and Manuela bought homegrown lettuce, carrots, sweet corn, and peppers. They bought tomatoes, Swiss chard, cantaloupe, and strawberries. Janine and Manuela found out that the tailgate market was held once a week. They decided to buy fresh vegetables and fruit there.

"It's my turn to cook tonight," said Janine on the way home. "How about stir-fried chicken and peppers with rice and a salad?"

* Success Tip

Tasty, healthy meals can be inexpensive and easy to prepare.

THINK CRITICALLY

1. What would you buy at the grocery store if you could buy anything you wanted?

2. How does what you eat affect how you feel?

OBJECTIVES

- Describe how the *MyPlate* food guidance system is used in choosing a healthful diet
- Identify your own recommended weight and daily calorie needs

KEY TERMS

- nutrition
- nutrient
- calorie
- sedentary
- basal metabolism

leungchopan/Shutterstock.com

Personal Decisions

Your school district has begun to provide more healthful lunches in the cafeteria. Lower calorie and lower fat entrees and more salad options are provided. In addition, junk food and sugary sodas have been removed from vending machines. They have been replaced with such things as baked chips, trail mix, and fruit juices. Some of the students are upset and are starting a petition to bring back the old menus and vending machines. You have been approached by one of your friends to sign the petition, but you actually favor the new food choices.

What would you do?

Eat Right

Sherri had not been feeling well for a long time. Her appetite was poor and she always seemed tired. She was spending a great deal of time in her room and had little interest in going out with her friends. She had frequent headaches. Sherri's parents became very concerned and took her to the doctor for a checkup.

After a complete exam and several tests, Dr. Williams sat down with Sherri to explain the results. "Well, Sherri," said the doctor, "I don't find any major problems. But I don't think you're in very good health."

The doctor's statement confused Sherri. Dr. Williams then explained to Sherri that being healthy means more than just being free from illness or disease. Good health involves a person's overall physical and mental well-being.

Dr. Williams told Sherri that achieving and maintaining good health depends on nutrition and diet, stress management, and exercise. Good health is related to your success and productivity at school and on the job.

Nutrition is the process by which plants and animals take in and use food. **Nutrients** are chemical substances in food that are needed for good health. Nutrients serve as fuel to provide energy, help regulate body processes, and furnish basic materials for building, repairing, and maintaining body tissues.

Nutrients are supplied by foods that people eat. Foods vary in the kinds and amount of nutrients they contain. Based on the most sound scientific information available, the federal government in 2010 published the 7th edition of the *Dietary Guidelines for Americans*. The *Guidelines,* which are mandated by Congress, form the basis of nutrition education programs funded by the federal government. They are used by health professionals to provide dietary advice to the general public.

The *2010 Dietary Guidelines* include 23 key recommendations for the general population and six additional recommendations for specific population groups, such as pregnant women. The full report is available at www.health.gov/dietaryguidelines. Following is a summary of several tips provided to help consumers translate the guidelines into their everyday lives:

- Enjoy your food, but eat less.
- Avoid oversized portions.
- Make half your plate fruits and vegetables.
- Switch to fat-free or low-fat (1%) milk.
- Compare sodium in foods like soup, bread, and frozen meals— choose the foods with the lowest sodium content.
- Drink water instead of sugary drinks.

In support of the *Dietary Guidelines*, the U.S. Department of Agriculture announced in June 2011 a new food icon called *MyPlate*. The icon, shown in Figure 11-1, serves as a simple visual reminder to make healthy food choices when you choose your next meal. *MyPlate* can help prioritize food choices by reminding you to make half of your plate fruits and vegetables and shows the other important food groups for a well-balanced meal: whole grains, lean proteins, and low fat dairy. An accompanying website at www.ChooseMyPlate.gov provides information and "how-to" materials about healthy eating. Interactive tools are also available like the customizable *Daily Food Plan* or *Food Tracker*.

MyPlate has been described as the first step in a multi-year effort by the federal government to raise awareness and encourage consumers to adopt healthier eating habits balanced with physical activity.

Childhood obesity rates in America have tripled over the past three decades. Nearly one in three children in American today are overweight or obese. If this problem isn't solved, one third of all children born in 2000 or later will suffer from diabetes at some point in their lives. Many others will face chronic obesity-related health problems like heart disease, high blood pressure, cancer, and asthma.

A companion effort to *MyPlate* is the *Let's Move* initiative advocated by First Lady Michelle Obama. *Let's Move* is a program dedicated

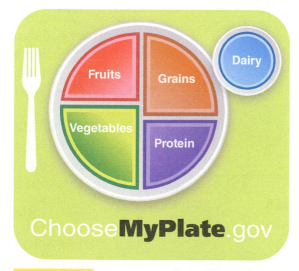

FIGURE 11-1 The MyPlate image and accompanying website provides information for a well-balanced meal.
Source: U.S. Department of Agricultrue

to solving the challenge of childhood obesity within a generation. A comprehensive website is available at www.letsmove.gov. The website provides information and ideas for individuals and organizations to help direct children to healthy lifestyle choices. The intent is to provide many options for solving the problem of childhood obesity.

Calories and Weight

Calories are units of energy produced by food when it is used by the body. Calories are needed for continuous body functions such as breathing, heart rate, and physical activities. How many calories you need depends on your age, your sex, your size, and your activity level.

For example, a 17-year-old male, who exercises between 30 and 60 minutes per day, should consume about 2,800 calories. A female of the same age and activity level would require 2,000 calories. If the girl exercises more than 60 minutes a day, her calorie level would increase to 2,400. As you can see, a person who is very active needs more calories than one who is sedentary, or inactive.

An important feature of the new *ChooseMyPlate* website is that you can get a personalized plan that provides you with specific food recommendations based on data you supply. To illustrate, a 17-year-old female who is 5'3" and weighs 120 lbs, and exercises more than 60 minutes a day should consume 8 ounces of grains, 3 cups of vegetables, 2 cups of fruits, 3 cups of milk, 6 1/2 ounces of meat or beans, and up to 7 teaspoons of oils.

When the foods you eat provide more energy than you need to meet the demands of the body, your body stores the extra energy as fat. If you regularly eat too much food, you gain weight. On the other hand, if your energy level requires more calories than you take in, your body uses stored fat. You then lose weight.

Body Mass Index (BMI)

Ideal weight varies among individuals. *Body Mass Index (BMI)* is a number that is calculated from a person's height and weight. BMI is an indicator of body fatness. The formula for BMI is

$$BMI = (\text{weight in lb} \div (\text{height in inches})^2) \times 703$$

As shown in Figure 11-2, the Centers for Disease Control and Prevention (CDC) provide guidelines for how adult BMI relates to weight status. The chart is for adults age 20 and older. The same chart is used for adult males and adult females. Figure 11-3 on the next page shows actual height, weight, and BMI levels.

Most individuals should try to maintain a BMI within the normal limits of 18.5 to 24.9. There will be some variations in BMI results that are related to sex, age, and race. Studies have shown that individuals who are overweight or obese may have an increased risk of getting certain diseases including hypertension, type 2 diabetes, and some cancers. If you are unsure about your BMI results or what the results mean for you, you should contact your doctor for additional information.

BMI	Weight Status
Below 18.5	Underweight
18.5–24.9	Normal
25.0–29.9	Overweight
30.0 and Above	Obese

FIGURE 11-2 BMI Chart that Correlates Adult BMI with Weight Status

Source: Centers for Disease Control and Prevention

BMI provides a reasonable guideline to assess weight and height ratios. There may be instances when BMI is not an accurate indicator of fitness. For example, a male with highly developed muscles may have a BMI that indicates he is obese. As muscle weighs substantially more than fat, the BMI formula can provide a distorted snapshot of the male's fitness.

As you try to decide what is an appropriate weight for your body, keep in mind that BMI provides an objective, consistent, scientific benchmark. When viewing the weight of celebrities and models, remember that many of them are unnaturally thin. As their livelihoods depend on their appearance, they may spend an above average amount of time and money trying to perfect their looks. They may use extreme, or even unhealthy methods, to achieve their weight goals.

Body Mass Index Table

	Normal						Overweight					Obese										Extreme Obesity											
BMI	19	20	21	22	23	24	25	26	27	28	29	30	31	32	33	34	35	36	37	38	39	40	41	42	43	44	45	46	47	48	49	50
Height (inches)												Body Weight (pounds)																				
58	91	96	100	105	110	115	119	124	129	134	138	143	148	153	158	162	167	172	177	181	186	191	196	201	205	210	215	220	224	229	234	239
59	94	99	104	109	114	119	124	128	133	138	143	148	153	158	163	168	173	178	183	188	193	198	203	208	212	217	222	227	232	237	242	247
60	97	102	107	112	118	123	128	133	138	143	148	153	158	163	168	174	179	184	189	194	199	204	209	215	220	225	230	235	240	245	250	255
61	100	106	111	116	122	127	132	137	143	148	153	158	164	169	174	180	185	190	195	201	206	211	217	222	227	232	238	243	248	254	259	264
62	104	109	115	120	126	131	136	142	147	153	158	164	169	175	180	186	191	196	202	207	213	218	224	229	235	240	246	251	256	262	267	273
63	107	113	118	124	130	135	141	146	152	158	163	169	175	180	186	191	197	203	208	214	220	225	231	237	242	248	254	259	265	270	278	282
64	110	116	122	128	134	140	145	151	157	163	169	174	180	186	192	197	204	209	215	221	227	232	238	244	250	256	262	267	273	279	285	291
65	114	120	126	132	138	144	150	156	162	168	174	180	186	192	198	204	210	216	222	228	234	240	246	252	258	264	270	276	282	288	294	300
66	118	124	130	136	142	148	155	161	167	173	179	186	192	198	204	210	216	223	229	235	241	247	253	260	266	272	278	284	291	297	303	309
67	121	127	134	140	146	153	159	166	172	178	185	191	198	204	211	217	223	230	236	242	249	255	261	268	274	280	287	293	299	306	312	319
68	125	131	138	144	151	158	164	171	177	184	190	197	203	210	216	223	230	236	243	249	256	262	269	276	282	289	295	302	308	315	322	328
69	128	135	142	149	155	162	169	176	182	189	196	203	209	216	223	230	236	243	250	257	263	270	277	284	291	297	304	311	318	324	331	338
70	132	139	146	153	160	167	174	181	188	195	202	209	216	222	229	236	243	250	257	264	271	278	285	292	299	306	313	320	327	334	341	348
71	136	143	150	157	165	172	179	186	193	200	208	215	222	229	236	243	250	257	265	272	279	286	293	301	308	315	322	329	338	343	351	358
72	140	147	154	162	169	177	184	191	199	206	213	221	228	235	242	250	258	265	272	279	287	294	302	309	316	324	331	338	346	353	361	368
73	144	151	159	166	174	182	189	197	204	212	219	227	235	242	250	257	265	272	280	288	295	302	310	318	325	333	340	348	355	363	371	378
74	148	155	163	171	179	186	194	202	210	218	225	233	241	249	256	264	272	280	287	295	303	311	319	326	334	342	350	358	365	373	381	389
75	152	160	168	176	184	192	200	208	216	224	232	240	248	256	264	272	279	287	295	303	311	319	327	335	343	351	359	367	375	383	391	399
76	156	164	172	180	189	197	205	213	221	230	238	246	254	263	271	279	287	295	304	312	320	328	336	344	353	361	369	377	385	394	402	410

Source: Adapted from *Clinical Guidelines on the Identification, Evaluation, and Treatment of Overweight and Obesity in Adults: The Evidence Report.*

FIGURE 11-3 BMI Chart that Shows Height, Weight, and BMI

People need to maintain a reasonable weight to height ratio. The BMI chart will help you determine what is reasonable. Focusing on liking yourself for who you are will be of greater long term value than trying to attain extreme thinness.

Balance Calorie Consumption

The number of calories used by the body each day to maintain weight is called the daily calorie need. Part of this is the minimum necessary for continuous body functioning and is called the **basal metabolism**. The remainder is used by the body as it carries out various work and leisure activities.

For good health, it is wise to maintain your recommended weight. Do this by controlling the amount and kinds of foods you eat (calories), your level of activity, or both. For you to maintain the same body weight, the amount of calories in the food you eat must balance the amount of calories you use. To lose weight, you need to take in fewer calories than your body needs (or use up calories through exercise). To gain weight, you must consume extra calories.

For each pound you want to gain or lose, you must take in about 3,500 more or fewer calories than the body uses. Although there is some variation in recommendations, a safe rate of weekly weight loss is from 0.5 to 1.5 pounds per week. At this moderate rate of weight loss, you are more likely to make lifestyle and eating changes that you can maintain for the long term. Faster weight loss can result in health problems or increase the chance of regaining the weight as soon as the diet is ended. Anyone who is considering a weight loss program should consult with their physician prior to beginning it. This is especially true for children who are still growing.

If you are interested in gaining or losing weight, the first step is to learn about the number of calories that various foods contain. Charts showing the calorie values of common foods appear in most cookbooks and can be found on the Web by searching for "calorie counter" or "food calorie chart."

If you are trying to gain or lose weight, remember that you still need proper nutrients. Even though the number of calories may vary, you need the appropriate number of servings from each part of *MyPlate*. It is a good idea never to go below 1,200 calories a day. If you take in fewer calories than that, you probably will not get the vitamins and minerals you need.

11-1 Assessment

1. Name the three functions that nutrients perform.
2. Name the five major food groups in the *MyPlate* food guidance system.
3. Calculate your height in inches and weigh yourself. Use Figure 11-3 to determine your weight status. Are you underweight, normal, overweight, or obese? If you are not in a healthy weight status, what steps can you take to get there?
4. About how many calories should you eat each day?
5. What is the purpose of the *Let's Move* initiative?
6. Why is childhood obesity such a serious problem?
7. Why is it important not to eat fewer than 1,200 calories a day?
8. Should you try to look like a model or celebrity? Why or why not?

High Growth Occupations
FOR THE 21ST CENTURY

Home Health Aides and Personal and Home Care Aides

 If you are interested in helping the elderly, disabled, and people who are ill, consider the occupations of home health aide and personal and home care aide. The two types of healthcare support occupations have similar duties. However, there are some small differences.

Home health aides go to the homes of elderly, disabled, or convalescing patients. Under the direction of the nursing or medical staff, home health care aides provide health-related services, which may include administering oral medications; checking patient's pulse rates, temperatures, and respiration rates; helping with simple prescribed exercises; helping patients get into and out of the bed; helping patients walk, bathe, and dress; and helping patients with personal grooming.

Personal and home care aides work in the patient's home or in residential care facilities to help patients have a better quality of life. Most of the patients are the elderly or disabled who need more extensive assistance than their families can provide. Other patients may be recently discharged from the hospital and need assistance for a limited time.

The duties of a personal and home care aide may range from housekeeping and routine personal care to cleaning patient's homes, doing laundry, and changing bed linens. Aides may plan meals, shop for food, and prepare the food. Aides also may help patients move from their bed and help them bathe, dress, and groom. Some aides may act as a guide and companion when patients need to go out of the home.

Home health aides and personal and home care aides are usually trained on the job by registered nurses, licensed practical nurses, experienced aides, or their supervisor. The specific requirements vary from State to State.

Aides should have a desire to help people. They should be responsible, compassionate, patient, emotionally stable, and cheerful. Because they work in private homes, aides should be tactful, honest, and discreet. A physical examination, criminal background check, and a good driving record also may be required for employment.

Lisa F. Young/Shutterstock.com

Sometimes people with health issues need medical assistance at home.

STRESS AND PHYSICAL FITNESS

OBJECTIVES

- Name and illustrate the three major ways to reduce or eliminate stress
- Discuss benefits of physical exercise
- Describe the three types of exercises that should be included in a workout

KEY TERMS

- stress
- stressor
- physical fitness
- aerobic exercise

Andresr/Shutterstock.com

▶ Personal Decisions

You have been studying all weekend for a test on Monday. You feel tense, and your neck and shoulders ache from leaning over a desk. One of your friends calls asking you to go to the recreation center for a workout. You would like to go, but you do not feel that you can take time away from studying.

What would you do?

Control Stress

Stress, an unavoidable part of life, is mental, physical, or emotional strain. Causes of stress, called **stressors**, may be events, activities, experiences, or situations. Stressors may be good or bad, and they may range from mild to severe. The following are the most common causes of stress:

- Daily activities, events, frustrations, and challenges cause stress. Examples include missing a bus to school, giving a speech, taking a test, overcooking dinner, or going on a blind date.
- Illness adds to stress because it forces the body to use its defenses. Stress also results when the body must heal an injury or adjust to conditions such as extreme heat, noise, or air pollution.
- A life change is often stressful. Examples might include moving into a new house, getting married, or changing schools. Such changes require many adaptations to new surroundings and situations.
- Life crises produce the greatest stress. These events might include the death of a parent, the loss of a job, or a divorce. The more serious the crisis, the greater the stress.

An event that causes great stress for one person may only be a minor problem for another. Your physical or mental condition influences your ability to handle a new stressor. Your response may also depend on whether you feel in control of the situation. A difficulty may cause little stress if you can predict it, overcome it, or at least understand it.

Most people are able to cope with life's everyday stresses. However, when stressors build up faster than you can deal with them, your capacity may be overloaded. Continual stress exhausts the body's resources that maintain energy and resist disease. The result may be anxiety, depression, or serious illness.

A well-balanced life can help you prevent or reduce stress. Ways of managing stress may include alternating mental activity with physical activity, sharing feelings with others, reading inspirational books, and having interests outside of school or work. In addition, cultivating positive emotions such as hope, confidence, faith, and love can enable you to develop a lifestyle that will help you resist daily life stresses. Worrying less and having a sense of humor also help a great deal. Three major ways to reduce or eliminate stress are to plan how to deal with stress, learn how to relax, and change your life.

Plan How to Deal with Stress

Some crises and other types of stressors cannot be predicted. For instance, a loved one may die suddenly. Other stressors such as taking a test, leaving home to go to school, or giving a speech, are known in advance. For those kinds of stressors, you can plan and prepare. For example, you can reduce stress associated with test taking by thoroughly studying the test material until you are confident that you know it well.

If possible, do not schedule several stressful activities during the same time period. When you know a stressful activity or event is coming up, learn to pace yourself. During stressful times, eat well, get plenty of rest, and exercise at an enjoyable pace.

Learn How to Relax

Because stress is unavoidable, it is very useful to learn a method that reduces or eliminates stress. One doctor suggests this very simple relaxation method. Sit or lie in a comfortable position in a quiet place where you will not be disturbed. Close your eyes, and silently repeat the word "one" over and over for 10 to 20 minutes. This activity seems to produce bodily changes that are the reverse of those stress causes. Muscle tension is reduced, and a variety of other changes occur in the heart and the circulatory and respiratory systems. To learn and use a meditation technique like this, you should practice it once or twice a day.

If meditation does not appeal to you, learn some other method that helps you relax and that has a calming effect. The activity may be jogging, listening to music, walking in a park, riding a horse, or sitting in a sauna. Use whatever works for you. Bear in mind that bodily changes associated with stress can be reversed if you take steps to do so.

Change Your Life

If the same stressor is always present, stress-release techniques may not be very beneficial. You may have a situation in your life that simply makes you miserable. This may be a class at school, a job, a conflict with a roommate,

Workforce Trends

Many employers are trying to improve productivity by reforming the way they organize work and motivate workers. To increase quality and lower costs, some firms encourage greater worker involvement and interaction. These innovative work practices include worker teams, total quality management, quality circles, peer review of employee performance, worker involvement in purchase decisions, and job rotation.

or some other ongoing problem. If the situation cannot be relieved through other means, your last resort may be to drop the class, quit the job, or find a new roommate. Of course, turning away from all stressful situations would be bad. But some situations and relationships are so stress-producing that it is often better to change them than to continue.

Physical Fitness

You cannot be healthy without physical fitness. People have different ideas of what fitness means. For some, it is not being ill. For others, it is having a trim body. **Physical fitness** refers to how well your heart and other organs function. Your physical fitness is determined by such factors as age, heredity, and behavior. Although you cannot control your age or heredity, your behavior can help you become physically fit. People vary greatly in their capacity for physical fitness, but almost anyone can improve by exercising regularly.

The years between adolescence and middle age are generally the peak period for physical fitness. However, people of all ages can stay fit if they maintain good health habits and get regular exercise. According to the American Medical Association, exercise

- Improves strength, endurance, and coordination, thus increasing the ease with which daily tasks are accomplished

- Aids in weight control, thus helping to ward off heart disease, arthritis, diabetes, and other ailments often associated with being overweight

- Helps ensure the proper growth and development of young bones and muscles

- Improves the ability to avoid and recover from illnesses and accidents

- Strengthens muscles that support the body, improving posture and appearance

- Increases poise by developing grace and ease of movement

- Reduces stress, thus acting as a natural tranquilizer

Types of Exercises

Your level of physical fitness depends largely on how often and how hard you exercise. The U.S. Surgeon General reports that a minimum of 30 minutes of moderate physical activity, such as brisk walking, on most days of the week can produce long-term health benefits.

To be beneficial, the exercise does not have to be difficult or strenuous. But, as your condition improves, you should increase the number of times that you do each activity. Every workout should include exercises for flexibility, endurance, and strength.

Flexibility Exercises

These exercises stretch the connective tissues and move the joints through a wide range of motions. Such exercises include touching the toes, swinging the arms in circles, rotating the upper body from the waist, and jogging slowly. Flexibility exercises should be performed before and after each workout.

Endurance Exercises

Aerobic exercises are exercises that condition the heart and lungs by increasing the body's ability to take in oxygen. Running, cycling, skipping rope, swimming, and brisk walking strengthen and speed up the action of the heart and lungs by increasing the body's ability to take in oxygen. They also strengthen the blood vessels.

Strength Exercises

Pull-ups, push-ups, sit-ups, weight lifting, and other exercises increase the strength and endurance of the body's major muscle groups. For example, lifting weights increases the strength of arms, shoulders, and back muscles.

Guidelines for Physical Fitness

Exercise is basic to healthful living. When beginning or maintaining an exercise program, keep the following guidelines in mind:

- Do not keep finding excuses not to exercise.
- Do not think of fitness as a crash program. To avoid injury and fatigue, start slowly and carefully increase the length of your workout.
- Enjoy yourself. Exercise can be fun.
- Do not set unrealistic expectations. Remember, you are not training for the Olympics.
- To avoid boredom, vary your exercise routine.
- Once you get in shape, continue with your exercise program. If you get lazy and quit, your fitness level can deteriorate rather rapidly. The longer you allow yourself to be inactive, the harder it is to get back in shape.
- Harmful health habits such as taking drugs, smoking, drinking alcohol, and not getting enough sleep can undo the benefits of regular exercise.

As a young person, you have most of your life ahead of you. The quality of that life will depend a great deal on your physical and mental health. Begin now to follow guidelines regarding nutrition and diet, reducing stress, and physical fitness. This will better allow you to live and enjoy your life to its fullest.

11-2 Assessment

1. Stress sometimes comes from a positive event. Give an example.
2. Do people respond in the same way to stress?
3. Name three major ways to reduce or eliminate stress.
4. Name four benefits of exercise.
5. Briefly explain the three basic types of exercises.
6. Name four unhealthy habits.

ACCIDENTS AND PERSONAL SAFETY

OBJECTIVES

- Describe the nature of accidents according to type and class
- Discuss rules for personal safety

KEY TERMS

- accident
- medically consulted injury
- safety
- electrocute

Workplace Decisions

It is your turn to work the Saturday evening shift. Normally, you do not mind working until 9:00 P.M. Tonight, though, you badly want to see the game. If you hurry, you may be able to see the last half. At quitting time, you quickly clean up. It only takes you a few minutes to wipe off the tables, clean the counter, and empty the trash. By 9:15, you are on your way. As you are heading through the door to the gym, you suddenly stop. Did you remember to lock the door before you left work? You think so, but you are not sure.

What would you do?

Accidents

An **accident** is defined as an unplanned event often resulting in personal injury, property damage, or both. Causes of death vary in frequency depending on age group. For the general public, accidents rank fifth behind heart disease, cancer, stroke, and chronic lower respiratory diseases as a cause of death.

Teenagers and young adults refer to people ages 15 to 24 years old. For teenagers and young adults, motor vehicle accidents were the leading cause of death in 2009 followed closely by homicides and suicides. In 2009, 10,568 teenagers died in motor vehicle accidents and 9,691 teenagers died as a result of homicides and suicides. Statistical data reported in this chapter are from *Injury Facts*, 2011 Edition by the National Safety Council.

Even though accidents are unexpected, this does not mean that they occur by chance. Almost all accidents can be prevented by eliminating unsafe behavior and conditions and by following basic safety rules.

A **medically consulted injury** is defined as an injury serious enough that a medical professional was consulted. In a typical year, accidents kill more than 128,000 Americans, and about 39 million more suffer medically consulted injuries. Accidents and injuries are estimated to cost the nation about $694 billion annually. There is no way to calculate the cost in human lives. Data on accidents are reported by cause and location.

Causes of accidents vary. The leading causes of accidental death in the United States are shown in Figures 11-4 and 11-5. Poisoning can occur from drugs, medicines, other solid and liquid substances, and gases and vapors. Poisoning is the leading cause of accidental death. Poisonings begin to rise in the teen years and peaks in the late 40s, after which poisonings decline through about age 70.

The second highest cause of accidental deaths for people under 35 is motor vehicles. For teenagers and young adults, about 59 percent of accidental deaths are caused by motor vehicles. Of these deaths, about 60 percent of these fatality victims are males. For people over 70, falls are the leading cause of accidental death, followed by motor vehicle accidents.

Locations of accidents vary. More accidental deaths occur in the home than in any other location. Accidental deaths in and on motor vehicles are second, followed by public places. Accidental deaths at work trail far behind.

If medically consulted injuries alone are classified by location, the home is the leading location, followed by public places, workplaces, and motor vehicles.

FIGURE 11-4 Major causes of accidental death in the United States

Source: National Safety Council, *Injury Facts* 2011 Edition

Types of Accidents	Number of Deaths
Poisoning	39,000
Motor vehicle	35,900
Falls	26,100
Choking	4,600
Drowning	3,700
Fires, flames, and smoke	3,200
Mechanical suffocation	1,800
All other types	13,900
Total	128,200

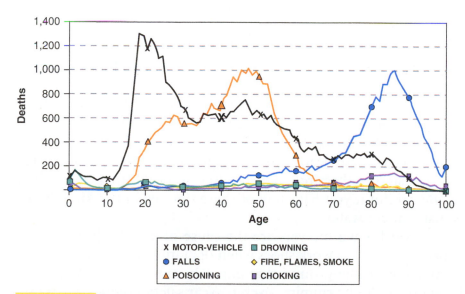

FIGURE 11-5 Unintentional Injury Deaths by Age and Event, United States, 2007

Source: National Safety Council, *Injury Facts* 2011 Edition

Rules for Personal Safety

Safety is freedom from harm or the danger of harm. The word safety also refers to the precautions taken to prevent accidents. There are many steps that can be taken to avoid or prevent accidents at home, at school, on the job, and elsewhere.

In the Home

More accidental deaths and medically consulted injuries occur in the home than in any other location. People spend more time at home than in any other location. Most poisonings occur at home.

Many poisoning deaths and injuries occur from taking illegal drugs and from overmedication. Misuse of drugs is a psychological, medical, and law enforcement issue in addition to a safety issue. Individuals having a drug problem should be encouraged and helped to seek treatment from a qualified medical professional.

Legal drugs and medications are found in most homes. Always follow the directions for taking prescription medications and over-the-counter drugs. Keep drugs and medications in a safe place inaccessible to young children and older adults having memory problems. The same precautions apply to household chemicals and cleaning supplies.

Good housekeeping is one of the most important safety defenses. Keep everything in its proper place. Do not leave shoes, toys, books, or other objects on the floor and stairs where someone could trip over them. Put kitchen knives, other utensils, tools, and household cleaners away immediately after you use them.

In many homes, the kitchen is the busiest and most dangerous room. Climbing and reaching cause many accidents. Use a ladder or a firm chair to reach objects in high places. Store appliances and other heavy objects on low shelves. Turn pot handles toward the back of the range to avoid burns and scalds. To prevent cuts, keep kitchen knives in a rack, not loose in a drawer. Kitchens often have types of floor coverings that can become very slick when wet. Immediately wipe up water, grease, or anything else spilled on the floor.

Falls are also one of the worst dangers in the bathroom. Install nonslip strips in the tub or shower and provide handrails to prevent falls while bathing.

Water is an excellent conductor of electricity. Dry your hands thoroughly before using a hair dryer or other electrical appliance. A plugged-in appliance could electrocute you if it falls into water. To electrocute is to cause death by electric shock. Do not use radios, televisions, and stereos that are plugged into electrical outlets in the bathroom. Be careful if you have any of these devices in the kitchen near areas that you use water.

In the yard, lawn mowers are the cause of many injuries. Wear a shirt, pants, and heavy work shoes when operating a mower. Be alert to anything lying on the ground that might be turned into sharp shards or flying projectiles by running over it. Wear safety goggles when using string-type weed cutters. Keep an eye out for nearby children or pets that might be at risk from the yard work you are doing.

At School

State and local laws require schools to meet certain health and safety standards. Beyond these, school officials try to make the environment as safe as possible. They conduct safety programs for students and teachers. Regular drills are carried out to prepare for fires, severe weather, earthquakes, or other types of emergencies. Teachers provide instruction regarding proper safety practices in their particular subjects.

Accidents in school most commonly occur in gyms, on athletic fields, in vocational shops, in science labs, and in art rooms. It is your responsibility to work with teachers and to follow their instructions in these types of classes. Accidents also occur in corridors, on stairways, and in regular classrooms. Many accidents result from students rushing to get to their next class or home. Stay to the right in corridors and on stairs. Do not run, crowd, or shove. In classrooms, keep your feet out of the aisles. Do not throw pens, pencils, or paper clips, which can cause serious eye injuries.

On the Job

Workplace safety has improved steadily over the years. For example, in 1992 there were 4.2 deaths per 100,000 workers. By 2009, the rate had dropped to 2.8 deaths per 100,000 workers. Still, about 3,582 deaths occurred at work in 2009 and about 5.1 million medically consulted injuries occurred on the job. The three most dangerous industries

Communication at Work — SAFETY WARNINGS

At work, safety warnings appear on everything from cleansers to metal stamping machines. Do people read them? You might be surprised to learn that even warning labels on prescription drugs can be confusing to medical professionals. In an effort to make prescription labels more easily understood, in 1992 the Food and Drug Administration (FDA) began a fourteen year process to improve the clarity of the labels on prescription drugs. In 2006, the FDA issued the final rules for prescription drug labeling. The goal of the new labeling requirements is to make it easier for medical professionals to prescribe the right drugs to patients. There are also legal requirements for how pharmaceutical companies will electronically maintain prescription information.

Warnings are the last resort of manufacturers to ensure that people use their products safely. If a product cannot be designed so as to be completely safe, and if safeguards to prevent its misuse cannot be built in, then warnings must be provided. To be safe at work, always read warnings thoroughly before using a product and be sure you understand them.

THINK CRITICALLY

1. Why is it important to always read safety warnings on products you use at work?
2. Who do you think would be responsible if, when you did not read a safety warning at work, your oversight caused your coworkers harm?

were agriculture, construction, and transportation, which accounted for about 51 percent of all workplace deaths. Your safety responsibilities as an employee are as follows:

- **Learn and obey rules** Supervisors and experienced workers have learned best how to do the job. Listen, observe, and follow their instructions. Always obey rules and regulations for shop or office safety practices.

- **Consult procedures** If you do not know how to do something, stop and consult the procedures manual or rules. Or ask your supervisor or experienced coworkers.

- **Watch for hazards** Many companies depend on employee assistance in identifying safety hazards and in changing safety procedures. Think about what you are doing. As you observe safety hazards or have ideas for improvements, make them known.

- **Report accidents and injuries** Accident reports are one of the best means of identifying safety hazards that need to be corrected. Participate in accident and injury reporting and investigation. Insurance benefits to the injured person sometimes depend on this.

- **Become involved** Encourage other workers to act and work safely. Try to set a good example. Volunteer to participate on the shop, department, or company safety committee.

- **Perform as trained** This is your most important responsibility regarding safety. Use the correct tools to perform your tasks. Allow enough time to finish a task safely. Avoid distractions. Follow operating procedures for using equipment and perform tasks according to training specifications. Do not operate machinery or drive under the influence of alcohol, drugs, or certain medications. Be neat and practice good housekeeping.

In Recreation

Many types of outdoor recreation have some element of possible hazard. The major causes of accidents are inexperience, overconfidence, and fatigue. General rules for safe recreation include keeping physically fit, learning the basic skills of the particular activity, selecting a safe area, using proper equipment and dress, avoiding overexertion, and never taking chances. Some activities present special problems.

Drowning is the third major cause of fatal accidents for teenagers and young adults. Anyone who goes in, on, or near the water should learn how to swim. Two important rules to follow are never to swim alone and always to be aware of your limitations.

Boating accidents have become an increasing problem. The chief causes of boating accidents are speeding, poor judgment, and recklessness. Operator fault is a factor in half the boating casualties. Boaters should know the safety limitations of their craft and never exceed the safe speed. The U.S. Coast Guard establishes and enforces boating regulations. A boat operator should learn to follow such regulations.

Rifles, pistols, and shotguns are deadly weapons. Never point a gun at anyone. Guns should be unloaded before cleaning or storing.

All firearms should be kept in a locked case or cabinet. Ammunition should be stored away from the firearms in a locked container.

If your friend wants to show you a gun, say you do not want to see it. If your friend persists, walk away.

On the Road

Today's automobiles and roadways are built to be safer than ever before. More vehicles are being equipped with air bags and more people are using seat belts and child restraints. It is estimated that the use of air bags, seat belts, and child restraints saved 12,713 lives in 2009.

Motor vehicle fatalities in the U.S. peaked in 1970 at around 53,000. Since then the numbers have dropped steadily to a total of 35,900 in 2009. Even more encouraging is the decrease of fatalities in relation to the number of miles driven. The current rate of about 1.2 deaths per 100 million miles of travel compares with the rate of about 7 deaths in 1950.

Traffic accidents are caused by a number of factors, the two most significant of which are speeding and alcohol. Excessive speed is a factor in 31% of all traffic fatalities and alcohol-impaired driving accounts for 32% of traffic fatalities.

A very worrisome trend is a significant increase in accidents resulting from the use of cell phones while driving. Drivers who use a cell phone while driving have a four times greater chance of being involved in a car accident. It is estimated that 23% of all traffic accidents are associated with drivers using cell phones to talk and text. Research indicates that there is no safety advantage of hands-free over handheld phone use.

Although motorcycles make up slightly less that 3% of all registered vehicles, they account for 13% of total traffic fatalities. Between 1999 and 2009, fatalities among motorcycle riders and passengers increased 80% from 2,483 to 4,462. On a positive note, motorcycle helmets are estimated to be 37% effective in preventing fatal injuries.

Pamela cannot wait for classes to begin next semester. She will be enrolled in driver education. She looks forward to learning how to drive and being able to use the family car. She is wise to take driver education. It is one of the most valuable tools in traffic safety. People who have taken driver education have fewer accidents.

You can help prevent auto accidents and injuries by following commonsense rules. Use seat belts every time you drive. Obey the speed limit. Adjust your speed to traffic and weather conditions. Be a courteous driver. Stay a safe distance behind other vehicles and signal when you plan to turn or change lanes. Do not use your cell phone when driving. Never drive under the influence of drugs or alcohol. Keep your car in good running order. If you drive a motorcycle, always wear a helmet.

Search the Net

Students Against Destructive Decisions (founded as Students Against Driving Drunk) or SADD is a peer leadership organization. It is dedicated to preventing destructive decisions, particularly underage drinking, other drug use, impaired driving, teen violence, and teen depression and suicide. Access www.cengage.com/school/working and click on the link for Chapter 11. Read the information on the website. Then write a paragraph discussing the value of this organization. If your school does not have a chapter of SADD, discuss having your class take the lead in starting one.

www.cengage.com/school/working

Bloodborne Pathogens

Blood and other body fluids can carry diseases. *Bloodborne pathogens* are microorganisms that are present in human blood and can cause disease. According to the American Red Cross, the most worrisome bloodborne pathogens are hepatitis B, hepatitis C, and HIV. If you encounter someone who is bleeding from an injury, you should know how to protect yourself if you decide to assist by administering first aid. The American Red Cross provides these guidelines:

- Avoid contact with blood and other body fluids.
- Use CPR breathing barriers when giving rescue breaths.
- When providing first aid, use protective coverings like disposable gloves and eyewear (in case the blood splashes).
- Cover any of your own sores before giving care.
- Remove hand jewelry before putting on gloves.
- Change gloves before assisting another victim.
- Remove soiled gloves without touching the soiled parts with your own skin.
- Wash your hands and other areas immediately after helping the victim.

Although it may not be practical to always have disposable gloves handy, consider keeping a few spare pairs in your car or backpack. You could also consider taking a basic first aid course. The decision of whether to help an accident victim is a personal one. If you have the proper protective gear and training, the decision may be easier.

11-3 Assessment

1. What is the leading cause of accidental death among teenagers and young adults?

2. What is the leading cause of accidental death in the United States? Where do most accidents occur?

3. Give three examples of how good housekeeping helps prevent home accidents.

4. What is the most important thing you can do on the job regarding safety?

5. Name the major causes of outdoor recreational accidents.

6. What two factors have been responsible for the decrease in motor vehicle fatalities?

7. What are the two major causes of traffic accidents?

8. What should you do if you are driving and see standing water in the roadway?

9. What first aid equipment should you consider keeping in your backpack or car?

NATURAL DISASTERS AND PUBLIC SAFETY

OBJECTIVES

- **Explain what to do in a flood, tornado, hurricane, and earthquake**
- **Name examples of government agencies and private organizations that promote public safety**
- **State the three E's of safety**

KEY TERMS

- natural disaster
- public safety

Personal Decisions

You had a great time at the picnic. The weather was good and the food was delicious. You enjoyed seeing your old friends. It is now time to hop in the car for the long drive home.

About halfway back to the city, the sky starts to darken. The wind begins to blow, and you see lightning in the distance. After a few more miles, the first drops of rain hit the windshield. The rain is soon coming down in torrents. It is only 4:30, but it is so dark that you have to turn on the headlights. The windshield wipers are going full speed. Even so, you can barely see the center line. You wonder what would happen if you had to stop suddenly. You would like to pull off the highway, but you are not very familiar with the road.

What would you do?

blyjak/iStockphoto.com

Natural Disasters

Many accidents and deaths result from natural disasters. A **natural disaster** is an uncontrollable event in nature that destroys life or property. Such tragedies often strike suddenly. Natural disasters differ from many other types of accidents in that they are not preventable. You can lessen the risks, however, if you know what to do during a flood, tornado, hurricane, or earthquake. Some safety rules apply to all natural disasters.

Flood conditions typically build up over hours and days. Leave a flood area as soon as a warning is announced. Do not be caught in a low-lying area.

As flash floods can occur quickly, do not drive through standing water on a roadway if you do not know the depth of the water and whether there is a current underlying it. According to the Federal Emergency Management Agency (FEMA), water just six inches deep

Natural disasters can cause damage violently.

can reach the bottom of most cars, can cause loss of control, and can cause stalling. Water that is twelve inches deep can float many cars. Two feet of rushing water can carry away most cars.

After returning from a flood, have electrical wiring and appliances checked before using them. Boil drinking water until health officials say that the water supply is safe.

Tornadoes occur most frequently in late spring and early summer. Be alert to threatening weather during these periods. If you are going to sleep while conditions are expected to worsen, consider sleeping with a slightly opened window so you can hear tornado warning sirens. If you live in a geographical area prone to tornados, consider purchasing a battery or crank operated weather radio that provides tornado alarm warnings. If you hear a warning or see a tornado coming, go to a basement or inside room without windows. If you cannot move to another room, get under a heavy table or lie flat on the floor. If you are in a car, do not try to outrun the tornado. Get out of the car and lie in a ditch.

Hurricane forecasting has improved tremendously in recent years. Weather bureaus work closely with local radio and television stations to broadcast information about hurricanes and other weather-related problems. After learning of a hurricane warning, keep your radio, television, or mobile device on for further information. Follow the instructions of local officials. After the storm, avoid loose electrical power lines and report them immediately to the power company.

Location	Type	Date	Number of Deaths
Galveston, TX	tidal wave	September 1900	6,000
Johnstown, PA	flood	May 1889	2,209
Florida	hurricane	September 1928	2,148
Central Gulf Coast	hurricane	August 2005	1,836
Ohio and Indiana	flood	March 1913	732
New England	hurricane	September 1938	657
Illinois	tornado	March 1925	606
Louisiana	hurricane	September 1915	500
San Francisco, CA	earthquake	April 1906	452
St. Francis, CA	flood (dam burst)	March 1928	450

FIGURE 11-6 These are the ten largest U.S. natural disasters in terms of fatalities.
Courtersty of National Safety Council

Earthquakes are the most sudden natural disaster. In an earthquake, you must react within seconds to the danger. If you are indoors, take cover under a table or desk. If you are outside, move away from buildings or other structures where you might be struck by falling objects. If you are in a car, stop immediately in a safe area and stay in the car.

Figure 11-6 on the previous page summarizes the ten largest U.S. national disasters in terms of fatalities.

Organizations That Promote Safety

Safety is everyone's business. Safe practices begin at the individual level. Each person is responsible for behaving safely. Some government agencies and private organizations promote public safety.

Public Safety refers to all efforts by federal, state, and local governments to protect persons and property. These efforts include legislation, such as traffic ordinances and building codes, and regulatory activities, such as control of air pollution. Police and fire protection services are devoted to public safety. School and public transportation systems also play important safety roles. For instance, if you have flown in a commercial airliner, you know that the flight attendants provide safety instructions before each departure. Since the 2001 terrorist attacks, federal air marshals are assigned to certain flights.

Police officers help maintain public safety.

JayLazarin/iStockphoto.com

Government Agencies

Many agencies of the United States government are devoted to safety. The Consumer Product Safety Commission protects consumers from unsafe household goods. The National Transportation Safety Board works to ensure the safety of all types of transportation. The Federal Aviation Administration creates and enforces air safety regulations. Safety in motor vehicles is the responsibility of the National Highway Traffic Safety Administration.

The Occupational Safety and Health Administration works to reduce hazardous job conditions. Most state, county, and city governments also have departments concerned with safety and health.

Homeland Security

After the 2001 terrorist attacks, the Department of Homeland Security was formed in 2003. Protecting the American people from acts of terrorism is the highest priority of the Department. The Department seeks to avoid terrorist acts in a variety of areas including preventing explosions in public areas, protecting cyber networks, and detecting biological warfare agents. The Department forms partnerships with state and local law enforcement to plan ways to fight terrorist threats.

Private Organizations

A number of nonprofit, private organizations engage in activities to promote personal and public safety. The National Safety Council collects and distributes information on every aspect of accident prevention. It publishes *Family Safety & Health* magazine and a variety of other print and online publications and aids in developing community safety programs. The American Red Cross conducts instruction in first aid and water safety. It also issues safety information. Underwriters Laboratories, which is often referred to as UL, tests and certifies electrical appliances, automobile and boat safety equipment, and burglar and fire alarms. Samples of UL marks are included in Figure 11-7.

FIGURE 11-7 A UL mark on a product or component means the product was tested and met UL's safety requirements. The marks featured here are for the U.S., for Canada, and a combined mark for both the U.S. and Canada.

Source: Underwriters Laboratories

The Three E's of Safety

The three E's of safety are engineering, education, and enforcement. Proper engineering of buildings, highways, machines, and appliances eliminates many accident hazards. Through education, people can be made aware of accident problems and ways to prevent them. Enforcement of safety rules prevents many accidents. The three E's of safety require expenditures of time and money. But these expenditures are small compared with the savings in human suffering, compensation costs, medical expenses, and lost time.

11-4 Assessment

1. Give two examples of government Public Safety efforts.

2. What are the three E's of safety?

3. How do natural disasters differ from other types of accidents?

4. Name three goals of the Department of Homeland Security.

Focus on the Workplace

Corporate Fitness/Wellness Programs

Faced with spiraling medical costs and insurance premiums, more companies are promoting preventive health care. This may include health screening for employees, educational seminars and workshops, and opportunities for physical activity.

Here is how preventive health care is being encouraged at one large corporation. The program offers classes on stress management and how to quit smoking. It teaches employees the importance of blood pressure testing, weight control, and exercise.

The company has a fitness center onsite. In the center, an aerobics instructor leads exercise classes before and after work and at lunchtime. The company distributes a monthly newsletter on fitness and sponsors regular seminars on good nutrition and other topics.

The program is voluntary, but incentives to participate are provided. For every 20 minutes of exercise, employees get a certain amount of "play money." They can use it to purchase exercise clothing, ankle weights, and other health-related items. Over half of the company's employees participate.

Other companies provide additional inducements for employees. Allowing employees to hold on-site meetings for weight loss programs, like Weight Watchers, is one incentive. Giving employees pedometers, which measure how many steps a person takes, is another way to encourage fitness.

Research has shown that fitness programs like this one pay off. There are fewer illnesses and accidents, reduced absenteeism, and a more vigorous, creative, positive workforce. In one company, it was found that the average yearly medical cost for exercisers was less than 50 percent of that for non-exercisers. Some companies even share the reduced medical costs with employees.

THINK CRITICALLY

1. Fitness programs result in "a more vigorous, creative, positive workforce." What does this suggest about the relationship between mind and body?
2. What are some other preventive health care programs that a company might adopt?

Mari/iStockphoto.com

Many corporations encourage employees to exercise.

Chapter Summary

11-1 Nutrition and Diet

A. The foods people eat provide nutrients needed for good health. To get the required nutrients, you need to eat a variety of foods each day. The MyPlate food guidance system is an easy-to-use daily food guide.

B. Calories are units of food energy needed for continuous body functions and for work and leisure activities.

C. Body Mass Index (BMI) gives an indication of your level of body fatness. For good health, it is wise to maintain your recommended weight. Do this by controlling the amount and kind of foods you eat (calories), your level of activity, or both.

11-2 Stress and Physical Fitness

A. Stress is mental, physical, or emotional strain. Continual stress exhausts the body's resources that maintain energy and resist disease. The result may be anxiety, depression, or serious illness.

B. A well-balanced life can help you prevent or reduce stress. Three major ways to reduce or eliminate stress are to plan how to deal with stress, learn how to relax, and change your life.

C. You cannot be healthy without physical fitness. This refers to how well your heart and other organs function. Physical fitness is determined by such factors as age, heredity, and behavior.

D. Your level of physical fitness depends largely on how often and how hard you exercise. Some experts recommend at least 30 minutes of moderate exercise daily. Every workout should include exercises for flexibility, endurance, and strength.

E. Harmful health habits such as taking drugs, drinking alcohol, smoking, and not getting enough sleep can undo the benefits of regular exercise.

11-3 Accidents and Personal Safety

A. An accident is an unplanned event. Accidents are the leading cause of death for teenagers and young adults. Almost all accidents can be prevented by eliminating unsafe behavior and conditions and by following basic safety rules.

B. Accidents are reported by cause and location. The leading cause of accidental death is poisoning. More accidental deaths and injuries occur in the home than in any other location.

C. Safety refers to the precautions you take to prevent accidents. Know and practice rules for personal safety in the home, at school, on the job, in recreation, on the road, and when dealing with possible bloodborne pathogens.

11-4 Natural Disasters and Public Safety

A. Natural disasters often strike suddenly. You can lessen the risks if you know what to do during a flood, tornado, hurricane, or earthquake. Some safety rules apply to all natural disasters.

B. Safety is everyone's business. Individuals and employers are responsible for personal safety. Many federal government agencies and a number of private organizations are devoted to public and personal safety.

C. The three E's of safety are engineering, education, and enforcement. The costs of safety are small compared with the savings in human suffering, compensation costs, medical expenses, and lost time.

Activities

1. For one full day, keep track of everything you eat and the approximate amount of each food. Then compare what you have eaten with the *MyPlate* guidelines by accessing www.cengage.com/school/working and clicking on the Web Links for *MyPlate*. How well does your diet compare with the recommendations? What foods, if any, are missing from your diet?

2. Access www.cengage.com/school/working and click on the Web Links for Daily Food Plan. Enter the requested personal information to determine your personal daily recommended food plan. Then create a one day menu using the suggested daily plan.

3. Learning a relaxation method can be helpful. For several days, practice the method described under "Learn How to Relax" in Lesson 11-2. In class, discuss whether you notice any difference in how you feel as a result.

4. Federal rules require food companies to put nutrition labels on their packaged food products. Labels must list calories, total fat, cholesterol, sodium, carbohydrates, and similar data. For many nutrients, the percentage of the recommended daily amount that the food contains is also provided. Bring a label from one of your favorite foods to class. Compare its nutritional value with the recommended daily intake shown on the label. Discuss how such nutritional information can help you make better food choices.

5. Consider several goals you might set in your life-span plan. Describe how your ability to achieve these goals might be affected by your health and therefore by your diet. Do you eat a healthful diet? Should you change your diet to protect your health?

6. Access www.cengage.com/school/working and click on the Web Links for Oprah's No Phone Zone Pledge. Read the information, watch Oprah's video, and then sign the pledge not to phone or text while driving. Encourage your friends and family to do the same.

7. Are you aware that the states often have different teen driving license requirements? Access www.cengage.com/school/working and click on the Web Links for State Driver's License Requirements to find the law in your state and compare it to neighboring states. Discuss why states are implementing Graduated Driver Licensing (GDL) requirements.

8. Assume you are at a party and some of the people have been drinking. The driver of your car has had too much to drink, but he insists on driving home. Do you allow him to do so? Do you ride with him? Role-play this situation with one person as the driver and the rest of the class as people at the party.

9. Assume that a cook trainee badly cut her hand in the kitchen. She had to be taken to the emergency room for stitches. Try to estimate the total cost of this accident. Include lost wages of the injured person and the driver, medical bills, lost productivity, and anything else you can think of. What should her coworkers do to protect themselves from bloodborne pathogens while helping her?

10. Imagine that you suffered a serious injury in an accident. How might such an injury affect your ability to achieve goals in your life-span plan? Describe what you can do now to protect your personal safety.

11. The instructor will divide the class into small groups. Each group should prepare a bulletin board display on workplace safety. As technology changes rapidly, research any new potential workplace hazards. The display should be changed periodically until each group has completed its assignment.

Word Power

On a separate sheet of paper, match each definition with the correct term. All definitions will be used, and a definition will be used only once.

a. accident
b. aerobic exercise
c. basal metabolism
d. calorie
e. electrocute
f. medically consulted injury
g. natural disaster
h. nutrient
i. nutrition
j. physical fitness
k. public safety
l. safety
m. sedentary
n. stress
o. stressor

12. An uncontrollable event in nature that destroys life or property

13. Exercises that condition the heart and lungs by increasing the body's ability to take in oxygen

14. All efforts by federal, state, and local governments to protect persons and property

15. Inactive

16. Freedom from harm or the danger of harm

17. Mental, physical, or emotional strain

18. An unplanned event often resulting in personal injury, property damage, or both

19. How well your heart and other organs function

20. Chemical substances in food that are needed for good health

21. Events, activities, experiences, or situations that cause stress

22. An injury serious enough that a medical professional was consulted

23. The minimum amount of energy (calories) necessary for continuous body functioning

24. To cause death by electric shock
25. The process by which plants and animals take in and use food
26. Units of energy produced by food when it is used by the body

Think Critically

27. It has been said that Americans are the most "overfed and under-nourished" people in the world. Why might this be true?
28. Eating disorders such as anorexia and bulimia have become serious health problems. What are some of the possible causes of these disorders?
29. In what ways may short-term stress be beneficial?
30. How does physical fitness differ from bodybuilding?
31. A good diet, control of stress, and physical exercise are all inter-related. Discuss how one may benefit the others.
32. Many government agencies and private organizations work in the field of personal and public safety. Select one of the following organizations. Read about it on the Web, or in another source and prepare a short, written report. Include your own reflections on the value of the services the organization provides.
    - National Transportation Safety Board
    - Federal Aviation Administration
    - National Highway Traffic Safety Administration
    - Consumer Product Safety Commission
    - Occupational Safety and Health Administration
    - Nuclear Regulatory Commission
    - U.S. Coast Guard
    - U.S. Forest Service
    - Mine Safety and Health Administration
    - National Safety Council
    - American Red Cross
    - National Fire Protection Association
    - Insurance Institute for Highway Safety
    - American Industrial Hygiene Association

Career Transitions Connection

Nutrition for Disease Prevention

Click on *Browse Career Paths*. Click on *Health Science*. Scroll down to locate and then click on *Dieticians and Nutritionists*. Click on *Career Videos* to watch the video. Why do you think nutrition is cited as one route to disease prevention? How do you think a national focus on losing weight, exercising more, and improving overall physical fitness will impact careers for dieticians and nutritionists?

12

Leadership and Business Ownership

> "*Good work habits help develop an internal toughness and a self-confident attitude that will sustain you through every adversity and temporary discouragement.*" —PAUL J. FLEYER

Blend Images/iStockphoto.com

12-1 Organizational Leadership

12-2 Parliamentary Procedure

12-3 Self-employment

12-4 Small Business and You

PREVIEW

Many people think of a particular person, such as a high government official, a sports figure, a person of wealth, or a prominent celebrity as a leader. But are all such people leaders? Of course not. Leadership definitions vary by situation. Some leaders are entrepreneurs who own their own business. People who start a small business share certain personality traits. There are many factors that help someone become a successful entrepreneur.

Taking/*Action* Leadership Opportunities

Tyrell and some friends in his business classes were wondering if there was a way that they could learn more about business and meet other students. They had heard about various national student organizations that they might join. They didn't know which group would be the right one. There weren't any organizations currently at their school.

Tyrell was talking about this with one of his business teachers, Mrs. Munoz. She asked if Tyrell was interested in forming a chapter of one of the national organizations at the school. If so, she said that it would take a lot of work. She volunteered to be an advisor or sponsor. She also gave Tyrell the names of some national organizations and information about each one.

Tyrell showed this information to his friends who were also interested in forming a chapter. They discussed the pros and cons of the various groups. At the end of the discussion, they had narrowed their choices to two organizations. Mrs. Munoz suggested that Tyrell and his friends contact nearby chapters of the two groups to set up a meeting with representatives. She also suggested having a set of questions ready.

The students followed Mrs. Munoz's advice. Tyrell telephoned the local chapters and arranged for several members to meet with him and his friends. The representatives were friendly and informative. They provided an overview of the local chapters' activities and discussed the benefits of membership. Tyrell and the other students had many questions, which the members readily answered.

After the meetings, Tyrell and his friends voted on which organization to join. Tyrell went to tell Mrs. Munoz about their choice. Mrs. Munoz said that she would contact the national organization to find out how to set up a new chapter. She also recommended to Tyrell that he run for president of the chapter.

THINK CRITICALLY

1. Why would a student want to join a national student organization?

2. Why would Mrs. Munoz recommend to Tyrell that he run for president of the chapter?

Rena Schild/Shutterstock.com

OBJECTIVES

- Explain what is meant by leadership and how it differs from management
- Describe the three most common leadership styles
- List the six traits or characteristics of effective leaders
- Explain the purposes of career and technical student organizations

KEY TERMS

- leadership
- management
- Career and Technical Student Organization
- code of ethics

CREATISTA/Shutterstock.com

▶ Personal Decisions

Several friends approach you saying that they would like to nominate you for office in a career and technical student organization. You are pleased that they respect your ability. If you were elected, it would mean extra work and responsibility. You are not sure that you have the time or could do the job.

What would you do?

What Is Leadership?

Dozens of books and hundreds of definitions have been written on the subject of leadership. One component of leadership is leadership within an organization.

Organizations are oriented toward achieving certain goals. An insurance company, for example, exists to sell insurance, meet the needs of its customers, and make a profit. **Leadership** is the process of influencing people in order to accomplish the goals of the organization.

The term management is often used as a synonym for leadership, but they are not the same thing. **Management** is the act of planning, organizing, and directing the activities of an organization. The leader's job is to set a direction for the group and to inspire and motivate. The manager's job is to direct people and resources according to the goals and values of the organization.

Even though they are different, leadership and management go hand in hand. In large organizations, the chief executive officer (CEO) is hired by the board of directors to lead and direct the management team and employees. In small organizations, one person (who is often the owner) may be both the leader and manager.

The leader of a group or organization may have a title such as CEO, President, Chair, or Team Leader. This individual is expected to carry out the role of leader. It is not unusual, however, for leadership to emerge at any level within a group or organization. You should be alert to opportunities as a group or team member, or as an employee, to exercise leadership.

Leadership Styles

The leader of an organization may carry out her or his role using different approaches or styles. Authors who write on this subject, mention three leadership styles as being the most common, which are authoritarian, participative, and delegative. These styles are described below:

- **Authoritarian**   This style is also known as autocratic. Authoritarian leaders tell their employees or group members what they want done and how they want it accomplished. They make decisions independently with little or no input from the group. This approach can work in situations where the leader is the most knowledgeable group member, there is little time for group decision making, and the members or employees are highly motivated. In many cases, however, the authoritarian leader is seen as bossy and dictatorial.

- **Participative**   This style is commonly known as democratic leadership. Participative leaders provide guidance to the group, but they also encourage and listen to input from other members or employees. This approach works best in situations where employees or group members are knowledgeable and skillful and can provide valuable input.

- **Delegative**   This style is also known as a hands-off approach. Leaders who use the delegative approach provide little guidance or direction to the group. This approach can work in situations where employees or group members are highly qualified and knowledgeable in a specific area. Frequently, however, delegative groups are less cooperative, less productive, and lack motivation.

In the majority of cases, the participative approach is the most effective leadership style. The authoritarian approach, however, often results in greater productivity. Overall, the delegative approach seems to be the least effective. An argument can probably be made that effective leaders over a long period of time probably combine all three leaderships styles in different combinations with different groups.

Leadership Skills

A number of very effective leaders can be identified throughout history who have achieved success and recognition in a variety of fields including government, business, industry, education, clergy, military, athletics, and the arts. Such leaders often share six common traits or characteristics that are described below.

- **Has a Vision and Goal**   Leaders understand why their organization exists and have a vision of where they want the organization to go. The vision needs to be clear to every employee. The vision should be accompanied by specific goals that can be measured to determine whether the vision has been achieved.

Life-Span
Plan

- **Is a Good Communicator** A vision and goal have little value unless the leader can communicate them to persons who have a direct or indirect stake in the organization. Leaders share information and use a variety of tools to communicate effectively. Good communication skills include good interpersonal skills. Successful leaders take the time and effort to interact with all members of the organization.

- **Sets High Standard** Leaders are ambitious and want to attain increasingly higher goals. They are not satisfied with mediocre performance from themselves or the organization. Leaders try to be good role models and an inspiration for employees.

- **Is Skilled and Competent** A leader is not necessarily the most intelligent person in the organization, but he or she should be recognized as having the knowledge and experience to move the organization forward. Being just a "nice gal or guy" won't take you very far in leading an organization if that is all you have to offer.

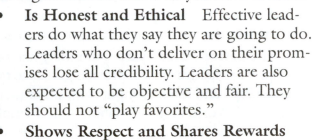
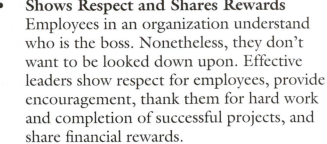

- **Is Honest and Ethical** Effective leaders do what they say they are going to do. Leaders who don't deliver on their promises lose all credibility. Leaders are also expected to be objective and fair. They should not "play favorites."

- **Shows Respect and Shares Rewards** Employees in an organization understand who is the boss. Nonetheless, they don't want to be looked down upon. Effective leaders show respect for employees, provide encouragement, thank them for hard work and completion of successful projects, and share financial rewards.

An effective leader has good communication skills that engage team members.

While these are generally common characteristics of successful leaders, keep in mind that a given leader might not be strong in all of them. Leaders may exhibit these characteristics in different ways.

Career and Technical Student Organizations

Career and technical student organizations (CTSOs) are nonprofit, national organizations with state and local chapters. They are supported primarily by student paid dues. Each organization is linked with an occupational area, such as business, family and consumer sciences, or health occupations. These organizations function as an integral part of career and technical education.

Specific goals and objectives vary from one organization to another. But all have similar overall purposes: to develop leadership skills and good citizenship. The organizations provide students with opportunities to function as junior members of the trade or profession. Students apply skills learned in the classroom and interact with others in the occupational area. A **code of ethics** is a set of rules for professional practice and behavior. Students develop a respect for the occupation and its code of ethics while participating in CTSOs. Other outcomes include providing service, developing decision-making skills, and building confidence.

The national organization generally produces written guidelines for teachers/advisors, student handbooks, and promotional materials. In addition, the organization may sponsor national conferences, leadership development workshops, competitions, and award programs.

There are many different CTSOs. A sample of a CTSO organizational structure is shown in Figure 12-1. A brief profile of each CTSO follows.

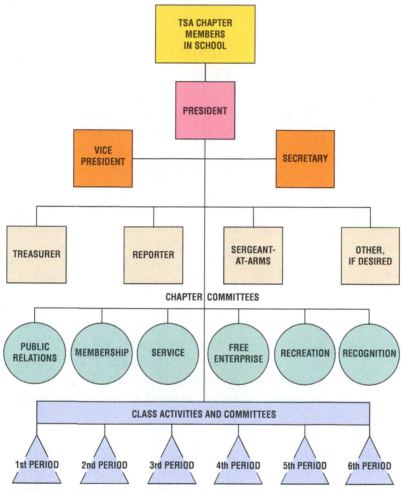

FIGURE 12-1 This charts shows how a local student organization might be structured

Courtesy of Technology Student Association

Business Professionals of America (BPA)

The BPA is for students pursuing careers in business management, office administration, information technology and other related career fields. Its mission is to help prepare a world-class workforce through development of leadership, citizenship, academic, and technological skills.

DECA

DECA prepares emerging leaders and entrepreneurs for careers in marketing, finance, hospitality and management in high schools and colleges around the globe. It also promotes understanding of and appreciation for the responsibilities of citizenship in a free enterprise system.

Future Business Leaders of America—Phi Beta Lambda, Inc. (FBLA-PBL)

FBLA-PBL seeks to bring business and education together in a positive working relationship through innovative leadership and career development programs. The association has four divisions: FBLA for high school students; FBLA-Middle Level for junior high, middle, and intermediate school students; PBL for postsecondary students; and Professional business people, alumni, educators and parents.

Student organizations provide opportunities to learn about occupations and to practice leadership and team building skills.

Robert Kneschke/Shutterstock.com

Future Educators Association (FEA)

The FEA is an international student organization that provides students interested in education-related careers with activities and materials that help them explore the teaching profession in a variety of ways. FEA helps students develop the skills and strong leadership traits that are found in high-quality educators.

Family, Career and Community Leaders of America (FCCLA)

FCCLA is for young men and women in family and consumer sciences education in public and private schools through Grade 12. It focuses on a variety of youth concerns and career exploration. Involvement in FCCLA offers members the opportunity to expand their leadership potential and develop skills for life.

Health Occupations Students of America (HOSA)

HOSA's two-fold mission is to promote career opportunities in the health care industry and to enhance the delivery of quality health care to all people. Activities focus on leadership, social skills, community service, career preparation, and fund-raising. HOSA is for secondary, postsecondary, and adult students in health occupations programs.

National FFA Organization

First known as the Future Farmers of America (FFA), this group was founded in 1928 as part of the high school vocational agriculture program. Today, the organization remains committed to the individual student, providing a path to achievement in premier leadership, personal growth and career success through agricultural education.

National Postsecondary Agricultural Student Organization (PAS)

PAS is an organization associated with agriculture/agribusiness and natural resources offerings in approved postsecondary institutions offering baccalaureate degrees, associate degrees, diplomas and/or certificates. The organization promotes individual growth, leadership, and strong personal ethics for students who are pursuing agricultural careers.

National Young Farmer Educational Association (NYFEA)

The mission of NYFEA is to promote the personal and professional growth of all people involved in agriculture. This group emphasizes leadership training, community service opportunities, strengthening communities, and improving the success potential of American agriculture.

Skills USA

Skills USA promotes leadership, teamwork, citizenship, and character development. It builds and reinforces self-confidence, work attitudes, and communications skills. Skills USA emphasizes total quality at work, high ethical standards, superior work skills, lifelong education, and pride in the dignity of work. The organization serves high school and college students and professional members who are enrolled in training programs in technical, skilled, and service occupations, including health occupations.

Technology Student Association (TSA)

TSA is a student organization devoted exclusively to technology education students. The organization is for students who are enrolled in or have completed technology education courses at the elementary, middle, and high school levels. Activities develop personal growth and leadership abilities. Skill development also occurs in technology, innovation, design, and engineering.

12-1 Assessment

1. How do the roles of a leader and a manager differ?
2. Which type of leadership style is generally the most effective? Why?
3. Leaders are good communicators. Explain how.
4. What does it mean for a leader to be a good role model?
5. In what ways do effective leaders show respect for employees?
6. What are the purposes of career and technical student organizations?
7. What types of activities are conducted by career and technical student organizations?

High Growth Occupations
FOR THE 21ST CENTURY

Accountants and Auditors

If you are good at math and are able to analyze, compare, and interpret facts and figures quickly, you might consider a career in business and financial operations. Two such occupations are *accountants* and *auditors*. They help to ensure that firms are run efficiently, that public records are kept accurately, and that taxes are paid properly and on time. They analyze and communicate financial information for various companies, individual clients, and Federal, State, and local governments.

Specific job duties vary widely among the four major fields of accounting and auditing: (a) *Public accountants* perform a broad range of accounting, auditing, tax, and consulting activities. (b) *Management accountants* are usually part of executive teams involved in strategic planning or the development of new products. (c) *Government accountants* and auditors work in the public sector, maintaining and examining the records of government agencies and auditing private businesses and individuals whose activities are subject to government regulations or taxation. (d) *Internal auditors* verify the effectiveness of their organization's internal controls and check for mismanagement, waste, or fraud.

Technology is rapidly changing the work of most accountants and auditors. With the aid of special software packages, these business and financial specialists summarize transactions in the standard formats of financial records and organize data in special formats employed in financial analysis. Because financial decisions are made on the basis of their statements and services, these workers should have high standards of integrity.

Most accountant and auditor positions require at least a bachelor's degree in accounting or a related field. Some graduates of junior colleges or business or correspondence schools, as well as bookkeepers and accounting clerks, can often obtain junior accounting positions. They can then advance to accountant positions by demonstrating their accounting skills on the job. Because many business processes are now automated, practical knowledge of computers and their applications is a great asset for job-seekers in the accounting and auditing fields.

mangostock/Shutterstock.com

Accountants rely on technology to perform job functions.

PARLIAMENTARY PROCEDURE

OBJECTIVES

- Demonstrate knowledge of how groups that follow parliamentary procedure are organized
- Explain what happens in a meeting under parliamentary procedure

KEY TERMS

- parliamentary procedure
- bylaws
- majority
- quorum
- order of business
- agenda
- motion
- precedence
- parliamentarian

Ethical Decisions

Your career and technical student organization has had a successful year fund-raising. You are meeting to discuss how to spend the chapter's money. A motion is on the floor to authorize spending it for a party. There is a lot of support for the motion. You would enjoy a party, but you think it is an inappropriate way to use the money. You are not sure if you should speak against the motion.

What would you do?

kentoh/Shutterstock.com

Basic Principles

Parliamentary procedure is a way to conduct a meeting in a fair and orderly manner. It is called parliamentary because it comes from the rules and customs of the British Parliament. The United States Congress and other lawmaking bodies follow parliamentary procedure. The rules are used in simpler form by business and professional groups, school organizations, and social clubs. The basic principles of parliamentary procedure are majority rule, protection of the minority, and the orderly consideration of one subject at a time.

Bylaws

An organization operating according to parliamentary procedure adopts a set of bylaws. The bylaws define the basic characteristics of the organization and describe how it will operate. They explain qualifications for membership and procedures for selection of members. The bylaws state the duties of officers and how they will be elected. They also explain how committees will be formed and what their functions will be. All members of an organization should be provided with a copy of the bylaws.

Officers and Committees

An organization usually elects a president (or chair), a vice president, a secretary, and a treasurer. Some groups also elect a sergeant-at-arms or other officers. The president presides at meetings and supervises the work of other officers and committees. The vice president assists the president and chairs meetings when the president is absent. The secretary notifies members of meetings, keeps the minutes, and takes care of all correspondence and committee reports. The treasurer keeps a record of income and expenses and prepares the financial reports. The sergeant-at-arms maintains order during meetings.

Most organizations elect officers once a year. This is often done at the first meeting of the new year. A member may nominate a fellow member. Usually, after two or more people have been nominated, the voting takes place by secret ballot. The person receiving the majority vote is the elected officer. A **majority** is a vote of at least one more than half of the people who vote. If no candidate receives a majority, balloting is continued until one receives a majority.

Most organizations have two types of committees. The *standing committee* deals with regular and continuing matters, such as membership and finance. A special committee is formed whenever it is necessary to work on a specific matter. Examples are to plan a social event or to revise the bylaws. Special committees dissolve when their task is done. Committees are appointed or elected according to the bylaws.

Holding a Meeting

Most organizations require that a quorum be present before a meeting may begin. A **quorum** is a majority of the total membership. An organization's bylaws usually provide for an **order of business**, which is the standard series of steps followed in a meeting. A typical order of business is shown in Figure 12-2 on page 295. An **agenda** is a list of items to be taken care of at a particular meeting. An agenda provides the sequence for discussing the meeting's topics. A typical agenda for a career and technical student organization is shown in Figure 12-3 on page 296.

An important part of any meeting is making, discussing, and disposing of motions. A **motion** is a brief statement of a proposed action. There are four types of motions:

- *Main motions* are the tools used to introduce new business.
- *Secondary motions* provide ways of modifying or disposing of main motions.
- *Incidental motions* arise out of business being conducted.
- *Privileged motions* deal with the welfare of the group, rather than any specific proposal.

The most common motions are summarized in Figure 12-4 on page 297. The motions are listed in order of **precedence**, or rank of priority. When the group is considering a main motion, secondary motion, or privileged motion, no motion listed below it may be introduced. Any motion listed above it may be introduced. Incidental motions have no precedence. They must be decided or disposed of before returning to

PARTS OF A CHAPTER MEETING

It is customary for every group to adopt a standard order of business for the meeting. When the organization's bylaws do not provide for or require a specific order, the following is in order.

1. Call to Order
"Will the meeting please come to order."

2. Roll Call
"Will the secretary please call the roll."

3. Reading and Approval of Minutes
"Will the secretary please read the minutes of the last meeting." The minutes are read and the chair asks:

"Are there any corrections to the minutes?" The chair pauses to hear any corrections offered, if there are none, the chair says, "There being no corrections, the minutes will stand approved as read."

If there are corrections, the chair recognizes the correction(s) and asks, "Are there further corrections to the minutes?" If there are none, the chair states, "There being no further corrections, the minutes will stand approved as corrected."

4. Adoption of Agenda
This step is provided to insure that (1) all persons are aware of what has been proposed for discussion at the meeting; (2) that all persons are given the opportunity to have whatever matter(s) they feel is (are) important to the organization placed on the agenda for discussion; and (3) to provide a limit to and order for the matters to be discussed at the meeting.

To achieve this, the presiding officer states, "The following items are proposed for discussion at this meeting." After reading the list of proposed agenda items, the presiding officer asks, "Are there other matters that should be discussed at this meeting?" If there are additional matters requiring discussion, the chair places them in their proper positions on the agenda.

The chair, after insuring that all pertinent matters will come before the meeting, reads the entire agenda and states, "There being no other matters that should come before this meeting, the agenda for this meeting will stand as read."

5. Report of Officers and Standing Committees
Officers, boards, or standing committees should be called upon to report in the order in which they are mentioned in the constitution or bylaws of the organization.

6. Report of Special Committees

7. Unfinished Business
"We have now come to unfinished business. Our agenda lists the following matters as unfinished business." The chair reads from the agenda and states, "We will hear these matters in the order in which they have been mentioned."

8. New Business
"We have now come to new business. Our agenda lists the following matters as new business . . ." The chair reads from the agenda and states, "We will hear them in the order in which they were mentioned."

9. Program
Programs such as exhibitions, demonstrations, etc., which are incidental to the business meeting, will be scheduled for presentation at this time.

10. Adjournment
Unqualified form:

Proposer moves for adjournment; motion is seconded; chair calls for a vote; action depends upon majority vote. The motion cannot be discussed.

Qualified form:

Proposer moves for adjournment within a definite time or adjournment to meet again at a specified time; motion is seconded; the chair calls for discussion; a vote is taken; action depends upon majority vote; can allow for legal continuation of the meeting.

FIGURE 12-2 Typical Parts of a Chapter Meeting
Courtesy of Technology Student Association

PLAN AND CONDUCT A MEETING

Planning and conducting a meeting are two tasks that every member should be able to perform correctly and with ease. To do this, certain knowledge and skills should become part of your repertoire.

The President, with assistance from the chapter officers, should meet prior to the time of the regularly scheduled meeting to plan the agenda. Minutes from the previous meeting should be examined so that any unfinished business can be noted for discussion at the upcoming meeting.

The agenda is a list of those activities to be engaged in and those items of business to be brought before the membership for discussion at the next meeting. A standard order of business is used when preparing an agenda. You should be aware of and apply the order of business in the planning and conducting of all meetings. A typical chapter agenda is shown below.

SCHOOL CHAPTER AGENDA

DATE ___September 16, 20--___

TIME ___1:30 p.m.___

PLACE ___Mills Godwin High School___

I. **CALL TO ORDER**

II. **OPENING CEREMONY** (Roll call, introduction of visitors)
   - Visitors: Mr. Joseph Long, Miss Laura East

III. **READING OF MINUTES**

IV. **OFFICER AND STANDING COMMITTEE REPORTS**
   - Treasurer's Report
   - Enterprising/Finance Committee to report on fundraising activities

V. **SPECIAL COMMITTEE REPORTS** (none)

VI. **UNFINISHED BUSINESS**
   - Halloween Dance to be held October 30–Selection of band

VII. **NEW BUSINESS**
   - The purchase of TSA blazers for chapter officers

VIII. **ANNOUNCEMENTS**
   - Members who have not turned in their money for the trip to Washington, D.C. must do so today.
   - The Executive Committee will meet on September 25 in the Technology Education Lab at 12:00 noon. Bring your lunch with you. Beverages will be served.

IX. **PROGRAM**
   - Miss Laura East, from the State TSA office, will speak on the Virginia TSA Annual Conference to be held in May.

X. **CLOSING CEREMONY**

FIGURE 12-3 A Typical Chapter Agenda
Courtesy of Technology Student Association

Action	Statement
Privileged Motions	
Adjourn the meeting	"I move that we adjourn."
Recess the meeting	"I move we recess until . . ."
Secondary Motions	
Postpone consideration of a matter without voting on it	"I move we table the motion."
End debate	"I move to end debate."
Have a matter studied further	"I move we refer this matter to a committee."
Amend a motion	"I move that this motion be amended by . . ."
Main Motions	
Introduce business	"I move that . . ."
Resume consideration of a previously tabled motion	"I move we take from the table . . ."
Reconsider a matter already disposed of	"I move we reconsider our action relative to . . ."
Incidental Motions	
Raise a question about parliamentary procedure	"Point of order."
Withdraw a motion	"I ask permission to withdraw the motion."
Seek information about the matter at hand	"Point of information."

FIGURE 12-4 Common Motions Listed in Order of Their Priority

the business under consideration. Each motion must be disposed of in some way before another item of business can be discussed.

Different rules apply to a motion regarding whether it needs to be seconded, whether the motion is debatable, and whether it can be amended. To *second* a motion is to state your support for it, so that discussion or voting may begin. A **parliamentarian** is someone who advises the presiding officer on matters of procedure. Even though motions differ, the general procedure is the same.

Chair is another term used to describe a presiding officer. To make a motion, a member obtains the floor by rising and addressing the chair. The chair recognizes the member by announcing his or her name. The motion is stated. Usually, it must be seconded by another member. The chair restates the motion for the benefit of all members. It is then open to discussion. *Debate*, which is another term for discussion, continues until all members who wish to speak have had an opportunity. Members then vote on the motion. Those in favor of the motion say "Aye." Those against the motion say "No." If the majority of members vote to accept the motion, it is approved.

Parliamentary procedure is not mysterious and complicated. However, it is something that takes time to learn. One of the best ways to learn it is to join and participate in a career and technical student organization.

12-2 Assessment

1. What are the three basic principles of parliamentary procedure?
2. Identify and explain the two types of committees.
3. Name and describe the four types of motions.
4. Explain how a motion is introduced for debate.

Focus on the Workplace

Trade and Professional Associations

Trade and professional associations are an important part of our economic, social, and working lives. A *trade association* seeks to advance common business interests of members. Some trade associations cover a business function, such as manufacturing, distribution, or retailing. For instance, several retail stores may form a trade association. Others are based on the types of goods or services produced. Peanut farmers, service station operators, or restaurant owners, for example, may form an association.

The most important goal of a trade association is to encourage members to generate ideas about how to produce more income from its products or services. Activities of trade associations may include advertising, sponsoring research on new products, and promoting high standards for products, services, or members. To get its message out, a group may produce pamphlets or sponsor tours. It may also publish a magazine for members and hold yearly conventions. To *lobby* for an issue is to try to persuade public officials to support the issue. For some trade associations, lobbying for favorable laws is a major activity. To pay for these activities, trade associations collect dues from members.

A *professional association* is made up of people with a common occupational background such as teacher, pilot, secretary, or chef. Members often need to have an academic degree, license, or certificate to join an association. Professional associations inform members about new developments and issues. They publish journals and hold meetings and conventions. Some associations have student memberships. If a professional association related to your occupation is available, join it. Most individual associations maintain websites that are easily located using a standard Internet search engine.

THINK CRITICALLY

1. What are some advantages of joining a trade or professional association besides those mentioned above?
2. Is lobbying a good idea? Why or why not?

kycstudio/iStockphoto.com

Trade and professional organizations work together to help all members of the organization improve their circumstances and knowledge.

SELF-EMPLOYMENT

OBJECTIVES

- Name contributions that small business makes to our society
- Discuss advantages and disadvantages of self-employment
- Show awareness of what it is like to own and operate a small business

KEY TERMS

- entrepreneur
- self-employed
- Small Business Administration (SBA)
- small business
- proprietorship
- partnership
- corporation
- creditors

Workplace Decisions

The company you work for is losing business to foreign competition. The owner says he cannot compete if he has to continue paying high labor costs. He is looking for a buyer. If he cannot sell the business, he is going to shut it down. A group of employees has been meeting to help find a solution. One option being considered is for the employees to buy the company and run it themselves. This has been done successfully in a few businesses.

What would you do?

Blend Images/Jupiter Images

Nature of Small Business

As a cooperative education or work experience student, you are probably working in a business owned or managed by someone else. In the future, you may continue to work as an employee for another person, or you may decide to become an entrepreneur. An **entrepreneur** is someone who runs his or her own business. An entrepreneur may or may not have additional employees. A small business owner without any employees is said to be **self-employed**.

Small businesses are found in agriculture, construction, health care, information technology, sales, services, and every other type of industry. They are located throughout the country. Many are in big cities, but a large number are in small towns. Small businesses are as scattered and different as the people who own them.

Small Business Statistics

The **Small Business Administration (SBA)** is a federal agency that encourages, assists, and protects the interests of small businesses. The SBA defines a **small business** as an independent business having fewer than 500 employees. The SBA is a very helpful organization for entrepreneurs. The SBA produces and distributes low-cost management assistance publications and conducts management workshops and courses. The agency also makes loans to small businesses. Some mentoring programs are available through the SBA. You can find the location of the nearest SBA office and other information by accessing www.cengage.com/school/working and clicking on the Web Links for Small Business Administration.

Small firms with less than 500 employees represent about 99.9 of all businesses. By examining the data associated with small businesses, it is easier to gain a better understanding of small businesses.

The data available from the U.S. Census Bureau indicates that in 2008 there were 27,281,452 business firms in the country. About 78% of these businesses were managed by self-employed individuals. This leaves 5,930,132 businesses that have one or more employees. Small businesses with various numbers of employees are shown in Figure 12-5.

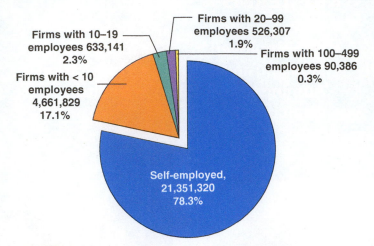

FIGURE 12-5 The majority of U.S. small business are self-employed.

Source: U.S. Census Bureau, Statistics of U.S. Business, 2008

Importance of Small Business

Small business makes many important contributions to society. One contribution is the creation of new jobs. As new businesses begin and expand, they hire new workers. Small businesses accounted for 65 percent, or 9.8 million, of the 15 million new jobs created between 1993 and 2009.

Another contribution is that small businesses often recycle old buildings. It is not unusual, for example, to find a restaurant or a dry cleaning business housed in what used to be a service station. Can you think of examples in your town or neighborhood?

A third contribution is that small business provides opportunities for women and minorities to get started in business. The SBA reported that women owned 29% of the 27.1 nonfarm businesses in 2007. Hispanic Americans owned 8.3%, African Americans owned 7.1%, and Asian Americans owned 5.7% of all U.S. businesses. The number of women- and minority-owned businesses is expected to continue to grow.

The most important contribution of small business comes from new inventions, products, and services. Many of the great success stories of American business have been the result of people who had a new idea or a better way of doing things. Following is information summarized by the SBA that illustrates how important small businesses are to the economy. Small firms

- Represent 99.7 percent of all employer firms
- Employ half of all private sector employees
- Pay 44 percent of total U.S. private payroll
- Create more than half of the nonfarm private gross domestic product

- Hire 43 percent of high tech workers including scientists, engineers, computer programmers, and others
- Are 52 percent home-based and 2 percent franchises
- Made up 97.5 percent of all identified exporters and produced 31 percent of export value in 2008
- Produce 13 times more patents per employee than large firms

Finally, being an entrepreneur is a goal that is achievable for a young person who is ambitious and willing to work hard. Thousands of individuals have started successful companies while in their teens and early 20s. What ideas do you have for starting a new business?

Forms of Organization

A business can be organized as a proprietorship, partnership, or corporation. Figure 12-6 shows percentages of how businesses are organized.

- **Proprietorship**   This is the simplest and most common form of business ownership. A **proprietorship** is a business owned by one person, who receives all the profits. The owner may have employees.
- **Partnership**   A **partnership** is a business that has two or more co-owners. Partnerships are often formed because proprietors need additional money or want help running their business. Owners in a partnership share in the company's management and profits.
- **Corporation**   A **corporation** is a form of business organization in which stockholders own the business. It is very different from the other two forms of business. A corporation pays the state a fee to receive a *charter*, which is a legal document that gives the corporation permission to conduct certain business activities. Stockholders have become partial owners of the business by purchasing stock or shares of ownership in the company. The stockholders elect a board of directors. The board makes major decisions about the company, such as hiring the company president.

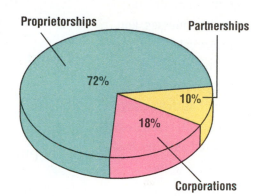

FIGURE 12-6   Proprietorships make up about 72 percent of all small businesses.
Source: The 2011 Statistical Abstract

Advantages and Disadvantages of Self-Employment

Being self-employed is different from working for someone else. Before starting a business, you should consider the advantages and disadvantages of working for yourself. Some entrepreneurs were interviewed about the benefits of self-employment. Their responses follow:

"I never liked working for other people. I like to try new things. That can be a problem when you are an employee. In my business, I can take full advantage of new ideas that appeal to me."

"Being self-employed, I can make my decisions quickly. I used to work for a large corporation in which decision making was very slow."

Workforce Trends

In order to encourage safety intervention at small businesses, the Ohio Bureau of Workers' Compensation provided grants to qualifying small businesses. Employers calculated the cost/benefits of the safety interventions. Many positive safety and health results were reported as a result of using the grants.

"I enjoy having a flexible schedule. Last week, my wife took two vacation days. I arranged my schedule so we could go camping."

"In the shop where I worked, I did only one task. Now I can work on a project from beginning to end. I can use all my skills. I am working toward goals that are important to me."

"I am proud to be a business owner. Four years ago, we opened this small supermarket. We now have three, which will belong to our kids someday."

"When you work for yourself, no one can fire you!"

All work situations have negative points. Self-employment is no exception:

"In the beginning, the appliance-repair business brought in little money. But we still had to pay rent and other expenses."

"I am a freelance graphic artist. My income varies a lot. It is either feast or famine, it seems."

"We are store owners in a one-industry town. As soon as the plant started layoffs, we were affected, and it wasn't our fault! If this keeps on, we may have to close. We could lose the money we have put into the business. We also could lose our house and other property. We are hoping for the best."

"Being self-employed is high-pressure. All the decisions are my responsibility. If I make a major mistake, all of us around here could be out of work."

"I often put in 60- or 70-hour weeks." Even when you are self-employed, you will not be your own boss entirely. No matter what business you choose, you must satisfy your customers, as well as your **creditors**, the persons or companies to which you owe money. Your competitors will also influence what you do. For instance, suppose the store down the street has a two-for-one sale. You may have to do the same at your store, too.

The law also impacts your business. Health authorities and insurance companies will expect you to meet certain standards and to follow certain regulations. You will have to abide by wage and hour laws and keep proper tax and business records as well.

No one person can represent the experiences of all entrepreneurs. The following case study, however, will give you a good idea of the advantages and disadvantages of self-employment. The workday of Ann Kirsten shows many of the freedoms, uncertainties, and responsibilities shared by small business owners.

Self-Employment Case Study

As an entrepreneur, Ann Kirsten does many types of work tasks. In a large business, each work task would probably be done by a single person. As you read this piece, which has been reprinted and slightly adapted from the *Occupational Outlook Quarterly*, keep in mind the variety of things that Ann has to be able to do.

The Day Begins On a typical workday, Ann Kirsten arrives at Country Gifts 'n' Crafts, her small gift and card shop, at about 10 A.M. Stepping inside, she takes a sharp owner's look around the store, which holds a miscellaneous assortment of wares: crystal salad bowls, candles, neckties, placemats, scented soap, and toys are among the many items in stock.

The store opens at 11 A.M. and Ann hurries to make sure everything is in order. She sets out a pitcher of orange juice and a tray of muffins—a bonus for early customers—and checks to see that the store's shelves are well stocked and tidy. Spotting a few gaps, she tells the two full-time salesclerks who have just arrived to shelve supplies of candleholders and cards. She also instructs the employees to unpack a recently arrived carton of stainless steel serving bowls, tag them with the prices she has determined, and display them near the crystal salad bowls.

Answering the Mail   Satisfied that everything is in order, Ann takes the morning mail upstairs to a small room filled with so many cardboard boxes that it looks more like a stockroom than an executive office. Sitting down at her desk, she opens the mail, taking special note of new merchandise catalogs, bills, and a customer check that has been returned by the bank because of insufficient funds. She pays a few bills, answers some letters, and files the rest into piles for future action.

Ann spends the rest of the morning in her office filling out several government forms required of self-employed persons. She is interrupted by a telephone call from a supplier who regrets that Ann's last order will be delayed for three weeks. A *supplier* is a person or agency that distributes goods to retailers, businesses like Ann's that sell directly to consumers. Annoyed, but unable to do anything about the shipment date, Ann shrugs off the incident.

Unexpected Visitor   A few minutes later, a sales representative walks in and tries to sell Ann a new line of paper placemats and napkins. Ann generally buys her merchandise from wholesale houses in New York City, which she visits about six times a year. *Wholesale houses* are businesses that sell to retailers rather than to consumers. Occasionally Ann does buy from a visiting salesperson. Today she declines, believing her current line of paper table items is adequate. Ann takes her time about making this decision, because her income hinges on her ability to make sound judgments about what her customers will buy. If she invests in an item that does not sell, she loses money.

Waiting on Customers   At 1 P.M., Ann goes back downstairs to relieve her clerks during their lunch hours. Before starting the store 7 years ago, Ann enjoyed a 15-year career in public relations. She likes working with people and enjoys waiting on and talking to customers.

The clerks return and Ann grabs a quick lunch before running a business errand at the post office. She then takes time out for a haircut. Because she is her own boss, Ann can take time off whenever she wants. Generally, however, she is reluctant to spend too much time away from the store, because there is always so much work to be done.

🔍 Search the Net

Access **www.cengage.com/school/ working** and click on the link for Chapter 12. Go to the SBA link. You will be directed to the "Starting Your Business" web page. Choose any one of the subtopics. "Writing a Business Plan," "Preparing Your Finances," and "Marketing a New Business" are examples of the topics you may choose. Read about one of the topics. Make notes as you read, and be prepared to explain your topic in class.

www.cengage.com/school/working

Bookkeeping Back at the office, Ann goes over the books with her accountant, who keeps track of income and expenses and evaluates the store's performance. Looking at recent sales income and expenses, Ann briefly remembers the days when she worked for other people. Back then, she regularly collected a paycheck from which her employers had withheld money for state and federal income taxes. Her share of payments for Social Security benefits, a health insurance plan, and other programs that assured her income during retirement or periods of sickness had also been deducted. Like most employers, the organizations for which she worked had paid part of the cost of these benefits.

Looking over the books, Ann is happy to see a good profit. If the store's income had not met expenses for the last several months, she would have had to make up the difference out of her own savings. This rarely occurs now, but like many new businesses, the store lost money during its first several months.

Ann recalls, too, how she had to borrow money to start the business and persuade a lender that she could succeed. Then there had been the years of meeting payments on the borrowed money as well as interest for its use. These payments had to be made regularly, for a merchant is helpless without a good credit rating. As she looks back, Ann is gratified to see that it has all paid off.

End of a Long Day Ann finishes conferring with her accountant at 6 P.M. and then goes downstairs to help wait on customers until the shop closes at 7. Several boxes of merchandise have arrived, and Ann stays for an hour after closing to unpack and shelve a few items. She generally puts in at least a nine-hour workday—not counting "time off" when she reads magazines to keep up with buying trends or thinks about new ideas for the store—and works six days a week.

Every once in a while, Ann remembers the days when she was salaried and worked a 40-hour, Monday-through-Friday week. She strongly believes, however, that the present freedom and challenge of being her own boss and the knowledge that her efforts are paying off in money that goes into her own pocket more than make up for the long hours and other disadvantages.

12-3 Assessment

1. Why isn't there such a thing as a typical small business?

2. What percent of U.S. business firms are self-employed?

3. Name four important contributions that small business makes to our society.

4. Briefly explain the three forms of business organization.

5. Give four advantages and four disadvantages of self-employment.

6. Name five work tasks performed by Ann Kirsten.

OBJECTIVES
- Identify ingredients necessary for a successful business
- Evaluate your own self-employment traits
- Describe factors to consider in choosing a business

KEY TERM
- franchise

Career Decisions

You are a very good auto mechanic and take pride in your work. You can diagnose difficult problems that other mechanics often cannot solve. Customers also know your work is good. Many of them specifically request that you work on their cars. This irritates some of your coworkers. Recently, several customers have remarked that you are too good a mechanic to work for someone else. They say you ought to consider starting your own business.

What would you do?

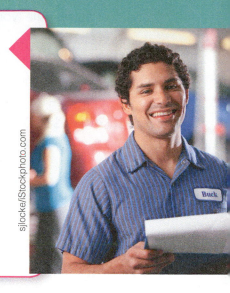

sjlocke/iStockphoto.com

Ingredients for Success

A successful business requires more than just interest and a desire to make money. Studies of businesses and conversations with business owners suggest that three things are necessary for a successful business: the right personality, know-how, and money.

Personality

Not everyone has the right personality for self-employment. Success in business is not based on wishful thinking. If you want to be your own boss, you need to be honest about your strengths and weaknesses. The traits needed by a self-employed person are as follows:

- Ability to take action when needed
- Ability to lead others
- Being dependable and trustworthy
- Being a good organizer
- Ability to work hard
- Ability to make good decisions
- Having a positive attitude
- Being honest and open
- Ability to accomplish goals
- Desire to succeed
- Willingness to take risks

Math Connection

You are thinking about starting a business that makes and sells unique drawer handles. Your fixed monthly expenses (loan payment, rent, utilities, salaries, etc.) would be $6,300. It would cost you $4 to make and ship each handle. You plan to sell the handles for $5.20 each. How many handles would you have to sell per month to break even (for your income to equal your expenses)?

SOLUTION

To determine how many handles you would have to sell per month to break even, first determine your markup on each handle (your net earnings).

Retail price − Cost = Net earnings
$5.20 − $4.00 = $1.20

Then divide your fixed monthly expenses by your net earnings per handle.

Fixed monthly expenses ÷ Net earnings = Number of handles
$6,300 ÷ $1.20 = 5,250

You would have to sell 5,250 handles per month to break even.

Know-how

Self-employed people need some knowledge in various areas of business. These areas include finance, economics, management, marketing, accounting, and commercial law. Business know-how is usually learned through coursework and on-the-job training. Before starting out on their own, most entrepreneurs have experience working in others' businesses.

Pat King started his own restaurant last year. He had worked for many years as a manager for a national chain before deciding to begin his own business. His restaurant management experience had taught him how to train employees, to order enough food to meet customer demand, how to provide exceptional customer service, and how to prepare and serve food safely.

Even after starting their business, many owners continue to expand their knowledge. They study on their own and enroll in management training programs and workshops.

Before starting a business in a trade, technical, or professional occupation, it is necessary to learn the required skills. For example, Kerry and Jill got training in electronics, worked for someone else, and then started their own electronics repair business.

Another way to get business know-how is to buy a franchise. A franchise is a contract with a company to sell its goods and services within a certain area. Some well-known franchises are California Closets, Dollar Discount Stores, Jiffy Lube, and Subway. Franchise fees range from several thousand to several hundred thousand dollars.

Money

The third key to successful self-employment is money. An entrepreneur must have enough capital, or money, to start a business. Money can be borrowed from banks and other lending institutions, or from friends or family. Business owners must pay rent, utilities, and other operating expenses. Equipment and supplies must be purchased. Retailers must be able to buy a large enough supply of merchandise to attract and hold customers. Employees must be paid. Most importantly, there must be enough left over for the owner's salary.

The cost of going into business depends on the type of business, the location, the size, and other factors. Often, the business that can be started with a small amount of money is the business with the least potential for profit. On the other hand, businesses with good profit potential are out of the reach of people because of the money required to begin.

Most small businesses start out slowly. It takes time for a new business to establish a reputation and build up a base of loyal customers. The Small Business Administration says it takes four to six months for some businesses to be self-supporting. Others take even longer. Unfortunately, about half of all new business start-ups fail within the first five years.

Are You the Type?

To succeed in business, you must honestly evaluate your strengths and weaknesses. You will be your most important employee. If you recognize that you are weak in a certain area, you may be able to improve yourself, to find a partner, or to hire an employee to help you. Answer the questions in Figure 12-7 to discover if you have the traits needed for self-employment.

How did you do? Count up the number of "Yes" answers. If most of your answers are "Yes," you may have what it takes to run your own business. Review your answers again. Make sure you did not answer "Yes" because of wishful thinking.

ENTREPRENEUR RATING SCALE

	Yes	Not Sure	No
1. I am a self-starter. I get things done.			
2. I like people. I can get along with just about anybody.			
3. I am a leader. I can get most people to go along when I start something.			
4. I like to take charge of things and see them through.			
5. I like to have a plan before I start. I'm usually the one to get things lined up when our group wants to do something.			
6. I like working hard for something I want.			
7. I can make up my mind in a hurry if I want to.			
8. People can trust me. I do what I say.			
9. If I make up my mind to do something, I'll see it through.			
10. I am always careful to write things down and to keep good records.			

FIGURE 12-7 Complete this exercise to see if you have the traits to be a successful entrepreneur. (Do not write in this book.)

Source: Starting and Managing a Small Business of Your Own, Small Business Administration

If you have several "No" or "Not Sure" answers, you should probably not risk your money and time starting a business. You should recognize, however, that you can take steps to improve yourself and increase your chances of success.

Choose a Business

If you are serious about going into business, you must first identify the business that is of interest to you. Be clear about the kind of business even though you may not know exactly which one you want to start. For example, you may be sure you want to go into retailing but not

Workplace Innovations

SEGWAY TOURISM

In 2001, inventor Dean Kamen introduced the Segway Human Transporter. His goal was to revolutionize urban transportation with a two-wheeled, upright, self-balancing electric-powered transportation device. The Segway hasn't lived up to Kamen's dream, but it has found an important role in the travel and tourism industry.

People take tours and vacations to locations that may cover many miles. Even though a walking tour can be very pleasant, there is a practical limit to what most people can or want to walk in a day. This is where the Segway comes into play. The easy to use vehicle allows tourists to go farther and see more in less time.

A typical example is the Museum of Science in Cambridge Massachusetts that offers a one-hour excursion through the city. Before the tour starts, riders are given a 30 minute Segway training lesson. Then, riders start out in groups of six led by a tour guide. They cruise along the Charles River at speeds up to 10 miles an hour and then slow down to navigate the sidewalks of the Massachusetts Institute of Technology. Riders tour the campus and learn about some of the famous architecture. The tour guide and riders can communicate through two-way headset radios. The tour covers about 3 miles during the one hour experience.

Segway guided tours are available in most major cities around the world. Other popular destinations are theme parks, vacation resorts, and state and national forests. In addition to travel and tourism, Segways are widely used by security firms and law enforcement agencies.

NET FOLLOW-UP

Search the Web for additional information on the Segway Human Transporter. Determine how Dean Kamen took his idea for a new product and developed a business. Are there any new products that have been recently used to start a new business? Be prepared to discuss you findings with the class.

Tourists can have fun while covering a lot of ground while using a Segway.

know what sort of store to open. Or you may decide that some other business is better than the one you originally considered.

Write a summary of your background and experience. Include what you have learned on jobs, in school, and from hobbies that relate to your business interests. Then write what you would like to do. Try to match up what you have done with what you would like to do. If you do not like the business you choose, your lack of interest will probably lead to failure.

The more experience and training you have, the better your chances of success. So pick a field you know a lot about. The best way to learn about a business is through actual experience. Seek a job working in the type of business you are considering. Try to choose a well-managed, successful company. Once hired, gather as much management know-how as you can.

Education will help, too. While there may be no educational requirements for starting your own business, the more schooling you have, the better equipped you will be. For example, in most businesses, you must know how to determine interest and discounts, keep simple and accurate records, and take care of correspondence.

Get all the facts you can about the kind of business you want to start. Find out what the appropriate trade association is, what it publishes, and what help it offers. Visit similar businesses for a firsthand idea of how they operate. Read magazines, newspapers, and newsletters on the subject. Collect as much information as possible, even from the competition. Talk with the local Chamber of Commerce, local business groups, and local banks.

Determine if customers need or want the type of business in which you are interested. Do not take anything for granted. Even if products and services meet certain needs, people may want something different.

The business you are thinking about should be in tune with the trends of the time. Choose a field in which growth is expected. You will need to study and seek advice from people who are in a position to know. Successful business owners are those who can make accurate predictions about the future.

12-4 Assessment

1. Name the three main ingredients necessary for self-employment.
2. What is the SBA? What does it do?
3. Why are the first six months often crucial in getting a new business started?
4. What proportion of new businesses fail in the first five years?
5. Are you the type of person who might be a successful entrepreneur? Why or why not?
6. Why is having a trade or a technical skill a good first step in becoming an entrepreneur?

Chapter Summary

12-1 Organizational Leadership

A. Leadership involves influencing people to accomplish organizational goals. Management is the act of planning, organizing, and directing the activities of an organization Three leadership styles are authoritarian, participative, and delegative.

B. Six common leadership traits are having a vision, being a good communicator, setting high standards, being competent, maintaining honesty, and showing respect and sharing rewards.

C. Career and technical student organizations provide students the chance to function as junior members of a trade or profession, apply skills learned in the classroom and interact with others in an occupational area.

12-2 Parliamentary Procedure

A. Parliamentary procedure is a way to conduct a meeting in a fair and orderly manner by applying the principles of majority rule, protection of the minority, and the orderly consideration of one subject at a time.

B. Bylaws define the basic characteristics of the organization and describe how it will operate.

C. An important part of any meeting is making, discussing, and disposing of motions. There are four types of motions: main, secondary, incidental, and privileged.

12-3 Self-employment

A. Small businesses are found in every type of industry. Self-employed individuals account for 78% of all business firms.

B. Small businesses make many contributions to society, including the creation of most new jobs. Small businesses provide opportunities for women and minorities to be entrepreneurs.

C. A business can be organized as a proprietorship, partnership, or corporation.

D. Self-employment has many advantages and disadvantages. Being one's own boss and having the opportunity to benefit financially from long hours and hard work motivates many entrepreneurs.

12-4 Small Business and You

A. Being a successful businessperson requires the right personality, know-how, and money. Before considering starting a business, you should honestly evaluate your strengths and weaknesses. Not everyone is suited to owning his or her own business.

B. If you are serious about going into business, pick a field you know a lot about. The more experience and training you have, the better your chances of success.

Activities

1. Acess www.cengage.com/school/working and click on the Web Links for Leadership 101: Youth. Watch the video. Concentrate on the messages presented. Then, watch the video a second time and write down the names of all the young people listed. Select a person of interest, and search the Web to learn more about them. Present a summary report to your classmates.

2. Find out the types of career and technical student organizations in your school. For each, list the qualifications for membership and invite a representative to talk to the class. Select an organization of interest and join it. Links to the eleven CTSOs described in this chapter may be found by accessing www.cengage.com/school/working and clicking on the Web Links for CTSOs.

3. Practice parliamentary procedure by role-playing a meeting. Elect a president, vice president, and secretary. The officers develop an agenda, which the secretary prepares and distributes. Conduct a meeting according to the agenda. Focus on making, discussing, and disposing of sample motions.

4. Suppose a member of your CTSO moves to end a debate. Two-thirds of those present must vote in favor of this motion for it to be approved. If 20 people are present, and 12 people vote for the motion, should it be approved?

5. List leadership skills that you think you currently possess. Explain how these skills can help you achieve goals in your life-span plan. Do you think you should work to improve your leadership skills? Describe how you might accomplish this.

6. Contact two or three small business owners in your community. Ask them to identify their main reason for going into business. In class, pool your findings and discuss the results.

7. Access www.cengage.com/school/working and click on the Web Links for Mind Your Own Business. The site was created by the U.S. Small Business Administration and Junior Achievement to encourage youth entrepreneurship. Explore the website. Discuss what you found to be the most interesting.

8. Acess www.cengage.com/school/working and click on the Web Links for Franchise and Business Opportunities Handbook. Select a franchise from the site. Print out a page of factual information about the franchise. Then, search the Web for additional franchise information about the company. Report your findings.

9. Download three copies of Figure 12-7 by accessing www.cengage.com/school/working and clicking on the Web Links for Entrepreneur Rating Scale. Complete one copy yourself. Give one to a parent or family member and one to your supervisor at work and ask them to rate you. Compare the ratings and discuss the results with your teacher.

10. You are thinking about buying a franchise to sell sunglasses. Your fixed monthly expenses would be $4,500. The sunglasses cost you $6 a pair. You plan to sell them for $15 a pair. How many pairs of sunglasses would you have to sell per month to break even?

Word Power

On a separate sheet of paper, match each definition with the correct term. All definitions will be used, and a definition will be used only once.

a. agenda
b. bylaws
c. career and technical student organization (CTSO)
d. code of ethics
e. corporation
f. creditor
g. entrepreneur
h. franchise
i. leadership
j. majority
k. management
l. motion
m. order of business
n. parliamentarian
o. parliamentary procedure
p. partnership
q. precedence
r. proprietorship
s. quorum
t. self-employed
u. small business
v. Small Business Association (SBA)

11. A contract with a company to sell its goods and services within a certain area
12. A business owned by stockholders
13. A majority of the total membership of an organization
14. Rules for professional practice and behavior
15. A business owned by one person
16. Printed information that defines the basic characteristics of an organization and describes how it will operate
17. A brief statement of a proposed action by a participant in a meeting
18. Nonprofit, national organizations with state and local chapters that exist to develop leadership skills and good citizenship among members
19. A standard series of steps followed in a meeting
20. An independent business having fewer than 500 employees
21. A vote of at least one more than half of the people who vote
22. In parliamentary procedure, the order of priority among the four types of motions used in a meeting
23. Persons or companies to which money is due
24. Federal government agency that encourages, assists, and protects the interests of small business
25. Not working for someone else; owning and operating one's own business
26. A list of items to be taken care of at a particular meeting
27. Formal rules used to conduct meetings fairly and orderly
28. A form of business organization in which two or more persons co-own the business
29. Planning, organizing, and directing the activities of an organization
30. A group member who advises the chair on correct parliamentary procedure
31. Someone who runs his or her own business
32. Influencing people in order to accomplish organizational goals

Think Critically

33. A characteristic of leaders is the ability to develop committed followers. There have been instances throughout history in which individuals have gained committed followers for illegal or immoral purposes. Think of some historic or present examples. Should such people be called leaders?

34. A person may be named head of an organization or be elected to an office without being a leader. Discuss some of the things, other than leadership, that allow people to rise in an organization.

35. Strong leaders may be scattered throughout an organization. Identify and discuss as many examples as you can.

36. You have probably been in meetings that dragged on without anything being accomplished. Discuss how parliamentary procedure might prevent this.

37. It has been said that "If you want to manage somebody, manage yourself." Discuss the meaning of this statement.

38. New businesses are often started because they provide something better or different. Name and discuss products and services that you are dissatisfied with that could possibly lead to the creation of a new business.

39. Think about recent trends and how society is changing. Discuss the types of businesses that are likely to be successful five years from now. Provide reasons for your predictions.

40. During the last several decades, dozens of young computer, software, and Internet whizzes became millionaires while still in their teens or early 20s. How were they able to accomplish so much at such a young age?

41. Consider several goals in your life-span plan that might best be achieved through self-employment. Do you think you are personally suited to being self-employed? Explain why or why not.

42. Select someone who has achieved success in a business that he or she started. After gathering information, write a two- to three-page biography. Turn in the paper to your teacher.

Career Transitions Connection

Jobs for Potential Entrepreneurs

Click on *Match Experience to New Careers*. From the *Explore Careers* tab, click on *A Day in the Life Videos*. From Architecture and Construction, click on *Electrician*. Watch the *Introduction, 21st Century Skills, Advice to Interested Students,* and *Education and Training* portions of the video. Nijaz's uncle, who has his own company, hired Nijaz to do electrical work. What information about the business does Nijaz have that could make him successful if he became an independent electrician? How will his advance apprenticeship training help Nijaz if he opens his own business?

13

Computer and Technology Skills

"Work is an inanimate thing and can be made lively and interesting only by injecting yourself into it. Your job is only as big as you are." —GEORGE C. HUBBS

Photodisc/Jupiter Images

PREVIEW

Computers are found in most workplaces. There are few jobs that do not require some computer skills, and new jobs involving computers are created every day. The better you understand computers, the more valuable you will be as an employee.

Taking/*Action* Computers Are Everywhere

Rei wakes up on a typical morning and gets ready for work. Every morning she checks her email and text messages. Her friends like to stay in touch using email, texting, and social media. Rei responds to a few emails and then remembers that she has to get gas that morning.

At the local gas station, Rei can use her credit card at the pump to pay for her purchase. Rei likes this because it saves her time. Since she pays her credit card bill in full every month, using her credit card does not cost Rei any extra money.

At work, Rei says hello to a few coworkers on the way to her cubicle. She works as a customer service representative for a major department store chain. Rei must log on to the computerized phone system to begin to take calls. The phone system keeps track of how many phone calls she takes, how long each call is, and when she logs off the system for a break.

Rei takes calls from salesclerks who are trying to open store credit accounts for customers. Customers usually want to have their credit applications processed in minutes. To do this, Rei takes the customer's credit information and enters it into her computer. A computer program accesses the customer's credit information. If the customer's information fits the acceptable credit guidelines, the application is approved. If not, the application may take longer to process or may be rejected.

Rei also logs credit application acceptances, rejections, and delays for further processing into a computer database. Her supervisor uses this database to track the results of credit requests.

At the end of the day, Rei stops at a local grocery store to pick up some groceries. She has a store card that gives her a discount at the checkout. She knows that when she uses her card, a computer is recording information about her buying habits, but that is fine with her. Rei receives coupons along with her grocery receipt for products she regularly buys.

THINK CRITICALLY

1. How would Rei's day be different without computers?
2. How do you use computers at work, school, or home?

takayuki/Shutterstock.com

OBJECTIVES

- Discuss the importance of keyboarding and related skills
- Summarize how a computer works

KEY TERMS

- computer literacy
- computer
- keyboarding skills
- program

carlofranco/iStockphoto

Personal Decisions

You don't have a computer at home because your family cannot afford one. You don't have a mobile phone either. Your mother says she barely earns enough in two jobs to pay the bills and put food on the table. You understand the family financial situation, but you would still like to have a computer. Your mother has suggested that there are places in the community where you can go to use a computer such as the public library and the "Y After School" program. You could do that, but it wouldn't be the same as having your own computer.

What would you do?

Keyboarding and Related Skills

Computer literacy is a general knowledge of what computers are, how they work, and what they can be used for. Virtually every type of industry and the majority of occupations involve using some type of computer.

Wayne graduated from high school without learning much about computers. He lost out on several good jobs after interviewers learned his computer skills were limited to surfing the Web. Wayne got the message and signed up for a keyboarding and computer applications course.

Wayne eventually got a job in the parts department of a plumbing supply business. In this job, he uses a computer more often than a pen. He orders parts, does billings, keeps inventory, and performs dozens of other tasks on the computer. He wonders what it must have been like in the parts department before the computers arrived.

A **computer** is an electronic tool. Like other tools, it helps people do various kinds of work. It can do simple arithmetic and can solve complex mathematical problems. With an optical device, it can read a printed page and display text and graphics on a screen. With a voice synthesizer, it can even "talk." It can direct equipment to do tasks. Unlike people, a computer can work 24 hours a day without getting tired. It runs on little electricity and seldom breaks down. It can store vast amounts of information and can communicate with its human user. Perhaps the computer's greatest benefit is its ability to work at very high speeds.

Like Wayne, you will need to learn keyboarding skills if you have not already. **Keyboarding skills** means the ability to type and to give commands to a computer using a keyboard. Keyboard operation varies a little depending on the type of computer and the software. Still, for all keyboards, the basic commands and procedures are similar. No matter what type of business or industry you work in, you will benefit by knowing how to use a computer keyboard.

You should also learn how to use touch pads, touch screens, track balls, and the mouse. Knowing how to use these devices will give you the confidence to learn how to use future tools. For example, one of the newest technologies is the 8pen spiral keyboard, which provides a method for entering text on a touch screen in a way that mimics the handwriting process. The 8pen spiral keyboard is becoming common on some smartphones and tablet computers.

Understand Computers

Regardless of whether you use a desktop, notebook, or tablet computer, they all work basically the same. In very simple terms, the computer works in three steps: (a) it receives instructions, (b) it does tasks according to these instructions, and (c) it shares the results.

Input → Processing → Output

The computer solves problems much as people do. For instance, compare how a person and the computer would add 20 + 43.

Input

You receive information by either reading or hearing the numbers. The computer receives information in the form of electronic signals.

Processing

You draw upon your knowledge of arithmetic in your memory. You bring together the data (20, 43) and the method (addition) and come up with the answer.

The computer draws upon a program stored in its memory. A **program** consists of instructions on how to solve a certain problem or do a certain task. Bringing the data from input and the instructions from memory, the computer adds the numbers.

Output

You report the result (63) by writing the answer or saying it out loud. The computer changes the result from electronic language to human language. It presents the result in print, sound, or another form.

Going beyond this simple explanation, the processing step is divided it into three parts—memory, arithmetic and logic, and control. The input–processing–output sequence now appears as follows:

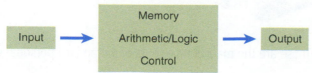

Input

Input devices let users enter information and change it into electronic signals the computer can use. The most common input devices are the keyboard and mouse. Other frequently used devices are the touch pad, touch screen, track ball, light pen, microphone, webcam, and USB port.

Three kinds of input are fed into the computer. One is programs. The others are data, which include text and numbers, and commands entered by the user. Input is sometimes sent to memory and sometimes to the arithmetic and logic section of the computer.

Memory

The memory is the part of the computer system that records and stores data and programs. These data and programs stay in memory until other parts of the computer need them.

The memory has several parts. One important part is *ROM*, which stands for read-only memory. The manufacturer pre-programs the ROM, which is permanent. The ROM tells the computer to do different things, depending on the uses of the computer.

Another important part is working memory. It is called *RAM*, which is random-access memory. This part of the computer stores programs currently being used and data being processed. When the computer is turned off, it erases everything in RAM.

Programs and files that are permanently stored on the computer are on the hard drive. They are loaded from here into RAM when they are needed. The hard drive is often considered a storage device rather than part of memory. Figure 13-1 provides details regarding the location of ROM, RAM, and other desktop computer components.

Arithmetic and Logic

The *arithmetic and logic section (ALU)* is the heart of the computer. It does the actual processing. As you might guess from the name, the ALU does this by means of math operations.

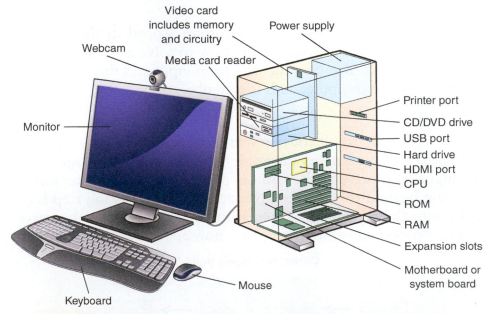

FIGURE 13-1 These are the main components of a standard personal computer.

The ALU adds, subtracts, multiplies, divides, and compares numbers. To do complex calculations, it combines the four operations into a number of steps as a program directs. It does these tasks in millionths of a second.

The arithmetic and logic section receives its input from memory and from input devices. After processing, the data are sent to memory or to an output device.

Computers are electronically complex and require maintenance from highly skilled technicians.

Control

Part of the program of instructions a computer receives goes to the control section. The control section directs the other four parts of the computer system. Based on the program, the control section decides when to accept data and from which input device. It chooses when to send information from input devices to memory and when to send it to the arithmetic and logic section. The control section decides when to call up a program and data from storage. It also decides when the computer's work should go to an output device.

Output

Output devices change data from electronic language into forms that people can understand. Most output is displayed, printed, or stored.

Output may appear on the computer monitor or screen, be printed, or listened to via a speaker or headphones. An internal hard drive is the most common storage device. Flash drives and CDs are frequently used external storage devices.

Certain business applications will output data on magnetic disks or tapes. Output can also consist of instructions that tell machines such as robots to do certain kinds of work.

13-1 Assessment

1. What are the three major steps in the operation of a computer?
2. List the five parts of a computer system. Briefly tell what each part does.
3. Name five input devices.
4. What is the difference between ROM and RAM?
5. Name three output devices.
6. Rewrite the following steps in the proper sequence: (a) processed data returned to memory, (b) numbers keyed, (c) processed data shown on monitor, (d) stored data moved for processing, (e) calculations performed, (f) keyed data stored in memory.

COMPUTER HARDWARE AND SOFTWARE

OBJECTIVES

- Identify computer hardware and types of computers
- Name and describe the two types of computer software and eight types of application software
- Explain cloud computing

KEY TERMS

- hardware
- microprocessor
- peripheral
- desktop computer
- mobile computer
- software
- icon
- graphical user interface (GUI)
- app
- cloud computing

beboy/Shutterstock.com

Personal Decisions

You have subscribed to a computer magazine to learn more about computers. You are saving money to buy a PC. The more you read, the more confusing it gets. There are so many different brand names and models from which to choose. When you get close to making a decision, you read that a more powerful and cheaper model will be out soon. Should you buy or continue to wait?

What would you do?

Computer Hardware

A computer consists of several interconnected pieces of equipment. The physical equipment that makes up a computer is called **hardware**. The most important piece of hardware is the *central processing unit (CPU)*, which does the actual processing or computing. The CPU is contained on a single tiny silicon chip called a **microprocessor**.

In addition to being the "brain" of a personal computer, microprocessors are used in hundreds of other applications. Special purpose microprocessors are used in automobiles, cameras, calculators, video game systems, toys, and home appliances. Any device that is electronic is almost certain to have a microprocessor imbedded in it.

The term computer is sometimes used just for the CPU, while the term computer system is used for the computer and its input and output devices. These devices are called **peripherals** because they are located outside of the CPU. The keyboard, mouse, and monitor are the most common peripherals. So too are printers, microphones, webcams, speakers, and external storage devices.

Types of Computers

Computers vary greatly in size, speed, storage, and cost. Computer users use either desktop or mobile computers.

A **desktop computer** is a PC intended for regular use at a single location. The typical desktop PC used in homes and businesses consists of a CPU (usually a tower), monitor, keyboard, mouse, and printer. One type of desktop computer combines the CPU and speaker into the same case as the monitor. It is called an all-in-one computer and usually has a webcam, touch screen, and a wireless keyboard and mouse.

A **mobile computer** is a PC that can be used on the move or at a remote location. There are many terms used to reference mobile computers including laptop and notebook. The primary advantages of a notebook PC are that all components (CPU, monitor, keyboard, hard drive) are integrated into a single unit and that it can be used in a variety of locations due to wireless Internet connectivity.

Significant mobile computing developments include the introduction of smartphones and tablet computers. A number of different manufacturers market a variety of smartphone options.

A *smartphone* is a mobile phone combined with a handheld computer. Smartphones run complete operating systems that allow users to perform essentially all of the same computing tasks as a desktop or notebook computer. In addition, smartphones are usually equipped with a camera and may have a *global positioning system*, or *GPS*, as well. Some smartphones have two way video call capabilities.

Smartphones will probably become the primary computing tool for most individuals and businesses. To overcome the keyboard and monitor limitations of a mobile device, most manufacturers will offer the option of a docking station connected to a keyboard, monitor, and printer.

The first popular tablet computers were introduced in 2010. A *tablet* is a fully functioning computer that is smaller than a notebook, but larger than a smartphone. Tablets are truly mobile devices having battery power and wireless connectivity. Most tablets are being used for entertainment purposes, to surf the Web, to stay connected to email and social media, to watch movies, and to take and view photos and videos. They are used in many jobs where mobile computing is a necessity.

Computer Software

Computer **software** is the instructions that tell the computer what to do. Software and programs mean the same thing. There are two main types of software. One is system software, which manages what happens inside the computer. The other is application software. These are the programs used to perform certain tasks, such as word processing.

System Software

A computer must have a program before it can do anything. Most computers are sold with operating system software installed. When you first "boot up" the computer, system software is loaded into the computer's main memory. Once booted, the computer is ready to receive the commands required to begin an application.

An **icon** is a small picture that a user can double-click on to give commands to software to perform specific functions. A **graphical user interface (GUI)** is an operating system that provides icons and menus from which the user can select commands. A mouse is often used to select GUI commands. Instead of keying a command, you can use a mouse to choose it from a menu or double-click on an icon.

Application Software

The widespread use of computers in the workplace is due to their ability to accomplish useful tasks. This is done through application software. Eight common types of application software are described below.

- **Word processing** One of the most common uses of PCs is for word processing. Word processing software lets you create documents such as letters, memos, and reports. This software provides many helpful features for editing and formatting documents. Like other application files, word-processed files can be printed, stored electronically, and recalled for future use.

- **Spreadsheet** Financial records kept by accountants and bookkeepers are called spreadsheets. Most problems in which data are put into rows and columns and used in calculations can be prepared with spreadsheet software. It is used for budgeting, sales forecasting, income projection, and investment analysis. As new data are added, calculations can be redone automatically. It can also be used to produce graphs, charts, and reports.

- **Database management** Magazine publishers, insurance companies, airlines, manufacturers, and many other businesses maintain large files of customer and inventory data. Your public library probably has its card catalog stored in a computer. This is done with database management software. Such software is used to organize, store, and retrieve information.

- **Personal information management** Personal information management software helps users organize their information. Features may include email, a calendar, an address book, and a task or assignment list.

- **Presentations** Electronic presentation software is used to create slide shows to accompany oral presentations. With this software, you can create slides that include text, graphics, sound, and even animation and video.

- **Communications** Transferring data from one computer to another is done with communications software. Traditionally, this software was used primarily for email and to search electronic databases on the Internet. Today, web browsers such as Apple Safari, Microsoft Explorer, Mozilla Firefox, and Google Chrome are commonly used for these tasks.

- **Software suites** Many types of application software are stand-alone programs. This means that they work by themselves. A user, however, often needs to switch between applications and use material from one application in another (for example, to create a bar chart from the statistical data in a spreadsheet for use in a presentation).

Workplace Innovations

ASSISTIVE TECHNOLOGY

The same types of hardware and software technologies commonly used by individuals and business are being widely used in education and training. Students with special needs are benefiting particularly from *assistive technology*. This term refers to those applications of technology that provide ways for students with sensory, cognitive, or physical disabilities to better access classroom instruction.

The number of students with disabilities has steadily increased. Depending on their type of disability, special needs students typically require more individualized instruction. Assistive technologies can free a teacher to help more students, while at the same time helping provide a disabled student with a sense of accomplishment and inclusion.

Among the most common assistive technology products are alternative computer input devices. These include electronic pointing devices used to control the cursor on the screen without the use of hands. Wands and sticks can be worn on the head or held in the mouth to press keys on the keyboard. Trackballs on top of a base can be used to move the cursor. And, touch screens allow activation of the computer directly without using any other device.

For visually-impaired students, Braille embossers transfer computer-generated text into Braille output and translation programs convert scanned-in text into Braille. Speech recognition programs allow students to give commands and enter data using their voices to create text documents, browse the Web, and navigate among applications. Screen readers can be used to translate everything on the screen into a computerized voice that is spoken aloud. These are among the many types of assistive technologies that are available to help disabled students become successful learners.

NET FOLLOW-UP

Use a search engine to explore the Web for additional information about assistive or adaptive technologies. Have you observed any students at your school using any adaptive technologies? If so, what impact have the technologies had on the students and teachers? Be prepared to discuss your observations in class.

To make this easier, integrated software suites have been developed. One popular suite includes word processing, spreadsheet, personal information management, and electronic presentation software. Integrated software has many advantages for home, office, and small business users.

- **Apps**   An **app** is a concise software program designed to perform a very targeted and limited function. Apps are used for a variety of purposes including gaming, social media, banking, and productivity. One type of productivity app is for grocery shopping. The app allows users to generate electronic grocery lists, use scanned bar codes to update grocery lists, rearrange grocery list items based on their location in the store, and help manage online coupons. Although many apps are developed by businesses for consumers to use, businesses also develop apps for other businesses. FedEx, for example, has an app that allows business and consumers to track a shipment, create shipping labels, and obtain cost quotes.

The cloud can help businesses save costs by eliminating the need for purchasing expensive computers. Flexible usage allows businesses to pay just for the computing time they need. Access **www.cengage. com/school/working** and click on the link for Chapter 13. Watch the video that explains cloud computing. Research cloud computing. What businesses do you currently use that provide services on the cloud? What other uses do you envision for the cloud?

www.cengage.com/school/working

The Cloud

In the past, individuals and businesses bought their own computers and their own software. The computers and software were stored on site, either in their home or at their place of business. Investing in the hardware and software was often quite costly.

Cloud computing is providing computer capabilities at a remote location that is accessible via the Web. Running software programs, hosting websites, and storing data files are a few examples of what can be done on the cloud. Hotmail, Gmail, and Facebook are three common examples of cloud computer services. It can be more efficient for individuals and businesses to use the cloud for computing needs. Just like when you need to turn on a light at home to see when it is dark, you can access the cloud when you need to use software or perform calculations. When the sun is shining, you turn out the light because you do not need it. In a similar way, you stop using the cloud when you are done with your task.

The cloud provides a flexible amount of computing capacity. You can use more when you need to and less when your computing needs go down. The cloud makes mobility easy. You can access needed software and files from any location. A *netbook* is a very compact and mobile computing device. Netbooks, which are less expensive than laptops, can perform many simple computer functions like accessing the Web. By using the cloud, businesses can save money on hardware and provide increased flexibility for their workers. Instead of purchasing a laptop and loading it with software, they can buy a netbook.

There are some concerns about using the cloud as a primary source of computing power and file storage. Reliability of the cloud including making sure files and computing power are always available is one concern. The security of proprietary and personal information that is stored at a remote location is another concern.

13-2 Assessment

1. What piece of hardware serves as the "brain" of a computer?
2. What three components make up a computer system?
3. List the three most common types of mobile computers.
4. Name and define the two types of computer software.
5. Identify the type of application software used for each of the following tasks: (a) storing inventory data, (b) writing a business report, (c) transferring data to another computer, (d) creating a slide show, (e) preparing a budget, and (f) preparing a grocery list.
6. What are two benefits of cloud computing? Two concerns?

High Growth Occupations
FOR THE 21ST CENTURY

Office Clerks

Do you like clerical tasks? Does working in an office appeal to you? If so, consider the occupation of general office clerk. People in this occupation usually do not perform a single specialized task, but they have responsibilities that vary with each job or employer.

Duties of a general office clerk may include filing or keyboarding, entering data into a computer, or operating office equipment such as photocopy and fax machines. They may also prepare office mailings, proofread mailings, and answer telephones, transfer calls, or take messages.

The type of office in which an office clerk works helps to determine required duties. For example, an office clerk who works in a doctor's office has different duties than an office clerk who works in the offices of a large financial firm. Some of the duties may be similar, such as those of sorting checks, keeping payroll records, taking inventory, and accessing information. Specialized duties could be organizing medications in a medical office or making slides for a presentation by a financial analyst.

Duties also may be determined by experience. Some office clerks may maintain financial or other records, set up spreadsheets, verify statistical reports for accuracy and completeness, handle and adjust customer complaints, work with vendors, make travel arrangements, take inventory of equipment and supplies, answer questions or departmental services and functions, or help prepare invoices or budgetary requests. General office clerks may be supervised by more experienced senior office clerks.

Most office clerks work a standard 40-hour week, with overtime during peak times. About one in four works part time. Most positions are entry-level administrative support, but some business or office experience may be required. Knowledge of word processing is helpful. Training is available through business education programs in high schools, community colleges, and postsecondary vocational schools.

Bobby Deal/RealDealPhoto/Shutterstock.com

Making copies is one of the responsibilities of office clerks.

OBJECTIVES

- Explain how the Internet works
- Discuss the possible future impact of computers

KEY TERMS

- network
- browser

Monkey Business Images/Shutterstock.com

▶ Workplace Decisions

You work for your grandparents in a small, family-owned business. After taking a computer course in school, you have become aware of what computers can do. You see a number of ways that a computer could be used in the business. You suggest to your grandfather that he buy a computer.

"We do not have the money for an expensive computer," he says. "Besides, the old-fashioned way has been working just fine for years." You are disappointed, but you still believe that a computer would be a wise investment.

What would you do?

The Internet

The Internet is one of the most significant technological developments of all time. It influences the ways in which people learn, work, communicate, spend leisure time, conduct business, and engage in many other aspects of their personal and professional lives.

When two or more computers are linked together by cable or wireless means, this is called a **network**. Networks enable computers to share software, data files, printers, and other equipment. For example, a high school might have dozens of computers connected in what is called a local area network (LAN).

The *Internet* is an "interconnected network of networks" that links millions of smaller computer networks worldwide. The cloud is made possible because of computer networks.

A Brief History

The Internet originated in the late 1960s through a project funded by the U.S. Defense Department. The purpose was to link government research facilities and other agencies in a network to share computer resources and data. The ARPANet, as it was called, was intended to serve only a few thousand scientists and computer specialists.

Throughout the 1970s, the ARPANet grew steadily. Other countries began to join the network, and other networks came into existence. In the early 1980s, the National Science Foundation began to create a national "backbone" network for supercomputers called the NSFNET. By the end of the decade, the Defense Department had shut down its network and moved over to the more advanced NSFNET. The collection of networks soon became known simply as the Internet.

Despite its growth, the Internet was difficult to use and was limited to communicating data and text-based information. This began to change in the early 1990s with development of the *World Wide Web*. The Web is a network within the Internet that provides sounds, pictures, and moving images in addition to text. The introduction of the Web helped make the Internet popular and easier to use.

The arrival of browser software in 1993 further simplified use of the Internet and began an era of explosive growth. A **browser** is a type of software used to locate and display information on the Web. Even though the Web represents only part of the Internet, most people now use the terms Internet, Net, and Web interchangeably.

How the Internet Works

To access the Internet, you instruct your communications software (which comes with most computers) to connect with an *Internet service provider*, or *ISP*. An ISP is a company such as AT&T, Comcast, Earthlink, Verizon, and others that provide Internet access for a monthly fee. To connect, you log in with a username and password. After the first login, you usually remain connected until you cancel or change the service. Most users connect at home to an ISP via cable or through their telephone line. *Wireless connectivity*, or *WiFi*, is also available from most of the same companies that provide cable and phone line connections.

To navigate the Web and view pages, users need a browser, like Apple Safari, Microsoft Internet Explorer, Mozilla Firefox, or Google Chrome. Most computers come with browser software. It can also be downloaded free from the manufacturer's website. See Figure 13-2 for a visual overview of the Internet.

Once a user is connected to the Internet, the user's computer can interact with other computers using a *client/server model*. The resources of the Internet, such as information and email services, are stored on host computers called *servers*. Your computer, called the *client*, requests the desired information from the server. Client and server software interact to deliver and display information

FIGURE 13-2 This diagram shows the various places information travels on the Internet.

Just 30 years ago, it was hard for people to imagine that computers would have anything to do with communicating at work. If you had to send a business letter, you wrote it out in longhand and then keyed it on a typewriter. You had to be careful because mistakes weren't easy to fix.

Now you can use word processing software to create the perfect letter. It offers different designs and even checks spelling and grammar. Desktop publishing software produces flyers and newsletters as attractive as if they came from a print shop. Communications software and the Internet makes possible email, videoconferencing, instant messaging, and chat.

In a short time, technology has created many new ways to communicate at work. Yet the fact that you can do more, more quickly, should be a caution. Taking care and time in your communication at work, both orally and in writing, is just as important as it always has been—perhaps even more so.

THINK CRITICALLY

1. What impact do you think the use of email has had on communicating at work?
2. How has the use of videoconferencing affected the way businesspeople approach preparing for meetings?

in the appropriate format. This is done simply and automatically because of the development of the World Wide Web and the use of web browsers.

Web Basics

Typically, when you connect to an ISP, your browser is launched and displays your home page. A *home page* is the starting point from which to begin navigating, or surfing, the Web. The home page might be the opening page of your school's or employer's website or of a popular web portal such as Yahoo or Windows Live. It might also be a social media page such as Facebook or Twitter.

The Web is made up of various sites, each of which has an electronic address called a *Uniform Resource Locator (URL)*. An example of a URL is www.whitehouse.gov/, which is the address for the website of the White House. To visit a specific website, you key the URL into the appropriate box in your browser window.

A *hyperlink* provides another way to go to a website. By clicking on a hyperlink, a user can jump from one page to another on the Web without keying the URL. A hyperlink can be text that is underscored or in a different color or

A great deal occurs behind the scenes to make your Web experience go smoothly.

Rob Marmion/Shutterstock.com

a graphic. The hyperlink is one feature that makes the Web so popular and easy to use.

The most common uses of the Internet are as follows:

Video conferencing is just one method of enhanced communication that is made possible with communication technologies.

- **Communication** Among the most popular uses of the Internet are email, texting, telephony, and multiple party video conferences. Billions of email and text messages are sent and received each day. *Telephony* refers to using a computer to place and receive telephone calls. Internet based videoconferencing services allow multiple users to simultaneously have face-to-face conversations with other people on a network. Groups of people can informally visit with each other online and have audio and video interactions. This is an Internet equivalent of dropping by a friend's house and visiting with mutual friends while there.

- **Research** The Internet can be regarded as a huge library that stores millions of files of information. Students, scientists, teachers, and other professionals use the Internet to access databases and share information. The average Web user uses the Internet to collect a variety of information, including airline schedules, consumer product reviews, medical information, recipes, stock quotes, tax forms, travel maps, and weather forecasts.

- **News and entertainment** For many individuals, the Internet is becoming the preferred source of news. Many newspapers, magazines, and television networks maintain web pages. On the Web, information can be updated continually throughout a 24-hour news cycle. The Web is also used to play interactive games, download videos, and view concerts live. As audio and video technologies improve and the growth of mobile computing continues, using the Web for news and entertainment will increase dramatically.

- **Consuming goods and services** Historically people shopped at a local store or used a mail-order catalog. To pay an electricity bill, you had to write a check. Now you are likely to use the Internet for shopping, purchasing, and even paying bills. Online banking has made many financial transactions paperless and postage free. Almost everything you can buy in your community can be purchased through the Internet.

Web 2.0

During the first decade or so following the introduction of web browsers, individuals used the Web basically as an electronic library. They simply viewed or downloaded content posted on the Web at portals and other

Web 2.0 allows users to customize their online content.

news and information sites. In "Web 1.0," there was little or no interaction between the viewer and the Web.

In 2003, the term "Web 2.0" began to be used to refer to a second generation of technologies. Web 2.0 is commonly associated with web applications that make possible information sharing and collaboration. Web 2.0 represents an important shift in the way digital information is created, shared, and manipulated. The shift, of course, is that users of the Web are creating more of the content and interacting with content in new ways.

In the Web 2.0 era, instead of simply reading a newsletter, you can create and publish your own blog. Instead of viewing photos online, you can upload and create your own photo and video galleries. Instead of opening a word processing program on your desktop, you can open a free word processing program online, create a document, and share it with a friend who is collaborating with you on a school project.

All of this is made possible by the development of web-based technologies and software that are free and easy to use. Some of the prominent names that have led this revolution include Flickr, Facebook, Google Apps, MySpace, Twitter, YouTube, and Wikipedia. This trend is also fed by the increasing use of mobile computing. Because the applications and data that make user interaction possible reside on the cloud, a variety of computer devices can access them.

Internet Issues

The development and increasing use of the Internet has brought with it a number of problems and issues. Not all of the information on the Web is accurate and appropriate. Some is intentionally misleading, hateful, violent, or presents adult content. Controlling access to inappropriate materials is an ongoing concern for parents and schools. Internet security and fraud are also serious issues.

There is a great deal of sophisticated math that is used in software and applications throughout the Internet. An *algorithm* is a process or set of rules to be followed in calculations or other problem solving operations. When your GPS system provides directions for the fastest route to go from point A to point B, an algorithm was used to calculate the route. When you search for information on the Web, an algorithm is working behind the scenes to provide you with answers that best match your search. Many of these algorithms are very advanced. Over the course of many searches, these algorithms begin to tailor your search results to match your preferences. For example, if prior searches revealed a preference for green shoes, new searches on related topics will focus on providing answers that include green shoes. In a similar way, advertisements that you see while looking at various websites will focus on green shoes. When search results are tailored to a user's known preferences, then users receive less diverse information.

Their view of the world becomes more targeted and less broad. This is a concern of some people who study Web usage patterns. Why do you think this concern exists?

Protecting Internet user's privacy and security are issues that are taken seriously by Internet Service Providers, browser developers, online retailers, financial companies, and other providers of Internet information and services. Many layers of protection have been built into the Internet to protect against viruses, fraud, spyware, hacking, and other threats.

Technology evolves so quickly that new threats can arrive at any time. Increased Internet connectivity among individuals, businesses, people in the U.S., and people throughout the world means that Internet viruses and security breaches can spread swiftly and efficiently. It is very important for you to continually educate yourself about such threats and to remain on your guard any time that you are online. On a regular basis you should search the Web using the topic "how to protect yourself online." Read and follow the guidelines suggested. Other smart ways to keep current on new threats is to read newspaper and magazine articles on the topic, listen to radio or television business news information, and discuss the topic with friends and coworkers.

The Future of Computers

The rapid development of computer technology should continue in the future. Computers will get smaller, more powerful, and less expensive. At the same time, they will become easier to use. Programming will be simpler. Technology for giving spoken commands to computers will continue to improve. All of these changes will have a great impact on the workplace. Predicting the future is risky. However, the following changes seem likely:

- The number of occupations that require computer literacy and keyboarding skills will continue to increase. Eventually, most occupations will involve computer use.
- Employment in areas involving computers and robots will increase dramatically. Computer technology will create many new industries and occupations.
- The use of industrial robots will expand from the assembly line to all phases of manufacturing. In the totally automated factory of the future, robots will replace humans for many tasks.
- The automation of offices and service industries will increase. In the office of the future, most communication will be carried out electronically. Electronic storage and transmission of information may finally lead to the "paperless office" that has long been predicted.
- Major shifts in job patterns will occur. Computers and robots may eliminate millions of jobs.
- Technology can also create jobs. Many experts believe that, in the long run, technology will produce more jobs than it takes away.
- Workers losing their jobs to automation will need to be retrained. To keep up with new technology, all workers will need continuing education and training.

Workforce Trends

Projected job openings are a measure of the total number of workers who will be needed to meet demand for a particular occupation. Job openings arise when new jobs are created from economic growth and also when workers who have permanently left an occupation need to be replaced. Although economic growth will create a substantial number of job openings over the 2008–18 projection period, the majority are expected to come from replacement needs.

With sophisticated computer programs, many factories can be automated.

- Employment in both goods and services industries will become more global and technology dependent. U.S. companies will export more jobs to foreign countries, and more foreign companies will establish a U.S. presence. Global economic competition will increase, particularly with India and China.
- Finally, some of the major advances in the world of computer technology have been completely unforeseen. There will be many more new advances in the future.

How much do you know about computers, and how much do you use them? If your knowledge and experience are limited, take a course or have a friend teach you keyboarding skills. Being unable to use a computer could hold you back in your career.

13-3 Assessment

1. Explain the basic idea of a computer network.
2. When you send an email message, what is the computer called on which an email is sent? What is the host computer called that receives the message?
3. What is meant by the acronym URL? Give an example of a URL for your school website or another website with which you are familiar.
4. What are the most popular uses of the Internet?
5. What is the difference between Web 1.0 and Web 2.0?
6. What difference does it make if browser search results are tailored to fit your particular interests?

Focus on the Workplace

Repetitive Motion Injury

We usually associate on-the-job injuries with occupations like police officer, coal miner, and farmer. One of the fastest-growing types of occupational injuries, however, is found among people who work with computers. It is called repetitive motion injury (RMI).

This disorder can arise when a person must repeat movements of the hands, fingers, or arms many times a day, day after day. Key-boarding is highly repetitive. Computer us-ers are more likely to develop RMI if they use incorrect keyboarding techniques, particularly not keeping the wrists straight. When a wrist is repeatedly flexed and extended, its tendons may become irritated and swell. The swelling presses on nerves, causing tingling and numb-ness in the fingers and hand. Pain may also occur in the arm, elbow, or shoulder.

RMI can often be avoided by setting up a computer workstation for maximum comfort and efficiency, using good keyboarding tech-niques, and taking frequent breaks. Here are some suggestions:

- Adjust chair height so thighs are horizontal and feet are flat on the floor. Sit back with your back and neck erect. Upper arms should be perpendicular to the floor and relaxed.
- Forearms should be parallel to the slant of the keyboard. Keep wrists straight and do not rest them on any surface.
- Adjust the computer screen height so that the top is at or just below eye level.
- Keep your fingers curved and upright. Strike each key lightly using the fingertip.

- Grasp the mouse loosely. Keep your fingers, hands, arms, and shoulders relaxed.
- Take a 15-minute break for every hour of intensive keying.

Working long hours at a keyboard does not necessarily mean that you will develop RMI. This disorder, like most on-the-job injuries, can be prevented.

THINK CRITICALLY

1. Think about your work, school, and per-sonal activities. Should you be concerned about RMI?
2. What, if any, changes should you make to the way you use a computer to reduce your chances of developing RMI?

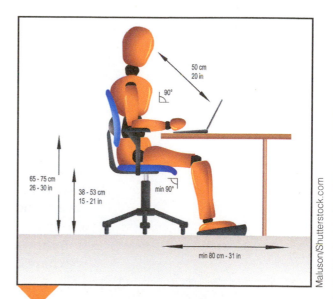

To avoid injury, it is important to use proper posture and positioning of your work area.

Chapter Summary

13-1 How Computers Work

A. Computer literacy is knowledge of how computers work. Computer keyboards are similar in terms of basic commands and procedures.

B. The input–processing–output sequence describes how a computer receives instructions, performs tasks according to instructions, and shares the results.

13-2 Computer Hardware and Software

A. A computer system consists of the CPU and peripherals. Computers vary greatly in size, speed, storage capacity, and cost. Desktops, laptops, and tablets are types of computers.

B. System software manages what happens inside the computer. Application software performs certain tasks, such as word processing.

C. Cloud computing provides remote access to computing power, software programs, and file storage.

13-3 The Internet and the Future of Computers

A. The Internet is a "network of networks" that links millions of smaller computer networks around the world. Servers host information. Clients request information.

B. Web 2.0 enables online information sharing and collaboration. Internet issues include inappropriate content, information security, and narrow search results.

C. Computer technology continues to develop rapidly. Occupations that require computer literacy and keyboarding skills will increase.

Activities

1. For these activities, access www.cengage.com/school/working, then click on Web Links.
   a. **Computer History Museum** Read about topics of interest. Your instructor may assign each class member a specific topic to research and summarize.
   b. **Rewiring Young Brains** and **Online, All The Time** Computers and the Internet are wonderful technologies. But their use can also have potential downsides. View videos from the PBS television show Frontline by clicking on the listed Web Links. After watching each video, your instructor will lead a class discussion.

2. Explain how strong Internet skills will help you achieve goals in your life-span plan.
3. Choose an occupation in which you are interested. Find out how workers in that occupation use computers. Present your findings in an oral report to the class.

4. Many software companies are updating software for use on the cloud. Examine the cost of buying a particular software package for use on your own computer and the cost for using it on the cloud. Which method is most cost efficient?

Word Power

On a separate sheet of paper, match each definition with the correct term. All definitions will be used. One definition will be used twice (there are two terms that mean the same thing).

5. Software used to locate and display information on the Web

6. A PC intended for regular use at a single location

7. The ability to type and to give commands to a computer using a keyboard

8. A feature of modern operating system software that provides icons and menus from which the user can select commands, typically with a mouse

9. The physical equipment that makes up a computer

10. Pieces of computer equipment attached to the main computer unit, such as the keyboard, mouse, and monitor

11. An electronic tool that can store and process data and can direct the work of other tools

12. A concise software program designed to perform a very targeted and limited function

13. A CPU contained on a single chip

14. Instructions on how to solve a certain problem or do a certain task; the instructions that tell a computer what to do

15. Small pictures that users can double-click on to give commands to software to perform specific functions

16. Providing computer capabilities at a remote location that is accessible via the Web

17. A PC that can be used on the move or at a remote location

18. Two or more computers linked together by cable or wireless means

19. A general knowledge of what computers are, how they work, and for what they can be used

a. app
b. browser
c. cloud computing
d. computer
e. computer literacy
f. desktop computer
g. graphical user interface
h. hardware
i. icon
j. keyboarding skill
k. microprocessor
l. mobile computer
m. network
n. peripheral
o. program
p. software

Think Critically

20. Some critics believe computers will take over most of what workers now do. Discuss in class the human costs and benefits of computers.

21. Many apps are available for free in a "lite" version. More complete versions of the same apps are available for a fee. Why do companies offer free "lite" versions of apps?

GETTY Images/iStockphoto.com

Co-op Career SPOTLIGHT

TV shows can have quite an impact on viewers. Just ask Jeff Simpson, who is pursuing a career in law enforcement, after spending some of his formative years watching a TV show about police officers. Jeff thought that if he worked in law enforcement, he would always have an interesting story to tell at the end of the day. Jeff, who is naturally friendly, open, and polite, has always been interested in interacting with people. Jeff plays intermural sports in college and likes skiing. He enjoys nature, children, and animals.

Jeff's first regular job was at a coffee shop with an indoor play area for children. He worked for minimum wage as a cashier and cook. Parents could eat while their children played nearby. The foods he cooked included coffee, small sandwiches, and macaroni.

During his senior year of high school, Jeff worked at a pet supply store. While working part-time as a stock person, Jeff stocked food and supplies on store shelves. He helped customers find the location of products and answered questions about specific products. He earned $8 per hour in this position.

Senior camp counselor was Jeff's next position. He maintained the safety and security of children between the ages of five and ten. His days were long, as campers were at camp from 7 a.m. until 6 p.m. Jeff coordinated and supervised arts and crafts, field trips, and guest speakers for the campers. To help keep campers well, Jeff acquired CPR certification and learned about basic first aid. If a camper was injured, Jeff filled out an incident report. This position paid $9.25 per hour.

Jeff used the combination of experience obtained during his part-time and seasonal positions to help earn himself a position as a Sleeping Bear Dunes National Lakeshore law enforcement intern. The Sleeping Bear Dunes National Lakeshore Park is located on Lake Michigan and has sand dunes that rise up to 400 feet. Within the park are two remote islands, accessible only by boat--North Manitou Island and South Manitou Island.

During his internship, Jeff lived on South Manitou Island. Jeff performed multiple safety patrols of swimming areas, boating docks, back country, hiking trails, and campsites. Jeff performed radio and telephone dispatch duties in support of district operations. He helped resolve minor problems that occurred on the campgrounds. Explaining rules and regulations to visitors was another part of the job. Jeff also helped with medical responses, law enforcement incidents, and visitor search and rescues.

Jeff spent ten days on the island and four days off the island. The internship, which paid $20 per day, included lodging. Jeff had to purchase his food with his wages. When he factored in the cost of gas for the four days he was off the island, he figured he was just about breaking even.

Although Jeff did not have the ability to save money during his Internship, he gladly accepted the position as it provided him with a start in government-based law enforcement. As he prepares to enter his final year of college, he hopes to leverage the combination of his experiences to obtain a position in law enforcement.

Jeff Simpson
Law Enforcement Intern

"The man who does not work for the love of work but only for money is not likely to make money nor find much fun in life." —CHARLES M. SCHWAB

The Economic World

Goodluz/Shutterstock.com

PREVIEW

The more than 150 million people employed in the workforce produce trillions of dollars' worth of goods and services a year. This activity occurs without the government telling people where to work or what to produce. Our system works well because people are free to make economic decisions and improve their financial condition. Each person has responsibilities both as a consumer and as a producer.

Jean is very excited. She just got her first job. The only problem is that she will have to buy a car to drive to work. Jean will have to get a used car, because she cannot afford a new one.

Jean uses the Internet to find out what to look for in buying a used car. Then she spends some time looking for different makes and models within her budget. She is even able to use the Internet to find several cars that interest her at two local dealers.

Jean visits the two dealers, as well as a third in the area. She looks at the cars she found on the Internet and at some other cars, too. Two of the dealers have similar cars that Jean would like. One car is priced higher than the other. Jean goes back and forth between the two dealers and is able to negotiate a price that is $250 less than the cost of the lowest-priced car.

Success Tip

In a free enterprise system, you can make many choices.

Jean also needs some new clothes for her job. She drives to a nearby mall and spends a few hours shopping. Some of the stores are having sales. By going to several different stores, Jean is able to find plenty of suitable clothes within her budget. The name-brand coat she wants for the fall is too expensive, however. Jean really likes the coat, so she decides to put it on layaway and pay for it a little at a time.

Jean is class treasurer, so she stays after school on Monday to attend a meeting. The class officers have to decide whether to spend class dues on a picnic at the beach or a trip to an amusement park. Jean thinks the beach would be more fun for everybody, so that's what she votes for, and that's what wins.

That evening, Jean watches the local news. There is a proposal to allow a second cable company to operate in the county. Those county council members who favor the proposal argue that this would bring cable prices down and improve the quality of service. Jean hopes the proposal passes. She thinks her family pays too much for cable TV, and the cable service doesn't carry some of the channels she would like.

THINK CRITICALLY

1. What are some examples of choices in this case study?

2. How might a second cable company bring prices down and improve service?

sixninepixels/Shutterstock.com

OBJECTIVES

- List the four factors of production
- Explain the circular flow of economic activity
- Illustrate how supply and demand influence market prices
- Name two types of economic systems

KEY TERMS

- economics
- need
- want
- production
- consumption
- market
- supply
- demand
- competition

AISPIX/Shutterstock.com

▶ Personal Decisions

A new brand of really attractive heels has just been introduced. These heels are "hot." Merchants can hardly keep them in stock. You go to the store to buy some. You love the shoes but are shocked by the price. They are about $30 more than what you usually pay. You would have to charge them since you do not have enough cash. Your mom suggests that you wait a few months until the price comes down. You doubt that they will be any cheaper in the future.

What would you do?

Factors of Production

Economics is the study of how goods and services are produced, distributed, and used. Economics is also concerned with how people and governments choose what they buy from among the many things they want. A need is a basic necessity of life, which includes food, shelter, and clothing. A want is something you would like to have because you would enjoy using it. Wants include portable music players, blu-ray dvd players, and a new set of discs for Frisbee golf.

You probably do not have much trouble spending your paycheck. The hard part involves making choices from among the many things you need and want. Federal, state, and local governments have the same types of choices to make. The most important economic decision faced by individuals and governments is how to choose between competing needs and wants.

The city of Centerville, for example, would like to build a new swimming pool at the city park. However, there is not enough money left in the budget after the city pays employees' salaries and bills. These expenses include street maintenance, garbage collection, and snow removal. A city, like an individual or family, has only so much money to spend.

Meeting the needs of people and nations from what is available leads to the economic activity called production. **Production** is making goods and providing services for human needs and wants. Production takes place when a farmer grows corn, a nurse cares for patients, or a barber cuts hair. In one way or another, all production involves the following four resources, or *factors*:

- **Natural resources**   Materials provided by nature are important to production. Soil, water, mineral deposits, and forests are all examples of a nation's resources. Human beings do not create them.

- **Labor**   Labor includes all of the people employed in the workforce. Both the skills of the workforce and the amount of labor help to determine the amount of production.

- **Capital**   Most people think of capital as money. To the economist, however, capital is any person-made means of production. Tools, machines, and factories are examples of capital goods. Capital used skillfully can greatly increase productivity. Sometimes capital is referred to as capital goods.

- **Management**   Management refers to the people who organize and direct the other three factors. Managers assume the risk of operating a business. The need for good organization and management applies to both single-person businesses and large corporations. Entrepreneurs represent a large proportion of managers.

The Circular Flow of Economic Activity

Several kinds of economic activities help people satisfy their needs and wants. Production is one such activity. **Consumption** is the process of using goods and services that have been produced. Buying a pair of shoes, drinking juice, and going to a movie are all different kinds of consumption. All of us are consumers.

There is a close relationship between consumers and producers called the *circular flow of economic activity*. The circular flow is illustrated in Figure 14-1. Here is how it works. Suppose that you work in business or industry. The inside bottom arrow in the figure shows that you give your services (your labor and skills) to a producer who employs you. The business or industry (producer) pays you a salary or wages for your work, as indicated by the outside bottom arrow. You also receive goods and services from producers, as the inside top arrow shows. For these goods and services, you pay money to producers, as indicated by the outside top arrow.

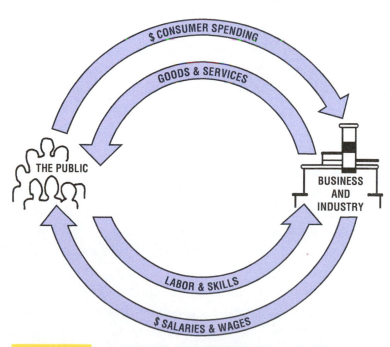

FIGURE 14-1 A circular flow of goods, services, and money takes place between consumers and producers.

Supply and Demand

Whenever goods and services are bought and sold, a **market** is created. A market may be a neighborhood grocery store or an international grain market. Buyers and sellers may meet in person, or they may conduct their business by telephone, mail, email, video conference, or the Internet.

In a free economy, market prices rise and fall according to supply and demand. **Supply** is the amount of goods or services available for sale. **Demand** is the willingness of consumers to spend money for goods and services. When demand is greater than supply, the seller will often raise the price of a product or service. This encourages the producer to provide a greater supply. Eventually, the supply begins to catch up with the demand. If the supply becomes greater than the demand, the seller may lower the price to help get rid of the excess supply. Can you provide an example of such a product or service?

In a market, competition helps to keep prices down. **Competition** refers to the efforts of sellers to win potential customers. Suppose there is only one seller for a product or service. Prices will be high. Consumers have no real choice. But if there are many sellers, each competes with the others. Shoppers benefit from the lower prices that result.

Workplace Innovations

SMART PARKING METERS

Local city and town governments use parking meters to help control on-street parking. For example, curbside meters are used near retail business to ensure turnover of parking spaces throughout the day. Requiring people to pay for parking discourages all day parkers.

The traditional coin-operated parking meter is gradually being replaced by various types of smart parking meters. One solar-powered device takes credit or debit cards or can be paid by mobile phone, in addition to accepting coins. Some meters allow motorists to use a prepaid key-like device that is inserted into a meter to pay for parking time. Another type uses RFID technology that allows a user to pay for parking by waving a card past the meter.

In addition to providing alternative payment methods, smart meters are capable of many other functions. For example, some meters will change hourly rates (say from $1 to $2 per hour) during the busiest part of the day. Some meters' time sensors reset to zero each time a car parks in the space. Meters linked by wireless networks have the ability to alert officers to parking violations and may even take a photograph of the license plate to provide evidence of a violation.

Meters in one major U.S. city have underground sensors that tell whether a vehicle is parked in a space. This makes it possible for motorists to use their mobile phones to find parking spaces online. Another city has removed the meters themselves and replaced them with a kiosk where you can buy a ticket for a pre-determined time and then place the ticket on the inside of your windshield to show evidence of payment.

NET FOLLOW-UP

Use a search engine to explore the Web for additional information on the topic of smart parking meters. Do you find the capabilities of the smart parking meters helpful or intrusive? Be prepared to discuss your observations in class.

Economic Systems

Countries do not solve their basic economic problems in the same ways. There are different economic systems. One major type is the *centrally planned economy*. Under this system, the people have no voice in economic decision making. A central authority, which is often the government, owns all resources and sets wages. The group in power also controls all production and distribution. For example, the central government decides how much production should be devoted to consumer goods, such as automobiles and washing machines.

A second major type of economic system is *free enterprise*. In such an economy, people and industries can do more or less as they please. Private individuals and industries own most of the resources and control production and distribution. People can work for themselves or they can sell their labor to someone else for a salary or wages. Consumers can buy and sell as they choose. Such buying and selling creates markets in which supply and demand influence prices.

In actual practice, neither of these economies is ever found in pure form. Historically, the former Soviet Union leaned heavily toward a centrally planned economy. In the late 1980s, however, the Soviet Union and the other 15 Communist nations of Eastern Europe began to relax government control of the economy. Private ownership of farms and factories were allowed and small business ownership began to increase. Only a few remaining centrally planned economies exist, including Cuba and North Korea.

The United States leans heavily toward a free enterprise economy. The government, however, owns many resources and runs various industries. It also controls prices for some items and regulates the manufacture and sale of certain products, such as drugs. Both the United States and the countries of the former Soviet Union, then, have what economists call *mixed economies*. Most of the other nations in the world also have mixed economies.

14-1 Assessment

1. What is the most important economic issue with which individuals and governments must deal?

2. All production involves four factors. Name them and briefly describe each one.

3. What phrase is used to describe the relationship between consumers and producers?

4. Explain how market prices rise and fall as a result of supply and demand.

5. Name two differences between a centrally planned economy and a free enterprise economy.

High Growth Occupations
FOR THE 21ST CENTURY

Do you want a rewarding career in medicine? If so, consider the occupation of registered nurse (RN). Registered nurses provide direct care to patients and assist physicians during examinations, treatments, and surgeries.

Responsibilities of registered nurses vary depending on the state laws and the setting in which the individual works. RNs work in hospitals, schools, nursing homes, clinics, physicians' offices, emergency medical centers, patients' homes, surgicenters (surgical facilities for operations not requiring a hospital stay), large companies, and in government and private agencies.

Registered nurses promote health, help prevent disease, and help patients cope with their illnesses. They observe, assess, and record symptoms, reactions, and progress. They also administer medications, and assist in convalescence and rehabilitation. Registered nurses may develop and manage nursing care plans and instruct the patient and their families in medications and proper care of the patient. Nurses who work in hospice care are part of a team that helps patients and families prepare for the patient's death.

Registered nurses who work in hospitals provide bedside care and medical requirements. Usually hospital nurses specialize in one area, such as surgery, maternity, pediatrics, the emergency room, or intensive care. Nurses who work directly in a physician's office, clinics, emergency medical centers, and surgicenters take care of the patients who come into the facility. Nurses who work in nursing homes care for residents, who are often elderly or in need of rehabilitation.

Nurses who work in home health care travel to patient's homes. Nurses who work in public health are in government agencies, schools, retirement communities, or other community arenas. Nurses who work in large companies, such as a manufacturing plant, are called occupational health or industrial nurses. They provide nursing care to employees and customers with minor injuries or illnesses in the workplace.

Education through a nursing school or college is required to become a registered nurse.

Blend Images/Shutterstock.com

Nurses can have a variety of specialties including surgery.

OBJECTIVES

- Summarize characteristics of the American free enterprise system
- Name three things required for economic growth
- Discuss types of economic freedoms that you enjoy

KEY TERMS

- monopoly
- prosperity
- recession
- depression
- inflation
- deficit

Personal Decisions

Warren Goldswain/Shutterstock.com

Business has been great at the shop where you work. You received a raise and are working a good deal of overtime. You are using the extra money to buy clothes and other things you have always wanted. One day at break, you show a coworker a picture of the new watch you put on layaway. "It is neat," he says. "But if I were you, I would not spend all of my paycheck. Good times will not last forever."

"I thought business was good," you say.

"It is," he responds. "This is the way it always is before things slow down and we get laid off."

You have not thought about that. You wonder whether or not you should buy the expensive watch.

What would you do?

Characteristics of Free Enterprise

The United States is said to have a free enterprise economy, even though it does not exist in a pure form. For the most part, the American economy runs by itself without government interference. People and industries make most of their own economic decisions.

Private Ownership

Suppose you go to a busy part of your town or city. You stop for an oil change at a shop owned by a friend. He says your car will be ready in half an hour. Since it is time for lunch, you go next door to a cafe to eat. The auto service shop and the cafe are two examples of private ownership. They are owned and operated by individuals who have risked their own money to make a profit. For the most part, people can set up any legal kind of business they wish.

Profit Motive

Business owners want to make as much money as possible. To stay in operation, businesses must make a profit. Not all of them succeed. Gino was surprised to learn that one of his favorite restaurants was going out of business. The restaurant had been owned by the same family for more than 30 years. The food was excellent and fairly priced. The restaurant seemed to have many loyal customers.

Gino wanted to own a restaurant, and checked into buying it. In examining the financial records of the business, Gino discovered why it was being sold. Mr. Colletti, the owner, may have known how to cook, but his knowledge of running a business was outdated.

Gino figured that the costs of operation were about 20 percent higher than they should have been. He concluded that by using good business practices, such as wholesale buying, quantity purchasing, and control of overhead, he could make a good profit. What's more, he could do it without sacrificing quality or service.

Competition

Jenny wanted to buy a certain brand and style of boots. Each store that carried the boots wanted a different price. Jenny bought from the store that offered the lowest price. If one company had a monopoly on

Communication at Work

CHARTS AND GRAPHS

Economic information is often presented in charts and graphs. These charts and graphs are seen in newspapers, in magazines, on the Web, and in TV news broadcasts. Economists and people in business use charts and graphs to present information. Being able to read and use charts and graphs is a valuable workplace skill. There are three common types:

- A pie chart is a circle divided into wedge-shaped parts. Pie charts are useful for showing the size of each part in relation to the whole. A pie chart is often used to represent a budget. Each wedge represents part of the budget. You can see a pie chart in Figure 12-5 on page 300.
- Bar graphs are useful for comparing items. A bar graph might be used to compare the amount of surplus (extra money) in the federal budget over several years. There would be one bar for each year. The bars would be different heights, depending on how much

money each represented. You will find several examples of bar graphs in Chapter 1 on pages 19, 20, and 21.

- Line graphs are also useful for making comparisons. They generally show trends or change. A line graph might show how much the federal government has spent over the past ten years. Amounts of money would be on the vertical axis. Years would be on the horizontal axis. Points would be plotted on the graph for the amount of money spent each year. These points would be connected with lines. Figure 11-5 on page 269 shows a line graph.

THINK CRITICALLY

1. Find an example of a pie chart, bar graph, and line graph in an outside source. Describe the function of each chart.
2. Why do you think being able to use charts and graphs is a valuable workplace skill?

the boot business, Jenny would not have had a choice. A **monopoly** is exclusive control over the supply of a product or service. Every pair of boots in all the stores would have been the same price.

Free enterprise needs competition. It forces producers to be efficient and encourages a wide variety of goods and services. Competition is so important to the American economy that the government has passed laws to forbid or regulate monopolies.

Freedom of Choice

People who have certain resources can start a business. They are not the only ones who have choices. Consumers and workers also have choices. Consumer choices influence the types of goods and services produced. For instance, if consumers stop buying a certain product, it will probably disappear from store shelves. Buyers also help determine the prices of goods. Marketers will price as highly as they think the market will bear. If they are wrong, prices will fall. Prices also go down if there is heavy competition.

A similar situation exists with workers. They seek to be paid as much as possible. In a free enterprise economy, they are able to work for whomever they choose. People who want to change jobs can do so.

Profit and competition help control this system. Some say that in free enterprise, markets are self-regulated. This means that supply and demand help set prices for goods and wages for workers.

Economic Growth

The United States economy has grown steadily throughout the years. In order for this growth to continue, several things must occur.

Capital goods, which include buildings, equipment, factories, and tools, are used to produce products. For economic growth to occur, a portion of the nation's resources must be used to produce capital goods. Individuals and businesses must use a portion of their income for savings and investments to help growth occur. Finally, the nation must use a portion of its resources for education and training.

Consumer goods and services are items that people use to fill their needs and wants. Consumer goods and services do not produce anything of further value. Four factors of production, natural resources, labor, capital, and management, are used by companies to provide capital goods and consumer goods and services. A country cannot grow if it uses all of its resources to produce consumer goods and services. Think about it. Once you buy them, a pair of jeans loses value. After using sunscreen lotion, the bottle is empty.

Capital goods, on the other hand, create future economic worth. Suppose a trucking company puts money into new rigs and loading docks. Workers use the docks over and over to load goods onto trucks. These, in turn, carry cargo to distant markets.

When buying new capital goods, businesses often borrow money. For example, Mrs. Luna decides to add on to her flower shop. She does not have all the funds she needs. The bank gives her a loan. Where does First City Bank get this money? It comes from deposits from people

FIGURE 14-2 Historical Inflation Rate, 1970–2010

Year	Annual Average Inflation
1970	5.7
1971	4.4
1972	3.2
1973	6.2
1974	11.0
1975	9.1
1976	5.8
1977	6.5
1978	7.6
1979	11.3
1980	13.5
1981	10.3
1982	6.2
1983	3.2
1984	4.3
1985	3.6
1986	1.9
1987	3.6
1988	4.1
1989	4.8
1990	5.4
1991	4.2
1992	3.0
1993	3.0
1994	2.6
1995	2.8
1996	3.0
1997	2.3
1998	1.6
1999	2.2
2000	3.4
2001	2.8
2002	1.6
2003	2.3
2004	2.7
2005	3.4
2006	3.2
2007	2.8
2008	3.8
2009	−0.4
2010	1.6

like you. When the savings rate is high, banks have more money to lend to businesses. The economy can grow.

Capital goods produce value. So do workers and managers. Offering training to employees benefits a business. Skilled workers and managers contribute to future production and growth.

Patterns of Economic Growth

A free enterprise economy goes through various cycles. Tracing these shifts is like following the path of a roller coaster. A period of expanding economic growth is known as **prosperity**. During these good times, unemployment is low. Workers receive steady pay raises because companies make high profits. Because so many people are working, they buy many consumer items. This leads to increasing production. The supply of goods meets the demand, so prices stay down.

A downturn in the economy is a **recession**. A recession can begin in many different ways. One reason a recession may begin is if there is a strong national feeling that the economy will turn bad. While concerned consumers save more of their incomes, goods pile up on shelves. Companies make production cutbacks, which lead to worker layoffs. Young people seeking their first jobs cannot find work. People then have less money to spend, so they buy even fewer goods.

If a recession gets worse, a depression can result. A **depression** is a severe recession marked by stagnant business activity. In this situation, very large numbers of people become unemployed. Consumers purchase only what they really need. Business failures increase. Production drops further and even more workers lose their jobs.

Major fluctuations in economic growth have occurred for decades. Yet there is much disagreement regarding causes and solutions. Many heated national debates result from disagreement among politicians and others over inflation, recession, and unemployment.

Inflation

Inflation occurs when prices of goods and services rise sharply. Inflation is a serious and frequent problem of our economic system. A slight upward trend in prices is very typical of free enterprise and is not very serious. Wages usually increase along with prices. When prices go up much faster than wages, though, money loses some of its value. This can happen for a variety of reasons.

Workers at The Jiffy Company do not think their wages are keeping up with the cost of living. Through their union, employees bargain for pay increases. To cover the raises, the company increases the prices of its products. Consumers buying a Jiffy food processor, for example, will now pay more for it. If there are price increases throughout the economy, Jiffy's workers will continue to seek higher wages.

What causes inflation? There is no easy answer. However, economists generally agree that the following factors contribute to inflation:

- Excessive consumer demand
- Government spending and deficits (A **deficit** is how much has been spent over budget or over what has been taken in.)

- Increased energy costs
- Decreased productivity
- Government regulations
- Fear of future inflation

The six factors listed above interact over time to produce varying rates of inflation as shown in Figure 14-2 on the previous page. From 2001 through 2010, for example, the average annual inflation rate was 2.4 percent (However, note that in 2009 the rate actually declined −0.4 This is called deflation.) But during the 1970s, it was over 7 percent. It seems likely that inflation will increase in the future as a result of high energy costs and government spending for national defense, homeland security, and Medicare and Medicaid. All segments of society—including government, business, labor, and consumers—must work together to keep inflation under control.

Economic Freedom

In a free enterprise system, individuals make most of the economic decisions. Another way of saying this is that people in a market economy enjoy economic freedom. Economic freedom consists of the following rights:

- The right to choose an occupation
- The right to change occupations or jobs
- The right to engage in business and to make a profit
- The right to spend money as you choose
- The right to offer goods or services at prices you decide
- The right to reject prices on goods or services you may want to buy
- The right to use property and wealth to produce income
- The right to succeed, limited only by your ambition and ability

Economic freedom is not available to everyone in the world. Like other freedoms, people often take economic freedom for granted. Economic freedom can be lost or weakened if individuals, businesses, and governments fail to act as responsible consumers and producers.

14-2 Assessment

1. List the four characteristics of free enterprise.
2. Why is it important for individuals and businesses to save and invest money?
3. Why is it important for companies to invest in training for workers and managers?
4. The economic growth of a free market economy goes through cycles like the path of a roller coaster. Give an example.
5. List six factors that economists generally agree contribute to inflation.

Focus on the Workplace

Counterfeit Goods Undercut the Economy

Few customers are aware that they may be buying counterfeit goods. Hundreds of fake products have flooded the market. These include jewelry, jeans, handbags, auto parts, toys, electronic appliances, perfumes, and even prescription medicines.

The economic toll is staggering. The International Chamber of Commerce estimates that counterfeit goods are responsible for five to seven percent of all goods traded world-wide. Counterfeit goods cut into company profits, reduce taxes paid, and cost jobs. Health and safety are also major concerns. Imagine driving around with fake brake shoes on your car! The death of a helicopter pilot was linked to the failure of a fake rotor assembly part. Many people are taking drugs and using health care products that contain ineffective or wrong ingredients.

Here is an example of how fake products are produced and distributed. A dishonest importer signs up a foreign manufacturer to make a shoddy oil filter. The manufacturer produces the filters. They are packaged into large crates generically labeled "oil filters" to pass U.S. Customs. The importer receives the filters and packs them in boxes printed with a real brand name. They are sold to a legitimate wholesaler as overstock (extra stock that is not needed). The wholesaler, who is unaware they are fake, sells the filters to reputable retail outlets. Consumers then come along and buy the phony filters at gas stations, auto dealers, and chain stores.

There are a number of things you can do to protect yourself. Be wary when looking for hard-to-get toys and other fad items. When shopping for a product having a high-status trademark, read labels carefully and pay close attention to workmanship. Look for sloppy printing, misspelled words, and altered logos on packages. Do not buy a product when the packaging is missing or not up to standard. Buy only at reputable places of business where, if you are accidentally sold a counterfeit item, you will be more likely to get a refund.

If prices seem really good, you should ask yourself why the merchandise can be sold so cheaply.

THINK CRITICALLY

1. Some people knowingly buy counterfeit products. Why would they do this?
2. What are some effects that counterfeit products have on the economy?

THE GLOBAL ECONOMY

OBJECTIVES
- Explain economic globalization
- Identify the major influences on economic globalization
- Describe the positive and negative results of economic globalization

KEY TERMS
- gross domestic product (GDP)
- globalization
- multinational
- outsource

Ethical Decisions

One of your favorite pastimes is to go shopping at the mall with your friends, Terri and Marla. Terri wanted to buy a new pair of sandals. After hours of shopping, she found a pair she liked at a large discount store. She tried them on and said, "Don't you guys think these are cute?" "Yes," said Marla, "but did you notice that the box said they were made in Thailand. I wouldn't buy anything imported because it hurts American workers." "I don't care where they come from," said Terri, "I like them, they are cheap, and I am going to buy them." You don't know what to say, as you think both points of view are reasonable.

What would you do?

Dmitriy Suzdalev/
Shutterstock.com

The Changing Global Economy

The market value of all final goods and services produced from a nation in a given year is the **gross domestic product**, or **GDP**. The economy of the United States is the world's largest national economy with a GDP in 2010 of approximately $14.7 trillion dollars. This figure represents about 23% of the total worldwide GDP.

In 2010, China jumped ahead of Japan in GDP to become the world's second largest economy. Leading economists predict that China will overtake the United States in terms of economic output by the early 2020s. Does this surprise you? If so, the next time you go shopping for hardware, tools, electrical appliances, toys, or other consumer goods, look on the box to see where it was manufactured.

What Is Globalization?

Globalization is defined as the process by which nations have become more interdependent. The economic growth over the last several

Workforce Trends

Globalization is continuing to increase. Changes in exports and imports are affecting the future of many industries. During the 2008-18 period, U.S. exports are expected to increase 3.9 percent. During the same period, imports are expected to increase 4.2 percent. Increased exports will benefit many businesses, ranging from agriculture and manufacturing to financial services. Increased imports will benefit some businesses. Certain businesses, such as apparel and textiles, are expected to be negatively affected by the rise in imports.

decades by such countries as China, Brazil, India, Russia, and other emerging economies is the result of globalization. Globalization occurs in language, politics, culture, travel, and finance.

Importing of manufactured goods from China is one example of globalization. Other examples are:

- The United States imports goods from many countries around the world. However, many goods are also exported including aircraft, agricultural commodities, chemicals, pharmaceuticals, and many other products.

- Many U.S. companies have become **multinational**, which means they have stores, offices, branches, or plants in different countries. This also holds true for foreign companies that have relocated to the U.S. Auto manufacturers from Japan, Germany, and South Korea have relocated some of their operations to the U.S.

- Some companies **outsource**, or contract with another company, to provide services that might be otherwise performed by in-house employees. Call center services or payroll services are examples of business functions that might be outsourced to foreign countries. Companies in India or Canada might provide services to U.S. firms.

- When a company closes down its U.S. operation and moves to another country, such as Brazil or Mexico, to reduce expenses, the company is said to be moving *offshore*.

- World financial markets actively trade in stock, bonds, and currencies. Foreign investments in other countries are also increasing, particularly in land, real estate, and commodities.

- Citizens of most countries around the world are able to travel freely from place to place for business and tourism.

- Individuals and businesses communicate throughout the world instantly via the Internet and other telecommunication methods.

As you may note, globalization has both positive and negative outcomes depending on your country of residence.

Influences on Globalization

Globalization has occurred throughout history beginning with the movement of people as they traveled to locations far from where they were born. As individuals and tribes migrated, they took ideas, customs, and products with them to new locations. This integration of outside influences has occurred slowly and steadily throughout history.

During World War II, the economies in Germany, Japan and many parts of Europe were nearly destroyed. The modern era of globalization began after World War II. Following the war, many world leaders joined together in the belief that interdependence would help prevent war. The belief was that reducing or eliminating barriers to international trade would increase living standards for everyone. The interdependence of nations, or globalization, has been assisted by three forces: changes in

Perov Stanisalv/Shutterstock.com

International cooperation is required for global markets to succeed.

transportation, new communication technology, and free enterprise.

Changes in Transportation

Individual nations are limited in terms of what they are able to produce. Countries trade with each other to meet consumer and business needs and wants. For example, the United States imports oil from the Middle East and coffee beans from Brazil, while it exports auto parts to Mexico and medical devices to Australia.

The development of modern transportation systems has supported and expanded globalization. The giant tanker, the container ship, and the airliner are the three major transporters of raw materials, manufactured parts and components, and finished goods throughout the world.

Airbus is the second largest manufacturer of passenger and cargo aircraft. At its website, Airbus explains how an A380 aircraft is built. This written narrative, along with photos and a video, illustrates both the nature of globalization and the extensive transportation network required to assemble a large jetliner.

Utilizing efficient methods of shipping, like loading ships with containers that may contain between 53,000 to 67,000 pounds of materials, helps international trade to be efficient. These containers can be unloaded from ships and loaded directly onto semi-trailer trucks.

A *sub-assembly* plant manufactures sub-assembled products. These products are manufactured at one location and then shipped to another location. A sub-assembled part is used in the manufacturing of a larger part. Sub-assembled parts are manufactured to very strict specifications. All sub-assembled parts need to fit precisely with other parts of the product.

Thousands of suppliers located in 30 countries are involved in construction of the A380 at some point. Parts for the aircraft are shipped to sub-assembly plants all across Europe. Sub-assemblies then travel by sea, river barges, outsized-load trucks, and large cargo planes to the final assembly line in Toulouse, France.

Even though they may not be as large and present the same transportation challenges as the A380 airbus, thousands of other products are manufactured in much the same way. Small parts and components are acquired from various suppliers. These parts and components are then fashioned into sub-assemblies at different locations. Sub-assemblies may then be shipped to different locations for assembly into finished products. Finished products may then be packaged and shipped via a host of carriers that include small trucks, semi-tractors and trailers, trains, cargo containers, boats and ships, and cargo planes before they reach the consumer. All of this may occur while someone at a computer monitor is tracking the product from its shipping origin, through warehousing, to its final destination.

New Communication Technology

Whereas transportation between continents may take hours, days, or weeks depending on the mode of transportation, communication may take only seconds. Perhaps, more so than transportation, communication technology has had a greater influence on globalization. In the last

Search the Net

Innovative companies can have a transformative effect on people. Access **www.cengage.com/school/working** and click on the link for Chapter 14. Read about Movirtu, a cellular phone company that has developed cell phones for use on the cloud. By furthering the concept of Mobile Identity Management, which means linking a mobile identity to a user instead of to a device, Movirtu has provided cloud phone service in geographically diverse areas ranging from rural sub-Saharan Africa to Afghanistan. Movirtu works to provide cloud phone service to people who live on less than two dollars per day. Research current developments at Movirtu. How is their technology improving the lives of people who are living on very limited budgets?

www.cengage.com/school/working

few decades new technologies have allowed instant communication, collaboration, and transfer of information. This instant communication has ushered in a new era of globalization.

With the Internet, broadband, telecommunications, wireless mobile devices, and other communication technology, the speed and scope of globalization has increased many times over. Remote workers throughout the world can now interact and collaborate as though they are located in the same office building.

A good illustration of the relationship between communication technology and globalization is the worldwide adoption of mobile phones. In 2012, there were about six billion mobile phone connections.

More importantly, from a globalization standpoint, the Asia-Pacific region including India and China is the main source of growth. These countries, which typically do not have land lines available in large parts of the region, account for more than a third of global mobile connections.

The availability of mobile phones has transformed life for many individuals in the developing world. One example is that poor farmers are now able to receive better prices for their crops because they can use mobile phones to access information on market prices. Another example is that mobile phones have created a number of small business opportunities, such as selling airtime and repairing or refurbishing phone handsets.

There are new mobile service options developing that free people from owning a cell phone. By assigning individuals unique phone numbers that are accessible on the cloud, individuals are able to access their phone accounts from any phone. Individuals can use their unique phone numbers to send and receive texts, make phone calls, and use mobile banking services. Groups of people, or entire communities, can share a few phones.

Free Enterprise

The free enterprise system is characterized by private ownership, profit motive, competition, and freedom of choice. A centrally planned economy is the opposite of free enterprise. A significant event occurred in 1978, when the leader of China, which had a centrally planned economy, began a period of reform that moved the country toward a market economy. This was followed in the early 1990s by economic reforms in India and the collapse of the Soviet empire. India (a socialist country) and the Soviet Union (a communist country) also had largely centrally planned economies. These events transformed the economic lives of about 2.8 billion people and moved three of the largest nations in the world toward greater globalization. Economic globalization has also spread throughout East Asia and much of Latin America.

Results of Globalization

Globalization has produced major economic changes throughout the world. Economists disagree whether the changes are good or bad. There is debate on both sides of the issue.

There is no doubt that globalization has stimulated international trade and expanded access to goods, services, investment capital, and innovation for billions of people. This in turn, has contributed to improvements in the standard of living for people in emerging economies, particularly in China, India, Russia, South Korea, and Brazil. Globalization has also brought big gains to developed countries as well. For example, consumers in the United States benefit from being able to purchase cheaper goods imported from overseas.

With globalization, products may be manufactured, sold, and purchased anywhere in the world.

Globalization has not worked well for everyone. More of the net capital has flowed from the developing countries to the richest countries. Many countries in Africa and Latin America have experienced few benefits from globalization and are falling farther behind the rest of the world economically. There has also been a downside to the United States. Consumer goods can be produced much more cheaply in developing countries. This has resulted in the loss of millions of manufacturing jobs in the U.S. and has tended to hold down the wages for remaining workers.

Perhaps the most negative result of globalization is potential damage to the environment. The worldwide demand for more manufactured goods has resulted in greater consumption of raw materials, deforestation, increased use of oil and coal, and competition for water resources. The increased burning of fossil fuels leads to greater global warming, which ultimately may have catastrophic consequences for the planet.

14-3 Assessment

1. Which three countries have the largest gross domestic product?
2. What is the primary reason that companies move offshore?
3. Name the three major types of transportation carriers involved in international trade.
4. Why are mobile phones being so quickly adopted in developing countries?
5. Give two examples of positive results of globalization.
6. What is probably the most negative result of globalization?

Chapter Summary

14-1 Principles of Economics

A. Economics is the study of how goods and services are produced, distributed, and used. It also explains how people and governments choose between competing needs.

B. Production involves meeting the needs of people and nations from what is available. Production involves four resources: natural resources, labor, capital, and management.

C. Consumption is the process of using goods and services that have been produced. The circular flow of economic activity links consumers and producers.

D. Whenever goods and services are bought and sold, a market is created. In a market, competition helps to keep prices down.

E. In a centrally planned economy, the government owns all resources and controls production and distribution. In a free enterprise economy, private individuals and industries own most of the resources and control production and distribution. A mixed economy contains elements of both central and free enterprise economies.

14-2 The American Free Enterprise System

A. The American free enterprise system has four main characteristics: private ownership, profit motive, competition, and freedom of choice. The system runs largely by itself without government interference.

B. For economic growth to continue, (1) a portion of the nation's resources must be used to produce capital goods, (2) individuals and businesses must use a portion of their income for savings and investments, and (3) the nation must use a portion of its resources for education and training.

C. A free enterprise economy goes through cycles. A period of expanding economic growth is known as prosperity. A downturn in the economy is called a recession. A very serious recession can lead to a depression.

D. Inflation is when prices of goods and services rise sharply. Causes of inflation include: excessive consumer demand, government spending and deficits, increased energy costs, decreased productivity, government regulations, and fear of future inflation.

E. Economic freedom is not available to everyone in the world. It can be lost or weakened if individuals, businesses, and governments fail to act as responsible consumers and producers.

14-3 The Global Economy

A. The market value of all final goods and services produced from a nation in a given year is called the gross domestic product, or GDP. The economy of the United States has the world's largest GDP.

B. Over the last several decades, the nations of the world have become more globalized, or interdependent. Globalization has both positive and negative outcomes.

C. Globalization has been assisted by three major forces: changes in transportation, new communication technology, and free enterprise.

D. Globalization has produced major economic changes throughout the world, but economists disagree whether the changes are good or bad. Perhaps the most negative result of globalization is potential damage to the environment.

Activities

1. As a class, identify the countries that maintain centrally planned economies. Then divide into small groups corresponding to the number of countries. Each group should collect information about the country and the current status of its economy and present a report to the class.

2. Divide goals you might set in your life-span plan into two lists: (a) goals that concern consumption, such as buying a house, and (b) goals that concern production of goods or services, such as working as an electrician. Explain how these lists show we are all consumers and producers in the economy.

3. For these activities, access www.cengage.com/school/working then click on Web Links to find the following:

   a. **Gross Domestic Product**   The definition of gross domestic product (GDP) includes the phrase "final goods and services." Why is the term "final" used? Give an example of a "final" good or service.

   b. **Literacy Test**   Test your own economic literacy by taking the 20 question online literacy test. After you finish, grade the test and compare your answers with classmates and others who have taken the test.

   c. **CPI Inflation Calculator**   This link will illustrate how inflation reduces purchasing power over time. Your instructor will explain how to use the calculator. The results can often be quite surprising. Discuss what happens if your earnings or savings do not keep up with the inflation rate.

   d. **National Geographic Globalization**   Explore the globalization trends by clicking on "Language," "Tourism," and "Global Travel." Discuss the pros and cons of each of these trends.

4. One person with a home computer and printer was flabbergasted when she called the toll free number listed by the manufacturer to reorder ink for her printer. Her call was sent to a call center in India. She knew the manufacturer had an ink distribution center about ten miles from her home. She placed the order with the representative in India. When the ink arrived, the return address on the mailing label was for a local address. Interview a few adults and ask if they have needed to work with any call centers in other countries. Ask how efficiently the matter was resolved. Try to determine whether it was more or less efficient for the customer to be served by a call center in another country. Summarize your results and be prepared to discuss as a class.

Word Power

a. competition
b. consumption
c. deficit
d. demand
e. depression
f. economics
g. globalization
h. gross domestic product (GDP)
i. inflation
j. market
k. monopoly
l. multinational
m. need
n. outsource
o. production
p. prosperity
q. recession
r. supply
s. want

On a separate sheet of paper, match each definition with the correct term. All definitions will be used, and a definition will be used only once.

5. How much has been spent over budget or over what has been taken in
6. The process by which nations have become more interdependent
7. The process of using goods and services that have been produced
8. Exclusive control of the supply of a product or service
9. A basic necessity of life, which includes food, shelter, and clothing
10. The willingness of consumers to spend money for goods and services
11. A severe recession marked by stagnant business activity
12. An area of economic activity created whenever goods and services are bought and sold
13. A period of expanding economic growth
14. Companies with headquarters in one country that have stores, offices, branches, or plants in different countries
15. The efforts of sellers to win potential customers
16. A sharp increase in the costs of goods and services
17. The study of how goods and services are produced, distributed, and used
18. The market value of all final goods and services produced from a given nation
19. The making of goods and services available for human needs and wants
20. A downturn in the economy
21. Contracting with another company, often in a different country, to provide some type of business service
22. The amount of goods or services available for sale
23. Something you would like to have because you would enjoy using it

Think Critically

24. In the early 1980s, large automakers lost billions of dollars. Thousands of autoworkers lost their jobs. Yet the price of new cars continued to rise. This seems to contradict the law of supply and demand. Discuss this situation in class. (Hint: see Figure 14-2)

25. Discuss how the following individuals might contribute to inflation: (a) a union leader negotiating a labor contract, (b) a merchant setting prices for goods, (c) a factory worker assembling car parts, (d) a consumer shopping for a smartphone, and (e) an elected official preparing a new budget.

26. What are some of the things the government often does during periods of recession to help stimulate the economy and relieve unemployment?

27. How have you, members of your family, your employer, or your community been affected by globalization?

28. During the summer of 2011 General Motors (GM) began production on the Chevrolet Sonic. This was a newsworthy event because the Sonic was the only subcompact car being manufactured in America. GM worked hard to make the Sonic manufacturing plant as efficient as GM plants located in Korea and Germany. GM also had to negotiate pay concessions from the United Automobile Workers (U.A.W.) union so that labor costs could be competitive with labor costs in other countries. Many of the Sonic workers agreed to work for $14 and hour even though the typical wage of a U.A.W. worker was $28 an hour. Research the Web to determine what other products are being manufactured in America that could be manufactured in other countries for lower costs. Find out how the American companies were able to manufacture the product at a cost that was competitive with other countries. Depending on the results of your research, determine whether you are hopeful or not hopeful that more manufacturing can return to the U.S. Summarize your results and be prepared to discuss as a class.

Career Transitions Connection

The Global Economy and Jobs

Click on *The Daily Leap*. Search on *"Global Economy"* in the search box. Read posted articles. How will global greening affect job opportunities? How has the U.S. economic recession impacted job opportunities? When other countries face challenges in their economies, how does that affect U.S. employment?

15

The Consumer in the Marketplace

"Take the best that exists and make it better. When it does not exist, design it. Accept nothing nearly right or good enough." —SIR FREDERICK HENRY ROYCE

DorianGray/iStockphoto.com

For Sale

PREVIEW

As a buyer, you will make decisions all your life. Today, you may choose between two brands of shampoo. In a few years, you may need to make more important choices, such as which house to buy. Making a mistake then could be very costly. By learning wise consumer skills now, you might save yourself problems later.

Taking/*Action* Consumer Choices

Mike goes to evening school and works part-time. Even though his job pays well, Mike never seems to have any money. In fact, he lives from paycheck to paycheck.

Mike cashes a paycheck for $190 every Friday. On payday, he pays $17 for dinner at a restaurant. He gives his parents $25 for room and board for the week. Mike goes to the mall with his buddies where he buys, on impulse, a $16 CD. With tax, his purchase comes to about $17.

Mike has to put gas in his car on Monday. Filling his car costs $56. He eats lunch out every day. It costs him $8 on Monday, about what he usually pays.

He's gotten in the habit of ordering water with lunch because it is free. On Tuesday, he goes out to lunch to celebrate someone's birthday. Mike's share of the bill is $15.

That evening, Mike's dad shows him the family cellphone bill. Mike is lucky. His parents are only charging him for the "additional phone line" cost of the bill and for his data plan. Although the phone line only costs $10 each month, the data plan costs $35. Are you keeping track? It is Tuesday, and Mike has just $7 left.

Mike's girlfriend, Janine, is coming home from college on Thursday for a long weekend. He wants to take her out. Mike decides to skip lunch for the rest of the week to save money. He asks his Mom if she can make a family meal on Saturday that would include Janine. Mike's Mom agrees to purchase the groceries if he agrees to make the salad, lasagna, garlic bread, and brownies. Mike doesn't really want to do all that work, but he thinks Janine would like a nice home-cooked meal. After dinner, he and Janine will watch a movie at Mike's house by streaming it through the family game console. Mike will use his $7 to treat Janine to a single dip ice cream cone after the movie. As Janine is also on a tight budget, he thinks she will understand how he is trying to take her out with limited funds.

When Mike is driving home on Wednesday, his front right tire blows out. Mike has known that he should replace the tire for some time, but he could never seem to find the money. Mike doesn't have any savings, so he has to borrow $65 from his parents to pay for a new tire. Mike can't believe his luck. The insurance and loan payments for his car are coming up, too. When will he ever be able to get ahead?

thefinalmiracle/Shutterstock.com

THINK CRITICALLY

1. What are some poor choices that Mike makes?
2. What are some ways that Mike could save money?

OBJECTIVES

- Give examples of goods and services that are consumed
- Name and describe the three stages involved in consuming goods and services
- Explain what is meant by planned and perceived obsolescence

KEY TERMS

- consumer
- good
- service
- generic product
- brand-name product
- comparison shopping
- warranty
- planned obsolescence
- perceived obsolescence

Monkey Business Images/Shutterstock.com

▶ Personal Decisions

You live in the city where you work and share an apartment with several friends. You all pool grocery money and take turns shopping and cooking. You are more thrifty than your roommates. You often buy store brands and generic products rather than more expensive brand-name foods. One day, as you are unloading groceries, one of your roommates comes into the kitchen.

"What is this stuff?" he bellows. "I am not eating this generic junk! We can afford to buy some decent food."

What would you do?

Goods and Services

A market is created whenever two or more parties come together to buy and sell. In earlier times, a typical market was a group of farmers selling produce out of the back of wagons in the town square. There were relatively few items to buy and few choices available. Today's market may be a department store, service station, grocery store, movie theater, or barbershop. All markets operate basically the same way. Sellers wish to attract buyers and then make a profit on a sale. Buyers, on the other hand, look for good quality at a low price.

A **consumer** is someone who buys or uses goods and services. **Goods** are articles that are produced or manufactured. Some goods, such as food, are used up almost immediately. Other goods, such as tools, last for many years. A house is also a type of good. If properly built and maintained, a house may last for a long time.

Services differ from goods. **Services** involve the payment of money to people and businesses for work performed. Having a suit dry-cleaned and getting a haircut are personal services. You pay fees to doctors, dentists, and lawyers in exchange for their knowledge and skills. Buying life insurance or obtaining a credit card involves the use of business services. Many common services are for maintenance and repair work, such as having an automobile tuned up or a television fixed. Entertainment and recreation are also types of services that are often purchased.

Money buys food, clothing, and other necessities. People also buy goods and services that they want but may not need. Designer jeans and a concert ticket are examples of things that you may want. People often use the term need when they really mean want. To say that you need a new pair of designer jeans is probably not true. You may want the jeans, but you do not actually need them. Needs are necessities; wants are luxuries.

What Is Consuming?

Being a consumer is more than simply paying money for something. Consuming involves three stages—choosing, buying, and using.

Make Choices

Buying always involves making choices. You have to eat in order to stay alive, so that really is not a choice. However, you do have to make decisions about what you eat. Do you eat a balanced diet or only pizza and soft drinks? Do you prepare meals at home? Or, like Mike, do you eat in restaurants or skip meals to have money for movie tickets?

Sometimes you have to choose between two similar products or services. Suppose you are going to buy a pair of shoes. The two pairs you like vary in price and quality. How do you decide which pair to buy?

Some choices involve different kinds of products or services. For example, what if you want to have both hair extensions and a sweater? But you only have enough money for one of these. Which will you decide to buy? Another type of choice is whether to spend your money or save it. This may be the most difficult choice of all. If you save some of your money, it will mean doing without some things that you would like to have now.

Buy Wisely

This stage begins once you have decided to buy. Knowledge and planning are very important to wise buying. There are several ways to learn about different products and services. You can talk with friends and family, attend special classes, do research on the Web, and read consumer magazines. *Consumer Reports* is perhaps the best-known consumer magazine. It rates various products in terms of price, quality, and other factors. Knowing which products are rated highly can save you shopping time as well as money. There are still other things you can do to be a good shopper.

Bill Martinez is a wise consumer. Bill never shops for food when he is hungry. He knows that when he is hungry he tends to buy food on impulse. To avoid exceeding his food budget, Bill plans what he will buy. He writes everything on a list and follows it. Bill knows the grocery stores in his town run sales on weekends, so he shops then when possible. He buys generic products when he can, because the quality is good and the prices are lower.

Workforce Trends

Gross Domestic Product (GDP) refers to the market value of all final goods and services produced in the United States. GDP is reported as either *nominal* or *real GDP*. Nominal GDP is based on the prices of goods and services in the year they were produced. Real GDP is the figure that has been adjusted for inflation or deflation. GDP is used as a measure of economic growth. For example, in a given year the nominal GDP increases by 5%. If the annual inflation rate were 3%, the real GDP would be 2%.

You are grocery shopping and need to get dry cat food. You can buy a 4½-lb bag for $4.29 or an 18-oz box for $1.49. Which is the better buy?

SOLUTION

Convert one of the weights so both are in the same units. Then divide the price by the weight. There are 16 ounces in a pound, so 4½ lbs = 72 oz.

$4.29 ÷ 72 = $.06 per ounce
$1.49 ÷ 18 = $.08 per ounce

The 4½-lb bag is the better buy.

Generic products state only the common name of the product on the label (grape juice). **Brand-name products** have a unique name given to them by the manufacturer (Welch's Purple 100% Grape Juice). Large sizes of food are often good buys. Bill chooses the large size when he is sure he will use up the product. If some of the food is wasted, a large size isn't a bargain. Last week, Bill saw some dented cans in a bin. He passed the bin without buying because the food might have been spoiled. Spoiled food, no matter how cheap, is no bargain.

Recently, Bill went to a department store to look for a new shirt. He found four he liked but rejected two right away. The care label on one said "dry-clean only." Dry cleaning can be expensive. The other rejected shirt was 100 percent cotton and would need to be ironed. Of the two remaining no-iron shirts, one was better-made than the other.

However, before buying the better-made shirt, Bill decided to do some comparison shopping. **Comparison shopping** means finding out the cost of a product or service at several different places before making a decision to buy. Bill first checked prices in an online catalog. They were slightly cheaper than the store's, but he would have to wait for the shirt to be delivered and pay postage. Then Bill saw a discount store's ad for shirts. When Bill reached the store, a clerk was putting shirts on a shelf. Two of them were exactly what Bill wanted. The labels showed they were brand-name shirts and they were on sale for 25 percent off.

Buying wisely also involves the careful use of credit. Some businesses sell products or services for less when you pay cash. If you charge a purchase, it is important to know how much more you will pay. Usually, if you pay within a certain amount of time, the credit is free. If you do not pay right away, though, credit may be expensive.

Use Goods and Services Properly

Wise consuming does not end after you bring a product home. If a product is ruined because of carelessness, you have wasted money. Treat products as if you want them to last forever. Suppose you just bought a new hair dryer. Save the receipt in case you have to return the product. Read the instructions carefully before trying it. Once you are sure the item works, check the packaging for the warranty card. A **warranty** is a guarantee or promise that a product is free from defects. Fill out the card, make a photocopy for your records, and send it in right away or register it online. Always use products according to the directions. If you misuse a product, you are responsible for any damage. Manufacturers will not honor warranties on misused products.

Being a wise consumer of services is also important. For example, the price of an oil change may vary by $10 or more. Watch for advertising by automobile dealers, discount stores, service stations, and tire and appliance service centers. Such businesses frequently lower the price on oil changes simply to increase business and get you into their shop. If you want to save the most money, buy the oil and filter at a discount store and change the oil yourself.

Product Obsolescence

The term *obsolescence* refers to something becoming out of date or no longer useful. When used in relation to the act of consuming, the phrases planned obsolescence or perceived obsolescence are frequently used.

Planned Obsolescence

Planned obsolescence refers to intentionally designing and producing products in order for them to be used up within a specific time period. You buy many types of products knowing they are designed for obsolescence, such as a paper coffee cup which is used once and then thrown away. Other products such as flashlight batteries, disposable razors, and light bulbs are designed for multiple, but still limited, use. Consumers are generally not bothered throwing out products that were designed to be used a limited number of times.

A lack of *backward compatibility* means that a new product will not work with older systems. This often happens when a consumer buys a new computer or gaming system and discovers that older software or games do not work on the new model. Another example is that new models of battery-operated power tools seldom work with older batteries and charging stations.

There are many other products that are designed and produced by manufacturers in such a way that they break down prematurely, are made to be difficult or costly to repair, or lack backward compatibility. What are some examples of planned obsolescence? It is difficult to prove that manufacturers of consumer products intentionally install parts designed to fail. There is, however, considerable truth in the saying that "you get what you pay for." A washing machine from a manufacturer that sells for half of what a higher-priced model sells for is usually cheaper for a reason. Part of the reason is that the cheaper model has parts and components of lesser quality that wear out sooner.

Many home appliances such as toasters, coffee makers, and food processors lack the ability to be repaired, or to be repaired at a reasonable price. When they fail it is usually cheaper

When appliances break down it can be time consuming and costly to fix them.

to discard them and buy a new one. Another example is MP3 players that have batteries which are difficult to replace without special tools. When a battery fails, the product may need to be returned to the retail store for repair. The replacement battery may cost as much as buying a new unit.

Perceived Obsolescence

There is another type of obsolescence called **perceived obsolescence**. This refers to the desire on the part of a consumer to replace a functional product because it is perceived or thought to be no longer stylish or appropriate. In other words, a product is replaced not because it fails or is worn out, but because the consumer wants something different.

The fashion industry is all about perceived obsolescence. Manufacturers of clothing and accessories continually change styles, colors, and materials to entice consumers to buy the latest fashion trends. The latest fashion trend is soon replaced by a new trend.

Consumer electronics is another area that experiences a great deal of perceived obsolescence. Computers, TVs, and mobile phones are good examples of this. People often replace computers every few years to gain faster speed, a larger hard drive, a bigger monitor, and other

Workplace Innovations

SMART CREDIT CARDS

We all love the convenience of taking out a credit card, swiping it through a reader, signing a receipt, and walking away with a purchase. This is made possible by a magnetic stripe on the back of the card which is read and authenticated by a magnetic card reader. What happens, however, if your card is lost or stolen? Or if the data is grabbed off your credit card by a fraud crime called "skimming." A lost or stolen credit card can be used by anyone to purchase merchandise or services until the credit card balance is reached or until the credit card company is notified. Another problem with magnetic stripe cards is that they cannot be used in many countries worldwide which use a different technology.

Credit cards issued in Europe and elsewhere use an integrated circuit card sometimes called a Chip and PIN card. Such smart cards are now starting to be issued by a number of U.S. banks and credit unions. Smart cards have a small computer chip imbedded in them which stores the account information in an encrypted format. Rather than swipe the card, it is inserted in a point-of-sale machine that reads the encrypted information. For additional security, the machine asks you to punch in a PIN, which provides identity authentication (in lieu of a signature).

Even though this type of card is more expensive to manufacture and requires replacing older magnetic readers, the additional security justifies the up-front costs. The security advantage of a Chip and PIN card along with its ability to be used for "contactless payments" and "mobile payments" almost guarantee that it will become the credit card of the future.

NET FOLLOW-UP

Use a search engine to explore the Web for additional information on the topic of "Chip and PIN cards."

features even though their existing computer is probably adequate. Or, they buy a notebook or tablet computer (or both) because they desire certain new features not present in their current desktop model.

Consumers used to keep TVs for years or even decades. In the early 2000s, individuals began to replace tube TVs for flat screen models. After owning a 32" flat screen model for a couple of years, some people can't resist buying a bigger 40" model with high definition. Next, the desire to own a 3D TV becomes the motivation to buy again. Upgrading from one TV model to another is a never-ending process.

Perhaps the best example of perceived obsolescence relates to the purchase of mobile phones. This is a very competitive market in which phone manufacturers introduce new models almost every six months. New features are constantly added to entice buyers to upgrade or to switch brands. Some people even buy a new phone in order to change their phone's color. Phone companies which sell service contracts also encourage consumerism by frequently changing plan features and pricing and by offering free or low-cost phones.

One of the newest gimmicks to increase perceived obsolescence is retail *buy back* programs. Retailers understand that consumers complain when a new electronic product is introduced soon after they have made a purchase. So, some of the largest retailers offer to buy back your old computer, TV, mobile phone, or other product for a certain percentage of the original cost within a certain time period. To qualify for a buy back you have to purchase a plan when you buy the product. For example, one company charges $99 for a HDTV that sells for $1,000. If you later trade in a product, you receive store credit rather than cash.

Electronic product buy back plans are basically a type of insurance. You pay a fee upfront for the right to trade in your product later. Plans have trade-in condition, time, and price restrictions based on the type of product. For a TV, you might get a 50 percent credit if traded in within six months. The percentage then drops steadily in six month increments. For a two year old TV, you might only get a 10 percent credit. Buy back plans are a good deal for retailers or they would not be selling them. However, many consumer organizations advise buyers against purchasing such plans.

15-1 Assessment

1. How are the goals of a buyer and a seller different?
2. What is a need? A want?
3. The process of consuming has three stages. Name and briefly describe them.
4. Give three reasons why Bill Martinez is a wise consumer.
5. Why should you use and care for a product properly?
6. Planned obsolescence is often referred to as "designed for the dump." Explain what this means.
7. Who benefits the most from retailer buy back programs—consumers or retailers? Explain your answer.

ADVERTISING AND THE CONSUMER

OBJECTIVES
- Explain advantages and disadvantages of advertising
- Identify different advertising techniques
- Describe sales traps to avoid

KEY TERMS
- advertising
- direct-mail advertising
- guarantee

sjlocke/iStockphoto.com

▶ Personal Decisions

You see an advertisement in the paper for an item you have been intending to buy. You put the ad in your pocket and head for the store. You find the item and take it to the checkout counter. The clerk rings it up at the regular price. You point out the item is on sale. The clerk brushes off your comment and says that the ad in the paper is in error.

What would you do?

Role of Advertising

Advertising is any type of public notice or message intended to aid in the sale of a product or service. Sellers of goods and services use advertising to attract potential buyers. It is all around you. It is in newspapers and magazines. Ads also appear on television, buses, signs, billboards, and the Web. **Direct-mail advertising** is advertising mailed directly to you. What types of ads do you receive in the mail? Direct-mail ads are being replaced rapidly by ads sent to your computer or mobile phone.

Advertising is important for both sellers and consumers. From a business point of view, the purpose of advertising is to aid in selling goods and services. For consumers, advertising provides information about goods and services for sale.

What are some ways that advertising helps you, the consumer? Suppose you see two newspaper ads for A-1 tents. One store's price is cheaper than the other's. Without leaving your home, you can decide where to buy the tent at the better price. This way, you do not have to go from store to store to check prices. You save time and money.

The next day, you hear a radio spot in which the announcer talks about a bargain tune-up at Smith's Garage. Later you see an ad in the window of Pope's Auto. On the same tune-up, Pope's offers a better price than Smith's. Again, by comparing advertising, you are able to save money.

Do you complain about ads on radio and television? Without advertising, many of your favorite programs would go off the air. This is because most of the costs of producing these programs are paid for by advertising. Newspapers, magazines, and websites are also operated with money made through advertising. Without advertising the world would be quite different. Advertising also has disadvantages. Consumers pay for it. The cost of advertising often ranges from zero to five percent of the selling price of a product or service. So $.50 of a $10 price tag could be advertising costs.

Advertising is any type of public message intended to aid in the sale of a product or service.

Advertising can be expensive in yet other ways. It can convince you to buy things you may not actually need. Jason knows this—now. He had been saving his hard-earned money for a used motorcycle. He already had $300. Last winter, he kept seeing ads for leather coats. Jason already had a nice coat, but many of his friends had leather ones. Jason thought they looked great. On the way to the bank one day, Jason was passing a clothing store. On an impulse, he went in. He entered with $300 and left with a leather coat and a few dollars. After several weeks, Jason was sorry he had not saved the money. He had to start saving for a motorcycle all over again.

Advertising Techniques

To get you to remember their products or services, advertisers use means such as pictures, slogans, and jingles (catchy tunes and slogans). In fact, you may often use a brand name to refer to a whole class of products. For example, how many times have you heard "Scotch tape" instead of "cellophane tape"? How about Kleenex tissues, Xerox copies, and Levi's jeans? Can you think of other examples?

Once people are familiar with a product's name, they may buy the product. But advertisers do not take chances. To achieve their aims, advertisers use proven methods, such as the following:

- **Endorsements**   Famous people present the advertising message. For example, a well-known athlete may tell you she uses a Whammo tennis racquet. If the racquet is good enough for her, it should suit you. Right? That is what the advertiser wants you to think.

- **Familiarity**   You hear a jingle over and over. The advertiser wants you to become familiar with a product and remember it.

- **Association**   This approach often is seen during the holiday season. Here is an example. A horse-drawn sleigh passes through a beautiful, snow-covered landscape. This pleasant scene is then associated with the product being advertised.

- **Goodwill**   Some advertisers work hard to create a good public image. They may provide health tips, donate money to worthwhile causes, or engage in other activities. One of the world's largest soft drink companies, for example, has helped sponsor every Olympic Game since 1928.

- **Successful living**   This approach appeals to people's desire for success, wealth, status, or beauty. For instance, one manufacturer of men's shoes uses the phrase "Shades of the Sophisticated Man" in its advertisements. The message is that you will be more sophisticated if you wear the shoes.

- **Emotional appeal**   Many ads contain messages related to happiness, friendship, and other pleasant emotions. "Buy a diamond for someone you love" is an example of a type of theme that frequently appears.

- **Economic appeal**   Messages about spending, saving, and making money are featured in many ads. An example is, "No money down. No payments until after the holidays!"

- **Conformity**   This approach encourages you to buy something because others have it. You may hear, "Our product is used by millions of satisfied customers." An example of a slightly different approach is, "By using this camera, you, too, can be an expert photographer."

- **Scare tactics**   We all want to avoid situations that are dangerous, embarrassing, or otherwise unpleasant. Who wouldn't want to prevent an auto accident? Sure-Grip tires will keep you from having one. This advertiser wants you to think you may have an accident if you do not use the product.

- **Intellectual appeal**   Many products claim to help you become more informed or better educated. Or they appeal to your intelligence. Perhaps the following sounds familiar: "Smart people have found this dishwashing soap to be the better product."

- **Health and comfort**   This approach is used in ads for products such as aspirin, skin creams, and vitamins. The ads tell you how the product will improve your health or make you feel better.

A *raincheck* is an offer to a customer to obtain an out-of-stock product at the advertised sale price when the product becomes available. To keep customers from getting angry, some stores may offer customers a raincheck when they run out of product. See Figure 15-1 on the next page for a sample raincheck.

Sales Traps

There is nothing wrong with advertising as long as it is honest. If you dislike an ad's message, you can choose not to buy. Problems occur when advertising is misleading. Be alert to the following deceptive, or misleading, practices.

- **False pricing**   When consumers see an item that has been marked down, they naturally believe it is a bargain. Sale prices

Sylvan's Department Store

RAINCHECK

ITEM _____

MODEL/SIZE _____

REGULAR PRICE _____ SALE PRICE _____

AD DATE _____ STORE NO. _____ QUANTITY _____

NAME _____

ADDRESS _____

CITY _____ STATE _____ ZIP _____

TELEPHONE _____

EMAIL _____

AUTHORIZED SIGNATURE _____

FIGURE 15-1 Merchants who sell out of an advertised product sometimes give rainchecks. What does a raincheck mean?

are usually lower than regular prices. However, some merchants raise the regular price before marking an item down. For example, there is a watch with a suggested price of $80. The seller changes the price tag to read "$120." The watch is then "marked down" to $80. A consumer buys the watch, believing that $40 has been saved. The truth is that the watch was bought at the regular price.

- **Bait and switch** This occurs when an ad offers a product or service that is not available. For example, a meat and cheese shop advertises a cut of meat at a bargain price. When you get to the store, you find that the meat has all been sold (or maybe they had none to begin with). The ad was used as bait to get you to the store. The clerk tries to sell you a more expensive cut, which is the switch.

- **Referral sales plans** A few sellers of services and expensive products use this technique. How does it work? Suppose someone contacts you about siding for your house. You are offered a "special introductory deal" on new siding. The seller explains that, although you will pay full price for the siding, you will receive a bonus of $200 for each new purchaser you refer. You then discover that it is very difficult to find customers for the company. (Its bad reputation is probably known. The seller may even have left town.) Most consumers are never able to earn their bonus money.

- **Unclear, untrue, and overstated claims** Some products are advertised as being "improved" or "lasting 50 percent longer." Look carefully at such ads. Are the advertisers keeping facts from you? Do they tell you how a product has been improved? If so, does what they say make sense? If a product is said to last longer, ask yourself, "Longer than what?" Your question might not

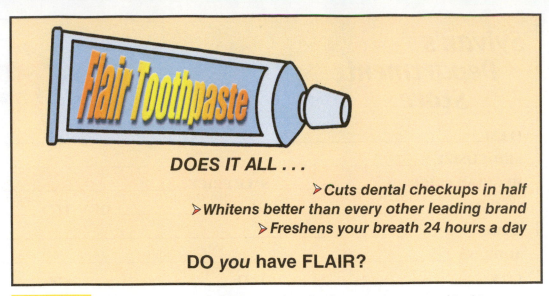

FIGURE 15-2 What advertising techniques and misleading practice are used in this advertisement?

have an answer. Other ads use descriptions like "stain-resistant" or "never needs ironing." Such descriptions may have several meanings. For example, a coat that is "stain-resistant" cannot be expected to resist all stains. A **guarantee** is a pledge that something is exactly as stated or advertised. Ads that say a product is guaranteed are often unclear and untrue. If you are told a product is guaranteed, make sure the guarantee is in writing. Another problem phrase is "lasts a lifetime." Few products do. If a product claim seems too good to be true, it probably is not true. Do the claims in Figure 15-2 seem justified?

- **Clever sales tactics** Salespeople use various techniques to get you to buy. Some use high-pressure or fast-talking approaches. Others flatter you or are very friendly because they want to make it difficult for you to say no. Sometimes, a salesperson who is having trouble getting you to buy will turn you over to a second salesperson. A favorite sales trick is to say, "The price is going up tomorrow." A similar line is, "This is the last item available."

15-2 Assessment

1. Advertising has advantages and disadvantages for consumers. Name two of each.

2. What does buying "on an impulse" mean?

3. Identify the advertising technique used in each of the following ads: (a) a famous person speaks for the product, (b) a company provides athletic uniforms with its name on them, (c) a company explains how its product will make you more attractive, (d) you are told how a certain service will save you money, (e) an accident or other dangerous situation is shown.

4. What is meant by "bait and switch"? Give an example.

High Growth Occupations
FOR THE 21ST CENTURY

Many people work in the personal appearance and beauty services industry including *barbers, cosmetologists* and *manicurists*. One of the fastest growing occupations in this field is *skin care specialist*. There are many reasons for this increase including an older population hoping to forestall the aging process, more people seeking advice in protecting or repairing sun damaged skin, and advances in medical science. New chemical treatments and procedures are also giving skin care specialists more products and tools to work with.

Skin care specialists, also known as *estheticians*, provide specialized beauty services that help clients look and feel their best. They cleanse and beautify the skin by giving facials and full-body treatments. They provide head and neck massages and they apply makeup. They may also remove hair by using waxing, electrolysis, or lasers.

Successful personal appearance workers should have an understanding of fashion, art, and technical design. They also must keep a neat personal appearance and a clean work area. Interpersonal skills, image, and attitude play an important role in career success. Business skills and the ability to be an effective salesperson are also important.

Most skin care specialists are employed in establishments such as beauty salons, barber shops, nail salons, day and resort spas, and doctor's offices. Beginning estheticians will typically work for a salon or spa as salaried employees until they build a client base and set themselves up for self-employment. About 44 percent are self-employed and rent space in a salon or spa. In this case, workers provide their own supplies, and are responsible for paying their own taxes and benefits.

Most states require that skin care specialists complete at least 600 hours of training. Each state has its own requirements to earn licensing. Specialists considering self-employment also need an awareness of sound business practices. These practices include knowing how to market services, manage inventory, retain clients while attracting new ones, negotiate rental contracts, and build a stable profit margin.

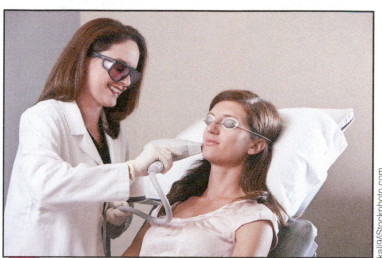

kali9/iStockphoto.com

Skin care specialists may use lasers to remove excess hair.

CONSUMER RIGHTS AND RESPONSIBILITIES

OBJECTIVES

- Discuss types of consumer rights
- Describe responsibilities of consumers
- Summarize steps to take in dealing with consumer problems

KEY TERMS

- recall
- assertive
- complaint

Monkey Business Images/Shutterstock.com

Ethical Decisions

You work part-time as a bagger at one of the well-known grocery store chains. The work is not difficult, but on weekends the store is so busy that you have to hustle to keep up with the long line of customers. As you are filling the third of what will be several more bags, you notice that a package of cookies has a small slit in the cellophane. Apparently, neither the customer nor the cashier noticed the tear. If you stop and inform the cashier, the checkout will be delayed for everyone in line. But, if and when the customer later discovers the tear, she will probably be upset.

What would *you* do?

Consumer Rights

Consumers have not always had rights. Until the last century, there were few laws to protect buyers. If consumers bought defective products, it was their problem. Because they had no legal responsibility, producers often paid little attention to safety and quality. After many consumers were harmed by unsafe products and faulty merchandise, the public began to demand tougher standards.

Laws now require manufacturers to make safety their concern. Consumers have a right to expect that what they buy is safe. Laws also protect consumers who buy faulty merchandise. After an item is sold, the producer must stand behind it. Areas covered by consumer rights include credit, interest rates, insurance, and housing.

Cathy bought a Cookbetter microwave. After she had used it for several months, she read a recall notice in the newspaper. A **recall** is a public request by a manufacturer for the return of a product that may be defective or contaminated. Many people had reported problems with the microwave. It had even caused several fires. When Cathy took the microwave back to the seller, she got a new one.

Laws protect buyers in another way. Free enterprise works best when consumers have choices. In the past, it was easy for a single company to control an industry, such as oil. The company could charge whatever it wanted and consumers had to pay. This is known as a *monopoly*. Today, strong federal laws regulate monopolistic practices.

Until the 1960s, there wasn't much information available about products and services. People often bought according to what they had heard from advertisers and friends. Now the government and many private associations and businesses provide a wide variety of consumer information and services. Historically, the primary consumer protection agency has been the Federal Trade Commission (FTC). You should become familiar with the FTC, especially the Bureau of Consumer Protection at www.ftc.gov. Smart shoppers take advantage of their right to obtain consumer information.

The Consumer Financial Protection Bureau (CFPB) has recently been established to focus on protecting consumers from complex financial products. The agency was established in response to the deceptive practices in the financial markets. These deceptive practices allowed mortgage fraud and credit card debt to increase rapidly. This combination of fraud and debt contributed to the 2008/2009 economic recession. According to their website, the primary mission of the CFPB is "to make markets for consumer financial products and services work for Americans—whether they are applying for a mortgage, choosing among credit cards, or using any number of other consumer financial products." You should become familiar with the CFPB by visiting their website at www.consumerfinance.gov/the-bureau.

Consumer Responsibilities

Along with consumer rights come responsibilities. First of all, you owe it to yourself to learn how to choose, buy, and use goods and services. Your study of consumerism is a lifelong process.

Assertiveness

To protect yourself and other consumers, you have a responsibility to speak out. Be **assertive**. This means being firm and positive in stating your position or point of view. If you think a business has not behaved properly, speak politely but firmly to a salesperson. If you are not satisfied with the salesperson's response, ask to see the manager.

Should you continue to receive poor products and services, take your business elsewhere. Buying goods and services is somewhat like casting a vote. Through the things that you buy or do not buy, you vote for or against a business.

Honesty

You expect businesses to be fair and honest with you at all times. As a responsible consumer, you should also be fair and honest. You may not realize it, but all consumers pay a penalty for a few dishonest people. When a person steals from a department store, for example, the store may suffer a temporary loss. However, to make up for this loss and others, the store will raise its prices.

Dishonest people increase costs for other shoppers. When stores lose merchandise to theft, stores recover their losses by charging more for their remaining products.

Consumer Complaints

Most of the time, you will be satisfied with goods and services you purchase. Sometimes, however, you may be disappointed. Here is a list of the most common consumer problems.

- Difficulties in getting a product repaired or replaced as promised in the warranty
- Misleading advertising, labeling, or packaging
- Defective products; for example, a cell phone may malfunction the first time you use it
- Being overcharged for a product or service
- Poor service or work of bad quality
- Goods that were ordered and paid for but never received
- Errors in computerized billing

Before Complaining

If you wish to make a **complaint**, or express your dissatisfaction with a product or service, review the whole situation and try to resolve it in the simplest manner possible.

- **Save everything**   Keep track of all paperwork related to what you buy. This includes copies of order forms, receipts, and warranties. It is difficult to settle a complaint without proof of purchase.
- **Think it through**   You may have a faded blouse or a broken tool, but who is at fault? The reason the blouse faded was because you washed it in hot water instead of cold. The tool broke because you used it improperly. You should not expect the seller or manufacturer to replace such a product. Many products do not work properly because people fail to follow instructions. This is often true for electrical appliances. If a product does not do what it should, reread the instructions. Look at the product again. Ask a friend or family member to do the same. Then return the item or call a service technician.
- **Give the seller a chance**   If you know there is a problem and you are not at fault, take the product back to where you bought it. Make sure you have the receipt and anything else you might need. Be prepared to explain the problem. Think over what you want the merchant to do. For example, do you want a replacement, a refund, or a repair? Ask to see someone who can handle your problem. Many larger stores have a complaint or customer service department. Explain your case to the person in charge. Do not be either too timid or too aggressive. Usually, if you are fair and reasonable, the other person will be also. You may be surprised at how quickly the problem is resolved. Sellers do not want to lose customers.

Make a Formal Complaint

If the seller cannot or will not help you, complain to the manufacturer. Get the name and address from the seller, the product, the Web, or a librarian can help you find it. When you do not have the name of a person to write to, address the letter to the customer service department. A sample letter appears in Figure 15-3 on the next page. The *Better Business Bureau (BBB)* is an organization that works to develop trust in an ethical marketplace. The BBB says a complaint letter should contain the following information:

- **What you bought** Describe the product. Does the item have a size and color? Is there a serial number?

- **Where you bought it** Give the complete address of the seller.

- **When you bought it** The date of purchase is important.

- **How you paid for it** Specify how you paid for the item. Did you use cash, a check, a credit card, or a money order? Attach copies of necessary papers. Never send originals. Paperwork may include receipts, cancelled checks, and sales contracts.

- **What the problem is** Let the facts speak for themselves.

- **What you want** Do you want a refund? Would you like the item repaired? Be clear.

Make a copy of the letter for yourself. You should receive a response within two or three weeks. If you do not, contact your local BBB or consumer rights group for help. To learn more about the BBB access www.cengage.com/school/working and click on the Web Links for Better Business Bureau.

436 Lincoln Rd.
Monroe, MI 48162-3459
June 12, 20—

Mr. Gerald Morris
Customer Service Manager
Barkley Tackle Company
1003 Seventh St.
Eau Claire, WI 54701-2845

Dear Mr. Morris

On June 7, 20—, I purchased a 5'6" Barkley casting rod (Model No. 96) at the Lunker Sporting Goods Store at 49 Washington Way in Monroe, Michigan. The selling price was $49.95, which I paid in cash. A photocopy of the receipt is enclosed.

Several days later when I used the rod for the first time, the rod tip snapped off during a routine cast. The rod had been in use for about an hour.

Upon returning the rod to Robert Stark, the manager at Lunker Sporting Goods, I was told the rod was not guaranteed. Although I had used the rod only once, he said there was nothing he could do.

I have never experienced problems with Barkley fishing products in the past. Perhaps there was a manufacturing defect in the product that I purchased. Please consider replacing my rod or sending me a refund. Please let me know if I can provide you with any additional information.

Sincerely

Brad Corder

Brad Corder

Enclosure

FIGURE 15-3 A Sample Letter of Complaint

15-3 Assessment

1. **What are your rights and responsibilities as a consumer? Name two of each.**

2. **How is buying a product or service similar to casting a vote?**

3. **What should you do before writing a formal letter of complaint?**

4. **What six points should be included in a complaint letter?**

5. **What is the purpose of the Better Business Bureau?**

Focus on Skills for Living

Buy a Used Car

Car ownership usually begins with buying a used car. In fact, used car sales far outnumber new car sales. Many people simply cannot afford a new car. Others, though, actually prefer a used car to a new one. They say that used cars are a much better value for the money.

The majority of used cars are bought from private owners, new car dealers, used car dealers and auto superstores (such as CarMax), and auto rental companies. A good car at a fair price may be found through any of the sources. New car dealers are often the best overall source.

New car dealers sell used autos that have been traded in for new ones. They usually keep only the newer and better cars on their lots. Cars are usually reconditioned and offered with some type of warranty. The dealer wants you to be satisfied and come back later to buy a new car. However, used car prices at a new car dealership are usually higher than elsewhere. This is because of the greater cost of doing business.

Before agreeing to buy, however, you will need to do some homework. Think about your needs, driving habits, and your budget. There is a wealth of information about used cars on the Web. Use a search engine and enter "used cars" as the key words. Many of these publications have details on the do's and don'ts of buying a used car. Several of these recommendations are summarized below.

Once you have located a car that interests you, make a careful inspection. You do not have to be an expert on cars to spot major problems. Look for body damage and signs of rust. Look under the car for holes in the exhaust system and for evidence of fluids leaking from the engine, radiator, transmission, or brakes. Drive the car and listen for noises, rattles, and vibrations. Note anything about which you feel suspicious or uncomfortable. Not all problems are serious. But find out what things will need to be fixed or replaced if you decide to buy.

A careful examination of a used car and a test drive should help you eliminate unacceptable cars. Before agreeing to buy, however, take these additional steps:

- **Get an idea of the price for the year and model car that you are considering.** Check prices of similar models using the NADA Official Used Car Guide, Kelley Blue Book, or Edmunds. com. Web addresses for these and related sources accompany this article.

- **Confirm the mileage and vehicle history.** The law requires that the seller provide the buyer with a signed statement indicating the current mileage. Anyone who illegally tampers with an odometer or fails to provide the required disclosure statement may be sued. A free CARFAX odometer check is available online. A complete vehicle history report can be purchased from CARFAX or AutoCheck. Many dealers will provide you a free copy of the vehicle history.

- **Check on defects and recalls.** After a new car is sold, it is not unusual for the manufacturer to discover problems and defects that may occur years later. Such problems are typically repaired free of charge by the manufacturer. The National Highway Traffic Safety Administration and the Center for Auto Safety provides information on safety defects, recalls, and service bulletins.

- **Take the car to a mechanic for an inspection.** You should not rely solely on your judgment about a car. Hidden problems in the engine, transmission, or rear axle are of the most concern because these are costly to repair.

- **Contact the previous owner.** Federal law requires dealers to have this information. Most reputable dealers will give you the name and phone number of this person. Call the person and explain that you are thinking about buying his or her car. You may be surprised at how honest this person can be.

- **Check out the warranty.** The Federal Trade Commission requires sellers of used cars (except private owners) to place a large "Buyers Guide" window sticker on each car. The guide makes clear what type of warranty is provided with the car. Many consumer experts recommend getting a warranty, even if it is just for 30 days. A warranty provides important financial and legal protection.

Now you are ready to finalize the deal. Most buyers and salespeople expect to haggle a little over the price. Do not expect the salesperson to lower the price much. Do not expect the seller to do free repairs as part of the deal. The margin of profit on a used car is fairly low.

Dealers try to make it easy for you to buy a car by providing financing. However, their rates will often be higher than you can find elsewhere. Do not be afraid to tell the salesperson that you will get your own financing. To hold the car, you may be required to leave a small deposit.

Once you pay for the car, it is yours. You will then need to arrange for insurance, license plates, and a new title. Drive carefully and do not text or talk on your mobile phone while driving.

There are many online sources available to help with buying a car. Access www.cengage.com/school/working. Then click on *Web Links* to find links for the following.

a. **Buying a Used Car, Federal Trade Commission** For general information
b. **NADA Guides, Kelley Blue Book, Edmunds.com** For used car pricing guides
c. **CARFAX, AutoCheck** For mileage and vehicle history
d. **The National Highway Traffic Safety Administration, Center for Auto Safety** For information regarding defects, recalls, and service bulletins
e. **Auto Loan Calculator** For calculating information on auto loans
f. **Consumer Guide Automotive, Insure.com** For auto insurance information

THINK CRITICALLY

1. Would you want to buy a used car? Why or why not?
2. What steps would you take to buy a used car?

Monkey Business Images/Shutterstock.com

Successfully buying a dependable car can be a gratifying.

Chapter Summary

15-1 You as a Consumer

A. A consumer is someone who buys or uses goods and services. Goods are articles that are produced or manufactured. Services involve the payment of money to people and businesses for work performed.

B. Being a consumer is more than simply paying money for something. Consuming involves three stages: choosing, buying, and using.

C. Obsolescence refers to something becoming out of date or no longer useful. There are two types of obsolescence: planned and perceived. Both types of obsolescence get in the way of smart consuming.

15-2 Advertising and the Consumer

A. For the seller, advertising aids in selling goods and services. For the consumer, it provides information about goods and services for sale.

B. Sellers use various advertising techniques to accomplish their purpose. You need to understand how and why they work.

C. There is nothing wrong with advertising as long as it is honest. Problems occur when advertising is misleading. Be alert to deceptive practices.

15-3 Consumer Rights and Responsibilities

A. Consumers are protected by laws on safety, faulty merchandise, and competition in the marketplace. Government, private associations, and businesses provide a variety of consumer information and services.

B. Along with consumer rights come responsibilities. Learn how to choose, buy, and use goods and services. Speak out regarding poor products and services. Be fair and honest in your business dealings.

C. Sometimes, you may have a complaint about a product or service. Try to resolve the problem in the simplest manner possible. Make a formal complaint if simpler approaches do not work.

Activities

1. Prepare a list of five different grocery items. Visit at least three stores and record the price of each item. At least one item should be a fruit or vegetable from the produce section. For packaged items, like cereal and yogurt, record the product's expiration date. For the fresh produce item, rate the item's freshness. What were your findings? Which store is the most expensive? The least expensive? Which store sold the freshest products? Which stores carry generic brands? Were those items priced lower than brand-name products?

2. Find examples of the advertising techniques discussed in this chapter. Print any online ads you find. Pool your ads with those

found by your classmates. Choose the best ads for a bulletin board display.

3. Using coupons is often a smart way to shop and save money. To find coupons, do a Web search using the phrase "best online coupon websites." Before your next shopping trip, check to see if any stores have online coupons available. Report to the class on any money saved.

4. Think of a problem you have had with a product or service. Write a sample complaint letter to the manufacturer. Follow the guidelines provided in this chapter. Turn in the letter to your teacher.

5. You can buy two 8-oz packages of cheese for $3 or a 24-oz package for $3.99. Which is the better buy? Why?

6. Evaluate your ability to consume wisely. Explain why this skill is essential to achieving many goals in your life-span plan.

Word Power

On a separate sheet of paper, match each definition with the correct term. All definitions will be used, and a definition will be used only once.

7. Advertising sent to potential customers through the mail

8. Any type of public notice or message intended to aid in the sale of a product or service

9. Work performed by individuals and businesses for others

10. Intentionally designing and producing products in order for them to be used up within a specific time period

11. An article that is produced or manufactured

12. A public request by a manufacturer for the return of a product that may be defective or contaminated

13. An expression of dissatisfaction with a product or service

14. Goods that state only the common name of the product on the label

15. The desire on the part of a consumer to replace a functional product because it is thought to be no longer stylish or appropriate

16. Firm and positive in stating one's position or point of view

17. Someone who buys or uses goods and services

18. A pledge that something is exactly as stated or advertised

19. The process of finding out the cost of a product or service at several different places before making a decision to buy

20. Goods given a unique name by the manufacturer

21. A guarantee or promise that a product is free from defects

a. advertising
b. assertive
c. brand-name product
d. comparison shopping
e. complaint
f. consumer
g. direct-mail advertising
h. generic product
i. good
j. guarantee
k. perceived obsolescence
l. planned obsolescence
m. recall
n. service
o. warranty

Think Critically

22. Think of a major purchase you made recently. Did you do comparison shopping? If so, explain how you went about it. If not, explain why not.

23. In the past doctors and lawyers were prohibited from advertising. It is still a controversial issue. What is your opinion of this practice?

24. Have you ever ruined a new product by failing to read or follow instructions? If so, discuss your experiences in class.

25. Have you ever been cheated by a dishonest seller or misleading advertising? If so, discuss your experiences in class.

26. In addition to those mentioned in the chapter, can you provide additional examples of planned obsolescence products? Which ones do you and your classmates dislike the most?

27. You or other members of the class have probably bought used cars. Share your experiences and discuss the following questions: Where was the car bought? Was a fair price paid? Were any hidden problems discovered after the sale? Was the car covered by a warranty? You can probably think of additional questions.

28. It is very common for cashiers to ask customers if they would like to buy an extended warranty on a product. Often the purchase of an extended warranty provides another year of warranty protection. If you think about it, the retailer is asking you how much confidence you have that the product you are purchasing will function reliably. On the one hand, the retailer is encouraging you to buy a product because you will like the performance of the product. On the other hand, the retailer is saying that, if the product breaks down prematurely, the extended warranty will offer you some financial protection. Discuss this concept as a class. Who do you think receives the greatest benefit from extended warranties?

29. Some retailers sell products with a popular or sought after brand name at a discount. Sometimes the products sold by these retailers are from a prior season. Other retailers may not have a popular brand name, but may sell current products at reasonable prices. What are the pros and cons of buying from each type of retailer?

30. Natasha works out at her health club four or five days each week. She enjoys both the classes and the company of other members. Sometimes, however, she gets a little discouraged at the poor maintenance of the club. The locker room is often dirty and some of the fixtures need replacing. Recently she decided to write a letter of complaint to the health club manager. She began the letter this way: "As I watched a cockroach climb through the rusted-out bottom of my locker, I began to wonder just how often this health club is cleaned. I also wondered how often broken items get fixed." Is this an effective way to write a letter of complaint? Why or why not? Be prepared to discuss this as a class.

31. Amid and his roommate sometimes go with their parents to a ware-house club where their parents are members. It is really tempting to buy large amounts of the food they like at prices that are cheaper than the grocery store. Lately Amid has noticed that the individually packaged chips they buy often have a flavor that neither of them likes. They usually end up either giving the chips to friends or tossing them when they go out of date. How should Amid and his roommate calculate the true cost of discounted foods? This true cost should include any food that is not consumed by either Amid or his roommate.

32. Conduct an election for your class's or school's favorite television commercial. Nominate candidates. Prepare an election ballot and circulate copies to classmates. Count the ballots and declare a winner. Discuss what elements of the commercial made it stand out. Send a letter to the winning company explaining what the class has done. You may be surprised by the response you receive.

33. There are federal and state laws that govern the sale and purchase of cars. Research the laws for buying and selling a used car in your state. You might want to check your state's website or the website of your state's Attorney General. Compare the summary of rules, which cover your rights as a buyer, with the Federal Trade Commission summary on buying a used car. Also compare with a summary from a different state. Prepare a report on the strengths and weaknesses of your state's laws. List improvements that could be made to your state's laws. Send your suggestion to the appropriate agency at your state. Ask that a written response to your suggestions be provided within three weeks. When your response arrives, be prepared to share it with the class.

34. Sometimes visitors to America who come from other countries are surprised by the number of choices Americans have when buying items. These choices range from buying cereal to buying deodorant to deciding what toppings to order on a burger. Why do you think manufacturers provide so many choices? How do you think all of these choices affect consumers?

Career Transitions Connection

Product Perception

Click on *Match Experience to New Careers*. From the *Explore Careers* menu, click on *A Day in the Life Video*. Within Marketing, Sales, and Service, click on *Assistant Manager*. View the *Introduction, Likes and Dislikes,* and *Education and Training* portions of the video. The focus of Keisha's job is to influence the way consumers perceive products. By making products seem desirable, sales can be increased. Why do companies hire people to strategically control how information about their products is conveyed in the marketplace? How do the efforts of marketing managers affect you as a consumer?

"I think we have to appreciate that we're alive for only a limited period of time, and we'll spend most of our lives working. That being the case, I believe one of the most important priorities is to do whatever we do as well as we can."—VICTOR KIAM

Banking and Credit

Blend Images/iStockphoto.com

PREVIEW

As you grow older, your use of money will probably change. Rather than pay cash for all of your purchases, you will find that it is often more convenient or necessary to write a check. Sometimes you may want to use credit. The credit may be in the form of a loan or a charge purchase. Knowing how to use checking, credit, and other financial services is an important life skill for everyone.

Taking /*Action* Give Yourself Credit

Nancy has had her first job for about two months. She lives with her parents. Whenever she has a bill or owes her parents money, she pays in cash.

Now Nancy is considering moving out on her own. Her friend Aurora has asked her if she would like to share an apartment. Nancy went with Aurora this morning to look at the apartment and liked it very much. After showing them around, Mr. Bellamy, the leasing agent, gave each of them a rental application. Nancy and Aurora thanked Mr. Bellamy and said that they would get back to him.

As Nancy reads the application at home, she realizes that the leasing company wants a lot of financial information about her. It wants to know where she is employed, if she has any debts, where she does her banking, and if she owns any assets. It also wants her permission to run a credit report.

![*] **Success Tip**

Checking accounts and credit can make your life easier, if you manage them well.

Because Nancy always cashes her paychecks and pays with cash, she knows she won't have a credit history with anyone other than her parents. She also does not have a checking account. Nancy wonders if these things are going to get in the way of getting the apartment. She calls Mr. Bellamy to ask him.

Mr. Bellamy is surprised to discover that Nancy has no credit history and no checking account. But he proposes a solution.

"You might be able to pay your rent in cash to your roommate, and she can write the rent check to us," he says. "Also, you can have just your roommate's name on the rental agreement if you are worried about your application being rejected."

Nancy explains Mr. Bellamy's suggestion to her parents. They both tell her that it is not a good idea. "If you are planning to rent this apartment with Aurora, both your names should be on the rental agreement," her mother says. Her father agrees. "Having your name on the agreement gives you important rights as a tenant."

"I guess it's time for me to get a checking account and start to establish a credit history," says Nancy. "Where do you think I should apply for a credit card?"

THINK CRITICALLY

1. How could a checking account help Nancy?
2. Why is it important to establish a credit history?

FINANCIAL INSTITUTIONS

OBJECTIVES

- Name and describe the four major types of financial institutions
- Discuss how electronic banking has changed money management
- Explain the recession, the housing market, and protections provided by the Federal Deposit Insurance Corporation

KEY TERMS

- full-service bank
- automated teller machine (ATM)
- electronic banking
- debit card

cartoons/Shutterstock.com

Personal Decisions

"Hey Fred, who were you talking to on the phone," said Gene. "You seem to be pretty upset." "My sister called to say that she read in the paper that our bank had been taken over this weekend by a new owner. I need to go down to the bank and see if I can get the money out of my savings account," declared Fred. "Wow," Gene stated, "that's where I have my checking account. I should probably go with you."

What would you do?

Types of Institutions and Services

A bank used to be the place to go to save money, borrow money, or open a checking account. Today, four major types of financial institutions provide these services.

Commercial Banks

Commercial banks may also be known as bank and trust companies or community banks. Commercial banks are the most common type of financial institution. They are **full-service banks**, which means that they offer customers a full range of financial conveniences and services. These services include checking and savings accounts, loans, safe deposit boxes, credit cards, drive-up windows, money orders, traveler's checks, and **automated teller machines**, or **ATMs**. An ATM is an electronic terminal which customers can use to withdraw cash, make deposits, or transfer funds to another account.

Mutual Savings Banks

Mutual savings banks began early in the 19th century in order to serve ordinary people that commercial banks often overlooked. In theory, a mutual savings bank is owned by its depositors. However, a board of trustees directs the bank's operations and acts on behalf of the depositors. Any profits that are earned are distributed to depositors as interest. There are only about 467 mutual banks in the United States.

These banks generally provide the same services as commercial banks. In addition, they offer some of the services of a savings and loan association. One of the main attractions of mutual savings banks is that they often pay a slightly higher rate of interest than commercial banks. Since the mid-1980s, many of these banks have become what are known as *stock savings banks*. Such banks are operated by a board of directors elected by shareholders. Profits are distributed to stockholders as cash dividends.

Savings and Loan Associations (S&Ls)

Other names for these institutions are building and loan associations, cooperative banks, savings associations, and homestead associations. They were started in the early 1800s by groups of people who pooled their savings so that each person, in turn, could borrow enough money to build a house. Savings and loan associations are now in all states. Several decades ago S&Ls made more loans to buy homes (*mortgages*) than all other lenders combined. Due to increased competition in the financial markets, a variety of lenders now provide mortgage financing.

Credit Unions

Credit unions (CUs) are nonprofit savings and loan cooperative associations. They are comprised of people who have something in common, like a place of employment or a union membership. For example, all employees of a particular school district might form a credit union. Members govern credit unions. They only accept savings from and make loans to people who belong to the credit union. At the end of the year, a well-run credit union often has a surplus of money to distribute to its members. Credit unions provide savings accounts, consumer loans, and financial counseling. A convenient feature of CUs is that members can often make deposits and loan payments through payroll deductions.

Applying for credit is necessary for most people at various times in their life.

Changes in Financial Institutions

During the last several decades, many banking laws have been changed to allow financial institutions to be more competitive. Now financial institutions can pay higher rates of interest than before. However, as a result of the 2008/2009 recession, interest rates dropped significantly. Another result of the changes is that the four major types of financial institutions have begun to offer similar services.

Financial institutions now actively compete for business. This is good news for the consumer. It means, however, that consumers should shop around and compare services, charges, and rates of interest.

The experience of Teresa Romero is a good example. When Teresa learned that her bank was raising the service charge on checking accounts, she began to ask about charges and services elsewhere.

She discovered that she was eligible to join the credit union where her mother worked. Teresa received no-cost checking and was paid monthly interest on her checking account balance.

Electronic banking allows you to conduct banking transactions at your convenience.

Electronic Banking

Electronic banking is a broad term used to describe various types of electronic fund transfers (EFTs). There are five common types of EFT services:

- **Automated teller machines (ATMs)** These 24-hour electronic terminals permit you to bank at your convenience. You simply insert your EFT card in the machine and enter your personal identification number (PIN). You can then withdraw cash, make deposits, or transfer funds between accounts.

- **Online banking** Banking through the Internet is very popular. Individuals can pay bills, transfer funds, check account balances, and generally manage their accounts completely online.

- **Mobile banking** With a smartphone, you can perform the same banking services that you can perform on a desktop or notebook computer. Checks can be deposited by taking a photo of the front and back of the check and sending the data to your account. Text banking, which allows you to perform multiple functions including checking account balances, is also available.

- **Direct deposits or withdrawals** You can arrange for sums of money that you receive on a regular basis, such as a paycheck, to be deposited automatically into your checking account. You can also have regular bills, such as rent payments and insurance premiums, paid in the same way, by automatic withdrawals from your account.

- **Point-of-sale transfers** These transfers let you pay for retail purchases with your EFT or debit card. A **debit card** is a plastic card used to immediately transfer funds for a purchase from a bank account to a seller. This is similar to using a credit card, except that the money for the purchase is immediately transferred.

Electronic banking can be very convenient. A possible disadvantage, however, is that your EFT card and PIN are used for all transactions. If they should be lost or stolen, you must immediately notify your bank. You also need to carefully examine receipts and monthly statements for errors. When you open an EFT account, your bank will provide you with written information on your rights and responsibilities.

Can You Trust Your Bank?

The median price of an American home has increased steadily almost every year since the mid-1940s. Because homes always seemed to be a good investment, a majority of Americans were encouraged to buy homes and later to trade-up to larger and more expensive homes. The demand for homes also encouraged builders to expand their businesses and build

Workforce Trends

At one time, classified ads for employment were divided into "men wanted" and "women wanted." It was unusual to see women or members of minority groups as television news anchors. Far fewer women or minority group members were in jobs as supervisors, firefighters, police officers, doctors, and college professors. Since the passage of the Civil Rights Act of 1964, minorities and women have made significant economic progress.

more and more homes and condominiums. There were also people who bought homes and condos with the idea that they could sell them a few years later for a profit. *Flipping* a home refers to the practice of purchasing a home with the specific intent of quickly reselling it for a profit. Economists call the housing boom leading up to 2006 a *housing bubble*.

The Housing Bubble Bursts

For many years common wisdom was that buying a house was a good investment. As houses generally increased in value over time, the house that you bought today would be worth a great deal more in later years. With a traditional thirty year mortgage, the amount of your monthly house payment stayed the same while the value of your house increased. When you finally sold your house, after living in it for a number of years, the difference between your selling price and your purchase price was the *profit*.

When the housing bubble burst, many homeowners lost their homes to bank foreclosure.

Prior to 2006, there were a number of unethical lenders who were trying to make money in the housing market by offering consumers loans that were above the consumers' ability to pay. The unethical lenders did not care if the homeowners would be able to pay off their mortgages because they were selling the mortgages to other investors. Because these lenders often sought out the most financially vulnerable consumers, these lenders are often referred to as *predatory lenders*. The most unethical lenders provided *liar's loans* to home buyers. Instead of making potential home buyers prove how much money they had in the bank and how much money they earned, these predatory lenders let home buyers claim whatever level of savings and income that they wanted to claim. These predatory lenders did not ask borrowers for any documentation to prove how much money they had. A number of consumers found the possibility of buying a home so tempting that they lied about their financial situation. After qualifying for loans that exceeded their ability to pay, many consumers found themselves living in homes that they could not afford. Banks began to foreclose on these homes.

Some opportunistic investors were looking for a quick way to make money. These opportunistic investors bought mortgages as an investment. However, investors who had purchased mortgages that were based on liar's loans realized that their investments had very little value. Investors, who used to purchase mortgages as an investment, no longer wanted to buy them. Soon the number of houses for sale far exceeded the number of qualified buyers.

Median home prices peaked in 2006 and then began to decline. As prices went down, it created financial problems for banks and investment companies that had made home loans. At this point, a number of financial institutions were holding home loans for more than the houses were worth. This problem was made worse by the fact that the American economy entered into a recession in December, 2007, causing a jump in unemployment. Many people who were unemployed could not make their house payments and lost their homes. As more and more homes were foreclosed, the value of existing homes dropped further. The housing bubble burst, the recession worsened, and the American economy was in a crisis.

Economic Crisis

In July, 2008, IndyMac Bank declared bankruptcy, which was the second largest S&L in history to fail. This was followed in September, 2008 by the failure of Washington Mutual, which was the largest S&L. Then the fourth largest investment bank, Lehman Brothers, failed. Most of the other large banks and financial institutions in the country were also in trouble. The United States financial system was on the verge of collapse when the federal government passed emergency legislation on October 3, 2008 to bail out the banking system. This law and later legislation helped the banking industry to stabilize and helped to prevent a more serious recession, or even a depression.

As a result of the economic crisis, many banks failed.

A total of 25 banks failed in 2008, 140 banks failed in 2009, and 157 banks failed in 2010. Contrast this with the fact that, between 2000 and 2007, only 32 U.S. banks failed. This period of economic crisis created a great deal of anxiety and personal financial problems for many Americans, including the loss of their homes.

Confidence in the Banking System

On a positive note, there are over 100,000 banks, S&Ls, and credit unions in the United States. The majority of these financial institutions are well managed and stable. Banking institutions have millions of satisfied customers. A 2010 study found that 87 percent of credit union customers and 86 percent of small bank customers are satisfied with their bank services.

If a Financial Institution Fails

What happens when a bank, S&L, or credit union does fail? About 90 percent of banking institutions are commercial banks. The process for closing most types of financial institutions is similar.

In the United States, banks are regulated by a federal agency called the *Federal Deposit Insurance Corporation (FDIC)*. Banks are required by the FDIC to provide regular data on their financial condition. The FDIC uses a scoring system to rank banks in terms of their "bankability." Those banks which have a low score are placed on a watch list which is published on the Web. If the condition of the bank deteriorates further, the FDIC takes it over.

The actual takeover of a bank is quite secretive. First, the FDIC quietly negotiates with another banking institution willing to buy the bank. Next, they assemble a team of accountants, computer experts, and support personnel who walk into the bank on Friday evening shortly before closing. They then announce to all employees that they are taking charge of the bank and turning it over to new owners.

FDIC employees and the new owners work with a handful of existing bank employees throughout the weekend to analyze and verify all financial records. The name is changed on the outside of the bank as well as on all inside references to the old bank. The bank then reopens on Monday morning with a new name. Many of the old employees now work for the new owner. Customers are notified about the change, but they can continue to write checks, deposit and withdraw cash, and use their ATM and credit cards as if nothing ever happened. All of this occurs without customers ever being at risk of losing a penny of their money.

Banks are insured by the FDIC. This means that the first $250,000 of total deposits that are held in a savings account, checking account, and certificate of deposits is guaranteed safe by the federal government. The same amount applies to S&Ls and credit unions. Even if a bank were to close permanently rather than be taken over, the FDIC would write or mail you a check for all of the money and interest you would be due. Federally-insured institutions often have their official seals displayed. See Figure 16-1 for some sample seals.

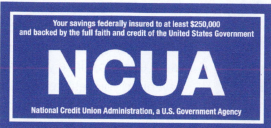

FIGURE 16-1 Look for these seals at your bank or credit union. The FDIC insures deposits in banks. The NCUA insures savings deposits in credit unions.

a. Courtesy of Federal Deposit insurance corporation b. Courtesy of National Credit Union Credit Union Administration

Sometimes FDIC maximum coverage changes. Periodically you should confirm the total amount of deposit coverage provided by the FDIC.

Even though a handful of large investment and mortgage banks helped create a financial crisis in 2008, most regional and community banks are trustworthy. As a banking customer, you can have confidence that money you have in a bank is backed by the "full faith and credit" of the United States.

16-1 Assessment

1. There are four major types of financial institutions. Name and briefly describe them.

2. Name and briefly describe the five types of EFT services.

3. What major factor led to the 2008 banking crisis?

4. What federal agency is responsible for regulating banks and insuring bank deposits?

5. How did predatory lenders contribute to the recession?

CHECKING ACCOUNTS

OBJECTIVES

- Describe types of checking accounts and how to open an account
- Illustrate how to write and endorse a check, maintain a check register, make a deposit, and reconcile a bank statement

KEY TERMS

- signature card
- postdating
- payee
- check register
- endorsement
- deposit ticket
- statement of account
- reconciling

ManuelVelasco/iStockphoto.com

▶ Personal Decisions

You like having a checking account, but the checkbook is just something else to carry. You often put it in the glove box of your car. This seems safe enough, since you always keep your car locked. After shopping one evening, you return to your car to find that it has been burglarized. Your stereo is gone, and so is your checkbook. You are very upset.

What would you do?

Understand Checking Accounts

Checking accounts are one of the most commonly used banking services. They have two main advantages: safety and convenience. Checks provide a safe and convenient way to pay bills. Some people pay all of their bills by check. However, it is becoming more common for people to use a combination of check writing and online bill payment. The methods used to manage a checking account and written checks can also be applied to managing online banking transactions.

It is unsafe to carry large amounts of cash. Keeping large amounts of money at home is unwise. Michael found this out. Michael never thought he needed a checking account. He liked to go to the bank on Friday evenings and cash his paycheck. He then paid for all of his purchases in cash. The cash he did not carry with him was kept in a tennis ball can that was stored on the hall closet shelf. No one would ever think of looking there for money, Michael thought.

Michael returned from a movie late Friday night to discover that his apartment had been burglarized. His television and DVD player were the only things that he noticed were missing. As he sat down on the couch to think about what to do, Michael remembered his money. He went to the hall closet. As he opened the closet door, an empty tennis ball can rolled off the shelf.

Michael had insurance to cover the cost of replacing the television and DVD player. But he was heartsick to lose the money he needed to live on. Needless to say, Michael opened a checking account the next time he got paid.

Checks are safer than cash, because only the person to whom a check is made out can get the money. A second advantage of checks is they make it easier to keep good financial records. A *canceled check* is a check that has been paid and is legal proof of payment. Canceled checks are electronically scanned and a copy may be returned to you with your bank statement or they are available online. Be sure to save images of your canceled checks.

Assume you take your car in for repairs and the bill comes to $65. Rather than pay the mechanic in cash, you write a check. That is, you write instructions to your bank, the American National Bank, to deduct $65 from your account and pay it to Joe's Garage. Joe then takes your check to his bank, Mid-America Bank, and deposits it in his account.

Mid-America Bank does not collect payment directly from the American National Bank. A bank scans its checks and sends the electronic copies to a centralized clearinghouse. The checks are added up at the clearinghouse each day. Each bank then receives just one daily payment from the clearinghouse. After the check has *cleared*, which means it has been authorized and credited to Joe's account, the electronic copy is returned to the American National Bank. This bank subtracts $65 from your account.

Types of Checking Accounts

Banks usually offer a variety of checking accounts. The names given to these accounts may vary, however, the two basic types of checking accounts are regular and special. A regular account, often called a *minimum balance account*, requires that the customer maintain a certain minimum balance. As long as the minimum balance is in the account, there is no extra charge. If the balance drops below the minimum amount, the customer will have to pay a service charge.

A second basic type of checking account is the *special account*, often called a cost-per-check account. With this type of account, you pay a flat monthly service charge plus a small amount for each check you write. Special accounts are for people who only write a few checks each month. A young person opening his or her first checking account should consider this type of account. Regardless of the type of checking account you have, there are many similar identifying characteristics of a written check. Refer to Figure 16-2 for a sample of a written check.

Another type of checking account is an interest-bearing account called a *negotiable order of withdrawal (NOW) account*. These accounts were first offered at savings and loan associations and are now available at many commercial and savings banks as well.

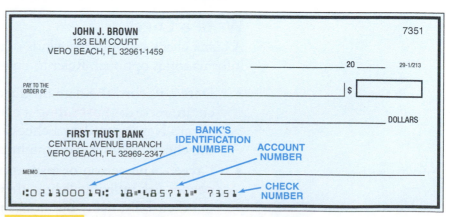

FIGURE 16-2 The coded numbers at the bottom of a check are read by a computer. This speeds up check processing considerably.

Evolving technology impacts the way banking activities are performed. As the paper trail of checks transitions to a digital trail of checks, it is important for consumers to understand their rights. Access and click on the link for Chapter 16. Read the summary of your rights on the Office of the Comptroller of the Currency website. Pay close attention to instructions regarding how to resolve errors if you do not have a paper copy of your check. Be prepared to participate in a class discussion regarding the best way to catch and resolve any errors in your checking account.

www.cengage.com/school/working

A withdrawal order is just like a check, except that it is written against a savings account rather than a checking account. Your money earns interest up to the day the order clears. Most NOW accounts require that you maintain a balance of at least several hundred dollars.

Most credit unions offer a type of checking account called a *share draft account*. It is very similar to a NOW account. You write drafts, or checks, against a credit union savings account. Your money earns interest until the draft clears. Many share draft accounts have no monthly service charges at all. However, for the account to earn interest, the credit union often requires a minimum balance of $500 to $750.

If used irresponsibly, a checking account can be very expensive. An *overdraft* occurs when you write a check for an amount of money that exceeds the amount of money in your account. An *overdrawn check*, which is a check you wrote that resulted in an overdraft, will be returned to you. Your bank will charge you a fee for every check like this that *bounces*. If you write a check to someone and decide to stop payment on it, or order your bank not to pay it, the bank will usually charge you for this as well. Request an information sheet that describes all of the institution's services and charges.

Open a Checking Account

Once you have decided on a bank and checking account, opening an account is very simple. You need only fill out a form known as a **signature card**. The signature card asks for your name, address, phone number, Social Security number, and similar data. At the end of the card, there is a place for your signature. The signature that you put on the card should be your legal name, not a nickname.

Manage a Checking Account

Maintaining an accurate, up-to-date checkbook requires knowledge and practice of a few important rules. Here are some guidelines to follow.

Write a Check

A blank check requires five kinds of information. One additional kind of information is optional. Refer to Figure 16-3 as you read about each part.

- **Date**   Record the date on the check. This will help you keep accurate records. **Postdating** a check is putting a future date on the check. Never postdate a check. If the party to whom you wrote the check cashes it, you might overdraw your account.
- **Payee**   The person or institution that you write the check to is the **payee**. Ask individuals how they would like the check made out. On their bills, many businesses indicate how to write the check. If the name is a long one, it is acceptable to abbreviate. However, use common abbreviations, such as "Inc.," "Co.," and "Assoc."

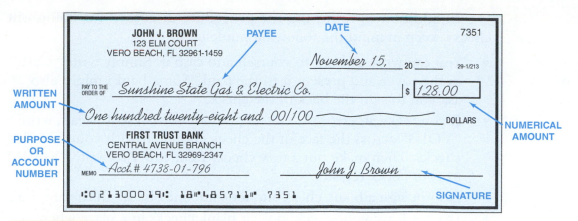

FIGURE 16-3 A Correctly Written Check

- **Numerical amount**   You record the amount of the check in two places. At the end of the line where you fill in the name of the payee, you write the amount of the check in dollars and cents; for example, "10.50." If the check is for under a dollar, put a zero in front of the decimal point and insert the word cents ("0.85 cents"). To keep someone from altering the check easily, place the figures close to the dollar sign.

- **Written amount**   On the long line near the middle of the check, is the word Dollars. Here you write in words the amount that you wrote in numerals earlier. Use this form: "Ten and 50/100" or "Fifty-three and 00/100." If the amount is less than one dollar, write in "Only eight-five cents" and draw a line through the word Dollars. If there is any blank space left, draw a wavy line between the written amount and the word Dollars. Otherwise, someone could alter the check. If there is ever a difference between the numerical amount and the written amount of a check, the written amount is the legal one. Generally, a bank will contact the account owner before it will accept a check with differing amounts.

- **Purpose or account number**   In the lower left-hand portion of a check, there is a space labeled "For" or "Memo." This space does not have to be filled out, but it is always a good idea to do so. This is where you indicate the purpose of the check; for example, "auto tune-up" or "gift." When you pay bills, some companies may ask you to write a policy or account number on the check. Next to "Memo" or "For," you would write "Acct. #4738-01-796" if that were your number. Routinely filling in this line can help you later as you review a budget or prepare an income tax return.

- **Signature**   The bottom right-hand portion of the check is where you sign your name. Sign it exactly as it appears on the signature card you filled out when you opened the account. Do not use Mr., Mrs., Ms., or Miss as part of a signature.

- **Use a non-erasable ink pen**   You should always use a non-erasable ink pen when writing a check. You should avoid pens with ink that is prone to smearing. Some check fraud has occurred when check recipients change the amount of the check. Protect yourself from this type of fraud by using reliable ink.

In addition to following the procedure discussed for filling out checks, keep in mind the following guidelines.

- You can write a check to yourself and cash it. Simply write "Cash" as the payee and present it to the bank. Some banks might also ask you to sign the back of the check.

- If you make an error on a check, do not correct it. Instead, write "VOID" across the face of the check and file it with your canceled checks. Then make out a new check. Remember to write "VOID" in your check register.

- Do not sign a blank check and let someone else fill in the amount.

- Do not leave your checkbook or blank checks in a place where someone can take them.

- Do not give a blank check to someone who has forgotten his or her checkbook. The bank's computer will read your electronic number and subtract the money from your account.

Keep a Check Register

After you open an account, you will receive a supply of imprinted checks and a check register. The **check register** is where you keep a record of checks written, deposits made, and other transactions. One checkbook style has a stub attached to each check. Another uses a carbon copy behind each check that provides customers with a record of the transaction. Figure 16-4 provides a sample of a carbon copy check.

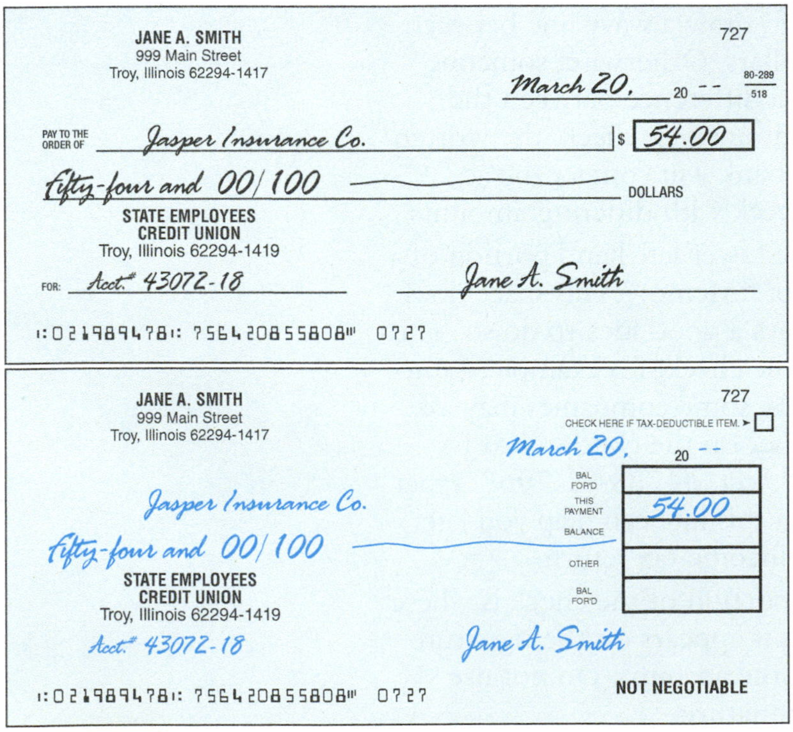

The most popular means of recording checks is to use the type of check register shown in Figure 16-5 on the next page. A common mistake people make in maintaining a checking account is not recording checks in the register. This often happens when someone is in a hurry. Another reason is that people who pay bills online often forget to record the transaction in their check register. Get in the habit of filling out the check register at the time you write a check or pay a bill online. If you don't, you won't know the correct balance and might overdraw the account.

Overdrawing a checking account can be very embarrassing. One day Jackie got a phone call from her friend Barbara who worked at The Clothes Rack. Barbara called about a check that Jackie had written to buy a new outfit. The bank had returned the check to the store because of insufficient funds. Jackie felt humiliated.

FIGURE 16-4 Some banks and credit unions use a carbon copy check that provides customers with a record of the transaction.

In looking over her check register, Jackie found that she had not recorded a check written to the gas company. It was near the end of

ONE-LINE ENTRY

		RECORD ALL CHARGES OR CREDITS THAT AFFECT YOUR ACCOUNT.									
										BALANCE	
NUMBER	DATE	DESCRIPTION OF TRANSACTION	PAYMENT/DEBIT (-)		✔ T	FEE (IF ANY) (-)		DEPOSIT/CREDIT (+)		$ 282	34
7341	3/25	Cash	$ 150	00		$		$ 255	67	388	01
7342	3/25	Sunshine State Telephone	25	00						363	01
7343	3/27	Unico Life Ins.	8	70						354	31
7344	3/27	ABB Ins.	5	78						348	53
7345	3/27	Payson Cable	19	75						328	78
7346	3/27	State Bank	400	00				305	67	234	45
7347	4/1	Mishiki Credit Corp.	257	62				485	45	462	28
7348	4/1	Feldspar Motel	68	00						394	28
7349	4/1	Buy-All Supermarket	36	11						358	17
7350	4/3	Kitchen and Bath Co.	90	91						267	26

TWO-LINE ENTRY

		RECORD ALL CHARGES OR CREDITS THAT AFFECT YOUR ACCOUNT.									
										BALANCE	
NUMBER	DATE	DESCRIPTION OF TRANSACTION	PAYMENT/DEBIT (-)		✔ T	FEE (IF ANY) (-)		DEPOSIT/CREDIT (+)		$ 282	34
7341	3/25	Cash	$ 150	00		$		$		150	00
		Car repair								132	34
Deposit	3/25	Deposit check						255	67	255	67
										388	01
7342	3/25	Sunshine State Telephone	25	00						25	00
		Telephone bill								363	01
7343	3/27	Unico Life Ins.	8	70						8	70
		Insurance								354	31
7344	3/27	ABB Ins.	5	78						5	78
		Insurance								348	53
7345	3/27	Payson Cable	19	75						19	75
		Cable bill								328	78

FIGURE 16-5 Keeping a check register up to date is not difficult. You just have to be accurate and pay attention to detail.

the month when she wrote a $53.46 check to The Clothes Rack. There was only $46.20 in her account and the check bounced. Jackie immediately took another check to Barbara.

Figure 16-5 shows two common ways to maintain a check register. Study each part of the illustration. Both ways work well; so choose the one that you prefer. The column next to the "payment/debit" column may be used to check off items when you balance a statement. Or, if you prefer, you can indicate in this column which items are tax-deductible (T).

Endorse a Check

Suppose a friend writes you a check. What do you do with it? You take it to your bank and endorse it there. An **endorsement** is your signature, sometimes with a brief message, on the back/left side of a check. You must endorse a check before you can cash it or deposit it. There are three common types of endorsements: blank, restrictive, and full. Each type of endorsement is shown in Figure 16-6 on the next page.

- A *blank endorsement* is simply your written signature. Once you have signed a check, it can be treated as cash. Anyone can then present it to the bank for payment. So, never endorse a check until you are ready to cash it.

- A *restrictive endorsement* is a message and a signature that restrict the use of the check. The most common restrictive endorsement

Blank Endorsement	Restrictive Endorsement	Full Endorsement
Jill Yount	*For Deposit Only* *Jill Yount*	*Pay to the Order* *of Sharon Weber* *Jill Yount*

FIGURE 16-6 Different forms of endorsements are used for different purposes.

is "For deposit only," followed by a signature. This is usually used when you wish to send a check by mail to a bank for deposit. With this message, the check can't be used for any other purpose.

- A *full endorsement* is used when you want to pay someone else with a check that is made out to you. This is done by writing "Pay to the order of," writing the person's name, and then signing your name. This endorsement transfers the right of payment from you to a new payee.

Endorse a check exactly as it is made out. Do this even if your name is written improperly or misspelled. When there is an error, you endorse the check first as is, followed by the correct way. For example, suppose a check to Sharon Robbins is made out incorrectly to "Sharon Robins." She would endorse it first as "Sharon Robins" and then as "Sharon Robbins." Similarly, a check written to Skip Turner would be endorsed as "Skip Turner," followed by "James A. Turner."

Federal law guarantees customers of financial institutions timely access to money they deposit. The law also requires customers to use uniform standards to endorse checks. Figure 16-7 on the next page summarizes these rules. If you fail to follow the rules for endorsing checks, you will still get your money. But it could take longer.

Make a Deposit

The process of putting money into a checking account is known as making a deposit. To do this, you fill out the preprinted deposit ticket that comes with your checks. A **deposit ticket** is a preprinted form used to deposit any combination of currency, coins, and checks. You can receive a portion of the deposit in cash. Figure 16-8 on the next page shows a completed deposit ticket.

When you make a deposit, the bank will return to you a receipt showing the amount of the deposit. Check this to make sure it agrees with the amount you wrote on the deposit ticket. Record the deposit right away in your check register.

Balance a Statement

A **statement of account** is a summary of all transactions completed in a checking account for a given period of time. Once a month, the bank will provide you with a statement of account and images of the canceled checks that you wrote. Some banks post monthly statements and cancelled check images online.

jonya/iStockphoto.com

It is necessary to fill out a deposit ticket when making a deposit into a bank account.

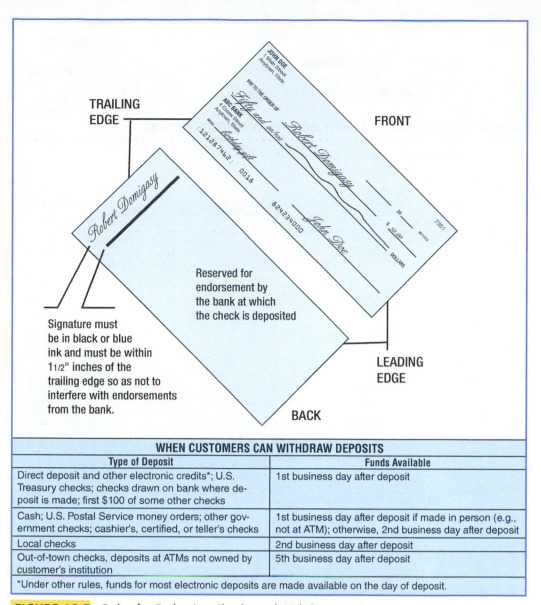

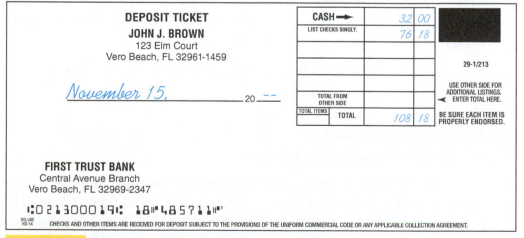

	FRONT
TRAILING EDGE	

Signature must be in black or blue ink and must be within 1½" inches of the trailing edge so as not to interfere with endorsements from the bank.

Reserved for endorsement by the bank at which the check is deposited

LEADING EDGE

BACK

WHEN CUSTOMERS CAN WITHDRAW DEPOSITS	
Type of Deposit	**Funds Available**
Direct deposit and other electronic credits*; U.S. Treasury checks; checks drawn on bank where deposit is made; first $100 of some other checks	1st business day after deposit
Cash; U.S. Postal Service money orders; other government checks; cashier's, certified, or teller's checks	1st business day after deposit if made in person (e.g., not at ATM); otherwise, 2nd business day after deposit
Local checks	2nd business day after deposit
Out-of-town checks, deposits at ATMs not owned by customer's institution	5th business day after deposit

*Under other rules, funds for most electronic deposits are made available on the day of deposit.

FIGURE 16-7 Rules for Endorsing Checks and Withdrawing Deposits

FIGURE 16-8 A Completed Deposit Ticket

FIRST TRUST BANK
Central Avenue Branch
Vero Beach, FL 32969-2347

JOHN J. BROWN
123 Elm Court
Vero Beach, FL 32961-1459

002 613 CY

13435711
6134357116

STATEMENT OF YOUR ACCOUNT(S) FOR PERIOD 11-15-XX THROUGH 12-13-XX

****

SUMMARY OF REGULAR ACCOUNT # 18 485711

BALANCE LAST STATEMENT	502.10	
DEPOSITS AND OTHER ADDITIONS	1910.78	
CHECKS AND OTHER SUBTRACTIONS	1306.12	
BALANCE THIS STATEMENT	1106.76	TAXPAYER ID NUMBER **123 45 6789**

DATE	TYPE OF TRANSACTION	CHECKS	SUBTRACTIONS	ADDITIONS	BALANCE
11-15	BEGINNING BALANCE				502.10
11-18	DEPOSIT			405.24	907.34
11-22	CHECKS POSTED (3)	67.20			840.14
11-23	DEPOSIT			650.15	
11-23	CHECKS POSTED (1)	17.75			1472.54
11-25	CHECKS POSTED (4)	519.45			953.09
11-28	CHECKS POSTED (1)	44.00			909.09
11-29	CHECKS POSTED (3)	47.20			861.89
11-30	DEPOSIT			305.24	
11-30	CHECKS POSTED (1)	50.00			1117.13
12-05	CHECKS POSTED (3)	363.27			753.86
12-06	CHECKS POSTED (1)	149.69			604.17
12-07	DEPOSIT			305.24	909.41
12-08	CHECKS POSTED (1)	4.00			905.41
12-09	CHECKS POSTED (1)	43.56			861.85
12-12	DEPOSIT			244.91	1106.76

CHECKS POSTED (* INDICATES SEQUENCE BREAK)

CHECK	AMOUNT	DATE	CHECK	AMOUNT	DATE	CHECK	AMOUNT	DATE
7242	50.00	11–30	7249	21.20	11–29	7255	16.00	11–29
7243	44.00	11–28	7250	8.70	11–25	7256	10.00	11–29
7244	17.75	11–23	7251	47.20	11–22	7257	13.27	12–05
7245	10.00	11–22	7252	10.00	11–22	7258	43.56	12–09
7246	400.00	11–25	7253	17.66	11–25	7259	300.00	12–05
7247	50.00	12–05	7254	93.09	11–25	7260	149.69	12–06
7248	4.00	12–08						

FIGURE 16-9 Every month your bank will provide you with a bank statement. This is a summary of all your transactions during that time period.

The statement (shown in Figure 16-9) is a summary of all your transactions for a given period. It includes the following:

- The amount of each check and the date the bank received it
- The deposits you made
- Any service charges
- Any interest earned
- Beginning and ending balances

Reconciling is the process of comparing the statement with your check register. *Balancing a checkbook* is the same as reconciling. The purpose of balancing a checkbook is to ensure that both you and your bank have recorded your checks, your deposits, and other activity in your account accurately. Instructions on how to balance your account are usually printed on the back of the statement. Sample instructions

It's Easy to Balance Your Account. Follow the instructions and use the reconcilement form below.

Reconcilement Instructions:
- Check off each paid check on your checkbook stub register.
- Be sure that all **checks posted** and **other subtractions** shown on your checking account have been subtracted from your checkbook balance and that all **deposits** and **other additions** have been added.
- List and total under "Checks Outstanding" all checks not paid by the bank during this statement period.
- Fill in the ending balance shown on this statement.
- Add the deposits made after the close of this period.
- Deduct the checks still outstanding.
- The result should be the same as the balance remaining in your checkbook.

Checks Outstanding						Reconcilement Form	
Check No. or Date	Amount	Check No. or Date	Amount	Check No. or Date	Amount		
	$	Total Forwarded	$	Total Forwarded	$	Balance as of this statement, shown on front	
							$
						Add deposits not yet shown on front.	
						Total	$
						Subtract total checks outstanding.	$
Total or Carry Forward		Total or Carry Forward		Total	$	This result should agree with your checkbook balance.	$

Please examine at once.

Your account will be considered correct if no report is received by our auditors in 14 days, except that matters involving your line of credit or electronic transfer(s) must be reported within 60 days.

FIGURE 16-10 You can keep your account balanced if you follow this step-by-step procedure.

are shown in Figure 16-10. Follow each step exactly as described. If you have a problem that you cannot figure out, do not wait until you receive the next statement. Rather, call or go to the bank right away and ask someone to help you.

After you have balanced your checkbook, make any necessary changes in the register. For example, you may need to record amounts for service charges, interest, or an overdraft fee.

16-2 Assessment

1. Name two main advantages of having a checking account.

2. Explain the basic difference between a regular checking account and a special checking account.

3. Name the five kinds of information you must write on a check.

4. What is a mistake people often make with their check registers? How can this mistake be prevented?

5. How should you endorse a check if your name is misspelled?

6. In simple terms, what is the purpose of balancing a checkbook?

7. Are banks required to provide you with printed monthly statements and paper copies of your checks? Why or why not?

High Growth Occupations
FOR THE 21ST CENTURY

Carpenters

An interest in working with tools and equipment and a willingness to do physical labor are important requirements for being a carpenter. Workers in this occupation construct, erect, install, and repair structures made from wood and other materials.

Each carpentry task is somewhat different, but most involve the same basic steps. Working from blueprints or instructions from supervisors, carpenters first do the layout involving measuring and marking. Next, they cut and shape wood, plastic, fiberglass, or drywall using hand and power tools. They then join the materials with nails, screws, staples, or adhesives. In the last step, carpenters do a final check of the accuracy of their work and make any necessary adjustments.

Carpenters may do many different tasks, or specialize in only one or two. Carpenters who remodel homes and other structures, for example, need a broad range of carpentry skills. As part of a single job, they might frame walls and partitions, put in doors and windows, build stairs, install cabinets and molding, and complete many other tasks. Well-trained carpenters are able to switch from residential building to commercial construction or remodeling work, depending on which offers the best work opportunities.

As is true of other building trades, carpentry work is sometimes strenuous. Prolonged standing, climbing, bending, and kneeling often are necessary. Carpenters risk injury working with sharp or rough materials, using sharp tools and power equipment, and working in situations where they might slip or fall. Additionally, carpenters who work outdoors are subject to variable weather conditions.

Learning to be a carpenter can start in high school by completing basic academic courses along with mechanical drawing and general shop. Some high schools have a building trades program where students construct an actual house. After high school, some individuals get a job as a carpenter's helper. At the same time, the helper might attend a trade or vocational school, or community college to receive further training. Some employers offer formal apprenticeships that combine on-the-job training with related classroom instruction.

Diego Cervo/Shutterstock.com

The duties of carpenters vary and include work on the outside of buildings as well as on the inside of buildings.

CREDIT AND ITS USE

OBJECTIVES

- Name and describe the two basic types of credit
- Discuss new credit legislation
- Calculate the cost of credit

KEY TERMS

- credit
- finance charge
- annual percentage rate (APR)

Personal Decisions

You got a good deal on your new car and the finance rate is reasonable. In going over the sales contract, you discover that financing includes charges for "credit life and disability insurance" and "extended warranty." You ask the salesperson about these items. He says that they are optional but that most people buy them. They only add a few dollars to the monthly payment. You are not sure whether you need them.

What would you do?

drbimages/iStockphoto.com

Types of Credit

Credit refers to the receipt of money, goods, or services in exchange for a promise to pay. People may get credit in the form of loans. This form is called loan credit. Sales credit is also available. With this type of credit, consumers can delay their payments for goods and services.

Loan Credit

Loan credit involves money borrowed in order to buy something. A borrower may not have cash on hand to pay for a house, car, or college education. The buyer usually gets a loan at one place and spends the cash in another. For example, you may secure a loan from a credit union. You will then use the money to buy a car at a local dealership.

Buyers generally pay back loan credit in equal installments over a fixed time period. In the case of a used car loan, for example, you might pay installments of $180 per month for 48 months.

Sales Credit

When using loan credit, you borrow money. *Sales credit*, however, allows you to purchase goods and services directly and delay paying until later. There are three main types of sales credit: open charge accounts, revolving charge accounts, and installment accounts.

Many retail businesses provide *open charge accounts* to customers with good credit ratings. A great deal of business to business sales are

In managing your own money and money at work, you will sometimes have to check numbers. Here are some tips that will help you do a good job and not make mistakes.

- Set aside some time to proofread when you are fresh and not in a hurry.
- If you have a rough copy and a finished copy, read one against the other, using two envelopes or pieces of paper to guide you line by line. Then read the finished copy straight through.
- Read numbers aloud. Read long lists with a partner.

- Try reading numbers in groups. For example, the telephone number 513-555-0116 can be read in three parts: five-one-three, five-five-five, zero-one-one-six.
- Double-check all calculations. For example, when you are adding numbers, add them once from top to bottom and then again from bottom to top.

THINK CRITICALLY

1. How would skill in proofreading numbers benefit you in your career?
2. How would skill in proofreading numbers help you in your personal life?

conducted using open charge accounts. Don uses his charge card at Polk's Store to buy two sweaters. He takes home his purchase. The bill arrives a few weeks later.

The *revolving charge* is probably the most common form of consumer sales credit. Revolving charge accounts are credit card accounts offered by retailers and banks. Common bankcards are Visa and MasterCard. You can charge many goods and services.

Like Don, credit card customers receive a monthly statement of all transactions. Don paid his entire bill. He could have made a minimum payment or sent some other amount. Had he done that, he would have paid a finance charge. **Finance charges** are the cost of credit and are the total dollar amount you pay for using credit.

Installment accounts are the third major type of sales credit. People may use them to buy items like furniture that exceed the credit line of revolving charge accounts (the amount of credit available).

The customer usually makes a small down payment. An installment contract detailing payment terms for the balance is signed. It typically calls for fixed monthly payments and a finance charge. Finance charges are often higher than those for revolving accounts.

Credit Legislation

In May 2009, President Obama signed into law legislation that provides credit card protection to consumers. The rules are summarized below:

- **Retroactive rate increases** Issuers can't raise rates on an existing balance unless a promotional rate expired. There are some exceptions. Read credit documents carefully.

Workplace Innovations

HIGH SPEED TRAINS

Extensive high speed rail systems are found in Europe, China and Japan. There are different standards for what is considered "high speed." In the European Union high speed trains travel 125 mph. In Japan, trains run at speeds of 185 mph. China's trains are the fastest, going over 215 mph.

High speed trains have several advantages over other forms of public transportation. Trains have the potential to relieve congestion. Trains are more energy efficient and produce less air pollution than other motor vehicles. In addition, trains reduce the amount of land used per passenger and train stations have a smaller ecological footprint than airports.

The United States has been slow to develop high speed train systems. The only line used for high speed rail in the U.S. is in the Northeast Corridor. Amtrak's Acela Express runs from Boston to Washington, D.C. It averages 68 mph for the entire distance, but can reach 150 mph during portions of the trip.

In February 2009, as part of the American Recovery and Reinvestment Act, Congress appropriated funds to be used for intercity rail projects including the development of high speed rail service. One of the first projects to begin construction is in California between Anaheim and San Francisco. Nine additional corridors have been identified for potential high-speed development.

NET FOLLOW-UP

Search the Internet for additional information on the topic of "high-speed rail." Are any new HSR systems under construction in the United States?

- **More advance notice of rate hikes** Consumers get 45 days' notice before rate increases take effect.
- **Fee restrictions** Cardholders will not face overlimit fees unless they elect to allow the creditor to approve overlimit transactions.
- **Restricts card issuance to students** Consumers under age 21 who can't prove an independent means of income or provide the signature of a co-signer over 21 won't get approved for credit cards.
- **Ends double-cycle billing** The practice of basing finance charges on the current and previous balance is banned.
- **Fairer payment allocation** Payments made above the minimum payments must now be applied first to the credit card balance with the highest interest rate.
- **More time to pay** Card companies must send statements 21 days (instead of 14) before a payment is due.
- **Gift card protection** Gift card holders now have at least five years before the card expires.

Access www.cengage.com/school/working and click on the Web Links for Credit Card Rules to see more explanations of these rule changes.

The Cost of Credit

The cost of credit varies from lender to lender. Fortunately, the law requires lenders to tell you in writing before you sign an agreement how much the charges will be.

	APR	Length of Loan	Monthly Payment	Total Finance Charge	Total Cost
Creditor A	14%	3 years	$205.07	$1,382.52	**$7,382.52**
Creditor B	14%	4 years	**$163.96**	$1,870.08	$7,870.08
Creditor C	**15%**	4 years	$166.98	$2,015.04	$8,015.04

FIGURE 16-11 The cost of credit varies according to the APR and the length of the loan.

The finance charge is the total dollar amount you pay for using credit. It includes interest, service charges, insurance premiums, and other fees. For example, borrowing $100 for a year might cost you $15 in interest and $2 in service charges. The finance charge will be $17.

The **annual percentage rate (APR)** is the percentage cost of credit on a yearly basis. Suppose you borrow $200 for one year and pay a finance charge of $20. If you keep the entire $200 for 12 months and then pay it back in one lump sum, you are paying an APR of 10 percent. However, if you repay the $200 and finance charge in 12 equal monthly installments (a total of $220), you do not really get to use the $200 for the whole year. In fact, you get to use less and less of the $200 each month. The $20 charge for credit amounts to an APR of 18 percent.

APR allows you to compare credit costs. Every lender must state the cost of their credit in terms of both the finance charge and the APR. The law says you must be aware of this information before signing a credit contract. To actually compare credit costs, you must take into account the APR and length of the loan. If you are buying a used car for $7,500, you will need to calculate the APR. You plan to pay $1,500 down and borrow $6,000. The relationship among three different credit arrangements is shown in Figure 16-11.

The loan with the lowest total cost is that offered by Creditor A. If you are looking for a lower monthly payment, you can get that by choosing Creditor B and paying the loan back in four years instead of three. However, the lower monthly payment will add $487.56 to the total finance charge. The 15 percent APR of the loan offered by Creditor C would add another $144.96 to the finance charge.

Consider all aspects of a loan, like the down payment size, before making a choice. The cost of credit is affected by many variables.

16-3 Assessment

1. Name and briefly explain the two basic types of credit.
2. What are the three main types of sales credit?
3. What does the finance charge include?
4. What is the practical purpose of the APR?

Focus on Skills for Living

Your Credit History

Potential lenders will usually request a credit report on you. A credit bureau is a private organization that provides information to businesses regarding the credit history of customers. The three nationwide credit reporting companies are Experian, Equifax, and TransUnion. Your credit file contains four major types of information:

- Your name, recent addresses, marital status, and number of dependents
- Household income information
- The status of your current accounts, what kinds of loans you now have, and whether you pay your bills in full and on time
- Any court judgments or liens against you. A *lien* is a charge against your property for failure to pay a debt. Accounts turned over to a collection agency are also noted.

The credit bureau only compiles information and provides it to the merchant or potential lender. That person (the merchant or lender) judges how creditworthy you are.

Federal law gives you the right to know what information is in your file. The Fair Credit Reporting Act (FCRA) guarantees you access to your credit report every 12 months for free from each of the three major reporting companies. Many companies claim to offer free credit reports. But, there is only one authorized source for the free annual credit report that is yours by law. The source is AnnualCreditReport.com which you can find on the Web. You can order your free credit reports by phone, by mail, or online.

If you are refused credit on the basis of a credit report, the merchant must give you the name and address of the bureau that provided the information. If you disagree with information in the file, the bureau must reinvestigate and remove information that cannot be verified. To correct errors in your report and to take advantage of all your rights under the FCRA, you must follow certain procedures. These procedures can be found by accessing www.cengage.com/school/working and clicking on the Web Links for Disputing Credit Report Errors.

You should look at your credit file annually. This will give you knowledge of the same information that a potential lender will receive. You can ask to have errors corrected, outdated information removed, and missing information added to the file.

THINK CRITICALLY

1. Why would a merchant want to review your credit file?
2. Why should you review your credit file annually?

If people have a bad credit rating, they are sometimes advised to destroy their credit cards.

GeraldConnell/iStockphoto.com

Chapter Summary

16-1 Financial Institutions

A. There are four major types of financial institutions: commercial banks, mutual savings banks, savings and loan associations, and credit unions.

B. Banks and consumers are transitioning to online and mobile banking.

C. Predatory lenders helped cause the recession. Most banks are trustworthy. FDIC insurance covers the first $250,000 in an account.

16-2 Checking Accounts

A. Checking accounts are safe and convenient.

B. When writing a check, include a date, payee, numerical amount, written amount, purpose or account number (optional), and signature.

C. The check register is where you keep a record of checks written, deposits made, and other transactions.

D. An endorsement is needed to cash, deposit, or transfer a check.

E. Balance your checkbook monthly.

16-3 Credit and Its Use

A. Credit refers to the receipt of money, goods, or services in exchange for a promise to pay. In May, 2009, credit protection legislation was passed.

B. The finance charge is the total amount you pay for credit. The APR is the annual percentage cost of credit. APR is used to compare credit costs.

Activities

1. As a class, count the financial institutions in your community, suburb, or region of the city. Classify each according to the four types of institutions discussed. Which is the most common type?

2. Ask an adult to let you do these tasks for him or her: write a check, record a transaction in a check register, and make a deposit to a checking account.

3. The instructor will provide a sample statement of account and check register. Download a copy of Figure 16-10 at www.cengage.com/school/working. Follow the procedure in Figure 16-10 to reconcile the statement.

4. Get a credit card application and read it carefully. Is an annual fee required? What is the APR? How is the finance charge figured? What is the credit limit? What is the minimum monthly payment required?

5. Compare interest rates being charged for consumer loans at several different types of financial institutions in your area. Which offers the best rates?

6. Identify a goal you might set in your life-span plan that could only be achieved through the use of credit. Discuss things you could do now that would improve your ability to borrow funds in the future.

Word Power

On a separate sheet of paper, match each definition with the correct term. All definitions will be used, and a definition will be used only once.

7. The process of comparing a bank statement with one's personal check register to verify accuracy

8. The total dollar amount paid for the use of credit

9. The percentage cost of credit on a yearly basis

10. A plastic card used in electronic banking to immediately transfer funds for a purchase from a bank account

11. A summary of all transactions completed in a checking account for a given time period

12. Various types of electronic fund transfers

13. The receipt of money, goods, or services in exchange for a promise to pay

14. Placing a date on a check that is ahead of the current date

15. A form that is completed to open a checking account

16. Banks offering many financial conveniences and services

17. The person or institution to which a check is written

18. Electronic terminals in which customers can insert a plastic card to withdraw cash, make deposits, or transfer funds

19. A booklet or forms for keeping a record of checking account transactions

20. A signature, sometimes with a brief message, on the back/left side of a check needed to cash, deposit, or transfer ownership of it

21. A preprinted form used to make a deposit in a checking account

a. annual percentage rate (APR)
b. automated teller machine (ATM)
c. check register
d. credit
e. debit card
f. deposit ticket
g. electronic banking
h. endorsement
i. finance charge
j. full-service bank
k. payee
l. postdating
m. reconciling
n. signature card
o. statement of account

Think Critically

22. Discuss advantages and disadvantages of electronic banking.

23. Some futurists are saying that society is headed for a "checkless" or "moneyless" society. Do you think that time will ever come?

24. Many people buy merchandise from catalogs or the Internet. Which method of payment is the safest and offers the greatest consumer protection: money order, check, or credit card? Why?

"Don't be afraid to give your best to what seemingly are small jobs. Every time you conquer one it makes you that much stronger. If you do the little jobs well, the big ones tend to take care of themselves." —DALE CARNEGIE

Budget, Save, and Invest Money

Photo_Concepts/iStockphoto.com

17-1 Budget Money

17-2 Save Money

17-3 Invest Money

PREVIEW

People often refer to someone's financial status with terms like rich, middle-class, and poor. Financial well-being, of course, is related to how much money you earn. The way you spend money, however, is also important. Many people who earn average incomes live comfortably and securely. Wise money management depends on knowledge and skill in budgeting, saving, and perhaps investing money.

Anna is frustrated. Even though she has a well-paying job, she cannot seem to make ends meet. At the end of the month, she has very little money left over after all her bills are paid. She doesn't know where all her money has gone.

To make matters worse, her parents and relatives keep advising Anna to save and invest for her future. She should save, they say, so that if an unexpected expense comes up, such as a car repair, she won't have to go into debt to cover the expense. Securing a comfortable retirement is another goal. Relatives have told Anna that she might need as much as $1 million saved for retirement by the time she is 65!

Success Tip

Find out how to save and invest.

"That's great in theory," Anna thinks. "I don't disagree. I just don't know how to save and invest when I can barely get by."

Anna has tried to limit her spending by not going to restaurants very often and not going to the mall to buy things for her new apartment. Although this strategy seems to be helping, it is still not enough.

Add to Anna's troubles that her car is not working very well. She will have to pay for expensive repairs or she will have to buy a new car within a year. She cannot get to work without her car.

Anna has not had a vacation in two years. One day she would like to buy a small house and fix it up herself. She would also like to begin donating to her favorite charities. All of these things take money. Anna wonders how anyone can afford to get ahead.

Anna has a cousin, Jose, who seems to understand saving and investing. Even though Jose earns less than Anna, he has been saving and investing for three years. Anna decides to ask him for advice.

THINK CRITICALLY

1. Why do you think Anna has trouble with saving?

2. What are some reasons that Anna might want to start a savings plan?

BUDGET MONEY

OBJECTIVES

- Identify your own personal income and spending patterns
- Name and describe the four steps involved in developing and using a budget, including distinguishing between regular and variable expenditures

KEY TERMS

- income
- expenditure
- budget
- savings
- regular expenditure
- variable expenditure
- allocation
- line item

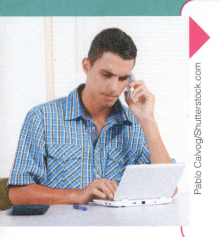

Pablo Calvog/Shutterstock.com

▶ Personal Decisions

You have done your best to develop and follow a budget. You are careful to stick to budget estimates, but every month there is an unexpected expense. It never seems to be the same type of expenditure. One month it is a car repair; the next month, it is a medical bill; and another month, it is an increase in insurance. You are very frustrated and about ready to pitch the budget.

*What would **you** do?*

Income and Spending Patterns

A good first step in learning how to manage money is to find out where your money is coming from and where it is going. **Income** is money that comes to you either through wages, investment interest, or gifts. An **expenditure** is money you spend to buy goods or services. You need to track your income and expenditures to effectively manage your money.

A simple form for tracking income and expenditures is shown in Figure 17-1 on the next page. You can track your income and expenditures for a week or any time period you choose. Begin by inserting the total amount of cash you have on hand at the beginning of the week. Don't include savings. Then start keeping detailed records of all income and expenditures. For income, include take-home pay as well as tips and any money you receive from gifts or allowances. List all expenditures, regardless of how small.

At the end of the week, total up all income and expenditures. How much money is left at week's end? It should equal initial cash on hand plus or minus income and expenditures. Say your initial cash on hand is $75.

You spend $50, and your aunt sends you $15 as a birthday gift. The end-of-week cash balance would be $40.

Once you have kept your records for a few weeks, figure your average income and expenditures. Add up all the income for the period and divide by the number of weeks covered. Do the same for expenditures. Keeping a record of income and expenditures over a period of time can help you understand your financial condition and spending habits. The data in Figure 17-1 show, for example, that the pattern of expenditures cannot continue much longer. You can use this information to set up a budget for yourself.

Develop and Use a Budget

A **budget** is a plan for managing income and expenditures. A budget will help you get the most benefit from your earnings. The four steps involved in developing a budget are as follows:

1. Establish goals
2. Estimate income and expenditures
3. Set up the budget, including distinguishing between regular and variable expenses
4. Follow and revise the budget

The process is similar for everyone—individuals and families, young people, and adults.

Establish Goals

Goals should be set before you prepare the details of your budget. Identify what you need and want. As you decide on goals, discuss them with your family. If the budget is for a family, all family members should participate. Goals should be kept realistic in relation to present and expected future income.

To focus on your goals, list them according to time periods. Be as specific as possible. Remember that there are short-range, medium-range, and long-range goals.

Naturally, goals change along with situations. For example, if you are single and live at home, your goals are probably different from what they will be when you leave home. If you marry, your goals will change

RECORD OF INCOME AND EXPENDITURES

Week _Feb. 4-10_ 20 --

Cash on hand ___$50.80___

Date	Item	Income	Expenditure
4	Allowance & lunch money	$30.00	
4	School lunch ticket		$10.50
5	Gas in car		$24.00
6	Babysitting	$42.00	
7	Basketball game		$4.25
	Snack afterward		$6.00
8	Movie w/friends		$8.50
	Pizza afterward		$6.00
9	Shopping (new music CD)		$16.75
10	Personal care items		$12.00

End-of-week cash balance ___$34.80___   Totals $72.00 $88.00

FIGURE 17-1 Records like these help determine patterns of income and expenditures for individuals, families, and businesses.

PERSONAL (OR FAMILY) GOALS

Goals for this year: _____

_____

_____

Goals for the next five years: _____

_____

_____

Long-term goals: _____

_____

_____

FIGURE 17-2 Write out your financial goals so you will know what you are working toward.

again, as they will if you have children. With two people working, the family goals may be different from what they would be if only one person was working.

Once you have decided on your goals, write them down, as in Figure 17-2. Save your list. You will need to refer to it as you plan the budget.

Estimate Income and Expenditures

Once you have decided on goals, estimate your income and expenditures. A budget may cover any convenient budget period. Most people like to plan a budget around how often they get paid, such as weekly, bimonthly, or monthly.

If you have kept records of income and expenditures for a four- to six-week period, you should be able to arrive at fairly close estimates. If the budget is for a family, records of income and expenditures should be kept over a three- to six-month period. Figure out your average income per budget period. Now review. Did you include all regular income, such as wages, salary, and tips? How about variable income, such as bonuses, gifts, interest, and dividends?

Individuals whose income varies may have special difficulty making estimates. Examples include seasonal workers, salespeople on commission, farmers, and other self-employed people. In these cases, it is usually better to base the budget estimates slightly below the average income. It is always easier to spend extra money than it is to come up with cash to cover a shortage.

Ann is a sales representative who earns most of her income from commissions. The more she sells, the more she earns. During the last six months, her income has been about 30 percent above normal. Business has been so good that she traded her car in on a new one. She can make payments with the extra commissions she is earning.

She got a call today from one of her best clients. "Hello, Ann, this is Cliff at Dramon Corporation. I'm afraid I'll have to cancel that big order you wrote up for me last week. My field representatives are telling me that business is slowing down. We could be moving into a recession."

What if an economic slowdown is on the way? Ann's future commissions will probably fall. Ann now wishes she had not gone in debt for the new car.

Your previous records should help you identify the major categories of spending. Next, review the list to make sure you have not left out a seasonal expenditure or some other item that does not show up in your records. A checkbook register together with bills and receipts can help you reconstruct past expenses.

Financial independence requires careful consideration of household priorities and savings goals.

Workplace Innovations
INTERACTIVE JOURNALISM

The traditional approach to journalism involved reporters collecting information and reporting a story that was read or listened to by an audience. As people began moving to the Internet for news and information, traditional journalism began to adapt and became more interactive. Interactive journalism is the use of digital technologies in ways that allow the user to participate in the media.

Interactive journalism is in use in most media outlets. Web links contained in online newspaper and magazine articles allow readers to find additional or related information. TV newscasts may announce a website where listeners can find information about weather-related school closings. Many live radio or TV broadcasts allow readers to email questions, send "tweets" to comment about a particular topic, or text to vote for or against a particular issue. Weather broadcasters often invite viewers to send photos or videos of weather events as they happen.

The explosion of information has resulted in the need for tools to analyze and visualize it. One of the more advanced forms of interactive journalism is information visualization or infovis. This refers to visual representation of information, data, or knowledge. A good example of infovis was in 2010 during the Gulf oil spill. As news of the oil spill was reported on network and cable news programs, several broadcasts also showed a live underwater feed of the oil flowing from the broken pipe. Dozens of additional websites added to the public's understanding of the extent of the oil spill. Satellite maps and computer modeling enabled daily, easy to visualize tracking of the spreading oil.

NET FOLLOW-UP

Use a search engine to explore the Web for additional information on the topics of interactive journalism or data visualization. Prepare a summary of your findings to use during a class discussion.

As you review your record of expenditures, decide whether to continue with your present spending pattern or to make changes. If you are satisfied with how you have saved your money, allow similar amounts in your budget estimates. Suppose your records highlight poor buying habits or overspending. In that case, you must decide to make changes.

Set Up the Budget

When you have established financial goals and estimated income and expenditures, you are ready to set up your spending plan. The sample budget form shown in Figure 17-3 on the next page consists of three main parts—savings, regular expenditures, and variable expenditures.

Savings

The first part of the budget is for savings. **Savings** is cash set aside in a bank account to be used for financial emergencies and goals. It is important to set aside this money as soon as you are paid. If you wait until the end of the budget period, there may be nothing left for savings.

You should save a regular amount of income for use in an emergency. For a family, the amount should equal at least one month's total income. Once you have reached your figure to set aside for emergencies, start shifting money to savings goals and investments.

Regular Expenditures

Regular expenditures, sometimes called fixed expenditures, are those essential monthly payments that are usually the same amount each month. Here is a list of common regular expenditures. Your regular expenditures may be slightly different.

- **Rent or mortgage payment**   This fixed expenditure covers your basic housing needs. Renters pay their landlord. Buyers of a property make payments to the lender that granted the mortgage. A mortgage payment usually includes property taxes and insurance.

- **Utilities**   These include services such as electricity, telephone, TV, Internet, gas, and water. Even though these amounts vary, you should list them as regular expenses because they are essential monthly payments. If you have trouble deciding how much to budget for utilities, check with the utility companies. Many have a plan that allows you to pay a fixed amount each month based on your average utility usage.

- **Insurance**   Include all insurance premiums not covered by payroll withholding and mortgage payments. Life and auto insurance are two common examples.

- **Auto payment**   You may not have an auto loan. However, many people do, and they make monthly installment payments on it.

- **Credit or loan payments**   These may include payments on charge accounts or student loans, for example. Not everyone has credit or loan payments.

Variable Expenditures

Variable expenditures are daily living expenses. They may change depending on the time of year, spending habits, and other non-regular needs.

- **Food and beverages**   This category includes food and beverages purchased for home use as well as essential meals

HOUSEHOLD BUDGET FORM

Month _Jan._ 20 _--_   Estimated Income $ _1,706_

Expenditure	Estimate	Actual	Difference (+ or −)
Savings Emergency reserve	$42	$42	0
Goals	$60	$36	+ $24
Regular Expenses Rent or mortgage payment	$360	$360	0
Utilities	$200	$235	− $35
Insurance	$120	$120	0
Auto payment	0	0	0
Credit or loan payments	$96	$96	0
Other ( )			
Variable Expenses Food and beverages	$420	$415	+ $5
Clothing	$60	$92	− $32
Transportation	$120	$114	+ $6
Household	$48	$48	0
Medical care	$36	$28	+ $8
Entertainment	$72	$82	− $10
Gifts and contributions	$36	$30	+ $6
Taxes	$36	$36	0
Other ( )			
TOTALS	$1,706	$1,734	− $28

FIGURE 17-3   Using a budget form like this can improve the quality of your life and help you meet future goals successfully.

eaten away from home, such as school lunches. Optional purchases, such as a snack after the game, should be listed under "Entertainment."

- **Clothing**   Include here the cost of buying and maintaining your clothes. Be sure to consider expenditures for repairs, alterations, dry cleaning, and laundry.
- **Transportation**   Include here the cost of using public transportation. If you own a vehicle, be sure to consider expenditures for insurance, gas, oil, repairs, tolls, parking, and license plates.
- **Household**   This includes the cost of buying and maintaining furniture and appliances. Furniture payments could instead be included in "Credit or loan payments." If you rent, the property owners may or may not provide furniture. Everyone must buy cleaning supplies. Homeowners may have extra expenses, such as paint and lawn care products.
- **Medical care**   You can plan ahead for some of your medical care. For example, you know if you have to take regular medication or have periodic checkups. Try to set aside some money for variable medical, dental, and eyecare expenses not covered by insurance.
- **Entertainment**   This category includes vacations, hobbies, concert tickets, and sporting events. If you have children, babysitting might be an entertainment expense.
- **Gifts and contributions**   Besides gifts, be sure to consider contributions to charity, political parties, and special causes.
- **Taxes**   Include here amounts for taxes not withheld from your paycheck or included in a mortgage payment. Keep in mind that it is often necessary to pay extra income taxes at the end of the year.

These are the expenditures most families have. Feel free to add or subtract items as necessary and arrange them in the way that works best for you. Once you have developed a list of expenditures, enter a dollar amount for each item. The total of all items in the Estimate column should equal the amount entered for Estimated Income.

Follow and Revise the Budget

Following a budget involves the **allocation**, or distribution, of income to the various items in the budget. It also involves keeping accurate records of expenditures. One way to allocate income is to deposit all or most of it in a checking account and then to write checks for items as necessary. Another common method is to cash your paycheck, divide the cash according to budget categories, and place it in separate envelopes labeled with your main budget headings. You can then take money out of the envelopes as needed.

A good choice is probably a combination of the two methods. Place most of your paycheck in a checking account. Write checks for larger and regular expenses. Keep the remaining cash on hand for smaller purchases. Regardless of which method you use, refer to your budget often. Otherwise, your spending plan is useless.

Keeping accurate records is an important part of maintaining a budget. If paid by check, major expenditures are easy to track. Be sure to write everything in your check register. Small cash purchases can be another matter. Because you make so many of them, it is tempting to ignore them. Failure to note these items makes your budget useless.

To account for cash purchases, use a form like the one shown in Figure 17-1. If it does not meet your needs, modify it or develop a new one. A number of software apps are also available for download that can be used for keeping track of daily expenses.

Another approach is to get an expandable manila file, label each pocket with a main budget heading, and file receipts in it. To jot down items for which you do not have a receipt, keep a notepad and pen near the file. All family members who spend money should get in the habit of saving and filing receipts.

At the end of the budget period, go over your receipts and records. Enter the information in the Actual column using the budget form in Figure 17-3. Write in the total amount spent for each line item in the budget. A **line item** is a single entry, or budgeted item. In the next column, record the difference between the "Estimate" and the "Actual" amounts. For example, if you estimated $120 for transportation but only spent $114, write "+$6." However, suppose you spent $135. In that case, you would write "−$15."

After you have filled in all the information, add the totals for the Actual and Difference columns. Now you must face reality. How does your spending compare to your estimates? If the figures are similar, you should be proud of yourself. If not, try to find the problem. Perhaps your estimates were not accurate or realistic. Or maybe the estimates were good, but you had trouble sticking to them. If there is a problem with the estimates, revise them. If the problem is with you, resolve to do a better job next time. Do not expect to have a perfect budget the first time you develop one. A budget is something you must keep working and reworking. Even after you arrive at a budget that is right for you, you will need to change it occasionally.

17-1 Assessment

1. Why should you keep a record of income and expenditures?
2. What four steps are involved in developing a budget?
3. Name two situations that might cause goals to change.
4. Why is it important to set aside money for savings as soon as you are paid?
5. Explain how to allocate income to budgeted items.
6. Name two reasons why actual expenditures might be quite different from budget estimates.

SAVE MONEY

OBJECTIVES

- Discuss the importance of setting aside a portion of income for savings
- Name and describe the two basic types of savings accounts
- Compute interest rate returns on savings

KEY TERMS

- liquidity
- certificate of deposit (CD)
- compounding
- annual percentage yield (APY)

Personal Decisions

You see an ad in the newspaper for the grand opening of a mutual savings bank. The bank is offering a camera to new customers who deposit a certain amount. You already have a passbook account and a certificate of deposit at another bank. But you are considering switching banks to get the free camera.

What would you do?

REDAV/Shutterstock.com

Why Save?

If all of your paycheck goes for bills, you are working for someone else! Ask Vikas. On the first of the month when he gets paid, Vikas writes checks for all of his monthly payments. Checks go for rent, a car payment, utilities, and various credit card accounts. After putting aside amounts for groceries and insurance, Vikas has little left. He keeps his fingers crossed every month. Vikas knows that an illness or emergency would be a financial disaster.

One weekend at a family gathering, Vikas was talking about his financial situation with his Uncle Sanjay. Uncle Sanjay, a banker, listened patiently until Vikas had finished. Then he said, "Vikas, you must learn to pay yourself first." What Uncle Sanjay meant was that Vikas should reward himself for working. He should take a portion "off the top" of his paycheck and put it into savings.

There are two reasons to set aside cash for savings. First, you will have some funds available to meet a financial emergency. Suppose Vikas follows his uncle's advice and opens a savings account. Then, should his old car suddenly break down, Vikas won't have to worry about how he will pay for repairs. Second, a savings account allows you to achieve financial goals. Vikas, for example, may want to save for new gaming components.

Commercial banks, mutual savings banks, savings and loan associations, and credit unions offer both checking accounts and savings accounts. It is not, however, necessary to have checking and savings accounts at the same place.

Do some comparison shopping. Teresa Romero did. You may remember from Chapter 16 how Teresa saved money by closing her old checking account and opening a new one at a credit union. When it came time to open a savings account, Teresa reviewed the material she had already collected about financial services at various institutions.

After comparing various plans and interest rates, Teresa decided to open a savings account at a mutual savings bank. It is close to her home and stays open until 8 P.M. on Friday evenings. Her money, on which she receives a good interest rate, is insured. She can withdraw funds at any time.

Because of changes in banking laws, financial institutions have begun to offer similar services. Shop carefully for the right services for you. Even within one institution, you may find a variety of savings plans. Your efforts will gain you more interest for your savings dollars.

Types of Savings Accounts

Financial institutions may advertise many different savings account plans. There are two basic types of savings accounts: regular savings accounts and time deposits. Sample deposit and withdrawal forms for these accounts are shown in Figure 17-4.

Regular Savings Accounts

Regular savings accounts, also called passbook accounts, are very convenient and flexible. You can make deposits and withdrawals at any time. A summary statement is mailed monthly or quarterly.

As a result of the Patriot Act, signed into law in 2001, the process of opening a bank account has changed. Banks are now required to use multiple documents and information to verify a customer's identification. These include name, date of birth, address, and ID number. For U.S. citizens, the ID number is their Social Security number. For non-citizens, a government issued document such as a passport or alien identification number is required. Banks may also require a driver's license or other form of photo identification. Banks are required to search whether the customer's name appears on a list of known or suspected terrorists or terrorist groups.

After legal requirements are met, you will be asked to sign a signature card and make a deposit. An individual account number will be assigned and you will probably be offered the option of receiving a bank credit/debit card.

Regular savings accounts offer safety, convenience, and liquidity. **Liquidity** refers to an

SAVINGS DEPOSIT FORM

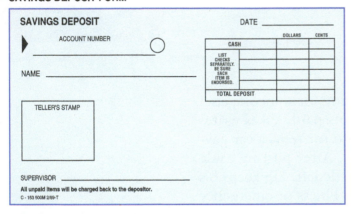

SAVINGS WITHDRAWAL FORM

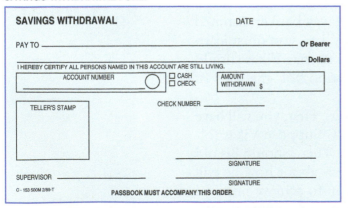

FIGURE 17-4 There are separate forms for making deposits to and withdrawals from a bank account.

asset that can be easily converted into cash. Depositors receive slightly less interest on regular savings accounts than on other types of accounts.

Time Deposits

If you can deposit a lump-sum amount for a longer period of time, you may be interested in time deposits. A **certificate of deposit (CD)** is a popular type of time deposit in which an amount of savings is deposited for a fixed period of time in return for a specified interest rate. Most time deposits work in the same way. A depositor puts in money for a fixed period of time. This may be six months, one year, or longer. The saver agrees not to withdraw money during that period. In return, the institution pays a higher rate of interest. The longer the saver agrees to keep the money in the account, the higher the rate of interest will be. Figure 17-5 provides examples of the relationship between increased length of investment and higher rates of interest. What if the depositor needs to withdraw the funds? It can be done, but the interest rate will be greatly reduced.

Time deposits are safe and provide a guaranteed rate of return for a fixed time period. On the negative side, they generally do not permit deposits and withdrawals and are not as liquid as regular savings accounts. Some accounts offer advantages of both regular savings accounts and time deposits. They have names such as Golden Passbook Account and Bonus Savings Account. These accounts have higher rates of interest than regular savings accounts but more flexible terms than time deposits. For example, they allow you to make withdrawals and additional deposits. Such accounts usually require a higher minimum balance than regular savings accounts.

First Trust Bank
Central Avenue Branch
Vero Beach, FL 32969-2347

SUBJECT TO CHANGE

TIME DEPOSIT RATES EFFECTIVE _____ May 3, 20--

THROUGH _____ May 9, 20--

Term	Minimum	Current Rates
32–91 days	$500	6.30
92 days–1 year	$500	6.55
13–18 months	$500	6.65
19–30 months	$500	7.25
31–48 months	$500	7.45
Over 48 months	$500	7.75

FIGURE 17-5 This is an example of how time deposit interest rates vary for different time periods.

Determine Interest Rates

Savings account interest rates fluctuate. In the early 1980s, for example, interest rates were over 10 percent. By the early 1990s, they had dropped below 3 percent. At the beginning of 2011, interest rates were barely above 1 percent. Rates also vary according to the type of savings plan. Determining the best interest rates for different savings plans requires effort on your part. To start, look at the newspaper ad in Figure 17-6. From the ad, you learn the annual interest rate (5.25%) and annual percentage yield (5.390%). University Bank also tells you how often interest is compounded (daily) and when it is paid (quarterly).

Annual Interest Rate

The law requires banks and other financial institutions to clearly state in their ads the true annual interest rate paid on savings. In the ad, 5.25%

Save more at University Bank: 5.25% interest compounded daily, paid quarterly on passbook savings. Yield 5.390%

FIGURE 17-6 A Sample Newspaper Ad for a Passbook Account

Math Connection

You just received $2,000 from your aunt. You want to put it into a savings account. If the interest rate is 6%, approximately how long will it take for your money to double?

SOLUTION

You can't do most compound interest problems in your head. But you can do this one by using the Rule of 72. Simply divide 72 by the rate of interest.

$$72 \div 6 = 12$$

It will take nearly 12 years for your money to double.

is the annual interest rate. This means that on each $100 of savings, the institution pays you $5.25 in interest. The interest calculation is below:

$$\text{Rate} \times \text{Time in years} \times \text{Principal} = \text{Interest}$$
$$0.0525 \times 1 \times \$100 = \$5.25$$

Frequency of Interest Compounding

You want the most interest. But the highest advertised annual rate may not be the best deal. **Compounding** is the process in which interest is earned on both the money put into an account and the interest periodically added to it, causing savings to steadily grow.

A 6 percent interest rate with interest compounded annually means the interest is added every 12 months. If $100 is in your account, $106 will be the balance after one year. At the end of the second year, you will have $112.36. The interest for the second year, $6.36, was figured on the new balance of $106. How much would you earn the third year?

If the interest rate is 6 percent but the interest is compounded semiannually, you will have $103 at the end of six months. After a year, you will have $106.09. At the end of two years, you will have $112.55. The more often the interest is compounded, the more money you make. Figure 17-7 shows how the value of a $1,000 deposit varies according to the frequency of compounding.

Frequency of Compounding	After 1 year	After 5 years	After 10 years	After 20 years
Daily	$1,053.90	$1,300.15	$1,690.40	$2,857.44
Quarterly	1,053.54	1,297.96	1,684.70	2,838.20
Semiannually	1,053.19	1,295.78	1,679.05	2,819.21
Annually	1,052.50	1,291.55	1,668.10	2,782.54

FIGURE 17-7 More frequent interest compounding results in higher returns. The figures are based on a $1,000 deposit at 5.25 percent.

5.25%, compounded	APY
Daily	5.39%
Quarterly	5.35%
Semiannually	5.32%
Annually	5.25%

FIGURE 17-8 The APY is the best indicator of how much interest you will earn.

Interest Pay Periods

How often does the financial institution credit interest to your account? The University Bank ad says the interest is compounded daily and paid four times a year (quarterly). Should you close the account in mid-quarter, you would lose all the interest for that three-month period. You may want to look for an account that pays interest from the day of deposit to the day of withdrawal.

Annual Percentage Yield

Annual percentage yield (APY) tells you the actual yearly interest rate per $100 left on deposit. It takes into account both the rate for annual interest and compounding. When comparing one savings account with another, it is useful to know the APY. The higher the APY, the better the deal you receive, as shown in Figure 17-8 on the previous page. The effects of compounding interest in the short and long terms are evident in Figure 17-9.

Just as the APR, which you learned about in Chapter 16, provides you with a means for comparing credit costs, the APY gives you a method for comparing the earnings of different savings account plans. Federal legislation nicknamed "Truth-in-Savings" requires banks and other savings institutions to provide this information to customers.

Weekly deposit	After 1 year	After 3 years	After 5 years	After 10 years	After 20 years
$ 5	$ 267.16	$ 845.95	$1,489.54	$ 3,431.69	$ 9,265.67
10	534.32	1,691.89	2,979.08	6,863.37	18,531.35
15	801.48	2,537.84	4,468.62	10,295.06	27,797.02
20	1,068.63	3,383.79	5,958.17	13,726.74	37,062.70
25	1,335.79	4,229.74	7,447.71	17,158.43	46,328.37

FIGURE 17-9 Over the years, a small amount of savings can add up to a large amount (figures based on 5.25 percent interest, compounded daily).

Interest rate	After 1 year	After 3 years	After 5 years	After 10 years	After 20 years
4.5%	$615.13	$1,932.88	$3,376.53	$7,618.34	$19,641.57
5	616.84	1,948.41	3,422.06	7,831.35	20,832.93
5.25	617.70	1,956.25	3,445.16	7,940.88	21,463.05
5.5	618.55	1,964.11	3,468.42	8,052.13	22,115.27
6	620.28	1,979.99	3,515.63	8,281.10	23,496.83
6.5	622.01	1,996.02	3,563.61	8,518.04	24,982.45
7	623.74	2,012.22	3,612.46	8,763.73	26,583.82
7.5	625.48	2,028.60	3,662.20	9,018.48	28,310.47
8	627.23	2,045.16	3,712.83	9,282.67	30,173.06

FIGURE 17-10 This table shows the importance of shopping for the highest interest rates (figures based on a $50 a month deposit, compounded daily).

Other Information

The four factors discussed here are not the only ones that influence savings interest. One bank ad, for instance, contained this statement: "Deposits made by the tenth of the month earn interest from the first. Interest is figured on the low balance per month and there must be a balance at interest-paying days in order to earn interest."

This illustrates only one of the many different methods that savings institutions use to compute interest. If you know the basic principles of figuring interest rates, you should be able to understand and compare the methods used by different institutions.

When shopping around, try to narrow down your choices to a few institutions offering the highest APY. Your best choice will be the institution having the highest APY and the fewest restrictions and penalties.

Following this advice will bring you financial rewards. Why settle for just any institution? It is your money. Study Figures 17-9 and 17-10 to see how different amounts of savings can grow according to different interest rates and time periods.

17-2 Assessment

1. What is meant by the expression "pay yourself first"?
2. There are two reasons to set aside savings. Name them.
3. Describe the two basic types of savings accounts.
4. Name two items APY takes into account.

High Growth Occupations
FOR THE 21ST CENTURY

Postsecondary Teachers

If you like the idea of being part of the educational community and like to teach others and be involved in research, take a look at the occupation of postsecondary teacher. These teachers instruct students in academic and vocational/technical subjects beyond the high school level. They work as college and university faculty and teachers in postsecondary career schools and technical education. Teachers in postsecondary education instruct students who are seeking a college degree or technical certificate, or students who want to improve their knowledge in specific skills.

The majority of postsecondary teachers are college and university faculty members who teach and advise students in both undergraduate and graduate schools. Many faculty members also are involved in research and add significantly to new developments in their fields and in the nation. Faculty members also may consult with governments, business, nonprofit, news, and community organizations as experts in their fields of study.

College and university faculty are organized into departments or divisions, which are based on academic subjects. Faculty members teach several different courses in related areas. For example, a faculty member in the field of humanities might teach a course in fine arts, philosophy, and speech communication. Classes are held on college or university campuses. Increasingly classes are being offered online.

Postsecondary vocational teachers are also known as postsecondary career and technical education teachers. They instruct students in disciplines that do not require a college degree, such as welding, or dental hygiene. Classes are taught in traditional schools, laboratories, and industrial settings. Hands-on education is important with vocational education. Traditional academic subjects may be incorporated into the curriculum.

Four-year colleges and universities require a doctoral degree for full-time faculty positions, but may hire master's degree holders or doctoral candidates for some disciplines or part-time positions. Two-year colleges require a master's degree. Postsecondary vocational schools usually require a bachelor's degree and several years of related work experience.

Golden Pixels LLC/Shutterstock.com

Post secondary teachers teach a wide variety of courses.

INVEST MONEY

OBJECTIVES

- Discuss advantages and disadvantages of investing
- Explain the following types of investments: stocks, mutual funds, bonds, exchange-traded funds, and money market funds

KEY TERMS

- investing
- stock
- broker
- commission
- dividend
- capital gain
- mutual fund
- bond
- exchange-traded fund (ETF)

Career Decisions

You were not looking forward to learning how to budget money, calculate savings account rates, and read about different types of investments. But, you are surprised to discover that it is actually interesting. You have always liked math and using financial software. You haven't made any firm plans for what to do after high school. You are now beginning to wonder about the types of occupations available in the finance area and how much training is required. "I think I should probably explore occupations in the finance career cluster," you think to yourself.

What would **you** *do?*

RichVintage/iStockphoto.com

Why Invest?

Investing is the process of using money not required for personal and family needs to increase overall financial worth. Investing is different from saving in that investing is a long-term financial strategy. Money for investing comes from funds left after meeting basic expenditures and short- and medium-range savings goals.

The investor wants to make as much money as possible. In order to make a lot of money, though, there is usually a risk of losing money. For example, buying stock in a new, unproven company is very risky. High-risk investments, however, can sometimes produce big payoffs. Another option is to buy bonds of a large, financially stable corporation. This type of bond involves a relatively low risk. However, lower-risk investments generally produce smaller profits.

When investing, you must learn to balance risks. Probably the best way to balance risks is to diversify investments. This means to spread out money over several different types of investment options.

Types of Investments

There are five popular types of investments: stocks, mutual funds, bonds, exchange-traded funds, and money market funds.

Stocks

A **stock** is a share of ownership in a company. Buying stock is one of the most popular forms of investment. When you buy stock in a company, you are buying shares of ownership in that company. Stock prices vary from a few dollars a share to a few hundred dollars. Stock may be bought in any number of shares, but hundred-share lots are common.

Stocks are usually bought from individuals or companies called **brokers** that specialize in selling stocks and other financial investments. Stock prices vary from day to day. The purchase price for a stock is the current selling price plus a fee, called a **commission**, charged by the broker. In recent years, many investors have chosen to buy stocks through the Web. Online investors can use full-service brokers that provide a range of services or discount brokers that provide fewer services but charge less. The Web is also a good resource for learning about investing, researching stocks, and checking stock prices.

You can make money on stocks through dividends, capital gains, or both. **Dividends** are profits a company divides among its shareholders. Consider what would happen if you bought stock in a company for $24 a share. If the company paid a $.50 per share dividend each quarter, you would make $2 a year on each share of stock that you owned. You can calculate the return on your investment by dividing the annual dividend for the year by the cost of a share of stock. The dividend return on your investment would be $2 divided by $24, or 8.3 percent.

Capital gain refers to an increase in the value of stock or another asset. It is only realized when the stock is sold. For example, suppose the stock you bought at $24 increased in price to $30 a share and you sold it. Your capital gain would be $6 per share. In this case, your capital gain return on investment would be 25 percent. Your total return on investment can be calculated by adding the $2 share dividend to the $6 capital gain and dividing by the initial cost of the stock. In this instance, $8 divided by $24 results in a total return of 33.3 percent. Be aware, however, that dividends and stock prices can go down. Know also that stock dividends and capital gains are subject to income taxes for the year in which they are earned.

Mutual Funds

Instead of buying individual stocks, you can purchase shares in a mutual fund. A **mutual fund** is an investment company that pools the money of thousands of investors and buys a collection of investments that may include stocks, bonds, and other financial assets. This is called a portfolio. Mutual funds have two advantages. First, they give you diversified investments less expensively than you could purchase them on your own. Second, your investments are professionally managed.

Like profits from stocks, profits from mutual funds can be derived from dividends, capital gains, or both. Any capital gains a fund realizes in selling assets must be distributed to investors. Mutual funds are generally recommended over individual stocks for beginning and small investors.

Workforce Trends

Workplace stress is an ongoing health issue. Studies indicate that three-fourths of workers believe there is more on-the-job stress than a generation ago. A wide range of health effects is attributed to stress, including increased risk of cardiovascular disease, psychological disorders such as depression and burnout, gastrointestinal disorders, and workplace injuries.

Bonds

You have learned that stock represents shares of actual ownership in a company. A **bond** represents a loan to a company or government agency. If a large corporation needs $10 million to expand its plant, there are two options available. One way to raise the money is to sell shares of stock in the company. Another way is to issue bonds. A bond is a pledge to repay the borrowed sum plus a certain amount of interest.

To be more specific, suppose Lunar Manufacturing Company issues $1,000 bonds that pay 6.5 percent interest, with a maturity date (date of repayment) of 2025. If you purchase one of these bonds, Lunar Manufacturing Company will pay you $65 in interest per year until 2025, at which time it will return your $1,000. Depending on the type of bond, interest may be paid periodically or be paid at the date of maturity.

Bonds issued by private companies like Lunar Manufacturing Company are called *corporate bonds*. Government agencies also issue bonds to raise money for roads, schools, sewer systems, and other public needs. Bonds issued by states, cities, counties, and other units of local government are called *municipal bonds*. When the federal government issues bonds, they are known as *government bonds*. The idea behind all bonds is the same. A bond is a certificate that represents a promise to repay a specific borrowed amount in the future and to pay interest.

Bonds can be purchased through the same brokers that sell stocks. Like stocks, bonds are available individually or through mutual funds that specialize in bonds.

Search the Net

Websites such as SmartMoney.com provide valuable information about how to go about investing your money. Access **www.cengage.com/school/working** and click on the link for Chapter 17. Surf the website and read a few articles that draw your attention. Then write a paragraph telling how this website would be valuable to investors.

www.cengage.com/school/working

Exchange-traded Funds

An **exchange-traded fund (ETF)** is a type of financial tool similar to a mutual fund but trades like a stock. What this means is that an ETF represents a collection of stocks like a mutual fund. For example the Standard & Poors 500 ETF holds shares in the 500 largest companies. ETFs offer the advantage of diversification like a mutual fund. There are hundreds of ETFs which allow you to make investments. With an ETF you can buy stocks from large, medium, and small company stocks. You can also use an ETF to purchase domestic bonds, international stocks or bonds, and commodities like gold, silver, and agricultural products.

An ETF is similar to a stock in the sense that you can buy or sell it anytime during the trading day. And, like a stock the share price of an ETF fluctuates throughout the trading day. Mutual funds, on the other hand, can only be bought or sold at the end of the trading day after the mutual fund share price has been determined. ETFs have many advantages and are becoming very popular types of investments. They are generally recommended only for experienced investors who thoroughly understand what they are buying.

Making decisions regarding how to invest your money wisely requires research and careful thought.

Money Market Funds

A *money market fund* is a type of mutual fund that invests in short-term, high-liquidity investments. These might include corporate or U.S. treasury notes (bonds that mature in one to ten years) and certificates of deposit. The objective is usually to earn the highest possible safe interest rate.

The main advantage of money market funds is that they provide a way for small investors to take advantage of the higher interest rates that were once available only to large investors. Most funds require a minimum deposit. However, as little as a few hundred dollars is often sufficient for a beginning investment.

Money market shares can be purchased directly from an investment firm, through a financial institution, or from a broker. The interest rates on these funds go up and down according to the general economy. Money market funds are not insured or guaranteed, but they are regarded as very safe. Shares in these funds can be sold, or redeemed, at any time. Money market funds have some of the same features as savings accounts.

Investment Planning

Investing is part of the overall process of budgeting and saving money. Decide on your personal or family goals and stick to them. Do not get greedy. Stay away from hot tips that promise instant wealth. To avoid losing money, educate yourself about investing, be wary, and research an investment very carefully before investing any money. Financial magazines and newspapers are good resources for researching investments. The Internet is another helpful resource for beginning investors.

17-3 Assessment

1. How is investing different from saving money?
2. Explain the two ways in which you can make money on stocks.
3. Name two advantages of investing in a mutual fund.
4. What is the basic difference between a stock and a bond?
5. Name the type of bond issued by a private company. Name the type issued by a local government.
6. An ETF is similar to both a mutual fund and a stock. Explain what this means.
7. What is the main advantage offered by money market funds?

Focus on Skills for Living

Credit Billing Blues

It is difficult enough to manage a budget without being billed for charges you do not owe. Problems can be taken care of, however, if you know how to use the Fair Credit Billing Act. To be protected under the law, here is what you need to do:

- Write the bank or merchant that extended the credit. A telephone call does not trigger the legal safeguards provided under the act. Your letter must be received within 60 days after the bill containing the error was mailed. Include in the letter your name and account number, the date, the type and dollar amount of the incorrect charge, and why you think there was a mistake.

- Send the letter to the correct place. Do not put your letter in the same envelope as your payment. Your bill will usually explain where you should address inquiries. You may wish to send the letter by certified mail to make sure the creditor receives it.

If you follow this procedure, the creditor is required to acknowledge your letter in writing within 30 days after it is received. The alleged error must be investigated. Within 90 days, the mistake must be corrected, or you must be given an explanation and proof of why the bill is accurate.

If you continue to have problems, you should contact your local or state consumer protection agency. Under the law, the creditor cannot close your account just because you disputed a bill.

THINK CRITICALLY

1. Why do you think the Fair Credit Billing Act does not cover complaints made by telephone?
2. A problem that leads to many billing disputes is identity theft—stealing personal information such as bank account, Social Security, and credit card numbers. How can you protect yourself from identity theft?

AVAVA/Shutterstock.com

Protecting yourself from credit card errors requires that you carefully review financial statements promptly.

Chapter Summary

17-1 Budget Money

A. A good first step in learning how to manage money is to maintain a record of income and expenditures. You can then use the information to develop a budget.

B. A budget is a plan for managing income and expenditures. A budget will help you get the most benefit from your earnings.

C. Realistic goals should be set before you work out the details of your budget. List short-range, medium-range, and long-range goals and use them to plan the budget.

D. Once you have decided on goals, estimate your income and expenditures. Base estimates on actual records. Budgets are usually planned around how often you get paid.

E. A budget consists of three main parts: savings, regular (fixed) expenses, and variable expenses. Items can be added, subtracted, and arranged in the way that works best for you.

F. Following a budget involves allocation of income to various budgeted items. Place most of your paycheck in a checking account. Write checks for larger and regular expenses. Keep the remaining cash on hand for smaller purchases. Keeping accurate records is an important part of maintaining a budget.

G. Do not expect to have a perfect budget the first time you develop one. A budget is something you must keep working and reworking.

17-2 Save Money

A. Savings refers to cash that has been set aside in a bank account. There are two reasons to set aside cash for savings: (1) to have funds for a financial emergency and (2) to achieve financial goals.

B. There are two basic types of savings accounts. Regular, or passbook savings accounts let you make deposits and withdrawals at any time. Time deposits, such as CDs, require you to deposit a lump sum for a fixed period of time in exchange for a higher rate of return. Some accounts offer advantages of both regular savings accounts and time deposits.

C. Interest earned on savings depends on the annual interest rate, frequency of compounding, and when the interest is paid. In comparing savings options, it is useful to know the annual percentage yield (APY). Generally the higher the APY, the better the deal.

17-3 Invest Money

A. Investing is the process of using money not required for personal and family needs to increase overall financial worth. Investing involves the risk of losing money. A good way to balance risks is to diversify investments.

B. There are five popular types of investments. Investing in stocks involves buying shares of ownership in a company. Mutual funds give you diversified investments and professional management. Bonds represent a loan to a company or government agency in return for interest. An exchange-traded fund is similar to a mutual fund but trades like a stock. A money market fund is a type of mutual fund that invests in short-term, high-liquidity investments.

Activities

1. Download a blank copy of the form in Figure 17-1 at www. cengage.com/school/working. Keep records for a week. Then, study them. List at least three things you noticed about your spending. Discuss your findings in class.

2. Think about your financial goals. Write your financial goals for the next year. Then note your financial goals for the next five years. Discuss your goals in class. How do they compare to your classmates' goals? Discuss how your goals might be different if you and your classmates were five years older.

3. Consider a family consisting of a couple and a young child. Assume the family's net monthly income is $3,000. As a group in-class activity, prepare an estimated budget for this family. Download a blank copy of the form in Figure 17-3 at www.cengage.com/school/working.

4. After completing Activity 3, invite a qualified person to class to examine and discuss the budget you have prepared.

5. Assume you deposited $500 in a savings account paying 2 percent annual interest. You do not disturb the money for a year. Interest is compounded quarterly. At the end of the year, how much money is in the account? What is the annual percentage yield? To help solve this problem, access www.cengage.com/school/working and click on the Web Links for Interest Rate Calculator.

6. Assume you bought 100 shares of stock at $25 a share. The stock pays a $.40 dividend each year. How much total dividend do you receive in two years?

7. Describe how you decide to use your earnings. Explain why creating and following a budget can improve your chance of achieving certain goals in your life-span plan.

8. This activity can be completed either with a printed newspaper or by accessing www.cengage.com/school/working and clicking on the Web Links for New York Stock Exchange (NYSE). Select a stock and answer the following questions.

   a. Does the stock pay a dividend? If so, how much, and what is the yield?

   b. How many shares were sold the previous day (newspaper users) or so far today (website users)?

   c. Newspaper users: what were the previous day's high, low, and closing prices, and what was the net change?

   d. Website users: what are today's high, low, and most recent trade prices, and what is the net change over yesterday's close?

9. You have inherited $5,000 from your uncle and are trying to decide how to invest it. You would like to have $10,000 nine years from now to open your own business. Approximately what interest rate will your investment need to earn for you to achieve this goal?

a. allocation
b. annual percentage yield (APY)
c. bond
d. broker
e. budget
f. capital gain
g. certificate of deposit (CD)
h. commission
i. compounding
j. dividend
k. exchange traded fund (ETF)
l. expenditure
m. income
n. investing
o. line item
p. liquidity
q. mutual fund
r. regular expenditure
s. savings
t. stock
u. variable expenditure

Word Power

On a separate sheet of paper, match each definition with the correct term. All definitions will be used, and a definition will be used only once.

10. An increase in the value of a stock or other asset that is only realized when the asset is sold

11. The process of using money not required for personal and family needs to increase overall financial worth

12. In budgeting, those essential monthly payments that are usually the same amount each month

13. A single entry in a budget; a budgeted item

14. In budgeting, day-to-day living expenses

15. Individuals or companies that specialize in selling stocks and other financial investments

16. A fee paid to a broker for purchasing stock for you

17. Money that is spent

18. Shares of ownership in a company

19. The distribution or assignment of something; for example, of income to the various items in a budget

20. Money coming in

21. An investment company that pools the money of thousands of investors and buys a collection of investments that may include stocks, bonds, and other financial assets

22. Cash set aside in a bank account to be used for financial emergencies and goals

23. The quality of being easily converted into cash; refers to assets

24. A certificate that represents a loan to a company or government agency in exchange for a pledge to repay the borrowed sum plus a certain amount of interest

25. Profit that a company divides among its shareholders

26. A popular type of time deposit in which an amount of savings is deposited for a fixed period of time in return for a specified interest rate

27. A process in which interest is earned on both the money put into an account and the interest periodically added to it, causing savings to steadily grow

28. A plan for managing income and expenditures

29. A financial tool that is similar to a mutual fund, but trades like a stock

30. This tells you the actual yearly interest rate per $100 left on deposit by incorporating annual interest rates and the effects of compounding

Think Critically

31. Philanthropy is the act of giving away money. How do you feel about giving money to charity?

32. A big problem for the federal government is staying within a budget. The government routinely spends more than it takes in. (This is called *deficit spending.*) Why do you think this is the case?

33. It is not unusual to read about the financial difficulties of high-paid professional athletes, entertainers, and other famous people. What are some of the problems created by fame and instant wealth?

34. What is the advantage of using payroll deductions to save and invest money? Are payroll savings and investment options available where you work?

35. Have you ever saved money over a long period of time and then used it to buy something? Describe how it made you feel to accomplish a savings goal.

36. There is an old saying that "you shouldn't invest more in stocks than you can afford to lose." How true do you think this statement is?

37. Why did the Patriot Act make it more difficult to open a bank account? How do financial accounts, like savings and checking accounts, affect the efforts of terrorists?

38. The recent recession has helped drive interest rates to extraordinarily low levels. If you manage to save money, how should you decide when to transfer money from a savings account that has very low interest to an investment that yields higher interest?

"Dreams never hurt anybody if you keep working right behind the dreams to make as much of them become real as you can."—FRANK W. WOOLWORTH

Insure Against Loss

Isaiah Shook/Shutterstock.com

PREVIEW

Deciding if you need insurance, evaluating different policies, and comparing costs and coverage can be difficult. This chapter will help answer your questions. The material will deal with the nature of insurance and then discuss the specifics of the four most important kinds of insurance: health, life, home, and auto.

Taking/Action Protect Against Loss

The tornado was only on the ground for two minutes as it moved through the town. But in that brief time, it injured 17 people and caused more than $2 million in property damage.

When he heard the warning sirens, Gary raced to an interior room of his apartment. As he passed a window, a tree branch smashed into it. Some of the flying glass injured Gary's arm. When the tornado had passed, a neighbor drove him to the hospital. Gary presented his insurance card. A few hours later, he left the hospital, having paid $25 for his emergency room visit. If he had had to pay himself, just going to the emergency room would have cost $350, and his treatment would have cost an additional $200.

Success Tip

Make sure to get the insurance coverage you need.

Maria had been at the mall when the tornado hit. She came outside afterwards to discover that her car had been damaged. One fender was badly dented and rubbed on the tire. Maria used her cell phone to call her insurance agent. By the next day, the car had been towed to a repair shop and Maria had gotten a rental car to use while it was being repaired. The bodywork on her car cost $1,800, the tow was $60, and the car rental was $180. After paying the first $350 towards repairs, Maria had no further charges.

Manuel had been at work. He returned to his house to find that the tornado had brought down power lines, which had started a fire. Manuel telephoned his insurance agent. Because there was too much damage for him to stay in his house, Manuel went to a motel. The next day, he met his insurance agent at his home. In a few days, he had a check for the damages.

Manuel chose a contractor that his agent had recommended, and repairs were quickly under way. He used the list of personal property that he had made and went shopping to replace the possessions that had been too damaged to keep. The repairs to Manuel's home took several weeks. During that time, he continued to stay at the motel and to eat at restaurants. Manuel's home insurance paid for everything. The bills amounted to $20,500.

THINK CRITICALLY

1. A tornado is an unlikely event. Should people pay for insurance against things that are not likely to happen? Why or why not?

2. Think of occasions when you or people you know have made insurance claims. What kind of service did you or they get?

Rob Byron/Shutterstock.com

OBJECTIVES
- Explain the basic idea of insurance
- Discuss health insurance, disability insurance, and COBRA
- Explain the Affordable Care Act

KEY TERMS
- risk
- catastrophe
- deductible
- stop-loss provision
- co-payment
- health maintenance organization (HMO)

Jiang Dao Hua/Shutterstock.com

> ## Workplace Decisions
>
> You are employed as a library assistant at a state university. You have received information about a new health insurance plan to be offered to all state employees. Beginning June 1, you will have the choice of continuing with the regular health insurance or switching to the new HMO option. The premium, which is paid mostly by the state, is the same for both plans. You are not sure which plan to select.
>
> **What would you do?**

The Nature of Insurance

Major purchases, such as a home or car, can be very costly. Once you have bought such items, you do not want to lose them. Things do happen, though. Suppose you purchase a new car. A week later, you park in the lot of a local grocery store. When you leave the grocery, the car is gone. The next day, the police call to say your car has been found. Your joy disappears upon learning the car was wrecked badly.

Throughout history, people have used insurance to protect themselves from **risk**, or the chance of a loss. Losses can result from fires, accidents, or other catastrophes. A **catastrophe** is a disaster or misfortune, often one that occurs suddenly. Few people can bear catastrophes without serious hardship.

Catastrophes can affect society as well. For instance, if a person is injured and does not have medical insurance, treatment costs will ultimately be paid by either charity, the government, or passed on to all other consumers of health care. When a building burns and a business is forced into bankruptcy, creditors lose money and employees lose their jobs.

The basic idea of insurance is that a large group of individuals pay money into a common fund. When disaster strikes one member of the group, the pooled funds pay for the loss. Insurance shifts the risk of loss from the individual to the group.

When you buy insurance, you are trading a known expenditure, which is your insurance premium, for protection against the risk of a large, uncertain loss. The kinds of risks against which people seek protection may be grouped in this way:

- **Personal risks**   These are catastrophes affecting individuals. Examples include accident, illness, disability, and unemployment.
- **Property risks**   There is always a possibility that property will be damaged or destroyed. Property losses can result from automobile accidents, natural disasters, fire, and vandalism.
- **Liability risks**   Liability risks are injuries to others or their property that you are responsible for or that occur on your property. Another person may be injured in a car accident you caused. Or a visitor might be hurt in your home.

In addition to providing protection against financial loss, insurance gives people greater peace of mind. Knowing that you have minimized your risks can contribute to your emotional security.

Jaimie Duplass/Shutterstock.com

Accidents that cause injury can happen unexpectedly at any time.

Types of Health Insurance

The purpose of health insurance is to pay expenses resulting from illness or accident. This is probably the most necessary form of insurance because the expenses resulting from illness or accident can be enormous. The costs of minor surgery and several days in a hospital are likely to be several thousand dollars. Fees for major surgery and an extended hospital stay can amount to tens of thousands of dollars.

Jim was painting his house. He fell about 20 feet from a ladder. Jim was badly injured. Over the next five years, he was in the hospital 22 times for surgery and other medical care. His total medical expenses were nearly a million dollars. This is a rare case, but it does show why insurance is so important.

Most people obtain health insurance through some type of group plan. This may be through an employer, union, or professional association. The group policy may only cover the individual enrolled, or it may include dependents as well. Persons not eligible for group coverage may buy individual plans. However, group plans usually provide more coverage and are less expensive than individual plans.

For full-time employees, employers often pay much or most of the cost of health insurance. In recent years, however, many businesses have increased the amount that employees must contribute towards health insurance because of rising premiums. There are two basic types of health insurance plans from which to choose.

Traditional Health Insurance Plans

In traditional health insurance plans, sometimes called fee-for-service plans, an insurance company pays a doctor or hospital for services performed in treating a patient who is ill or injured. Routine office visits are not covered. A **deductible** is the amount of money an insured person must pay on medical expenses before the insurance company begins to pay. A typical plan might have a deductible that requires you to pay the first $100 for a hospital stay and 20 percent of the remaining amount. Many policies contain a **stop-loss provision**, which prevents your out-of-pocket expenses from rising above a certain amount.

There are four kinds of fee-for-service coverages. They are usually sold together in various combinations.

- **Hospital expense**   This coverage provides for hospital charges such as room and meals, operating room use, laboratory fees, and medications. The policy may specify a certain maximum-per-day room charge or may limit the number of days a person may stay in the hospital.

- **Surgical expense**   This covers a wide variety of medical procedures and operations, ranging from using stitches to close a cut to replacing a heart valve. Procedures may be performed on an inpatient or outpatient basis, depending on the procedure. A policy may contain a list of covered surgical procedures and the amount that will be paid for each one.

- **Medical expense**   Medical expense, also known as physician's expense, is usually combined with hospital and surgical insurance. The three together form what is known as basic coverage. Medical expense coverage pays for a doctor's medical visits while a patient is in a hospital. Some policies provide benefits for home and office visits as well.

Communication at Work

GET INFORMATION

You will sometimes need to get information from others in order to make good personal choices. Deciding on a health insurance plan is an example. Suppose you have several plans to choose from. You have carefully read the information about each plan. You have made a checklist to compare the plans. Still, you have questions and need advice.

Find out who can help you. Make up a brief list of specific questions, and contact the person. Organize your list and outline important points. For telephone calls, follow the advice in Chapter 4 on using the telephone.

If you think you can get the information you need over the telephone, begin by explaining the purpose of your call and asking if this is a good time. If it is not, arrange a time that is. Other people are usually glad to give you information if you are considerate of their time.

THINK CRITICALLY

1. What types of people could you call to get information about health insurance?

2. Why should you write a list of questions before calling someone for help?

- **Major medical expense** This type of insurance protects against huge expenses resulting from a serious illness or accident. Covered expenses generally include the same types as those for basic coverage. Major medical contains a co-insurance, or **co-payment**, feature that requires a policyholder to share in the expenses beyond the deductible amount.

One of the most common plans is an 80–20 policy in which the insurance company pays 80 percent and the policyholder takes care of the other 20 percent. In one group plan, for example, the insurance company pays 80 percent of the first $50,000 of covered expenses and 100 percent thereafter, up to a maximum of $500,000.

Health Maintenance Organizations (HMOs)

The **health maintenance organization (HMO)** is an alternative to traditional health insurance. Members in an HMO, or their employers, pay a regular fee as they would for an insurance policy. However, HMOs cover all health care, including regular office visits and checkups as well as treatment for illness and accidents. Members typically pay a small co-payment for services and prescriptions. An office visit, for example, might cost $20.

Unlike traditional health insurance plans, HMOs do not require patients to fill out insurance forms for payments to be made. All paperwork is handled through the HMO.

HMOs often require members to choose a primary care physician. This doctor provides most of the person's medical care and makes referrals to specialists when needed. Usually, the HMO has a list of doctors from which members must choose.

Which Plan to Choose?

Individual plans can vary widely, so carefully read the information for the plans you are considering. It is a good idea to make a list of items that are important to you. For example, do you have a particular doctor that you like to see? What medical needs do you anticipate? Do you have a spouse and children who will need to be covered on your plan? How much will each plan cost, both in premiums and in out-of-pocket expenses?

Make sure the plan you choose has a stop-loss provision. Both traditional health insurance plans and HMOs may include this coverage.

Both types of plans have advantages and disadvantages. Traditional plans let you choose doctors. With most HMOs, you must choose a doctor that is on the plan. HMOs cover preventative services like checkups and immunizations. Traditional plans usually do not. Fee-for-service plans require a deductible before paying benefits, and you may have to file your own claim forms.

Some hybrid plans are available. A *Point of Service Plan (POS)* is an HMO type plan that gives you more personal choices. With a POS plan you can select health care services without getting a referral from your primary care physician. A *Preferred Provider Organization (PPO)* negotiates lower rates with a network of health care providers. With a PPO, you can either choose a provider within the network or outside of the network. With either of these options, when you stay in network, your fees are less

A single fall can cause severe injuries.

than if you go out of network. The details of each plan will vary. It is important to thoroughly understand the coverage provided by your plan.

Disability Coverage

Paying benefits to someone unable to work because of illness or injury is the purpose of *disability insurance*. This coverage is sometimes called loss-of-income insurance. Disability coverage is not usually part of traditional health insurance or HMOs. You must purchase it separately. A typical policy may pay between 50 and 75 percent of the worker's normal earnings for a specified period.

Helen was in a hurry to get to work and failed to notice that a light rain had fallen and then frozen during the night. As she stepped from her covered porch onto the sidewalk, she slipped and fell. She cried out in pain. A neighbor who was leaving for work at the same time saw her fall. He ran to help her and called an ambulance. Helen's injury was diagnosed as a broken hip. Surgery was required, followed by a long period of rest and physical therapy. It was six months before Helen was able to return to work. Fortunately, her disability insurance policy provided her with income while she could not work. Without the disability policy, she would have had to dip into her retirement savings.

Disability insurance is an important type of coverage for workers to consider. It may not be as important for people already covered by such benefits as paid sick leave, workers' compensation, and Social Security.

What is COBRA?

In 1986, Congress passed the Consolidated Omnibus Budget Reconciliation Act, also known as *COBRA*. COBRA is designed to help bridge the gap between using employer-provided health insurance and using health insurance purchased directly by you from an insurance provider. For example, what happens if you are working for a company that provides you with health insurance and you are laid off and lose your health insurance? In this instance, COBRA may be an option for continuing your health care coverage.

A company with 20 or more employees is required by law to inform laid off workers in writing about their rights under COBRA. The law gives workers the right to purchase health insurance coverage from their former employer at the previous group rate. The laid off worker, however, must pay 100 percent of the premium.

COBRA provides individuals and families an option to continue coverage that they might not be able to obtain because of preexisting conditions. But the reality is that most individuals who are out of work cannot afford the cost. However, as a result of recent legislation discussed in the following section, all individuals will have the option of purchasing more affordable coverage at new "health insurance exchanges" beginning in 2014.

The Affordable Care Act

On March 23, 2010, President Obama signed the Affordable Care Act. This is a comprehensive health insurance reform law that will affect every American. Some reforms started immediately, with most reforms taking place over four years and beyond. So important is this new law, that you owe it to yourself to become fully informed about its contents. A website has been set up at www.healthcare.gov to explain the legislation and keep everyone informed regarding new developments.

One section of the website is addressed to "Young Adults." According to the website, here are the "Top 5 Things to Know" for individuals age 18–25.

- You can continue to be insured as a dependent on your parent's health insurance plan until age 26.
- New health plans must now cover certain preventive services without cost sharing.
- Starting in 2014, if you're unemployed with limited income up to about $15,000 per year for a single person, you may be eligible for health coverage through Medicaid.
- Starting in 2014, if your employer doesn't offer insurance, you will be able to buy insurance directly in an *Exchange*. An Exchange is a new competitive insurance marketplace where individuals and small businesses can buy affordable health insurance plans.
- Starting in 2014, if your income is less than the equivalent of about $43,000 for a single individual and your job doesn't offer affordable coverage, you may get a tax credit to help pay for insurance.

These are only five of many important parts of the Affordable Care Act that you may need to know about. Visit the HealthCare.gov website often to learn and stay informed. Be aware that Congress and/or the Supreme Court can change or eliminate some or all parts of this legislation.

Workforce Trends

When workers do not get enough sleep, productivity goes down. Nearly one third of American employees admit that being sleepy during the workday keeps them from performing at their peak during work. Reasons that workers may not get enough sleep include work demands that occur 24/7. Although technology provides workers with flexibility, it can also make it hard for a worker to stop working while at home. One study estimated that lost productivity due to tired workers ranges from about $2,500 to $3,100 per employee.

18-1 Assessment

1. Explain how insurance shifts the risk of loss from the individual to the group.

2. Insurance protects against three kinds of risks. Name them.

3. What is meant by basic health insurance coverage? What is major medical coverage?

4. Which individuals are most in need of disability coverage?

5. What is the purpose of COBRA? Explain the primary disadvantage of COBRA.

6. When you graduate from high school, and if you go on to college or a job, can you be covered by your parent's health insurance policy?

OBJECTIVES

- Discuss the advantages and disadvantages of term and cash-value life insurance
- Outline different characteristics of homeowner's insurance

KEY TERMS

- face value
- premium
- beneficiary
- homeowner's insurance
- peril
- liability

michaeljung/Shutterstock.com

> ## Personal Decisions
>
> You just moved into an apartment with two friends. One of your room-mates asks if you have purchased renter's insurance. You laugh and say that you do not have enough possessions to worry about insurance.
>
> "You would be surprised," says your roommate. "It would cost quite a bit of money to replace everything in this room."
>
> "I will think about it," you say. "But I cannot afford insurance for a couple of months."
>
> **What would you do?**

Life Insurance

Life insurance involves a contract written between an insurance company and a policyholder. The document specifies an amount of money, or **face value**, to be paid in the event of the policyholder's death. The **premium** is the price of the policy. The **beneficiary** is the person to whom the death benefits are to be paid. Sometimes there are multiple beneficiaries for a single policy. For example, a parent with grown children may name each of the adult children as a beneficiary of the policy. The policy's face value, premium, and beneficiaries are all listed within the policy. The main purpose of life insurance is to provide financial security for dependents after the insured's death.

Individuals differ in terms of their need for life insurance. A young, single person without dependents, for example, has little need for life insurance. All that may be required is a small policy to pay funeral expenses and to cover outstanding debts.

People with children have the greatest need for life insurance. If the wage earner or earners should die, the family would need an income to pay daily living expenses. Insurance would help a family member or friend raise surviving children and perhaps provide them with higher education. Even a person not working outside the home should be insured to cover added expenses in the event of death.

As with health insurance, both group and individual life insurance policies are available. Many employers offer some free life insurance to their employees. Most life insurance, though, is in the form of individual policies. The two basic types of life insurance are term and cash value.

It is important to carefully consider what type of insurance coverage to purchase.

Term Insurance

Term insurance is often called pure insurance because it provides protection only. The policy has no cash value or loan value. People buy term insurance for a specified period of time. Under term insurance, you pay as long as you need the coverage. Then you drop the policy or it terminates automatically. For example, you might purchase a 25-year policy to provide protection while you are making big house payments and your children are growing up.

As you grow older, the likelihood of your dying increases. This is why term insurance premiums increase as you age. Premiums are low at first and then increase steadily throughout the course of your life. By the time you reach age 60, you may be paying 15 times what the same amount of protection cost you at age 18.

In this example, the face value of the policy remains steady and the premium increases yearly. Such insurance is called *level term*. Another type, called *decreasing term* insurance, works differently. The premium remains steady, but the face value decreases yearly. In Year 1, for example, your policy might have a face value of $50,000. In Year 2, it might drop to $48,000; in Year 3, to $46,000; and so on.

Cash-value Insurance

Under *cash-value insurance*, protection is teamed with gradual buildup of a savings account. Cash-value insurance is also called permanent insurance because when the policy is paid up after a certain number of years, the policyholder owns the insurance. For example, if you purchase a plan called "Life Paid-Up at 65," you pay premiums until you are 65. At that point, you have a permanent policy that will pay the face value upon your death. Other names for cash-value insurance are whole, ordinary, and straight life insurance.

The premium and the face value for cash-value insurance remain the same each year. You pay the same premiums for as long as you live. Or you can purchase plans that are paid up in 20 or 30 years. A portion of the premium is set aside and accumulates in a type of savings account. The interest rate, however, is usually less than for other forms of savings. If the policy is dropped, the cash value is returned to the policyholder.

Which Type to Buy?

There are advantages and disadvantages to both types of insurance. The primary advantage of term insurance is that it is less expensive. But with cash-value insurance, you have protection combined with savings.

Most experts on the subject who do not work for insurance companies seem to agree that term insurance is the better value. They point out that the main purpose of life insurance is protection. About the only way young people can realistically afford the amount of insurance necessary to protect their families is to purchase term insurance. You may want to buy term insurance and save the difference between that and cash-value insurance. Later, you may want to consider cash-value insurance as part of an overall life insurance program. Do not purchase a big policy with a large premium at a time when you can least afford it.

How Much Will You Need?

The amount of life insurance coverage you should purchase depends on your personal situation and what you want to protect. The needs of a young, single person are very different from those of someone with a family or a middle-aged couple who have their home paid for and their children raised. Some insurance agents provide the general guideline that you need insurance equal to about four to eight times your annual income.

Unexpected natural disasters, like flooding, can make homes uninhabitable.

Rufous/Shutterstock.com

Homeowner's Insurance

For most people, a home is the largest expenditure in their budget. In addition to the home itself, household furnishings and personal belongings represent a sizable investment. For this reason, it is very important to protect a home and the contents against damage or loss. **Homeowner's insurance** provides coverages for perils and liabilities for people who own or rent a home. A **peril** is a possible damage against which a house is insured. The basis for all homeowner's insurance policies is coverage against the various damages or perils shown in Figure 18-1 on the next page.

Another important feature of homeowner's insurance policies is the provision for living expenses. For example, the Alfanos' home was damaged by a storm and they could not live in it. The insurance company paid for the family's lodgings, meals, and related expenses elsewhere, until the house was livable again.

Liability coverage is another important part of homeowner's insurance policies. **Liability** refers to legal responsibility for something, such as damages or costs. The most important type of liability coverage is personal liability, which protects you against a claim or lawsuit resulting from an accident or injury occurring on your property. The same coverage will also protect you if someone in your family causes an injury away from home.

You may purchase various kinds of homeowner's insurance, depending on the type of coverage desired and whether you live in a house, apartment, condominium, or other dwelling.

Rebekah and Koby were newlyweds who had just moved into their first apartment. They were awakened one night by a fire alarm. They got up quickly, threw on coats, grabbed the puppy, and fled the apartment. As they raced down the back exit, they heard the siren of a fire truck. The fire was on the floor above theirs.

The fire company put out the blaze in a few minutes. It was not a serious fire, but there was a lot of smoke and water damage. All of Rebekah's and Koby's clothes and upholstered furniture was ruined.

The next day, the couple went to the apartment manager's office to find out about getting their clothes and furniture replaced. The manager told them that his insurance only covered damage to the building. Apartment tenants should carry insurance on their personal property. Rebekah and Koby were upset. They had assumed that the building owner carried insurance that also covered their property. They should have had a renter's policy. The fire was a costly lesson for Rebekah and Koby on the need to understand homeowner's insurance.

1. Lightning or fire
2. Property loss due to perils including fire
3. Automobiles
4. Hail or windstorm
5. Explosions
6. Theft
7. Smoke
8. Broken glass that is part of a building's structure
9. Airplanes
10. Riots
11. Vandalism
12. Objects that fall
13. Power surges and other damage resulting from electrical malfunctions
14. Ice, sleet, or snow that causes damage due to it's weight
15. Frozen pipes and appliances
16. Buildings that collapse
17. Fluids that accidentally leak from pipes or appliances
18. Physical breakdown of heating or steaming systems
19. Perils except for nuclear accident, earthquake, flood, and war. (These exclusions vary by policy.)
20. Antiques, jewelry, and art, as well as coverage for sewer back up, can be added to a policy for an additional fee.

FIGURE 18-1 A basic homeowner's insurance policy provides protection against these types of disasters.

18-2 Assessment

1. **Describe an advantage and a disadvantage of term and cash-value insurance.**

2. **Which type of term insurance has the same face value throughout the life of the policy?**

3. **What four things are usually covered by homeowner's insurance?**

4. **What is the purpose of renter's insurance?**

High Growth Occupations
FOR THE 21ST CENTURY

Physical Therapist Assistants and Aides

 **Health Science** Do you like working with people? Do you want to help people improve their quality of life? You might find the occupation of *physical therapist assistant* or *physical therapist aide* is a good fit for you. Both assistants and aides support the physical therapist in a variety of tasks that aid in the treatment of patients.

Treatment and services provided by a *physical therapist* may include helping patients who have injuries from an accident, relieving patients' pain, and preventing or limiting permanent physical disabilities of patients who suffer from injuries or disease. Patients may include individuals injured in accidents and individuals with cerebral palsy. They also include individuals with disabling conditions such as lower back pain, arthritis, heart disease, fractures, and head injuries.

Responsibilities for *physical therapist assistants* may include assisting patients with exercise, or performing massage, electrical stimulation, paraffin baths, hot and cold packs, traction, or ultrasound treatments. All treatments performed by assistants are under the direction of the physical therapist. Assistants also record how the patient responds to, and the outcome of, treatments. *Physical therapist aides* also work under the direction of a physical therapist. Responsibilities may include keeping the treatment area clean and organized. Aides prepare the treatment area for each patient and help patients move from one treatment area to another, either by pushing a patient's wheelchair, or by lending a shoulder for the patient to lean on. Duties also include clerical tasks, such as ordering supplies, answering the phone, or filling out insurance forms and other paperwork. *Physical therapist assistants* usually require state licensing. Programs offering certification are available through community colleges or private schools. *Physical therapist aides* do not require licensing. They receive on-the-job-training. About two-thirds of the assistants and aides work in hospitals or private medical offices. Others work in nursing and personal-care facilities, out-patient rehabilitation centers, offices and clinics of physicians, and home health agencies.

monkeybusinessimages/iStockphoto.com

Physical therapists help patients regain strength and relearn physical skills.

AUTO INSURANCE

OBJECTIVES

- **Name and describe the six types of auto insurance coverage**
- **Identify factors that influence the cost of auto insurance**
- **Explain no-fault insurance**

KEY TERMS

- auto insurance
- no-fault insurance

Ethical Decisions

You just bought your first used car that you will use to commute to Northwest Community College. Your auto insurance estimate may cause you to reevaluate your plans. Your friend Dan said that he has his car titled and insured in the name of his brother. "The cost is about half of what I would pay on my own," Dan explained. "You ought to do the same thing."

What would you do?

ftwitty/iStockphoto.com

Types of Coverage

The topic of auto insurance is very important to young people. Unfortunately, they are the ones who most need it. According to the National Safety Council, drivers under age 25 account for about 13 percent of all licensed drivers, but are involved in about 27 percent of all auto accidents.

Everyone who drives a motor vehicle is responsible for operating it safely and paying for any damage the vehicle might cause. All states now have what are called financial responsibility laws that require drivers to pay for damages they cause to people or property. Rather than risk having to come up with thousands of dollars as a result of an accident, most people buy insurance to show proof of financial responsibility. About half of the states have laws specifically requiring registered automobile owners to have liability insurance of some kind.

Auto insurance provides liability and other coverages for the operation of a motor vehicle. An auto policy may provide six basic types of coverage:

- **Bodily injury liability**   This coverage applies if you kill or injure someone in an accident in which you are at fault. The person may be a pedestrian, a rider in your car, or someone in another car. The policy covers bodily injury expenses and claims, including your legal expenses if you are sued.

- **Property damage liability**   What if you damage another person's car or property? This type of insurance won't pay for repairs to your car, but it will cover repairs to the other person's car or

Inattentive drivers cause many accidents.

property. Property damage liability also pays for legal expenses should you be taken to court.

- **Protection against uninsured motorists** This coverage applies to bodily injuries that you may suffer as a result of a hit-and-run accident. The policy also covers you in the event of an accident in which the other driver does not have insurance.

Shriram was sitting in his car at a stoplight waiting for the light to change. Suddenly, a car from the next lane smashed into him. The other driver was adjusting the radio and not paying attention. Shriram's car was badly damaged. The police came and filled out an accident report. They gave Andy, the other driver, a traffic citation for reckless driving. Shriram and Andy exchanged information regarding addresses, phone numbers, and emails. Andy said that he could not remember the name of his insurance company but that he would call Shriram later with the information. The call never came.

In the meantime, Shriram contacted his insurance company. The representative he spoke to told him to have his car fixed. His insurance company would collect from Andy's. As it turned out, Andy lacked auto insurance. However, since Shriram was covered by uninsured motorists protection, his insurance company paid for the car repairs.

Andy was found to be in violation of the state financial responsibility law. His driver's license and automobile registration were revoked. In order to get them back, Andy will have to pay Shriram's insurance company the $2,200 it cost to repair Shriram's car.

- **Medical payments** Under this coverage, your insurance company agrees to pay medical expenses resulting from accidental injury. This insurance covers you and family members whether injured in your car or someone else's. It also applies if you are struck by a car. Payment is made regardless of who is at fault.

- **Auto collision** Your car is covered by this type of insurance. The insurance company will pay to have your car repaired or replaced regardless of who is at fault. Collision insurance does not cover repairs that cost more than the actual cash value of the car. Collision is the most expensive form of coverage. Most collision insurance is sold with a deductible, usually $200 or $250.

- **Auto comprehensive** This coverage protects your car against loss from theft, vandalism, fire, and other perils. If your car is damaged in an accident, collision, not comprehensive, will cover it.

The Cost of Auto Insurance

Basic rates for automobile insurance vary from area to area. Each state is divided into rating territories that indicate the losses paid in various parts of the state. The price of insurance is set based on the loss experience of the rating territory. This means rates in an area having heavy losses will be higher than those in places where losses are not so great.

Many other factors influence the price of insurance. These include the year, make, and model of the car. The sex, age, marital status, and driving record of the driver are also factors. In addition, driving a car a long distance every day will raise premiums. Even though you cannot do much about influencing basic insurance rates, you do have some control over the final cost.

Many states have set minimum amounts of insurance that you must purchase. It is important to know that these minimums would not come near covering the costs of a serious accident. For liability and uninsured motorists coverage, many experts recommend buying significantly more than the minimum state coverages. Buying more insurance is less expensive than you might think. The more you buy, the less you have to pay for the amount of coverage you get.

In considering medical payments coverage, check carefully to see whether it would duplicate coverage that you already have under your medical insurance.

Whether you purchase collision or comprehensive depends on how much your auto is worth. It would be foolish to have collision on an old car worth only a few hundred dollars. You can also reduce the cost of car insurance by choosing higher deductibles in these categories. For example, raising the deductible on collision or comprehensive coverage from $100 to $250 can save you about 20 percent.

Shop around for insurance coverage and compare rates. Premiums can vary by hundreds of dollars. You can save money by having a parent add you to his or her policy and by not being the principal driver of the car. You may also pay less if you spend part of the year away at school without a car.

Be sure to ask whether the company offers any discounts that might apply to you. Many insurance companies offer discounts to drivers who complete an approved driver's education course. Good grades entitle you to a discount from most insurance companies. Some give discounts for safe driving over a period of years. If your car has automatic seatbelts and airbags, if you carpool, and even if you don't smoke, you may be able to save money on coverage.

More important than price is the quality of service the company provides. You can find reviews of insurance companies at a library or on the Internet. Word of mouth is another good way to find out about insurers.

Motorcycle insurance is similar in coverage to that for cars. If you know the basics of auto insurance, you should have no trouble understanding policies covering motorcycles.

Search the Net

Access **www.cengage.com/school/ working** and click on the link for Chapter 18. According to this web page, what are the five distinct parts of a personal auto policy? Why is it important to read and understand your auto insurance policy?

www.cengage.com/school/working

No-fault Insurance

A problem for insurance companies is determining who is at fault in an accident. This process often requires the service of lawyers. It may lead to long delays in having bills paid and vehicles repaired, as well as expensive legal fees. Courts award generous compensation to some victims. Others receive little or nothing.

Workplace Innovations

GEOSPATIAL TECHNOLOGY

You have probably used a Global Positioning System (GPS) in your vehicle or on your smart phone to help you find the route to a desired location. GPS and several related technologies are becoming widely used in agriculture, natural resource management, environmental science, and other industries.

Geospatial technology (GS) is a broad phrase used to describe a combination of GPS, Geographical Information System (GIS), remote sensing, field sensors and specialized software to collect, map, manipulate, and display all forms of geographic information. One application of GS is "precision farming."

Farmers use fertilizer, herbicide, and pesticide spreaders to uniformly apply such materials over an entire field. Now, using GS, a farmer can turn on a GPS monitor to pinpoint his exact location. He can press a button to display a series of GIS maps that can identify soil fertility and weed, insect, and disease problems. He uploads these data into an onboard machine that automatically regulates the application of fertilizer and chemicals to a precise location. Some areas of the field get more, some less.

There are many additional uses for GS technology including mapping the best locations for wind farms, monitoring plant inventories at nurseries, and studying urban growth to evaluate environmental impacts. GS is being used in the study and implementation of how to capture carbon dioxide and improve air quality.

NET FOLLOW-UP

Use a search engine to explore the Web for additional information on the topic of "geospatial technology" or "precision farming."

In order to reduce time and costs and provide fair settlements to victims, twelve states have developed **no-fault insurance**. Under the no-fault system, each person's losses and expenses are paid for by his or her insurance company regardless of who caused the accident. Lawsuits are permitted only under certain conditions.

No one enjoys paying insurance premiums, especially for something that you do not see or may never use. Do not be tempted to take a chance and go without insurance. You only have to have one big loss to realize why it is so important to have insurance protection.

18-3 Assessment

1. What percentage of auto accidents is caused by drivers under the age of 25?
2. Name four factors that influence the cost of auto insurance.
3. What factor should you consider in deciding whether to purchase collision or comprehensive auto insurance?
4. Explain the idea underlying no-fault auto insurance.

Focus on Health and Safety

Medical Urgent Care and Convenient Care Clinics

What would you do if you severely cut yourself while slicing vegetables or if you woke up on a Sunday morning with a bad earache and high fever? You would probably head for the emergency room of the nearest hospital. There is, however, another option. It is called the *urgent care* or *walk-in medical clinic*.

These health clinics are one of the choices in medical care. Thousands of them are available across the country. Regional and nationwide chains exist just like fast-food restaurants. They are legitimate medical facilities staffed by licensed doctors and other professional personnel. They provide competition and are changing the way decisions are made about medical treatment.

The clinics take patients without appointments. They are often open 12 to 16 hours a day, seven days a week. Some clinics remain open 24 hours a day. They can treat most typical illnesses or accidents. But they do not do major surgery or handle serious emergencies like auto accidents. Fees for a normal visit are the same as or slightly less than those for a regular doctor. For emergency services, however, clinics can cost substantially less. Treatment of a cut requiring stitches, for example, can be a third to a half of what is charged by a hospital emergency room. Health insurance usually covers such emergency treatment.

A similar health care option is *convenient care clinics* located in retail stores. The three largest providers are CVS, Walgreens, and Target. Clinics at these facilities offer a variety of services ranging from allergy care to flu shots to school physicals. A major difference between urgent care and convenient care clinics is that the latter are usually staffed by nurse practitioners or physician assistants rather than physicians. These facilities allow consumers the opportunity to take care of some routine medical needs conveniently.

Cost and convenience, however, are not the whole story. In today's mobile society, many people do not have a regular physician. When they need a doctor, walk-in clinics can provide that service.

THINK CRITICALLY

1. What are some reasons that walk-in clinics are so popular?
2. List several possible disadvantages of using walk-in clinics for health care.

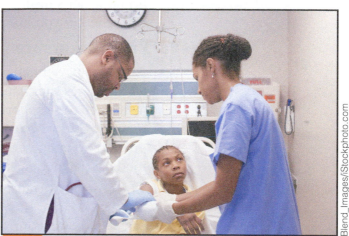

Patients need access to medical care at whatever time of day or night, including holidays, that injuries or illness occurs.

Chapter Summary

18-1 Health Insurance

A. Insurance shifts the risk of loss from the individual to the group. The basic idea of insurance is that a large group of individuals pay a yearly premium that goes into a common fund. When disaster strikes one member of the group, the pooled funds pay for the loss.

B. The purpose of health insurance is to pay expenses resulting from illness or accident. There are two basic types of health insurance plans: traditional or fee-for-service plans and HMOs.

C. Disability insurance is usually sold separately. It provides income to people who are unable to work because of illness or injury.

D. COBRA is the name of a law that gives laid-off workers the right to purchase health insurance from their previous employer at group rates.

E. The Affordable Care Act passed in 2010 is a comprehensive health insurance reform law that has the potential to expand affordable health insurance coverage to millions of Americans.

18-2 Life and Home Insurance

A. The main purpose of life insurance is to provide financial security for dependents after the insured's death. The two basic types of life insurance are term and cash value. The amount of life insurance coverage you need depends on your personal situation and what you want to protect.

B. For most people, a home and its contents are their most valuable investment. For this reason, it is very important to protect a home and its contents against damage or loss. There are various kinds of homeowner's insurance, depending on the type of coverage desired and whether you live in a house, apartment, or other dwelling.

18-3 Auto Insurance

A. All states have financial responsibility laws requiring drivers to pay for damages they cause to people or property. Most people buy insurance to show proof of financial responsibility. An auto policy may provide six basic types of coverage: bodily injury liability, property damage liability, protection against uninsured motorists, medical payments, auto collision, and auto comprehensive.

B. The cost of auto insurance varies from one geographic area to another. Many other factors influence the price of insurance. You can have some control over the final cost of insurance by purchasing sensible limits for the different types of coverage, comparing rates, and asking about discounts.

C. Twelve states have no-fault auto insurance that pays for losses and expenses regardless of who caused the accident.

Activities

1. Mrs. Owen has just recovered from an illness. Her hospital stay resulted in a bill of $12,340. She has health insurance that contains the following provisions:
   - $100 deductible for each hospital visit
   - Co-insurance in which the plan pays 80 percent of the next $5,000 and 100 percent of the costs thereafter

   How much of the bill does Mrs. Owen have to pay?

2. As a class, obtain a policy or descriptive information about disability insurance. What types of illnesses and injury does the insurance cover? How much will the policy provide? What is the cost of the policy?

3. There are many online sources available to help you learn about insurance. Access www.cengage.com/school/working and click on the link for Chapter 18. Then click on the Web Links for the following.

   a. **Insurance Needs for Young Adults** Watch the video that addresses the insurance needs of young adults. What did you learn from watching the video that is the most meaningful in your situation?

   b. **Graduated Driver Licensing** Most states now have some form of Graduated Driver Licensing (GDL) which has been found to be effective in reducing auto accidents and helping to hold down the cost of auto insurance. Find out the requirements in your state and in other states. Discuss the benefits of the GDL program, even though some teens may not like it.

   c. **Auto Insurance Cost** There are 18 different factors that may affect the cost of your auto insurance. Find out what they are. Your instructor may assign different members of the class a topic to explore and provide an oral summary to the class.

4. As a class, obtain cost estimates on three different life insurance policies with a $50,000 face value of the following types:
   a. 5-year renewable level-term plan
   b. 30-year decreasing term plan
   c. 30-year cash-value plan

   What is the annual cost for each plan at ages 20, 30, 40, and 50? What is the average yearly cost for insurance over the 30-year period? Is this a fair way to compare the cost of life insurance? What other factors (if any) need to be taken into consideration?

5. Obtain a policy or descriptive information about renter's insurance. What does the policy cover? How much is the annual premium? Does a young person moving into an apartment for the first time need such insurance? Why or why not?

6. Learn your state's requirements for auto insurance coverage. You can call the department of motor vehicles or, in many states, visit its website. Also find out whether no-fault insurance is available in your state.

7. Consider goals you might set in your life-span plan. Explain how health insurance can improve the likelihood of your achieving these goals.

Word Power

On a separate sheet of paper, match each definition with the correct term. All definitions will be used, and a definition will be used only once.

a. auto insurance
b. beneficiary
c. catastrophe
d. co-payment
e. deductible
f. face value
g. health maintenance organization (HMO)
h. homeowner's insurance
i. liability
j. no-fault insurance
k. peril
l. premium
m. risk
n. stop-loss provision

8. A provision of health insurance in which the insured person is required to share in the expenses of health care

9. A type of insurance in which all health care is provided for a fixed fee

10. For life insurance, the person to whom the death benefits from a policy are to be paid

11. A condition of health insurance that limits the amount of the bill for which the insured person is responsible

12. For insurance, the cost of a policy

13. Regarding life insurance, the amount of money that is paid in the event of the insured's death

14. The chance of a loss; for example, an accident

15. For home insurance, the possible damages from which one seeks protection through the purchase of insurance

16. In traditional health insurance, a certain initial amount that the insured person is required to pay before the insurance company pays the balance

17. Legal responsibility for something, such as damages or costs

18. A disaster or misfortune, often occurring suddenly

19. Provides liability and other coverages for the operation of a motor vehicle

20. Each party in the accident has losses and expenses paid for by his or her insurance company regardless of who caused the accident

21. Provides coverages for perils and liability for people who own or rent a home

Think Critically

22. Hospitals have traditionally been operated as nonprofit community agencies. More and more hospitals and clinics are now being operated as private businesses. Why have these changes occurred? What is your opinion of health providers becoming businesses operated for profit?

23. People differ in terms of their need for life insurance. Identify and discuss family situations in which there is a great need for life insurance.

24. Home insurance perils are related to where you live. Identify and discuss different perils that are more common in one part of the country than another.

25. Under the Affordable Care Act, starting in 2014, most individuals who can afford it will be required to obtain basic health insurance coverage. The Supreme Court is likely to rule on whether this is constitutional. This so-called "individual mandate" has a number of supporters and opponents. Find out the current status of this health care requirement and discuss your thoughts in class.

26. Some primary care physicians charge an annual fee to be part of their practice. What is included in this fee may vary from one physician to another. Typical services that are included are: getting questions answered over the phone, getting prescription refills, and getting priority when scheduling an appointment. Doctors say they have resorted to this annual fee to help offset their losses due to lower insurance reimbursement rates. Do you think this system is fair to patients? Why or why not?

27. During an auto accident, motorcycle drivers are more likely to incur serious injuries than someone driving a car in a similar type of accident. Do you think motorcyclists should pay a proportionally higher rate of insurance because of this? Why or why not?

28. Insurance funds come from the pool of policy holders who pay into the fund. Claims against the fund result in money being paid out of the fund. The insurer needs the amount of money coming into the pool to exceed the amount of money leaving the pool in order to be profitable. Therefore, if a policyholder engages in risky behavior that results in a claim, all of the policyholders are affected by their behavior. (Because if the pool of money is lowered due to excessive claims, insurers will raise the rates for all policyholders.) Do you think it is all right for laws to be in place to require drivers to behave responsibly? Do you think it is all right for motorcycle riders to be required to wear helmets? Are enforced seat belt laws all right? What other reasons, besides insurance costs, might there be to pass vehicle safety laws?

Career Transitions Connection

Insurance Appraisers

Beginning with *Browse Career Paths*, a series of consecutive clicks will be required. Click *Finance*, then *Insurance*, then *Insurance Appraisers*, *Auto Damage*, then *Career Videos*. Watch the *Career Overview* video. Whose interests do insurance appraisers represent? If you are involved in an auto accident, what steps should you take to make sure your settlement is sufficient to meet all the expenses that arise from the accident? Are these steps the same whether you caused the accident or if another person caused the accident?

"I find that the harder I work, the more luck I seem to have."—THOMAS JEFFERSON

Taxes, Taxation, and Retirement Planning

Garry L./Shutterstock.com

19-1 Taxation

19-2 File an Income Tax Return

19-3 Social Security

19-4 Individual Retirement Accounts

PREVIEW

As you begin work, you will need to pay income taxes and file an income tax return. This chapter will help you to understand more about the purpose of taxes, the different types of taxes, and what taxes you can expect to pay. You will also learn about Social Security, which is a broad state and federal effort consisting of various types of social programs. Finally, you will be introduced to individual retirement accounts and learn the importance of investing money for your later retirement years.

Taking/*Action* Understand Taxes

Jack Pate had just completed two weeks on his new job. He could hardly wait to get his first paycheck. His supervisor handed him the check as he was leaving on Friday afternoon. He took the paycheck and put it into his jacket pocket, not wanting to appear too excited.

After he got on the bus headed for home, Jack unfolded the paycheck and looked at it. He was disappointed. He had known that deductions would be taken from his paycheck. But he had not realized the amount would be so large.

When he got home, Jack asked his mother why he had to pay taxes. "After all," he said, "I don't make very much money." Jack's mother explained how every citizen is expected to pay part of the cost of government. Mrs. Pate also explained the types of taxes and Jack's future need to file an income tax return.

That night, Jack went to dinner with his older sister, Emily, who worked as a camera operator at a television station downtown. She asked a lot of questions about his new job. Jack answered her questions. Then he told Emily how he had felt about getting his first paycheck.

"I know," Emily said. "I felt that way, too. But I don't mind the amount of taxes I have to pay, really. I pay more than you do because I earn more. But that doesn't bother me. It seems to me that if you earn more than somebody else, you should pay more taxes. And if you think about it, we get a lot of services for the money we pay."

"I'll have to file an income tax return next year," Jack thought . "Is it as hard as everybody says?"

"I never bother with it," she replied. "I have a tax preparer do it for me. I have dividends and capital gains income from stock I invest in through work. I also deduct interest I pay on my student loan. Every year I kick myself for spending the money on a tax preparer—but you know how bad I am at organizing! Not like you." She smiled.

"Maybe when you get yours done next year, you can help me do mine!"

THINK CRITICALLY

1. What sorts of services do people get for their tax money?

2. What other taxes do taxpayers pay besides income taxes?

Mark Stout Photography/Shutterstock.com

OBJECTIVES

- Explain the purpose of taxes
- Identify and explain the major types of taxes
- Illustrate the difference between a graduated tax and a flat tax

KEY TERMS

- taxation
- tax
- revenue

Workplace Decisions

You are working about 15 hours a week as part of a work experience program. In looking over your pay statement, you find that money has been withheld for federal and state income taxes. You try to think back to when you filled out Form W-4, the Employee Withholding Allowance Certificate. You think that you claimed exemption from withholding because you did not expect to owe any taxes this year. Perhaps you made a mistake on Form W-4.

What would you do?

Christopher Meder-Photography/Shutterstock.com

The Purpose of Taxes

The local, state, and federal units of government provide a wide variety of services. Supporting schools, building and maintaining roads, and providing for the nation's defense are examples. The process by which the expenses of government are paid is called **taxation**.

A **tax** is a compulsory, or required, contribution of money people make to government. Calling a tax compulsory helps to distinguish it from other types of payments. For example, when you buy a postage stamp, you are paying for a government service. The difference between that purchase and taxation is that you are not required to buy a stamp. The main purpose of taxation is to raise **revenue**, or money, to pay the cost of government. Most taxes are revenue taxes.

A *direct tax* is paid directly to the government. Examples include income taxes and property taxes. If you buy gasoline, you pay an *indirect tax*. The oil company pays tax on the gasoline it produces. These increased costs are then passed on to you at the pumps. Passing on taxes to the consumer is known as *shifting the tax burden*.

Sometimes, a direct tax can become an indirect tax. Karen's landlord told her that the rent was going up by $20 a month. When she asked why, Karen learned that property taxes on the building had risen by about $600 the previous year. Property tax is a direct tax the owner is required to pay. The owner passed the property taxes on to Karen and other renters in the form of an indirect tax.

The consumer is often aware of indirect taxes. When you buy gas, the price you pay for excise tax is clearly shown on the pump. When you buy tires, the bill lists the amount of federal excise tax. *Excise taxes* are a sales tax placed on specific items. They are one of the most common types of indirect taxes.

Some kinds of indirect taxes are hidden. The price you pay for a mobile phone includes taxes paid on the labor and raw materials used to produce the product. Taxes were collected on the factory and equipment used in manufacturing. Shipping costs to get the product to market include taxes paid by the transportation company. In fact, hidden taxes make up 20 percent or more of the cost of goods you buy.

Search the Net

The IRS website has a web page for students. Access this page by clicking on the link for Chapter 19 at **www.cengage.com/school/working**. Which of the categories of taxable income for students do you have now or do you anticipate having in the next four years? Read the categories that apply to your situation. Make a list of questions that occur to you as you read.

www.cengage.com/school/working

Types of Taxes

Individuals and businesses pay a variety of direct and indirect taxes for the purpose of raising revenue.

Income Taxes

You pay taxes on the money you earn, and businesses are taxed on their profits. The federal government, most state governments, and a few local governments collect income taxes. You pay income taxes on salary, wages, and tips, and on savings and investment income as well.

Payroll Taxes

Payroll taxes only go to support Social Security insurance programs. If you work for an employer covered by Social Security, both you and the employer make a contribution. These funds will help provide you with a retirement income, health insurance, and other benefits. Some workers, such as teachers and government employees, pay into a state retirement program rather than into Social Security.

Sales and Excise Taxes

Most state governments and some local ones have a sales tax. When you buy something, a few cents per dollar is added to the amount of the sale. Taxes on large items, like a car, can be high.

Excise taxes are often placed on quantities of certain items such as gasoline, tires, tobacco, alcohol, and amusements. Why do you suppose the government taxes these things?

Estate, Inheritance, and Gift Taxes

When a person dies, the government may collect two types of taxes. An *estate tax* is assessed on the value of the dead person's wealth and property before it passes on to the heirs of the estate. In addition, an *inheritance tax* may be taken out of each person's share of the will. The

Math Connection

federal government collects only an estate tax. Some state governments levy both inheritance and estate taxes. You may wonder why people do not just turn over large sums while living so heirs can avoid these taxes. Gifts up to a certain amount are tax-free. Beyond that amount the person giving the money must pay a gift tax.

The Federal Income Tax

In 1913, Congress passed the 16th Amendment to the Constitution, which gave the government the right to tax income. Since 1913, income tax laws have changed many times, and income tax rates have increased greatly.

In 1911, Wisconsin became the first state to administer an income tax. The success of this tax led many states to pass similar laws. By the mid-1970s, almost all states had passed some form of income tax law. After World War II, many cities also adopted income taxes.

Who Must Pay?

Unless excused by law, individuals, corporations, trusts, and estates generally must pay income tax. For example, the government does not tax individuals and families who have low incomes. Nonprofit organizations such as churches, charities, and many hospitals are also tax-exempt.

Aliens, or citizens of other countries, who live and earn income in the United States must pay income taxes. All corporations are subject to income taxes. Small businesses do not pay corporate taxes unless they have been incorporated. Instead, owners of such businesses pay individual income taxes on their shares of the business income.

Graduated Income Tax and Flat Tax

The income tax is seen by most people as being the fairest type of tax. People who earn more money should be able to pay more. A system in which taxes are tied to one's income is called a *graduated tax*. Figure 19-1 on the next page shows the relationship between the federal income tax rate and income.

Filing Status and Income Tax Rates 2011

Tax Rate	Single	Head of Household	Married Filing Jointly or Qualified Widow(er)	Married Filing Separately
10%	$0–8500	$0–12,500	$0–$17,000	$0–8500
15%	$8,500–34,500	$12,150–46,250	$17,000–69,000	$8,500–34,500
25%	$34,500–83,600	$46,250–119,400	$69,000–139,350	$34,500–69,675
28%	$83,600–174,400	$119,400–193,500	$139,350–212,300	$69,675–106,150
33%	$174,400–379,150	$193,500–379,150	$212,300–379,150	$106,150–189,575
35%	over $379,150	over $379,150	over $379,150	over $189,575

FIGURE 19-1 The rate at which you pay tax is based on the amount of taxable income you earn and your filing status.

Each taxpayer is allowed a certain level of tax-free income, which is dependent on marital status and number of dependents. For the 2011 tax year, a single person without dependents paid no taxes on her first $9,500 of earned income. Marie and Frank, a married couple with two children, paid no taxes on their first $26,400 of earned income.

People with very low incomes pay nothing. Large families generally pay less in taxes than small families. At one time, married couples paid less than a single person. Legislation passed in 2003 has largely eliminated the so-called "marriage penalty." A single person and a married couple filing a joint return now pay taxes at the same percentage rate.

Most state and local income taxes are graduated. Some state and local governments, however, use a *flat tax*. This means that all taxpayers have the same tax rate regardless of income. A flat tax is usually 1 to 6 percent. If the flat rate were 5 percent, a person with a taxable income of $20,000 would be assessed $1,000 in taxes.

Many provisions have been written into the tax laws that allow people who meet certain requirements to reduce the amount of income on which they are taxed and thereby pay less tax or to avoid paying tax altogether. For example, people who have a home mortgage loan can subtract the interest they pay on the loan. But people paying rent have no similar means of reducing their tax. Such provisions are often criticized because they are regarded by some people as unfair.

19-1 Assessment

1. Why do all taxpayers need to pay taxes?
2. What is revenue?
3. Is an excise tax on tires a direct or an indirect tax?
4. Name and describe the seven major types of taxes.
5. Do aliens working in the U.S. have to pay income taxes?
6. What is a flat tax? How is a graduated tax different?

FILE AN INCOME TAX RETURN

OBJECTIVES

- Summarize the general process by which the amount of income tax is determined
- Complete a Form 1040EZ

KEY TERMS

- adjustments to income
- individual retirement account (IRA)
- adjusted gross income
- deduction
- exemption
- taxable income
- tax credit
- tax evasion
- filing

Blend Images/Shutterstock.com

Personal Decisions

You are in the process of filling out your income tax return. The next line on the form deals with charitable contributions. You review your canceled checks and discover several that qualify as deductions. You can remember a few other cash contributions, but you do not have the receipts. Also, you had some out-of-pocket expenses for church activities. These are allowable deductions. But you do not have records for them, either. You are not sure how much you should claim for charitable contributions.

What would you do?

Determine Your Income Tax

Your total income for a given year consists of money you earned from your job plus income from savings, investments, and other sources. But you do not have to pay taxes on your total income. Figure 19-2 on the next page shows the process you use to determine how much of your income is subject to tax.

First, you subtract certain nontaxable items called **adjustments to income**. Some examples of adjustments to income are alimony paid and contributions to an **individual retirement account (IRA)**, which is a plan that lets individuals save money for retirement and receive special tax benefits. After you subtract adjustments to income, you are left with an **adjusted gross income**.

Next, you subtract various nontaxable items called **deductions**. For example, mortgage interest, property taxes, and contributions to charity or churches can be deducted.

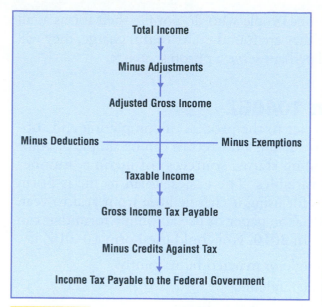

FIGURE 19-2 This is the general process used to determine the amount of federal income tax owed. The actual process varies among individuals.

After that, you may subtract a set amount for yourself and each dependent. These are your **exemptions**. A married couple with one child, for example, would have three exemptions. Subtraction of amounts for deductions and exemptions leaves you with your **taxable income**, the amount on which you pay tax.

Determine the amount of tax owed by using the appropriate tax table. A sample tax table is shown in Figure 19-3. For example, suppose you are married and filing a joint return. If you made $41,438 in taxable income, the tax is $5,376. A single person earning the same amount would owe $6,538.

A **tax credit** is a reduction in the amount of income tax owed. Your figure from the tax table may be reduced by any tax credits for which you are eligible. Tax credits are offered for child care and certain other expenses. The amount left after subtracting credits will be the amount of federal income tax you owe.

A final step in determining your tax is to compare the amount owed with the tax you have already paid. Because your employer withheld taxes from each paycheck, most or all of your tax obligation should be satisfied. If too much tax has been withheld, you can claim a *refund*. However, if too little has been withheld, you will have to pay an additional amount.

You must sign and mail your return and any attachments by April 15. In signing your name, you signify that everything on the form is accurate and truthful. If you mail the form late, you will have to pay interest and perhaps a penalty. **Tax evasion** is illegally avoiding payment of some or all

If line 43 (taxable income) is—		And you are—			
At least	But less than	Single	Married filing jointly	Married filing separately	Head of a household
			Your tax is—		
41,000					
41,000	41,050	6,438	5,316	6,438	5,556
41,000	41,100	6,450	5,324	6,450	5,564
41,050	41,150	6,463	5,331	6,463	5,571
41,150	41,200	6,475	5,339	6,475	5,579
41,200	41,250	6,488	5,346	6,488	5,586
41,250	41,300	6,500	5,354	6,500	5,594
41,300	41,350	6,513	5,361	6,513	5,601
41,350	41,400	6,525	5,369	6,525	5,609
41,400	41,450	6,538	5,376	6,538	5,616
41,450	41,500	6,550	5,384	6,550	5,624
41,500	41,550	6,563	5,391	6,563	5,631
41,550	41,600	6,575	5,399	6,575	5,639
41,600	41,650	6,588	5,406	6,588	5,646
41,650	41,700	6,600	5,414	6,600	5,654
41,700	41,750	6,613	5,421	6,613	5,661
41,750	41,800	6,625	5,429	6,625	5,669
41,800	41,850	6,638	5,436	6,638	5,676
41,850	41,900	6,650	5,444	6,650	5,684
41,900	41,950	6,663	5,451	6,663	5,691
41,950	42,000	6,675	5,459	6,675	5,699

FIGURE 19-3 Sample Tax Table (tax year 2010)

of one's income tax obligation. People who do not file their forms at all are practicing tax evasion. If they are found guilty of this charge, they will have to pay a heavy fine and perhaps serve a prison sentence.

Complete a Form 1040EZ

The term **filing** is used to refer to the process of completing and submitting an income tax return. Filing a tax return can be simple or complex, depending on your filing status, source(s) of income, number of deductions, and other variables. The easiest form to file is Form 1040EZ. The qualifications for using it change little from year to year. You can fill out Form 1040EZ on paper or use an online form that can be submitted electronically. In 2010, you could use Form 1040EZ if:

- Your filing status was single or married filing jointly.
- You did not claim any dependents.
- You did not claim any adjustments to income.
- You claim only the earned income credit and the making work pay credit.
- You (and your spouse if filing a joint return) were under age 65 and not blind.
- Your taxable income was less than $100,000.
- You had only wages, salaries, tips, taxable scholarships or fellowship grants, unemployment compensation, or Alaska Permanent Fund dividends, and your taxable interest was not over $1,500.
- You did not receive any advance earned income credit payments.
- You did not owe any household employment taxes on wages you paid to a household employee.
- You are not a debtor in a chapter 11 bankruptcy case filed after October 16, 2005.
- You do not figure your standard deduction using Schedule L.

You may remember Jack Pate from the beginning of this chapter. Jack now needs to fill out his first personal income tax form. In 2011, Jack worked afternoons after school and all day Saturdays at an ice cream parlor. During the summer, he worked a full 40-hour week. As reflected in Figure 19-4 on the next page, Jack received a *Form W-2 Wage and Tax Statement* from his employer in early 2012. This is an Internal Revenue Service (IRS) form that your employer prepares and sends to you by January 31 of the following year. The form shows your total earnings for the previous year and the total amount of federal income tax that was withheld from your pay.

When Jack got his W-2, he went online at www.irs.gov and downloaded a copy of Form 1040EZ and the instructions for the form. IRS forms and publications are also available in many public buildings, including libraries and post offices.

Jack read through the instructions. He filled out the form, using the information from his W-2. He also used a statement from his bank that reported the interest income he had earned on his savings during 2011. After completing his income taxes and checking his work,

Form W-2 Wage and Tax Statement (2011)

Field	Value
a Employee's social security number	
OMB No. 1545-0008	Safe, accurate, FAST! Use IRS e-file
	Visit the IRS website at www.irs.gov/efile
b Employer identification number (EIN)	37-5732196
1 Wages, tips, other compensation	8750.00
2 Federal income tax withheld	312.50
c Employer's name, address, and ZIP code	Ice Cream Parlor, 1640 W. Main Street, Carbondale, IL 62901-1409
3 Social security wages	8750.00
4 Social security tax withheld	542.50
5 Medicare wages and tips	8750.00
6 Medicare tax withheld	127.00
7 Social security tips	.00
8 Allocated tips	
d Control number	315-20-4024
9	
10 Dependent care benefits	
e Employee's first name and initial Last name Suff.	Jack V. Pate, 1612 Fredrick St., Carbondale, IL 62901-1482
11 Nonqualified plans	
12a See instructions for box 12	
13 Statutory employee / Retirement plan / Third-party sick pay	
12b	
14 Other	
12c	
	12d
f Employee's address and ZIP code	
15 State Employer's state ID number	IL 0348-4321
16 State wages, tips, etc.	8750.00
17 State income tax	335.04
18 Local wages, tips, etc.	8750.00
19 Local income tax	
20 Locality name	

Form **W-2** Wage and Tax Statement **2011** Department of the Treasury—Internal Revenue Service

Copy B—To Be Filed With Employee's FEDERAL Tax Return.
This information is being furnished to the Internal Revenue Service.

FIGURE 19-4 A Form W-2, Wage and Tax Statement, will be sent to you by your employer in late January following each year that you worked.

Jack determined that he owed $70 in taxes. A copy of Jack's completed return is shown in Figure 19-5 on the following two pages.

It was not difficult for Jack to file an income tax return. Not all returns are as simple as this. Because Jack's older sister, Emily, had dividend and capital gains income from stock and deductible student loan interest, she had to use Form 1040A. Jack's parents used a third common type of form, Form 1040, because they itemize instead of taking the standard deductions and they also receive income from a property they rent.

In the process of completing his Form 1040EZ, Jack discovered that he enjoyed this type of work. When he asked his sister and parents if he might help them with their forms, they quickly accepted his offer. By helping to fill out their forms, Jack learned a great deal more about income tax returns. Why don't you offer to help a family member or friend with income tax preparation? You will probably learn a lot, too!

19-2 Assessment

1. Based on Figure 19-3, how much tax does a married couple filing jointly owe on an income of $41,743? How much does a single person owe on the same amount?

2. What is the difference between "adjusted gross income" and "taxable income"?

3. What happens if you have earned income and fail to file an income tax return?

4. If you are married, can you use Form 1040EZ to file your federal income tax return?

Form **1040EZ**	**Income Tax Return for Single and Joint Filers With No Dependents** (99)	**2011**	OMB No. 1545-0074

Your first name and initial	Last name	Your social security number
Jack V.	Pate	315 : 20 : 4024
If a joint return, spouse's first name and initial	Last name	Spouse's social security number

Home address (number and street). If you have a P.O. box, see instructions.   Apt. no.

1612 Fredrick St.

▲ Make sure the SSN(s) above are correct.

City, town or post office, state, and ZIP code. If you have a foreign address, also complete spaces below (see instructions).

Carbondale, IL 62901-1482

Foreign country name	Foreign province/county	Foreign postal code

Presidential Election Campaign
Check here if you, or your spouse if filing jointly, want $3 to go to this fund. Checking a box below will not change your tax or refund.   ☒ You   ☐ Spouse

Income

Attach Form(s) W-2 here.

Enclose, but do not attach, any payment.

1	Wages, salaries, and tips. This should be shown in box 1 of your Form(s) W-2. Attach your Form(s) W-2.	**1**	8750
2	Taxable interest. If the total is over $1,500, you cannot use Form 1040EZ.	**2**	78
3	Unemployment compensation and Alaska Permanent Fund dividends (see instructions).	**3**	—
4	Add lines 1, 2, and 3. This is your **adjusted gross income.**	**4**	8828
5	If someone can claim you (or your spouse if a joint return) as a dependent, check the applicable box(es) below and enter the amount from the worksheet on back. ☒ **You** ☐ **Spouse** If no one can claim you (or your spouse if a joint return), enter $9,500 if **single**; $19,000 if **married filing jointly.** See back for explanation.	**5**	5800
6	Subtract line 5 from line 4. If line 5 is larger than line 4, enter -0-. This is your **taxable income.** ▶	**6**	3028

Payments, Credits, and Tax

7	Federal income tax withheld from Form(s) W-2 and 1099.	**7**	313
8a	**Earned income credit (EIC)** (see instructions).	**8a**	—
b	Nontaxable combat pay election. 8b		
9	Add lines 7 and 8a. These are your **total payments and credits.** ▶	**9**	313
10	**Tax.** Use the amount on **line 6 above** to find your tax in the tax table in the instructions. Then, enter the tax from the table on this line.	**10**	303

Refund

Have it directly deposited! See instructions and fill in 11b, 11c, and 11d or Form 8888.

11a	If line 9 is larger than line 10, subtract line 10 from line 9. This is your **refund.** If Form 8888 is attached, check here ▶ ☐	**11a**	10
▶ b	Routing number	▶c Type: ☐ Checking ☐ Savings	
▶ d	Account number		

Amount You Owe

12	If line 10 is larger than line 9, subtract line 9 from line 10. This is the **amount you owe.** For details on how to pay, see instructions. ▶	**12**	70

Third Party Designee

Do you want to allow another person to discuss this return with the IRS (see instructions)? ☐ **Yes.** Complete below. ☐ **No**

Designee's name ▶	Phone no. ▶	Personal identification number (PIN) ▶

Sign Here

Under penalties of perjury, I declare that I have examined this return and, to the best of my knowledge and belief, it is true, correct, and accurately lists all amounts and sources of income I received during the tax year. Declaration of preparer (other than the taxpayer) is based on all information of which the preparer has any knowledge.

Joint return? See instructions.

Keep a copy for your records.

Your signature	Date	Your occupation	Daytime phone number
Jack V. Pate	2/20/12	fast food worker	
Spouse's signature. If a joint return, **both** must sign.	Date	Spouse's occupation	If the IRS sent you an Identity Protection PIN, enter it here (see inst.)

Paid Preparer Use Only

Print/Type preparer's name	Preparer's signature	Date	Check ☐ if self-employed	PTIN
Firm's name ▶			Firm's EIN ▶	
Firm's address ▶			Phone no.	

For Disclosure, Privacy Act, and Paperwork Reduction Act Notice, see instructions.   Cat. No. 11329W   Form **1040EZ** (2011)

FIGURE 19-5A Most young workers can use Form 1040EZ.

Use this form if	• Your filing status is single or married filing jointly. If you are not sure about your filing status, see instructions. • You (and your spouse if married filing jointly) were under age 65 and not blind at the end of 2011. If you were born on January 1, 1947, you are considered to be age 65 at the end of 2011. • You do not claim any dependents. For information on dependents, see Pub. 501. • Your taxable income (line 6) is less than $100,000. • You do not claim any adjustments to income. For information on adjustments to income, use TeleTax topics 451–453 and 455–458 (see instructions). • The only tax credit you can claim is the earned income credit (EIC). The credit may give you a refund even if you do not owe any tax. You do not need a qualifying child to claim the EIC. For information on credits, use TeleTax topics 601, 602, 607, 608, 610, 611, and 612 (see instructions). • You had only wages, salaries, tips, taxable scholarship or fellowship grants, unemployment compensation, or Alaska Permanent Fund dividends, and your taxable interest was not over $1,500. But if you earned tips, including allocated tips, that are not included in box 5 and box 7 of your Form W-2, you may not be able to use Form 1040EZ (see instructions). If you are planning to use Form 1040EZ for a child who received Alaska Permanent Fund dividends, see instructions.
Filling in your return	If you received a scholarship or fellowship grant or tax-exempt interest income, such as on municipal bonds, see the instructions before filling in the form. Also, see the instructions if you received a Form 1099-INT showing federal income tax withheld or if federal income tax was withheld from your unemployment compensation or Alaska Permanent Fund dividends.
For tips on how to avoid common mistakes, see instructions.	Remember, you must report all wages, salaries, and tips even if you do not get a Form W-2 from your employer. You must also report all your taxable interest, including interest from banks, savings and loans, credit unions, etc., even if you do not get a Form 1099-INT.

Worksheet for Line 5 — Dependents Who Checked One or Both Boxes	Use this worksheet to figure the amount to enter on line 5 if someone can claim you (or your spouse if married filing jointly) as a dependent, even if that person chooses not to do so. To find out if someone can claim you as a dependent, see Pub. 501.
	
	A. Amount, if any, from line 1 on front . . . .
	           + 300.00 Enter total ▶ A. _**9050**_
	B. Minimum standard deduction . . . . B. _**9000**_
	C. Enter the **larger** of line A or line B here . . . . C. _**9050**_
	D. Maximum standard deduction. If **single,** enter $5,800; if **married filing jointly,** enter $11,600 . D. _**5800**_
	E. Enter the **smaller** of line C or line D here. This is your standard deduction . . . . E. _**5800**_
	F. Exemption amount.
	    • If single, enter -0-.
	    • If married filing jointly and —
	      —both you and your spouse can be claimed as dependents, enter -0-.
	      —only one of you can be claimed as a dependent, enter $3,700. } F. _**0**_
	G. Add lines E and F. Enter the total here and on line 5 on the front . . . . G. _**5800**_

(keep a copy for your records)	**If you did not check any boxes on line 5,** enter on line 5 the amount shown below that applies to you. • Single, enter $9,500. This is the total of your standard deduction ($5,800) and your exemption ($3,700). • Married filing jointly, enter $19,000. This is the total of your standard deduction ($11,600), your exemption ($3,700), and your spouse's exemption ($3,700).
Mailing Return	Mail your return by **April 17, 2012.** Mail it to the address shown on the last page of the instructions.

Form **1040EZ** (2011)

FIGURE 19-5B   Form 1040EZ (Continued).

OBJECTIVES

- Define social security
- Describe six major federal and state social insurance programs
- Explain who is eligible for Social Security and how the program is financed
- Show awareness of issues related to the future funding of Social Security, Medicare and Medicaid

KEY TERMS

- social security
- Social Security
- benefit
- pension
- lump-sum payment
- work credits
- Federal Insurance Contribution Act (FICA)
- wage base

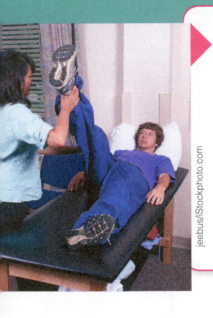

jeebus/iStockphoto.com

▶ Ethical Decisions

You injured your leg badly in a warehouse accident. It will probably be months before you can go back to work. You are glad you have workers' compensation benefits.

Your coworkers stop by to see you. During one visit, you remark that you cannot wait to go back to work. Your buddy laughs and says if he were you, he would lie about the leg hurting and stay home as long as possible. He says a lot of people do it.

What would you do?

What Is Social Security?

You know that your employer withholds money from your paycheck for federal, and perhaps state and local, income taxes. Money is probably also withheld for Social Security taxes. In general terms, social security refers to government programs that help people meet social and economic needs. Social Security is also the name of a particular set of government programs, the federal system of retirement benefits, survivors payments, hospital insurance for the elderly, and other services. The word benefits refers to financial help in times of sickness, old age, disability, or the like.

At one time, most Americans lived in rural areas and were farmers. Rural families lived off the land. They built their own homes; raised their own food; and traded or sold surplus food, crops, and livestock. Families and neighbors helped each other during difficult times. Gradually, the country began to change from an agricultural economy to an industrial one. Increasing numbers of people moved to cities and took jobs in factories. Instead of living off the land, families began to depend on wages paid by an employer. If the income stopped for some reason, such as a worker's illness or old age, the whole family suffered.

The Great Depression of the 1930s showed on a large scale the painful effects of unemployment. To help deal with unemployment and the many other social problems brought on by the Depression, Congress, in 1935, passed the Social Security Act. This law provided for a system of old-age (retirement) benefits, unemployment insurance, aid for dependent children, benefits for the blind, and assistance for a few other groups and purposes. Over the years, Congress has made a number of changes in the act. Medicare was added in 1965. Other changes include the extension of benefits to more groups, an increase in tax rates, raising the retirement age from 65 to 67, and the option to enroll in a prescription drug plan.

There are two types of social security programs. One type aids the needy regardless of their work record. Public assistance, or welfare, is an example. General taxes finance public assistance.

The second type is social insurance programs. The federal Social Security system is an example. Unlike public assistance, the federal Social Security program pays benefits to people who have earned them by working and paying Social Security payroll taxes. In some cases, a worker's family can receive benefits.

In many ways, social insurance programs are similar to other types of insurance. During your working years, you and your employer pay taxes that go into special funds. The risks and costs are spread among many people. When your earnings stop because of retirement or certain other situations, you receive benefits. If you die, payments are made to your survivors.

Major Social Insurance Programs

National and state systems of social security have changed greatly from the way they were in 1935. The six major social insurance programs in the United States are shown in Figure 19-6 on the next page. The general nature of each of these programs is described in this chapter. As some of the rules are quite technical, no effort is made to explain all details regarding eligibility and payments. For federally administered programs, more specific information can be obtained from your local Social Security Administration (SSA) office or on the Web at www.ssa.gov/.

Retirement Payments

This is the best-known program in the federal Social Security system. It provides a monthly pension to retired workers when they reach full retirement age. A **pension** is a regular payment of money to a person, usually a retired person. Individuals may choose to retire and begin receiving benefits as early as age 62. If they retire early, however, their monthly payments will be reduced to compensate for the longer period over which they will be paid. The amount of monthly benefits received is based on your average annual earnings.

Benefits are also payable to the spouse of the retired worker. A spouse's benefits equal about 50 percent of the worker's benefits. Under certain conditions, unmarried children of the retired worker may also be eligible for benefits.

Monkey Business Images/Shutterstock.com

It is important to make financial plans for later in life so that you can have the opportunity to enjoy your retirement years.

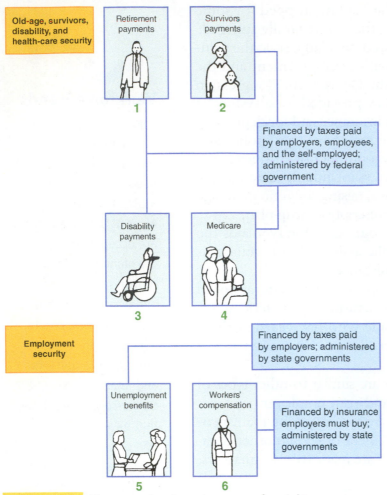

Retirement payments

Survivors payments

Financed by taxes paid by employers, employees, and the self-employed; administered by federal government

1

2

Disability payments

Medicare

3

4

Employment security

Financed by taxes paid by employers; administered by state governments

Unemployment benefits

Workers' compensation

Financed by insurance employers must buy; administered by state governments

5

6

FIGURE 19-6 These are the six major types of social insurance programs in the United States.

Retirement-age rules were changed as a result of revisions made in 1983 to the Social Security Act. The retirement age has been gradually increasing from 65 to 67 based on one's date of birth. Individuals born after 1960 will not be eligible to receive full retirement benefits until age 67. You can still retire at age 62, but you will get only 70% of what you would get at age 67. If you retire at age 65, you will get 86.7% of the monthly benefit you would get at age 67.

Survivors Payments

If you have worked and paid into Social Security, when you die (either before or after retirement) your dependents may be eligible for survivors payments.

There are two types of payments your survivors may be eligible for. A **lump-sum payment** is a one-time payment of money. Survivors may receive a small lump-sum payment. Your dependents may also be eligible for a monthly survivors benefit.

Monthly payments may be made to a surviving spouse age 60 or older. Under certain conditions, surviving unmarried children and dependent parents may also receive payments. The amount of monthly payments is based on the benefits the worker was getting at the time of death. If the person had not yet retired, the survivor would be entitled to the benefits the deceased worker would have received.

Disability Payments

If you are unable to work because of a severe physical or mental disability, you may be eligible for benefits. The disability must have lasted at least 12 months or be expected to last that long. Payments can start upon the sixth full month of disability.

Benefits may also be paid to a disabled worker's spouse. Unless he or she gets a higher Social Security benefit, a spouse may collect full benefits at age 65 or reduced benefits at ages 62–64. Unmarried children under 18 can receive benefits. If a worker has a disabled child, special benefits may apply.

Medicare

In 1965, Congress added hospital and medical insurance benefits to the Social Security program. This coverage, known as Medicare, is for people age 65 or older. (This is sometimes confused with Medicaid, which is a health service program for people with low incomes or special needs.)

Disabled workers under age 65 who have received disability benefits for two years are also eligible. So are people with certain kidney diseases.

Medicare consists of hospital insurance and supplementary medical insurance. Hospital coverage, referred to as Part A, pays for nursing care as well as for hospital, hospice, and some home health care expenses. *Hospice* programs provide care for the terminally ill. The insured person must pay an initial amount, or a deductible, for each hospital stay. Medicare then pays the rest of the hospital expenses for up to 60 days. If a stay lasts more than 60 days, additional limitations apply.

The hospital insurance part of Medicare is automatically provided to eligible workers and spouses. However, the medical coverage, which is referred to as Part B, is an optional health insurance plan. It pays the cost of doctors' fees and other medical services not included in hospital insurance. If you want medical coverage, you must pay a monthly premium for the service. You must pay a deductible each year. The program then pays 80 percent of most remaining expenses.

Starting January 1, 2006, Medicare began offering insurance coverage for prescription drugs. The plan is referred to as Medicare Part D and is designed to help Medicare-eligible individuals save on their prescription drug costs. Insurance companies and other private companies work with Medicare to offer these plans. The plan requires enrollees to pay a monthly premium and co-pays for each prescription. Out-of-pocket costs may vary depending on the plans.

Disability insurance can provide financial assistance to injured workers while they recover.

Unemployment Benefits

Unemployment insurance, which was included as part of the original 1935 Social Security Act, is not a federal program. The purpose of the law was to motivate states to pass their own laws. Each state finances and administers its own unemployment insurance program within guidelines established by federal law. In most states, the system is financed by payroll taxes paid by employers.

Unemployment insurance provides weekly payments to workers who have lost their jobs. Paul Miller, for instance, was laid off from his job at the Black Gold Coal Mine. He had to go to the local state employment service office to register for unemployment benefits. Paul has started receiving weekly checks amounting to half of his normal full-time pay. He is eligible to receive payments for up to 26 weeks. However, during the time he is receiving unemployment benefits, Paul is required to accept any suitable job that the employment service has available.

The amount of the weekly payment and the number of weeks of eligibility vary from state to state. Otherwise, state programs of unemployment insurance operate in the same general manner.

During periods of unusually high unemployment, the federal government has traditionally stepped in with emergency measures to provide extra weeks. The most recent instance was in February 2009 when Congress passed legislation to provide many unemployed workers up to 99 weeks of unemployment insurance benefits. As this book goes to press, millions of unemployed workers have exhausted their benefits, while Congress is deadlocked over providing any further assistance.

Workers' Compensation

Every state has a workers' compensation law, which helps people who are injured or who develop a disease as a result of their job. The program pays the cost of medical care and helps replace lost income. Workers' compensation also pays death benefits and pensions to spouses and dependent children of workers killed on the job.

Benefits vary among states. How much workers receive depends on the type and duration of the disability and on the worker's weekly earnings. States have minimum and maximum benefit limits and benefit periods. Injured workers typically receive about two-thirds of what they would have earned. In return for compensation, workers give up their right to sue an employer for damages arising from their disability.

In most states, employers are required to participate in a workers' compensation program and to purchase insurance coverage that pays for it. However, many states do not cover farm workers, household workers, and employees of small firms. Some states refuse to extend protection to workers in dangerous jobs.

Eligibility and Financing

As a review of Figure 19-6 will highlight, there are four federally administered Social Security programs and two state-administered ones.

Who Is Eligible

To be eligible for Social Security benefits, you must earn a certain number of **work credits**, or points earned in jobs covered by Social Security. Work credits were previously called "quarters of coverage." In 2011, a worker received one credit for each $1,120 of annual earnings. The amount of earnings needed for a credit increases periodically. You are limited to four credits per year no matter how much money you earn. The number of credits you need to be eligible for benefits depends on your age and the type of benefit. To be eligible for retirement benefits, you must earn 40 work credits. The number of credits required to earn disability benefits depends on how old you are when you become disabled.

Finance the Program

You and your employer share the cost of financing federal Social Security by paying the **Federal Insurance Contributions Act (FICA)** tax, also known as the payroll tax. Your employer deducts your share of FICA tax from your paycheck. Your employer then adds an equal contribution and sends the Treasury Department the total amount monthly or quarterly. The department distributes the money among the various funds that will pay benefits.

Up to a certain limit, taxes are figured on your gross annual salary or wages. The salary limit is called the **wage base**. In 1937, when the first FICA taxes were collected, both the worker and the employer paid a 1 percent tax on the first $3,000 of earnings. In 1937, $3,000 was the wage base. In 2011, the wage base had increased to $106,800. Earnings in excess of the wage base are not subject to FICA tax. However, you must continue to pay 1.45% for Medicare on all earned income.

FICA taxes are collected at a rate of 7.65% on gross earnings paid by both employer and employee (6.2% for FICA and 1.45% for Medicare). In 2011, Congress passed a one-year 2% reduction in FICA taxes for employees from 6.2% to 4.2%. Employers continued to pay 6.2%. The 2% reduction in payroll taxes for employees was designed to help stimulate the economy. it is unknown whether the reduction will be extended or allowed to return to the higher 6.2% rate.

Future of Social Security, Medicare, and Medicaid

Social Security and Medicare are paid for by payroll taxes contributed by employers and employees. Both programs are administered by the federal government. Medicaid is a state-administered program that provides health insurance and other benefits for low income people. Medicaid is financed jointly by the states and the federal government. The exact amount varies somewhat from state to state, but the federal government pays about 50 percent of the cost of Medicaid.

In 1935, when the Social Security Act was passed, the life expectancy for men was 58 and 62 for women. The relatively small number of people who survived to age 65 received Social Security for only a few years. As a result, the Social Security System was able to build up a pool of reserve funds, the *trust fund*, to pay out to retirees and for other benefits. In the last few decades it has become apparent that the pool of money is decreasing at a steady rate. Each year the Social Security and Medicare trust funds are required to report on their financial status. The report is published on the Web at www.ssa.gov/oact/trsum/index.html.

The 2011 annual report stated that "Projected long-run program costs for both Medicare and Social Security are not sustainable under currently scheduled financing..." Population aging is the largest single factor contributing to cost growth in both programs. People are living longer and are consuming more health services and prescription drugs. The average life expectancy in 2011 for men was about 77 and for women was about 81. Further contributing to the funding problem is the fact that the large baby-boom generation began to retire in 2008, which has added considerably to the size of the older population.

The same factors putting pressure on Social Security and Medicare funding are also being felt in Medicaid funding. As more people live longer and longer, many more require skilled nursing care and have to move to a nursing home. These facilities are very expensive, which few people can afford. As a result, they have to apply for Medicaid support.

There is wide recognition by citizens and government leaders that something must be done to address these problems. Potential solutions include raising taxes, cutting benefits, eliminating waste and fraud, and operating health care programs more efficiently.

There is no quick or easy answer to the future of Social Security, Medicare, and Medicaid. You can do your part by being informed about the issues, by leading a healthful life, by voting for government leaders whose policies seem to offer balanced solutions, and by encouraging your family, friends, and fellow citizens to do the same.

Workplace Innovations

CLOUD COMPUTING

The typical computer user has a computer with word processing, accounting, e-mail, and other software. To create a letter, the word processing software is opened, the document is created, and a file is stored on the computer hard drive. The hard drive may also be used to store photos, videos, and music.

This traditional approach results in duplication of software on each computer, software installation and maintenance, and ever increasing demand for more storage capacity. In large businesses, information technology (IT) staff install and maintain hardware and software and manage the local computer network, all of which can be quite expensive.

A new technology is now in place called "cloud computing." This refers to moving application software and file storage to the Internet. Large data centers are located throughout the country which house data servers. Instead of downloading an application from your desktop, you download it from your web browser. Instead of storing a file on your hard drive, you store it on a remote server.

Cloud computing has many advantages for individuals and businesses. Many people have a desktop computer, notebook, tablet computer, and smartphone. By keeping software, email, music, videos, and other files on the cloud, software and files can be accessed from any one of multiple personal computer devices. For businesses, the advantages are even greater. They can eliminate software purchases and upgrades, eliminate storage servers, reduce IT staff, and devote resources spent on technology to other business uses.

NET FOLLOW-UP

Use a search engine to explore the Web for additional information on the topic of cloud computing. How do you feel about storing personal information, including your contact list and your online calendar, at remote locations?

19-3 Assessment

1. When was the Social Security Act passed? When was Medicare added?
2. List and briefly describe the six major social insurance programs.
3. Name the three types of Medicare insurance. Which type is automatically provided to eligible workers?
4. How are state unemployment benefits and workers' compensation financed?
5. How is federal Social Security financed?
6. Why are Social Security, Medicare, and Medicaid facing such difficult financial pressures?

High Growth Occupations
FOR THE 21ST CENTURY

Construction Laborers

Most construction laborers do physically demanding work. This entry-level job is one to consider if you are physically fit, can tolerate hard work, and are willing to work in sometimes difficult conditions. An advantage of this occupation is that employment opportunities are expected to grow much faster than average.

Construction laborers can be found on almost all construction sites, performing a wide range of tasks from the very easy to the hazardous. They can be found at building, highway, and heavy construction sites; residential and commercial sites; tunnel and shaft excavations; and demolition sites.

Most workers start by getting a job with a contractor who provides on-the-job training. Entry-level workers generally help more experienced workers, by performing routine tasks such as cleaning and preparing the worksite and unloading materials. When the opportunity arises, they learn from experienced construction trades workers how to do more difficult tasks, such as operating tools and equipment.

Construction laborers also may choose or be required to attend a trade or vocational school, association training class, or community college to receive further trade-related training. Some laborers receive more formal training in the form of an apprenticeship. Workers who use dangerous equipment or handle toxic chemicals usually receive specialized safety training.

Through training and experience, laborers can move into other construction occupations. Laborers may also advance to become construction supervisors or general contractors. For those who would like to advance, it is increasingly important to be able to communicate in both English and Spanish in order to relay instructions and safety precautions to workers with limited understanding of English.

Construction supervisors and contractors need good communication skills to deal with clients and subcontractors. They also need good math skills to estimate the quantity of materials needed to complete a job and accurately estimate how long a job will take to complete and what it will cost. Computer skills also are important for advancement as construction becomes increasingly mechanized and computerized.

There is an ongoing need for a variety of construction workers.

INDIVIDUAL RETIREMENT ACCOUNTS

OBJECTIVES

- Explain the purpose of an individual retirement account (IRA)
- Name and describe the two types of IRAs

KEY TERMS

- Roth IRA

OtnaYdur/Shutterstock.com

> ### ▶ Personal Decisions
>
> You work for a large company that employs hundreds of workers. Every several months, the human resources department conducts "brown-bag" lunches for interested employees on such topics as investing and tax planning. A blast email is sent indicating that next week's brown-bag lunch will discuss IRAs. You are supposed to register online if you are interested. You do not think you will go. You can't imagine giving up seeing your friends today at lunch to plan for a retirement that is at least 40 years in the future.
>
> **What would you do?**

Purpose of an IRA

The Social Security retirement program is designed to provide a minimum standard of living for retired workers. Social Security was never designed to meet all of a retired person's financial needs. To live reasonably well in retirement, it will be necessary for you to supplement Social Security retirement income with income from other sources. These might include savings, investments, or private pensions.

About 94 percent of all workers are in jobs covered by Social Security. But less than half of all workers have some type of private pension plan. An individual retirement account (IRA) is a voluntary private pension plan that allows employed individuals to save a certain amount annually toward retirement and receive special tax benefits. To encourage more people to save for their retirement, Congress passed legislation in 1981 making almost every working person eligible to make contributions to an IRA.

Two Types of IRAS

There are two types of IRAs. The first is a traditional IRA. Anyone who earns income from working and is under age 70½ can open one of these IRAs. In 2011, most workers were eligible to put up to $5,000 a year into it. For married couples, a non-working spouse could also invest up to $5,000 in an IRA.

Tax Benefits

A traditional IRA has two big tax benefits. First, people can deduct IRA contributions from their income tax. The amount of the deduction depends on income level, age, marital status, and whether you are covered by another pension plan at work. Below are simplified examples that cover the majority of young adults.

In 2011, if you did not participate in a retirement plan at work, you could deduct up to $5,000 regardless of your income level. If you participated in an employer-sponsored retirement plan at work, however, you could deduct up to $5,000 only if your *modified adjusted gross income (MAGI)* was no higher than $56,000. As your income increases, the amount that you can deduct is reduced. If your MAGI is more than $66,000, the amount you can deduct drops to $0. If you are married, both you and your spouse can deduct $5,000, unless you have unusually high incomes.

Age Open IRA	Age 65	Age 70
18	$288,680	$395,675
19	270,870	371,634
20	254,097	348,994
25	183,793	254,097
30	131,710	183,793
35	93,125	131,710
40	64,540	93,125

FIGURE 19-7 This table shows what an IRA would be worth at retirement based on a $1,000 annual contribution at 6 percent compounded daily.

For another example, consider a married couple that files jointly and has a taxable income of $48,000. By placing $4,000 into an IRA, they would only pay taxes on $44,000. In 2011, this would have resulted in a tax savings of $600. It would have cost this couple, in effect, $3,400 to make a $4,000 investment. For people earning higher incomes, the savings are even greater.

The second tax benefit of a traditional IRA is that interest and other earnings are not taxed until they are withdrawn. This allows an investment to compound at a much greater rate than if taxes were deducted. Examples of how an IRA investment can multiply are shown in Figure 19-7. You can see that it is possible for a young person like you to accumulate several hundred thousand dollars before retirement. The amounts shown would increase dramatically if you put in the full amount and you earned a higher yield. Remember, however, that inflation may also increase over the years.

Even if you cannot put the full amount into an IRA, try to put in what you can afford. The key to getting the most from an IRA is to start early, put in as much as you can, and make a contribution every year.

Roth IRA

A Roth IRA differs from a traditional IRA because contributions are not tax-deductible, but they grow tax-free. The Roth IRA, which is named after the senator who sponsored the legislation, became available in 1998 as another retirement option. The $5,000 investment limit for a Roth IRA is the same as the investment limit for a traditional IRA. In 2011, a single person making less than $107,000 was eligible to contribute to a Roth IRA. For a married couple to make a Roth IRA contribution, the upper income limit was $169,000.

In simple terms, a traditional IRA provides a tax deduction and tax-deferred income. A Roth IRA provides no tax deduction but tax-free income. To illustrate, if you earn $50,000 a year and put $2,000 in a traditional IRA you would pay taxes on $48,000 in income. The funds in a traditional IRA grow tax-free, but you have to pay income tax when you later withdrawal the funds.

On the other hand, if you put the same $2,000 in a Roth IRA, you would not receive the income tax deduction. The funds in a Roth IRA grow tax-free and you do not have to pay income tax when you withdrawal the funds. Which type of IRA is better? A number of individual factors need to be taken into consideration before answering this question. Experts on this subject say that the Roth IRA makes more sense in most situations.

Open an IRA

Deciding whether to open a traditional IRA or a Roth IRA requires a lot of study. Many types of financial institutions can advise you in making a decision and in opening an account. Institutions that offer IRAs include banks, savings and loan associations, insurance companies, brokerage firms, credit unions, and mutual fund companies. To open an account, you only have to complete a simple application form and make an initial deposit. In most cases, you can make contributions to the account anytime during the year and in any amount.

Once you open an IRA, you will need to decide which type of investments you want to purchase with your IRA funds. The type of investment you select can vary widely. You can purchase certificates of deposit, U.S. treasury securities, bonds, stocks, mutual funds, and many other types of investments. You may even choose several different types of investments and build up a diversified account. You are allowed to switch from one investment to another as you wish. Because selecting the investments to make with an IRA is a complex decision, you should consider getting professional advice to help you decide the best way to balance your portfolio.

In addition to opening an IRA, be sure to learn about and take advantage of retirement plans at work. Employee benefits may include tax-deferred savings, employer investments, and matching employer contributions. Traditional pension plans, offered less frequently today, provide a fixed income at retirement, paid for by the employer.

19-4 Assessment

1. Why did Congress pass legislation creating the individual retirement account (IRA)?

2. Do research to determine how much money can be contributed in the current year to an IRA for the following circumstances: a) a single worker, b) a married couple in which both people work, and c) a married couple in which only one person works.

3. What are the two tax benefits of having a traditional IRA?

4. Roth IRA contributions are not tax-deductible, but they are tax-free. Explain what this means.

Focus on Health and Safety

Job Stress and Workers' Compensation

In the early 1900s, several states passed laws to provide benefits for industrial workers injured on the job. Over the years, the idea of workers' compensation expanded to include all states, most occupations, and most job-related accidents and illnesses.

In 1955, workers' compensation took a new turn. Two men had been working on a scaffold when a rope broke. One fell to his death. The other was caught by the rope and dangled in the air until he was rescued. His most serious injury was a rope burn. But the man was too afraid to get on a scaffold ever again. So he filed a claim for workers' compensation. After a lengthy legal battle, Texas courts upheld an award for the man.

Since then, some state courts have allowed compensation for three new categories of workers: (1) those who suffer a physical injury that leaves a psychological after-effect; (2) those who suffer mental trauma that leads to a physical ailment; and (3) those who suffer mental strain that leads to more serious mental problems. The last type is the most controversial. Here is an example.

The department in which an employee worked was eliminated. The employee transferred to another job. She developed chest pains and suffered an emotional breakdown. She quit working and filed a workers' compensation claim against the company. She argued that the job transfer caused her breakdown. Ultimately, the state supreme court awarded her payment of medical bills and two-thirds of her salary.

Job-stress cases such as this have mushroomed in recent years. Since workers' compensation is governed by state law, states often differ in recognizing everyday mental stress as grounds for covered benefits. This is likely to remain a hot issue for a long time to come.

THINK CRITICALLY

1. It can be difficult for employees to win job-stress cases. Why do you think this is so?
2. Why might job-stress cases have mushroomed in recent years?

Sometimes daily job stresses can be overwhelming.

CREATISTA/Shutterstock.com

Chapter Summary

19-1 Taxation

A. The process by which the expenses of government are paid is called taxation. A tax is a compulsory contribution of money people make to government. Most taxes are revenue taxes.

B. A direct tax is paid directly to the government. An indirect tax is included in the cost of goods and services you buy.

C. Individuals and businesses pay a variety of direct and indirect taxes. The major types are income, payroll, sales, excise, estate, inheritance, and gift.

D. Unless excused by law, individuals and corporations generally pay income taxes. Income from a small, unincorporated business is taxed as individual income rather than as corporate income.

E. A graduated income tax is one in which the amount of tax paid is tied to income. The more you earn, the more you pay. Some state and local governments use a flat tax. This means that all taxpayers are taxed at the same rate regardless of income, usually 1 to 6 percent.

19-2 File an Income Tax Return

A. To determine your income tax, subtract from your income any adjustments, deductions, and exemptions for which you are eligible. Figure your tax based on this amount. You may be able to reduce your tax by subtracting tax credits.

B. Most young workers can use Form 1040EZ, the easiest tax form to file.

19-3 Social Security

A. Government programs that help people meet social and economic needs are called social security. Social Security is also the name of a particular set of programs, the federal system of retirement benefits, survivors payments, hospital insurance for the elderly, and other services.

B. There are two types of social security programs. One aids the needy regardless of their work record. An example is welfare, which is financed by general taxes. The second is social insurance programs such as Social Security. It is financed by taxes on earnings paid by workers and employers.

C. The four Social Security programs administered by the federal government are retirement payments, survivors payments, disability payments, and Medicare. The two state-administered social insurance programs are unemployment benefits and workers' compensation.

D. To be eligible for federal Social Security benefits, you must earn a certain number of work credits in jobs covered by Social Security. A fully insured worker has earned 40 credits and is eligible to receive complete benefits.

E. Federal Social Security programs are financed by payroll taxes on earnings. Both you and your employer contribute similar amounts. In most states, unemployment benefits are financed by payroll taxes paid by employers, and workers' compensation is financed by insurance that employers must purchase.

F. Social Security, Medicare, and Medicaid trust funds are decreasing at a steady rate. This is due largely to the fact that people are living longer and are therefore consuming more medical services and prescription drugs. There seems to be no quick or easy solution to the funding problems.

19-4 Individual Retirement Accounts

A. To live comfortably in retirement, most people will find it necessary to supplement Social Security with private retirement savings. An excellent way to provide for retirement is to establish an IRA.

B. In 2011, individuals could contribute up to $5,000 to either a traditional or a Roth IRA. Each type of IRA has different features and requirements. An IRA started at an early age can grow to a large amount of money by the time you retire.

Activities

1. Get a copy of and instructions for Form 1040EZ. Fill out the form using the following figures: wages of $15,178, tips of $1,132, and $220 in interest income. Federal income tax in the amount of $1,596 was withheld. What is the amount of tax? Your instructor may assign additional problems.

2. If your state has an income tax, obtain a copy of the income tax form and instructions. Using the amounts shown in Figure 19-4 (except for state income tax), complete the form. Ask your instructor to check the figures.

3. You earn $370 a week. Each year you pay $2,884 in federal income tax, $578 in state income tax, $262 in sales tax, $88 in property tax, $1,472 in FICA tax, and $158 for other taxes. How much do you pay for taxes during the year? How many weeks must you work just to pay taxes?

4. Suppose you earned an annual salary of $27,000 and your spouse earned $32,000. If there were a flat tax on income of 5%, how much income tax would your family have to pay?

5. Have you ever worked at a job in which FICA tax was withheld from your paycheck? If so, prepare a list of all such jobs and the length of time you were employed in each. Then, figure out how many work credits you have accumulated to date. Compare your results with those of your classmates.

6. Last year, Shirley James earned $26,700. The FICA tax rate was 7.65 percent. How much money was withheld for Social Security from Ms. James's income? What was the total FICA tax paid by Ms. James and her employer?

7. Three single workers had taxable incomes of $21,000, $25,000, and $29,000, respectively. Each plans to make a $3,000 contribution to a traditional IRA this year. Using a current federal tax table, figure how much tax each person will save. Compute how much the contribution costs each person.

Word Power

On a separate sheet of paper, match each definition with the correct term. All definitions will be used, and a definition will be used only once.

a. adjusted gross income
b. adjustments to income
c. benefit
d. deduction
e. exemption
f. Federal Insurance Contributions Act (FICA)
g. filing
h. individual retirement account (IRA)
i. lump-sum payment
j. pension
k. revenue
l. Roth IRA
m. social security
n. Social Security
o. tax
p. tax credit
q. tax evasion
r. taxable income
s. taxation
t. wage base
u. work credit

8. The federal system of retirement benefits, survivors payments, hospital insurance for the elderly, and other services

9. A required contribution of money people make to government

10. Unlike a traditional IRA, contributions are not tax-deductible, but they grow tax-free

11. Items that can be subtracted from total income when filing an income tax return to arrive at adjusted gross income

12. A voluntary private pension plan that lets employed people save money annually toward retirement and receive special tax benefits

13. Various nontaxable items that can be subtracted from adjusted gross income when filing an income tax return

14. The amount on an income tax form that results after you subtract adjustments from total income

15. The amount of income on which you pay taxes

16. Money that is raised through taxes to pay the cost of government

17. The illegal practice of avoiding payment of one's income tax obligation

18. Points used to determine eligibility for Social Security benefits; linked to amount of earnings

19. The process by which the expenses of government are paid

20. Financial help in times of sickness, old age, disability, etc. (benefits)

21. Set amounts for yourself and each dependent that are subtracted from adjusted gross income when filing an income tax form

22. A one-time payment of money

23. The process of completing and submitting an income tax return

24. Reductions in the amount of income tax owed

25. The amount of gross annual wages subject to Social Security tax

26. A regular payment of money to a person, usually retired

27. The federal law requiring employers to deduct an amount from workers' paychecks for Social Security and to contribute an equal amount

28. Government programs that help people meet social and economic needs

Think Critically

29. Why do you think some people dislike paying income taxes? How do you feel about it?

30. Which do you think is more fair, a graduated tax or a flat tax?

31. In what ways might the federal income tax system be improved? Give specific illustrations.

32. Have you ever heard of the "underground economy"? To what does it refer? Give examples.

33. Assuming they have no house or rent payment, about how much monthly income do you think a retired couple would need to live comfortably in your area?

34. Why is inflation such a major concern for most retired people?

35. Make a list of taxes you currently pay and those that you expect to pay in the future. Evaluate how these taxes, and the government services they support, will affect your ability to achieve goals in your life-span plan.

36. Identify a goal you might set in your life-span plan that you would expect to achieve in your later years, after the age of 67. Discuss how Social Security benefits might make this goal easier to achieve.

Career Transitions Connection

Financial Advisors

Click on *Browse Career Paths*. In the box preceded by *I'm interested in learning about this career* enter *Financial Advisors*. Click on *Financial Advisors* from the list of options offered. Click on *Career Videos*. Click on *A Day in the Life: Financial Advisor 1*. Click on the *Introduction* to watch an overview of the Financial Advisor's job. Why do you think parents, who would risk their lives to step between their children and danger, will pause before thinking of giving their money to their children? Why do you think accurately reading people's body language is an important part of the Financial Advisor's success?

UNIT 6 Independent Living

484

Co-op Career SPOTLIGHT

Business, Management & Administration

Kelley Holsopple's grandmother was a physical therapist. Talking to her grandmother about her work helped Kelley understand that taking care of people could be a satisfying career.

During her senior year of high school in Florida, Kelley was in a dual enrollment program at the Charlotte Vocational Technical Center. Each morning she attended nursing classes and each afternoon she attended high school. After six months in the dual enrollment program, Kelley obtained her Certified Nursing Assistant certificate. For the rest of her senior year, Kelley worked during the morning in a nursing home and attended high school classes during the afternoon.

After graduation, Kelley had a few different jobs in the medical field. Kelley then accepted a position as a medical assistant in a urology office. Her initial duties included blood draws, taking patient's vitals, performing bladder ultrasounds, catheterizing patients, and assisting with patient treatments for prostate and bladder cancers. During her ten years at this office, Kelley was repeatedly promoted. When she became an office manager, her duties included staffing and office planning. Her growing abilities were financially rewarded. During the ten years that Kelley was at the urology office, her hourly rate of pay increased from $11 per hour to $19.51per hour.

Kelley, her husband, and their three young daughters relocated to Kentucky after her husband suffered a severe back injury.

Kelley Holsopple
Administrative Co-op

Kelley was often frustrated that she was unable to obtain a Kentucky job that was equivalent to her Florida job because she lacked a college degree. This frustration propelled Kelley to enroll at Gateway Community and Technical College. Kelley takes "Learn on Demand" online courses. Kelley is able to complete courses as quickly as her schedule allows. With the help of Gateway's Co-operative education program, Kelley was able to obtain a coveted co-op position with Procter & Gamble as an administrative co-op. Kelley, who is now studying business administration, works 40 hours a week, from 6:30 a.m. until 3 p.m.

Part of Kelley's education is being funded by a Pell Grant. However, as she takes classes more quickly than the Pell Grant allocates funding, she pays for many classes herself.

Kelley is able to juggle the demands of school and working due to the support of her husband and her father. Her family temporarily moved in with her father during their transitional period from Florida to Kentucky. Her husband cares for their young children while Kelley is at work or studying. Her schedule is fairly rigorous. She gets up each weekday at 5 a.m. and usually gets to bed between 10:30 and 11:30 p.m.

Kelley hopes her achievements will serve as a positive role model for her daughters. She wants them to understand that anything in life is possible and that you can start on a new path at any point in your life.

"The marvelous richness of human experience would lose something of rewarding joy if there were no limitations to overcome. The hilltop hour would not be half so wonderful if there were no dark valleys to traverse." —HELEN KELLER

The Legal System

LeggNet/iStockphoto.com

PREVIEW

Law is concerned with many everyday matters. Understanding laws and the court system is an important part of informed citizenship. It is also necessary to know how to find legal help. It is good to learn this before needing such services.

Janice Lee is very upset. Several months ago, she took her car to a local auto repair shop to have the clutch checked. It had been slipping quite a bit.

The manager, Mr. Jacobs, called her that afternoon and said that the clutch would need to be replaced. The new clutch cost Janice $450. It was the first big expense she had had on her car, which she had bought used and was now 12 years old. Janice did not mind very much. The car ran well and had never caused her any trouble.

Soon after Janice got her car back, the clutch began slipping again. She called Mr. Jacobs and took the car back to the shop. Mr. Jacobs said that the clutch pedal was out of alignment. When Janice expressed surprise that the pedal had gone out of alignment that quickly, Mr. Jacobs asked if Janice had very much experience driving a car with a manual transmission. He suggested her driving habits might be responsible.

When the clutch began slipping a third time, Janice took her car to another mechanic whom a friend had recommended. The mechanic told her that the new clutch had been improperly installed. He said that it was already showing signs of wear and would probably need to be replaced in a few years. Janice knew that clutches usually last many years.

Janice went home and wrote a letter to Mr. Jacobs. She explained what the other mechanic had said and requested that the shop reimburse her for the new clutch, the adjustment, and the other mechanic's inspection.

Mr. Jacobs did not reply to Janice's letter. She wrote several more letters, which also received no response. Then Janice contacted the Better Business Bureau. Mr. Jacobs's shop was not a member of the Bureau, and he refused to cooperate in resolving the dispute.

Now a coworker has suggested that Janice get a lawyer. Janice does not know any lawyers, so she looks online. She calls three lawyers. They all recommend that Janice take Mr. Jacobs to small claims court.

Janice has heard of small claims court, but she does not know much about it. She decides that she will find out, though. Janice believes that she is in the right. She wants her money refunded.

THINK CRITICALLY

1. What are some ways that Janice might prove that she is in the right?

2. What do you know about small claims court?

elewynn/Shutterstock.com

> ### ✳ Success Tip
>
> Understanding the law and the legal system can help you in your everyday life.

OBJECTIVES

- Explain the difference between civil and public law
- Describe the general process by which laws are enforced

KEY TERMS

- law
- common law
- statute law
- warrant
- arraignment
- grand jury
- indictment
- bail

Stockbyte/Jupiter Images

Personal Decisions

You go to answer the door. You open it and are surprised to find a police officer. It seems that a car like yours was seen last night leaving the scene of a gas station holdup. The officer wants you to come to the station to answer some questions.

What would you do?

Civil and Public Law

Hopefully, you will never become involved with the legal system through breaking the law. Even if you never break the law, though, you might sometime be accused of a crime that you did not commit. Or you may become an innocent victim of crime.

Not all law deals with crime. For example, Faron and Susie adopted a baby. To finalize the adoption, they had to hire a lawyer and appear before a judge in a court of law.

Law is the body of enforced rules by which people live together. If all people did as they pleased, society could not function. For example, what would happen if everyone drove an auto as fast as they wanted or an employer decided to ignore safety rules? The law defines and makes clear the relationships among individuals and between individuals and society. Law tries to give as much freedom to each person as possible, while protecting the freedom of others.

There are two main sources of law in the United States. In deciding a case, a judge will often look at how similar cases in the past were decided. These decisions are known as **common law**. The second source of law is **statute law**, or legislation. This refers to laws made by Congress and other government bodies.

The two main branches of law are civil and public.

- **Civil law**   Sometimes called private law, civil law determines a person's legal rights and obligations in activities that involve other people. Examples include making credit purchases, renting an apartment, and signing an employment contract. Judges and lawyers spend most of their time on civil matters. Most civil law cases are settled out of court. Even so, more than a million lawsuits are tried yearly in U.S. courts.

- **Public law** Public law defines citizens' rights and responsibilities under local, state, federal, and international laws. Criminal law is the most familiar kind of public law. Public law also deals with different divisions of government and their powers. An example of public law is the requirement that all cars have seat belts. Workers' wages and hours and public safety also come under public law.

Law Enforcement

Most people obey laws. But what about people who do not? The police may arrest anyone they see violating the law. They may also arrest someone they reasonably believe has committed a crime. In some cases, a warrant is required. A **warrant** is a court order that authorizes a police officer to make a search, seizure, or arrest.

After the suspect has been arrested, a charge is entered in the arrest book. The criminal evidence is turned over to a government attorney, or prosecutor. An **arraignment**, which is a hearing in which a prosecutor, police officer, or citizen brings charges against the arrested person, is then held before a judge. A **grand jury** is a group of citizens selected to determine if there should be a trial. For more serious crimes, the prosecutor usually presents the evidence to a grand jury instead of to a judge. If the grand jury decides in favor of a trial, it prepares a formal statement charging the person with the offense. This is called an **indictment**.

The person being held can answer the charges. If the individual pleads guilty, the judge gives a sentence or sets a future date for sentencing. If the accused pleads not guilty, a trial must be held. Rather than remain in jail until the trial, an individual is usually released on **bail**. This is money deposited with the court to guarantee that the person will show up for trial. If the person does not, the bail is forfeited. For certain serious crimes, someone may be held without bail. A person without bail remains in jail until the trial. If he or she cannot afford an attorney, the judge ensures that one is provided.

The purpose of a trial is to determine the guilt or innocence of the accused. Attorneys for both sides present their evidence. A decision of guilty or not guilty is then made, usually by a jury. If the defendant is found guilty, the judge imposes a sentence.

Criminal laws generally specify the minimum and maximum prison terms for which a criminal can be sentenced. Not everyone goes to jail, however. In certain cases, the judge may decide to release a person on probation instead. In such instances, the person must report regularly to a parole officer. For some crimes, the judge may impose a fine as part of the sentencing.

Any law enforcement officer, such as a police officer, sheriff, state trooper, or game warden, can make an arrest. What if a law enforcement officer wants to arrest you? Do not physically resist. Your guilt or innocence can be determined later. If the arrest is legal and you resist, you may be guilty of the crime of resisting arrest.

Workforce Trends

The BLS assigns each occupation to a category based on the typical amount of education or training required. The categories range from "short-term on-the-job training" to "first professional degree." In 2008, about 30% of jobs were in occupations requiring some form of postsecondary degree. During the period 2008–18, it is projected that about 50% of all new jobs created will require a postsecondary degree.

Workplace Innovations

BIOMETRICS

Since the September 11, 2001 terrorist attack, considerable attention has been given to homeland security and the use of biometric techniques. *Biometrics* is a term used to describe a measurable biological characteristic that can be used for automated recognition. Common biometrics include fingerprint, palm print, iris, face, and voice recognition.

A simplified biometric system is comprised of three components. A sensor is used to collect the data and convert it into digital form. A data storage component keeps information that the data input will be compared to. Special mathematical software is used to compare the data input with the data base to arrive at a decision (match).

Facial recognition is a good illustration. Several pictures are taken of a subject (voluntarily or while under surveillance) at different angles and with different facial expressions. Such things as the distance between the eyes, nose, mouth, and jaw; depth of the eye sockets; shape of the cheekbones; length of the jaw line; and the shape, structure, and proportions of the face are recorded. This information is then stored as a biometric template.

At the time of verification and identification, another image is taken and compared to those previously recorded. Some systems are capable of processing 8 million faces in one second. A benefit of facial recognition technology is that it can be done at a distance without the subject being aware they are being scanned. One novel application is a camera placed on a police officer's shirt that allows scanning individuals during a traffic stop for immediate identification of a security risk to that officer.

NET FOLLOW-UP

Use a search engine to explore the Web for additional information on the topic of biometric recognition technology. How would you feel if an employer wanted to use some of your biometric information as part of the company's security system? What if your company wanted to use a retina scan or your fingerprints as a way to check your attendance at work?

An officer may stop you if he or she has reason to believe that you have committed or are about to commit a crime. The officer may ask for your name and address and for an explanation for your actions. You may be searched for weapons if the officer is fearful for his or her safety.

20-1 Assessment

1. Why are laws necessary?
2. Name the two main branches of law. List one area each covers.
3. What happens if a person is arrested and cannot afford to hire an attorney?
4. If you are stopped by a police officer and arrested for a crime you did not commit, how should you act?

THE COURT SYSTEM

OBJECTIVES
- Describe the two parts of the court system
- Summarize how a court works

KEY TERMS
- plaintiff
- defendant
- summons
- judgment
- decree

Personal Decisions

In sorting through the day's mail, you find a postcard that says you have been chosen for jury duty. You are instructed to appear at the courthouse next Wednesday at 9 A.M. for possible jury selection. "I can't go," you think to yourself. "I have to work."

What would you do?

gosphotodesign/Shutterstock.com

State and Federal Courts

The court system is the branch of government having the power to settle disputes. Courts are an essential part of government. Without courts to interpret them, laws would be meaningless. Although they differ in some ways, most courts decide civil disputes between individuals or other parties, determine the guilt or innocence of accused persons, and impose punishment on the guilty. The court system has two parts: state and federal.

State Courts

Each state has its own court system. The lowest or first courts are the police or magistrates' courts in cities and the justices of the peace in villages and rural communities. There may also be various special and municipal courts. Above the lowest level of courts are general trial courts. These courts, also known as county or circuit courts, deal with civil and public law matters.

Many states have an intermediate appellate court, which is between the general trial courts and the state supreme court. Appellate courts hear appeals from the trial courts. The highest appellate court in a state is usually called a supreme court. Several judges (usually five to seven) sit on a state supreme court.

Federal Courts

The United States Constitution provides for a federal court system. Federal courts handle cases involving the Constitution, violations of federal laws, suits between citizens of different states, and cases in which the U.S. government is a party.

The lowest courts of the federal system are the U.S. district courts. The trial of both civil and public cases begins in the district courts. The

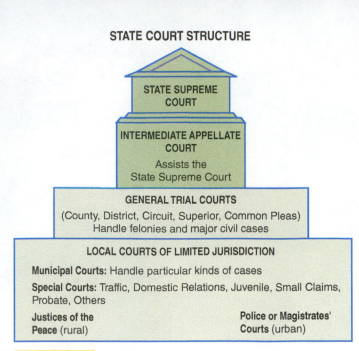

STATE COURT STRUCTURE

STATE SUPREME COURT

INTERMEDIATE APPELLATE COURT
Assists the State Supreme Court

GENERAL TRIAL COURTS
(County, District, Circuit, Superior, Common Pleas)
Handle felonies and major civil cases

LOCAL COURTS OF LIMITED JURISDICTION

Municipal Courts: Handle particular kinds of cases

Special Courts: Traffic, Domestic Relations, Juvenile, Small Claims, Probate, Others

Justices of the Peace (rural)

Police or Magistrates' Courts (urban)

FIGURE 20-1 Although court systems vary from state to state, this pattern is typical.

manner of arrest, indictment, trial, and appeal is very similar to that of state courts.

Above the trial level are the circuit courts of appeal. These courts operate about the same way as state appellate courts. Each appeal is heard by a panel of three judges. A typical pattern of court hierarchy is shown in Figure 20-1.

The highest federal court is the United States Supreme Court. This court has nine justices, or judges. The Chief Justice of the United States presides over the court. Most cases the Supreme Court hears are appeals from the circuit courts and appeals from state supreme courts if they present questions of federal or constitutional law.

How a Court Works

Disputes may arise between two or more persons over money, personal injury, property, or many other issues. A **plaintiff** is a person who files a complaint with the court. A **defendant** is a person who has a complaint filed by someone else against them. After a plaintiff files a complaint against a defendant, the court clerk issues a **summons**, which is an order that commands the defendant to appear in court on a certain day.

The defendant then submits a written report that tells his or her side of the story. If grounds for a suit are present, the judge sets a trial date. When the trial is held, attorneys for the plaintiff and for the defendant present evidence. Part of the evidence may be supplied by *witnesses*. The judge or the jury decides factual disputes and reaches a verdict.

When the case is decided, the judge makes a **judgment**, which is a decision in favor of either the plaintiff or the defendant. The terms *guilty* and *not guilty* are not used in civil cases. If the case is decided in favor of the plaintiff, the judgment depends on the nature of the original complaint. One type of judgment is the award of a sum of money to the plaintiff. Another is a solution for the dispute, such as cancellation of a contract. A third type of judgment is for the court to issue a **decree**, which is an order requiring the defendant to stop doing whatever he or she was doing that harmed the plaintiff.

20-2 Assessment

1. **What are the three basic things that most courts do?**

2. **What are the two parts of the court system?**

3. **In a court case, whom does the prosecuting attorney represent? Whom does the defense attorney represent?**

4. **Give an example of a judgment that might result from a court case.**

High Growth Occupations
FOR THE 21ST CENTURY

Retail Salespersons

Do you like to talk to people? Do you like to sell things? If so, take a look at this occupation—*retail salesperson*. Individuals in this occupation sell a wide variety of products, such as clothing, electronic equipment, vehicles, and just about everything else that satisfies the consumer's wants and needs. The retail salesperson, as the representative for the business, must provide courteous and efficient service in order for the business to remain competitive. Consumers form their impression of a business through their contact with retail salespersons.

Responsibilities of the retail salesperson include assisting customers in finding what they are looking for and trying to interest them in buying the merchandise. Individuals in this occupation must be able to describe a product's features, demonstrate its use, and show various models and colors. Some retail sales positions may require special knowledge or skills. Salespeople who sell vehicles, for example, must be able to explain the features of different models of vehicles, provide information about warranties, and explain the types of options and financing available.

Additional responsibilities may include making out sales checks; receiving cash, checks, and charge payments; bagging or packaging purchases; giving out change and receipts; counting money in the register; separating charge slips, coupons, and exchange vouchers; and making deposits. Some individuals in this occupation may open or close the store and the cash registers.

Most retail salespersons work weekends and evenings, especially during the peak retail season from Thanksgiving through the beginning of January, or during special sales and other peak seasons.

A high school diploma or equivalent is preferred, but no additional education is required. Retail salespeople need to enjoy working with others, be able to communicate clearly and effectively, and have the skill and patience to be able to deal with difficult customers. A neat appearance is also helpful.

iofoto/Shutterstock.com

Customers form opinions about businesses based, in part, on their interactions with retail sales personnel.

OBJECTIVES

- Identify situations that may require legal advice
- Explain how to choose a lawyer
- Name the three types of legal fees

KEY TERMS

- small claims court
- contingency fee

Andresr/Shutterstock.com

► Ethical Decisions

"Hey Andre, have you heard this new song?" Andre listens for a few moments and comments, "that's cool, where did you buy it?" "What do you mean buy it? I have a friend that showed me a website where I can download music for free." "But isn't that illegal?" Andre says "Nah," you say "everybody does it. Do you want a copy of the song?"

What would you do?

Decide if You Need a Lawyer

During your lifetime, you will probably face many legal problems. You may be able to resolve some of them yourself. If you cannot, you will need an attorney.

Whether or not you need a lawyer depends on your situation. The following are some types of situations that may require legal advice:

- Being charged with a crime
- Buying a house
- Starting a business
- Suffering an accident or injury
- Buying a faulty consumer product or service
- Being discriminated against in employment
- Preparing a will
- Declaring bankruptcy
- Getting a divorce

A lawyer is not absolutely necessary in all these cases. The more you learn about the law and legal services, the better able you will be to decide whether you need a lawyer.

A **small claims court** is one of the lowest levels of courts in the state court system and it allows you to sue someone without using an attorney. Small claims courts, sometimes called people's courts, have been around since 1913. One use of small claims court is for unpaid wages. For example, what if you worked two days for Ms. Adams, a local businessperson, who then refused to pay you. To get your money, you could file a claim in small claims court.

The amount of money that can be recovered in small claims court varies among states. The amount is usually limited to several thousand dollars. You cannot generally sue for lost time, nor can you sue for hurt pride, and you cannot collect damages beyond your loss.

Choose a Lawyer

Lawyers, like doctors, are in either a general or a specialized practice. Most lawyers are general practitioners who handle a variety of legal work. For most situations, a general attorney will be adequate. General lawyers who cannot handle a particular problem will usually refer clients to a specialist.

Choosing a lawyer is similar to selecting a doctor, banker, or other professional. Ask enough people and the same name may come up repeatedly. This is a good sign that you are on the right track.

The American Bar Association (ABA) is the largest voluntary professional association in the world. The ABA has nearly 400,000 members, the majority of whom are practicing lawyers and law students. Among its services is the maintenance of the Lawyer Referral Directory. Access www.cengage.com/school/working and click on the Web Links for Lawyer Referral Directory. You can use this online directory to locate an attorney in your particular state and locality who specializes in various fields of practice.

Another way to choose a lawyer is through advertising. Refer to Figure 20-2 to see a few sample ads. Lawyers are allowed to advertise their services, although few do so. If you read or hear an ad that you like, give the attorney a try. Many attorneys provide a free initial consultation. Before deciding on an attorney, it may be wise to meet with several different ones.

FIGURE 20-2 Lawyers now advertise their services.

You should always inquire about legal fees prior to hiring an attorney.

Once you have identified a few lawyers that might meet your needs, visit the website for their firm. Many firms have websites that are menu driven and allow you to select the specialty that you need. If you are not sure what specialty you need, try searching the site for keywords related to your need. When you compare a few different websites, you will start to get a feel for the firms.

If you cannot afford a lawyer, you have several options. In a criminal case, the court will ensure that a lawyer is provided for you. For civil cases, there are hundreds of free legal services and defender programs in the United States. You can find such agencies by looking up "Legal Aid" or "Legal Assistance" in the phone book. Another source is the Directory of Legal Aid and Defender Offices, which is available in many libraries.

Legal Fees

The fees lawyers charge vary depending on the type of situation you have. Do not be afraid to ask about fees at your first meeting. You are entitled to know in advance the approximate cost of legal services.

Lawyers may charge a flat fee, an hourly fee, or a contingency fee. A *flat fee* often covers routine services that take about the same amount of time in all instances. Examples might be a real estate closing or an uncontested divorce. An *hourly fee* is a specific amount paid for each hour the lawyer spends on your case. Rates may range from about $100 to several hundred dollars per hour.

A **contingency fee** is based on whether or not a case is won. If a case is won, you pay the attorney. If the case is lost, you do not pay the attorney. If the attorney does win, you must pay a certain percentage of the amount awarded. A one-third contingency fee is common. For example, if you receive $75,000 in a legal judgment, the attorney will receive $25,000. The contingency fee is used for certain kinds of cases, such as personal injury or medical malpractice.

20-3 Assessment

1. Name three situations that may require legal advice.
2. Explain the purpose of the Lawyer Referral Directory.
3. If you cannot afford a lawyer in a criminal case, what option do you have? In a civil case, what are your options if you cannot afford a lawyer?
4. Explain the three methods of paying for legal services.

Focus on Skills for Living

Common Law

The system of law used in the United States is called common law, except in Louisiana where the Code Napoleon is followed. Common law originated in England as a way of settling disputes.

The law at first was based on customs. That changed in the twelfth century, when the king's courts began to take over the settlement of disputes from the local customary courts. The decisions of the king's justices were supposed to be based on customs. On occasion, there were no customs. The courts then had to reach a decision based upon logic and reason. As a result, a body of common law grew up from the judges' decisions.

The early colonists who settled in America brought with them the practices of common law. After the American Revolution, the tradition of English common law continued. Over the years, American judges gradually changed the common law to make it more suitable for our society.

As new conditions arose, common law often did not apply. A new source for law emerged. This was statute law, or legislation. Statute law is that type of law made by Congress and state legislatures. In present-day society, legislation and judge-made law are equally important.

THINK CRITICALLY

1. In Chapter 19, you read about workers' compensation. As the United States became more industrialized, an increasing number of workers sued employers for work-related injuries or diseases. This was their right under common law. Soon lawsuits bogged down the court system. Partly to address this problem, workers' compensation laws were written. Why was legislation rather than common law the solution to this problem?

2. Some people believe that there are too many laws in the United States, that they harm business and interfere in people's private lives. Do you agree? Why or why not?

Common law originated in England.

Chapter Summary

20-1 The Nature of Law

A. Law is the body of enforced rules by which people live together. The law defines and makes clear the relationships among individuals and between individuals and society. The two main branches of law are civil and public.

B. The police may arrest anyone they see violating the law or reasonably believe has committed a crime. At an arraignment or before a grand jury, charges are brought against the person. If the accused pleads not guilty, a trial is held. If he or she is found guilty, the judge imposes a sentence.

C. If a law enforcement officer wants to arrest or search you, do not physically resist. Your guilt or innocence can be determined later.

20-2 The Court System

A. Most courts decide civil disputes between individuals or other parties, determine the guilt or innocence of accused persons, and impose punishment on the guilty.

B. In a civil case, the plaintiff files a complaint and the defendant receives a summons. The defendant submits a written report of his or her side of the story. If there are grounds for a suit, the judge sets a trial date. Attorneys present evidence, a verdict is decided, and the judge makes a judgment.

20-3 Legal Services

A. If you cannot resolve a legal problem yourself, consult with a lawyer.

B. You may sue someone in small claims courts without using an attorney.

C. The Lawyer Referral Directory helps people get legal assistance.

D. Lawyers may charge a flat, hourly, or contingency fee, depending on the type of situation. Ask about fees at your first meeting.

Activities

1. Identify a recent Supreme Court decision. Investigate this decision and prepare a short oral report to present to the class.

2. Invite a member of SADD (Students Against Destructive Decisions) to discuss the legal issues surrounding drunk driving.

3. Research how to file a complaint with your local small claims court. Try to obtain a copy of any written guidelines and forms on how to file a complaint. What types of situations may be taken to small claims court?

4. In legal terms, what does the term "bar" refer to?

5. "Sexting" using your mobile phone can be a very serious criminal offense. What does sexting refer to? Search for information on the Web, including the legal consequences of sexting.

6. Identify and explain a goal you might set in your life-span plan that will be easier for you to achieve because of our system of civil law.

Word Power

On a separate sheet of paper, match each definition with the correct term. All definitions will be used, and a definition will be used only once.

7. A main source of law in the United States; previous cases

8. A court order authorizing a police officer to make a search, seizure, or arrest

9. A low level court that allows you to sue without using an attorney

10. A hearing before a judge during which formal charges are brought against an arrested person

11. The complaining party in a lawsuit

12. A grand jury's formal statement charging a person with an offense

13. The judge's decision in a civil suit in favor of either the plaintiff or the defendant

14. Money deposited with a court to guarantee that an accused person will show up for trial

15. The body of enforced rules by which people live together

16. An order commanding a party to a lawsuit to appear in court

17. A person required to answer charges in a lawsuit

18. An order issued by a court; for example, requiring a defendant to stop doing whatever is harming the plaintiff

19. Laws made by Congress and other government bodies

20. A group of citizens to which a prosecutor presents evidence of a serious crime who must determine if there should be a trial

21. Whether you pay the attorney depends upon whether the case is won

a. arraignment
b. bail
c. common law
d. contingency fee
e. decree
f. defendant
g. grand jury
h. indictment
i. judgment
j. law
k. plaintiff
l. small claims court
m. statute law
n. summons
o. warrant

Think Critically

22. How might you be affected in the future by having a criminal record?

23. What is meant by "white-collar" crime? Should white-collar criminals be treated differently than other criminals?

24. In what types of legal situations would you probably need a specialized lawyer, as opposed to a general lawyer?

25. The widespread use of smartphones and other electronic mobile devices has resulted in more illegal activities such as downloading music, copying files, sexting, harassment, and cyberbullying. Discuss how you can protect yourself from these practices.

"You gain strength, experience, and confidence by every experience where you really stop to look fear in the face. . . . You must do the thing you cannot do."
—ELEANOR ROOSEVELT

Where to Live

Jason_ViStockphoto.com

21-1 A Housing Plan

21-2 Apartment Life

PREVIEW

At some point in your life, you will probably leave your parents' home. When that time comes, deciding where to live will become important to you. The choice is a difficult one that involves both personal and financial considerations. Young people who have never before lived away from home may not know what is involved in renting or buying their own place. They may also underestimate the total cost of a house or an apartment.

Taking/Action A First Apartment

Ezra's life is changing very rapidly. In a few weeks, he will graduate from high school. He has accepted a job as a mechanic at Porter Tire and Auto. Although he does not mind living at home, he would like a place of his own.

Ezra and his brother have shared a room since Ezra was five years old. When Ezra thinks about an apartment, he thinks it would be great to have it all to himself. He knows, though, that apartment living is less expensive if you have a roommate.

Ezra has noticed an apartment complex near his job. He calls to find out how much it would cost to rent a one-bedroom and a two-bedroom apartment.

The one-bedroom apartment would be too expensive, but he could afford the two-bedroom apartment with a roommate.

Ezra talks to his best friend, Lonnie, about renting an apartment together. Ezra and Lonnie have been friends for years. Lonnie does not have a job yet, though, so he is not planning to look for an apartment for some time.

Then Ezra thinks about furnishing an apartment. His parents would let him take his bed, dresser, and desk, but he does not have any other furniture. Maybe his Aunt Lorraine has some pieces he could borrow. He calls her.

"I have a kitchen table and chairs, an armchair, and an old sofa that you can take and keep," his aunt tells him. Ezra figures he can fill in the gaps for other apartment needs by picking up a few things from Craigslist.

Then she describes some of her experiences in renting apartments. One apartment manager had told her that an air conditioner would be installed in an apartment she was planning to rent. When his aunt moved in, there was no air conditioner. She asked the manager about it. The manager replied that air conditioners were not in the rental agreement and refused to install one.

Ezra thinks some more about renting an apartment. He is not so sure it is a good idea. He might continue to live with his parents and save his money for a while.

THINK CRITICALLY

1. What are some things to consider when deciding whether to rent an apartment?

2. What steps should you take to find and rent an apartment?

manzrussali/Shutterstock.com

▶ Interpersonal Decisions

You want to get an apartment closer to work but have not located anything you can afford. You post on Facebook that you are looking for an apartment. Lana, who is a friend's friend, replies that her roommate has left and she is looking for someone to move in and share expenses. You've never met Lana, but you have seven mutual friends. You are uneasy about the idea of sharing an apartment with someone you do not know.

What would you do?

Choose a Type of Housing

If you decide to get a place of your own, housing will probably be the largest single expense in your budget. In many areas, rents and home prices are high and costs continue to increase. But cost is not the only problem. Many desirable communities have housing shortages.

Because housing is such a major expense, plan carefully. Begin by analyzing your needs and wants. Based on what you learn, you can then decide whether buying or renting is best for you.

Housing Needs and Wants

The perfect place to live may not be available or affordable. So it may be necessary to make some compromises that suit you and your budget. Nonetheless, it will be important to consider needs and wants in a place to live. Identify your needs and wants before you start looking.

It is a good idea to make a list of the features you think are essential or important in a place to live. That way you will not be attracted by some eye-catching feature that you do not really need or want. Know the difference between essential and important.

Rosanna is looking for an apartment. She does not want a long commute to work. For Rosanna, being near her office is essential. She also thinks having a garage is important.

Individuals and families differ greatly in how they feel about housing. For some people, a house or apartment is simply a place to stay.

For others, their lifestyles, hobbies, and goals revolve around their home.

Housing Alternatives

Different types of housing are available. One alternative is the single-family detached house. This kind of house usually offers more space, a larger yard, and more privacy than other types of housing. Many people consider a house the most convenient and desirable place to raise children. A detached house is often the most expensive type of housing. Attached houses, also called **townhouses**, are common in some communities. This kind of housing often includes a small yard. The houses may share common properties such as a pool and tennis courts.

Housing is also available in apartments. These may range in size from one room to many rooms. An apartment usually does not include a yard. A **cooperative** is part of a property jointly owned by residents. A **condominium** is an individually owned unit with shared ownership of common facilities, like the grounds. A townhouse or apartment may be a cooperative or a condominium.

Mobile homes are another alternative. They are usually located on small lots in mobile home parks in or near a city.

Renting an apartment may allow you to live in a central part of a city without making a permanent commitment to the location.

Rent or Buy?

Now that you have analyzed your needs and wants and considered the types of housing available, consider whether you should rent or buy.

Buying and renting have advantages and disadvantages. In deciding which is best for you, you will want to consider various factors. These include the number and ages of the people in your family, your financial situation, your lifestyle, and the housing alternatives available in your community. Remember that buying generally means making a down payment and then a mortgage payment every month for 15 to 30 years. A **mortgage** is a loan, typically for 30 years, obtained from a financial institution to buy housing.

Considerations When You Rent

Some advantages of renting follow:

- Rent is usually a fixed amount for the term of the lease. A **lease** is the rental agreement between a **tenant**, or renter, and a **landlord**, who is the owner or manager of the property. Renters face fewer unexpected costs.
- Renting only obligates you for the length of the lease. If you want to move, you can make other arrangements when the lease expires.
- Renters are not responsible for taxes and repairs.
- Expenditures for renters are usually lower than those for buyers.
- If you obtain a job opportunity in another city, it is easier to move if you are renting.
- When new to an area, renting gives you the chance to learn about the community.
- When future housing needs are uncertain, you can postpone a decision by renting.

Renting may involve different costs and responsibilities depending on what you rent. If you rent a detached house or a townhouse, you will probably have to pay all the normal expenses for running a home in addition to rent. You may also be responsible for maintenance and repairs.

If you rent an apartment, you will generally not be responsible for maintenance or repairs. They will be taken care of by the landlord. If you do not want to buy furniture, you can find apartments where the major pieces are provided. Renting an apartment is often more economical than renting other types of housing or buying. For all these reasons, renting an apartment is often a common choice of young people who are living away from home for the first time.

Some disadvantages of renting include:

- If the property is sold while you are a tenant, you may be forced to move or have your rent increased even though you are within the terms of your lease.
- If your landlord decides to renovate your apartment, you may have to live through the renovation process and all the accompanying inconvenience and mess.
- If you have rental units above you, and water leaks either from a water heater, a sink, or a commode, the water will leak into your apartment.
- You are at the mercy of your least responsible neighbor. For example, if your neighbor goes to work while leaving an appliance on and a fire results, your apartment may also be affected by the fire.

Considerations When You Buy

The advantages of buying a home include

- Spending money to buy a home is a fairly safe form of investment. Unlike most investments, a home can be used.

Communication at Work — DO RESEARCH

The need to do research does not end when you finish school. You may need to shop for the best price for a computer part or compare printers to see which one your company should buy. A customer may ask you what type of gas logs you recommend for his fireplace. You may be looking for an apartment, deciding where to open a savings account, or choosing an IRA. You can do some of these things without research, but research will almost certainly result in a better recommendation or decision.

Like research for school, research for work might mean going to a library or using the Internet. But it might mean other things as well.

Suppose you work for a landscaping company. Your boss might ask you to plant several different kinds of grasses and observe them over time to see how well each grows.

Take notes as you do your research. Once you have finished, organize your information. Then examine it carefully. What conclusions can you draw?

THINK CRITICALLY

1. Why is it important to take notes as you do your research?
2. How might you conduct research to find out about different types of gas logs?

- During inflationary times, property values rise. If you have a mortgage, you will be paying it off with cheaper dollars.
- Owning your home saves money on income taxes through deductions for mortgage interest and real estate taxes.
- The **equity**, or money invested in a home above the amount owed on a mortgage, can be used as security for a loan.
- Home ownership can improve your credit rating.
- When you own your own home, you can decorate, remodel, and landscape the way you wish.

Buying involves different costs and levels of responsibility depending on what you buy. Homeowners pay not only the mortgage but also all expenses for home operation, upkeep, taxes, insurance and repairs. Performing maintenance and repairs is also your responsibility.

When you buy a cooperative or a condominium, you are sharing with others the responsibilities, obligations, and maintenance costs. Very often, cooperative and condominium owners form a homeowners' or maintenance association. Owners pay monthly fees to the association. The money is used to provide for maintenance and improvements to common properties such as grounds and tennis courts. Maintenance fees may be substantial.

Mobile homes are much less expensive to buy than houses. Mobile homes allow more people to enjoy the benefits of home ownership. However, mobile homes do not increase in value as much over time as houses, cooperatives, and condominiums generally do. Mobile homes may also be unsafe in storms and high winds.

Some disadvantages of buying a home include:

- Buying a home means that you have to make an initial down payment and take out a mortgage.
- Monthly costs of owning a home are variable. What happens if your furnace or water heater has to be replaced?
- If you get sick or lose your job and can't make monthly payments, the lender can call the loan and you could lose the home.
- Owning a home usually makes moving more difficult and complicated if your job or family situation changes.
- Traditionally, owning a home has been a good investment. However, after the real estate bubble collapsed in 2007, many home prices dropped 25% or more.

21-1 Assessment

1. What is the first step in deciding where to live?
2. What are the four major types of housing alternatives?
3. Explain how inflation may contribute to the value of a home?
4. Name three advantages of renting and buying.

High Growth Occupations
FOR THE 21ST CENTURY

Nursing Aides, Orderlies, and Attendants

 Numerous entry-level jobs in the health care field are available for nursing aides, orderlies, and attendants. These occupations provide hands-on care and perform routine tasks under the supervision of nursing and medical staff. Many workers start their careers in these occupations and later leave to attend training programs for other healthcare occupations.

Nursing aides, also known as *nurse aides, nursing assistants, certified nursing assistants, geriatric aides, orderlies,* or *hospital attendants*, handle many aspects of a patient's care. They often help patients eat, dress, and bathe. They also answer calls for help, deliver messages, serve meals, make beds, and tidy up rooms. Aides sometimes are responsible for taking a patient's temperature, pulse rate, respiration rate, or blood pressure. They also may help provide care to patients by helping them get out of bed and walk, escorting them to operating and examining rooms, or providing skin care.

Psychiatric aides, also known as *mental health assistants or psychiatric nursing assistants*, care for mentally impaired or emotionally disturbed individuals. They work under a team that may include psychiatrists, psychologists, psychiatric nurses, social workers, and therapists. In addition to helping patients to dress, bathe, groom themselves, and eat, psychiatric aides socialize with them and lead them in educational and recreational activities. They accompany patients to and from therapy and treatment.

Work as an aide can be physically and emotionally demanding. Aides spend many hours standing and walking, and they often face heavy workloads. Aides also perform tasks that some may consider unpleasant and the patients they care for may be disoriented, irritable, or uncooperative.

Nursing and psychiatric aide training is offered in some high schools, vocational-technical centers, nursing care facilities, and community colleges. Many employers provide classroom instruction for newly hired aides, while others provide informal on-the-job instruction by a licensed nurse or an experienced aide. Such training may last from several days to a few months. Some states require psychiatric aides to complete a formal training program.

Gina Sanders/Shutterstock.com

Nursing aides perform many tasks that contribute to patients' comfort.

APARTMENT LIFE

OBJECTIVES

- Name and describe factors to consider when finding an apartment
- Summarize items included in an apartment lease
- Explain rights and responsibilities of landlords and tenants

KEY TERMS

- security deposit
- sublet

Personal Decisions

You come home from work to discover the landlord leaving your apartment. He seems surprised and says that he was checking on the furnace. Several times over the next month, you notice little things that suggest someone has been in the apartment. You are aware that the landlord has the right to enter your apartment for emergencies and for maintenance. But you are upset by the thought that he may be in the apartment for other reasons.

What would you do?

Piotr Marcinski/Shutterstock.com

Find an Apartment

You might decide to rent an apartment. Available rental housing is often listed with a real estate agency or an apartment-finding business that charges fees for its services. More often, people find an apartment by checking the newspaper classified ads, searching the Web, following through on tips from friends or coworkers, or just walking or driving through a particular neighborhood. College students can often find an apartment through the school's housing office.

Things to Consider

Suppose you and a friend are looking for separate places to rent at the same time. What you consider important may not be important to your friend. But both of you will need to be concerned about certain things.

Location   The neighborhood in which an apartment is located is important. However, the location may not be as critical to a renter as it is to a homebuyer. Renters have no financial investment in the property. So their interest is limited more to convenience factors. Finding an apartment that is close to work or school, has nearby shopping, and is accessible to public transportation may be important to you.

Safety   You should pay careful attention to safety. Well-lit and uncluttered entrances, hallways, and stairways contribute to security. A locked

Bed bugs are a complication of modern life. Bed bugs, which bite sleeping people, are so tiny that they are dwarfed by a penny. Their size makes them difficult to spot. Bed bugs can be brought into a home on luggage, backpacks, furniture, framed pictures, and clothing. Bed bugs can travel within a building on pipes, vents, and electrical wiring. Access **www.cengage.com/school/working** and click on the link for Chapter 21 to learn more about bedbugs. Scroll through the brochure posted by the New York City Department of Health and Mental Hygiene to learn how to detect the presence of bed bugs in a building. How should you inspect a potential apartment for bedbugs? Research the requirements in your state or city for any requirements landlords have in relation to informing tenants about bedbugs and about treating bedbugs.

www.cengage.com/school/working

outside entrance is another good feature. Apartment doors should be securely constructed and have deadbolts or other types of strong locks. Basement or first-floor apartments should have special window grilles or locking features in addition to regular window latches.

Another aspect of safety is fire protection. Each apartment should have one or more smoke detectors in good working order. The kitchen area ought to have a fire extinguisher available. (Buy one yourself if it doesn't.) Check to see if the apartment has an external fire-escape exit. If not, is there an evacuation plan to follow in case of fire?

Privacy and noise   Find out about the people who currently live in the building. If possible, meet and talk with some of the tenants. Remember that you may be sharing a relatively small area with dozens or even hundreds of other people. Because apartment residents live closely together, noise can be a real problem. Noise can come from outside streets and parking lots or from within other apartments. Buildings should be soundproofed to dampen the sounds of talking, plumbing, and music between apartments and between hallways and apartments. Noises from apartments above are usually more noticeable than sounds from apartments below.

Scott and Tasha Foster, for instance, have an upstairs neighbor who works from 3:30 P.M. to midnight. He usually wakes them up about 12:20 A.M. when he gets home and opens the apartment door. A few minutes later, he is heard taking a shower. Off and on throughout the night, Scott and Tasha are awakened by sounds of footsteps, closing doors, music, and TV. Their neighbor is not unusually loud or inconsiderate. He just happens to have a different lifestyle than they do.

Ventilation   Can air enter easily? Most apartments that have air-conditioning are well ventilated. Without this feature, cooking odors and stagnant air may be problems. Does the stove have an exhaust fan? Is the number of windows adequate, and do they all open easily?

Other considerations   Check appliances such as refrigerators, stoves, and dishwashers. Be sure you know who pays for utilities. Is the electricity your responsibility? How about heat? Is basic cable provided? How is cellphone reception in the apartment? Ask for an estimate of typical costs for utilities and other services for which you will be responsible. Notice how well the landlord keeps up the property. Does he or she keep the lawn cut, the hedges trimmed, and the hallways clean?

Take notes on the condition of the apartment. Include items such as chipped paint, marked-up walls, and worn or stained carpeting or other flooring. Check the bathroom and kitchen for water leaks and make sure all the drains work properly. Look for signs of rodents, like mice. Determine if there are any signs of bugs, like cockroaches. Look inside all the closets and cabinets to see if there is any damage. If you are renting a furnished apartment, list each piece of furniture and write down a description of its condition. Take pictures of anything that is not in good repair. Write up an inventory from your notes and photos. Go over it with your landlord, and make sure it is part of the rental agreement.

You probably have friends or relatives who live in apartments. If so, ask them to describe how they found their living quarters.

How to Approach a Landlord

Looking for a place to live is similar to getting a job. As with a potential employer, it is important to make a good impression on the landlord or apartment manager. Be courteous when applying for an apartment.

Most landlords will ask you to fill out an application. The landlord is interested in checking your past rental record and credit references. Fill out the application form honestly and completely. Do not leave any blank spaces.

Some landlords charge an application fee. Before you pay such a fee, ask if you will get it back. Also find out if you must rent the unit if your application is accepted. Be sure you know when you will be notified of the landlord's decision.

Find out whether you will be required to pay a security deposit. A **security deposit** is a sum of money, usually equal to one month's rent, which the landlord holds during the time you rent the apartment. It is intended to be used for any damage you cause. If the apartment is clean and in good condition at the time you leave it, your security deposit should be refunded.

The Rental Agreement

The lease is a written legal contract between you, the tenant, and the landlord. For agreeing to pay rent and following the lease's rules, you are allowed to rent the apartment. The lease is often a preprinted form that contains most or all of the following parts and rules:

- Landlord name, tenant name, and property's address
- The beginning and ending dates of occupancy
- The amount of rent and when and where it is to be paid
- The amount of any security deposit
- Limits on the number of renters
- Any rules regarding pets
- Who is responsible for normal maintenance and repairs. The renter must pay for any damage caused by carelessness.
- Who is responsible for electricity, trash pickup, and other routine items
- An attached inventory that describes the condition of the apartment and lists and describes the condition of any furnishings
- To **sublet** an apartment is to be a tenant in an apartment and then lease the apartment to someone else. Is subletting allowed?
- The conditions that allow the landlord to enter the apartment.
- The procedures to be followed when the tenant wishes to end the lease. An automatic renewal clause may also be a part of the lease.

Workforce Trends

During periods of high unemployment, job seekers often relocate. However, home prices have dropped substantially since 2007. Many people now owe more on their homes than they are worth. Adding to the problem, potential employers are cutting back on the amount of relocation assistance they will provide. Therefore, many people are both unemployed and stuck in a home they cannot afford to sell.

Any special arrangements between you and the landlord should be written into the lease. An example would be any repairs that the landlord agrees to make and a date when they will be completed.

Read the lease very carefully before signing it. When you put your name on a lease, you say that you understand and accept all conditions contained in it. Make sure you are provided with a signed copy of the agreement.

Landlord-tenant Relationships

The relationship between you and a landlord is a legal one. Both of you have certain rights and responsibilities.

Rights and Responsibilities of Landlords

The landlord has the right to set reasonable rules and regulations for the management of rental units. Unless you have agreed to repair or maintain the property, the landlord must keep it in reasonable repair. This means the landlord must keep the premises in a clean, safe condition.

Rights and Responsibilities of Tenants

Your rights as a tenant are essentially the reverse of the landlord's responsibilities. You pay rent for housing, and you expect to receive a safe and livable apartment. If something goes wrong, it should be repaired in a reasonable amount of time. You are entitled to peace, quiet, and privacy.

You have the responsibility to follow the rules in the lease. These basically deal with paying the rent on time, keeping your area clean and safe, and not abusing the landlord's property or the rights of other tenants. Try to maintain a proper business relationship with the landlord. Report all problems as they occur. In addition, have in writing all communication with the landlord, and make copies of everything. Communicating by email is one easy way to generate copies. This will protect your rights.

A landlord-tenant relationship is like any other personal or business association. For the relationship to work, both parties must fulfill their obligations. Do your part by understanding your obligations and then carrying them out.

21-2 Assessment

1. How do most people locate an apartment?
2. What two types of fire protection devices should be in an apartment?
3. Explain how renting an apartment is similar to getting a job.
4. What is the purpose of a security deposit?
5. What should be attached to a lease?
6. What are the responsibilities of landlords and tenants?
7. Why should you maintain a business relationship with the landlord?

Focus on Skills for Living

Roommate Relationships

Most people have a roommate at one or more times in their lives. Living with a roommate is a business relationship because money is exchanged. But it is also an emotional relationship.

Before choosing or becoming a roommate, you should have a serious discussion with the other person. Items you will need to agree on in advance include housework and laundry, food supplies, overnight guests, the security deposit and how it will be refunded, pets (and who takes care of them), boyfriends or girlfriends, and shared electronic devices, like TVs. Particularly important are the terms for moving out. It is a good idea to have a written agreement to give each other a 30- or 60-day notice.

Unless the tenant is allowed to sublet, all roommates should sign the lease. Be wary of any arrangement that does not involve you signing a lease. A roommate whose name is not on a lease does not have the same legal rights as a tenant that has signed the lease.

Privacy is an important issue in a society that has countless social networks and the ability to post messages, pictures, and videos instantly. Before agreeing to become roommates, establish ground rules regarding respecting each other's privacy for any electronic postings.

Because many people use electronic methods for banking, purchasing, and bill payment, you need to also make sure your roommates are trustworthy. You should store all electronic passwords in a safe location.

Here is how one group of four roommates have been able to get along. Before they rented the apartment, each person signed a separate form outlining all the financial responsibilities involved and what would be shared. Each person contributes a fixed amount each week for household staples. Each person takes turns going out to buy what is needed. Apart from this, the roommates buy their own food and do their own dishes. They occasionally cook a meal together for a holiday or special event.

Utility bills are divided equally. Each roommate has a separate phone, and no one answers anyone else's phone. Every two weeks, the group meets to discuss any problems.

Sharing living space can be difficult. But many roommate crises can be easily prevented or resolved. Set ground rules from the start. Discuss your feelings and expectations with your roommate. And always be willing to negotiate and compromise.

THINK CRITICALLY

1. What should roommates discuss before signing a lease?
2. What are some keys to living successfully with a roommate?

nullplus/iStockphoto.com

Proactively making an agreement regarding how food and meals will be handled is one way to reduce possible conflicts between roommates.

Chapter Summary

22-1 A Housing Plan

A. At some point in your life, you will probably move from your parents' home. When that time comes, deciding where to live will become important to you. The choice is a difficult one that involves both personal and financial considerations.

B. Since housing is such a major expense, plan carefully. Begin by analyzing your needs and wants. It may be necessary to make compromises that suit you and your budget. Your housing alternatives may include a detached house, townhouse, condominium, apartment, or mobile home.

C. Buying and renting have advantages and disadvantages. Become familiar with these. Renting an apartment is probably the most common choice of young people who are living away from home for the first time.

22-2 Apartment Life

A. When looking for an apartment, you need to be concerned about many variables including location, personal safety, fire protection, privacy, noise, ventilation, and furnishings. Looking for a place to live is a great deal like getting a job. It is important to make a good impression on the landlord or apartment manager.

B. Most apartments are rented according to an agreement called a lease. It is a written legal contract between you and the landlord. Know what to expect in a lease. Read it carefully before signing.

C. You and the landlord have certain legal rights and responsibilities. The landlord must keep the property in reasonable repair. Your rights as a tenant include receiving a safe and livable apartment. You are also entitled to peace, quiet, privacy, and fair treatment. You have the responsibility to follow the rules in the lease. Deal with the landlord in a businesslike manner.

Activities

1. Assume you are going to move to a nearby town in a few months to begin a new job. A friend who works for the same company is also moving there. The two of you decide to share a place to live. Prepare a list of what you need and want in housing. Turn the list in to your instructor. Then discuss this subject in class.

2. Check local classified ads or search the Web to find out the cost of renting in your area.

3. Lease and rental agreement laws may differ from state to state. Access www.cengage.com/school/working and click on the Web Links for Rental Agreements. Locate the link for your state. In addition to

information about laws, this page also contains related information on leases and rental agreements. Your instructor may assign different topics to class members to read and present an oral summary in class.

4. Find out if your state or city has a tenancy law, tenant ordinance, or housing code (not building code). What is the warranty of habitability? Can a tenant be evicted from an apartment? How may a tenant resolve complaints with a landlord?

5. Consider the housing alternative that you think you would set as a goal in your life-span plan. Explain why other people may set different housing goals in their individual life-span plans.

Word Power

On a separate sheet of paper, match each definition with the correct term. All definitions will be used, and a definition will be used only once.

6. A townhouse or apartment that is part of a property jointly owned by residents

7. The owner or manager of a rental property

8. An individually owned townhouse or apartment with shared ownership of common facilities, like the grounds

9. Renter; the person who rents an apartment

10. A rental agreement between a tenant and a landlord

11. Individually owned houses that are attached to other houses on one or both sides

12. To lease a property as a tenant to another person

13. The value of (money invested in) a home above the amount owed on a mortgage

14. A loan, typically for 30 years, obtained from a financial institution to buy housing

15. A sum of money, usually equal to one month's rent, which a landlord holds while you rent an apartment

a. condominium
b. cooperative
c. equity
d. landlord
e. lease
f. mortgage
g. security deposit
h. sublet
i. tenant
j. townhouse

Think Critically

16. Sharing an apartment with others is a good way to economize on housing. However, living with roommates can be difficult at times. What do you think might be the most common problems with roommates? How can they be avoided?

17. Does your community have a neighborhood watch, neighborhood patrol, or other type of citizen-oriented crime prevention program? Discuss how such programs operate.

18. The price and availability of housing are often important factors in the decision to accept a first job or to relocate in another job. Discuss and provide illustrations of this.

22

"Careers, like rockets, don't always take off on schedule. The key is to keep working the engines."
—GARY SINISE

The Rest of Your Life

Lisa F. Young/Shutterstock.com

PREVIEW

One of your most important roles in life is that of citizen. Citizenship is a part of daily living. It involves participation in home, school, community, and work life.

Education and training beyond high school can make you a more valuable employee and can open many career opportunities. Lifelong learning, continually pursuing education and training, and understanding how to evaluate financial opportunities that support education, are part of the process of keeping your employment skills up-to-date.

Taking/*Action* Learn to Earn

Cid is interested in becoming a bookkeeper or an accountant. He is having a difficult time deciding which occupation is right for him. He will be graduating next year, so he needs to make a decision soon.

Cid decides to ask his Uncle Roberto, who is a bookkeeper, for advice. He visits him at work one day. Uncle Roberto shows Cid around and demonstrates the accounting software that he uses. Then the two go out to lunch together.

"How long does it take to learn to become a bookkeeper?" Cid asks. "What kinds of courses do you have to take?"

"That depends," Uncle Roberto replies. "You should call some potential employers and find out what their job requirements are and what kind of accounting software they use. Then, check with your business department at school or the local community college for courses."

"Actually, if I were you," he continues, "I would seriously consider becoming an accountant instead. You could make more money. You could continue your education by becoming a certified public accountant or certified financial planner, which might increase your earning potential even more. You might be able to become your own boss one day."

"That sounds great," says Cid, "but I need to get a job as soon as possible. I don't have much money for college, and I do not want to go into debt."

"You can start by taking accounting classes now at your high school. Then you could work and go to school part-time. But think carefully about applying for a student loan or other assistance and going to college full-time. Federal student loans have long repayment periods and low interest rates. There are some things that are worth going into debt for. You should talk to your school career counselor and get more information before you make this decision."

Cid thanks Uncle Roberto for his advice. Cid knows what he needs to do next.

✳ Success Tip

Find out the educational and training requirements for occupations that interest you.

THINK CRITICALLY

1. What does Cid need to do next?

2. Think of an occupation that interests you. What education and training does it require?

RidoFranz/iStockphoto.com

OBJECTIVES

- Explain the four responsibilities of citizenship
- Summarize the process of registering to vote and casting a ballot
- Discuss the importance of voting in local, state, and national elections

KEY TERMS

- citizenship
- precinct

icyimage/Shutterstock.com

▶ Personal Decisions

The school board has voted to make drastic cuts in the district's career and technical education program. The board says that it is too expensive to operate. Many students are very upset. A group of them is meeting after school to discuss what they might do. You have been asked to come to the meeting. You are concerned about the cuts, but you are not sure you want to get involved.

What would *you* do?

Responsibilities of Citizenship

Citizenship is membership in a community, state, county, or nation. It also means carrying out the duties and responsibilities of a citizen. The responsibilities of citizenship involve personal, economic, political, and national-defense activities.

On the personal level, good citizens are considerate of the needs of others. They help develop and preserve basic institutions such as community. They adhere to the customs and laws of society. Good citizens stand up for what they believe is right and take action against what they know is wrong.

Economically, being a good citizen means producing efficiently and consuming wisely. It also means helping to protect the rights of others to work. Good citizens use their talents and abilities to further the economic welfare of the society.

In the political area, every citizen of age should be a registered voter and should participate in all elections. A good citizen keeps up with local, national, and international issues and informs elected representatives of his or her opinions. People can serve the government directly in such ways as performing jury duty when ordered. Contributing to national defense is another way to serve the government.

Some full-time workers belong to the military reserve. Darius Hartley, for instance, is a member of the Air National Guard. His regular job is working as a cabinetmaker. Darius attends monthly reserve meetings and spends two weeks at reserve summer camp. In a national emergency or military conflict, Darius could be called into active duty.

Vote

Voting is both a privilege and a right. In many countries, people have no say in how they are governed or in the laws that are passed. You have the responsibility to vote in local, state, and national elections. If everyone refused to vote, self-government would come to a standstill. "What difference will my vote make?" you ask. Election outcomes often hinge on a few votes. Yours might make the difference!

Voting Qualifications and Procedures

In all states, voters must be U.S. citizens and at least 18 years old. They must also meet the residency requirements of their state. As soon as you meet these three conditions, you should register to vote. Every state except North Dakota has some form of voter registration. A complete listing of each state's voter laws and registration deadlines is available by accessing www.cengage.com/school/working and clicking on the Web Links for State Voting Laws.

In the registration process, a person's name is added to the list of eligible voters. Voters may register in person or by mail. Several states offer online registration. Registration forms can be obtained at a

Communication at Work — PERSUASIVE WRITING

Thomas Jefferson said that his intention in writing the Declaration of Independence was "to place before mankind the common sense of the subject, in terms so plain and firm as to command their assent." That is the purpose of good persuasive writing. You have a cause that requires the support of others. It may be raising funds to extend library hours on weekends or getting a company to clean up pollution. You may need to write a proposal, letter to the editor, or other persuasive document.

Persuasive writing begins with research. Find out the best way to accomplish the change. Pay special attention to costs involved and how your plan will affect others. Gather facts and statistics. Find respected authorities that support your position. Learn and determine ways to address them. Here is one way to organize your writing:

1. Introduce the topic. Say what you think needs to be done.
2. Explain why it should be done. State your strongest reasons in order starting with the best. Support each with facts, examples, and other information.
3. Address objections. List major objections and respond to them.
4. Conclude by summarizing the issue and restating your position.

THINK CRITICALLY

1. Choose a controversial business-related topic.
2. Write a persuasive document addressing the topic using the organization method listed above.

variety of locations including election offices, driver's licensing offices, high schools and universities, and on the Web. Many public buildings have them. Each state varies in the locations that provide voter registration forms. To be eligible to vote in an election in most states, you must register at least 30 days prior to the election.

In most states, registration is permanent unless the voter moves to another town. Many states may cancel registration if a voter fails to vote for several years. If you move to a different place in the same county, notify the appropriate county office. It will need to update its records.

Voter registration has become a contested issue in recent years. Many states have become more proactive about purging voter registration rolls. If you are unsure if your voter registration is current, check your status with your local board of elections at least two months before the next election. If you discover that your registration is not current, this should give you time to correct your registration status before the election.

Cast a Ballot

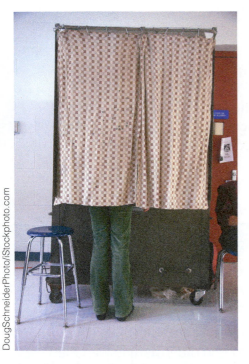

Americans have the right to cast a secret ballot.

In the United States, each county, ward, city, or town of a state is divided into voting districts called **precincts**. A person must vote at the polling place for the precinct in which he or she lives. The polling place may be a public building such as a school, a place of business, or even a private home. At the polling place, election officials check eligibility for voting, distribute ballots, and count the votes after the polls close.

Basic to the United State's voting system is the right to cast a secret ballot. At every polling place, some type of private booth is provided. Only one voter at a time is permitted to be in the voting booth. The voting itself is made as easy as possible. Voters either mark a printed ballot or use some type of voting machine.

When voting for various offices, people may vote a straight ticket or split their ballots. Voting a *straight ticket* is when someone simply votes for all candidates of a particular party. *Splitting a ticket* is voting for some candidates of one party and some of another. For example, someone might vote for a Democratic candidate for president and a Republican candidate for governor. In most states, people may also write in the name of someone whose name is not on the ballot. Issues and questions on the ballot require only a yes or no vote.

Election of Candidates

In most elections, the candidate with the most votes is the winner. Suppose that in a class election Leroy Johnson receives 98 votes; Tiffany Anderson, 95 votes; and Eric Washington, 80 votes. Leroy Johnson would be the winner.

In some elections, though, a candidate must have a majority of the votes cast. If that were the case in the class election, Leroy Johnson would not be the winner. He failed to receive at least half of the 273 votes. When no candidate receives a majority, a *runoff* election is usually held between the top two candidates. Johnson would run against Anderson. The person with the most votes is the winner.

Voter Behavior

Our ancestors struggled to earn the right to vote. Unfortunately, too many people now take this privilege for granted. Middle-aged and older citizens are much more likely to vote than are young adults. Only a minority of the people under age 25 vote. In the 2000, 2004, and 2008 presidential elections, an average of about 39 percent of 18- to 24-year-olds voted. On a positive note, however, the percentage of young voters has increased in each of the last three elections. Fewer youth vote in the non-presidential election years. For example, only about 20 percent voted in 2010. Females across all age groups are slightly more likely to vote than males. In 2008, 60 percent of females voted compared to 56 percent for males.

Too many people are like Roger's friend, Felipe. On election day, Roger awoke before the alarm sounded. He got up and dressed quickly. This was the first election in which he was old enough to vote. After breakfast, he headed off to the polling place. On the way, Roger saw Felipe jogging on the sidewalk.

"Hey Felipe," said Roger, "Do you want to go with me to vote?"

"Are you nuts, man?" exclaimed Felipe. "It doesn't do any good to vote. Those politicians don't care about anyone except themselves."

Roger was very disappointed in Felipe's reaction. He went on to the polling place. There was a short line in front of the building, but no one seemed to mind. People quietly chatted among themselves until it was their turn. Roger signed the register and got in line.

Several minutes later, a booth became available. Roger entered and marked his ballot. After he finished, Roger fed the ballot into the machine that read ballets electronically. He left the polling place with a feeling of satisfaction. He was glad he had voted, but he could not help but think about Felipe. "I wonder what I could do to change Felipe's mind," he thought.

Because of the publicity of a national campaign, more people vote in a presidential election than in any other. On average, fewer voters participate in elections for state and local officials. People's lives are influenced directly by the actions of their state and local officials.

🔍 Search the Net

The U.S. government has developed a website called Answers.USA.gov to provide a single location for information produced by the federal government. Access **www.cengage.com/school/working** and click on the link for Chapter 22. Explore the various topics available on the Answers.USA.gov site. Write a paragraph explaining ways in which this website is helpful to U.S. citizens.

www.cengage.com/school/working

22-1 Assessment

1. Name the four types of citizenship responsibilities.
2. Give three examples of how citizens might exercise economic responsibilities.
3. What would happen if all but a very few people failed to vote?
4. In order to vote in an election, what must you do beforehand?
5. What is it called when a person votes for candidates of different political parties?

High Growth Occupations
FOR THE 21ST CENTURY

Food Preparation and Serving Workers

Jobs in the food service industry are plentiful, offer part-time opportunities, and have few educational requirements. As a result, many young people begin their work history as food preparation and serving workers.

Cooks and food preparation workers prepare, season, and cook a wide range of foods. *Cooks* prepare and cook meals while *food preparation workers* assist cooks by performing tasks, such as peeling and cutting vegetables, trimming meat, preparing poultry, and keeping work areas clean and monitoring temperatures of ovens and stovetops.

The number, type, and responsibilities of cooks vary depending on where they work.

Food service workers must know how to store foods safely to avoid foodborne illnesses.

Institution and *cafeteria cooks*, for example, work in the kitchens of schools, cafeterias, businesses, hospitals, and other institutions. *Restaurant cooks* usually prepare a wider selection of dishes, cooking most orders individually. *Short-order cooks* prepare foods in restaurants and coffee shops that emphasize fast service and quick food preparation. *Fast food cooks* prepare a limited selection of menu items in fast-food restaurants.

Food and beverage serving and related workers are the front line of customer service in full-service restaurants and casual dining eateries. The largest group of these workers are *waiters* and *waitresses*. These workers greet customers, escort them to seats and hand them menus, take food and drink orders, and serve food and beverages. They also answer questions, explain menu items and specials, and keep tables and dining areas clean and set for new diners.

Other serving occupations include *bartenders* who fill drink orders. *Hosts* and *hostesses* welcome guests and maintain reservations and waiting lists. Dining room and cafeteria attendants and bartender helpers—sometimes referred to collectively as the *bus staff*—assist waiters, waitresses, and bartenders by cleaning and setting tables, removing dirty dishes, and keeping serving areas stocked with supplies.

Although most cooks, food preparation workers, and serving workers learn on the job, students with an interest in food service may be able to take high school or vocational school courses in kitchen basics as well as food safety and handling procedures.

THINK CLEARLY

OBJECTIVES
- List sources of facts on candidates and issues
- Identify and describe those things that get in the way of clear thinking

KEY TERMS
- rumor
- opinion
- prejudice
- allegation
- bias
- propaganda

Ethical Decisions

An election will be held in a couple of weeks for class officers. Small groups of students have organized to push for certain candidates. Campaign workers are putting up posters, passing out literature, posting support for candidates on Facebook, and even sending Tweets about candidates. The campaign is starting to get dirty. A representative of one group has come to you asking that you not vote for Christine because "we do not want a girl for president."

What would you do?

AISPIX/Shutterstock.com

Gather the Facts

It is not always easy to choose between two political candidates or to decide which position on an issue is the correct one for you. Many issues such as alternative energy, federal spending, climate change, and the role of labor unions are not clear-cut. To clarify your thinking, gather all the facts you can. Newspapers, magazines, websites, television, and radio news programs are good sources of information.

The League of Women Voters is a national organization that works to encourage the informed and active participation of citizens in government. Its state and local chapters issue printed newsletters before an election describing the candidates and issues. Access www.cengage.com/school/working and click on the Web Links for the League of Women Voters to find more information.

Many people use the Internet to prepare for an election. A growing number of websites provide candidate biographies, information on issues, voting records, campaign finance data, and other relevant information.

Recognize the Facts

Facts can be proven. It is fact, for example, that the earth is round and not flat. The following are a number of things that are frequently confused with facts.

Rumor

A **rumor** is a popular report or story that has not been proven. Most rumors are spread by word of mouth. People often treat rumors as if they are fact.

Opinion

An **opinion** is one person's views about something. A person reveals an opinion when a preference is shown for a certain candidate or when he or she takes a particular side in an issue. Although opinions may be based on fact, they are not fact in themselves.

Workplace Innovations

CAPSULE ENDOSCOPY

Medical doctors have many external and internal ways to examine and diagnosis patients for injuries or diseases. Problems and diseases of the small intestine, however, are difficult to evaluate using existing methods.

A new technology called "capsule endoscopy" has been developed in which the patient swallows a capsule containing a small camera that takes pictures of the inside of the body. The capsule is about the size of a large vitamin pill and contains a small camera, or video chip. The capsule also contains a light bulb, battery, and a radio transmitter.

The patient swallows the pill with some water. As the capsule travels down the esophagus, stomach, and small intestine it takes photographs rapidly. Once it is swallowed, the patient is unaware of the capsule. The capsule passes naturally through the digestive tract and the small and large intestines. The photographs it takes are sent by radio transmitter to a small receiver worn on the waist of the patient.

At the end of the painless procedure, the capsule is passed by the patient into the toilet and flushed away. The data recorder worn on the belt is returned to the physician who downloads the data into a computer where the images can be evaluated.

In addition to small cameras contained in capsules, medical scientists have also developed miniature video cameras so small that they can be inserted into an artery to examine blockages or used as a visual aid in surgery. The development of new medical diagnostic procedures and surgical techniques are expected to continue, due in large part to collaboration between medical scientists and engineers.

NET FOLLOW-UP

Use a search engine to explore the Web to determine the benefits and risks of capsule endoscopy. Be prepared to discuss the benefits versus risks as a class.

©David Bleeker Photography.com/Alamy

The small camera in the capsule endoscopy pill travels through the digestive system while recording images on a portable monitor worn by the patient.

Prejudice

A **prejudice** is an opinion that is based on insufficient information. A *prejudgment* is one form of prejudice. People might express prejudice about a person's sex, race, or religion, or about some other characteristic. Prejudice frequently causes great harm to people and is the opposite of clear thinking.

Allegation

An **allegation** is an unproven statement about someone or something. For example, you might state that Elliot Chemical Company dumps hazardous waste into the river. Making an allegation is very serious. You

Spreading rumors or making false allegations can cause people to distrust each other.

should never make an allegation unless you have the supporting facts. You could be hurting an innocent party. You could also be sued.

Bias

When you have a tendency to favor something because of familiarity or preference, you have a **bias**. You might then make exaggerated claims. For example, even though running is good exercise, some runners overstate its benefits. Biases are not necessarily harmful. Everyone has them. But, when making choices and decisions, carefully keep in mind who is saying what.

Propaganda

Propaganda involves any organized effort or movement to spread certain information. The information may be true or false. Like biases, propaganda is not always negative. For example, the American Heart Association uses propaganda to convince people of the hazards of smoking.

22-2 Assessment

1. List six sources of facts on candidates and issues. Include sources for national, state, and local elections.

2. A prejudice can be thought of as a prejudgment. Give an example.

3. Why should you be careful in making an allegation?

4. Having a bias may be positive or negative. Give one example of each (other than ones mentioned in the chapter).

EDUCATION AND TRAINING OPTIONS

OBJECTIVES

- Discuss why education or training beyond high school may be needed
- Illustrate how the amount of required preparation varies among occupations
- Name and describe six common types of education and training

KEY TERMS

- career ladder
- proprietary school
- major

INSAGO/Shutterstock.com

Career Decisions

After several years in your present job, you have reached a dead end. You cannot advance without additional training. But you never were a very good student. You are a poor reader, have difficulty memorizing, and nearly panic whenever you have to take a test. You do not want to admit it, but you are scared by the thought of taking a course.

What would you do?

Invest in Your Future

One day Lionel and several of his friends were discussing what they were going to do after high school. "I can't wait to get my diploma," said Lionel. "I'm sick of school."

"I'm going to get a job in a factory," remarked Marty. "That way, I don't have to go on with school."

"Yeah," said Henry, "who wants to get more education? I have a cousin who graduated from college and she can't get a job."

"I think all of you are wrong," said Samantha. "Most jobs require some type of education or training. And there is a lot of competition for jobs, even among people who have degrees or training."

The conversation among these students shows some truths and some misunderstandings about the relationship between education and employment. As illustrated in Figure 22-1, it is true that about 39% of the projected job openings during the period 2008–18 will be in occupations that require short-term on-the-job training. These jobs tend to be low-paying and have little job security. The majority of projected job

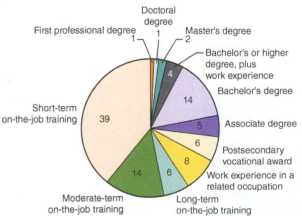

FIGURE 22-1 Percent of Projected Job Openings by Required Level of Education or Training, 2008–18
Source: *Occupational Outlook Quarterly*, Winter 2009–10, page 15

openings, however, will require more extensive on-the-job training, work experience, or formal postsecondary education or training.

It is also true that getting a college degree will not automatically guarantee you a job. Some types of degrees do not lead directly to employment. For instance, to get a job in psychology, most students will need at least one graduate degree. With some programs, there are more graduates with degrees than there are available jobs. These graduates take jobs requiring less education. These are often jobs that high school graduates usually fill. So competition for lower level jobs increases.

On the other hand, it is a mistake to think that you will not need more education or training after high school. Most entry-level jobs in factories, retail stores, healthcare, transportation, food service, and other workplaces require on-the-job training. If you want to advance in a company, you will probably have to continue learning throughout your lifetime. Your attitude toward future schooling is one of the things your employer is likely to consider in judging you for a promotion or raise.

Lydia and Vicki were in the same high school graduation class. After graduating, they were both hired as assemblers at General Electronics. Their work involved putting together electrical components for motherboards.

General Electronics has an agreement with Northwest Community College to offer courses at the plant. Classes start at 4 P.M. after employees get off work. The company pays the tuition. Lydia enrolled in the program because she wanted a more challenging, better-paying job. Vicki ignored the program, saying that the courses were a waste of time.

New jobs at General Electronics frequently open up at all levels from assemblers to supervisors. Employees with two years of experience may apply for higher-level jobs. As soon as they were eligible, both Lydia and Vicki applied for the first available job in the records department. Lydia got the job. The personnel manager was impressed by the fact that she had the initiative to continue her education. Vicki has since been passed over for several other jobs. Could it be due to her feelings about further training?

Career ladders exist in most industries. A **career ladder** is a group of related occupations with different skill requirements organized into ranks like steps on a ladder. Two examples of career ladders in the food service industry are shown in Figure 22-2. It is possible to start at the bottom of a career ladder and climb to the top. To do so, however, a person will need on-the-job experience and additional training.

Even though you are looking forward now to completing high school, do not turn your back on education at a later time. Some type of education or training program will probably be suited to your interests and abilities. Think it over carefully. Additional education and training will be one of the best investments you can make in your future.

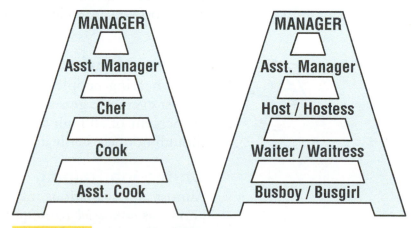

FIGURE 22-2 These career ladders show how workers can progress in the food service industry. They master one job and then move up to the next.

Courtesy of Educational Foundation of the National Restaurant Association

Prepare for an Occupation

Do you have any idea of how you might go about becoming a hotel manager? A toolmaker? A computer programmer? A pilot? The first thing you would have to do for each of these occupations is learn a set of skills. To work as a hotel manager, you would have to learn about accounting, hiring, employee relations, and food service management. Toolmakers need to know machining operations and math. They also need to be able to read blueprints and use machine tools and special measuring instruments. To work as a computer programmer, you would have to learn how to translate ideas into language the computer could understand and write instructions it could follow. To become a pilot you would have to learn how to fly a plane.

Like a hobby or a sport, every occupation involves knowledge and skills that must be learned. The amount of preparation needed varies among occupations. Deciding how much time and effort you are willing to put into education or training is important to career planning. It does not make sense to aim for a career as a veterinarian, for instance, unless you do well in school, are interested in science, and are willing to put in at least eight years of hard work and study after high school.

The best way to begin a career is to complete high school. High school courses teach basic skills that will help you be a better worker, consumer, and citizen. A high school diploma is necessary if you want to go to college. You will usually need a diploma to get into trade schools, technical institutes, apprenticeship programs, or the military. Most employers prefer to hire people who are at least high school graduates.

The choices that are open to you after high school are shown in Figure 22-3. As you can see, many options are available to get the necessary education and training. The path you choose depends on the kind of occupation you want—and the time and effort you are willing to put into your education and training.

FIGURE 22-3 Several different paths may lead to your career goal.

Types of Education and Training

From hearing people talk, you may sometimes get the feeling that almost everyone gets a college education. That is not so. More than 70 percent of all high school graduates do continue their schooling, though not necessarily in college.

On-the-job Training

Almost all occupations involve some sort of learning by doing, also known as *on-the-job training (OJT)*. A skilled worker teaches you as you watch. You then do the task under that worker's supervision. An advantage of OJT is that you are paid while you learn. Some jobs are almost always learned through OJT. Examples include cashiers, retail salespersons, stock clerks, and security guards. Generally, OJT is given for jobs that take more than a few days to learn, but less than a formal apprenticeship would require.

OJT is often combined with short-term classroom training. A power truck operator, for example, may take a safe driving course lasting several days. In some cases, OJT takes a few years. Air traffic controllers, for example, need two or three years of training and work experience before they are considered fully qualified.

Apprenticeship

As explained in Chapter 3, an apprenticeship is a formal on-the-job program during which a worker, who is called an apprentice, learns a trade. Extensive OJT and related instruction are involved. The top occupations for apprenticeship are listed in Figure 22-4.

The main drawback to apprenticeship is the stiff competition to get into a program. Generally, program sponsors seek people who seem to have the greatest chances of completing the program. To get your name placed on an apprenticeship register, or waiting list, you usually have to take an aptitude test, have an interview, and meet the necessary physical requirements. Once you are on the register, the wait can last months or even years.

- Able seaman
- Carpenter
- Chef
- Child care development specialist
- Construction craft laborer
- Dental assistant
- Electrician
- Elevator constructor
- Fire medic
- Law enforcement agent
- Over-the-road truck driver
- Pipefitter

FIGURE 22-4 These are the top occupations that are associated with the Registered Apprenticeship program.
Source: United States Department of Labor

Career and Technical Schools

Many types of schools offer training to teach skills used on the job. Career programs are offered by high schools, career high schools, and area career centers. Common areas of study include business, office, and marketing education; family and consumer sciences; technical and technology education; health occupations; and agriculture/agribusiness.

Other sources of training include trade schools, technical institutes, business schools, and correspondence or home-study schools. Privately run schools such as these are often called **proprietary schools**. In classes lasting from several weeks to several years, these schools will teach you cosmetology, barbering, flying, office procedures, computer operations, fashion design, locksmithing, and many other skills. A proprietary school is often more expensive than a public institution such as a community college.

In a career or technical school, you will practice in the classroom the skills you will need on the job. In business school, you might do word processing, file, use office equipment, or keep financial records. In programs for health occupations, you might operate medical equipment. People learning to be mechanics and repairers would take classes in blueprint reading and shop math.

When you complete your program, you will receive a certificate. You will then be ready to begin work, though your employer may also want to give you some on-the-job training.

Community and Junior Colleges

These two-year colleges provide two types of programs. One is the college transfer program, a two-year general education program for students who plan to transfer to a four-year college. General education

You are considering two occupations: office assistant and dental hygienist. You would not require any further training to become an office assistant, and you would earn $10 an hour. To become a dental hygienist, you would have to go to school for two years, but you could make $20 an hour to start. You have a relative who will pay your tuition. Five years from now, assuming you work 40 hours per week for 50 weeks of the year, in which job will you have earned more income before taxes?

SOLUTION

To calculate the amount of income, you must multiply the hourly wage, the number of hours worked per week, the number of weeks worked per year, and the number of years worked.

Total income for office assistant position $= \$10 \times 40 \times 50 \times 5 = \$100,000$

Total income for dental hygienist position $= \$20 \times 40 \times 50 \times 3 = \$120,000$
(with two years spent in school)

You would earn $20,000 more working for three years as a beginning dental hygienist than you would working for five years as an office assistant.

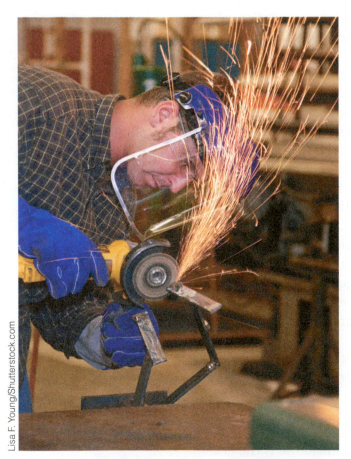

Among courses offered by community and junior colleges are practical training in skills like welding.

Lisa F. Young/Shutterstock.com

courses include English, history, science, art, and music. The other is the occupational or career program, which offers specialized skill training leading directly to employment. Though a typical occupational program lasts two years, some, such as licensed practical nurse, can be learned in one year.

A community or junior college offers training in many occupational areas. Examples include computer service technician, dental hygienist, forestry technician, emergency medical technician, recreation leader, auto mechanic, and welder.

Community and junior colleges offer two main advantages. First, they have close ties with local business and industry and try to tailor their training programs to the needs of the local area. This makes it easier for students to find jobs after training. Another advantage is that these colleges are usually less expensive to attend. Since they are supported by local property taxes, many community and junior colleges charge lower tuition.

Colleges and Universities

Colleges and universities are four-year institutions that vary widely in terms of whether they or their different programs of study are intended to prepare students for specific occupations. Some are primarily liberal arts schools that offer a broad, general education. Others are very specialized and are oriented toward engineering and technology. Still others, such as large state universities, offer a combination of general and specialized education.

A typical state college or university offers 100 or more areas of study called **majors**. Common majors include business and administration, journalism, education, engineering, political science, chemistry, economics, plant and soil science, art, theater, and psychology.

By and large, college does not prepare you for one particular occupation. Instead, most undergraduate programs give you a foundation upon which many careers can be built. In four years of college, you can expect to gain a basic education in your chosen field of study. In addition, you will be expected to broaden your knowledge of literature, mathematics, science, history, the fine arts, and many other areas. One advantage of college is that you usually have a lot of freedom in choosing courses that interest you.

Kurt is attending a state university. His major is Administration of Justice. Within his major, he takes courses in law enforcement, correctional management, juvenile justice, and delinquency prevention. Administration of Justice graduates get jobs as police officers, corrections counselors, and parole officers. Kurt plans to get additional training and hopes to become an FBI agent.

Military Training

Another way to get education and training is to join a branch of the Armed Forces—Army, Navy, Air Force, Marines, or Coast Guard. The military prepares people for a variety of occupations in which civilians also work. These include cook, nurse, computer operator, mechanic, firefighter, and hundreds of others. While in the service, you can learn occupational skills and gain work experience. Then, when you get out, you can use your skills to get a civilian job. Or you may decide to make a career of military service.

22-3 Assessment

1. Give three reasons to get education or training beyond high school.

2. What is the best way to begin a career?

3. Identify six common types of education and training.

4. What is the difference between OJT and apprenticeship?

5. Which is more expensive to attend, a community college or a proprietary school? Why?

6. Community and junior colleges provide two main types of programs. Name them.

7. Why is the information in Figure 22-1, that correlates level of education with projected job openings, important?

Focus on Skills for Living

Citizen Lawmakers

Most laws are passed by national, state, and local legislative bodies. However, through a method called an *initiative*, citizens can introduce a law. The initiative is used primarily at the state and local levels. Twenty-four states provide for initiatives.

In states or cities that use initiatives, anyone can draw up a proposed law. The next step is to collect a specific number of signatures on a petition favoring it. Once the initiative petition has qualified, it is voted on.

An initiative may be direct or indirect. In the first case, the proposed law is placed on a ballot and goes directly to the voters. In an indirect initiative, the proposed law goes first to the legislature. Should the legislative body approve the initiative, it goes into law. In some states, the question is ended if the legislature votes the bill down. In other states, a rejected bill is submitted to the people. If they vote for it, the bill

becomes law. In most states, the governor cannot veto a bill passed in this way.

In 2008, 174 statewide ballot propositions were voted on in 37 different states, including 153 ballot measures that appeared on the November 4 ballot. Following are several examples:

- **Alaska**   Prohibit shooting of wolves and grizzly bears by aircraft
- **Colorado**   Create state education fund savings account
- **Hawaii**   Reduce the age at which someone could be elected Governor or Lt. Governor from 30 to 25 years old
- **Masachusetts**   Repeal state income tax
- **Ohio**   Would allow one $600,000,000 resort/casino in state
- **Oregon**   15% of lottery profits for crime preventions, investigation and prosecution

Initiatives work in much the same way in a city as they do in a state. Whether at the state or local level, an initiative enables people to take direct political action if their elected representatives ignore their wishes.

Richard Seeley/Shutterstock.com

▸ Due to a successful ballot proposition in Alaska, it is no longer legal to shoot grizzly bears from aircraft.

THINK CRITICALLY

1. Citizen initiatives have been described as "direct democracy." What do you think this means?
2. Opponents say that citizen initiatives are not democratic because they infringe on the power of legislatures to make laws and do not protect minority rights. Do you agree or disagree? Give reasons for your answer.

EDUCATIONAL AND FINANCIAL AID INFORMATION

OBJECTIVES

- Know sources of information regarding education and training
- Know sources of information regarding financial aid

KEY TERMS

- financial aid
- scholarship

Career Decisions

You notice an advertisement in the paper for Whitney Business College. The ad states, "Flexible hours, credit for life experiences, tuition financing arranged, guaranteed job upon graduation." The school is not too far from your home.

"This could be just what I am looking for," you say to yourself. "I think I will give them a call."

What would you do?

STEEX/iStockphoto.com

Education and Training

To make a good educational decision, get information on various schools—their courses of study, admission requirements, and costs.

At the end of every occupational description in the *OOH*, a section titled "Sources of Additional Information" appears. Write to the sources listed or visit their websites. The information you receive will frequently list places where education and training are available.

Both private and government publishers offer guides to education and training programs. A collection of these guides should be available at your school guidance office or career center, your local public library, and on the Web. Use the most recent edition.

Colleges and universities have websites. For colleges of interest, click on the link for "Prospective Students," "Student Admissions," or something similar that will provide you with essential information.

Your local One Stop Career Center is probably the best source of apprenticeship information. In some cities, Apprenticeship Information Centers (AICs) furnish information, counseling, and aptitude testing. They also direct people needing more specific help to union hiring halls, Joint Apprenticeship Committees, and employer sponsors. You can also contact your state office of apprenticeship by accessing www.cengage.com/school/working and clicking on the Web Links for State Office of Apprenticeship.

Workforce Trends

The BLS makes forecasts of trends and explains what factors influence these trends. Their latest projections are for the period 2008–18. Their 2008 projections are tentative since this was during a recession. The impact of the recession will not be known until the recovery is well underway. Therefore, some of the projections reported may be higher than the BLS originally forecast. This is because part of the employment growth may be due to the recovery of jobs lost during the recession.

For information about education and training in the Armed Forces, access www.cengage.com/school/working and click the Web Links for Armed Forces. Each service has information available describing its specific programs. Be aware that during times of conflict, you may be required to serve in combat areas.

Financial Aid

The cost of education or training is an important consideration in making educational decisions. Think about how much training you and your family can afford as well as how much you would like to get. Sometimes there is great variability in the training requirements for a specific occupation. Different occupational alternatives for nursing that require different levels of education and training follow:

- Nursing aide, which requires a minimum of 75 hours of training.
- One year of training is required for a licensed practical nurse.
- A registered nurse can obtain a two-year associate degree, a three-year diploma, or a four year BS degree in nursing.
- Master's and Ph. D. nursing degrees are available.

Financial aid is a broad term that includes all forms of financial assistance including scholarships, loans, and grants to individuals pursuing postsecondary education. About two-thirds of all students who graduate from college use student loans and other financial aid.

You need to be informed about loan terms, interest rates, and repayment options before applying for a loan. An organization entitled "The Project on Student Debt" recommends that students and their families exhaust all of their federal aid options before considering riskier private student loans. Access www.cengage.com/school/working and click on the Web Links for Student Debt. The information provided may help you make better decisions about loan options.

Federal student loans are available to almost all students who are U.S. citizens or permanent residents, and who are attending college at least half-time. Congress sets federal loan terms and conditions and they are the same for all borrowers regardless of their income, their credit score, or where they go to school. Some students may avoid having to repay a portion of the amount borrowed.

The process of applying for federal student aid is shown in Figure 22-5 on the next page. A school counselor or financial aid officer can help you. Access www.cengage.com/school/working and click on the Web Links for Financial Aid to view a government website that can answer your questions.

It takes time to complete the financial aid process. Start early and make sure that you understand the school and state aid deadlines. A **scholarship** is financial aid awarded to a student on the basis of outstanding academic achievement. If you have good grades and good standardized test scores, you may be eligible for a scholarship.

Take advantage of educational opportunities. Whether you take formal course work, learn on the job, or study on your own, you benefit as a worker and human being by continuing to learn and grow.

Steps to Federal Student Aid

The following figure will help you keep track of what you need to do when applying for federal student aid.

STEP 1 Get free information and help from a school counselor, the financial aid office at the college or trade school you plan to attend, or the U.S. Department of Education at **www.studentaid.ed.gov** or **1-800-4-FED-AID (1-800-433-3243)**. Free help is available any time during the application process. You should never have to pay for help.

STEP 2 Get a Federal Student Aid PIN, a personal identification number. A PIN lets you apply, "sign" your online *Free Application for Federal Student Aid* (FAFSA℠), make corrections to your application information, and more—so keep it safe. Go to **www.pin.ed.gov** to get one.

STEP 3 Collect the documents needed to apply, including income tax returns and W-2 forms (and other records of income). A full list of what you need is at **www.fafsa.gov**. Tax return not completed at the time you apply? Estimate the tax information, apply, and correct information later.

STEP 4 Complete the FAFSA between Jan. 1, 20___, and June 30, 20___ (no exceptions to either date!). BUT, apply as soon as possible after Jan. 1 to meet school and state aid deadlines (see note after step 7). Apply online at *FAFSA on the Web*℠ (the faster and easier way) by going to **www.fafsa.gov**. If you don't already have your PIN, you can get it when you complete the online FAFSA.

STEP 5 Within a few days, the U.S. Department of Education will send you your *Student Aid Report* (SAR)—the result of your FAFSA. Review your SAR and, if necessary, make changes or corrections and submit your SAR for reprocessing. Your complete, correct SAR will contain your Expected Family Contribution (EFC)—the number used to determine your federal student aid eligibility.

STEP 6 The college or trade school that you plan to attend might request additional information from you. Be sure to respond by any deadlines, or you might not receive federal student aid.

STEP 7 **All applicants:** The college or trade school will tell you how much aid you can get at that school. Contact the school's financial aid office if you have any questions about the aid being offered. **First-time applicants:** Review award letters from schools to compare amounts and types of aid being offered. Decide which school to attend based on a combination of (a) how well the school suits your needs and (b) its affordability after all aid is taken into account.

Note: *You also might be able to get financial aid from your state government, your school, or a private scholarship. Research nonfederal aid early (ideally, start in the spring of your junior year of high school). You can find a free scholarship search at* **www.studentaid.ed.gov/scholarship**. *Be sure to meet all application deadlines!*

FIGURE 22-5 Follow these steps to apply for student aid.
Source: Funding Education Beyond High School: The Guide to Federal Student Aid, 2011–12. U. S. Department of Education, Federal Student Aid, The Guide 3

22-4 Assessment

1. **List three types of information that you will need to make a good educational decision.**

2. **Give two sources of information about apprenticeships.**

3. **Provide an original example of how education or training requirements may vary for an occupation.**

4. **Why should you start early to apply for student aid?**

22 Assessment

Chapter Summary

22-1 Be a Citizen

A. Citizenship is a part of daily living. The responsibilities of citizenship involve personal, economic, political, and national-defense activities.

B. You have a responsibility to vote in local, state, and national elections. In all states, voters must be U.S. citizens and at least 18 years old. They must also meet state residency requirements. To be eligible to vote, you must register beforehand.

C. A person must vote at the polling place for the precinct in which he or she lives. At every polling place, some type of private booth is provided. People may vote a straight ticket or split their ballots.

D. Too many people take the privilege of voting for granted. About 39 percent of the people under age 25 vote in presidential elections. On the average, fewer voters participate in elections for state and local officials than in presidential elections.

22-2 Think Clearly

A. It is not always easy to choose between two political candidates or to decide which position on an issue is the correct one for you. To clarify your thinking, gather all the facts you can.

B. Facts can be proven. A number of things are confused with facts. These include rumor, opinion, prejudice, allegation, bias, and propaganda.

22-3 Education and Training Options

A. Some jobs require little or no additional schooling. Such jobs tend to be low-paying and have little job security. It is a mistake to think that you will not need more education or training after high school. Additional education and training will be one of the best investments you can make in your future.

B. Every occupation involves knowledge and skills that must be learned. But the amount of preparation needed varies among occupations. Deciding how much time and effort you are willing to put into education or training is important to career planning.

C. Six common education and training options are on-the-job training, apprenticeship, career and technical schools, community and junior colleges, colleges and universities, and military training.

22-4 Educational and Financial Aid Information

A. To make a good educational decision, you will need information on various schools. Private and government publishers produce guides to education and training programs. Such material is also available on the Web.

B. The cost of education or training is an important consideration in making educational decisions. Many students use loans and other sources of financial aid to help cover the cost of their education.

C. Education is never wasted. You will benefit as a worker and human being by continuing to learn and grow.

Activities

1. Identify someone, perhaps a friend or relative, in your community who is a naturalized citizen. Invite the person to class to talk about why he or she chose to become a U.S. citizen. Prepare a list of questions to ask.

2. Research the residency requirements for voting in your community or city. Find out how you go about registering to vote where you live. Discuss your findings in class.

3. Newspaper and magazine editorials are a special type of opinion. Bring editorials of interest to class. Discuss them. Are there any about which the class disagrees? If so, compose a class opinion and send it to the proper source. Follow the persuasive writing guidelines in Lesson 22-1.

4. Bring to class a brochure or other statement that can be considered propaganda. Identify the main idea that the propaganda is attempting to communicate. Then, discuss the following questions: (a) Who wants you to believe this? (b) Why does the person or group want you to believe it? (c) Are there arguments on the other side?

5. Explain why you would, or would not, include being a good citizen as a goal in your life-span plan. Describe how practicing good citizenship might help other people achieve goals in their life-span plans.

6. Select an entry-level occupation of interest. Develop a career ladder for the occupation similar to those in Figure 22-2. You will probably need to ask people in related occupations for assistance.

7. There are many online sources available to help with the financial aspects of post-secondary educational process. Access www.cengage.com/school/working and click on Web Links to find links for the following.

   a. **Financial Aid** A variety of information and activities to help you prepare for your education are available. Your instructor may assign you a specific task to complete.

   b. **Educational Tax Credits** A number of tax credits, deductions, and savings plans are available to taxpayers to assist with the expense of higher education. Tax information changes from time to time. So, make sure that you have the most recent information, which is contained in IRS Publication 970.

8. Ask your local One Stop Career Center what types of information it has about apprenticeship. Identify the location of the nearest Apprenticeship Information Center.

9. Identify a school or college that interests you. Use one of the resources in this chapter to find the following information: (a) What are the entrance requirements? (b) How long does it take to complete the program you are interested in? (c) How much does it cost to attend? (d) Is financial aid available? (e) Does the institution provide job-placement services? Prepare a written report summarizing your findings and submit it to your instructor.

10. Identify types of education or training you expect to complete after you graduate from high school. Explain how this training can help you achieve goals in your life-span plan. Also explain why it is unreasonable to think you can learn everything about an occupation.

Word Power

On a separate sheet of paper, match each definition with the correct term. All definitions will be used, and a definition will be used only once.

a. allegation
b. bias
c. career ladder
d. citizenship
e. financial aid
f. major
g. opinion
h. precinct
i. prejudice
j. propaganda
k. proprietary school
l. rumor
m. scholarship

11. Privately operated postsecondary vocational, technical, or business schools

12. Divisions of a county, ward, city, or town for election purposes; voting districts

13. Any organized effort or movement to spread certain information

14. One person's views about something

15. A broad term that includes all forms of financial assistance (scholarships, loans, grants, and so on) to individuals pursuing postsecondary education

16. Membership in a community, state, county, or nation; carrying out the duties and responsibilities of a citizen

17. A tendency to favor something because of familiarity or preference

18. Primary areas of study chosen by students for a college or other degree

19. A group of related occupations with different skill requirements that can be arranged in a ladder-type fashion from low to high

20. Financial aid awarded to a student on the basis of outstanding academic achievement

21. A popular report or story that has not been proven

22. A prejudgment; an opinion that is based on insufficient information

23. An unproven statement about someone or something

Think Critically

24. If you were an employer, how might you feel if several of your employees were called away for emergency military reserve duty?

25. Citizens may be of three types. One type is like a stone that stays where it is, neither hearing nor responding. A second type is like a

sponge that absorbs and retains but does not respond. The third type is like a generator that converts energy into power. Generators are the people who get things done. What percentages of students in your school, do you think, fall into each of these three groups? In which group do you belong? Discuss your answers in class.

26. Why do you think so few young adults vote? What can be done to increase the number of young voters?

27. Many companies encourage their employees to pursue additional education. How does this benefit the employer?

28. If you are working now, find out what type of education or training you would need to move ahead in your job. Discuss this in class.

29. Federal student loan default rates have been climbing. As reported in the *New York Times* in 2010, 15 percent of students at for-profit schools defaulted on their loans. In 2009, default rates were 11.6 percent. Although only about ten percent of the nation's students are enrolled in for-profit schools, the federal loan default rate at these schools represents nearly half of the defaults. Although a weak economy was cited as one reason for the default rates, student recruiting abuses were cited as a strong contributing factor. Work in two teams. Each team should research and report on one of the following topics.

   a. **Investigate recruiting abuses.** For example, registering a recently hospitalized war veteran who has traumatic brain injury and who may not be able to study effectively is one type of recruiting abuse. Provide examples of other recruiting abuses and what government actions, if any, have been put in place to stop them.

   b. **Some schools recruit students who will not have good job prospects.** Despite poor job opportunities, the schools enroll students and help them access loans that result in a very high debt level upon graduation. Research two for-profit schools and their published job placement rates. Compare anticipated salaries with anticipated loan amounts. Determine what the monthly loan repayment levels will be and whether anticipated salaries would be sufficient to pay off the loans in a timely fashion.

Career Transitions Connection

Research Higher Education

Click *Search Schools & Programs*. Enter your course interest and your geographic location as requested. The results include a listing for School, Location, Type, Cost, and Programs. Hit on the links for three schools of interest. Develop a chart that summarizes the program offered, tuition costs, funding options, and the time it takes to earn a degree. You will need to independently calculate either transportation costs to commute or room and board costs if you would live on campus. Prepare a possible plan of action that would allow you to study in one of these programs. Submit your work to your instructor.

Glossary

accident An unplanned event often resulting in personal injury, property damage, or both (p. 268)

adjusted gross income For income tax purposes, total gross income minus certain specific adjustments to income (p. 462)

adjustments to income Items that can be subtracted from total income when filing an income tax return to arrive at adjusted gross income (p. 462)

advertisement A public notice or message intended to aid in the sale of a product or service (p. 75)

advertising Any type of public notice or message intended to aid in the sale of a product or service (p. 368)

aerobic exercise Exercises that condition the heart and lungs by increasing the body's ability to take in oxygen (p. 267)

affirmative action A set of policies and programs designed to correct past discrimination (p. 177)

agenda A list of items to be taken care of at a particular meeting (p. 294)

allegation An unproven statement about someone or something (p. 523)

allocation The distribution or assignment of something; for example, of income to the various items in a budget (p. 417)

allowance The number of tax exemptions to which one is entitled (p. 146)

alternative Options to choose from in making a decision (p. 34)

annual percentage rate (APR) The percentage cost of credit on a yearly basis (p. 406)

annual percentage yield (APY) The annual percentage amount earned on a savings deposit (p. 423)

anxiety A feeling of concern, worry, or unease (p. 136)

app A concise software program designed to perform a very targeted and limited function (p. 323)

appraise To evaluate someone or something, such as a potential employer (p. 114)

apprentice A person enrolled in a formal on-the-job training program for a specified period to learn a trade or craft (p. 70)

apprenticeship Formal-on-the-job training (p. 70)

apprenticeship register A waiting list for entry into an apprenticeship program (p. 72)

aptitude Things that you are good at doing; natural talents or developed abilities (p. 11)

area The number of square units of space on the surface of a figure enclosed by the perimeter (p. 247)

arraignment A hearing before a judge during which formal charges are brought against an arrested person (p. 489)

assertive Firm and positive in stating one's position or point of view (p. 375)

authority The power or rank to give orders and make assignments to others (p. 139)

auto insurance Provides liability and other coverages for the operation of a motor vehicle (p. 447)

automated teller machine (ATM) Electronic terminals in which customers can insert a plastic card to withdraw cash, make deposits, or transfer funds (p. 386)

automatic raise A regular pay raise received by all employees (p. 188)

bail Money deposited with a court to guarantee that an accused person will show up for a hearing or trial (p. 489)

barcode A series of lines of varying width, printed on a label that can be read by an optical scanner (p. 213)

barrier Any condition that makes it difficult to achieve an objective (p. 115)

basal metabolism The minimum amount of energy (calories) necessary for continuous body functioning (p. 261)

beneficiary For life insurance, the person to whom the death benefits from a policy are to be paid (p. 442)

benefit Financial help in times of sickness, old age, disability, etc (p. 468)

bias A tendency to favor something because of familiarity or preference (p. 523)

body language Unspoken communication through physical movements, expressions, and gestures (p. 123)

bond A certificate that represents a loan to a company or government agency in exchange for a pledge to repay the borrowed sum plus a certain amount of interest (p. 427)

brand-name product Goods given a unique name by the manufacturer (p. 364)

broker Individuals or companies that specialize in selling stocks and other financial investments (p. 426)

browser Software used to locate and display information on the Web (p. 327)

budget A plan for managing income and expenditures (p. 413)

Bureau of Labor Statistics (BLS) A federal agency that measures labor market activity and working conditions (p. 17)

bylaws Printed information that defines the basic characteristics of an organization and describes how it will operate (p. 293)

calorie A unit of energy produced by food when it is used by the body (p. 260)

capital gain An increase in the value of a stock or other asset that is only realized when the asset is sold (p. 426)

career The combination of all the occupations and jobs held throughout your work life (p. 9)

career and technical student organizations (CTSO) Nonprofit, national organizations with state and local chapters that exist to develop leadership skills and good citizenship among members (p. 288)

career guidance Programs and activities designed to assist students in career planning and decision making (p. 46)

career ladder A group of related occupations with different skill requirements that can be arranged in a ladder-type fashion from low to high (p. 525)

cash discount A reduction in price, often of several percent, offered to a buyer to encourage early payment on an account (p. 241)

catastrophe A disaster or misfortune, often occurring suddenly (p. 436)

certificate of deposit (CD) A popular type of time deposit in which an amount of savings is deposited for a fixed period of time in return for a specified interest rate (p. 421)

character The combination of qualities and traits that defines who you are (p. 96)

check register A booklet or forms for keeping a record of checking account transactions (p. 396)

chronological resume Organizes your experience around the jobs you have had (p. 97)

circumference The perimeter of a circle (p. 246)

citizenship Membership in a community, state, country, or nation; carrying out the duties and responsibilities of a citizen (p. 516)

civil service test A pre-employment test that is administered to a job applicant seeking a government job (p. 105)

cloud computing Remote storage of computer software and data that are accessible via the Web (p. 324)

code of ethics Rules for professional practice and behavior (p. 289)

commission A fee charged by a financial institution for certain transactions such as the purchase or sale of stocks and bonds (p. 426)

commitment A duty or obligation to do something (p. 114)

common law A main source of law in the United States; judge-made law (p. 488)

comparison shopping The process of finding out the cost of a product or service at several different places before making a decision to buy (p. 364)

compatible Pleasant or agreeable (p. 122)

compensation The total amount of income and benefits received for a job (p. 185)

competition The efforts of sellers to win potential customers (p. 342)

complaint An expression of dissatisfaction with a product or service (p. 376)

compounding A process in which interest is earned on both the money put into an account and the interest periodically added to it, causing savings to steadily grow (p. 422)

computer An electronic tool that can store and process data and can direct the work of other tools (p. 316)

computer literacy A general knowledge of what computers are, how they work, and for what they can be used (p. 316)

conditions of employment The specific details of a job offer, such as working hours, salary or wages, and fringe benefits (p. 127)

condominium An individually owned townhouse or apartment with shared ownership of common facilities, like the grounds (p. 503)

confidentiality Keeping a customer's or patient's data or information private (p. 142)

confirm To verify or make firm, such as calling to check on an appointment (p. 119)

consumer Someone who buys or uses goods or services (p. 362)

consumption The process of using goods and services that have been produced (p. 341)

contingency fee One type of legal fee charged by an attorney based on whether the case is won (p. 496)

cooperation Getting along with and working well with others (p. 155)

cooperative A townhouse or apartment that is part of a property jointly owned by residents (p. 503)

co-payment A provision of health insurance in which the insured person is required to share in the expenses of health care (p. 439)

corporation A business owned by stockholders (p. 301)

cover letter A letter of application accompanied by a resume that is sent to a potential employer (p. 301)

credit The receipt of money, goods, or services in exchange for a promise to pay (p. 403)

creditor Person or company to which money is due (p. 302)

debit card A plastic card used in electronic banking to immediately transfer funds for a purchase from a bank account (p.388)

decision making The process of choosing between two or more alternatives or options (p. 34)

decision-making style Typical ways in which people make decisions (p. 39)

decree An order issued by a court, for example, requiring a defendant to stop doing whatever is harming the plaintiff (p. 492)

deductible In traditional health insurance, a certain initial amount that the insured person is required to pay before the insurance company pays the balance (p. 438)

deduction A certain amount that is withheld from the paycheck of an employee (p. 187); Various nontaxable items that can be subtracted from adjusted gross income when filling an income tax return (p. 462)

defendant A person required to answer charges in a lawsuit (p. 492)

deficit The amount spent over budget or over what has been taken in (p. 348)

delegate Assign a task or responsibility to others (p. 140)

demand The willingness of consumers to spend money for goods and services (p. 342)

deposit ticket A preprinted form used to make a deposit in a checking account (p. 398)

depression A severe recession marked by stagnant business activity (p. 348)

desktop computer A PC intended for regular use at a single location (p. 321)

direct-mail advertising Advertising sent to potential customers through the mail (p. 368)

discretion Behaving or speaking in such a way as to avoid causing offense or revealing private information (p. 217)

discrimination Favoring one person as compared to another (p. 176)

dividend Profit that a company divides among its shareholders (p. 426)

due process The legal right to be notified of a complaint against you and to state your case or point of view before a decision is made (p. 142)

economics The study of how goods and services are produced, distributed, and used (p. 340)

electrocute To cause death by electric shock (p. 270)

electronic banking Various types of electronic fund transfers (p. 388)

employee handbook A booklet given to new employees that contains an explanation of company policies and rules (p. 140)

employee orientation program Training for a new employee about the company and its policies and procedures (p. 136)

employment practice The manner and method by which an employer deals with employees (p. 175)

endorsement A signature, sometimes with a brief message, on the back/left side of a check needed to cash, deposit, or transfer ownership of it (p. 397)

enthusiasm Eagerness; a strong interest in something (p. 156)

entrepreneur Someone who runs his or her own business (p. 299)

entry-level job Job requires little or no experience (p. 75)

enunciation How distinctly or clearly one speaks (p. 205)

environment One's surroundings, including neighborhood, family, friends, and the like (p. 41)

equal employment opportunity The idea, supported by law, that employers, unions, and employment agencies cannot discriminate against people because of age, race, color, religion, sex, disability, or national origin (p. 176)

equity The value of (money invested in) a home above the amount owed on a mortgage (p. 505)

ergonomics The scientific study of people at work and how the work is performed (p. 182)

exchange traded fund (ETF) A financial tool that is similar to a mutual fund, but trades like a stock (p. 427)

exempt To be free of something, such as not having to pay taxes (p. 146)

exemption Set amounts for yourself and each dependent that are subtracted from adjusted gross income when filing an income tax return (p. 463)

expenditure Money that is spent (p. 412)

experience What you do and what happens to you in your environment (p. 41)

face value Regarding life insurance, the amount of money that is paid in the event of the insured's death (p. 442)

Federal Insurance Contributions Act (FICA) The federal law requiring employers to deduct an amount from workers' paychecks for Social Security and to contribute an equal amount (p. 472)

fee A sum of money charged by a private employment agency for helping someone find a job (p. 77)

filing The process of completing and submitting an income tax return (p. 464)

finance charge The total dollar amount paid for the use of credit (p. 404)

financial aid A broad term that includes all forms of financial assistance (scholarships, loans, grants, and so on) to individuals pursuing postsecondary education (p. 532)

follow-up letter A thank-you letter sent to an interviewer following a job interview (p. 126)

franchise A contract with a company to sell its goods and services within a certain area (p. 306)

full-service bank Banks offering a broad range of financial conveniences and services (p. 386)

functional resume Organizes your experience around skills rather than job titles (p. 98)

generic product Goods that state only the common name of the product on the label (p. 364)

globalization The process by which nations have become more interdependent (p. 351)

good Articles that are produced or manufactured (p. 362)

goods-producing industry Companies and businesses such as manufacturing, construction, and mining which produce some type of product (p. 18)

goodwill Acts of kindness, consideration, or assistance (p. 228)

grammar A set of rules about correct speaking and writing (p. 205)

grand jury A group of citizens to which a prosecutor presents evidence of a serious crime who must determine if there should be a trial (p. 489)

graphical user interface (GUI) A feature of modern operating system software that provides icons and menus from which the user can select commands, typically with a mouse (p. 322)

grooming Maintaining a neat, attractive appearance (p. 159)

gross domestic product (GDP) The market value of all final goods and services produced by a nation during a specific period of time. (p. 351)

gross pay The amount of salary or wages earned during a certain time period before deductions are withheld (p. 187)

guarantee A pledge that something is exactly as stated or advertised (p. 372)

hardware The physical equipment that makes up a computer (p. 320)

health maintenance organization (HMO) A type of insurance in which all health care is provided for a fixed fee (p. 439)

homeowner's insurance Provides coverages for perils and liability for people who own or rent a home (p. 444)

honesty A refusal to lie, steal, or mislead in any way (p. 156)

human relations Interactions among people (p. 223)

hypothetical Imagined or pretended (p. 117)

icon A small picture or symbol on which a user can double-click to give commands to software to perform specific functions. (p. 322)

income Money coming in (p. 412)

indictment A grand jury's formal statement charging a person with an offense (p. 489)

individual retirement account (IRA) A voluntary private pension plan that lets employed people save money annually toward retirement and receive special tax benefits (p. 462)

industry In the NAICS system, all places of employment, regardless of the type of product produced or service provided (p. 17)

inflation A sharp increase in the costs of goods and services (p. 348)

information communications technology (ICT) Electronic tools and equipment that store, retrieve, manipulate, transmit, or receive information in digital form (p. 212)

interest Something that you like to do (p. 11); A feeling of excitement and involvement (p. 156)

interpersonal attraction A tendency to be drawn to another person, often because of similar characteristics and preferences (p. 226)

intuition A feeling or hunch (p. 39)

investing The process of using money not required for personal and family needs to increase overall financial worth (p. 425)

invoice A bill for goods (p. 240)

job A paid position at a specific place or setting (p. 8)

job application form Used by employers to collect personal, educational, and employment information (p. 91)

job bank Electronic data base of jobs searchable by a computer (p. 78)

job interview A face-to-face meeting between a job seeker and a potential employer (p. 114)

job portal Job boards or company website containing job banks and various kinds of job search information (p. 79)

job-lead card A card on which to record information and notes about a job lead (p. 80)

journey worker A skilled, experienced, worker who has completed an apprentice training program (p. 70)

judgment Thinking about a problem and making the right decision (p. 153); The judge's decision in a civil suit in favor of either the plaintiff or the defendant (p. 492)

keyboarding skills The ability to type and to give commands to a computer using a keyboard (p. 317)

landlord The owner or manager of rental property (p. 503)

law The body of enforced rules by which people live together (p. 488)

leadership Influencing people in order to accomplish the goals of the organization (p. 286)

lease A rental agreement between a tenant and a landlord (p. 503)

letter of resignation A letter written by an employee notifying an employer of the intent to quit a job (p. 193)

liability Legal responsibility for something, such as damages or costs (p. 444)

line item A single entry in a budget; a budgeted item (p. 418)

liquidity The quality of being easily converted into cash; refers to assets (p. 420)

loyalty Faithfulness; believing in and being devoted to something (p. 156)

lump-sum payment A one-time payment of money (p. 470)

major Primary areas of study chosen by students for a college or other degree (p. 529)

majority A vote of at least one more than half of the people who vote (p. 294)

management Planning, organizing, and directing the activities of an organization (p. 286)

markdown A reduction in the selling price of a product (p. 243)

market An area of economic activity created whenever goods and services are bought and sold (p. 342)

markup An amount added by a retailer to the cost price of goods that allows it to cover expenses and make a fair profit (p. 242)

measurement The act of determining the dimensions, quantity, or degree of something (p. 245)

medically consulted injury An injury serious enough that a medical professional was consulted (p. 269)

merit raise A pay raise based on the amount and quality of an employee's work (p. 188)

microprocessor A CPU contained on a single silicon chip (p. 320)

minimum wage By law, the lowest hourly wage that can be paid to an employee (p. 175)

minor A person who has not yet reached full legal age (p. 69)

mobile computer A PC that can be used on the move or at a remote location such as a smartphone, tablet computer, or notebook (p. 321)

monopoly Exclusive control of the supply of a product or services (p. 347)

monitor To keep track of or to watch over (p. 64)

morale A mood or spirit, such as the attitude and emotion of employees (p. 141)

mortgage A loan, typically for 15–30 years, obtained from a financial institution to buy housing (p. 503)

motion A brief statement of a proposed action by a participant in a meeting (p. 294)

multinational Companies with headquarters in one country that have stores, offices, branches, or plants in different countries (p. 352)

musculoskeletal disorder (MSD) A broad term describing a variety of workplace injuries and illnesses caused by repetitive motion, fatigue, and overuse of muscles and joints (p. 181)

mutual fund An investment company that pools the money of thousands of investors and buys a collection of investments that may include stocks, bonds, and other financial assets (p. 426)

natural disaster An uncontrollable event in nature that destroys life or property (p. 275)

need A basic necessity of life, which includes food, shelter, and clothing (p. 340)

net pay The amount on a paycheck; the take-home pay of an employee after deductions are subtracted from gross pay (p. 187)

network Two or more computers or other electronic devices linked together by cable or wireless means (p. 326)

no-fault insurance Each party in the accident has losses and expenses paid for by his or her insurance company regardless of who caused the accident (p. 450)

North American Industry Classification System (NAICS) A grouping of different workplaces according to the type of product produced or service provided (p. 17)

nutrient A chemical substance in food that is needed for good health (p. 258)

nutrition The process by which plants and animals take in and use food (p. 258)

obsolete No longer produced or used; out-of-date (p. 63)

occupation The name given to a group of similar tasks that a person performs for pay (p. 7)

occupational description Explains what the work in an occupation is like including the tasks involved, the working conditions, and the earnings (p. 22)

Occupational Outlook Handbook (OOH) A reference source produced by the federal government that provides occupational information and data (p. 17)

Occupational Safety and Health Administration (OSHA) The government agency that sets and enforces standards for safe and healthful working conditions (p. 179)

occupational search Collecting information about an occupation of interest using one or more printed resources or databases (p.22)

occupational skill Skills needed to perform tasks or duties of a specific occupation (p. 43)

One Stop Career Center A system of public employment offices (p. 77)

opinion One person's views about something (p. 522)

order of business A standard series of steps followed in a meeting (p. 294)

outsource Contracting with another company, often in a different country, to provide some type of business service (p. 352)

overtime pay The wage received for working more than 40 hours a week, usually 1½ times the normal hourly wage (p. 186)

paperless office A work environment in which the use of paper and traditional forms of communication are eliminated or greatly reduced (p. 212)

parliamentarian An officer of a group who advises the chair on correct parliamentary procedure (p. 297)

parliamentary procedure The formal rules used to conduct a meeting in a fair and orderly manner (p. 293)

partnership A form of business organization in which two or more persons co-own the business (p. 301)

patron A customer of certain service-producing businesses or institutions (p. 228)

payee The person or institution to which a check is written (p. 394)

pension A regular payment of money to a person, usually retired (p. 469)

perceived obsolescence Refers to the desire on the part of a consumer to replace a functional product because it is perceived or thought to be no longer stylish or appropriate (p. 366)

performance evaluations The process of judging how well an employee is doing on the job (p. 164)

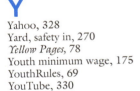